FileMaker®
Pro 8.5 Bible

FileMaker® Pro 8.5 Bible

Dennis R. Cohen
Steven A. Schwartz

WILEY

Wiley Publishing, Inc.

FileMaker® Pro 8.5 Bible

Published by
Wiley Publishing, Inc.
111 River Street
Hoboken, NJ 07030-5774
www.wiley.com

Copyright© 2006 by Wiley Publishing, Inc., Indianapolis, Indiana

Published by Wiley Publishing, Inc., Indianapolis, Indiana

Published simultaneously in Canada

ISBN-10: 0-470-08277-1

ISBN-13: 978-0-470-08277-5

Manufactured in the United States of America

10 9 8 7 6 5 4 3 2 1

1O/QY/QS/QW/IN

For general information on our other products and services or to obtain technical support, please contact our Customer Care Department within the U.S. at (800) 762-2974, outside the U.S. at (317) 572-3993 or fax (317) 572-4002.

Wiley also publishes its books in a variety of electronic formats. Some content that appears in print may not be available in electronic books.

Library of Congress Control Number: 2005936652

About the Authors

Dennis R. Cohen has been developing software and writing about it since the late 1970s. Starting in the Jet Propulsion Laboratory's Deep Space Network (DSN), through stints at Ashton-Tate, Claris, and Aladdin Systems, he was involved in creating and maintaining such packages as the DSN Station Scheduling System, dBASE III, dBASE Mac, FileMaker, ClarisWorks, Claris Resolve, and many others.

During this time, Dennis wrote numerous articles appearing in a variety of different publications, including *Personal Computing, Macintosh Today, Macworld,* and *MacTutor.* The author (or co-author) of over a dozen books, including *AppleWorks 6 Bible, AppleWorks 6 For Dummies, Mac OS X Bible, iLife Bible, Teach Yourself Visually iLife '04, FileMaker Pro 7 Bible, The Xcode 2 Book* (all Wiley), and *Mac Digital Photography* (Sybex), Dennis has also been the technical editor for over 100 titles, including all editions of *FileMaker Pro Bible* prior to *FileMaker Pro 7 Bible.*

Dennis resides in Sunnyvale, California, with his best friend — a Boston terrier named Spenser. You can find out more about him at his Web site at `http://homepage.mac.com/drcohen`.

In 1978, **Dr. Steven Schwartz** bought his first microcomputer, a new Apple II+. Determined to find a way to make money with it, he began writing software reviews, BASIC programs, and user tips for *Nibble* magazine. Shortly thereafter, he was made a contributing editor.

Over the past 20 years, Steve has written hundreds of articles for more than a dozen computer magazines. He currently writes for *Macworld* magazine. He was also a founding editor of *Software Digest* as well as a business editor for *MACazine.* From 1985 to 1990, he was the director of technical services for Funk Software.

Steve is the author of more than 40 books, including all editions of *Macworld ClarisWorks/AppleWorks Bible* and the *FileMaker Pro Bible* (Wiley); *Running Microsoft Office 2001* (Microsoft Press); *Visual QuickStart Guide for Internet Explorer 5 for Windows, Internet Explorer 5 for Macintosh, Entourage 2001 for Macintosh, CorelDraw 10 for Windows,* and *Office v.X for Macintosh* (Peachpit Press); and dozens of popular game strategy guides.

Steve has a Ph.D. in psychology and presently lives in the fictional town of Lizard Spit, Arizona, where he writes books and complains about the heat. His official Web site is `www.siliconwasteland.com`.

Credits

Acquisitions Editors
Terri Varveris/Tiffany Franklin

Senior Project Editor
Paul Levesque

Associate Project Editor
Jean Rogers

Technical Editor
Michael E. Cohen

Senior Copy Editor
Teresa Artman

Editorial Managers
Leah Cameron, Kevin Kirschner

Editorial Director, Development
Mary C. Corder

Vice President, Publisher
Andy Cummings

**Vice President & Executive
Group Publisher**
Richard Swadley

Project Coordinator
Kristie Rees

Graphics and Production Specialists
Beth Brooks
Andrea Dahl
Lauren Goddard
Denny Hager
Joyce Haughey
LeAndra Hosier
Stephanie D. Jumper
Barbara Moore
Alicia B. South

Quality Control Technician
John Greenough

Proofreading
TECHBOOKS Production Services

Indexing
Richard T. Evans

To my friends and family: in particular, Spenser—DRC

To my family—SAS

Preface

FileMaker Pro is a mature database product. We're not talking about some company's latest brainchild that is being foisted bug-laden onto an unsuspecting public. In its various incarnations and from its various publishers, this product has been known as FileMaker, FileMaker 2, FileMaker IV, FileMaker Pro, FileMaker Pro 2, 3, 4, 5, 5.5, 6, 7, 8 . . . and now, FileMaker Pro 8.5. FileMaker Pro has been around the block — and we've been in lock step with it.

Unlike many computer products that are periodically redefined by having drastic changes made to the program's focus (changing a simple text editor into a desktop publishing program, for example), FileMaker Pro's versions have all shown steady progression. This means that if you've used any version of FileMaker Pro — even one that is several years old — the information and experience that you've gained haven't been a waste of your time. Much of your knowledge can be applied directly to the current version of the program.

Although we've reviewed computer programs for more than 20 years for magazines such as *Macworld* and *PC World,* only a surprisingly few products have impressed either of us enough to stick with them over the years. FileMaker Pro is such a program. Apparently, much of the computer community agrees with this assessment because FileMaker Pro currently owns the vast majority of the Mac database market, and it's making steady inroads into the world of Windows. Because we assume that you own or use a copy of FileMaker Pro, you're in excellent company.

About This Book

FileMaker Pro 8.5 Bible is a different kind of computer book. First, it's not a manual. Many people don't like computer manuals — perhaps because they feel obligated to read a manual from cover to cover, or perhaps because manuals are designed to explain how features work rather than how to make a program work for you. *FileMaker Pro 8.5 Bible* is not a book you *must* read. Rather, it's a book we hope you'll *want* to read and reference because it provides easy-to-find and easy-to-understand explanations of the common tasks for which you bought or use FileMaker Pro in the first place. When you want to know how to use a particular program feature, you can use the extensive table of contents or the index to identify the section of the book you need to read.

Second, like previous incarnations of *FileMaker Pro Bible,* this is a cross-platform book. Whether you use a Macintosh or a Windows PC, the material in this book is applicable to you. Windows- and Mac-specific materials are clearly delineated so you never have to guess whether a particular procedure or explanation is relevant to you.

Note When commands, dialog titles, or other program elements are different between the two platforms, they are shown as *Macintosh item/Windows item* (such as ⌘+L/Ctrl+L).

Third, although we hope you'll find some of the material in this book entertaining, the primary mission of *FileMaker Pro 8.5 Bible* is to inform. We really want you to understand how FileMaker Pro works and to make it do what you want it to do. No matter where you turn in this book, if you find yourself with a puzzled look on your face after reading a section, we haven't done our job.

Finally, the philosophy of this book — as well as the other books in the *Bible* series from Wiley — is that you don't want or need a handful of books to learn all about a computer program: One book should suffice. *FileMaker Pro 8.5 Bible* is an all-in-one book that gives you a well-rounded knowledge of FileMaker Pro and FileMaker Pro 8 Advanced. You don't just learn *how* to perform an action; you also learn *when* and *why* you would perform that action. You can find almost anything you want to know about FileMaker Pro in this book.

Whom This Book Is For

FileMaker Pro 8.5 Bible is for anyone who uses version 8 or version 8.5 of FileMaker Pro or FileMaker Pro Advanced:

✦ If you're a beginning FileMaker Pro user, step-by-step instructions help you get up to speed quickly with explanations of how to use common (and not-so-common) FileMaker Pro features and procedures.

✦ If you're an intermediate or advanced FileMaker Pro user — someone who doesn't need much handholding — tips and insights in each chapter will help you get the most from FileMaker Pro. And you'll find the information provided in the sidebars to be handy additions for your FileMaker Pro toolbox.

How This Book Is Organized

Each chapter is self-contained. When you must perform a particular FileMaker Pro task, scan the table of contents to locate the chapter that addresses your needs. You can also flip through the pages of the book to find the chapter you need quickly. *FileMaker Pro 8.5 Bible* is divided into the following parts.

Quick Start: What's New in FileMaker Pro 8.5?

In this special Quick Start, we introduce the new features in FileMaker Pro 8.5 — namely Web Viewer objects and the script steps and functions that accompany them. Although Web Viewer objects are the only real feature update to the software, we think you'll find them quite powerful after you familiarize yourself with how they work. The examples in this Quick Start will help you develop your own creative uses for Web Viewer objects, and the steps walk you through the process of employing the new functions and script steps to achieve results not previously possible within FileMaker Pro. Flipping to this Quick Start is easy; just look for the largest section of gray along the pages' edges.

Part I: The Fundamentals

This part is a gentle introduction to database concepts, essential FileMaker Pro concepts and procedures, and what's new in FileMaker Pro 8.

Part II: Database Design Basics

This part instructs you in using the various design tools to construct databases and design different types of layouts.

Part III: Working with Databases

Here you will learn about working with databases: entering and editing data, searching for particular records, sorting, designing reports, and printing.

Part IV: Putting FileMaker Pro to Work

This part covers material that helps you make more productive use of FileMaker Pro. It isn't essential to learn about these features immediately, but you will want to tackle them after you're comfortable with the FileMaker Pro basics.

Part V: Mastering FileMaker Pro

Material in this part will interest more experienced FileMaker Pro users and would-be developers, including information on using relations and lookups to link databases; using FileMaker Pro in a network workgroup and setting security options; publishing databases on the Internet or a company intranet; sharing data via ODBC, JDBC, and XML; and enhancing FileMaker's capabilities with plug-ins.

Part VI: Developing Databases for Others to Use

This is where we tie together the pieces, advising you how to put together databases that others can use, either as custom solutions or commercial (including shareware) products. We discuss FileMaker Pro 8 Advanced's additional features and capabilities as well as how they augment your development efforts.

Part VII: Appendixes

The appendixes present all keyboard shortcuts for the Macintosh and Windows versions of FileMaker Pro 8; explain all the FileMaker Pro built-in functions; list additional resources to which you can turn to learn more about FileMaker Pro; and explain common computer, system software, database, and FileMaker Pro terms that you might not know.

Conventions Used in This Book

The book contains the following icons:

The New Feature icon identifies new features found in FileMaker Pro 8 and higher. All other features are available to FileMaker Pro 7 users.

The Note icon highlights a special point of interest about the topic being discussed—information that is not necessarily vital to performing a task. Look here if you're interested in achieving a more well-rounded knowledge of FileMaker Pro.

The Tip icon marks a timesaving shortcut or technique that will help you work smarter.

The Caution icon alerts you that the action or operation being described can cause problems if you aren't careful.

Mac icons make it easy to identify material that is specific to the Mac computer platform. All other material is relevant to *all* supported platforms.

Ditto for Windows, 2000 or XP.

This icon informs you that something discussed here can be found on the Web site that accompanies the book. Point your browser to www.wiley.com/compbooks/ filemaker8.5bible.

We use the Cross Reference icon to point you to a discussion elsewhere in the book where you can find additional information relevant to the current topic or task.

How to Use This Book

We won't tell you how to read this book. Reading and learning styles are all very personal. When Steve gets a new computer program, he frequently reads the manual from cover to cover before even installing the software. Of course, he'll be flattered if you read *FileMaker Pro 8.5 Bible* the same way—but we'll be surprised. Dennis, on the other hand, generally looks through any Read Me or QuickStart file that accompanies the software and does a quick scan of the manual while the software is installing. He expects that you will probably fall somewhere between his style and Steve's.

This book is written as a reference to all things FileMaker Pro. When you want to learn about defining fields, there's a specific chapter to which you can turn. If you just need to know how to use the spelling checker, you can flip to the table of contents or the index and find the pages where this feature is discussed. Most procedures are explained in step-by-step fashion so you can quickly accomplish even the most complex tasks. Thus, you can read this book like you would a novel, read just the chapters that interest you, or just use it as a quick reference to learn about a particular feature or procedure.

For those who prefer a little more direction than *whatever works for you,* some general guidelines are suggested in the following sections — arranged according to your level of computer expertise and FileMaker Pro experience.

However, we do make one general suggestion: *If at all possible, read this book with FileMaker Pro running and onscreen.* Sure, you can read about editing a user dictionary for the spelling checker while relaxing in the tub, but unless you have exceptional recall, what you read will be more meaningful if you're sitting in front of the computer. Additionally, many tasks involve multiple interface elements (dialogs, tools, and controls), and following along is a lot easier if you actually see the items being referenced.

For the beginner

Like the manuals of most computer programs, this book assumes you have a general grasp of the procedures necessary to use your computer, such as using the mouse, choosing commands from menus, using the Finder/Windows Explorer, and printing documents. If FileMaker Pro is your first program and you have not yet taken the time to work through the manuals that came with your computer, stop reading now. It's time to drag out the manuals for your computer, printer, and system software. After you fill in the gaps in your computer education, you'll feel more confident and comfortable tackling FileMaker Pro and any other programs you eventually use.

If you're relatively new to computers and FileMaker Pro, start by reading all of Part I. This part will acquaint you with database concepts and the FileMaker Pro basics. Next, work through the tutorial presented in Chapter 4. This chapter gently leads you through the process of creating your first database, which is a relatively full-featured address book in which you can record your business and personal contacts. Finish by reading the remaining chapters of Part II (Chapters 5–7) and at least the next three chapters of Part III (Chapters 8–10). This material will provide you with a sufficient grounding in FileMaker Pro concepts and features to enable you to tackle basic database projects. Then, as you find it necessary to explore additional program features, such as printing or creating calculations, you can simply jump to the appropriate chapter.

The more advanced stuff is saved for Parts IV and V. Although you'll eventually want to check out the material in those parts, too, we've purposely separated the advanced matters from the basics in order to keep new users from being overwhelmed. Finally, if you're planning to create databases for others to use, check out Part VI. In fact, much of the material in Part VI can be useful to you for personal database projects, assuming that the projects are fairly complex.

For the more experienced computer user

If you're familiar with databases, you can safely skip Chapter 1. The material in this chapter is very basic and is probably second nature to you. If FileMaker Pro is your first database program, however, you should at least skim through the material in Chapter 1.

Chapter 2 is a must-read for every FileMaker Pro user. Many FileMaker Pro tasks, such as using the tools, are discussed here.

Parts II and III contain the real meat-and-potatoes chapters for new FileMaker Pro users. Many of the topics covered in these parts are at least touched upon in Chapter 4. After completing this tutorial chapter, you might feel sufficiently confident to tackle some of your own database projects. You can treat the remainder of the book as reference material and read it as needed.

For an owner of a previous version of FileMaker Pro

As mentioned earlier, FileMaker (in its various incarnations) has always worked basically the same. Through the years, however, new features and capabilities have been added. If you are familiar with an older version of FileMaker, you should pay particular attention to material in the following chapters:

- ✦ The Quick Start covers all the new features in FileMaker Pro 8.5. Before you get started with these features, you should be familiar with creating and modifying layouts (Chapter 6). However, to experience fully the flexibility and power that Web Viewer objects offer, you should be familiar with creating calculations (Chapter 14) and using ScriptMaker (Chapter 15).

- ✦ Chapter 3 provides a brief description of all changes and new features introduced in FileMaker Pro 8.

- ✦ Chapter 14 explains how to create calculations. For a complete reference to all FileMaker Pro built-in functions, you should review Appendix C as well.

- ✦ Chapter 15 discusses ScriptMaker and explains how to automate many common tasks.

- ✦ Chapter 16 explains the procedures for moving data between FileMaker Pro and other programs.

✦ Chapter 18 discusses FileMaker Pro's relational and lookup capabilities, enabling you to use data in the current database from another table, either in the same database file or in an external database file.

✦ Chapter 19 explains how FileMaker Pro works on a network and also shows how to create accounts and privilege sets to control accessibility for different users.

✦ Chapter 20 tells how to use Instant Web Publishing to host databases on the World Wide Web or a corporate intranet.

✦ Chapter 21 delves into more advanced database connectivity and import/export issues, explaining how to use ODBC, JDBC, XML, and XSLT to share data with non-FileMaker data sources.

✦ Chapter 22 shows you how to use plug-ins to expand FileMaker's capabilities.

✦ Chapter 23 introduces the things you should consider when creating a database for others to use.

✦ Chapters 24, 25, and 26 cover the additional capabilities present in the FileMaker Pro 8 Advanced version of FileMaker. This includes the Script Debugger, Database Design Reports, custom functions, file maintenance, and the Developer Utilities.

Example Files

We've included the critical files for this book as well as other examples from FileMaker, Inc., on the Web site accompanying this book. You can download these files by browsing to www.wiley.com/compbooks/filemaker8.5bible. See Appendix F for more details.

Acknowledgments

There are many other people who should get some credit and are too numerous to mention by name, but especially deserving of thanks are Michael Cohen for a fastidious technical review, Paul Levesque and Jean Rogers for coordinating the project so smoothly, and Teresa Artman for her careful copy edit. As a group, Dennis would like to thank all the folks at FileMaker, Inc. (especially his friends on the development and testing teams) for producing such a great enhancement of the product. The new features and continued high reliability make this, at least in his opinion, a great polishing of the FileMaker Pro 7 product, which in turn was the biggest single advance in FileMaker's power since the initial release—and you made it even easier to use.

Contents at a Glance

Contents

What's New in FileMaker Pro 8.5?

Usually, when FileMaker, Inc., introduces an upgrade (as opposed to an update) for FileMaker Pro, the user community encounters numerous enhancements offering new functionality and, occasionally, a few changes impacting existing databases.

FileMaker Pro 8.5 is a little different in that there is only *one* enhancement (okay, two if you include a universal binary offering native performance to owners of Intel-based Macintoshes). But that one new feature, the Web Viewer layout object, is so significant an advance that we think most users will find what it offers a compelling reason to upgrade.

The thrust of this Quick Start is to discuss the new FileMaker Pro 8.5 Web Viewer functionality. After briefly introducing Web Viewer layout objects, we walk you through creating, using, customizing, and leveraging them.

Note
Before you get started with the new features in FileMaker Pro 8.5, you should be familiar with creating and modifying layouts (Chapter 6). However, to experience fully the flexibility and power Web Viewer objects offer, you'll also find it helpful to understand creating calculations (Chapter 14) and using ScriptMaker (Chapter 15).

Although Web Viewer objects are new, we already see some revolutionary possibilities for their use. But no one (and that includes us) has a corner on the imagination market, and breakthrough functionality really blooms when it gets out into the "real world." We're sure that some of you will come up with applications for Web Viewers that neither we nor FileMaker, Inc., have foreseen — and that still others will build upon.

Introducing the Web Viewer Layout Object

In its most simplistic guise, a Web Viewer is just a rectangular object on your layout that displays a Web page. This basic use means that you no longer need a script that tells the user's default Web browser to display a specified page, and while using a database, you don't have to switch from FileMaker Pro to the Web browser application. Figure QS-1 shows how much more compact and convenient a Web viewer makes displaying associated Web content compared to the "old" method.

 Note

Just because a Web Viewer displays Web content like a browser doesn't mean that it *is* a browser. You don't get History or Address Bar functionality, nor does it spawn additional Web Viewers (if the Web page spawns a new window, that window opens in the user's default Web browser).

Different uses for Web Viewers

The kind folks at FileMaker include a sample database (Web Viewer Example, in the Extras folder within your FileMaker Pro 8.5 application directory), that exemplifies some of the myriad cool things you can do with Web Viewer objects, such as

- ✦ Using data in your tables to access maps and driving directions via Google Maps or MapQuest
- ✦ Tracking shipments via FedEx
- ✦ Checking on stock activity via Google Finance

Similarly, you can use a Web Viewer to chart data without having to export it to Excel (or some other spreadsheet/charting application) or to display Flash and PDF content.

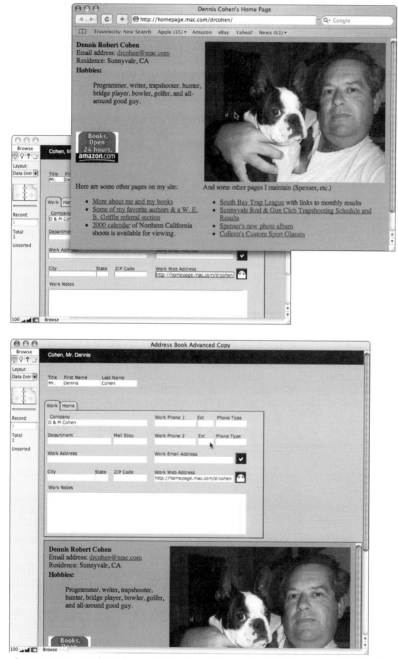

Figure QS-1: A FileMaker window for data and a Web browser window for the Internet component (top) versus one window for your data and an associated Web page (bottom).

Figures QS-2 through QS-5 show just a few of the demonstrations available via the Web Viewer example database, located in the English Extras/Examples subdirectory of the FileMaker Pro 8.5 application directory.

In the following examples, you see:

✦ Address data that's connected to a MapQuest search

✦ A Web viewer that displays updated information about a stock

✦ Tracking information for a FedEx shipment

✦ A Web viewer that displays a data chart

Figure QS-2: The Web Viewer Example Database showing a MapQuest display for a record's address data.

Figure QS-3: The Web Viewer Example Database reporting a stock's performance.

Figure QS-4: The Web Viewer Example Database tracking a FedEx shipment.

Figure QS-5: The Web Viewer Example Database charting data without leaving FileMaker.

To give you a starting point when including Web Viewers in your layouts, FileMaker includes templates for the example viewers (and a few others) as predefined choices in the Web Viewer Setup dialog, which we visit in great detail later in this Quick Start.

Working with Web Viewer objects in scripts

Generically, a Web Viewer is a rectangle with an associated calculation that resolves to a URL. FileMaker even encodes the URL string for most basic cases (encoding spaces, percent signs, and so on) for you.

The addition of a new layout object property, Name, makes accessing Web Viewer objects via script steps easy. FileMaker 8's (and earlier versions') very useful Size palette has morphed into FileMaker 8.5's Info palette, adding an Object Name field to the top, as shown in Figure QS-6. It is accessible via the View ⇨ Object Info menu choice.

Note   Object names must be unique within a given layout. FileMaker will warn you if names are not unique and focus will be returned to the Info palette's Object Name field. If you close the Info palette with a name that is not unique, that name will not be committed. The maximum length for an object name is 100 characters.

Figure QS-6: The Size palette has evolved into the Info palette.

By adding the Name property to layout objects, FileMaker 8.5 does more than just make Web Viewer objects accessible. You can now navigate, via scripting, to any layout object, such as a button object or a tab control. The script step that leverages named objects is the brand new *Go to Object* script step. Additionally, the new *Set Web Viewer* script step allows you to control a Web Viewer's behavior in your scripts.

Additionally, five new functions have been added to the Calculation dialog:

✦ **LayoutObjectNames (filename; layoutName)** returns a list of all named objects of the specified layout in the referenced file.

✦ **Get(ActiveLayoutObjectName)** returns the name of the active layout object on the layout currently referenced in the calculation.

✦ **GetLayoutObjectAttribute(objectName; attributeName {; repetitionNumber; portalRowNumber})** returns the attributes specified by attributeName for the objectName object on the layout currently referenced in the calculation.

✦ **GetAsURLEncoded(text)** returns URL encoding of the passed text.

✦ **List(field {; field...})** returns a carriage return–delimited list of the (non-blank) values in the referenced field(s).

We delve into the details of these new functions later in this Quick Start.

Creating a Web Viewer Layout Object

You create a Web Viewer object on your layout in pretty much the same way you create any other layout object. You enter Layout mode and select the layout to which you wish to add the object (from the Layout pop-up menu/drop-down list) or create a new layout (Layouts ➪ New Layout). Then you select the tool from the Tools palette for the object you wish to create and drag out the bounding rectangle for your object on the layout surface. (For a more detailed look at working with layouts, see Chapter 6.)

At this point, FileMaker walks you through specifying your object's characteristics. The following steps walk you through a very simple example of creating a layout with a Web Viewer object that displays the Work URL (if one exists) for entries in your Address Book Advanced database (available from the book's Web page, if you haven't walked through creating the Address Book Advanced database in Chapter 4 of this book).

STEPS: Creating a Layout with a Web Viewer

1. With Address Book Advanced open, switch to Layout mode either by choosing View ➪ Layout Mode, by clicking the Layout button in the Tools sidebar, by choosing Layout from the Mode pop-up, or by pressing ⌘+L/Ctrl+L.

2. Choose Layouts ➪ New Layout/Report (or press ⌘+N/Ctrl+N).

   The New Layout/Report Assistant appears (see Figure QS-7).

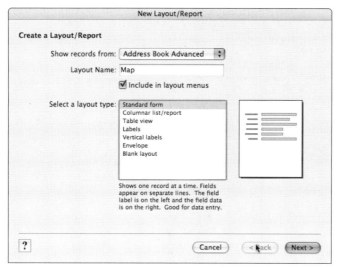

Figure QS-7: The opening screen of the New Layout/Report Assistant.

3. Type **Map** in the Layout Name text box.

   This will be the name of the layout you'll employ to view a map of your contact's location.

4. Because you want FileMaker to format the fields for you as well as set the background colors, select Standard form as the layout type and then click Next to continue.

5. On the Specify Fields screen (see Figure QS-8), select and move the following fields to the Layout Fields list: First Name, Last Name, Work Address, Work City, Work State, and Work ZIP Code.

   To move a field to the Layout fields list, select the field and click the Move button. You can also move a field by double-clicking its name. To simultaneously move multiple contiguous fields, hold down Shift as you select the first and last fields; then click Move. You can also ⌘+click to select multiple fields one at a time.

   You can combine these selection techniques as follows: Click Title, Shift+click Work Notes, and then ⌘+click/Ctrl+click Last Modified and Full Name to select all the fields at one time. Then click Move.

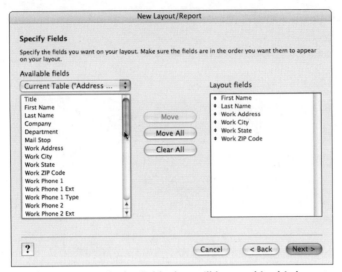

Figure QS-8: Specify the fields that will be used in this layout.

6. Click Next to continue.

> **Note**
>
> In this and other FileMaker Pro dialog lists, you reorder items by dragging the small, double-headed arrow to the left of the item you're repositioning.

7. On the Select a Theme screen (see Figure QS-9), choose a color scheme and field styles.

   For this database, we selected the Soft Gray Screen. Feel free to choose a different screen theme if you want, but be aware that different themes might employ different fonts and sizes, so the placement and arrangement of items might not match our example.

8. Click Finish, and the new layout is generated for you.

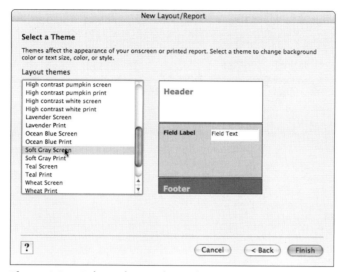

Figure QS-9: Select a layout theme here.

9. To make room for displaying the map, make the Body section taller by clicking Body and then clicking and dragging the dotted dividing line between the Body part and the Footer part.

10. Select the Web Viewer tool (the globe between the tab control and button tools) in the Tools sidebar and drag out a rectangle to enclose your map. The Web Viewer Setup dialog appears.

11. We're going to use the Google Maps (US) template from the Choose a Website list. We construct the Web Address calculation by clicking the arrow buttons to the right of the Address, City, State, and Zip Code text boxes, choosing Specify Field from the pop-up menu that appears, and selecting the appropriate field for each from the Specify Field dialog boxes that appear (Work Address for Address, Work City for City, Work State for State, and Work ZIP Code for Zip Code).

The Web Viewer Setup dialog should now look like Figure QS-10.

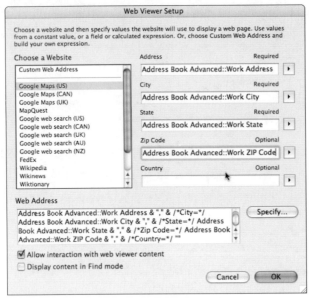

Figure QS-10: Fill in the text boxes for the Google Maps template.

12. Click OK and the calculation appears in the rectangle that you drew in Step 10. Your layout should now resemble Figure QS-11. Notice that FileMaker displays the URL template to be used in the Web Viewer rectangle.

13. Return to Browse mode (View ⇨ Browse Mode, ⌘+B/Ctrl+B, click the Tool sidebar's Browse button, or choose Browse from the mode pop-up menu at the bottom of your layout's window).

Note   If you haven't set your FileMaker Preferences to automatically save layout changes, FileMaker will prompt you to save your changes before switching to Browse mode.

Now, when you access a record that includes a Work Address, you will see a layout resembling that shown in Figure QS-12. (You'll see a different address and map, of course.)

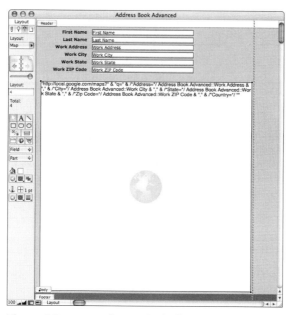

Figure QS-11: Your layout, including your new Web Viewer object.

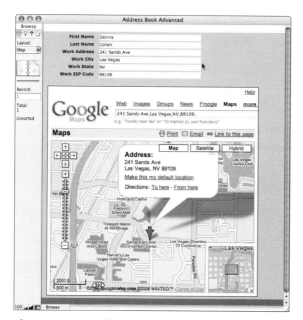

Figure QS-12: Voilà! Your layout now displays a map to the contact's work address.

Displaying a map in a contact database is, inarguably, a useful feature. But maps are just the tip of the iceberg. FileMaker supplies the templates for a number of very popular sites, including Google Maps, MapQuest, FedEx, Wikipedia, Google Web Search, Wikinews, Wiktionary, Wikibooks, and Wikisource. By taking advantage of the Custom Web Address selection and a knowledge of the query for a Web site whose template isn't included, you can employ a Web Viewer to suit your particular desires. For example, to find a movie title in the Internet Movie Database (IMDb), your URL could be "`http://www.imdb.com/find?q=`" & Title & "`;s=tt`". A very simple layout demonstrating this custom implementation is shown in Figure QS-13. The sidebar, "Inside the Web Viewer object," fills you in on how your calculation is encoded before being passed to your platform's Web engine (IE on Windows and Safari on Mac).

Figure QS-13: If you know the query format for other Web databases, you can create custom Web queries.

Tip You can copy graphics from the page displayed inside your Web Viewer objects to container fields on your layout. Mac users can use drag and drop, and both Mac and Windows users can employ copy and paste. Just right-click (or Control+click on a Mac with a one-button mouse) the graphic in the Web Viewer and choose Copy Image from the shortcut menu that appears. Then click in your container field and choose Edit ⇨ Paste (⌘+V/Ctrl+V).

Note When creating a Custom Web address calculation, FileMaker still displays the last template chosen rather than an empty calculation box. Clear any part of that template you don't wish to employ in your custom calculation (up to all of it) and specify your calculation. Clicking the Specify button displays a standard Specify Calculation dialog containing the template, ready for your modification. The URL must include the protocol (for example, `http://` or `file://`) and must be enclosed in quotes.

Inside the Web Viewer object

A Web Viewer object is defined by two things: its bounding rectangle and a calculation that, when evaluated, produces a URL to be loaded into that rectangle. FileMaker includes a simple URL encoder to remove the hassles of encoding certain characters (such as spaces to `%20`, percent signs to `%25`, and the like) to conform with URL encoding. We say "simple" because it doesn't attempt to handle every conceivable case, just the everyday ones. The rules for encoding are as follows:

✦ Letters, digits, and the following punctuation characters will never be encoded:
`-_.~!*'();:@=+$,/?[]`

✦ Ampersands (&) will be encoded only when followed by a space.

✦ Pound signs (#) will be encoded only when followed by a digit.

✦ Backslash (\) and percent (%) characters will always be encoded.

✦ Any character not included in the above will always be encoded.

Scripting Web Viewer Objects

The good folks at FileMaker, Inc., didn't stop with just supplying Web Viewer objects. They included two new script steps, one useful with all layout objects (Go to Object) and one specific to Web Viewer objects (Set Web Viewer). Both of these script steps rely on yet another new FileMaker 8.5 feature, *layout objects,* for their specification. Additionally, five new functions (which I introduce earlier in "Working with Web Viewer objects in scripts,") are available in the Calculation Editor to deal with named layout objects, and all these new functions can prove quite useful when scripting Web Viewers.

For example, you might use a script to retrieve the name of the currently active layout object and have the script override the Web Viewer's default URL calculation based on the active object (for example, use home address fields for the map if your Address Book Advanced database is displaying home data and work address fields for the map when on the Work tab). But, you have an easier way to achieve this goal. The following steps walk you through a simple example of using the new GetLayoutObjectAttribute function to display the map appropriate to the Home or Work address, depending upon which tab is frontmost.

STEPS: Creating a Conditional Web Viewer Display

1. With Address Book Advanced open, switch to Layout mode either by choosing View ⇨ Layout Mode, by clicking the Layout button in the Tools sidebar, by choosing Layout from the Mode pop-up, or by pressing ⌘+L/Ctrl+L.

2. Choose the Data Entry layout from the Layout pop-up menu/drop-down list in the Tools sidebar if it isn't already showing.

3. Choose Layouts ⇨ Duplicate Layout.

   A new layout, Data Entry Copy appears.

Note The layout duplication happens so quickly that you may think nothing occurred, but checking the Layout pop-up menu/drop-down list will show you that you're now working on a copy of the layout.

4. If the Info palette isn't visible, choose View ➪ Object Info.

5. Resize the layout's body part, making it tall enough to hold your Web Viewer object (we made ours 14 inches tall). The fastest way to resize the body part is to click the Body label and enter **14** in the Info palette's height field, as shown in Figure QS-14.

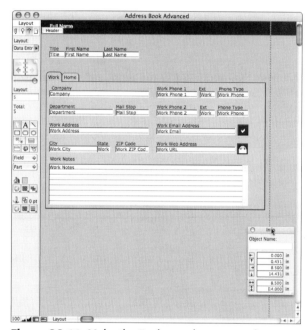

Figure QS-14: Make the Body part large enough to accommodate your Web Viewer object.

6. Click the Work tab of your layout's tab control and enter **WorkTab** in the Info palette's Object Name text box.

Note

If the Work tab is not frontmost, you'll need to click twice — once to make it frontmost and once to select it.

7. Click the Home tab and enter **HomeTab** in the Info palette's Object Name text box.

8. Create a Web Viewer object using the Google Maps (US) template (as described earlier in "STEPS: Creating a Layout with a Web Viewer"). In the Web Viewer Setup dialog that appears, click the arrow to the right of the Address text box and choose Specify Calculation from the pop-up menu that appears.

9. In the Specify Calculation dialog that appears, select the If function from the list of functions in the righthand list.

10. For the *test* parameter, select the GetLayoutObjectAttribute function, filling its parameters as shown in Figure QS-15 (**"WorkTab"** and **"isFrontTabPanel"** — remember to enclose the arguments in quotes). For *resultOne*, select the Work Address item from the field list, and for *resultTwo*, select the Home Address item from the field list.

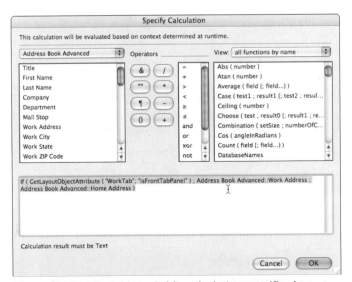

Figure QS-15: The Address field's calculation specification.

11. Repeat Steps 9 and 10 for the City, State, and Zip Code text boxes, using the work and home city, state, and ZIP fields in place of the address fields.

When you're done, the following settings appear in your Web Viewer Setup dialog:

- **Address:** Advanced::Home Address)
- **City:** Advanced::Home City)
- **State:** Advanced::Home State)
- **Zip code:** Advanced::Home ZIP Code)
- **Web Address text box:** The code you see appears as follows:

```
"http://local.google.com/maps?" & "q=" & /*Address=*/ If
( GetLayoutObjectAttribute ( "WorkTab"; "isFrontTabPanel") ; Address
Book Advanced::Work Address ; Address Book Advanced::Home
Address ) & "," & /*City=*/ If ( GetLayoutObjectAttribute ( "WorkTab";
"isFrontTabPanel") ; Address Book Advanced::Work City ; Address
Book Advanced::Home City) & "," & /*State=*/ If
( GetLayoutObjectAttribute ( "WorkTab"; "isFrontTabPanel" ) ; Address
Book Advanced::Work State ; Address Book Advanced::Home State) &
"," & /*Zip Code=*/ If ( GetLayoutObjectAttribute ( "WorkTab";
"isFrontTabPanel" ) ; Address Book Advanced::Work ZIP Code ;
Address Book Advanced::Home ZIP Code) & "," & /*Country=*/ ""
```

Tip

If you want the Web Viewer to be functional in Find mode, select the Display Content in Find Mode check box at the bottom of the Web Viewer Setup dialog.

12. Click OK.

13. Set your Web Viewer's dimensions to 8 inches by 6 inches, 0.667 inches from the left and 6.25 inches from the top of your layout if you want to match our layout.

Figure QS-16 shows the Info palette display when our Web Viewer (map) is selected.

Note

If the Info palette isn't open, open it by choosing View ➪ Object Info.

Figure QS-16: The Web Viewer object's Info palette.

Now, when you save your layout and enter Browse mode, your layout will display the map appropriate to the frontmost tab panel (Work or Home), as shown in Figure QS-17.

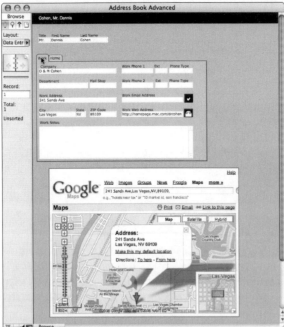

Figure QS-17: The Web Viewer displays the map for the frontmost tab panel's address (Home or Work).

Note

We apologize for the 75% zoom-factor views used for some of the screen shots in this Quick Start; however, production constraints limit the screen resolution we're allowed to employ to 1024x768, and that's a pretty small screen by today's hardware standards and for the amount of data that will be displayed without scrolling on the Web pages accessed via the FileMaker-supplied Web Viewer templates. We want to illustrate the salient features in the example layouts, and reducing the zoom factor is the only way we can fit the material into the permissible dimensions.

Of course, there's more than one way to skin a cat. This particular feline—selecting from two or more URLs for your Web Viewer to send—can also be accomplished via a script. The following steps walk you through using a script to override a Web Viewer's default URL based on which tab panel is frontmost.

STEPS: Scripting a Conditional Web Viewer Display

1. Perform Steps 1 through 7 in the previous steps list, "STEPS: Creating a Conditional Web Viewer Display."

2. Create a Web Viewer that uses the Google Maps (US) template, but you don't need to specify any parameters to the calculation.

Note

You can, of course, specify a default address if you want to. For example, your application might default to the Work Address if the layout's most frequent use will be for work locations.

3. Name your Web Viewer object map in the Info palette's Object Name text box and size it to 8 inches by 6 inches, 0.667 inches from the left, and 6.25 inches from the top of your layout.

4. Choose Scripts ➪ ScriptMaker.

   The Define Scripts dialog appears.

5. Click the New button to open the Edit Script dialog, shown in Figure QS-18.

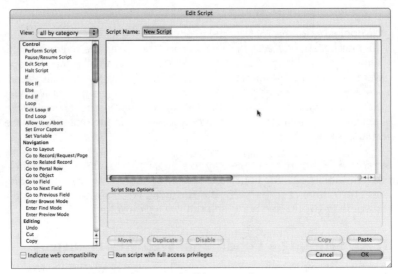

Figure QS-18: This is where you build your script.

6. Enter a name for your script in the text box at the top of the dialog. (We called ours Scripted Map.)

7. Double-click the If script step in the script step list on the left side of the Edit Script dialog.

8. Click Specify to call up the Specify Calculation dialog.

9. Double-click the GetLayoutObjectAttribute function in the function list on the right.

10. Replace the *objectName* placeholder with **"homeTab"** and the *attributeName* placeholder with **"isFrontTabPanel"**. Remove the braces and optional *repetitionNumber* and *portalRowNumber* parameters.

Your calculation should now look like the one shown in Figure QS-19.

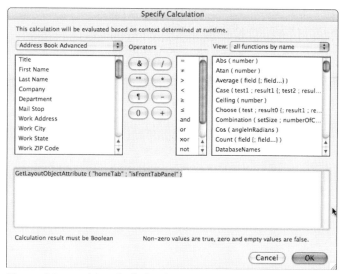

Figure QS-19: This calculation lets your script select the URL to generate.

11. Click OK to return to the Edit Script dialog; then add the Set Web Viewer script step (in the Miscellaneous category).

12. Click Specify to open the "Set Web Viewer" Options dialog, shown in Figure QS-20.

Figure QS-20: The "Set Web Viewer Options" dialog.

13. Enter **map** in the Object Name text box and choose Go to URL from the Action pop-up menu/drop-down list.

    The "Set Web Viewer – Go to URL" Options dialog, shown in Figure QS-21, appears. Notice that this dialog is virtually indistinguishable from the Set Web Viewer dialog with which you're already familiar.

14. Fill in the Address, City, State, and Zip Code text boxes with the Home Address, Home City, Home State, and Home ZIP Code fields, respectively.

    That is, choose Specify Field from the pop-up menu that appears when you click the arrow to the right of the text box, select the appropriate field from the Specify Field dialog's field list, and then click OK.

15. Click OK to dismiss the "Set Web Viewer – Go to URL" Options dialog.

16. Click OK to dismiss the "Set Web Viewer" Options dialog.

17. Add an Else script step.

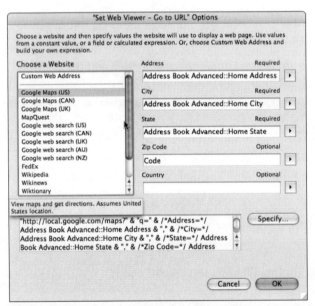

Figure QS-21: Set your destination URL options in this dialog.

18. Repeat Steps 11 through 16, replacing the Home fields with the corresponding Work fields in Step 14.

19. The Edit Script dialog should now look like Figure QS-22.

20. Click OK to dismiss the Edit Script dialog and OK to dismiss the Define Scripts dialog.

21. Add a button to the layout. In the Button Setup dialog that appears, select the Perform Script action and click the Specify button.

See Chapter 15 for more on creating buttons on the layout.

22. In the "Specify Script" Options dialog that appears, select the Scripted Map script you just created and click OK. Then click OK to dismiss the Button Setup dialog.

23. Put a label on your new button. (We call ours Map It.)

24. Your layout should now look similar to Figure QS-23, the degree of similarity depending upon how you size and place your button. Return to Browse mode to try it out.

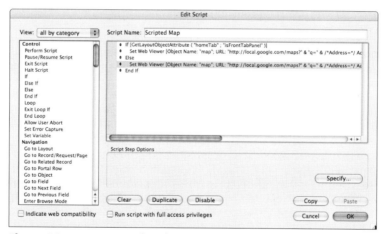

Figure QS-22: Your completed script.

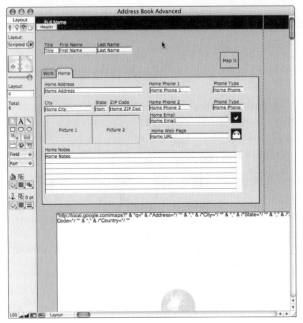

Figure QS-23: Your layout is ready for use.

You'll notice that, initially, the Map shows Google's default map of North America with a note that you haven't entered an address it can resolve. When you click the Map It button, your Web Viewer recontacts Google Maps (US) and updates the display to reflect the address in the current record. This map display will remain until you change records (at which point the default Google map reappears) or you click the Map It button.

We believe that the conditional approach is best suited to this particular example, but the scripted variation could be more useful in situations in which more than two options are possible, particularly if you supply a default Web Viewer URL (maybe a map to a company's corporate Web Site with the script providing maps to branch offices for individual employee's personnel records).

New Functions and Script Steps in FileMaker Pro 8.5

As noted earlier in this Quick Start, five new functions are available for use in calculations. You've seen one example of using the GetLayoutObjectAttribute function in the above conditional Web Viewer demonstrations and have also seen one use of the Set Web Viewer script step. We now present the specifications for the new functions and script steps.

Presenting FileMaker's five new functions

You might think, "Only five new functions in this upgrade? What a rip!" But you would be underestimating just how much new functionality these five functions bring to you, the FileMaker user. The following function descriptions are followed by simple examples in a FileMaker database (`NewFunctions.fp7`) that is available on this book's Web site. The functions are as follows:

✦ **LayoutObjectNames (** *filename*; *layoutName***)** returns a carriage return–delimited list of named objects on the specified layout. The database *filename* must be open on the computer where the function is evaluated (but can be opened as a client).

If the object is a group, tab control, or portal containing other named objects, those subordinate objects will be enclosed within angle brackets (<>).

✦ **Get (***ActiveLayoutObjectName***)** returns the name of the active object on the current layout (or an empty string if the active object is unnamed).

✦ **GetLayoutObjectAttribute (** *objectName* ; *attribute* {; *repetitionNumber* ; *portalRowNumber* } **)** returns the value of the requested attribute for the specified object on the current layout. If the option *repetitionNumber* and/or *portalRowNumber* parameters are specified for a field or portal object, the result applies to that repetition or portal row. FileMaker 8.5's implementation of GetLayoutObjectAttribute supports the following attributes:

- **objectType:** Tells FileMaker to return (in English) one of the following text literals: `field`, `text`, `graphic`, `line`, `rectangle`, `rounded rectangle`, `oval`, `group`, `button group`, `portal`, `tab panel`, `web viewer`, `unknown`.

- **isFrontTabPanel:** Tells FileMaker to return True (1) if the object in question is the frontmost tab panel in its tab control object.

- **hasFocus:** Tells FileMaker to return True (1) if the specified object has the focus (that is, is the object on which copy, paste, and keyboard activity operate). Only fields, tab panels, portals, button groups, and Web Viewer objects can have the focus. Note that if a portal row is selected, hasFocus returns True for the portal. (hasFocus is not supported by Instant Web Publishing.)

- **containsFocus:** Tells FileMaker to return True (1) if the object has the focus or contains an object that has the focus. (This attribute isn't supported by Instant Web Publishing.)

- **left:** Returns the object's left edge coordinate (in pixels).

- **right:** Returns the object's right edge coordinate (in pixels).

- **top:** Returns the object's top edge coordinate (in pixels).

- **bottom:** Returns the object's bottom edge coordinate (in pixels).

- **width:** Returns the object's width (in pixels).

- **height:** Returns the object's height (in pixels).

- **rotation:** Returns the object's rotation (in degrees).

- **bounds:** Returns the left, top, right, and bottom edge coordinates and the rotation for the object as a space-separated list.

- **startpoint:** Returns the horizontal and vertical coordinates for a line object's startpoint.

- **endpoint:** Returns the horizontal and vertical coordinates for a line object's endpoint.

- **source:** Returns the current URL of a Web Viewer, the fully qualified field name for a field, the text of a text object, the table name of a portal, the image (as container data) in a graphic, or an empty string for any other object.

- **content:** Returns the contents of an object (HTML source and images for a Web Viewer object, the formatted data within fields, the text of a text object, the image data as a container data type for graphics, and an empty string for any other object).

- **enclosingObject:** Returns the name (if the object is named) of the enclosing layout object (which can be a group, tab panel, or portal).

- **containedObjects:** Returns a list of named objects within the requested object (only groups, portals, and tab panels can contain other objects).

Note

The hasFocus, containsFocus, source, and content attributes behave slightly differently when GetLayoutObjectAttribute is called via Instant Web Publishing. Rather than the focus being current based upon a user tabbing to another field, editing a field, and so on, Instant Web Publishing returns the value based upon when the Web browser last loaded the page. Additionally, source and content both return the same value, a URL.

✦ **GetAsURLEncoded (*text*)** returns the URL encoding of the *text* parameter. Characters in *text* are first converted to UTF-8 and then encoded in compliance with URL encoding standards as described at www.w3.org/ International/0-URL-code.html. A side effect of the encoding operation is that any applied text styling (size, color, and so on) is removed.

✦ **List (*field { ; field...} *)** returns a carriage return–delimited list consisting of the contents of the (non-container) fields passed as arguments. If any arguments are repeating fields, the list consists of repetitions, each repetition in the list consisting of the corresponding repetition(s) of the arguments.

Introducing FileMaker 8.5's new script steps

In addition to the five functions listed in the preceding section, FileMaker 8.5 adds two new script steps: Go to Object and Set Web Viewer.

Go to Object

Purpose: To allow you to position the focus to any named layout object.

Options: Specify

Like the Go to Field and Go to Layout script steps, Go to Object is grouped in the Navigation category. When you add this script step and click its Specify button, the "Go to Object" Options dialog appears (Figure QS-24). You can enter either a literal value (such as the default **1** that appears in the Repetition text box) or click the corresponding Specify button to create a calculation that resolves to an object name (a text value) and/or a repetition number (a numeric value).

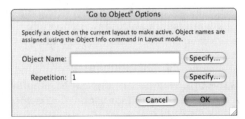

Figure QS-24: The "Go to Object" Options dialog.

Set Web Viewer

Purpose: To provide control over a Web Viewer object by (re)loading the viewer's default URL, loading a new URL, moving backward or forward through the viewer's session history, or reloading the currently viewed URL.

Options: Specify

Located in the Miscellaneous category, Set Web Viewer allows your script to control any instance of a (named) Web Viewer object. When added to your script, clicking the step's Specify button calls up the "Set Web Viewer" Options dialog shown in Figure QS-25. You choose your desired Web Viewer action from the Action pop-up menu/drop-down list and use either the Object Name text box or its associated Specify button to designate the Web Viewer object you wish to control.

Figure QS-25: The "Set Web Viewer" Options dialog with its Action pop-up menu displayed.

Using the New Functions and Script Steps

As promised previously, we include a sample database (NewFunctions.fp7) on the book's Web site. The following discussion walks you through the database's design and usage.

The NewFunctions database is a little unusual (okay, more than a little) in that its purpose is not the storage and retrieval of records. Rather, its sole layout functions more like a spreadsheet or calculator. You enter a value into an input field and click a button to display results in the other two fields. Figure QS-26 shows the NewFunctions database's layout in Layout mode.

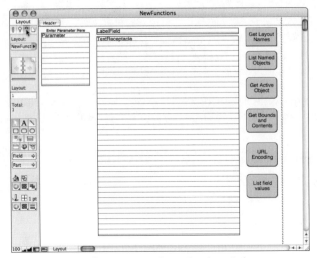

Figure QS-26: The NewFunctions database's layout.

The LayoutObjectNames function

The Get Layout Names button doesn't directly demonstrate a new FileMaker 8.5 function but returns the list of layouts in the Web Viewer Example database that accompanies FileMaker 8.5 (you must have the Web Viewer Example database open when clicking Get Layout Names or List Named Objects).

Assuming that FileMaker, Inc., has not modified the Web Viewer Example database between the time we wrote this and the time you got your copy, clicking Get Layout Names results in the display shown in Figure QS-27.

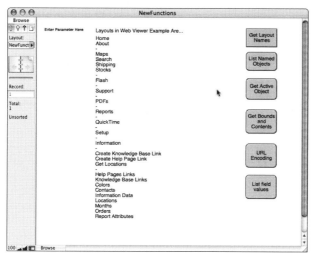

Figure QS-27: The list of layouts in Web Viewer Example appear here.

Either type, paste, or drag the layout name that interests you into the Enter Parameter Here field and then click List Named Objects to see how many objects FileMaker, Inc., named in that layout and what they were named.

As you'll note, not that many were named — actually, only the Web Viewer objects — and they weren't given very descriptive names. We trust you'll give your objects more meaningful names, as well as naming more navigable objects (tab panels, buttons, and so on). Figure QS-28 shows the result of clicking List Named Objects for the Maps layout.

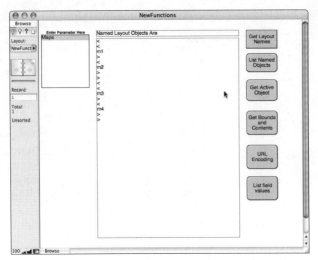

Figure QS-28: The Web Viewer Example Maps layout's named objects.

The List Named Objects button performs the ListNamedObjects script, shown in Figure QS-29. We could have shortened the script a bit by consolidating some Set Variable and Set Field steps, but we believe storing the function's result in a variable is better from a pedagogic perspective and, as you'll see in later examples, allows more flexibility when using the result. The script steps are as follows:

1. Set a label variable to a descriptive string.

2. Go to the parameter field, which contains the name of the layout you want to examine.

3. Set a layout name variable to the contents of the active field.

4. Set a named objects variable to the result of calling the new LayoutObjectNames function.

5. Store the label variable's contents in LabelField.

6. Store the namedObjects variable's contents in the (large) TextReceptacle field.

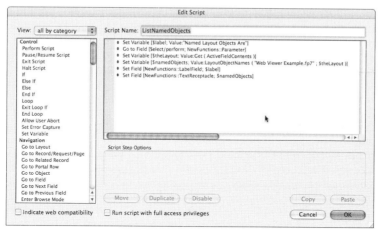

Figure QS-29: The ListNamedObjects script.

The ActiveLayoutObjectName script

We now move on to the examples that do not depend on Web Viewer Example being open. The Get Active Object button performs the ActiveLayoutObjectName script, shown in Figure QS-30.

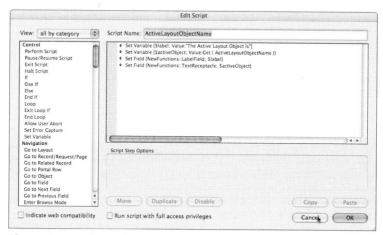

Figure QS-30: The ActiveLayoutObjectName script.

The ActiveLayoutObjectName script returns, in the TextReceptacle field, the name of the active object on the current layout (an empty string is returned if the active object is not a named object).

ActiveLayoutObjectName is a very simple script that does the following:

1. Sets a variable to hold a description of what the script returns.

2. Sets a second variable (activeObject) to hold the result of calling Get (ActiveLayoutObjectName).

3. Sets LabelField and TextReceptacle to hold the two results, respectively.

Note We have named the NewFunctions layout fields. inputField is the field in which you enter an argument, and Receptacle is the field where the results are displayed.

As you can see in Figure QS-31, if the parameter field is active, clicking the Get Active Object button results in the following message:

```
The Active Layout Object is inputField.
```

If you have the cursor in the Text Receptacle field, you see the following result instead:

```
Receptacle
```

If the label field holds the focus, an empty string is returned.

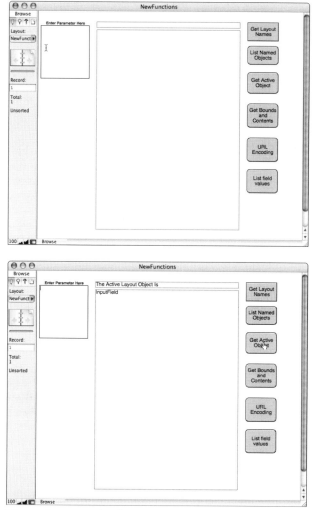

Figure QS-31: Make the parameter field active (top) and click Get Active Object to see (bottom) that the parameter field object is named inputField.

The GetLayoutObjectAttribute function

Our candidate for the single most powerful and useful new function is GetLayoutObjectAttribute. As outlined earlier in this chapter, it offers a number of options for which attribute to retrieve. The NewFunctions layout's Get Bounds and Contents button demonstrates two options for whichever layout object is currently active by calling our example's GetAttributes script. You can see the GetAttributes script steps in Figure QS-32.

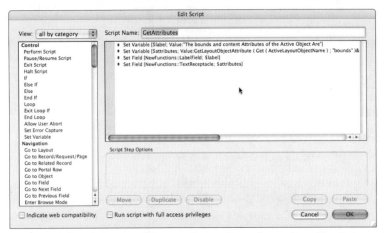

Figure QS-32: The GetAttributes script retrieves the active object's bounds and content

As is our practice, we load a descriptive text label into a local variable ($label) and then load another local variable with the result of our calculation:

```
GetLayoutObjectAttribute ( Get(ActiveLayoutObjectName) ; "bounds") & ¶ &
GetLayoutObjectAttribute ( Get(ActiveLayoutObjectName) ; "content")
```

We then set the label and TextReceptacle fields with the values of our local variables. Notice that one effect of employing a local variable to receive the function results is that we can evaluate multiple attributes, adjust the intermediate results, and so forth before modifying the content of any field. Figure QS-33 shows the result of clicking Get Bounds and Contents when the TextReceptacle field already contains data (in this example, the names of your authors).

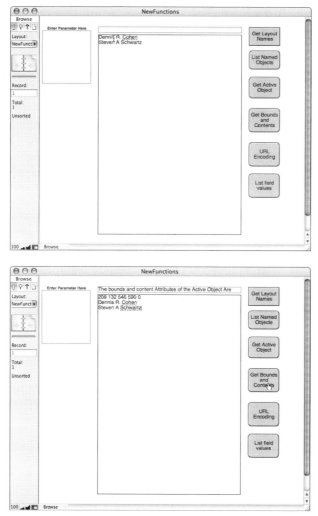

Figure QS-33: Clicking the Get Bounds and Contents button with the authors' names in the TextReceptacle field (top) produces the pictured result (bottom).

In an earlier example, employing a modification to this book's Address Book Advanced example database, we demonstrate how the isFrontTabPanel attribute might be used to determine which page to load. A simple but diverse use of the various attributes would be to create a "poor (wo)man's database design report" — for those users with FileMaker Pro rather than FileMaker Advanced. You could use GetLayoutObjectAttribute to create a report describing your layout objects.

Tip This is as much a rant as a general tip. GetLayoutObjectAttribute recognizes so many attributes that you will probably need to keep a reference list handy just to make sure you have the desired attribute and that it is spelled correctly. Maybe, with enough user feedback, FileMaker will add a method for the program to let you select from the recognized values rather than having to remember them.

The GetAsURLEncoded function

Although the GetAsURLEncoded function is intended to massage a URL into a string that will pass the standard tests for URL encoding compliance, you can also use it to convert arbitrary strings into compliance — something you might want to do when constructing a URL to embed in your own HTML code. Figure QS-34 shows the URLEncode script.

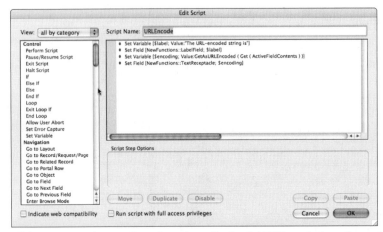

Figure QS-34: The URLEncode script calls GetAsURLEncoded on the active field's contents.

This script places a descriptive string telling what the result will be in the label field and then encodes the contents of the currently active field and places that result into the TextReceptacle field, as shown in Figure QS-35.

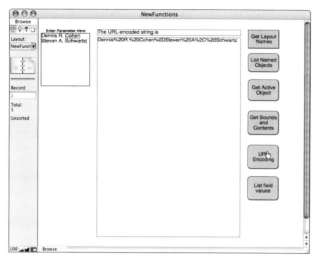

Figure QS-35: Clicking URL Encoding converts the active field's contents into a form that conforms to the specifications for URL text (though not necessarily a valid URL).

The List function

The final button on our NewFunctions layout is List Field Values. Not surprisingly, this button invokes a script demonstrating the new List function—the script is shown in Figure QS-36.

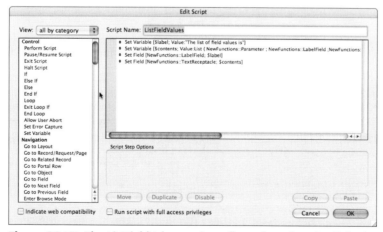

Figure QS-36: The ListFieldValues script collects the values in all the layout's fields.

As usual, the script loads a local variable with the string that we will place in the Label field and then loads a local variable with the result of a calculation using the List function we wish to demonstrate. Finally, we set the Label and TextReceptacle fields to the respective variables. Figure QS-37 shows the before and after of this script (we include all three fields' contents in the list).

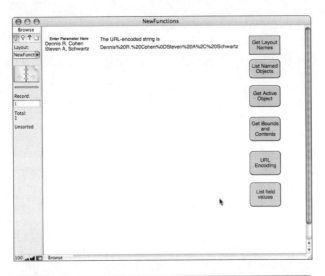

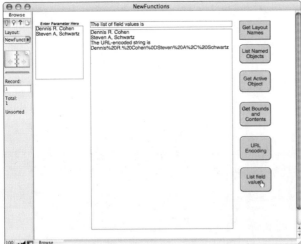

Figure QS-37: The layout before (top) and after (bottom) clicking List field values.

Some Cool Web Viewer Uses

FileMaker's Web Viewer example database includes a diverse collection of possible Web Viewer applications. The most complex of these (at least in our opinion) is the Generate Custom Report script, invoked by the Generate Report button on the Reports example's Report Builder tab. To understand this script in its entirety involves understanding HTML (actually XHTML) coding and thus is beyond the scope of this book.

However, if you have HTML markup knowledge and are curious, you should peruse this script to see how the HTML for a Web page can be dynamically generated to match user specifications, such as what data the user wants to see and how the user wants the data to be formatted. The generated HTML is then placed in a field, that field exported to a file on disk, and that disk file loaded into a Web Viewer object. By employing variations on this theme, you can empower your users to customize reports without you having to manually design each conceivable variation in its own layout. And all this can occur without your Web Viewer ever actually accessing the Internet!

Another useful demonstration leverages the powerful GetLayoutObjectAttribute function — Save Knowledge Base Page (invoked by the Save Page button on the Support example's Knowledge Base tab). This relatively short script, shown in Figure QS-38, asks the user to enter a title for a new record, retrieves the source (the URL) for the Knowledge Base page being displayed, and stores that information in a record so that you can later retrieve the particular article without having to navigate FileMaker's Knowledge Base Web pages to find the information — one click and it loads in a Web Viewer object, as demonstrated by the Open Knowledge Base Page script.

A couple of obvious uses for this technique would be to save Internet Movie Database (IMDb) links to the titles in your DVD or videotape collection for rapid loading or to link to product pages in a catalog Web site to retrieve information concerning frequently (or occasionally) ordered items.

Note Web links can grow stale as Web sites evolve. Some links, such as product catalogs, tend to become outdated more rapidly than others (such as historical references). These Web links are just like Web browser bookmarks and, like bookmarks, you will occasionally need to refresh them.

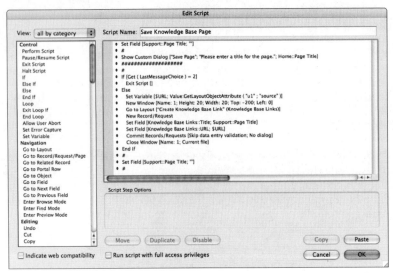

Figure QS-38: The Save Knowledge Base Page script shows how easily you can save a link to a page perused in a Web Viewer object for later access.

Although FileMaker supplies templates for many of the most popular reference sites, such as Google and the various Wikis, a wealth of other sites have content that is accessible in a similar manner. The Internet Movie Database, Amazon, and the GCD (Grand Comic Book Database) are just a few. For example, the GCD (www.comics.org) employs Lasso (a very popular Unix-based Web server) to host its content, and Lasso has a search function. So to find all the comic books with *Superboy* as part of the title, you would form the following query:

```
http://www.comics.org/search.lasso?type=title&query=Superboy&sort=alpha&Submit
=Search
```

Your Web Viewer will now display a page similar to that shown in Figure QS-39. The Custom Query we created is shown in Figure QS-40. By using a little experimentation and deductive reasoning, you can derive similar queries for sites you access frequently.

Figure QS-39: Search the Grand Comic Book Database for titles containing *Superboy*.

Note

It would surely be nice if the Choose a Website list were extensible (as label templates are). We have submitted a feature request for this extensibility. If you agree with us, please submit a similar request to the good folks at FileMaker, Inc.

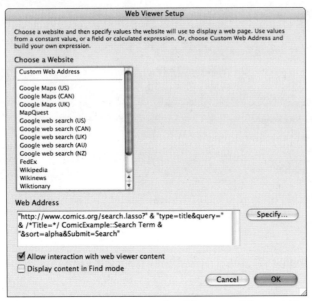

Figure QS-40: The Custom Web Address used for our title search term example.

New Feature Limitations

Both the Web Viewer object and Object Names have some limitations. These limitations are logical, but you should be aware of them.

For example, when a Web page link opens a new page in a new window, that window won't be in your FileMaker layout. After all, a layout exists, by definition, within a single window. The spawned page will open in your Web browser. One side effect of this spawning behavior becomes particularly annoying if you access pages that spawn pop-up ads — those ads are unexpected, at least in general, and having random browser windows appear, obscuring your layout, can get really old really fast. Less disconcerting, but of more practical consequence, are those links that tell your browser to open the linked page in a new window (or tab, if you're using a tabbed browser such as Safari). The newly opened page is not in your Web Viewer object and thus denies you the opportunity to employ such techniques as using GetLayoutObjectAttribute to store the page's URL (source attribute) in a field.

Object names have the limitation that they must be unique within a given layout. For example, you can have as many objects named *mapViewer* as you have layouts, but only one can be on any given layout. Requiring unique names within a layout makes the Go to Object script step possible. A side effect is that naming multiple instances of a single field on a layout (possible, but generally not a good idea) allows you to specify *which* instance of the field you wish to give the focus.

The Web Viewer Gallery

FileMaker, Inc. offers a page (www.filemaker.com/products/fmp/wvg) on its Web site hosting additional Web Viewer example databases. Numerous examples were available on the day FileMaker 8.5 was released, and more appear as the FileMaker user community makes them available to FileMaker, Inc. for sharing. We believe that there is no faster way to hone your skills than to understand and build onto or modify existing examples.

✦   ✦   ✦

The Fundamentals

What Is a Database?

Before exploring FileMaker Pro 8, you must understand what a database is. A *database* is an organized collection of information, usually with one central topic. In a computer database (as opposed to a paper database), the program that you use to enter and manipulate the data is either a *database program* or a *database management system (DBMS)*.

The word *organized* is a key part of this definition. Otherwise, a shoebox stuffed with business receipts might be considered a database. In general, if you must look at every scrap of data until you find the one for which you're searching, you don't have a database. You just have a shoebox full of stuff.

Even if you've never used a computer database management system, you're already familiar with many examples of paper (and probably computer) databases:

- ✦ Address books and business card files
- ✦ TV schedules
- ✦ Employee records
- ✦ Recipe card files
- ✦ Telephone books
- ✦ Holiday greeting card lists

Note

You also encounter special-purpose databases on your computer all the time. For example, iTunes is a database that tracks your music files and the information about them. Likewise, iPhoto and Photoshop Album are both databases; and your e-mail programs, such as Apple Mail or Microsoft Outlook, are databases. Even the disk directories that keep track of your hard disks' files and their sizes, locations, and icons are databases (as is the Windows Registry).

Every database—whether on paper, in a hand-held electronic organizer, or in a computer—is composed of records in tables. A *record* contains information that has been collected on one individual or entity in the database. A *table* holds the records that you create, and the database encompasses the tables. For example, in the Employee Records database example given in the preceding list, you might have one table containing the employees' ID numbers, names, addresses, dates of birth, and dates of hire. Another table might include salary information, and another might include personnel actions (such as review dates and performance history).

In the previous list of examples, a record would hold all the address data on one friend or business associate (the address book or business card file example); the title, channel, start/end times, and episode description for one television show (the TV schedule example); the employment information on one employee (the employee records example); the ingredients and cooking instructions for one recipe (the recipe card file example); the name, street address, and phone number for one person or business in the area (the telephone book example); and the name of one person or family from whom you previously received a card or want to send a card to (the holiday greeting card list example).

Note   A database containing more than one table of related information is a *relational* database. Each related table contains a field in common with the table(s) to which it is related, such as the Employee ID number. FileMaker Pro is a relational database management system (RDBMS).

Records are divided into fields. A *field* contains a single piece of information about the subject of the record. In an address database, for example, the fields might include first name, last name, street address, city, state, ZIP code, and phone number. Figure 1-1 shows the relationship among the components of a database.

What distinguishes a database from any old hodgepodge of information is that the data within each record is organized. *Fields* are responsible for this organization. The fields appear in the same place on every record and are reserved for a particular type of information. In the example in Figure 1-1, the field for the last name is always in the upper-left corner of the address card, and it always contains a person's last name. No matter which address card you pull, you will find a last name at that spot on the card.

Of course, in some paper databases, maintaining this level of organization can be difficult. When you are writing or typing an address card, for example, you might occasionally reverse the order of the last and first names or enter a company name in that spot. Organization in informal paper databases comes exclusively from your own consistency—or lack thereof.

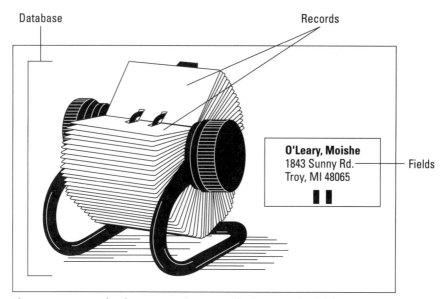

Figure 1-1: Every database comprises records that contain fields.

When consistency is critical, such as when you're recording information on employees or filling out a customer invoice, records are often designed as forms. Spaces on the form have labels so that you always know which piece of information belongs where. You can still type a phone number in the space labeled *Social Security number,* but at least the labels make catching and correcting mistakes easier. Forms help organize the data in much the same way that a computer-based database does. In fact, this type of paper database is frequently the basis for a computer database.

Note

As we describe in Chapter 5, you can establish field options that help prevent users entering a telephone number (usually seven or ten digits) into a Social Security number field (nine digits). Field validation options are yet another advantage that computerized database management systems have over manual entry systems on paper.

Paper Databases versus Computer Databases

What's wrong with paper databases? After all, many homes and businesses rely on them. In the following sections, we discuss some shortcomings of paper databases and explain how computer databases can help avoid these limitations.

Limitations of paper databases

First, consider some of the shortcomings of paper databases:

✦ *Making data-entry errors is easy to do.* Even when you're using a typeset form, nothing prevents you from entering the wrong data in a field or forgetting to fill in a critical field, such as the hire date or medical history.

✦ *Maintenance can be difficult.* For records to be easy to locate, they must be in some rational order. Whenever you return or add a record to a folder or the filing cabinet, you must place it in the correct spot. If you put the vendor file for Alpha Corporation in the Q folder, you might never find it again!

✦ *Updating records can be time-consuming.* Because of changes in information (such as addresses, phone numbers, and salaries), few databases are static. Updating a paper record could require several steps, including finding the record, erasing the old information, writing in the new information (or typing a whole new record), and returning the form to the filing cabinet. Making an across-the-board change — such as granting an incremental salary increase to all employees — can take a long time.

✦ *Sorting records, selecting subgroups of records, and creating reports are cumbersome tasks.* Suppose the boss walks into your office and says, "We're thinking about putting in a day-care center. How many of our 149 employees have kids under the age of five?" Or you might be thinking of sending a direct mail piece to your local customers. To determine printing and postage costs, you must know how many customers are in the target ZIP code or are within a particular range of ZIP codes.

In either case, you probably have to examine every record in the paper database. Whenever a task requires sorting, organizing, or summarizing the data in a different way, you can look forward to a nightmare of paper shuffling — hoping that you didn't overlook something important. And when you're through, you have to restore all the records to their original order.

✦ *Sharing records is difficult.* When a supervisor borrows some employee records, for example, the office manager no longer has easy access to those records unless you decide to kill some trees by photocopying the paperwork. (They're no longer in the file drawer.)

✦ *Information is hard to reuse.* If you want to use the information in a paper database for any purpose other than just reading it (addressing envelopes, for example), someone has to drag out the typewriter. Photocopying an address and then taping it onto a letter is considered bad form (unless you're creating a ransom note).

Advantages of computer databases

Computer databases, on the other hand, offer the following benefits:

✦ *Entering error-free information is easier.* Most database programs have features that speed data entry. Setting default values for some fields can save an incredible amount of typing time and ensure that information is entered consistently. (Using `CA` as the default entry for a State field, for example, ensures that you don't end up with records that variously contain CA, Calif., and California in the same field.) Other useful data-entry features include

  • Auto-incrementing fields (which automatically assign invoice or record numbers to new records)

  • Field types (which, for example, can prevent you from entering alphabetic information in a field that was designed to record salary data)

  • Range checking (which accepts only numbers within a particular range)

  • Required fields (which warn you if you don't fill in a critical field)

✦ *You can easily add, delete, or change data.* Making a change to a record merely involves bringing the record up onscreen, editing it, and then closing the file or moving to another record. Because you make all changes on a computer, you don't need to search through file drawers or hunt for an eraser. And if you need additional copies of records, you can quickly print them. The ease with which you can manage data is one of the key reasons for buying and using a database program such as FileMaker Pro.

✦ *Finding records is simple.* A Find feature enables you to quickly locate the record or records of interest.

✦ *You can specify criteria for sorting data.* Arranging records in a different order is as simple as issuing a Sort command. You can rearrange records in order of salary, record creation date, or any other field that's in the database. Most database programs also enable you to sort by multiple fields simultaneously. For example, you can sort a client database by state and by city within each state.

✦ *You can work with discrete groups of records.* Using the database program's record selection tools, you can select a subgroup of records that's based on any criteria you want. You might, for example, want to see only recipes that have chicken as the main ingredient or perhaps group employee records according to salary ranges or by department.

✦ *Database programs can perform calculations, frequently offering many of the same calculation capabilities that spreadsheet programs offer.* Instead of using a hand calculator to compute the sales tax and total for an invoice, you can have your database program automatically make the computations. In addition to performing computations within individual records, database programs can also generate summary statistics across all records or for selected groups of records. For example, you can easily summarize the efforts of different sales teams by calculating sales totals and averages by region.

✦ *Many people can simultaneously access the database.* If several people in a company need to view or modify the information in a database, you can use a database program on a network. Some database programs — including FileMaker Pro — also enable you to publish and share your data over the Web or a company intranet.

✦ *You can readily use information for multiple purposes.* For example, you can use the address information in records to print mailing labels, envelopes, a pocket-sized address book, or personalized form letters.

✦ *You can create custom reports.* Only you are in a position to decide which reports are essential to running your business, department, class, bowling league, or home. In most database programs, you can create your own reports and lay them out in any format that meets your information needs. Because you can save report formats on disk, you can reuse a format whenever you want to generate a current report.

✦ *You can use data from one program in another program.* Most database programs can import and export data.

  • *Importing* enables you to bring information into the database from other programs. For example, you might already have an address book program in which you've recorded the addresses of friends and business associates. Rather than retyping those addresses in your database program, you can export them from the original program (creating a file that your database program can read) and then import them into a database.

  • *Exporting,* on the other hand, enables you to use fields and records in a database to create a file that other programs can understand. For example, you can easily export numeric data so that you can graph it with a spreadsheet program, such as Microsoft Excel.

When should you use a database program?

Not every database is a good candidate for computerization. Specifically, when deciding between using a paper database and using a computer database, you must ask yourself the following questions. (The more Yes answers you give, the more reasons you have for using a database program.)

✦ *Will the contents of individual records change frequently?* If the information for each record isn't static and editing is often necessary, choose a computer database.

✦ *Is much of the information repetitive?* A database program can have default entries for fields. If much of the information that you'll enter is repetitive, using a database program can help you avoid unnecessary typing.

✦ *Must the records be grouped or sorted in different ways?* Database programs can quickly re-sort and select records for even very large collections of data.

✦ *Are calculations necessary?* The more complex the calculations, the more you need a database program.

✦ *Is printed output required?* Unless photocopies are satisfactory, use a database program.

✦ *Are reports necessary?* Database programs excel at summarizing information. If your reports go beyond simple record counts, a database program might be the best choice.

Flat-File and Relational Databases

You can roughly classify every database program as either *flat-file* or *relational,* according to the program's *relational capabilities:* that is, its capability to simultaneously draw information from more than one table on the basis of shared fields.

That explanation is quite a mouthful, isn't it? A couple of definitions and an example might make it easier to swallow:

✦ *A flat-file database* always consists of a single table. All required fields must be contained within that table.

✦ *A relational database* consists of at least two interrelated tables that have at least one key field in common.

When you're creating a relational database, instead of designing a single customer table that contains all your customer information (as you would in a flat-file database program), you might create several smaller tables. For example, you could create one table called Addresses to contain just customer addresses, and another called Orders to hold information about the customers' previous orders. To link the records in the two tables, you could assign a unique identification number to each customer. By placing this ID field in both tables, you can relate the two sets of information. For example, you can generate a statement from entries in the Orders table and instruct the program to pull the customer's mailing address from the Addresses table after finding the record that contains the matching ID number, as shown in Figure 1-2.

Both types of database programs have advantages. Conceptually, flat-file database programs are easier to understand and learn to use. All the important data is in a single table. If you must record additional information, you just add more fields to the table.

On the other hand, because of the multitable approach that relational database programs use, the tables tend to be smaller and, hence, faster to work with for common tasks, such as sorting and searching. Because of their power and flexibility, relational database programs are frequently used for large record-keeping projects or projects that have complex requirements. Another significant advantage of relational databases is their ability to reuse (or repurpose) data. For example, a high school might maintain a series of databases for extracurricular activities but draw all the name and address information from a single, student registration database.

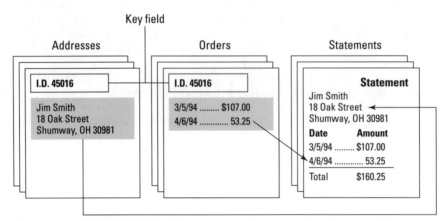

Figure 1-2: Relational database programs can create a report by extracting information from several tables.

Learning to use a relational database program can be difficult because of the complexity of the relational concept and the fact that much of the program's power frequently comes from a programming language that you must use to create advanced databases. In addition, designing relational databases often requires substantial planning. You must usually decide on the relational (or key) fields ahead of time and determine what data will be collected in each file. Unlike a flat-file database, a relational database isn't easy to toss together.

Introducing FileMaker Pro

Because this book is about FileMaker Pro, you might well be asking yourself where it fits into the "relational versus flat-file" classification scheme. Up through FileMaker Pro 2.1, FileMaker Pro was a flat-file database program with some relational capabilities. Specifically, you could use its Lookup feature to look up information in a secondary file and then copy that information into the current file's table.

Since version 3.0, however, FileMaker Pro has had full relational database capabilities. In addition to lookups, you can define relationships between tables that merely display the related data from a secondary table rather than copy it into the primary table. Depending on the nature and extent of your data, you can save loads of hard disk space by creating related databases instead of relying on lookups.

Note

Until FileMaker Pro 7, each FileMaker Pro database file contained a single table, which resulted in solutions that could comprise dozens of files. Beginning with FileMaker Pro 7, a single database file can contain multiple tables, eliminating Desktop clutter and making your task still easier because you no longer have to ensure that all the related files are present for a specific task. Of course, you can still relate separate files; however, maintaining separate files is no longer mandatory.

If you run a business, you might already have an invoice database, for example. Instead of retyping a customer's name and address (or using a series of lookups to copy this information from another file) whenever he or she places another order, you can store the address information in a separate, customer address database and then merely reference it in the invoice file. No matter how many invoices you create for a customer, the name and address information is recorded only once and is always current.

FileMaker concepts

Before you sit down to try out FileMaker Pro, understanding a few key concepts and features is important. Although all database programs have much in common with each other (as we explain earlier in this chapter), FileMaker Pro has distinct ways of doing things that clearly distinguish it from other programs. (These differences explain — at least partially — why FileMaker Pro has long been the database program of choice for Macintosh users and is making great strides in the Windows world.) In the remainder of this chapter, we introduce you to these key concepts and explain how you can use FileMaker Pro to tackle many database needs, both in the business and home arenas.

Understanding layouts

Much of the power of FileMaker Pro comes from its layout feature. A *layout* is an arrangement of a set of database fields. Every layout is a view or window into the contents of a database, and different layouts present different views (frequently using different groups of fields). You can create separate layouts for doing data entry, generating reports (onscreen or printed), and printing labels or envelopes. And you can have as many layouts for each database as you need.

New Feature

FileMaker Pro 8 introduces tabbed layouts that allow you to partition your layouts, whether to eliminate scrolling or because previous input makes a subset of the fields unnecessary. (For example, in a movie collection, you might want to display different fields for videotapes than you display for DVDs.) We demonstrate the use of tabbed layouts in Chapter 4.

Whenever you create a new database and define its fields, FileMaker Pro automatically generates a layout that is a standard arrangement of all the fields that you have defined (see Figure 1-3). If a quick-and-dirty database is all you need, you can use this standard layout to start entering data immediately.

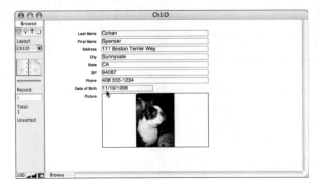

Figure 1-3: A standard database layout.

On the other hand, you can customize a database layout by doing any of the following:

✦ Changing the placement of fields (to create a columnar report, for example).

✦ Eliminating fields from the layout that you don't want to display (while still being able to use them in other layouts where they *will* display).

✦ Creating separate tabs that contain subsets of your layout's fields.

✦ Removing some or all the field labels or moving the labels to different positions. (Field labels aren't attached to fields.)

✦ Embellishing the layout by adding text and graphics and by modifying the font, style, color, pattern, or border for fields.

✦ Eliminating layout parts (which we explain later in this chapter) that aren't needed, or adding parts that display summary statistics or present information that repeats on every page.

Figure 1-4 shows a custom layout for the database previously shown in Figure 1-3. The data entry screen is more attractive because of the rearrangement of the fields, changes in font sizes and styles, and addition of color and graphics. To make it even easier to create attractive custom layouts, FileMaker Pro offers layout themes. When creating a new layout, you can optionally select a theme from the ones supplied by the program, automatically setting the background colors and field borders.

Note   Themes apply only while creating the layout. You cannot assign a theme to an already existing layout.

Every layout that you create for a database is separate from every other layout, but it draws from the same set of fields. When you design a new layout, you select only the fields that you need. In a customer database, for example, you can use one layout to display invoice information, such as the customer's name, address, items, or services purchased, and a total. A second layout might contain only name and address information that's formatted as a mailing label. You can create a third layout to print or display a client phone book or monthly client purchase totals. Figure 1-5 shows two different layouts for the same database.

Figure 1-4: A custom layout.

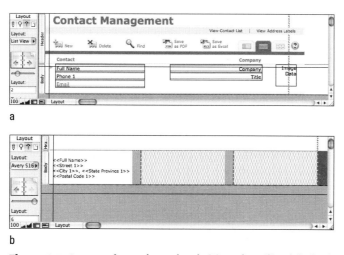

a

b

Figure 1-5: Layouts for a phone book (a) and mailing labels (b).

No practical restrictions limit the number of fields that you can use in a layout. Data entry screens, for example, frequently have many fields so that you can easily enter all the important information for a record in a single layout. At the other extreme, a help screen or menu layout might contain only static text and buttons — no fields at all.

When you design layouts for a database, you might need to create additional fields that are specific to a single layout. For example, a field that shows a total for each customer order is important in an invoice layout but unnecessary (or pointless) in an address label layout. Conversely, you do not have to place every field that you define on a layout. You might want to create a field to use only as a test for a calculation (determining whether another field is blank, for example) but not place it on any layout.

Keep in mind that data you enter in one layout automatically appears in any other layouts that use those same fields. And although you can — and usually will — create an all-encompassing layout for data entry, you can use the other layouts for data entry, too.

Because you can make new layouts whenever you like (even after a database contains records), you can design additional reports, labels, and data entry screens as the need arises. And if you didn't originally remember to create a field that is critical to a layout, you can also add fields as you need them.

Remember the following important points about layouts:

✦ Every database can have as many different layouts as you need.

✦ Every layout can use as many or as few of the defined fields as you like.

✦ A database can have fields that aren't included in any layout.

✦ Like with the process of defining new fields, you can create, modify, or delete layouts whenever the need arises.

Understanding layout parts

Layouts are divided into parts. Like a word processing document, a layout can have a body, header, and footer. Each of these elements is a *part*. Every part can contain database fields, graphics, static text, and other embellishments. (As you will learn in Chapter 5, information in some parts is visible both onscreen and in reports, but you can see information in other parts only when you print a report or use the Preview command.)

The following layout parts are available to you:

✦ *Title header and title footer:* This special header or footer appears only on the first page of a report. It substitutes for any other header or footer part that has been defined for the layout.

✦ *Header and footer:* Headers and footers appear at the top or bottom, respectively, of every page of a report or other type of layout. (If you create a title header or footer, it replaces the normal header or footer on the first page of the report.) Page numbers, logos, and the current date are popular items to place in a header or footer.

✦ *Body:* Unlike other layout parts, information in the body appears in every record in the database. For this reason, you normally place most fields in the body.

✦ *Sub-summaries:* You use sub-summary parts to summarize groups of related records after you have sorted the database by the contents of a particular field. For example, after sorting an address database by city, you can use a sub-summary field to display a count of records in each city. Sub-summaries can appear above or below each group of records, and their content is visible only in Preview mode and in printed output. (Preview and other FileMaker Pro modes are discussed in the next section.)

✦ *Grand summaries:* Statistics that appear in a grand summary apply to all records that are currently visible. A grand summary can appear at the beginning (leading grand summary) or end (trailing grand summary) of a report. Its content is visible in Browse and Preview modes and in printed output.

Prior to FileMaker Pro 7, grand summaries did not display their content in Browse mode.

When you first create a layout, it starts with only a body, header, and footer. You can remove unnecessary parts and add other parts, as you like. Figure 1-6 shows a layout that has several parts. The figures illustrate the relationship between the layout and an onscreen preview of the report.

Understanding modes

FileMaker Pro has four modes of operation: Browse, Find, Layout, and Preview. The mode that you use at any given moment governs the types of activities that you can perform:

✦ *Browse mode:* You use this mode to create and delete records as well as to enter and edit data. You perform all data entry in Browse mode.

✦ *Find mode:* In Find mode, you can search for or hide records that meet criteria that you specify.

✦ *Layout mode:* You design, edit, reorder, or delete database layouts in Layout mode.

✦ *Preview mode:* You use Preview mode to preview a report or layout onscreen (usually prior to printing).

Preview your documents before printing

Use Preview mode to check your reports before printing them. When examining a report or other type of layout in Preview mode, whatever is shown on the preview screen is precisely what will be sent to the printer. If your printout doesn't look like what you expected, use Preview mode to check your changes until the printout's preview display is correct. This saves time, ink or toner, and paper when printing data records, labels, and reports.

Note   The four modes are indicated by small, iconic buttons in the Tool area at the top left of a FileMaker window. Browse is the pencil, Find is the magnifying glass, Layout is the T-square, and Preview is the dog-eared piece of paper. The selected mode is highlighted, and its name appears in the text box above the buttons.

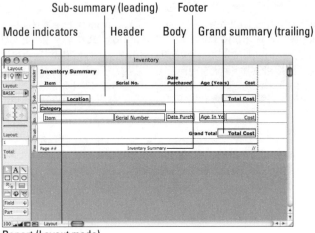

Report (Layout mode)

Report (Preview mode)

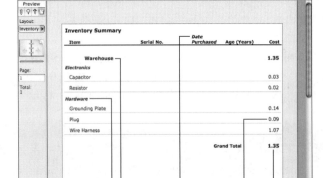

Figure 1-6: Layout parts (as displayed in Layout and Preview mode).

Thus, when you want to enter a new record, you must switch to Browse mode. To modify any portion of a layout (to add or resize a graphic; edit a field label; or move, format, add, or delete a field, for example), you have to be in Layout mode. If you're not sure what mode you're in, you can check the Mode button in the window's status area or the Mode indicator at the bottom of the database window. Alternatively, you can open the View menu and see which mode has a check mark next to it.

Getting "The Big Picture"

Now that you understand what a database program is and does, and how to determine when it's the right tool for the job, you might be facing a problem common to anyone who buys a new type of program. You probably wonder what you can do with FileMaker Pro. (Yes, many of us often purchase software solutions before clearly defining the problems they were intended to solve.)

Although FileMaker Pro is a wonderful piece of technology, it's only as useful as you make it. And, like so many other things in life, understanding how something works isn't the same as knowing when to use it. If you've ever taken an advanced math or statistics course, you understand what we mean. Memorizing formulas isn't the same as knowing when to apply them.

If you've already experimented with the sample files and templates included with FileMaker Pro 8, you probably also already know that they aren't meant to serve all your database needs. Before long, you'll be faced with the prospect of designing and using your own databases. And if you're new to databases, your biggest initial problem won't be learning how to use the program but rather what to use it for.

To get you into the proper mind-set, this chapter concludes with a list of some uses to which FileMaker Pro can be put — some general and some very specific. Hopefully, these examples will give you ideas for databases that you might want to create, moving you from the thinking stage to the doing stage.

Business uses for FileMaker Pro

Because of the ease with which you can create functional, useful databases (regardless of your prior database experience), FileMaker Pro has long been a favorite program among business users. Here are a few of the things you can do with FileMaker Pro:

✦ *Automate business forms.* Most businesses rely on forms, and many of these forms are perfect candidates for databases. A petty cash voucher system is one example. Rather than just fill out a slip of paper that gets tossed into a cash box or drawer, you can duplicate the voucher as a FileMaker Pro data entry form. Features such as date-stamping and assigning serial numbers can be automatically applied to each new voucher. And by creating appropriate report layouts, you can break down disbursements by time periods, departments, or individuals.

✦ *Improve shipping records.* Rather than frantically searching for a shipping receipt or bill of lading whenever a shipment goes astray, you can use FileMaker Pro to help you keep track of incoming and outgoing shipments. The program's search capabilities make it easy to locate any shipping documentation that normally might be tucked away in a file drawer. FileMaker Pro can also help you organize your receipts and create appropriate reports — grouping them and showing total shipments to each customer, for example.

✦ *Reuse existing customer data.* For many businesses, the customer list is its most valuable asset. Sadly, many businesses — both small and large — still attempt to maintain their customer records on paper only. Entering customer information into a database makes it possible to do mass mailings to announce sales, easily update and correct information (a change of address, for example), examine customer buying patterns, and determine when an additional sales call or purging from your list is appropriate.

✦ *Track rental information.* Small businesses that do rentals are excellent candidates for FileMaker Pro. By creating necessary formulas, scripts, and reports, you can instruct the database to find all rentals that are late, calculate late charges, and determine who your best customers are.

✦ *Examine employee performance.* Although a database program is not the best choice for project tracking (many programs are designed specifically for this task), you can certainly create a simple assignment-oriented database that records each assignment you hand out, including its due date, progress notes, and completion date. By adding fields for "quality of work," the database can help you perform (and document) the dreaded salary review.

✦ *Schedule company resources.* Conference rooms, audiovisual equipment, and other limited company resources are often in high demand. If you're the office manager, consider creating a database of resource requests. You can then sort by resource, date, and time to quickly flag duplicate requests.

✦ *Share information between branches.* FileMaker Pro's ability to host multi-user databases on the Internet or a company intranet provides an ideal way for you to share data between distant branches of your company or among the users on your corporate local area network (LAN).

Home uses for FileMaker Pro

FileMaker Pro isn't just for business. In fact, home users make up a substantial portion of those who purchase and use FileMaker Pro for their data recording needs. Here are some ways you can use FileMaker Pro for your own record keeping:

✦ *Maintain a home inventory.* If you know anyone who has had a large casualty loss due to a burglary, fire, or natural disaster, you understand the pressing need for documenting everything you own. An inventory database can be used to conveniently list your possessions along with their serial numbers, purchase date, and cost. A similar database that lists insurance policies, credit cards, and other important documents (and their locations) can also be very useful.

✦ *Track a collection.* A database program is perfect for recording purchases and catalog values for any set of collectibles, such as stamps, coins, baseball cards, comic books, paintings, books, wines, Pez dispensers, or Beanie Babies. ***Hint:*** You can also include graphics images of the items in your database.

✦ *Record credit card and checking account activity.* If you don't already have a home accounting program, you can use FileMaker Pro to create one. Every transaction (a check, deposit, charge, or payment) can be treated as a separate record.

✦ *Keep track of who has your property.* Do you have neighbors, friends, and relatives who are great at borrowing but not at returning items? Use a database to track what was lent, when, and to whom. By including a simple date calculation, you can automatically determine how long it has been since each item was lent, too. Even if you don't throw this information in the borrower's face ("Bill, you borrowed my hedge clippers 47 days ago!"), at least you'll always know where your things are.

✦ *Get a handle on your investments.* Say you just sold some stock but don't remember what you paid for it. The IRS expects you to record this information in order to determine capital gains. FileMaker Pro can help you keep track of your buy/sell costs and dates. And with its calculation capabilities, you can also use FileMaker Pro to compute gains and losses (in dollars and percentages), the number of days an investment was held, and so on.

Summary

✦ Every database is composed of tables — collections of records — one per person or entity in the database. Records are divided into fields, which are each designed to hold one particular piece of information.

✦ A database program, such as FileMaker Pro, enables you to store information for rapid retrieval and organize the data in ways that are extremely cumbersome and time-consuming if attempted with a paper database.

✦ Paper databases are most useful when the data collected is relatively static, the amount of data is fairly small, and your reporting requirements are minimal. A database program is a better choice when data frequently changes, when you must use the information for multiple purposes, or when you want to be able to print the information. A database program is also a better choice when you want to perform calculations on the data, select subsets, reorder the records based on different criteria, or when you need summary information or reports.

✦ Layouts are arrangements of database fields. Different layouts enable you to view and present information in different ways. You can have as many layouts for a FileMaker Pro database as you like.

✦ Layouts are divided into sections called parts. Depending on the parts in which you place fields, text, and objects, they're printed once for every record in the database (body), only at the top or bottom of each report page (header or footer), only at the top or bottom of the first report page (title header or title footer), once before or after each group of records sorted on the sort-by field (leading or trailing sub-summary), or once before or after all the records being browsed (leading or trailing grand summary).

✦ You do all work in FileMaker Pro in one of four modes: Browse, Find, Layout, or Preview, you can enter data only when the database is in Browse mode. If you're ever unsure of the current mode, check the Mode indicator at the bottom of the database window.

✦   ✦   ✦

FileMaker Pro Basic Operations

✦   ✦   ✦   ✦

In This Chapter

Starting up and
quitting FileMaker
Pro

Performing basic file-
handling procedures

Issuing commands

Using FileMaker Pro's
tools and palettes

Using toolbars

Getting help

✦   ✦   ✦   ✦

In Chapter 1, you learned that FileMaker Pro is a *mode-oriented program*. That is, the mode you're in (Browse, Find, Layout, or Preview) determines the types of operations you can perform. Now that you understand the fundamental FileMaker Pro concepts of modes and layouts, you're ready to explore the basic, essential procedures for performing common operations.

Starting Up

You can start FileMaker Pro by using one of two methods. The method you use depends on whether you also want to open one or several databases as you're starting up.

Note   When books, magazines, or manuals discuss *starting up* a program, they sometimes use the terms *run, launch, or open.* All four terms mean the same thing.

STEPS: Launching FileMaker Pro without Opening an Existing Database

1. Locate the FileMaker Pro program icon on your hard disk (see Figure 2-1).

   If the program is stored on a disk whose window is closed, double-click the disk icon to open its window. Similarly, if the program is stored in a folder that isn't open, double-click the folder to display its contents. Continue opening folders as necessary until you see the FileMaker Pro icon. (Note that in some operating systems or with certain preference settings, it might be necessary to just single-click a folder to open it.)

Figure 2-1: The FileMaker Pro program icon.

If you have Windows, you can launch FileMaker Pro by choosing its name from the Start ➪ All Programs menu and then going to Step 3. As an alternative, you can create a shortcut for FileMaker Pro and drag it onto the desktop or onto the Quick Launch bar (to the right of the Start button). The FileMaker Pro installer program also asks whether you wish a shortcut created in either the system tray or on the desktop.

The FileMaker Pro installation program for OS X offers you the option of placing FileMaker Pro's icon on your Dock for easy access, as shown in Figure 2-2. If you avail yourself of that option (we do), you need only click the FileMaker Pro icon on the Dock to launch the program or to make an already running copy your active (front-most) application.

If you've recently run FileMaker Pro on your Mac, you can launch it by choosing its name from the ⌘ ➪ Recent Items submenu. You might also find it helpful to make an alias of FileMaker Pro and then drag the alias to a convenient location, such as the Desktop or the main (root) level of your Home directory. You can then launch FileMaker Pro by double-clicking its alias. To make the alias, select the FileMaker Pro program icon and press ⌘+L.

We work with the Dock on the right-hand side of the Desktop, so if you operate with the Dock on the bottom or left, adjust your viewpoint accordingly.

2. Double-click or click the FileMaker Pro program icon (depending on your operating system, its configuration, and whether the program icon is in a folder, on the Windows taskbar, or the Mac OS X Dock).

   FileMaker Pro opens, presenting you with the New Database dialog (see Figure 2-3).

3. Select the appropriate radio button in the New Database dialog.

   • To create a new database from one of the included templates, select the Create a new file using a template radio button, choose a template category from the pop-up menu (drop-down list on Windows), and then select a database template from the list below the pop-up (drop-down).

   • To create a new database from scratch, select the Create a new empty file radio button.

   • To open an existing database, select the Open an existing file radio button and then traverse the Mac or Windows Open dialog that appears to locate your existing database.

Figure 2-2: In OS X, you can add FileMaker Pro to the Dock, enabling you to quickly launch it whenever you want.

Figure 2-3: The New Database dialog appears when the program starts.

4. Complete your choice by clicking OK.

- If you select Create a new file using a template, FileMaker Pro automatically generates a new, empty copy of the chosen database template — after you give it a name.

- If you select Create a new empty file, a Save file dialog appears, like the ones shown in Figure 2-4. Type a name for the new file, select a location on disk in which to store the database, and click Save. The Define Database dialog appears, with the Fields pane showing, enabling you to complete the initial database definition.

  Define the necessary fields and click Done. A standard layout is created for you, the first record of the database is displayed, and you are switched into Browse mode, where you can begin entering data for the first record. (Chapters 5 and 6 contain the details of defining fields and designing layouts.)

- If you select Open an existing file, an Open file dialog appears. Navigate to the drive and folder that contains your database, select its name in the file list, and then click Open.

Tip   If you prefer, you can just dismiss the New Database dialog by clicking the Cancel button. You can then choose commands from the File menu to create new databases (New Database) or open existing databases (Open). Note that New Database and Open work the same whether you select them in the New Database dialog or choose their commands from the File menu.

FileMaker Pro and memory usage

When you launch FileMaker Pro and open a database, the entire database isn't always loaded into memory — in fact, unless it is very small, it will almost never be entirely loaded into memory. FileMaker Pro, like most powerful applications (Word, Excel, iMovie, iDVD, and so on) uses a disk-caching scheme, loading only the data it requires at the moment (based on your find requests, the layout in use, and so on). When the program needs to display additional records or a different layout, it reads the information from the disk, replacing the data that was previously in memory with the new data. This way, you can open a 1GB database with a computer that has only 256MB of RAM, for example. Disk caching is common to many programs that deal with large quantities of data and is in addition to your Mac or Windows virtual memory. The amount of caching done, though, like the amount of virtual memory page-swapping, will vary inversely with the amount of real memory available.

If you're using FileMaker Pro with a laptop computer, you'll notice an important consequence of this disk-caching scheme. With large databases, you can expect more disk accesses than normal, which more quickly uses up the battery charge. If you are running on battery power, you're well advised to restrict your work to smaller databases or to use larger databases sparingly — closing them as soon as you accomplish the task at hand.

Enter a new database name here.

Mac OS X (10.4)

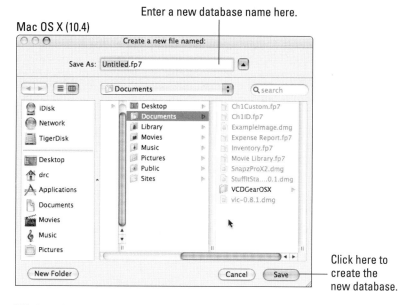

Click here to create the new database.

Windows XP

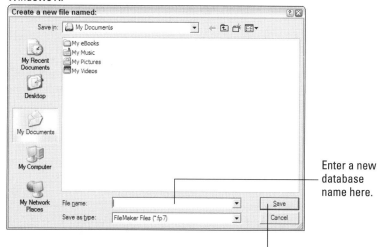

Enter a new database name here.

Click here to create the new database.

Figure 2-4: This Create a new file named: dialog appears when you create a new database. The specific dialog you see depends on your computer's operating system.

Dealing with the New Database dialog can be a nuisance — and totally unnecessary if the database you want to work with already exists. You can simultaneously launch FileMaker Pro and open a database by double-clicking the database's file icon. FileMaker Pro launches, and the database automatically opens.

Tip　You can stop the New Database dialog from appearing at startup by selecting the No longer show this dialog check box (refer to Figure 2-3).

STEPS: Simultaneously Launching FileMaker Pro and Opening One or More Databases

1. Locate the file icons of the databases that you want to open.

   To open more than one database simultaneously, you must have all the database files on the same disk and in the same folder (or in the root directory of the same disk). (Note that if you have a Mac and view the files in list view, they need only be on the same disk. You can select files in different folders by expanding the folders as needed.)

2. Select the databases to be opened by dragging a selection rectangle around their icons (either platform), Shift+clicking or ⌘+clicking their icons (Mac), or Ctrl+clicking their icons (PC).

3. Open FileMaker Pro and the databases you've selected, as follows:

   • *Macintosh:* Choose File ⇨ Open, press ⌘+O, or Ctrl+click one of the icons and choose Open from the shortcut menu that appears.

   • *Windows:* Right-click one of the selected files. Choose the Open command from the shortcut menu that appears.

   FileMaker Pro launches, and all the selected databases open.

Tip　Create aliases (Mac) or shortcuts (Windows) for frequently used databases so that you can easily find and open them.

FileMaker Pro and the power switch

Just like it's a bad idea to shut down your Mac or PC by simply cutting the power instead of using the Shut Down command, turning off the juice is also a poor substitute for using a program's Quit/Exit command. Although FileMaker Pro does indeed save your work automatically and even has a command that can be used to recover a damaged database file, you shouldn't take unnecessary risks with your data. Unless circumstances beyond your control prevent you from doing so (your system crashes; lightning strikes; or you roll a chair over the computer's power cord and cut it), you should always use the Quit/Exit command to end a FileMaker Pro session.

Quitting

When you're ready to end a FileMaker Pro session, choose the Quit/Exit command:

✦ *Mac OS X:* FileMaker Pro ➪ Quit FileMaker Pro (⌘+Q)

✦ *Windows:* File ➪ Exit (Alt+F4 or Ctrl+Q)

Any open data files are closed as part of the Quit/Exit process. Because FileMaker Pro automatically saves changes to files as you work with them, you don't need to issue any Save commands. (For more information on how FileMaker Pro saves data, see "Saving files," later in this chapter.)

File-Handling Procedures

While you're working in FileMaker Pro, you might want to open additional database files, create new files, close files, or make a backup copy of a database you are using. The information in this section explains how to perform these common procedures.

Opening, creating, and closing databases

You use the File menu or a keyboard shortcut to open an existing database, create a new database, or close a database.

STEPS: Opening an Existing Database

1. Choose File ➪ Open (or press ⌘+O/Ctrl+O).

   A standard file dialog appears, as shown in Figure 2-5.

2. Navigate to the drive and folder where the database file is stored.

3. Open the file by double-clicking its filename or by selecting the filename and then clicking the Open button.

   You can have several FileMaker Pro databases open at the same time, if you like. To open additional databases, simply repeat these steps.

Tip   The FileMaker Pro Open dialog has a Show pop-up menu/Files of Type drop-down list that filters the file list to display only particular types of files. By default, FileMaker Pro Files is selected. Select a different file format, such as Tab-Separated Text Files, only when you want to convert another type of file into a FileMaker Pro 8 database. The procedure for doing this is described in Chapter 16.

Mac OS X (10.3)

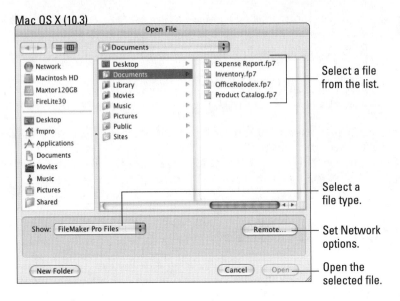

Select a file from the list.

Select a file type.

Set Network options.

Open the selected file.

Windows XP

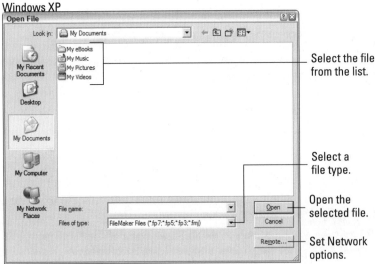

Select the file from the list.

Select a file type.

Open the selected file.

Set Network options.

Figure 2-5: One of these file dialogs appears when you choose the Open command. The exact appearance of the dialog depends on the operating system installed on your Mac or PC and possibly the appearance theme you're employing.

FileMaker Pro includes a feature making it simple to open any recently used database. You can choose a database to open from the list that appears in the File menu's Open Recent submenu. To enable this feature or change the number of recent files displayed, choose Edit ➪ Preferences (Windows) or FileMaker Pro ➪ Preferences (Mac OS X). Then mark the check box for Show recently opened files in the General pane of the Preferences dialog (see Figure 2-6). The number you specify for this option determines the number of recent files that will be listed in the File ➪ Open Recent submenu.

Mac OS X

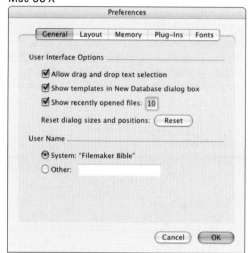

Figure 2-6: To make it easy to open recently used databases, enable the Show recently opened files option.

Windows XP

To create a new database file from scratch or from a FileMaker-provided template, choose File ➪ New Database. A (very slightly) modified version of the New Database dialog appears (refer to Figure 2-3), with the Open an existing file option eliminated. Follow the instructions that we present in the section "Starting Up" (earlier in this chapter) for working with the New Database dialog.

Note Windows determines which program is associated with a given file by the file's *extension* — a (usually) three-character suffix, such as .doc or .zip. When you create a FileMaker Pro 8 database in Windows, the filename automatically includes an .fp7 extension, such as Sales.fp7. Mac filenames, on the other hand, do not absolutely require extensions. But if you want a Mac database to be recognized by the Windows version of FileMaker Pro or if you want to store the database on a disk that is not formatted with a Mac file system, add the .fp7 to the end of the filename. FileMaker Pro 8 will include the extension for you. In general, it's safer simply to add the extension, regardless of your platform. (Note that Windows databases created with FileMaker Pro 3.0–4.1 had an .fp3 extension, FileMaker Pro 5.0–6.0 had an .fp5 extension, and FileMaker Pro 7–8 employ the .fp7 extension. FileMaker Pro 8 can convert the .fp3 and .fp5 files and open the result. Conversions are permanent, so make a copy before converting if you wish to continue using the database with an earlier version of FileMaker Pro.)

When you're through working with a database, you can close its file by performing any one of the following actions:

✦ Choose File ➪ Close (or press ⌘+W/Ctrl+W).

✦ Click the file's Close box or button. In Mac OS X, it's the small, red button in the upper-left corner of the document window. In Windows, the Close box is the tiny *x* in the upper-right corner of the document window.

✦ Quit from FileMaker Pro (as described in "Quitting," earlier in this chapter). Quitting automatically closes any open database files and records any unsaved changes.

Note When you're working in FileMaker Pro, remember that you don't have to close *any* files. You can have as many open files as will fit in your computer's available memory.

Saving files

In most programs, the procedure for saving a new file or for saving changes you've made to an older file is to choose the File ➪ Save or File ➪ Save As command. In FileMaker Pro, however, it doesn't work that way. In fact, if you check the File menu (see Figure 2-7), you'll see that it doesn't have Save or Save As commands. They're missing because FileMaker Pro automatically saves changes as you work with a file. And when you close a file or quit the program, you never see a dialog asking whether you want to save your changes — the program has already saved them.

Figure 2-7: The File menu (Mac OS X).

Tip

You can, however, exert some control over *when* FileMaker Pro saves files. Choose Edit ➪ Preferences (Windows) or FileMaker Pro ➪ Preferences (⌘+, [comma] in Mac OS X). The Preferences dialog appears. Click the Memory tab. You can instruct FileMaker to save only during idle time or every so many minutes. The latter option is most useful if you're using a notebook or laptop and running from battery. When you set the minutes between saves to a relatively high number, you can conserve battery power by reducing the frequency of hits on the internal hard disk (or floppy) drive. Select a setting with which you're comfortable. For instance, if you set 15 minutes as the Save period, you risk losing as much as 15 minutes' worth of data in the event that FileMaker Pro crashes before the data is saved. Don't worry if you quit before the time is up, though. FileMaker Pro automatically saves all data when you quit.

You can also increase or decrease the size of the cache — forcing more- or less-frequent saves — by entering a new number in the Attempt to set file cache to text box (see Figure 2-8).

Because the integrity of your data is paramount, FileMaker Pro's approach to saving goes a long way toward reducing the risk of data loss. The only negative side to autosaving is that FileMaker Pro saves *all* changes — both good and bad — that you make to a database. For example, if you experiment with a layout, FileMaker Pro instantly records the changes — whether or not you want to save them. Two options are available for recovering from inadvertent changes:

✦ Immediately choose the Edit ➪ Undo command (or press ⌘+Z/Ctrl+Z).

✦ Create a backup of the file before you make the changes (as discussed in the next section).

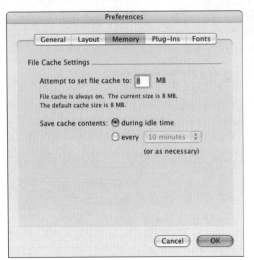

Figure 2-8: You can alter the frequency with which FileMaker saves changes within the Memory section of the Preferences dialog.

The Undo command has two limitations:

✦ You can undo only the most recent modification made to the database. (The wording of the Undo command automatically changes to reflect the most recent action that you can undo.) For example, if you delete some text from a field and then type information into another field, you cannot undo the deletion. (However, as long as you have not switched to a different record, you can use the Records ➪ Revert Record command to undo *all* changes made to an individual record.)

✦ Some commands simply cannot be undone. When you can't use the Undo command, it toggles to Can't Undo. Actions that can't be undone include using most of the Delete commands, such as Delete Record, Delete All Records, Delete Layout, and the Delete command in the Define Fields dialog.

The moral is that relying on the Undo command to save you from major mistakes can be a major mistake itself. The safest approach is to keep backups of important files, ensuring that you can recover from even horrendous mistakes or a computer calamity.

Making a backup copy of a file

Don't trust computers! Although you might have spent thousands of dollars on your computer and programs, they're not infallible. Regardless how many times they hear this, most computer users appear to feign deafness. Then they wake up one morning to find that their hard disk has bit the dust, the kids deleted the folder that contained the family's financial records (you can minimize this possibility by giving the kids their own account that doesn't have access to your files), or a thief has walked off with the computer. Without a backup of your important data, you're back at square one.

Because your data and layouts are important to you, FileMaker Pro provides several ways to make backup copies. In the event that something happens to the original file, you can use the backup copy to get the database up and running again. In addition to using the backup procedures provided by FileMaker Pro, you can make copies by using the Finder (Macintosh), Windows desktop, or a commercial backup program, such as Retrospect from EMC Dantz (www.dantz.com).

In particular, you might want to make a backup copy of a file for the following reasons:

✦ As a general precaution against data loss caused by user error, hardware failure, or software problems (a crash, for example)

✦ When you're planning to make a major change to a database, such as deleting records or modifying a layout

✦ When you want to create a database template for someone else or for your own use

You can make an exact duplicate of a database file (containing all the data and layouts) from the Finder/Windows desktop, using a commercial backup program, or from within FileMaker Pro. However, you can make *templates* (databases without data) only from within FileMaker Pro.

STEPS: Duplicating a FileMaker Pro Database File from within FileMaker Pro

1. In FileMaker Pro, open the database that you want to copy.

2. Choose File ➪ Save a Copy As.

A file dialog appears, as shown in Figure 2-9.

3. Click the Type pop-up menu /Save As drop-down list, and select the type of file you want to create:

- *copy of current file:* Use this choice when you want an exact duplicate of a database, including all the layouts and data it contains.

- *compacted copy (smaller):* This choice produces a usable copy of a database, but the copy is compressed to save disk space. This option is particularly useful when you are *archiving* a database (storing it for posterity or as a backup) or when a database is too large to fit on your backup medium.

Figure 2-9: This dialog enables you to save a copy of a FileMaker Pro database in any of three formats.

> • *clone (no records):* Select this option when you want to create a template from the database. All formulas, field definitions, and layouts are retained in the new file, but it contains no records.

4. Enter a new filename for the copy or leave the displayed default name as is.

   The default name that FileMaker Pro presents is one of the following, depending on the type of file you selected in Step 3:

   > • *Current filename* Copy (if you chose *copy of current file* or *compacted copy*)
   >
   > • *Current filename* Clone (if you chose *clone*)

Note

For cross-platform compatibility, the .fp7 extension is automatically added to the end of the filename regardless of whether you're using a PC or a Mac.

5. Using standard file dialog procedures, navigate to the disk and folder in which you want to save the copy.

New Feature

FileMaker Pro 8 includes two new check boxes specifying whether the new file is to be opened automatically subsequent to the save and whether your default e-mail program should be invoked with a new message created and the file copy attached.

6. Click Save (or press /Return/Enter).

   The copy is saved in the format you selected.

More about clones

A FileMaker Pro *clone* is similar to a template or stationery file created in most other programs. It's an empty database, ready for you to begin adding records. However, unlike icons for templates or stationery files that you might create in other programs, the icon for a clone looks exactly like the icon for any other FileMaker Pro database file, so recognizing that it's a clone is difficult. And because it's not a real template or stationery file, when you open a clone, you aren't opening a copy of it: You're opening the actual file. Any data you add to the clone is automatically saved as part of the file. If you want to preserve the clone, make a copy of it (or make a second clone) and then make changes to the copy rather than to the original.

Clones are particularly useful when you have databases that you routinely start over from scratch (for example, a bookkeeping database that you clear monthly or annually), when you want to experiment with a layout or scripts, or when you want to provide a template for other users but don't want them to have your data.

When you open a clone for the first time, it will not contain any records. To begin using the file, choose Records ⇨ New Record (⌘+N/Ctrl+N).

Automatic backups

If you're worried about making inadvertent changes to a database or concerned that something catastrophic might happen to it, you can create a FileMaker Pro script that automatically creates a backup every time you open the database. You can add a copy of the Automatic Backup script to the Scripts menu so that you can create backups during a session, too. (Yes, we know we're getting ahead of ourselves. Scripting is covered much later in this book. If you don't feel comfortable with scripting at this moment, return to this section when you do. You'll find it surprisingly easy.)

STEPS: Creating an Automatic Backup Script

1. Launch FileMaker Pro and open the database.

2. Choose Scripts ⇨ ScriptMaker.

   The Define Scripts dialog appears (see Figure 2-10). The dialog displays all scripts that have been defined for the database.

3. Click the New button to display the Edit Script dialog, as shown in Figure 2-11.

4. Type a name for the new script in the Script Name box.

5. Scroll down the Steps list on the left until the choice Save a copy as appears. (It's in the Files category.)

6. Choose Save a copy as and then click the Move button.

   The Script step is copied to the Script list on the right and is automatically highlighted, displaying a Specify button in the options area.

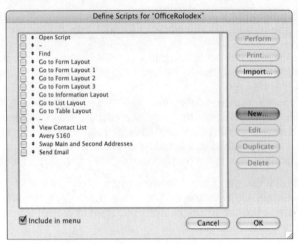

Figure 2-10: The Define Scripts dialog.

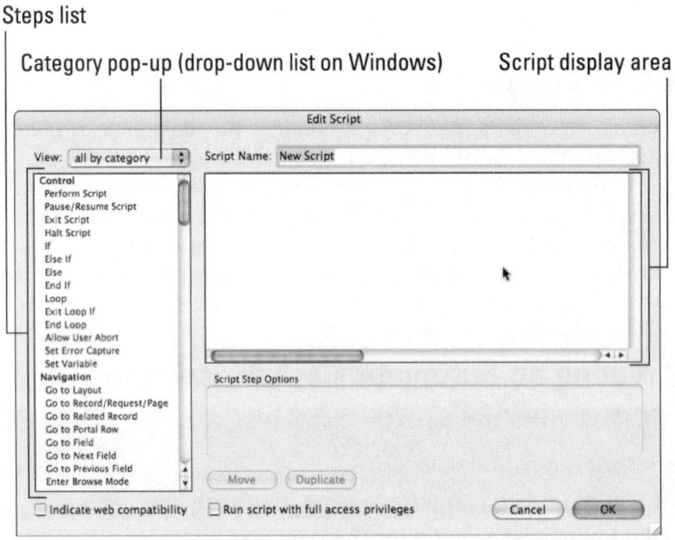

Steps list

Category pop-up (drop-down list on Windows)   Script display area

Figure 2-11: The Edit Script dialog.

7. Click the Specify button.

The Specify Output File dialog appears, as shown in Figure 2-12.

8. Click the Add File button to make a standard file dialog appear. (Refer to Figure 2-4.)

Figure 2-12: The Specify Output File dialog.

Note

You can also type in a path as described by the examples at the bottom of the dialog, making Steps 8 and 9 unnecessary.

9. Navigate to the drive and folder where you intend to store the backup files made by the script.

   By default, FileMaker Pro offers to name the backup file *filename* Copy, but you can change the name of the file by using normal editing techniques.

10. Click Save.

11. To complete the script, click OK in the Edit Script dialog and then in the Define Scripts dialog.

Note

Make sure that Include in menu is selected in the Define Scripts dialog so that the script is added to the bottom of the Scripts menu.

12. To make the script execute automatically whenever you open the database file, choose File ➪ File Options.

   The File Options dialog appears, as shown in Figure 2-13.

13. Click the Open/Close tab (if it isn't already selected).

14. Mark the Perform script check box in the When opening this file section of the dialog.

15. Choose the Automatic backup script option from the pop-up/drop-down list that appears.

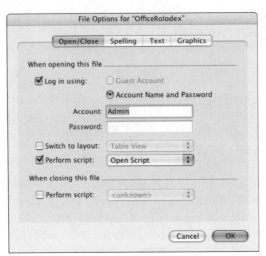

Figure 2-13: The File Options dialog.

16. Click OK.

The changes are recorded, and the dialog disappears.

Note

In versions of FileMaker Pro before FileMaker 6, a new script automatically included a set of standard steps, such as setting Browse mode and preparing for printing. To save you the trouble of manually having to clear any irrelevant steps, FileMaker Pro no longer makes such assumptions about default script steps; *none* are provided for you. That is, the Edit Script dialog (refer to Figure 2-11) is initially empty.

Keep the following in mind when you're using this backup script:

✦ Each time a new backup is created, it writes over the previous backup file. If you need to keep multiple generations of backups, you should return to the Desktop and manually rename the backup before or at the end of each FileMaker Pro session. You might add the backup date to the filename, for example.

✦ Remember that the backup file is an *exact* copy of the original. Thus, it also contains the automatic backup script. If you ever need to use the backup file, be sure to rename it or copy (or move) it to another folder before opening it in FileMaker Pro. Otherwise, an error dialog will appear, informing you that FileMaker was unable to create a backup (because the script is attempting to make a copy of the currently open database, using its own name).

✦ Because you selected the Include in menu option in Step 11, you can also execute this script by choosing its name from the Scripts menu. If you intend to run the script more than once during a session, be sure to rename each backup immediately after you create it.

Note

As you probably noted in Step 14, you can also choose to make the backup script automatically run each time you close the database. Whether you run the script on opening or closing is entirely up to you.

Issuing Commands

Issuing commands in FileMaker Pro is no different from issuing them in any other program. For those of you who are new computer users, the following discussion will be helpful.

To issue a command in FileMaker Pro — to create a new record or add formatting to a field, for example — you can use the mouse to choose the command from a menu or, if the command has a keyboard equivalent, you can press a special combination of keys. Figure 2-14 shows an example of choosing a command from a menu.

Figure 2-14: Choosing the Print command from the File menu.

Some menu commands might be dimmed. *Dimmed commands* aren't available, usually because they aren't relevant to the operation you're attempting to perform. For example, when you're operating in Browse mode and a field isn't currently selected, commands and the heading for the Format menu are dimmed. This is because you can execute formatting commands only when you've selected something that you can format. Dimmed commands become available only when they're relevant to the current state of the database and what you're doing at the moment.

STEPS: Choosing a Menu Command

1. Click the menu title that contains the command you want to issue.

The menu drops down, exposing the commands within it.

2. Click the command you want to execute.

The command executes.

Note   You can also select a menu command with the up- and down-arrow keys and then press Return/Enter.

You can issue any menu command that is followed by a letter, number, or symbol without using the mouse or the menus. Such a command is said to have a *keyboard shortcut* or a *keyboard equivalent*. (Both terms mean the same thing.) Sometimes the Shift key is used in conjunction with platform-specific modifier keys.

On a Mac, a propeller-shaped symbol and a character follow some menu commands. This symbol represents the Command key (shown on most keyboards as either ⌘ or a hollow Apple shape). The Option key is often used in conjunction with the ⌘ key and is denoted in menus by this symbol: ⌥. In rare cases, the Control key might also be employed as a modifier — it will be denoted by a caret (^). The Mac version of FileMaker Pro 8 does not use the Control key modifier.

On a PC, the Ctrl or Alt keys are the keys used for keyboard shortcuts.

STEPS: Issuing a Keyboard Shortcut

1. Press and hold the modifier key (or keys) that precedes the letter, number, or symbol in the menu.

The modifier keys that FileMaker Pro uses for Mac menu shortcuts include the Shift, Option, and ⌘ keys. In the Windows version, these modifier keys are the Ctrl, Alt, and Shift keys. They are called *modifier keys* because they have an effect only when you press them in combination with a letter, number, or symbol key. They modify the meaning of that key. Figure 2-15 shows the symbols used to represent these keys on the Mac.

Commands with ellipses and triangles

If you browse through FileMaker Pro's menus, you'll notice that two unusual elements are tacked onto the end of some commands: ellipses and triangles.

An *ellipsis* is a series of three dots. It indicates that the command displays a dialog to which you have to respond (such as File ➪ Print...). In contrast, menu commands that do not have ellipses are executed immediately.

A triangle following a menu command indicates a hierarchical menu (also called a *submenu*). When the mouse pointer slides over one of these menu commands, another menu pops out to the side of the original menu. Click to open the menu and then slide the pointer until you highlight the appropriate command in the submenu. Then click once to choose the command.

Option   **Figure 2-15:** Modifier key symbols as displayed in Mac FileMaker Pro
                 menus.

Shift

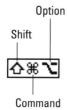

Command

2. While holding down the modifier key (or keys), press the letter, number, or
   symbol key that completes the keyboard shortcut.

   The command executes.

See Appendixes A and B, respectively, for a complete list of the Mac and Windows
keyboard shortcuts available in FileMaker Pro 8.

You can also use keyboard shortcuts in some dialogs. For example, you can click
the default button in dialogs by pressing Return/Enter, and you can choose the
Cancel command by pressing Esc (and, on a Mac, ⌘+. [period]). If you're running
Windows, you can execute any command or select any choice in a dialog containing
an underlined letter by pressing Alt in combination with the underlined letter. For
instance, in the Define Database dialog's Fields pane, you can choose or click all
buttons in this manner.

Using Tools and Palettes

This section provides a brief introduction to the tools and palettes that are available in FileMaker Pro 8. The tools and palettes are described in greater detail in
later chapters.

Figure 2-16 shows FileMaker Pro in Layout mode. This figure shows all tools except
the few that are specific to Find mode.

The following list briefly describes the basic FileMaker tools and palettes:

✦ *Layout pop-up menu* (available in all modes): Click this pop-up menu to display a
   menu of the names of all layouts that have been created for the current database. Selecting a different layout from the menu switches to that layout. (Note
   that the database's designer can optionally *hide* layouts, making them unavailable in the Layout menu. Such layouts are accessible only while in Layout mode
   or when a relevant script is performed that switches to the layout.)

✦ *Book:* In Browse mode, you use the Book tool to switch to different records.
   In Find mode, you use it to switch between multiple find requests. In Layout
   mode, you use it to switch to different layouts. In Preview mode, you use it to
   switch between different pages of a multipage report.

Part tool

Layout pop-up menu

Tools palette

Mode
selector Book Field tool

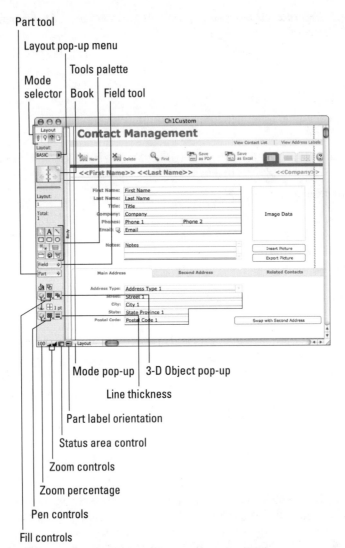

Mode pop-up | 3-D Object pop-up

Line thickness

Part label orientation

Status area control

Zoom controls

Zoom percentage

Pen controls

Fill controls

Figure 2-16: The FileMaker Pro tools and palettes.

✦ *Tools palette* (Layout mode only): From the top left, these tools are used to select objects (the Pointer tool), add or edit text (the A tool), draw lines (the Line tool), draw rectangles and squares (the Rectangle tool), draw rounded rectangles and rounded squares (the Rounded Rectangle tool), draw ellipses and circles (the Ellipse tool), create buttons, create check boxes and radio buttons, create tabs, and create portals to display fields from a related database.

✦ *Field and Part tools* (Layout mode only): These tools enable you to place additional fields and parts on a layout.

✦ *Fill and Pen controls* (Layout mode only): You use the Fill controls to set fill colors and patterns for objects. You use the Pen controls to set line and border colors. Figure 2-17 shows the pop-up palettes that appear when you click the fill, pattern, line width, and 3-D effect controls.

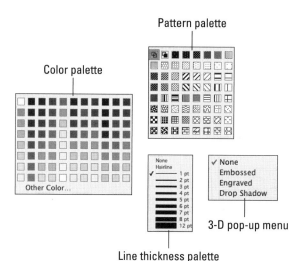

Pattern palette

Color palette

Figure 2-17: Select a color, pattern, line width, or 3-D effect by clicking in these palettes.

3-D pop-up menu

Line thickness palette

Note

The number of colors shown in the Fill palettes is dependent on a setting in the Layout section of the Preferences dialog. It can display 88 (System subset), 256 (Standard system palette), or 216 (Web palette) colors.

✦ *3-D object pop-up* (Layout mode only): This control enables you to add 3-D embossing, engraving, or a drop shadow to any selected object.

✦ *Zoom percentage* (all modes): This box shows the current zoom level. (*Zooming* enlarges or shrinks your view of what's onscreen.) Click the box to switch between the current zoom level and 100 percent.

✦ *Zoom controls* (all modes): Click the left icon to reduce the view to a bird's-eye perspective. Click the right icon to increase the document's zoom (magnification) level.

✦ *Status area control* (all modes): Click this control to show or hide the status area (on the left side of the window), including all tools.

✦ *Part label control* (Layout mode only): Click this control to switch between displaying layout part labels horizontally and vertically.

✦ *Mode pop-up* (all modes): This displays the current mode. You can click the mode selector to display a pop-up menu (see Figure 2-18) that enables you to switch between the four program modes: Browse, Find, Layout, and Preview.

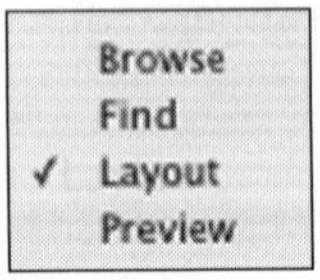

Figure 2-18: The Mode pop-up menu.

In addition to these tools, a few special tools are introduced in Find mode, as shown in Figure 2-19.

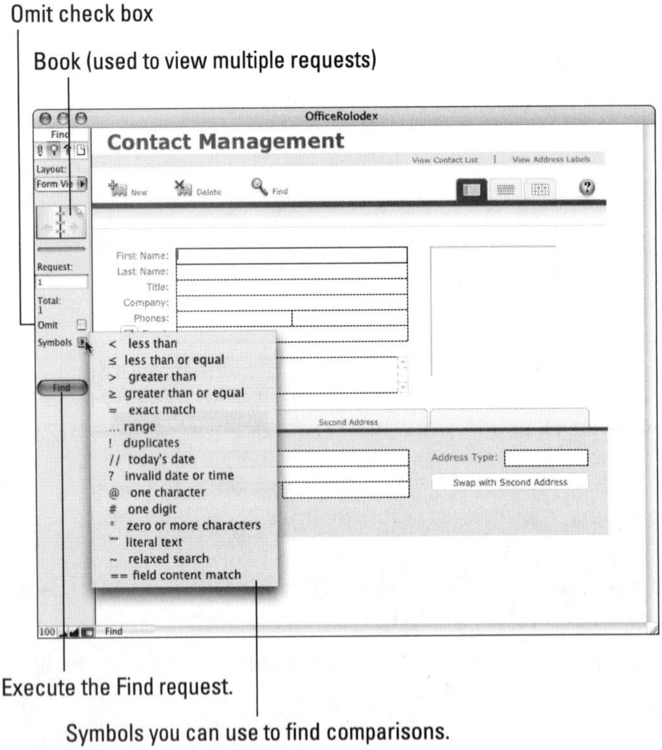

Omit check box

Book (used to view multiple requests)

OfficeRolodex

Contact Management

View Contact List   View Address Labels

New   Delete   Find

First Name:
Last Name:
Title:
Company:
Phones:

Request:
1
Total:
1
Omit
Symbols

< less than
≤ less than or equal
> greater than
≥ greater than or equal
= exact match
... range
! duplicates
// today's date
? invalid date or time
@ one character
# one digit
* zero or more characters
" literal text
~ relaxed search
== field content match

Second Address

Address Type:

Swap with Second Address

Find

100   Find

Execute the Find request.

Symbols you can use to find comparisons.

Figure 2-19: The tools in Find mode.

Overcoming keystroke conflicts

If using a keyboard shortcut produces an unusual effect (a dialog appears that seems to have nothing to do with FileMaker Pro or a program launches, for example), you probably have a utility running in the background that conflicts with FileMaker Pro. Many background programs constantly scan for the particular key combination that activates them.

Several options are available for overcoming conflicts of this sort:

✦ Reconfigure the utility so that it responds to a different key combination.

See the utility's manual or consult Help for instructions. Assuming reconfiguration is possible, this is the best solution. To avoid additional conflicts, try to choose key combinations that are unlikely to conflict with your main programs.

✦ If you cannot reconfigure the utility, turn it off when using FileMaker Pro. (Again, see the manual for details.)

No matter how helpful utilities are, few of them are as critical as the work you do in a major application, such as a database, word processing program, or spreadsheet. If a utility gets in the way, temporarily shut it down. If you can't reconfigure it or shut it down, get rid of it.

✦ When a conflict occurs, restrict yourself to using FileMaker Pro's menus to choose the command.

You use the Find tools as follows:

✦ *Omit check box:* Select this check box to exclude records from the found set that match the find criteria. For example, if the criterion is Sales > 100000, you can create a found set of records that includes everyone *except* salespeople with sales of more than $100,000.

✦ *Symbols pop-up menu:* Instead of typing conditional symbols and special characters when entering find criteria, you can choose them from this pop-up menu.

✦ *Find button:* Click this button when you're ready to perform a Find request (or multiple Find requests).

Using Toolbars

FileMaker Pro 8 has four toolbars (see Figure 2-20). The toolbars are referred to as Standard, Text Formatting, Arrange, and Tools.

You can click buttons in the Standard toolbar to issue common FileMaker Pro commands, such as opening a file, deleting the current record, or summoning Help. The icons in the Standard toolbar change to reflect the mode you're in (Browse, Find, Layout, or Preview).

Text formatting toolbar

Standard toolbar

Arrange toolbar

Tools toolbar

Figure 2-20: The FileMaker Pro toolbars.

You can click the icons in the Text Formatting toolbar to format selected text or to set a paragraph alignment. You can change the font or size of currently selected text by choosing options from the drop-down menus.

The Arrange and Tools toolbars are available only when you're in Layout mode. The Arrange toolbar duplicates commands in the Arrange menu. The Tools toolbar duplicates many of the Layout mode tools and is useful if you choose to hide the Tools sidebar to give yourself more screen real estate when working on a layout.

If you're not certain what a toolbar icon does, let your cursor rest over it for a moment. A tiny description automatically appears. To hide or show a toolbar, choose the toolbar's name from the View ➪ Toolbars submenu. When a check mark appears beside the name, the toolbar is visible.

Getting Help

The manual doesn't cover all the FileMaker topics. To make it simple for you to find the help information that you need while running FileMaker Pro, the program provides an extensive Help system.

Help for Windows users

If you're using the Windows version of FileMaker Pro, you can obtain the following types of online Help:

> ✦ *Toolbar help:* When FileMaker Pro 8 toolbars are displayed, rest the cursor over any toolbar button or menu for a few seconds. A pop-up label for the button will appear.

✦ *Context-sensitive help with dialogs:* You can summon context-sensitive help when working in a FileMaker dialog by pressing the F1 key or clicking the Help button (if one is available).

Many FileMaker Pro dialogs have a question mark (?) in the upper-right corner, just to the left of the Close box. Click it to change the cursor into a question mark, and then click any element in the dialog for a brief explanation of the element (see Figure 2-21).

Help button

Figure 2-21: Click the button with the question mark for help with a dialog.

✦ *General help:* You can browse through the FileMaker help information by choosing Help ➪ FileMaker Pro Help or pressing the F1 key. The Help Topics window appears, open to the Contents, Search, or Favorites tab. (By default, the window opens to the last tab you used.)

- To browse Help by topic, click the Contents tab. Expand items until you find a topic of interest. Highlight the topic to view the help information for that topic.

- Click the Favorites tab to add or remove Help topics to a collection that you feel the need to frequently reference. (This is especially useful for some of the functions you might use in calculations.)

- To search Help for a particular topic, click the Search tab. Enter your search string in the Type in the word(s) to search for text box, click List Topics, select the closest matching term in the list that appears, and then click Display.

Note

The first time you click the Find tab, the Help information is indexed for you. This can take a while, depending on the speed of your computer and disk.

✦ *Web help:* If you have an active Internet connection, you can visit the FileMaker Web site. Choose Help ➪ FileMaker on the Web. A standard Web page opens in your default browser. Click the Visit the FileMaker Website link to go to the support area of the FileMaker Web site.

Help for Macintosh users

If you're using the Macintosh version of FileMaker Pro, you can obtain the following types of online Help:

✦ *Toolbar help*: When FileMaker Pro 8 toolbars are displayed, rest the cursor over any toolbar button or menu for a few seconds. A pop-up label for the button will appear.

✦ *Help with dialogs:* You can summon context-sensitive help when working in a FileMaker dialog by choosing Help ➪ FileMaker Pro Help, pressing ⌘+? (question mark), or pressing the Help key (if you have an Extended or Pro keyboard). You can summon help when working with some assistants by making the same menu choices or by clicking the Help (?) button.

✦ *General help:* You can browse through the FileMaker help information by choosing Help ➪ FileMaker Pro Help, pressing ⌘+?, or pressing the Help key (if you have a Pro or Extended keyboard). Help Viewer launches and displays the main page of the FileMaker Pro Help window (see Figure 2-22).

Figure 2-22: The FileMaker Pro Help window in OS X.

Click the underlined text to expand items and select topics to view. You can search for specific information by typing a search word, phrase, or question into the text box at the top of the window and then pressing Return/Enter. To move backward or forward through recently viewed Help information, click the Back or Forward buttons.

✦ *Web help:* If you have an active Internet connection, you can visit the FileMaker Web site. Choose Help ➪ FileMaker on the Web. A standard Web page opens in your default browser. Click the Visit the FileMaker Website link to go to the support area.

Tip   Help Viewer is a separate program and is responsible for displaying all general and context-sensitive FileMaker Pro help information, as well as the help information for Mac OS X and other applications. When you quit FileMaker Pro, Help Viewer doesn't automatically quit. To quit Help (either to end a help session or to free up some additional memory), press ⌘+Q or choose Help Viewer ➪ Quit Help Viewer.

Summary

✦ Double-clicking a database icon on the Desktop is the quickest way to launch FileMaker Pro and simultaneously open the database.

✦ Changes you make to a database are automatically saved for you. If you want to preserve a database, you can use the Save a copy as command to make a backup copy.

✦ You can issue commands by choosing from menus and, in some cases, by pressing keyboard shortcuts.

✦ FileMaker Pro makes extensive use of tools and palettes, especially for designing database layouts.

✦ FileMaker Pro 8 has four toolbars that enable you to issue common commands, format text, arrange items in Layout mode, and create/edit layouts.

✦ FileMaker Pro offers several different types of Help information. You can summon Help when working in most parts of the program by choosing a command from the Help menu, pressing a keyboard shortcut, or clicking a Help button in a dialog.

✦   ✦   ✦

What's New in FileMaker Pro 8?

A s it has in the past, FileMaker Pro 8 builds upon the capabilities and features of previous versions of the program. If you've used FileMaker Pro in any of its earlier incarnations, the information in this chapter will help smooth your transition to FileMaker Pro 8 by pointing out the changes and additions you need to learn about. In the sections in this chapter, we briefly describe the new features. Some of these feature additions and changes are fairly advanced and might not make a lot of sense to someone unfamiliar with previous versions.

Note A section at the end of this chapter covers features introduced in FileMaker Pro 7. This section will be especially useful to those of you coming from an even earlier version of FileMaker Pro. FileMaker Pro 7 was, arguably, the most comprehensive re-engineering of the product, at least on par with FileMaker Pro 3 (which made FileMaker Pro a relational database).

The FileMaker Pro 8 Product Family

As was the case with FileMaker Pro 6 and 7, FileMaker Pro 8 consists of a line of interrelated products, each designed to address a specific database need.

Note In the past, FileMaker, Inc. introduced its base product, FileMaker Pro, first. Then, the remaining products in the line were usually released over the six- to nine-month period that followed. However, with version 8, FileMaker has managed almost simultaneous releases of both the main and Server versions of its product. At the time of this writing

(October 2005), FileMaker Server shipped very shortly after FileMaker Pro 8; FileMaker Pro 8 Mobile is coming soon and will be available by the time this book makes it to the bookstores. Although this book covers only FileMaker Pro 8 and FileMaker Pro 8 Advanced, we feel that you should be aware of the other parts of the product family.

✦ *FileMaker Pro 8:* Regardless of how you will eventually use a FileMaker Pro database (as a single-user database, shared on a network, or published on an intranet or the Web), you design and modify it by using FileMaker Pro 8 or FileMaker Pro 8 Advanced. To work with any FileMaker Pro database (other than those published on the Web or those created as standalone or run-time solutions), each user must have his or her own copy of FileMaker Pro. Web-published databases are viewed and modified by using a browser, such as Internet Explorer, Safari, Firefox, or Netscape Navigator.

Note FileMaker Pro 8 can share files only among small workgroups. If more than five users need to simultaneously share a database on a network, they must host the database with FileMaker 8 Server or FileMaker 8 Server Advanced.

✦ *FileMaker Pro 8 Advanced:* Although developers can easily create databases for their companies or for resale with a standard copy of FileMaker Pro 8, Advanced offers special developer tools as well as the ability to create standalone databases that Mac or Windows users who don't have a copy of FileMaker Pro can run.

✦ *FileMaker Server 8*: FileMaker Server 8 is used to host databases on a network where more than ten users must simultaneously be able to access the database. Server 8 supports up to 250 simultaneous guests. Each user must also have his or her own copy of FileMaker Pro (either FileMaker Pro 7 or FileMaker Pro 8).

Note FileMaker Pro 7 and 8 databases cannot be served by FileMaker Server 6 or earlier versions.

✦ *FileMaker Mobile 8:* Mobile 8 lets you use a Palm OS-based or PocketPC PDA (personal digital assistant) in conjunction with simple FileMaker Pro databases. If you need to view, add, or edit FileMaker data while away from your computer, Mobile is the solution.

Changes Introduced in FileMaker Pro 8

FileMaker Pro 8 leverages the structural changes introduced with FileMaker Pro 7 (described later in this chapter) and shares the FileMaker Pro 7 file format. The thrust of FileMaker Pro 8's enhancements are centered around database layout features and the sharing of data.

The most important new and enhanced features in FileMaker Pro 8 are discussed (very) briefly in the next few pages. All these additions and changes, as well as others, are covered in greater detail elsewhere in this book.

Operating system requirements

FileMaker Pro 8 requires a fairly recent version of Mac OS X or Windows. If you're running on a Mac, you need to run Mac OS X 10.3.9 or later — commonly known as Panther (10.3.x) and Tiger (10.4.x). Windows users must run Windows XP with Service Pack 2 or Windows 2000 with Service Pack 4 or later.

Database design enhancements

As your databases become larger and more complex, managing the tables and the relationships between them becomes more difficult. FileMaker Pro 7 introduced the Relationships Graph, which was a huge step forward. FileMaker Pro 8 enhances the Relationships Graph in a number of ways to facilitate your management efforts. Among these enhancements are these helpful tools:

✦ Place notes on the graph to document features.

✦ Click a table and instantly see its related tables.

✦ Use alignment tools to more coherently present your graph.

Layout enhancements

Even though computer screens are getting bigger and bigger, supporting higher and higher resolutions, you never seem to have quite enough screen real estate to present all the fields and other layout elements your databases require — at least, not without scrolling. Traditionally, the shortage of space has been addressed either by scrolling the layout window or by creating two or more layouts. Our Address Book example in Chapter 4 used to follow the latter approach, as you can see in last edition's Chapter 4 PDF file on the companion CD-ROM. The addition of *tab controls,* which we employ in this edition's Chapter 4, lets you use a portion of your layout for groups of layout elements, only some of which are visible at a given time. This is very similar to the tabbed dialogs with which we're all familiar in Preferences dialogs or the tabbed approach to Web browsing. Figure 3-1 shows a layout containing a tab control with three tabs.

A more minor enhancement, but one that should be very popular in solutions that involve a lot of date fields (or even just a few date fields in databases with a lot of records), is the addition of drop-down calendars for date fields. Now, when you place a date field in the layout, you can specify that it be displayed as a Drop-down Calendar, resulting in the interface shown in Figure 3-2. You can still enter dates by typing, but you can also move around in the calendar display to select a date.

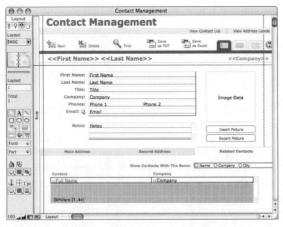

Figure 3-1: Your layouts can now contain tabs, separating fields into logical groups.

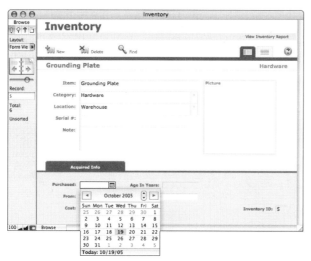

Figure 3-2: Drop-down calendars make date fields even
easier to fill in.

Note

Not only are the new layout capabilities available when you're running FileMaker Pro 8, but they're even available in databases you share via Instant Web Publishing, as are the tooltips that you can add to a database if you're using FileMaker Pro 8 Advanced. (See the upcoming section, "Advanced enhancements.")

Data entry enhancements

To help you catch typographic errors (or just protect against inferior spelling skills), FileMaker Pro 8 introduces a *live spellchecker,* which places a dotted underline — while you type — beneath those words not in your dictionary. You can use a shortcut menu (accessed by Control+clicking/right-clicking the marked word) to gain access to all your customary spell-checking functionality without having to display any dialogs.

Until now, finding a record with matching data required going into Find mode, creating a query, and executing it. With FileMaker Pro 8's Fast Search capability, you can Control+click/right-click a field's contents and choose Find Matching Records from the shortcut menu that appears — making very common and basic searches much faster and easier than ever before.

Tip

Control+clicking/right-clicking a field lets you find records that match the field's contents. Control+clicking/right-clicking a selection within the field finds matches for the selection.

Additionally, entering dates has long been a source of confusion to users, as they wonder in what format they need to enter the date. FileMaker Pro 8 includes an option to attach a drop-down calendar to date fields on a layout. When the field is so formatted, all a user need do is select the date from the calendar and FileMaker deals with the formatting.

Data sharing enhancements

Although there are undoubtedly some databases from which you don't want to produce any reports or summaries, most databases are used to store, retrieve, and communicate information. Three features added in FileMaker Pro 8 make the communication easier and save a few trees in the process.

FileMaker incorporates Datalogic's Adobe PDF support library, letting you create PDF files directly within FileMaker, retaining all the formatting and appearance of your report while supporting PDF security features, such as password access and disallowing printing.

FileMaker is a great database management, but like other database managers, it focuses on entering, storing, and retrieving information, leaving analysis of the data to other applications (or to the human element). Probably the world's most heavily used data analysis application is Microsoft Excel. FileMaker Pro 8 lets you save records in Excel format—outputting one record or the current found set as an Excel worksheet so that you can apply Excel's analysis and modeling tools to your data.

And closely tied to both the PDF and Excel support just mentioned is the new ability to send your PDF or Excel output as an e-mail attachment.

ScriptMaker enhancements

FileMaker Pro 8 introduces *script variables,* which allow you to define variables that can be either local or persistent, to hold and receive intermediate values. This eliminates the cumbersome (and distracting) use of global storage fields that proliferated in many solutions.

This and other ScriptMaker changes are covered in greater detail in Chapter 15.

Advanced enhancements

Formerly known as FileMaker Pro Developer, FileMaker Pro 8 Advanced introduces the ability to copy and paste tables between database files as well as import tables, including their schemas. You can also copy scripts from one database file to another.

Modern applications and operating systems employ a modeless form of user assistance known as *tooltips,* which are little text bubbles that appear when the mouse hovers over interface elements. You can now attach tooltips to your layout elements, providing customized help to your users in a familiar paradigm.

Debugging scripts has become even easier with the new capabilities of disabling/re-enabling specific script steps, monitoring field and variable data while debugging in the new Data Viewer, and tracing the script's calling structure for subscripts.

Also introduced in Advanced is the ability to further customize your solutions by defining and implementing your own menu structures, (almost) completely replacing the standard FileMaker menus. In addition to defining your own menu items and what they do, you can group menus into sets that can be linked to specific layouts.

Changes Introduced in FileMaker Pro 7

FileMaker Pro 7 was the most extensive revamping of the FileMaker product since its initial release in the mid 1980s. The most important new and changed features in FileMaker Pro 7 are discussed (very) briefly in the next few pages.

FileMaker Pro 7 introduced several changes that are not specific to a particular mode or program state.

Operating system requirements

For the first time in our memory, a FileMaker Pro version release was incompatible with most older operating system versions on both Mac and Windows. To use FileMaker Pro 7 on a Mac, you needed Mac OS X (v. 10.2.8 or later). Windows users need to run Windows 2000 (SP 4) or Windows XP to employ FileMaker Pro 7.

File format changed

The file formats for FileMaker Pro 5, 5.5, and 6.0 databases were identical and used the .fp5 file extension. Databases created in FileMaker Pro 7 employed a new format and bear the extension .fp7. The .fp7 file is not usable with any previous version of FileMaker Pro.

> **Note** FileMaker Pro 8 uses the same .fp7 extension (and file format).

When you used FileMaker Pro 7 to open a database created with an earlier version, a new copy of the database was created in FileMaker Pro 7 format. If you needed to access the database with an earlier version, the original was still available but did not reflect any subsequent changes you made to the data, layouts, or scripts with FileMaker Pro 7. In short, you ended up with two databases, each containing overlapping but not identical records.

Multiple tables per file

In all previous incarnations, FileMaker Pro supported only (and exactly) one table per file. The FileMaker Pro 7 format supported zero or more tables per file. With multiple tables per file, you can create a complete relational system in a single desktop icon, significantly lowering the application and system overhead of simultaneously handling multiple files and reducing your organizational work by keeping all components together and in synchronization.

New relational model

Your relationships were no longer constrained to being *unidirectional* (parent-children). By introducing a new graphical view of all tables and relationships, FileMaker 7 relationships were *bidirectional* (sibling or peer), where related records from any table in the graph are accessible. Each file's relationship graph was independent and could refer to tables in any other file. Among other things, this means that a file might contain no tables of its own, tying together tables from other files. Thus, layouts and scripts could be separated from the data/tables they reference.

Another relational model enhancement was the addition of more complex relationships. Not only could a relation be based upon equality of key: It could be based on inequality, comparison, or cross-product.

New Database Definition dialog and Field options

In all previous versions of FileMaker and FileMaker Pro, defining a database involved just specifying the fields (name, type, and options). With FileMaker Pro 7's relational model supporting multiple tables per file came a significantly expanded Define Database dialog with three tabs: Tables, Fields, and Relationships. The three tabs are displayed in Figure 3-3.

Global storage fields could be calculated fields and have all the other characteristics of normal fields, such as auto-enter and range validation. Note that this did not mean that global field values propagated to the host computer in a distributed system — they were still maintained locally.

Repeating fields allowed for specification of the starting and ending repetition to display as well as summarization.

New Accounts methodology eliminates groups

A new account/access-level model replaced the old user/group model. Instead of assigning privileges directly to an account, you specified a privilege set that defined the account's access level.

Tables

Fields

Relationships

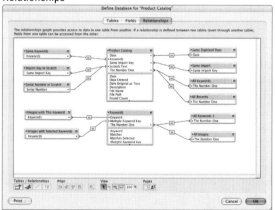

Figure 3-3: The Define Database dialog's three tabs.

Note   If you're running in Mac OS X, the privilege mechanism was supported by its Keychain.

If you attempted to open a secured database, there was a new login dialog in which you entered your account name and password. Autologin and Guest access were still supported.

Three new Get functions were available to scripts to return the current user, all enabled extended privileges, or the current user's privilege set. See Chapter 19 for a breakdown of what this all means.

New calculation features

FileMaker Pro 7 used a new fixed-point math library, totally eliminating rounding errors and supporting up to 400 decimal digits on either side of the decimal point.

Note   Trigonometric functions still used operating system routines (Mac or Windows) and were limited by the precision those provide.

Functions were added to programmatically control font face, size, style, and color.

Local variable support (Let function) allowed for temporary local variables in scripts, which improved performance by letting you store instances of a calculation or reference for repeated use.

The Evaluate function let you perform a complete calculation but was otherwise analogous to the GetField function.

Type conversion functions replaced existing GetAsText functions. You can find a complete list, with descriptions, of all FileMaker Pro functions in Appendix C.

In FileMaker Developer 7, you could create your own custom calculation functions. These custom functions could be called by a user in FileMaker Pro 7 but only in the file in which they were stored. They could not be imported into another file but could be copied/pasted if the user had that privilege specified.

C/C++ style comments could be included in a formula for documentation and future reference.

FileMaker Pro 7 also featured numerous other new functions and function changes. Refer to Chapter 14 and Appendix C for a detailed breakdown and enumeration of the available functions and, where pertinent, changes to them.

ScriptMaker enhancements

All options were editable in ScriptMaker on a step-by-step basis. This allowed multiple Find/Sort/Print operations in a single script, each with its own options. You no longer had to create a new script for each Find/Sort/Print operation to be called as a subscript.

Button scripts supported all steps other than conditional and repetition (flow-of-control). In other words, loop and If steps weren't supported in button scripts.

Calculations could be used as arguments to a script step. Further, scripts could take a parameter string.

ScriptMaker changes are covered in greater detail in Chapter 15.

Enhanced Instant Web Publishing (IWP)

Web Companion support was extended to over 70 script steps. The Web Publishing engine could directly execute ScriptMaker scripts, allowing you to build a reusable library. Additionally, Instant Web Publishing and FileMaker Pro used consistent terminology (that is, no more Find Records versus Search Records).

Unicode support

FileMaker Pro 7's text engine was based on Unicode, which means that there was only one FileMaker Pro 7 application worldwide, with the user determining which language resources to install. Another result of Unicode support was the elimination of separate file formats (Japanese) to handle multibyte character encodings.

New and updated templates

FileMaker Pro 7 included new and updated templates, with the Business category split into more manageable chunks: Finance, General, People & Assets, and Projects. The new and relocated templates were Document Library (Business – General, formerly Education), Issue Trading (Business – Projects), Lending Library (Business – People & Assets), Movie Library (Home), People Management (Business – People & Assets), Registration (Business – General), Research Notes (Business – General, formerly Education), Resource Scheduling (Business – Projects), and Task Management (Business – Projects).

✦   ✦   ✦

Database Design Basics

Creating Your First Database

When we first conceived this chapter, we imagined walking you through the steps of creating a simple FileMaker Pro database. But the more we thought about it, the more pointless that approach seemed. The purpose of this book is to give you a solid understanding of FileMaker Pro's features and capabilities — not just a quick glimpse of them. So the chapter took a dramatic turn.

Instead of helping you design a simple database in this chapter, we step you through the creation of a full-featured database called *Address Book Advanced,* which is a database featuring multiple layouts, buttons, scripts, and reports. Figure 4-1 shows the data entry layouts for the completed database and points out some of its features. The only major FileMaker Pro 8 features that we don't cover here are multiple tables and relations, but we get to those in subsequent chapters (in particular, Chapter 18).

Note   For those of you who have encountered the Address Book Advanced example in previous editions, we have made a major change by employing FileMaker Pro 8's new tab controls on a single layout rather than creating separate layouts for Work and Home information.

This extended exercise will help you become familiar with many of the important functions of FileMaker Pro while you create a database that you might actually want to use. After you finish making the database, you will have at least a passing familiarity with how FileMaker Pro works and its many capabilities. In later chapters, we provide in-depth instructions on using the program features discussed in this chapter.

Pop-up list   Switch to Home tab   Send e-mail   Pop-up list

Date stamp   Go to URL   Scrolling field

Work layout

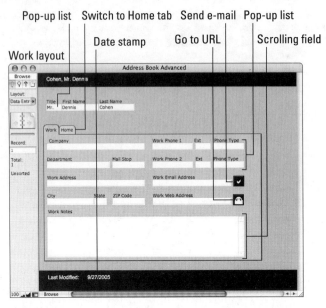

Home layout

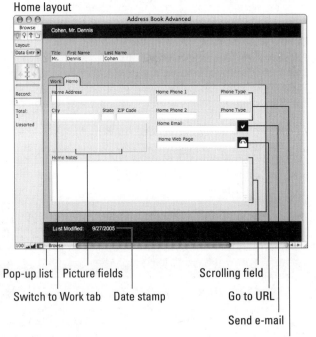

Pop-up list   Picture fields   Scrolling field

Switch to Work tab   Date stamp   Go to URL

Send e-mail

Pop-up lists

Figure 4-1: The data entry layout for Address Book
Advanced — both tabs.

Designing a database that does exactly what you want (collecting the proper data and presenting it in ways that meet your specific needs) is seldom a linear process. Unless you spend an inordinate amount of time planning a database before you begin the actual construction work in FileMaker Pro (or any other database management system), you're likely to add fields, delete some fields (that in retrospect, you didn't really need), design additional reports, and tweak the layouts (trying out different fonts and alignments, for example). In the design process, you'll repeatedly bounce among Layout, Browse, and Preview modes, as well as in and out of ScriptMaker.

Like most tutorials, this one is in a step-by-step, linear format, but don't be fooled. This relatively simple database took a full day to construct, and the process was far from linear. So don't be surprised if the process you go through in designing your own databases doesn't match the Step 1 ➪ Step 2 ➪ Step 3 approach that you find in this chapter. (Of course, planning *does* help. The more time you spend deciding which fields, reports, and scripts you need, how to format fields, and what you want the layouts to look like, the faster the creation process will go.)

Note Even if you've gone through this tutorial in a previous edition of this book, we strongly recommend that you at least read through this material. You'll find many useful tips for creating better databases; a number of interface elements have changed; and, as noted earlier, we show you how to use tab controls rather than separate layouts.

Step 1: Create a New Database

The first step depends on whether FileMaker Pro is running.

✦ *If FileMaker Pro isn't already running,* double-click the FileMaker Pro icon to launch the program. To begin the process of creating the database, select Create a new empty file from the New Database dialog and then click OK.

✦ *If FileMaker Pro is already running,* choose the File ➪ New Database command. The New Database dialog appears. Select Create a new empty file and then click OK.

In either case, a file dialog appears. Select the disk and folder in which you want to store the new database, enter a name for it (**Address Book Advanced** or **Address Book Advanced.fp7**), and click Save. The Define Database dialog appears, displaying the pane associated with the Fields tab (see Figure 4-2).

Table containing these fields   List of fields appears here.

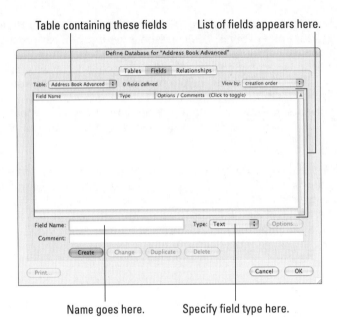

Name goes here.   Specify field type here.

Figure 4-2: The Define Database dialog's Fields pane.

Step 2: Define Fields

Like with any new database, the first task is to define the fields the database will use to store and present the data. A *field definition* consists of the field's name, the type of information the field will contain (for example, text, number, date, time, picture, or calculation), and any special options you want to set for the field.

Defining fields for a database often requires several steps. You normally begin by defining all the fields you think you will need. In the process of designing the database, however, you'll often discover that you should have created additional fields or find that you don't need some of the fields you've already defined. Making a change in the fields isn't a problem. You can add or remove fields even after you've created records and entered data.

To keep things simple, we've used only a few field types in this database: Text, Date, Calculation, and Container. (Container is the type representing multimedia content, such as pictures, video, or sound.) Table 4-1 lists the database fields you need to define. Don't worry if you don't understand the Options column right now; we deal with that later.

Table 4-1
Field Definitions for Address Book Advanced

Field Name	Type	Options	Field Contents
Title	Text	Value list	Person's title
First Name	Text		First name of contact
Last Name	Text		Last name of contact
Company	Text		Company affiliation
Department	Text		Department
Mail Stop	Text		Mail stop
Work Address	Text		Street address
Work City	Text		City
Work State	Text		State
Work ZIP Code	Text		ZIP code
Work Phone 1	Text		Area code and phone number
Work Phone 1 Ext	Text		Phone extension
Work Phone 1 Type	Text	Value list	Phone type
Work Phone 2	Text		Area code and phone number
Work Phone 2 Ext	Text		Phone extension
Work Phone 2 Type	Text	Value list	Phone type
Work Email	Text		E-mail address
Work URL	Text		Web address
Work Notes	Text		Notes
Home Address	Text		Street address
Home City	Text		City
Home State	Text		State
Home ZIP Code	Text		ZIP code
Home Phone 1	Text		Area code and phone number
Home Phone 1 Ext	Text		Phone extension
Home Phone 1 Type	Text	Value list	Phone type
Home Phone 2	Text		Area code and phone number
Home Phone 2 Ext	Text		Phone extension

Continued

Table 4-1 *(continued)*

Field Name	Type	Options	Field Contents
Home Phone 2 Type	Text	Value list	Phone type
Home Email	Text		E-mail address
Home URL	Text		Web address
Home Notes	Text		Notes
Picture 1	Container		Picture
Picture 2	Container		Picture
Last Modified	Date	Modification Date	Date the record was last altered
Full Name	Calculation	Indexed	Full name (displayed in header)

Note   Early database applications often required that you define all fields and set options for them at the same time. Like most modern database applications, however, FileMaker has no such requirement. You can return to the Define Database dialog's Fields tab whenever you want to add and delete fields, set and change field options, and so on.

You need to set options for only two fields initially: Last Modified and Full Name. Although you can set field options when you are defining the field, for this example, you define all the fields first and then set all necessary field options.

Text or number fields?

Although the phone number, extension, and ZIP code fields contain numbers, these fields are defined as text fields rather than number fields in Address Book Advanced. In FileMaker Pro, you should define a field as a number field for the following reasons:

✦ You intend to use the contents of the field in a calculation.

✦ You want to restrict the contents of the field to numbers only.

Because you aren't going to base a calculation on any of these fields and because they can legitimately contain letters or special characters—such as (619) 443-5555, 1-800-SUCCESS, and N9B 3P7 (a Canadian postal code)—treating them as text rather than defining them as numbers makes better sense. In addition, some U.S. ZIP codes start with a 0, which wouldn't show up in a Number field. Furthermore, nine-digit ZIP codes contain an embedded dash.

To define the first field, type **Title** in the Field Name text box of the Define Database dialog's Fields pane. Because Text is already chosen as the field type and you aren't assigning any options to the field, click the Create button. The field is added to the scrolling list at the top of the dialog. (Later in this chapter, we'll describe how to create a value list and associate it with a field definition.)

To create the First Name field, type **First Name** in the Field Name text box and click Create again. Continue this process, defining every text field in Table 4-1 (the First Name field through the Home Notes field).

Tip

You can make the field definition process go faster by pressing Return (Enter) immediately after you type each field name. Whenever the Create button—or any other button in a dialog—has a blue highlight (Mac)/a drop shadow (Windows), you can choose it by pressing Return (Enter). Of course, you can still click the button with the mouse if you prefer.

Now create the two picture fields: Picture 1 and Picture 2. Set the field type for each of them to Container.

Next, create the Last Modified field. Type **Last Modified**, choose Date as the field type, and click Create.

Finally, create the Full Name field. Specify Calculation as its field type, and then click Create. The Specify Calculation dialog appears. Enter the following formula *exactly* as shown in Figure 4-3:

```
Last Name & ", " & Title & " " & First Name
```

The formula works by *concatenating* each person's last name, title, and first name into a single text string while inserting the necessary punctuation. Last Name is immediately followed by a comma and a space (" , ") the Title (such as Mr. or Ms.), another space (" "), and then the first name. Our names, for example, would be calculated as **Schwartz, Dr. Steven** and **Cohen, Mr. Dennis**. The & symbols in the formula are concatenation symbols; they're used to combine text strings.

To complete the formula, choose Text as the Calculation result type. Click the Storage Options button, set Indexing to All (see Figure 4-4), and click OK. (The purpose of enabling indexing for this or any other field is because you intend to frequently sort or search on this field. Indexing speeds up this process.) Click OK again to dismiss the Specify Calculation dialog. Don't dismiss the Define Database dialog yet, though—you still have more to do in it.

Note

The Define Database dialog can be resized by clicking and dragging its bottom-right corner. This comes in handy for examining fields that have multiple options, as well as for lengthy Calculation fields. FileMaker Pro 8 features a large number of resizable dialogs.

Field list   Operators   Function list

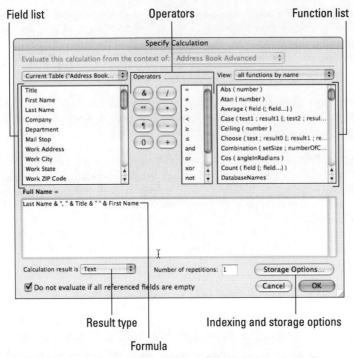

Result type

Formula

Indexing and storage options

Figure 4-3: Specifying the formula used to calculate the Full Name field.

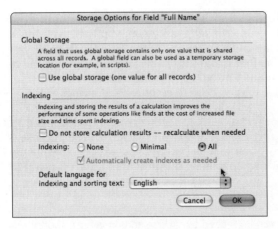

Figure 4-4: Setting storage options for the Full Name field.

Step 3: Set Field Options

You can use various field options to help you automatically enter information (such as the current date or a serial number), verify that only appropriate data has been entered, or create repeating fields. To give you a sample of these capabilities, this section shows you how to define options for the Last Modified field.

Select the Last Modified field in the Define Database dialog's Fields pane, and then click the Options button. The Options for Field Last Modified dialog appears.

Note Regardless of the field for which you are setting options, the dialog always looks the same. However, the name of the dialog changes to reflect the name of the field for which you're setting options.

Click the Auto-Enter tab at the top of the dialog (if it is not already displayed) and then choose Date from the pop-up menu (drop-down list) to the right of the Modification check box (see Figure 4-5). FileMaker Pro will automatically mark this check box. Click OK to return to the Define Database dialog. You'll see that the Last Modified field now lists Modification Date in the Options column. (When you set options for any field, they are noted in the Options column.)

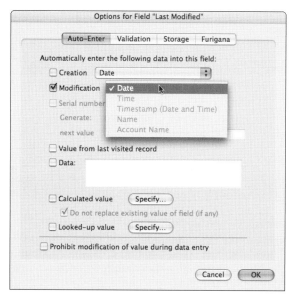

Figure 4-5: Setting an auto-entry option for the Last Modified field.

Note Note that the Last Modified field is automatically filled in with today's date. This happens whenever you create a new record or edit an existing one. Be aware that when you first enter Browse mode after defining the fields, no record exists until you choose Records ⇨ New Record.

After you've defined all the fields and set their options, click OK to dismiss the Define Database dialog. A standard layout is automatically created for you, as shown in Figure 4-6. As you can see, a *standard layout* is a vertical arrangement of all the database fields. Each field includes a label that matches whatever you named the field in the Define Database dialog; initially, all fields are the same size.

Figure 4-6: The initial database arranged in a standard layout.

Note

As you can see in Figure 4-6, we had to reduce the magnification to 75% to make all fields visible to you on a full-screen (1024 x 768) layout without scrolling the window. (One of the benefits of the higher-resolution monitors that are becoming so common is that you don't have to "zoom out" quite so often.)

If you're interested in only a quick-and-dirty database, you can stop right here. Address Book Advanced is ready to receive data. However, in keeping with the goal of this chapter — to teach you how to create a full-featured database — the next step involves rearranging the fields, adding field formatting, and including some color to make this layout more visually appealing.

Cross-Reference

When you'd like to learn more about defining fields and setting field options, see Chapter 5.

Step 4: Design the Layout

If you want to take a standard layout beyond the functional stage — all the way to attractive and pleasant to use — you might find that you spend more time on this task than on any other database development task. Frankly, however, not every database is worth the extra effort required to "pretty it up." Many databases, such as those intended only for your personal use, need never evolve beyond the functional stage. A database that you use daily or one that you intend to distribute to others, on the other hand, should look good and contain scripts making it easy to perform common tasks. In this step, you'll do the work that's required to create an attractive layout.

Creating a new layout

Normally, the standard layout that FileMaker Pro automatically creates is a good starting point for a database. You can often rearrange the fields, add graphics, and come up with an attractive result. However, because FileMaker Pro 8 includes a variety of attractive layout themes that set background colors, field styles, and text fonts, you can often get much closer to a final layout by letting FileMaker Pro help you generate it.

Note

You cannot apply a theme to an existing layout. Themes are *initial* settings for a layout during its creation via the New Layout/Report Assistant only.

STEPS: Creating the Data Entry Layout

1. With Address Book Advanced open, switch to Layout mode either by choosing View ➪ Layout Mode, clicking the Layout button in the Tools sidebar, choosing Layout from the Mode pop-up, or pressing ⌘+L/Ctrl+L.

2. Choose Layouts ➪ New Layout/Report (or press ⌘+N/Ctrl+N).

   The New Layout/Report Assistant appears (see Figure 4-7).

3. Type **Data Entry** in the Layout Name text box.

   This will be the name of the initial data entry layout that you'll use to record each person's mailing addresses, e-mail addresses, and so on.

4. Because you want FileMaker to format the fields for you as well as set the background colors, select Standard form as the layout type and then click Next to continue.

5. In the Specify Fields screen (see Figure 4-8), select and move all the fields. (To move a field to the Layout fields list, select the field and click the Move button. You can also move a field by double-clicking its name. To simultaneously move multiple contiguous fields, hold down Shift as you select the first and last fields, and then click Move. You can also combine these techniques as follows: Click Title, Shift+click Work Notes, and then ⌘+click/Ctrl+click Last Modified and Full Name to select all the fields at one time. Or, as in this example, you can move all the fields by clicking the Move All button.)

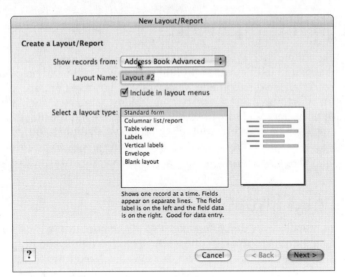

Figure 4-7: The opening screen of the New Layout/Report Assistant.

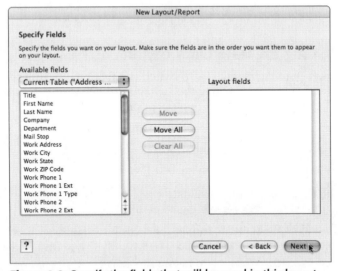

Figure 4-8: Specify the fields that will be used in this layout.

6. Because the fields will initially be arranged according to the order set in the Layout fields list, you can save a little work by dragging the Full Name field up

to the top of this list. (The person's full name will be displayed in the header.) Click Next to continue.

Note

In this and other FileMaker Pro lists, you drag an item by dragging the small, double-headed arrow at the left of the item's name.

7. In the Select a Theme screen (see Figure 4-9), choose a color scheme and field styles.

For this database, we select the Ocean Blue Screen. (Feel free to choose a different screen theme, if you want, but be aware that different themes might employ different fonts and sizes, making placement and arrangement not match our example.)

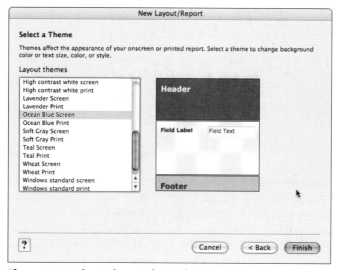

Figure 4-9: Select a layout theme here.

8. Click Finish.

The new layout is generated for you, as shown in Figure 4-10.

When FileMaker Pro creates a standard layout, it automatically generates three basic sections (called *parts*) for the layout: header, body, and footer. As your needs dictate, you can remove unnecessary parts and create additional parts, such as a title header (for the first page in a report layout) and sub-summary parts (for numerically summarizing data across records in the database). The data entry layout will use all three standard parts but not require any others, so you don't have to delete or add parts.

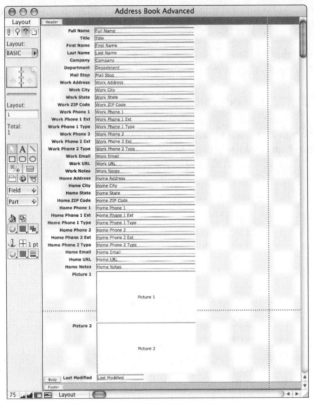

Figure 4-10: The generated Work layout.

Setting field attributes

Instead of immediately moving the fields and labels to their final resting places on the layout, you'll use the initial stacked format to select the fields and assign text attributes (font, size, style, alignment, and color) and field borders to them, as described in the following sections.

Text attributes

All the field labels are displayed in the finished database with the same font and format, so start by selecting them. In the initial Data Entry layout, the fonts and sizes for the labels and fields are the same. One difference is that the labels automatically appear in the boldface, which you're going to remove.

To select multiple objects, first select the Pointer tool by clicking its icon in the Tools palette. Then do either of the following:

✦ Drag a selection rectangle that completely surrounds the objects of interest.

✦ Hold down the Shift key and click every object that you want to include in the selection.

You can also combine the two approaches. In this case, however, because the field labels are all stacked in a nice, neat column, the first approach is simplest. The selected labels should look like the ones in Figure 4-11.

Tip   Another way to select multiple items on a layout is to hold down the ⌘/Ctrl key as you drag the selection rectangle. Rather than having to surround the objects you're selecting, merely touching them with the selection rectangle is sufficient.

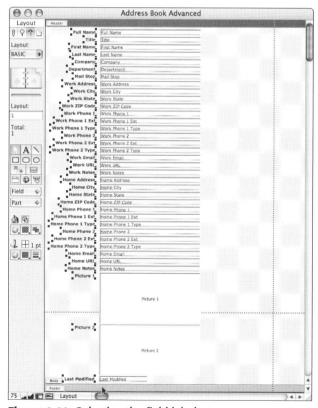

Figure 4-11: Selecting the field labels.

Preselecting text-formatting settings

Whenever you enter Layout mode and set a new font, style, color, and so on without first selecting a field or object to which the formatting will be applied, those formatting options become the new defaults. The next field, label, or object you create will automatically use your preselected settings. You can use this trick to preselect the text formatting for fields, saving yourself the trouble of having to reformat each field manually after FileMaker Pro generates the layout. (Pressing ⌘/Ctrl and clicking a field or object also changes the default setting to that of the clicked field or object.)

To remove the boldface from the field labels, either choose Format ⇨ Style ⇨ Bold (Shift+⌘/Ctrl+B) (each Style command works as an on/off toggle), choose Format ⇨ Style ⇨ Plain Text (this removes *all* styles from the selected text), or click the B icon (Bold) on the Text Formatting toolbar (if the toolbar is visible). The fields and labels should now all have the same format: 10 point (pt) Verdana, no styles. (If your computer doesn't have this font installed, feel free to choose another easy-to-read font, such as Arial or Helvetica.)

You might also have noticed that every field label is right-aligned. Because you'll want them to line up with the fields beneath them (refer to Figure 4-1), they should all be left-aligned. While the labels are still selected, choose Format ⇨ Align Text ⇨ Left, click the Align Left button on the Text Formatting toolbar (if present), or press ⌘+[/Ctrl+[. (Because the label text boxes are sized to perfectly fit the enclosed text, you won't see a change unless you resize the text boxes.)

The Full Name and Last Modified fields will eventually be placed in the Header and Footer parts, respectively. To make them stand out from the data, you can assign their labels and fields a different font and size. Select the Full Name and Last Modified fields and labels by Shift+clicking the four items. Set the font and size to 12 pt Arial. (If you don't like Arial, you can use Times or any other font that you find attractive.)

Another way to quickly format fields is to use the Format Painter, which works in a similar fashion as the Format Painter in Microsoft Word. You simply select an object or text whose format you want to copy, choose Format ⇨ Format Painter or click the Format Painter icon (the paintbrush) on the Standard toolbar, and then click the object or text that you want to format. The format from the initial object or text is instantly copied to the destination object or text. In the previous example, after formatting the Full Name label as 12 pt Arial, you could have used the Format Painter to copy that formatting to the Last Modified label, and then used the same technique to copy the field formatting between the two fields.

Note, however, that you generally will not want to use this technique to copy formats between fields and field labels. In this database, for example, the fields have background colors and borders. If you selected the reformatted Full Name label and copied its format to the field, although the font and size would be correct, the field borders and background would vanish.

Placing the fields

The two major field-arrangement tasks that you have before you are placing the fields in their proper places on the layout and resizing them. In Layout mode, you can alter the size of fields, field labels, and graphic objects in a layout in two ways:

✦ *Manually:* By selecting an object and dragging one of its handles in the appropriate direction

✦ *Precisely:* By entering one or more dimensions in the Size palette

Note

A *palette* is a tiny, special-purpose window provided by some programs to display options that you need to use frequently, such as color, pattern, and other attributes. Palettes float freely onscreen and can be moved (by dragging the title bar) or closed (by clicking the Close button/box) whenever you wish. Palettes have an appearance that immediately distinguishes them from normal windows.

To see the Size palette (see Figure 4-12), choose the View ➪ Object Size command.

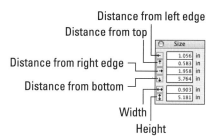

Distance from left edge
Distance from top
Distance from right edge
Distance from bottom
Width
Height

Figure 4-12: The Size palette enables you to see and change the dimensions and location of any selected object.

Similarly, you can change the position of objects on a layout either by manually dragging objects to new positions or by entering specific numbers in the Size palette (specifying the distance from the page edge to the top, bottom, left, or right edge of the currently selected object).

Because your task in this tutorial is to duplicate the layout shown in Figure 4-1 — rather than make a rough approximation of it — you can use the Size palette to avoid all the manual dragging and resizing. However, because most of the databases you'll design from scratch won't have a template that you're attempting to match, you also need to explore the manual method.

Manually placing and sizing objects on the layout

Because the Body part is currently cluttered with fields and labels, start by moving everything out of the way. Expand the layout until it is the full width of the screen. Select all the fields and labels by choosing Edit ➪ Select All (⌘+A/Ctrl+A). Then drag them to the right until they cross the vertical dashed line that marks the page break (see Figure 4-13).

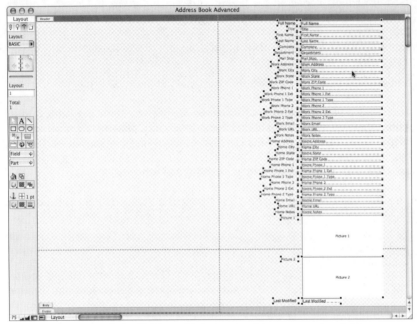

Figure 4-13: Drag all the fields and labels out of the way to the right.

Before creating layout tabs or moving any of the objects to their final positions, you might want to turn on some of the helpful tools in the View and Arrange menus. For example, Arrange ➪ Object Grids (⌘/Ctrl+Y) simplifies creating equal-size fields and arranging them in a uniform manner by restricting field movements and adjustments to those coinciding with invisible grid coordinates. With Object Grids on, you'll find it simpler to align objects as well as to evenly distribute them.

The T-Squares tool (choose View ➪ T-Squares [⌘/Ctrl+T]) can help you make sure that fields properly align with one another in straight rows and columns. You might also want to choose View ➪ Show ➪ Text Boundaries. This command places a bounding box around every field label and text object on the layout, enabling you to visually determine whether these objects are correctly positioned and aligned with other objects.

The graphic rulers (choose View ➪ Graphic Rulers) are an enormous help when placing and aligning objects. As you drag any object, its exact position is shown on the horizontal and vertical rulers. Finally, you might also find it useful to display the ruler lines (choose View ➪ Ruler Lines). Use as many or as few of these tools and visual indicators as you like.

Manually placing an object is a simple task. Click anywhere within the center of the object and drag it to a new spot on the layout. As you drag, FileMaker Pro displays an outline of the object so that you can easily see the object's precise location before you release the mouse button.

Tip   You can nudge any selected field, label, or other selected object slightly by pressing any arrow key. This technique works even when the Object Grids command is in effect.

Take another peek at Figure 4-1 to see approximately where each field and label should go on the Work layout, as well as the width of each field. (For the time being, ignore the graphics and buttons; you'll add those later.)

Begin by dragging the Title field into position. Because the Title field will contain only a short text string (Mr., Mrs., Ms., or Dr.), it's much too long and should be resized. To manually resize an object — whether it's a field, a label, or another layout object — you always start by clicking the object with the Pointer tool to select it. (A selected object has a black dot called a *handle* at each of its corners.) To change a field's size or shape, drag any handle to a new location. Dragging options include the following:

✦ *Dragging:* This normal dragging procedure enables you to change the height, width, or both dimensions as you drag. (If the Object Grids feature is on and you're reasonably careful, making sure that only one dimension changes is fairly easy.)

✦ *Shift-dragging:* If you press the Shift key as you drag, you restrict size changes to one dimension: horizontal or vertical. When you want to keep all text fields the same height (as is the case with the majority of the fields in this example), this technique is ideal for ensuring that only the field's width changes.

✦ *Option-dragging/Ctrl-dragging:* Depending on the shape of the object you're resizing (and the size of the layout), pressing the Option/Ctrl key as you drag forces the object's final shape to a square, a square with rounded corners, or a circle.

To shorten the Title field, click either of the field's handles on the right edge and drag to the left until the field is a little less than half an inch wide. (If you want to avoid inadvertently changing the field's height, hold down Shift as you drag.) Now use the same procedure to place the First Name field beside the Title field, and then resize its width to an inch or so. Finally, repeat this procedure for the Last Name field, making it about the same size as the First Name field.

Now drag the three field labels into position above the Title, First Name, and Last Name fields. You'll immediately note that (with Object Grids on) the labels are all too close or too far away from the fields and that aligning them with the left edge of each field is impossible. To nudge them into position, select the labels and then press the appropriate arrow key. Each key press will move the selected field label 1 pixel in the direction indicated by the key.

At this point, it is time to create the tab control and the two tabs on which the work-related and home-related fields will reside. Select the Tab Control tool and drag a rectangle enclosing the area where you want the tabs to reside. The Tab Control Setup dialog appears, as shown in Figure 4-14.

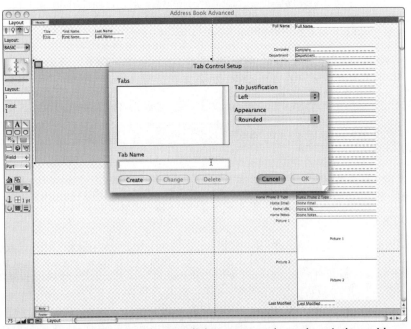

Figure 4-14: The Tab Control Setup dialog appears above the window with your new tab control.

Create your two tabs, **Work** and **Home**. Type the tab's name in the Tab Name text box and then click Create. We opted for rounded tabs (by choosing Rounded from the Appearance pop-up menu) and left tab justification (by choosing Left from the

Tab Justification pop-up menu), but you can make other choices as your aesthetic sense directs. After you've defined your tabs, click OK to dismiss the Tab Control Setup dialog.

Drag the work-related fields and labels (Company through Work Notes) into position on the Work tab, resizing them as necessary. You'll note that several of the field labels shown in Figure 4-1 have been edited, either because they were too long or because they weren't sufficiently descriptive. Each field label is merely a static text string, so you're free to edit them (or even delete them) as you see fit. Select the Text tool (the A), click within the labels, and make the changes listed in Table 4-2.

Tip   Double-clicking a text label with the Pointer tool selected automatically switches to the Text tool, facilitating your editing efforts. And, when you're finished editing, pressing Enter reselects the Pointer tool.

Note   The width of a static text string, such as a field label, does not change if you shorten its text. If some labels are now too wide, you can adjust their widths by clicking a handle and dragging. (Although being too wide doesn't hurt anything, you'll probably find it easier to work with the labels if each one is an appropriate width.)

Table 4-2
Edited Field Labels for the Work Layout Tab

Initial Label	Edited Label
Work City	City
Work State	State
Work Zip Code	Zip Code
Work Phone 1 Ext	Ext.
Work Phone 1 Type	Phone Type
Work Phone 2 Ext	Ext.
Work Phone 2 Type	Phone Type
Work Email	Work Email Address
Work URL	Work Web Address

When you're done making these changes, the only fields and labels that should still be on the right side of the screen are the Home-related fields plus Full Name and Last Modified. The layout should look similar to Figure 4-15.

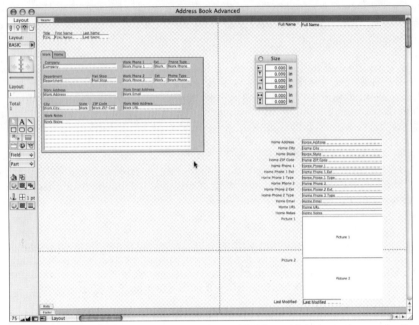

Figure 4-15: The manually placed and resized fields and labels on the Work tab.

Aligning objects on the layout

After resizing and rearranging the fields and labels, you might also want to try out FileMaker Pro's alignment commands. To keep things nice and uniform, you can use Align and Set Alignment to align the edges of any group of fields or to align fields and their labels, for example. These commands are especially helpful when you have nudged several objects with the arrow keys or have been aligning objects by using the *eyeball method* — as in, "Hmm . . . looks like the First Name and Last Name fields are lined up now."

STEPS: Aligning Selected Objects

1. Select the objects that you want to align with each other by drawing a selection rectangle around the objects with the Pointer tool, Shift+clicking the objects, or using a combination of the two selection methods.

2. Choose Arrange ➪ Align.

3. Select an option from the submenu for the alignment you seek.

   For example, to align the left-most fields and labels along their left edges, you would select Left Edges (Option+⌘+←/Alt+Ctrl+←).

FileMaker Pro executes the chosen alignment option. If the result is not what you intended, you can restore the objects to their previous locations by immediately choosing Edit ➪ Undo Align (or by pressing ⌘+Z/Ctrl+Z).

In this layout, you can use the Align submenu commands to make sure that each row of fields and each row of labels is aligned along their bottom edges. You can also align each label and its associated field along their respective left edges.

New Feature

Prior to FileMaker Pro 8, aligning objects was a much more laborious process, requiring that you invoke the (now defunct) Set Alignment dialog and establish your settings. Then, you could choose the Arrange ➪ Align menu command to repeat whatever your last settings were. Any change, and you had to go through the dialog yet again.

Using the Size palette to size and place objects

Now, if you'd like to make your layout match ours *exactly,* you can use the Size palette (refer to Figure 4-12) to set the precise placement and dimensions of the fields and labels. On the other hand, if *close enough* is good enough for you, it's okay to leave the Work tab as it is. You should at least read this section, though, so you'll understand the capabilities and power of the Size palette. Note that if you choose "close enough," you'll need to make some slight adjustments when following along later in this chapter.

You can use the Size palette to perform the following functions:

✦ Determine the exact location and dimensions of any object on a layout.

✦ Move an object to a precise location.

✦ Change the dimensions of an object.

Instead of using the Align command to arrange several fields in a perfect column, for example, you can select each field and then enter the same distance to the left edge of the page in the first text box in the Size palette. Also, by clicking several objects one by one, you can check to make sure they're all exactly the same distance from a particular edge or that they're all the same height or width.

In this tutorial, however, your use of the Size palette will be a bit unorthodox. You'll combine the second and third uses of the Size palette from the preceding list to size and precisely place every field and label on the layout — and do *both* at the same time. Using the Size palette in this manner is very much like having a robot slave who happily and mindlessly pushes the fields around the page for you.

Although this exercise doesn't have a practical application — after you start designing your own databases, that is — it does serve two important purposes. First, it enables you to match the placement of fields and labels with those in the finished

Address Book Advanced database. Second, it will make you an expert on using the Size palette. When you have a real need for it, you won't have to flip through the manual or this book to see how the Size palette works.

To resize and place the fields and labels, read the following instructions for using the Size palette and then, using the information in Tables 4-3 and 4-4, enter the appropriate numbers in the palette's text boxes to size and place the fields and field labels, respectively.

Tip   Although you don't have to perform manual Save operations when creating records, you do have to save your layout editing changes. FileMaker Pro will prompt you to save changes when you switch from Layout mode to another mode, or you can select the check box to make saving changes on leaving Layout mode automatic. You should consider choosing Layouts ⇨ Save Layouts (⌘+S/Ctrl+S) frequently during the following exercise and during your normal layout creation activities.

STEPS: Using the Size Palette to Resize and Place Objects

1. If the Size palette isn't visible, choose View ⇨ Object Size.

   The Size palette appears (as previously shown in Figure 4-12). If you want to change the measurement units for the Size palette, click one of the units to the right of any number entry in the palette. Each mouse click chooses one of the three possible measurement units: inches, centimeters, or pixels. Note that any visible text or graphics rulers will simultaneously change to reflect the chosen unit.

Tip   Using pixels is frequently the best units choice for creating layouts meant for onscreen use. Inches or centimeters are more appropriate for layouts that will be printed.

Note   When graphic rulers are displayed, the current measurement unit is also displayed in the intersection of the ruler bars.

2. Select the object whose placement or size you want to modify.

   Handles (black dots) appear at the object's corners to show that it is selected.

3. To change the position of the selected object, type numbers into any of the top four text boxes in the Size palette. In order, these boxes represent the distance from

   • *Left:* The left edge of the object to the left edge of the layout

   • *Top:* The top edge of the object to the top of the layout

- *Right:* The right edge of the object to the left edge of the layout
- *Bottom:* The bottom edge of the object to the top of the layout

Tip
You can precisely set the location of any object by specifying any pair of vertical and horizontal numbers, such as the distance from the left and distance from the top. As you make changes to the chosen pair of figures, the numbers in the other pair automatically change to reflect the object's new location.

4. To change the dimensions of the selected object, type numbers into the bottom two text boxes: width and height.

5. *To execute the changes on a Mac,* press Tab or Return to move to the next text box, press Enter to stay in the same text box, or use the mouse to click in a different text box.

   To execute the changes on a Windows PC, press Enter, or press Tab to move to the next text box.

Because the distance to the top of the layout is directly affected by the height of the Header part, you *must* resize it before using any of the figures in the following tables to set the positions of the fields and field labels. To resize the Header, click its part indicator and type **.417** in the height text box of the Size palette. Because the Footer part will be a matching height, set its height to **.417** in the same manner.

To get a feel for using the Size palette, set the size and location of the Title field and the other fields in the Body of the Work tab by following these steps:

1. Using the Pointer tool, select the Title field.

2. In the Size palette, type the numbers shown in the First Name row of Table 4-3.

   Move from one text box to another by pressing Tab or clicking in the next box with the mouse.

3. Next, without closing the Size palette, individually select each additional field and — one by one — enter the appropriate settings from Table 4-3.

Table 4-3 lists the size and placement for the fields in the Address Book Advanced database. Note that the height dimension remains constant for most of the fields. This consistency is natural because most fields contain data that is formatted with the same font and size.

Table 4-4 contains the data you need to position the field labels. It doesn't include width and height dimensions because every label is already the correct size. One by one, select each field label listed in Table 4-4 and enter its pair of placement figures in the Size palette.

Table 4-3
Work Tab: Field Size and Placement (In Inches)

Field Name	Left Edge	Top Edge	Width	Height
Title	.514	1.000	.431	.222
First Name	1.014	1.000	1.181	.222
Last Name	2.264	1.000	1.181	.222
Company	.514	2.25	3.264	.222
Work Phone 1	4.014	2.25	1.347	.222
Work Phone 1 Ext	5.431	2.25	.514	.222
Work Phone 1 Type	6.014	2.25	1.014	.222
Department	.514	2.833	2.097	.222
Mail Stop	2.681	2.833	1.097	.222
Work Phone 2	4.014	2.833	1.347	.222
Work Phone 2 Ext	5.431	2.833	.514	.222
Work Phone 2 Type	6.014	2.833	1.014	.222
Work Address	.514	3.417	3.264	.222
Work Email	4.014	3.417	2.597	.222
Work City	.514	4	1.597	.222
Work State	2.181	4	.431	.222
Work Zip Code	2.681	4	1.097	.222
Work URL	4.014	4	2.597	.222
Work Notes	.514	4.583	6.514	1.306

Table 4-4
Tab: Field Label Placement (In Inches)

Field Label	Left Edge	Top Edge
Title	.514	.806
First Name	1.014	.806
Last Name	2.264	.806
Company	.514	2.083

Field Label	Left Edge	Top Edge
Work Phone 1	4.014	2.083
Ext	5.431	2.083
Phone Type	6.014	2.083
Department	.514	2.667
Mail Stop	2.681	2.667
Work Phone 2	4.014	2.667
Ext	5.431	2.667
Phone Type	6.014	2.667
Work Address	.514	3.25
Work Email Address	4.014	3.25
City	.514	3.833
State	2.181	3.833
ZIP	2.681	3.833
Work Web Address	4.014	3.833
Notes	.514	4.333

Adding the finishing touches

In designing the Work tab, a few small tasks remain:

✦ Setting the final size of the layout

✦ Specifying colors for the layout parts

✦ Formatting and adding the Full Name and Last Modified fields to the header and footer

✦ Setting additional field options (pop-up lists, scrolling text boxes, and within-field data selection)

✦ Adding a line to separate each person's name from the other data

✦ Deleting the original, default layout (Layout #1)

✦ Creating the scripts and placing the buttons that enable you to switch between the Work and Home tabs, address e-mail, and view a Web page

In the following sections, we address all but the final point. Creating the scripts and buttons are covered in "Step 6: Create the Data Entry Buttons and Scripts."

Setting the final size of the layout

Because you will use the Data Entry layout only for data entry and never to view more than one record at a time, the layout will look better if you eliminate the unnecessary blank space in the Body part below the tab control.

STEPS: Resizing the Body Part

1. If the part designators (Header, Body, and Footer) at the bottom-left of each layout part are not horizontal, click the Parts icon (Part label control) at the bottom-left corner of the database window. (You can also switch the orientation of the part designators by ⌘/Ctrl+clicking any of them.)

2. Click the Body indicator once to select it. (When selected, a part indicator turns dark.)

3. Drag the Body indicator upward by clicking on and dragging the bottom edge (using the Pointer tool) until only a small gap exists between it and the Footer.

Note   If you find that you can't drag the Body indicator upward, it's probably because the fields and labels (off to the right) are preventing you from doing so. To correct this problem, drag those fields and labels upward and *then* resize the Body.

Your version of the Data Entry layout should now look similar to the one shown in Figure 4-16.

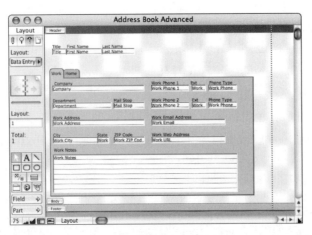

Figure 4-16: The resized Data Entry layout.

Specifying colors for the layout parts

Like many other aspects of layout design, color choices are subjective. Although many might consider the initial color choices attractive, we'll show you how to change them to a combination that we prefer.

To create backgrounds for your layouts, you can either color the layout parts or add colored graphics. To add color to the Work layout, use the first approach. To embellish the Home layout (described later in this chapter), use the second approach.

STEPS: Coloring Layout Parts

1. Click the Header part indicator to select it.

   After you've selected a part indicator, you can apply a color to it.

2. Click and hold down the Fill Color tool in the status area and select a deep shade of navy blue from the Fill Color palette that appears (see Figure 4-17).

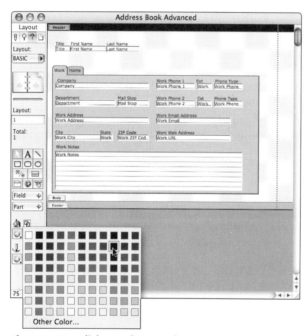

Figure 4-17: Click to select a color from the Fill Color palette.

The specific palette you'll see depends on your setting in the Layout section of the application Preferences. The palette shown in Figure 4-17 is the System subset (88 colors).

3. Select the Footer part indicator and apply the same color to it that you did for the Header.

4. In some themes (such as this one), the body part isn't a solid color; it's a combination of color and pattern. To remove the pattern, select the Body indicator and then click the solid pattern in the Fill Pattern palette (see Figure 4-18).

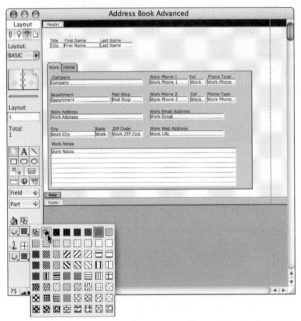

Figure 4-18: Removing the pattern from the Body.

5. Using the Fill Color palette, change the body to a shade of blue that's easier on the eyes. With the Body indicator still selected, choose the light blue that's immediately to the right of the original color selection (assuming you used the same theme we did).

Adding fields and text to the header and footer

Okay. You probably thought we'd completely forgotten about the Full Name and Last Modified fields. Well, now it's time to move them into position.

You won't be using the Full Name label, so you can start by selecting it and pressing Delete, Backspace, or Del to remove it. Now drag the Full Name field into the header and position it near the left edge. (If you still have the Size palette open, place the field 0.514 inches from the left edge, aligning it with the fields beneath it in the body.)

You'll note that the field is rather cramped. Expand the header by dragging the Header indicator down until there's a little extra blue showing. Now resize the Full

Name field so that it's centered vertically within the header, leaving the left edge at 0.514. (After you've set the header to the desired height, you might as well set the footer's height to match. Click the Header indicator and check its height in the Size palette; ours was 0.417. Now click the Footer indicator and enter the same height number in the Size palette.)

To format the Full Name field, you need to remove its background, color, special effect, and the surrounding line, as well as change the text color to white. Make sure that the field remains selected throughout the entire procedure. The following steps describe the editing changes that remove these attributes.

STEPS: Formatting the Full Name Field

1. Select the field and choose Format ⇨ Field/Control ⇨ Borders (Option+⌘+B/ Alt+Ctrl+B). In the Field Borders dialog, remove the check marks and click OK.

2. The field was also formatted as Engraved. To remove this effect, choose None from the Effects pop-up menu (the third Fill Tools palette, as shown in Figure 4-19).

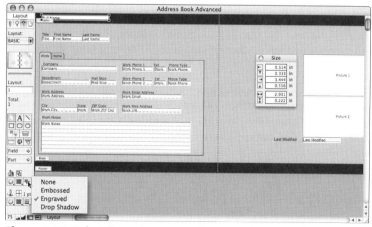

Figure 4-19: Select None to remove the engraving special effect.

3. Remove the field's color by selecting the transparent icon (the first icon) in the Fill Pattern palette.

4. Eliminate the line surrounding the field by choosing Format ⇨ Field/Control ⇨ Borders and choosing None from the Field Borders dialog's Line Width pop-up menu and click OK.

5. To set the text color, choose Format ⇨ Text Color and then click the white square in the palette-like submenu that appears.

Completing the footer

You've already set the color and height of the footer. All that's left is to move the Last Modified field and label into position. Select both items and drag them into the footer area, close to the left edge. With the items still selected, enter **0.514** in the Left edge text box of the Size palette. This will line up the label with the fields and labels in the body.

Use the Format Painter to copy the format from the Full Name field in the header to the Last Modified label and to the Last Modified field (changing both items to white, unembellished text). To finish up, edit the label by appending a colon to it (Last Modified:), and move the Last Modified field a few pixels to the right so that it isn't so close to the label.

Deleting Layout #1

There's a rule when designing FileMaker databases: *You must always have at least one layout.* Thus, you cannot delete the initial layout until you've created an additional one. You don't need the default layout that was generated when you created this database—Layout #1—so you can now delete it.

Switch to Address Book Advanced (the original default layout) by choosing it from the Layout pop-up/drop-down menu (right above the Book icon). When FileMaker Pro 8 prompts you to save changes to the Data Entry layout, do so. When Address Book Advanced is displayed, choose Layouts ➪ Delete Layout and then click the Delete button in the confirmation dialog that appears.

Caution

Be *sure* that you have Address Book Advanced displayed when you choose the Delete Layout command. Like the other deletion commands, there is no Undo if you mistakenly delete the wrong layout. FileMaker Pro 8 hints that Undo will be unavailable by using the word *Permanently* in the confirmation dialog.

Step 5: Design the Home Tab

You will use the Home tab control that you're about to configure to record home address, phone, and related information for each person in your database. As you see in Figure 4-1, the Work and Home layouts are almost identical. In fact, you should position and size corresponding fields in the Home tab identically to their counterparts in the Work tab, as described previously in this chapter.

As you can see, the Home tab contains some gaping holes where the Work tab had Company, Department, Mail Stop, and the two phone extension fields. Use the Pointer tool to select all four address fields and labels and drag upward, holding down the Shift key, until they're level with the phone fields. If you'd rather do it the easy way (not that we'd blame you), after selecting the fields and labels, all you have to do is enter **2.083** in the Size palette's second text box (distance from top).

Adding the picture fields

The gap beneath the address fields leaves a spot in which you can insert two Container fields: Picture 1 and Picture 2. For each record, you'll be able to insert a picture, sound file, or QuickTime movie into these fields. Finally, you'll align each picture field to match the top of the Home Email Address field label and the bottom of Home URL field.

STEPS: Adding the Picture Fields to the Home Tab

1. Drag the Picture 1 field onto the tab, releasing the mouse button when the field's left edge and top are in the approximate position you want.

2. Select the field and make the necessary changes to the Size palette, as shown in Figure 4-20.

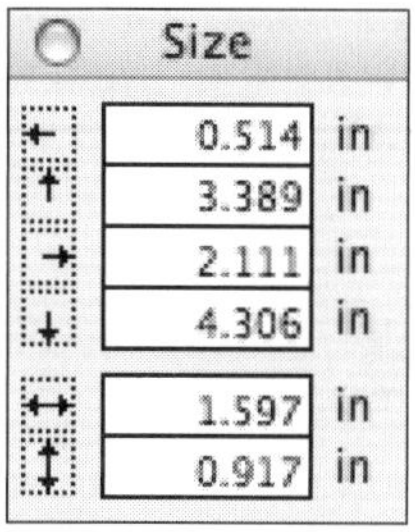

Size		
←	0.514	in
↑	3.389	in
→	2.111	in
↓	4.306	in
↔	1.597	in
↕	0.917	in

Figure 4-20: Specifications for the Picture 1 field.

3. To help the picture fields blend in, set their background color to match that of the tab's background — you can find out the tab background color by selecting the tab control and clicking the Fill Color tool to see what color is selected. Select the Picture 1 field and then choose the color and pattern that matches. Repeat for the Picture 2 field.

4. To complete the field's formatting, select the Picture 1 field and choose Embossed from the Effects pop-up menu. Repeat for the Picture 2 field.

5. Drag Picture 2 into position to the right of Picture 1. Be sure that it aligns with the top of Picture 1 and is aligned with the edges of the State and Zip Code fields directly above it.

Your Home tab should now look like what's shown in Figure 4-21.

Note

We don't want extension fields on the Home telephone numbers, so those fields should be removed from the layout.

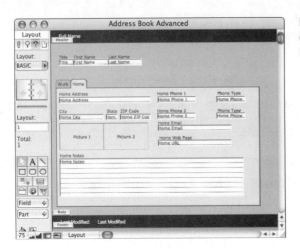

Figure 4-21: The current state of the Data Entry layout's Home tab.

Adding data entry enhancements

FileMaker has many features that help speed up data entry as well as ensure the integrity of the data. In this section, we demonstrate how a few of them work and apply them to the Work and Home layouts. These features include

- ✦ Adding a scroll bar to the large Notes text fields
- ✦ Preventing the Full Name and Last Modified fields from being modified by the user
- ✦ Creating two value lists that are presented as pop-up lists whenever you tab into or click any of the Title or Phone Type fields
- ✦ Specifying a tab order for each data entry tab

Scroll bars for text fields

Usually, if you type more text than will fit within the width and height of a given field, the excess text is hidden from view until you click or tab into the field again. Although this isn't a problem with most types of data and can often be fixed by slightly increasing the size of the field, this isn't a practical solution for fields designed to hold a lot of text — the two Notes fields, for example. Although they're already large text boxes, if you add a scroll bar to the side of the field, you can easily view any additional data that might not fit within the displayed box.

To add a vertical scroll bar to the Work Notes field, switch to Layout mode, choose the Work tab, select the field, and then choose Format ➪ Field/Control ➪ Setup. In the Field/Control Setup dialog (see Figure 4-22), choose Edit Box from the Display as pop-up menu/drop-down list, select the Include vertical scroll bar check box, and then click OK. Switch to the Home tab and use the same procedure to format the Home Notes field. In Browse mode, whenever you tab or click into either of these fields, the vertical scroll bars will appear.

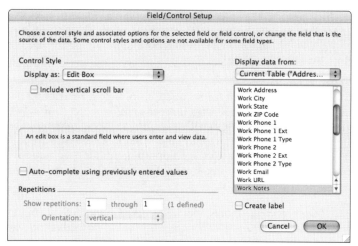

Figure 4-22: The Field/Control Setup dialog displays the currently selected field's display attributes.

 Tip   When in Layout mode, double-clicking a field on the layout will also present the Field/Control Setup dialog.

Preventing fields from being modified

If you switch to Browse mode, you'll note that nothing prevents you from manually changing the information in the header or footer — altering the data in the Full Name or Last Modified field. These two fields are intended for display only, so you need to prevent users from directly modifying their contents. Switch to Layout mode, select the Full Name field in the header, and choose Format ➪ Field/Control ➪ Behavior (Option+⌘+K/Alt+Ctrl+K). In the Field Behavior dialog (see Figure 4-23), remove the check mark from the Allow field to be entered In Browse mode check box and then click OK. Do the same for the Last Modified field in the footer. When entering data, you'll no longer be allowed to tab into or click these fields. You will, however, be able to search (do a Find) on the contents of these fields: That's why you left the check mark on the In Find mode option.

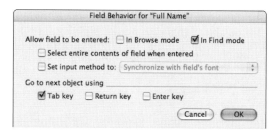

Figure 4-23: The Field Behavior dialog shows how and when the currently selected field can be entered.

In FileMaker Pro versions prior to FileMaker Pro 7, there was no Field Behavior menu option or dialog; this functionality was in the (far more-crowded) Field Format dialog. FileMaker Pro 7 and 8 split out and extends this functionality.

Formatting fields to use value lists

Freeform data entry is a good thing, but for some types of fields, restricting data to a specific set of choices is often better. Rather than ask someone to manually type the day of the week, you can provide them with a list of the days and simply ask them to choose one. FileMaker Pro can present such a list of choices (a *value list*) as a set of check boxes, a set of radio buttons, a pop-up menu, or a pop-up list. In addition to speeding data entry, presenting a value list can also ensure that every entry is worded and spelled consistently.

Note   Value lists are *field-independent:* That is, they are created independently from the fields. You can associate a given value list with as many or as few fields as you wish. You can even associate them with fields in other databases!

For this database, create two value lists that will be associated with six fields: Title (a list of titles) and Phone Type (a list of phone types). You can name the value lists anything you want. Generally, however, the more descriptive a name is, the better.

STEPS: Creating and Assigning Value Lists

1. To create a value list, choose File ➪ Define ➪ Value Lists.

   The Define Value Lists dialog appears (see Figure 4-24).

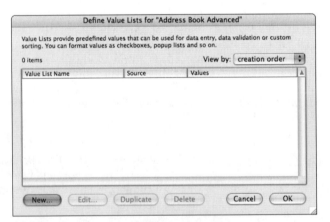

Figure 4-24: The Define Value Lists dialog.

2. Click the New button.

   The Edit Value List dialog appears (shown in Figure 4-25), in which you create and edit value lists.

Figure 4-25: The Edit Value List dialog.

3. For the first value list, enter **Title** in the Value List Name text box, make sure that the Use custom values radio button is selected, and type the following text strings in the list box to the right: **Mr., Ms., Mrs., Dr.**. Type each one on a separate line (see Figure 4-26), pressing Return (Enter) at the end of each line *except the final line.* The list should look like this:

```
Mr.
Ms.
Mrs.
Dr.
```

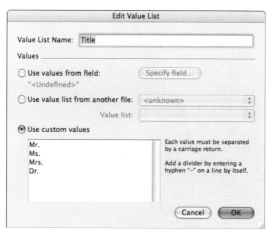

Figure 4-26: Your Titles value list.

4. Click OK when you're finished.

The Define Value Lists dialog reappears and now includes the definition of this value list.

5. Repeat Steps 2–4 to create a second value list named Phone Type. Enter the following values in the list box: **Direct**, **Switchboard**, **Cell**, **Fax**, **Pager**.

> **Note**
>
> Custom value lists are not alphabetized when they're presented to you. They're shown in the same order in which you originally typed them. If you later find that you prefer a different order (alphabetized, for instance), you can return to the Define Value Lists dialog, select the value list, click Edit, and rearrange items in the list by cutting and pasting.

6. Click OK to dismiss the Define Value Lists dialog.

   Now it's time to associate the value lists with the appropriate fields.

7. Enter Layout mode, select the Title field, and choose Format ⇨ Field/Control ⇨ Setup. In the Field/Control Setup dialog, choose Drop-down List as the format and choose Title as the value list to use from the Display values from pop-up menu/drop-down list (see Figure 4-27). Click OK.

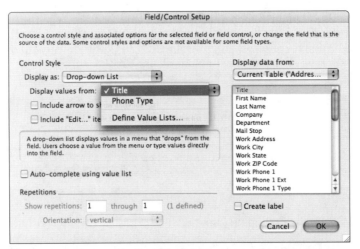

Figure 4-27: Formatting the Title field to use a value list.

8. Switch to the Work tab, if necessary, and repeat this process to associate the Phone Type value list with the first Phone Type field — as a drop-down list. Do the same for the second Phone Type field.

> **Tip**
>
> You can select multiple fields and simultaneously associate a single value list. Most times, you won't have multiple layout elements sharing a single value list, but occasionally (as here), you can save a little time by taking advantage of multiple selection.

9. Switch to the Home tab and repeat Steps 7 and 8 for the two Phone Type fields.

When you tab into or click any of these fields in Browse mode, a list will drop down (as shown in Figure 4-28).

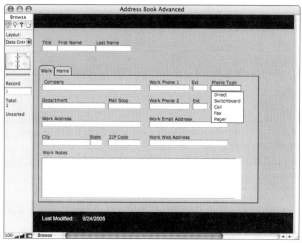

Figure 4-28: Example of a drop-down list.

Setting the tab order

When you get ready to start entering data (feel free to create a few sample records whenever you wish), most people press the Tab key to move from field to field. However, as you place and rearrange fields, the tab order invariably gets messed up, often causing the cursor to jump from field to field in what appears to be a random or nonsensical order. To correct this, you can specify a particular tab order to be used for any layout.

STEPS: Setting the Tab Order

1. Switch to Layout mode and display the Work tab.

2. Choose Layouts ➪ Set Tab Order.

   The Set Tab Order dialog appears, and each of the 21 fields on the layout is marked with a numbered arrow that indicates its present position in the tab order. The Home tab is also numbered, giving you 22 numbered items when the Work tab is selected.

3. Edit the numbered arrows as indicated in Figure 4-29. Note that the arrows in the header (for Full Name) and in the footer (for Last Modified) should be blank because you don't want users to be able to tab into or modify either of these fields.

4. Click OK in the Set Tab Order dialog.

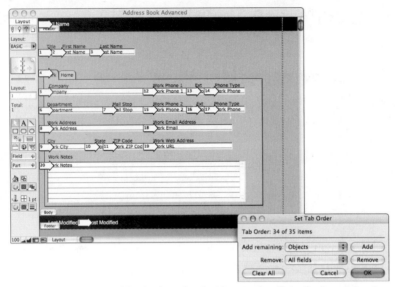

Figure 4-29: The modified tab order for the Work tab control and the Set Tab Order dialog.

5. If you'd like to test the new tab order, switch to Browse mode, click the Title field of an existing record (or create a new record), and press Tab repeatedly.

6. Repeat this procedure to set the tab order for the Home tab. Switch to the Home tab and perform Steps 2–5. See Figure 4-30 for the tab order settings.

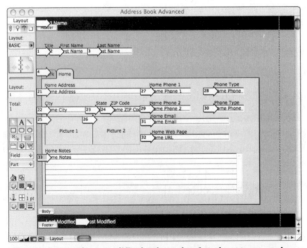

Figure 4-30: The modified tab order for the Home tab control.

Step 6: Create the Data Entry Buttons and Scripts

Strictly speaking, you could quit right here and still have an extremely functional database. However, by adding scripts that automate database operations, you can transform this functional database into an easy-to-use, time-conserving database. Carefully chosen scripts can eliminate an enormous amount of wasted effort. What's the point of constantly re-creating a particular find request or set of sort instructions, for example, when all you have to do is design a small script that performs these actions at the touch of a button?

Because the term *script* smacks of programming, many users shy away from the ScriptMaker feature. The simple but powerful scripts that we present in this section show you what those users are missing and demonstrate just how easy ScriptMaker is to use. And no programming is required!

Address Book Advanced uses scripts in two ways: Some are assigned to buttons, and others are available only as commands in the Scripts menu. Some of the scripts contain several steps, and some execute only a single command. By looking at the ways in which scripts are incorporated into this database, you can get an idea of what you can do with scripts in your own databases.

The script definition process

When creating a script, the first step is to use menu commands to perform all the actions that the script will eventually handle. Doing so sets up the database so that all necessary command options are already selected. That is, while you're executing the steps you intend to include in the script, you set the correct Sort, Find, Page Setup, Print, Export, and Import options, for example. Setting these options is essential because you cannot specify sort fields, find logic, print options, or settings for other commands as you create the script. In fact, the following methods are the only ones you can use to set options for commands used in scripts:

✦ Instruct the script to present a dialog allowing the user to verify the current settings or enter different ones.

✦ Instruct the script to use the command settings in effect at the moment the script was created.

If you are creating a generic sort, find, or export script, the first approach works well. Each time the script step is executed, the user can enter the appropriate settings in the dialog that appears.

In many cases, however, you want scripts to perform steps that have preset options. For example, you could create a script that switches to a particular layout, finds only the records of employees who have arrived late more than three times in the last month, sorts the found records by salary, sets the print orientation to landscape, and then prints the resulting report. Although you can instruct FileMaker Pro to present a dialog for each of the last four actions (Find, Sort, Page Setup, and Print), doing so is a waste of time. Because you intend to use the same options every time you execute this script, incorporating the command options within the script steps is much simpler. Doing so adds consistency to the script's performance, and it ensures that no matter who runs the script (such as a temporary worker or an assistant who is sitting in for you), the result will always be the same.

After creating the necessary scripts in the following sections, you'll assign some of the scripts to buttons. Other scripts will be available only as commands in the Scripts menu.

The Data Entry layout scripts

Address Book Advanced contains five scripts. Each of the four data entry–related scripts is described in detail in this section. (The final script — Phone Directory — creates a phone directory report from the records in the database. It's related to a second layout that you have yet to create, which we describe later in this chapter.)

Note　Before you start creating scripts, spend a few minutes entering some sample records for the database. You can more easily determine whether your scripts are working correctly if you have records in the database. To create a new record, enter Browse mode and choose Records ➭ New Record. When you're ready to use your own data with Address Book Advanced, you can delete the sample (sometimes called *dummy*) records.

First, you'll create a button enabling you to automatically address an e-mail message to the person represented by the current record. Create this one-step script button as follows.

Revealing a script's Sort and Find instructions

You can easily reveal the Sort and Find instructions that are used in scripts in other people's databases. Perform the script and then immediately choose the Records ➭ Sort (⌘+S/Ctrl+S) and Records ➭ Modify Last Find (⌘+R/Ctrl+R) commands.

When you're examining the sort instructions and find requests, performing the actual sort or search isn't necessary or even desirable. You simply use these commands to determine what options the creator of the database set for the scripts.

You can exit the Sort Records dialog by clicking Sort or Cancel and exit Find mode by choosing View ➭ Browse Mode (or by pressing ⌘+B/Ctrl+B), choosing Browse from the Mode pop-up menu, or clicking the Browse mode button in the Tools sidebar (the one that looks like a pencil).

STEPS: Creating the Send Email Button

1. Switch to Layout mode and display the Work tab.

2. Click the Button tool (the finger pressing a button) and drag a small rectangle to the right of the Work Email Address field.

   Don't worry about the size or color — you'll adjust those later.

3. When you release the mouse button, the Button Setup dialog appears, as shown in Figure 4-31.

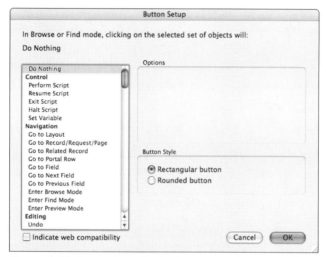

Figure 4-31: Set options for the button you just created on the layout.

4. In the Button Setup dialog, select the Send Mail script step from the scrolling list (in the Miscellaneous section). Options for the Send Mail script step appear in the Options section at the right of the dialog.

5. Click the Specify button to present the "Send Mail" Options dialog. In the To section of the "Send Mail" Options dialog (see Figure 4-32), choose Specify Field Name from the pop-up button on the right and set Work Email as the field from the Specify Field dialog that appears.

6. Click OK twice to dismiss the two dialogs.

7. In the Button Setup dialog (see Figure 4-33), ensure that the Perform without dialog check box is marked and then click OK.

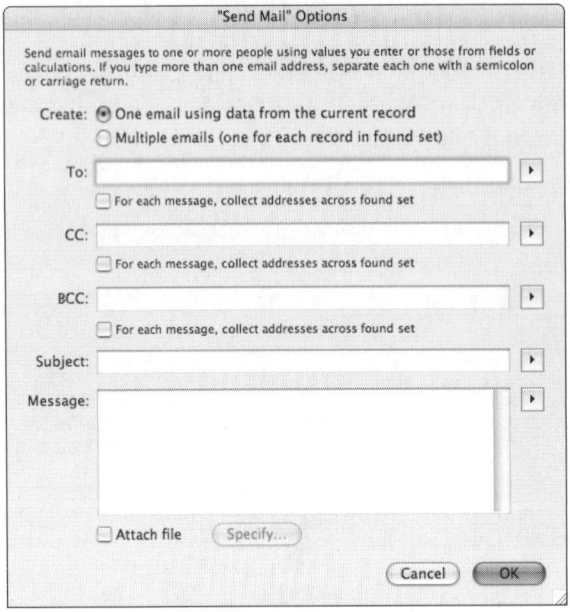

Figure 4-32: Instructing FileMaker Pro to use the e-mail address found in the Work Email field to address a new message.

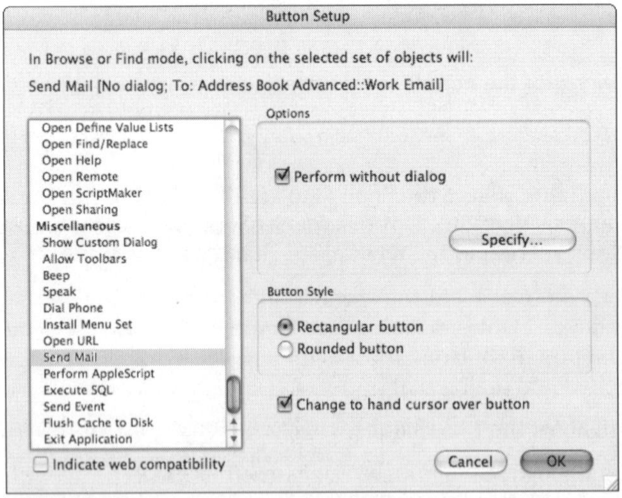

Figure 4-33: Tell FileMaker Pro to execute the script without a dialog.

8. Click OK to return to the Work tab and name the button using a single character, such as Option+v (a check mark symbol when typed on a Mac), a dingbats
font symbol (a lower-case *a* in Webdings looks like a check mark), or a Zapf
Dingbats character. Set the button's color to the same navy blue used in the
header and footer and the text color to a light color (or white) for contrast.
Size and position the button as follows: height = 0.347, width = 0.347, left =
6.681, top = 3.278 (see Figure 4-34).

Figure 4-34: The Send Email button.

Because this e-mail button will also be used on the Home tab, copy it here
(Edit ➪ Copy), paste it into the Home tab, and then move it to the same posi-
tion. Double-click the button on the Home tab, click Specify, choose Specify
Field Name from the To pop-up menu, and select Home Email (rather than
Work Email) from the field list. Click OK three times to get back to the layout.

Note

When you click the button, FileMaker attempts to launch your default e-mail program and addresses a message to the e-mail address specified in the Work Email
or Home Email field. However, even though the Send Mail script step works with
many Mac and Windows e-mail programs, it doesn't work with all of them.
Depending on which supported e-mail application you use, the addressed message will either be waiting for you in the Drafts folder (in Microsoft Entourage or
Outlook Express, for example) or be open in its own window. In either case, you
must then complete the message and send it as you normally would. (If you want
to use the database to send pre-prepared messages without further intervention
from you, modify the script by marking the Perform without dialog check box and
specify the subject, message text, and any necessary attachments in the "Send
Mail" Options dialog.)

Now create the buttons for launching the default Web browser and visiting a person
or company's Web site. The procedure is identical to the one specified for creating
the Send Email button.

STEPS: Creating the Open URL button

1. You can use a copy of the Send Mail button as the basis for the URL button.
Copy and paste the button into the layout and then align it with Work URL
field (left = 6.681, top = 3.875).

If you want to display a different symbol on the face of the URL button, click
the Text tool and then edit the button's text. (We used the lowercase *u* in
Webdings.)

2. Double-click the button, select Open URL from the script step list, click Specify, click Specify in the Open URL Options dialog, double-click Work URL in the field list of the Specify Calculation dialog that appears, and then click OK three times.

3. Copy the URL button and paste it into the Home tab. Move it into the same position as it was in the Work tab. Double-click the button and where you chose Work URL above, select Home URL as the referenced field.

The Open URL script step works with many types of Internet prefixes, such as HTTP and FTP. To ensure that FileMaker understands that you are requesting a Web site, you should enter a *full* URL for every Web address, such as `http://www.siliconwasteland.com` (rather than just `www.siliconwasteland.com`).

That completes the Data Entry layout. Compare yours with the one shown in Figure 4-1.

Step 7: Design a Report Layout

Although the Data Entry layout, with its two tabs, is excellent for its intended purpose (entering contact information), you probably won't want to use this layout to create reports. Unless you have designed an all-purpose layout for a database or think that a Table view will suffice, you're usually better off creating a separate layout for data entry and other layouts for reports.

If you're curious, open Address Book Advanced, make sure that the Data Entry layout is selected, create a few records, and then choose View ➪ Preview Mode. Preview mode shows what you would get if you printed the current layout. As you can see, only one record fits on a page, and the information in each record is arranged in exactly the same way it looks when you're in Browse mode. Pretty, but not very functional, with one tab hidden.

As an example of the kinds of reports you can produce from Address Book Advanced, you will now create a layout for a phone directory. The Business Phone Directory layout is a columnar report layout. As with most such layouts, you can print reports that you generate from the layout or view them on the monitor in Preview mode. The finished layout looks like the one in Figure 4-35.

STEPS: Creating the Business Phone Directory Layout

1. Change to Layout mode by choosing View ➪ Layout Mode (or pressing ⌘+L/Ctrl+L), choosing Layout from the Mode pop-up menu, or clicking the Layout mode button in the Tools sidebar.

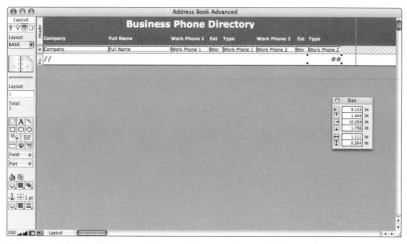

Figure 4-35: The Business Phone Directory layout (viewed in Layout mode).

2. Choose Layouts ⇨ New Layout/Report (or press ⌘+N/Ctrl+N).

   The opening screen of the New Layout/Report Assistant appears.

3. Type a name for the layout in the Layout Name text box. (In this case, type **Business Phone Directory**.)

Note
Instead of accepting the default name for the layout (Layout #2, in this example) or naming it later in the process (as you generally do with Layout #1), you can name this layout as you create it.

4. Choose Columnar List/Report as the layout type, remove the check mark from the Include in layout menus check box, and then click Next.

5. Select the Columnar list/report radio button but leave the Constrain to page width check box cleared.

Note
Leaving the Constrain to page width check box cleared corresponds to the Extended Columnar layout in FileMaker Pro 4.1 and earlier. If you wanted to restrict the width of the report to a single page width, select the Constrain to page width option (corresponding to the old Columnar report layout).

6. Click Next.

   The Specify Fields screen appears, as shown in Figure 4-36.

7. Select fields in the left side of the dialog and then click Move to transfer them to the Layout fields list on the right. When you've finished, click Next. (Note that instead of selecting a field and clicking Move, you can also simply double-click the field you want to move.)

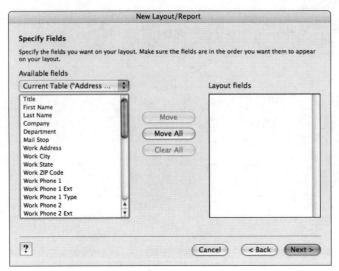

Figure 4-36: The Specify Fields screen.

The Specify Fields screen has two functions. You use it to select the initial set of fields you want to appear in the layout, as well as to set the order in which the fields appear. For the Business Phone Directory layout, select and move the following fields (in order): Company, Full Name, Work Phone 1, Work Phone 1 Ext, Work Phone 1 Type, Work Phone 2, Work Phone 2 Ext, and Work Phone 2 Type.

Tip   You can also move contiguous fields (such as Work Phone 1 through Work Phone 2 Type) as a block by Shift+selecting them all and then clicking Move.

8. The Sort Records screen appears. Move the following fields (in order): Company and Full Name. Both sort fields should be set for ascending order. (Three bars, increasing in height from left to right, denote ascending order.)

9. Click Next.

   The Select a Theme screen appears.

10. You're going to make this an onscreen report, so add some features to make it more visually appealing. Choose Lavender Screen and click Next.

    The Header and Footer Information screen appears.

11. In the Header section, click the Top center pop-up menu and choose Large Custom Text. Type **Business Phone Directory** in the dialog that appears, and click OK.

12. In the Footer section, choose Current Date from the Bottom Left pop-up menu and Page Number from the Bottom Right pop-up menu. (The settings are shown in Figure 4-37.) Click Next.

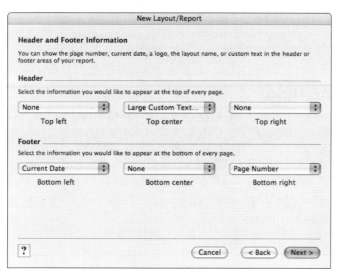

Figure 4-37: Specify header and footer information that you want to display on every page of the report.

The Create a Script for this Report screen appears.

13. Select the Create a script option and then click Next.

Although it will need some modification, the assistant-generated script will serve as a good starting point for the script that you'll use to create the report.

The final screen appears.

14. Select View the report in layout mode and then click Finish.

The report layout is generated.

If you scroll the Phone Directory layout from side to side or expand it to the full width of your screen, you'll see that it extends beyond the current page width. Three possible solutions are available:

✦ Delete some of the fields.

✦ Change the report from *portrait* (right-side up) to *landscape* mode (sideways).

✦ Change the layout by reducing the size of some fields and sliding them to the left.

Assume that you have your heart set on producing a phone directory that includes every one of the chosen fields. That leaves the second and third options. The simplest change is to switch the report to landscape mode because it doesn't involve resizing or moving fields and labels. Choose File ➪ Page Setup/Print Setup, set landscape as the orientation, and click OK to dismiss the dialog.

Unfortunately, although it helped, the fields still don't fit in a single row. Now you have to proceed with the second option—reducing field sizes and sliding them left so that they'll fit within the width of a single landscape page.

Resizing the fields

Try using the *eyeball approach* (best approximation) to resize and move the fields manually so that they fit on the layout. You can refer to Figure 4-35 and use it as a rough guideline for how wide the fields should be. (Unless you're feeling adventuresome, however, leave the column headings where they are. In the next section, we show you an easy way to move them.)

When you alter the width of each field, hold down the Shift key as you drag. Doing so ensures that only one dimension of the field will change: the width, in this case. Because the same font is used in every field, the height of each field is already correct.

When you're through manually resizing and shuffling the fields to the left, check your results against the Size palette settings shown in Table 4-5. Please note that no settings are right or wrong. As long as you leave sufficient room for each field to display its intended contents, the layout is fine. However, if the data from any record doesn't fit within a field's new dimensions (a record might contain an extra-long company name, for example), the extra characters will be *truncated* (chopped off) when the report is printed. When setting field widths, err on the plus side if possible.

As before, to examine or alter the dimensions or placement of any field, select the field on the layout and then check its size and location in the Size palette.

Table 4-5		
Field Dimensions (In Inches) for the Business Phone Directory		
Field Name	*Distance from Left Edge*	*Field Width*
Company	0.389	2.250
Full Name	2.667	2.000
Work Phone 1	4.694	1.250
Work Phone 1 Ext	5.958	0.417
Work Phone 1 Type	6.389	1.083
Work Phone 2	7.486	1.250
Work Phone 2 Ext	8.750	0.417
Work Phone 2 Type	9.181	1.083

Formatting the header

In a columnar report, the field labels for the columns are normally placed in the Header part rather than in the Body part. That way, when you scroll the report onscreen or print it, you can be assured that the column headers (that is, the field labels) are always visible. As you've seen, the New Layout/Report Assistant automatically placed the labels in the header. Thus, all you must do now is align each label with its matching field.

STEPS: Aligning the Company Label with the Company Field

1. Select the Company field and its matching label by Shift+clicking the two elements.

2. Choose Arrange ⇨ Align ⇨ Left Edges.

   The two fields are aligned.

After you set the proper alignment options, you can quickly align the remaining fields and labels by selecting each pair and pressing Option+⌘+←/Alt+Ctrl+← (the keyboard shortcut for the Align Left Edges command). Be aware that when you set Left to Right alignment options, the objects align with the position of the leftmost object. Similarly, top-to-bottom alignment is based upon the position of the topmost object.

The labels now have only one thing wrong with them: Some are longer than their matching fields. Select the Text tool (the A) from the Tools palette. Change the wording of the Work Phone 1 Ext and Work Phone 2 Ext labels to Ext. Change the Work Phone 1 Type and Work Phone 2 Type labels to Type. Then shorten their widths by clicking and dragging. Next, change the width of any additional label that's too long.

Tip Aligning before shortening works for us here because we're left-aligning text that is left-justified. The same would be true if we were top-aligning a row of labels. You should consider performing your editing and resizing operations before aligning the labels in most situations.

Finally, the report's title (Business Phone Directory) is no longer centered. Drag it until it's in the middle of the report. (In landscape mode, depending on the font and size of the title, its left edge should be approximately 3.25 inches from the left side of the layout.)

Formatting the footer

Like every other layout generated by FileMaker Pro, this one already has space reserved for a footer. Footers are often useful in report layouts. They can be used to present any information you want to see on every page, such as the page number, date, name of the database, or name of the user who created the report. While creating the layout, you specified that date-stamp and page number placeholders be included.

If you had decided to add these elements after closing the New Layout/Report Assistant, all you'd do is choose Insert ➪ Date Symbol and Insert ➪ Page Number Symbol. The date symbol is represented by a pair of slashes (//), and the page number symbol is represented by a pair of pound signs (##).

To complete the footer, all you must do is align the left edge of the date symbol and the right edge of the page number symbol with the data fields above them. Set the date at left = 0.389 inches and the page number at right = 10.264 inches.

Cross-Reference   For more information on working with layout parts, see Chapter 6.

Modifying the Business Phone Directory script

The script generated by the New Layout/Report Assistant is good but not exactly what you need. So here we show you how to make two important changes to the script:

✦ Ensure that the report is always displayed in landscape mode.

✦ Maximize the screen to the full width and height of your monitor when displaying the report, and then resize it when returning to the Work or Home layout.

STEPS: Editing the Business Phone Directory Script

1. Choose Scripts ➪ ScriptMaker.

   The Define Scripts dialog appears.

2. Select the Business Phone Directory script and click Edit.

   The Edit Script dialog appears, displaying the script that was generated by the assistant. (See Figure 4-38 for the list of script steps that will be in the edited script.)

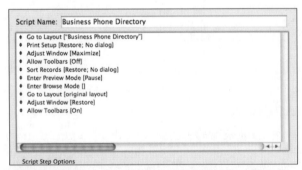

Figure 4-38: The steps in the revised Business Phone Directory script.

3. Move the Print Setup step into the script and then drag it up so it becomes the second step. When a script step is selected, its options appear in the Edit Script dialog's Script Step Options area, Select both the Perform without dialog and Specify page setup options, if they are not already selected.

Because you previously chose File ➪ Page Setup and selected landscape mode, this step assures that the report will be displayed in landscape mode.

4. Move the Adjust Window step into the script and then drag it up so that it becomes the third step. From the Specify pop-up menu, choose Maximize.

This step will automatically enlarge the database window so that it fills the screen of whatever computer it happens to be running on.

5. Because you've maximized the window size, part of it will be hidden behind any toolbars that are currently visible. Move the Allow Toolbars step into the script as the fourth step and mark the Off radio button.

6. Move a second copy of the Adjust Window step into the script (or select the one that's already in the script and click Duplicate). With the second copy of the step selected, choose Restore from the Specify pop-up menu. Make this the script's penultimate step.

This step will restore the screen to its original size in the Work or Home layout, whichever one you were in when you executed the report this time.

7. Move a second copy of the Allow Toolbars step into the script as the final step, with the On radio button selected.

This restores any previous toolbar display.

8. Click OK to close Edit Script dialog and then click OK to close the Define Scripts dialog.

Generating a report

Whenever you want to view or print a copy of the phone directory, choose Scripts ➪ Business Phone Directory or press the keyboard shortcut that FileMaker assigned to the script (as indicated in the Scripts menu). The report automatically pauses in Preview mode. If you want to view it onscreen, click the Book pages. Each page represents a different page of the report. If you'd like to print the report, choose File ➪ Print while the preview is displayed. When you're done viewing or printing the report, click the Continue button. You'll automatically return to your previous layout, the database window will be resized, and any toolbars will be restored.

Step 8: Set Startup Actions

To complete Address Book Advanced, you can add one last option to make the database even easier to use. You can specify startup actions that will occur whenever you open the database. For example, you can make the Work layout automatically appear, regardless of the layout you last used.

STEPS: Setting Database Startup Actions

1. Choose File ➪ File Options.

   The File Options dialog appears (see Figure 4-39).

Figure 4-39: The File Options dialog.

2. To set the open/close preferences for the current database, click the Open/ Close tab at the top of the File Options dialog (if it is not currently displayed).

3. Select the Switch to layout check box in the dialog's When Opening This File section and then choose Data Entry from the pop-up menu/drop-down list.

4. Click OK.

   The dialog closes, and the changes are recorded.

By choosing Data Entry from the Switch to layout pop-up menu/drop-down list, you ensure that the database will automatically open to the Data Entry layout, regardless of the layout you were using when you last closed the database.

Tip   To further ensure that the database opens in the manner that best suits your needs, you could also create a script for it that automatically executes whenever you open the database (an *opening script*). The script might change to a particular layout and sort the database by Company and Full Name, for example.

Tips for Using the Database

When you're ready to use the database to store actual contact information, start by deleting any sample records you may have entered. (You must be in Browse mode for this operation.) To simultaneously delete all records, choose Records ➪ Delete All Records. (If the status area indicates that only some of the records are currently visible, you should first choose Records ➪ Show All Records.) If you want to delete only specific records while leaving others, display each one you want to delete and choose Records ➪ Delete Record or press ⌘+E/Ctrl+E.

Here are some helpful tips for working with the database:

✦ To create a new, blank record, choose Records ➪ New Record or press ⌘+N/Ctrl+N.

✦ The person's Title, First Name, and Last Name can be entered regardless of whether the Work or Home tab is foremost.

✦ When tabbing or clicking into a field that contains a drop-down list (Title or Phone Type), most people select the item they want by clicking it with the mouse. However, you can also select an item with the up- and down-arrow keys or by typing the first letter of the item. To complete the selection and move to the next field, press Return (Enter).

✦ To insert a picture into either of the Picture fields on the Home tab, either tab into or click the field and then choose Insert ➪ Picture. A file dialog appears that enables you to choose an image file from disk. Selecting the Store only a reference to the file check box is often a good idea because it results in FileMaker merely making a note of the picture's location on disk. Storing actual images, on the other hand, can quickly cause the database to balloon in size because even though the images are tiny, FileMaker stores them in their actual size.

Caution

The downside of storing a reference is that if you ever move the database to another disk, you can break the link between the database and the picture, so you have to remember to move the pictures as well and re-create the links.

✦ You can also insert pictures in a Container field by Ctrl+clicking/right-clicking the field and choosing Insert Picture from the contextual menu that appears.

✦ If you prefer this database to another contact application or database you might be using, you might be able to export your old data to a format that FileMaker can read (such as tab-delimited text). Then choose File ➪ Import Records ➪ File to add that data as new records in Address Book Advanced. For more information on importing data, refer to Chapter 16.

Summary

✦ Creating a database can be as simple as defining fields and then using the default layout that FileMaker Pro provides. However, taking the time to enhance the database by creating custom layouts, adding graphics, and designing scripts can greatly improve a database's functionality and ease of use.

✦ Each field in a database is a specific type. The field type determines the kind of information the field can contain, such as text, numbers, dates, or pictures.

✦ You can resize and move fields as necessary. You can also apply different formatting options to fields, such as fonts, styles, sizes, and colors.

✦ A database can have as many different layouts as are needed to collect and display the data in the ways you want. For example, creating one layout specifically for entering and editing data and other layouts for generating reports and mailing labels is a common practice. Every layout draws on the same information contained in the database; FileMaker simply arranges and displays the data in a different way.

✦ Scripts enable you to automate common and not-so-common database procedures. ScriptMaker sets many script options for you by "watching" the actions you perform.

✦ You can use graphic or text objects on a layout as buttons, or you can use the Button tool to create 3-D buttons. When you click a button, it executes the script or script step that has been attached to it.

✦ To make it simple to create new layouts, FileMaker Pro provides the New Layout/Report Assistant. You can use the assistant to create layouts that conform to an overall style as well as to specify sorting instructions and create a basic script to print or preview the layout as a report.

✦   ✦   ✦

Defining Fields

As explained in Part I of this book, *fields* are the elemental building blocks from which databases are constructed. In this chapter, you'll learn all about defining fields, selecting field types, and setting field options.

Setting Field Definitions

Until you define fields for a table, you cannot store data in that table. (Technically, it isn't even a table until fields have been defined, and you can't have a database until you have at least one table.) After you select the disk and folder in which you want to store the new database and give the database a name, the next step is to specify a table and define that table's fields. The process of defining a field includes the following:

+ Naming the field

+ Setting a type for the field (the type of information the field will store)

+ Setting options for the field (data validation procedures, auto-entry options, and so on)

The first two steps, naming the field and selecting a data type for the field, are required. Setting options is (naturally) optional. You create all fields in the Define Database dialog's Fields pane, shown in Figure 5-1.

You can access the Fields pane in one of two ways:

+ Create a new file. When you create a new database file (by selecting Create a new empty file from the New Database dialog or by choosing File ⇨ New Database), the Define Database dialog's Fields pane automatically appears after you name the new database.

Table containing fields   Field order viewing options

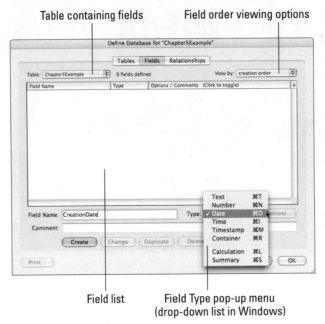

Field list   Field Type pop-up menu
                      (drop-down list in Windows)

Figure 5-1: The Define Database dialog's Fields pane.

✦ Open an existing database and choose File ➪ Define ➪ Database (or press Shift+⌘+D/Shift+Ctrl+D) and click the Fields tab in the Define Database dialog that appears if it isn't already selected. When you want to create new fields or examine, edit, or delete existing field definitions, choose the Define Database command and use the Fields pane.

STEPS: Defining a Field

1. Do one of the following:

   • To create a new database when launching FileMaker Pro, select Create a new empty file in the New Database dialog. Enter a filename for the database in the file dialog that appears and then click Save.

   • To create a new database when FileMaker Pro is already running, choose File ➪ New Database and then choose Create a new empty file from the New Database dialog. Enter a filename for the database in the file dialog that appears and click Save.

   • For an existing database, choose File ➪ Define ➪ Database (or press Shift+⌘+D/Shift+Ctrl+D). Then select the Fields tab if it isn't already selected.

   In all these cases, the Define Database dialog then appears.

2. Type a name for the new field (up to 60 characters long) in the Field Name box.

If you think that you might want to use the field in a calculation formula, be sure that the name does not start with a numeric digit or a period nor contain a comma, semicolon, colon, ampersand, parenthesis, square bracket, quotation mark, math symbol, or logical keyword (AND, OR, XOR, or NOT). In addition, the name cannot be the same as any of the FileMaker Pro built-in functions. (Refer to Chapter 14 or Appendix C for the names of FileMaker Pro functions.) Such symbols and words will be improperly interpreted as being part of the formula. To prevent such occurrences, FileMaker Pro routinely warns you if you enter an improper name, as shown in Figure 5-2. FileMaker Pro will warn you if you violate any of these strictures but will let you proceed — you just won't enjoy the consequences.

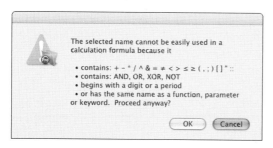

The selected name cannot be easily used in a calculation formula because it

• contains: + – * / ∧ & = ≠ < > ≤ ≥ (, ;) [ ] " ::
• contains: AND, OR, XOR, NOT
• begins with a digit or a period
• or has the same name as a function, parameter or keyword. Proceed anyway?

OK   Cancel

Figure 5-2: This warning appears if you enter an improper field name.

3. Choose a data type for the field from the Type pop-up menu/drop-down list.

As Figure 5-1 shows, a field type can also be selected by pressing the keyboard equivalent, such as ⌘+D/Alt+D for a Date field. We explain field types in the section, "All about field types," later in this chapter.

4. Click Create (or press Return/Enter).

If you select Calculation or Summary as the field type, another dialog appears in which you specify additional required settings (such as a formula). For any other field type, the basic definition process ends when you click Create, unless you click the Options button and select Global Storage.

5. To define additional fields, repeat Steps 2–4. Click OK when you're through defining fields.

Tip   If you intend to publish the database on the Web or use it in conjunction with Open Database Connectivity (ODBC) or Java Database Connectivity (JDBC), as described in Chapter 22, use underscore characters rather than spaces when creating field names (for example, Sales_Total rather than Sales Total). If you don't like using underscores, you might consider intercapping (SalesTotal).

After you create a field, you can set options for it, as we describe in "Setting Field Options," later in this chapter.

Breaking up complex fields

When you're defining fields for a database, think seriously about dividing complex fields into their logical components. For example, instead of defining a single Name field, you might want to define Title, First Name, and Last Name fields (possibly even a Middle Name or Middle Initial field). This approach makes sorting by last name simple. If you attempt to sort a single Name field, on the other hand, FileMaker Pro will list everyone alphabetically by first name or (worse yet) by title, such as Mr., Dr., or Ms.

Using different fields for Title, First Name, and Last Name also makes performing a mail merge easy. You can create the salutation by combining the Title and Last Name fields, as in

```
Dear <<Title> <<Last Name>:
```

rather than

```
Dear <<Name>:
```

Thus, instead of inserting Dear Dr. John Abrams:, the form letter would read Dear Dr. Abrams:.

As you can see, combining specific fields is much simpler than attempting to dismantle or work with a single general field. Plan ahead.

When creating a database, many people normally begin by defining all its tables and fields. You should note, however, that you are not locked in to this initial set of fields. You can later add new fields, delete fields, set and change field options, or even change field types (from Number to Text, for example). You can change field definitions at any time by choosing File ⇨ Define ⇨ Database (or pressing Shift+⌘+D/Shift+Ctrl+D) and selecting the Fields tab. For additional information, see "Modifying Field Definitions, Names, and Options," later in this chapter.

All about field types

Every field in a FileMaker Pro database must have a field type. The *field type* determines the kind of data you can enter and store in a field. Number fields, for example, store numeric data. Because Number fields contain numbers, you can (and usually do) use them to perform calculations, such as SALE * .05 for a field that computes a commission.

FileMaker Pro 8 has eight field types from which you can choose: Text, Number, Date, Time, Timestamp, Container, Calculation, and Summary. Each field must be defined as being one—and only one—type.

In order to improve the speed of executing Find requests and sorts, FileMaker Pro can keep track of data that has been entered in any field and maintain an index for that field. Depending on the field type you assign to a field and the indexing option you select, FileMaker Pro indexes all data for that field, only part of the data, or no data at all, as Table 5-1 summarizes and the following sections describe.

<table>
<thead>
<tr>
<th colspan="3" align="center">Table 5-1
Field Type Specifications</th>
</tr>
<tr>
<th>*Field Type*</th>
<th>*Field Content and Restrictions*</th>
<th>*Indexed Information*</th>
</tr>
</thead>
<tbody>
<tr>
<td>Text</td>
<td>Up to 1 billion characters of any type</td>
<td>First 100 alphanumeric characters of every word</td>
</tr>
<tr>
<td>Number</td>
<td>Up to 400 digits on either side of the decimal point (must be on one line)</td>
<td>Up to 400 digits, ignoring non-numeric contents</td>
</tr>
<tr>
<td>Date</td>
<td>One date between year 1 and 4000</td>
<td>Entire date (10 characters — month, day, and year — plus separators)</td>
</tr>
<tr>
<td>Time</td>
<td>One time</td>
<td>Entire time (9 characters — hours, minutes, and seconds separated by colons, the ninth character being an optional negative sign)</td>
</tr>
<tr>
<td>Timestamp</td>
<td>A combination of date and time, separated by a space</td>
<td>Entire value</td>
</tr>
<tr>
<td>Container</td>
<td>One picture, QuickTime movie or audio clip, sound, or OLE object (Windows only)</td>
<td>Not indexed</td>
</tr>
<tr>
<td>Calculation</td>
<td>One formula with a text, numeric, date, time, or container result</td>
<td>Calculation result (the amount of data indexed corresponds to the result type)</td>
</tr>
<tr>
<td>Summary</td>
<td>Result of one summary function</td>
<td>Not indexed</td>
</tr>
</tbody>
</table>

In addition, field data used in any of the following manners is automatically indexed unless you specifically turn off indexing for the affected fields:

✦ Finding duplicates

✦ Using a value list

✦ Validating fields that have the unique or existing value validation criterion set for them

✦ Matching fields in a lookup, related, or master file (based on a relationship)

You might, depending upon the amount of data being indexed, note a delay (with a progress dialog) when the field is initially indexed. After the index exists, FileMaker Pro will keep it up to date.

Text fields

A Text field can store any type of information: text, numbers, and other characters. With a maximum of one billion Unicode characters, Text fields are ideal for handling large amounts of information, such as comments and notes. If indexing has been turned on for a given Text field, searching for any word in the field is easy because FileMaker Pro automatically indexes *every* word — not just the first one. However, indexing (especially on large Text fields) can significantly increase the size of the database file. For this reason, you are better off either disabling indexing on large Text fields that you do not intend to use in searches or setting it to Minimal. Because you can enter any type of data in a Text field, a preponderance of database fields are usually defined as Text fields.

Number fields

Although its name implies otherwise, you can also enter anything in a Number field — text and symbols, in addition to numeric characters, unless `Strict` data type is set in the field's Validation options. Number fields, however, have greater restrictions than Text fields. They can contain no more than 800 characters, and you must enter data on a single line. If you attempt to press Return (Enter) when typing an entry in a Number field, FileMaker Pro beeps and ignores the Return. Because the numeric information in Number fields is readily accessible for use in formulas and computations, the contents of Number fields are frequently used as the basis for Calculation fields (discussed later in this chapter).

When indexing is turned on for a Number field, text and other characters are ignored. If you enter both text and numbers in a Number field, individual numbers in the field are combined to form a single number. As an example, suppose you have entered the following address in a Number field:

```
23 East Elm Street, Apt. #7
```

For indexing purposes, FileMaker Pro treats this field as though it contains the number 237. (It appends the 7 to the end of the number 23.) This method of operating also affects searches (performed with the Find command). If you enter **23** or **7** as the search string, the search will fail. Similarly, because text in a Number field is not indexed, searching for Elm also fails. On the other hand, searching for 237 — the concatenated digits — successfully finds this record. If you were to create an Employee ID field or Social Security number field as a numeric field, this would allow indexing on only the numeric characters, ignoring parentheses, dashes, and other characters.

This discussion of concatenation leads to an important point. If you think you will need to enter both text and numeric information in a field, you might be happier if you define it as a Text field rather than as a Number field. If you're just interested in making sure that only legitimate numbers can be entered into a Number field, you can set the Numeric Only validation option for the field. See "Setting Field Options," later in this chapter, for instructions.

Tip

Even if you believe the field will contain only numeric digits, you should often consider defining the field as Text rather than Number if you won't be performing calculations. For example, ZIP code and Serial Number fields often have leading zeros as part of their value—those leading zeros will be lost if the field is defined as a Number field.

Date fields

Date fields are reserved for dates. Each date can contain up to eight characters plus separators (MM/DD/YYYY, such as 10/07/1952), and the entire date is indexed as a single string (when indexing is turned on for the field). When you type dates, you must use only numbers and the following separators: slash (/), hyphen (–), period (.), or a space. Thus, all the following dates are proper FileMaker dates: 11/19/98, 3/20/1950, 5-24-1960, 7.30.1928, and 5 7 1929. Leading zeros (as in 07/09/99) are optional. The year portion of the date must be between 1 and 4000.

When you enter the month or day part of a date, you can use one or two digits. As shown in Table 5-2, the allowable number of digits in the year portion of a date depends on which year it is when you enter it (we'll assume 2005 in the following table).

<table>
<tr><th colspan="3">Table 5-2
Entering Years in Dates</th></tr>
<tr><th>*For a Year in This Range*</th><th>*Enter This*</th><th>*Example*</th></tr>
<tr><td>1–9</td><td>Two or three zeros, followed by a single digit</td><td>004 or 0004</td></tr>
<tr><td>10–99</td><td>One or two zeros, followed by two digits</td><td>057 or 0057</td></tr>
<tr><td>100–999</td><td>Three or four digits</td><td>756 or 0756</td></tr>
<tr><td>1000–1974</td><td>Four digits—the actual year</td><td>1847</td></tr>
<tr><td>1975–1999</td><td>Two or four digits</td><td>94 or 1994</td></tr>
<tr><td>2000–2075</td><td>One, two, or four digits</td><td>2, 02, or 2002</td></tr>
<tr><td>2076–4000</td><td>Four digits—the actual year</td><td>3217</td></tr>
</table>

Tip   Although Table 5-2 suggests that entering dates can be terribly confusing, here's a shortcut. Any year within the 30 years prior to entry or the 70 years subsequent to entry may be entered as a two-digit value. Any other year — as well as that same span of years — can be entered by using four digits. To avoid any potential confusion, we encourage you to set all Date fields to use Strict data type: 4-Digit year date as a validation criterion. Alternatively, you can use the new calendar drop-down for date fields, allowing your users to click a date on a calendar rather than typing.

The manner in which the date is displayed, on the other hand, is determined by the format you've set for the field in Layout mode by using the Format ⇨ Date command (see Chapter 6). Note that when you base a Find request on the contents of a Date field, you must enter a date that is in keeping with the restrictions listed in Table 5-2.

Tip   Here's another way to avoid some typing. When you enter a date for the current year, you don't have to include the year at all. If you type **10/17**, for example, FileMaker Pro 8 fills in the current year for you.

Time fields

Like Date fields, a Time field can hold one time (up to eight characters in length), and it is indexed as a single string (if indexing is turned on for the field). You can enter times as hours (5); hours and minutes (5:12); or hours, minutes, and seconds (5:12:43). To enter minutes and seconds, it is necessary to enter an hour value as well (00:05:12 for 5 minutes and 12 seconds). When you enter data in a Time field, you should separate the parts of the time with colons. Leading zeros are optional. (Both 05:07 and 5:7 are acceptable, for example.) You can also append AM or PM to the end of a time string. You can set a display format for a Time field by using the Format ⇨ Time command (see Chapter 6).

Note   In addition to using Time fields to record a specific time of day (such as 12:45 P.M.), you can also use them to record time durations. When formatting such a Time field, select Leave data formatted as entered or 24-hour notation, using Format ⇨ Time for that field (in Layout mode). Either formatting option will enable you to enter times greater than 24 hours, such as 147:12:17 (147 hours, 12 minutes, 17 seconds).

If you enter a single integer, FileMaker Pro interprets that as a number of hours. If you enter a decimal number, FileMaker Pro interprets your input as a number of seconds. Figure 5-3 shows the field as entered on top, then displayed in hh:mm:ss format below.

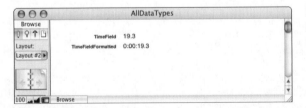

Figure 5-3: FileMaker treats a fractional time entry as a number of seconds.

Timestamp fields

FileMaker Pro 7 introduced a new field type: Timestamp. The Timestamp field is a specialized data type specifying a moment in time — a date *and* a time. For example, noon on 20 March 1950 would be entered as 03/20/1950 12:00:00 p.m. Timestamp fields can hold any value between 12 a.m. on 1 January 0001 and 11:59:59 p.m. on 31 December 4000. Like time fields, when used in a calculation, timestamp fields have a resolution of seconds (and fractions thereof). For example, if you wished to increment a timestamp field by 30 days, you would add 2,592,000 seconds.

If you enter data that does not meet the requirements for a timestamp field (a date and a time), you see the alert shown in Figure 5-4.

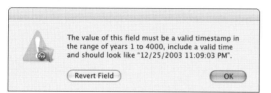

The value of this field must be a valid timestamp in the range of years 1 to 4000, include a valid time and should look like "12/25/2003 11:09:03 PM".

Revert Field   OK

Figure 5-4: This message appears when an incorrectly formatted timestamp value is entered (when you tab out of the field or otherwise leave the field).

Note   If you choose Insert ➪ Current Date, only the date portion will be entered. You will need to enter a time value as well to avoid the alert shown in Figure 5-4. Choosing Insert ➪ Current Time inserts both the date and time.

Container fields

A Container field can store one of four types of material: a picture, a QuickTime movie/audio clip, a sound recorded in FileMaker Pro, or an arbitrary file.

In the Windows version of FileMaker Pro 8, a Container field can also store OLE (Object Linking and Embedding) objects.

You can play movies and sounds from within a database by double-clicking the Container field in which the data is stored. You can also play QuickTime movies and audio by clicking the Play button in the QuickTime control bar, as shown in Figure 5-5. You can copy pictures and QuickTime movies and paste them into the field, or you can add them by choosing a command from the Insert menu. (See Chapter 16 for instructions.) You can record sound clips directly into a Container field if you have the necessary hardware.

Information in a Container field is not indexed, so you cannot perform a Find operation based on the contents of the field. Of course, this limitation makes sense because the information in the field isn't labeled in any way — there's nothing for which to search. If you want to search for a particular picture, sound, or movie, create a separate Text field (or two, or more) to store a title or set of keywords that describe the picture, sound, or movie, and then base your Find request on the contents of the Text field.

Figure 5-5: A QuickTime movie in a Container field.

Inserting OLE objects into Container fields

If you use Windows, you can insert an OLE object into a Container field in one of two ways. You can embed the object in the field, or you can link the object to the field. *Embedding* objects results in a "portable" database: That is, when you give a copy of the database to someone, the person gets all the actual objects. However, if the objects are large, the database file can become huge. *Linking* an object simply stores a pointer to where the object is stored on your hard drive or network. Linking saves space in the database file, but it makes it difficult to transfer the database to someone else.

Another difference between linked and embedded objects is that linked objects can be set to update automatically whenever the original object is modified. (Browse the relevant record and choose Edit ➪ Objects ➪ Links to set update options.) Embedded objects, on the other hand, are static. Even if the original object changes, the embedded object remains the same.

You'll quickly discover many types of OLE objects, such as Adobe Acrobat documents, Paint Shop Pro images, and WordPad documents. FileMaker Pro 8 enables you to insert OLE objects from a file or create them from scratch (as long as you have the necessary program).

To insert an OLE object into a Container field, follow these steps:

1. In Browse mode, click to select a Container field.

2. Choose Insert ➪ Object (or right-click the field and choose Insert Object from the contextual menu that appears).

   The Insert Object dialog appears. (Refer to the top half of the following figure.)

3. To create a new OLE object, select the Create new radio button and then select an object type from the scrolling list. (Refer to the top half of the following figure.) If you want to display an icon in the field rather than the actual object, select the Display as icon check box. Click OK.

The creator program opens (assuming that you have the program). Design the object or document.

or

To insert an existing object into the field, select the Create from file radio button. (Refer to the bottom half of the following figure.) To insert a link to the object's file rather than embed the object, click the Link button. Select the file to insert by typing its path or by clicking the Browse button. If you want to display an icon in the field rather than the actual object, select the Display as icon check box. Click OK.

You can view or modify the original OLE object by double-clicking the Container field that holds the object (or by right-clicking the field and choosing the Edit or Open command from the contextual menu that appears). Windows launches the application in which the object was created (if it's available), enabling you to view or edit the object. When you are done, you can close the creator application and update the FileMaker Pro record.

Note that when opened in either of the Macintosh versions of FileMaker Pro 8, OLE objects appear as graphics. Mac users can view, cut, copy, and paste OLE objects, but they can neither insert nor edit them.

Creating a new OLE object

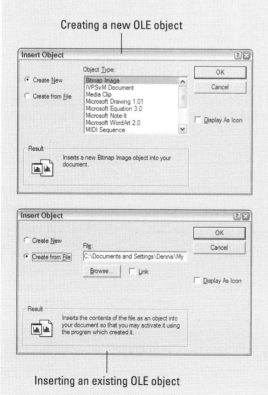

Inserting an existing OLE object

Calculation fields

Calculation fields perform numeric, text, date, time, or timestamp calculations within each record. A calculation can include constants, any of FileMaker Pro's built-in functions, and references to other fields, as well as any combination of these items. The capability to perform calculations elevates a database from a nicely arranged stack of note cards to a powerful information source. For example, you can use any word processing program to type an invoice. But an invoice database that has Calculation fields can also, for example, automatically total the purchases, compute the sales tax, and show you the number of days a payment is overdue.

You specify the formula for a Calculation field in the Specify Calculation dialog, which appears automatically when you select Calculation as the field type. You need to specify the result type for each Calculation field. A result can be text, a number, a date, a time, a timestamp, or a container. Table 5-3 gives examples of some of calculations you can perform.

Table 5-3
Examples of Calculations

Formula	Result Type	Explanation
SalesTotal * .08	Number	Multiply the value in the SalesTotal field by 0.08 to compute the salesperson's commission.
First & " " & Last	Text	Concatenate each person's first and last name to show the full name. (First and Last are separated by a space.)
EndTime – StartTime	Time	Compute the amount of time spent on a particular task.
DueDate – Today	Number	Subtract today's date (Today) from the due date to determine the number of days that remain.
If (State="CA", Picture 1, Picture 2)	Container	If the state is California, display the image stored in the Picture 1 field; otherwise, use the image stored in the Picture 2 field.

By default, the results of Calculation field formulas are automatically stored on disk as part of the database. For calculations that change frequently, you can turn off the storage setting for the field, thereby instructing FileMaker Pro to calculate the formulas only as needed. For example, if a project management database has a field that computes the number of days until each project is due, you might want to turn off automatic storage for the field because the field will have to be recalculated whenever you open the database.

To avoid erroneous results, FileMaker Pro will not let you modify the contents of a Calculation field. To emphasize this fact, Calculation fields are automatically skipped when you tab from field to field. However, if you want to copy the contents of a Calculation field, you can click the field, select the data, and then choose Edit ⇨ Copy (or press ⌘+C/Ctrl+C).

You cannot edit the results in a Calculation field, but you can auto-enter a calculation's result in any Text, Number, Date, Time, or Container field. Unlike a result in a Calculation field, auto-entered calculation results *can* be edited. Whenever you create a new record, the auto-enter calculation is used to create a default value for the field. You might, for example, want to use today's date plus one day as a default entry in a Homework Due Date field. See "Setting Field Options," later in this chapter, for details.

Chapter 14 presents the details of creating formulas for Calculation fields, as well as descriptions of FileMaker Pro's built-in functions. Additional instructions for defining a Calculation field are in the section "Defining Calculation, Summary, and Global fields," later in this chapter.

Tip

You might be wondering how a Container could be the result type for a Calculation. As an example, in an address database, you could display a small state map that corresponds to the state in which each person lives. To do this, store the map images in a separate table whose records include a state abbreviation and a Container field for the map image or 50 Global fields (one per state). Then use a Case function to specify the match between state abbreviations and the GlobalStorage field in which each image can be found, as in the following:

```
Case (State = "AZ", MapAZ, State = "AK", MapAK)
```

Summary fields

Instead of performing calculations within each record as Calculation fields do, Summary fields perform calculations *across* records. For example, in a database that tracks customer purchases, you could define a Summary field named Grand Total to total all the purchases by all customers.

A Summary field is based on the contents of a single Number, Date, Time, or Calculation field, and it summarizes the records you are currently browsing. When all records are visible, the Grand Total field provides the total of all purchases by all customers. If, on the other hand, you issue a Find request to restrict the visible records to only customers from Boston, the Grand Total field shows total purchases by Boston customers rather than by the entire database.

You can place Summary fields in any layout part: header, body, footer, and so on. If you place a Summary field in a sub-summary part and sort the database by a particular field, you can generate group statistics, such as computing the average rainfall for cities in country A, country B, and so on. (Chapter 6 discusses the sub-summary and other layout parts.)

FileMaker Pro automatically recalculates Summary fields whenever necessary. When you change the contents of a field on which a summary is based or when the set of browsed records changes, the summary figure is recalculated.

Functions for Summary fields include Total, Average, Count, Minimum, Maximum, Standard deviation, and Fraction of total. Defining Summary fields is discussed in the section, "Defining Calculation, Summary, and Global fields," later in this chapter.

As it does with Calculation fields, FileMaker Pro prevents you from tabbing into a Summary field. However, you can click a Summary field and copy its contents. Summary fields are not indexed, nor can you base a Find on the contents of a Summary field.

Global fields

A Global field is any (nonsummary) data field used to hold the same value for all records in a table (a commission percentage, for example). It can also be used to store script results temporarily. Each Global field is stored only once for the entire table. If placed in a layout, a Global field shows the same value in every record.

Note   In versions of FileMaker Pro previous to FileMaker Pro 7, which introduced support for multiple tables in a file, Global fields were used far more often for such things as a sales tax percentage. You now have more flexibility using a related table of sales tax percentages (or map images, as in the example of container fields earlier in this chapter), leaving Global fields primarily as temporary storage fields.

To define a field as Global, name and type it as described previously, click the Options button, and specify Use global storage in the Options dialog's Storage tab, as shown in Figure 5-6. You can also make it a repeating field by entering a number greater than 1 for the maximum repetitions that the field will require. Additional instructions for defining a Global field are in the section, "Defining Calculation, Summary, and Global fields," next in this chapter.

Defining Calculation, Summary, and Global fields

You normally define field types by simply naming them, selecting a field type, and clicking Create. The definition procedure is slightly different for Calculation, Summary, and Global fields, however, as described in the step-by-step instructions in this section.

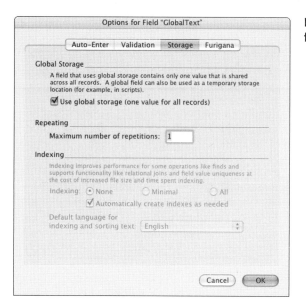

Figure 5-6: Setting options for a Global field.

STEPS: Defining a Calculation Field

1. In the Define Database dialog's Fields pane (refer to Figure 5-1), type a name for the new field (up to 60 characters) in the Field Name box.

2. Choose Calculation from the Type pop-up menu/drop-down list (or press ⌘+L/Ctrl+L).

3. Click Create.

The Specify Calculation dialog appears, as shown in Figure 5-7.

4. Enter the formula for the field in the large text box in the center of the dialog.

You can select field names, special symbols, operators, and functions by clicking the appropriate items in the upper part of the dialog. You can also type directly into the Formula text box.

To make it easier to find the appropriate function in the list on the right side of the dialog, you can set a different viewing preference by clicking the View pop-up menu/drop-down list, as shown in Figure 5-8.

By default, FileMaker lists the fields from the current file. If you've defined relationships for this file and want to base a calculation on a field in a related database, choose the name of the relationship from the pop-up menu in the upper-left corner of the dialog. All fields from the related file are then displayed. (You can also create relationships by choosing Define Relationships from the same pop-up menu. We cover defining relationships in Chapter 18.)

Current table

Field list   Operators   Relationships   Function view options

Function list

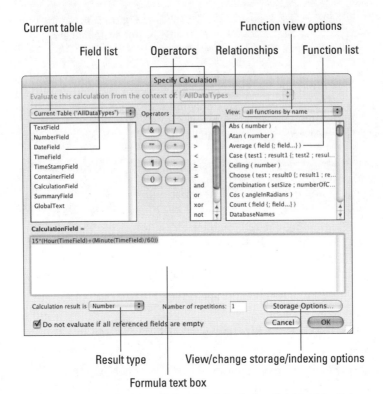

Result type

View/change storage/indexing options

Formula text box

Figure 5-7: Create a formula for the Calculation field in this dialog.

Figure 5-8: The View pop-up menu (drop-down list on Windows).

5. Choose a result type for the formula.

You must choose a result type for every formula. Choose Text, Number, Date, Time, or Container from the Calculation result is pop-up menu/drop-down list.

6. By default, the Do not evaluate if all referenced fields are empty check box is marked. If you want the calculation to *always* be performed — even if all the referenced fields are blank — click the box to remove the check mark.

> **Note**
>
> The point of this option is to make sure that every displayed calculation shows a non-zero value. If you select the Do not evaluate if all referenced fields are empty check box, FileMaker Pro performs only the calculation if at least one referenced field contains an entry. However, this also means that if *some* of the referenced fields are empty, FileMaker Pro will still perform the calculation, often resulting in a misleading and potentially incorrect computation. (It's too bad there isn't an option to keep the calculation from being performed if *any* of the referenced fields are blank although you often can work around that limitation by nesting IF tests to ascertain the presence of values in necessary fields.)

7. *Optional:* If you want the field to be a repeating field, enter a value greater than 1 in the Number of repetitions text box, specifying the maximum number of repetitions you want the field to have.

   See "Repeating fields," later in this chapter, for more information.

8. *Optional:* To set indexing or storage options for the results of the calculation, click the Storage Options button.

9. Click OK.

   FileMaker Pro evaluates the formula and reports any errors it detects. When the formula is syntactically correct, it returns you to the Define Database dialog.

10. You can define additional fields by repeating Steps 1–9, or you can click OK to dismiss the dialog.

> **Cross-Reference**
>
> For greater detail about the process of creating Calculation fields, check out Chapter 14. Appendix C contains definitions and examples for each of the built-in functions.

STEPS: Defining a Summary Field

1. In the Define Database dialog's Fields pane, type a name for the new field (up to 60 characters) in the Field Name box.

2. Choose Summary from the Type pop-up menu/drop-down list (or press ⌘+S/ Ctrl+S).

3. Click Create.

   The Options for Summary Field *Field Name* dialog appears, as shown in Figure 5-9.

4. Choose a summary function by selecting one the radio buttons there.

   See Table 5-4 in the next section, "Understanding summary functions," for a description of the summary functions and their options.

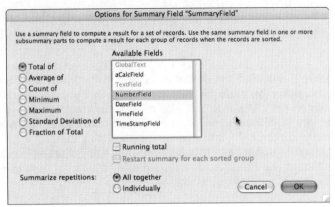

Figure 5-9: Select a summary function in this Options dialog.

5. From the scrolling field list, select a field on which to base the summary.

   Ineligible fields, such as Global and Container fields, are *dimmed* (unselectable).

6. *Optional:* At the bottom of the dialog, many of the summary functions provide an option that you can select by marking the check box and, if required, choosing a field from the new list that appears (see Table 5-4). The option displayed depends on the summary function chosen.

7. Click OK to accept the definition or click Cancel to ignore the settings you have selected.

Understanding summary functions

Table 5-4 lists the available summary functions and their options.

Table 5-4	
Summary Functions and Options	
Summary Function	*Option*
Total	Running total
Average	Weighted by field name
Count	Running count
Minimum	None
Maximum	None
Standard deviation	By population
Fraction of total	Subtotaled (when sorted by field *x*)

The following descriptions of the summary functions and their options can help you select the most appropriate function for any Summary field:

✦ ***Total/Running Total:*** The Total function totals a selected field across all records that are being browsed.

Example: In a household expense database, you can create a Total Summary field that shows total expenses for the entire database. You can place the Total Summary field in a sub-summary part and then sort by Expense Category to calculate separate totals for each type of expense.

Select the Running Total option if you prefer to see a cumulative total for the field as you flip from one record to another. To calculate subtotals for groups of records, place this Summary field in a sub-summary part and then sort by the appropriate field.

✦ ***Average/Weighted Average:*** The Average function calculates a simple numeric average of a selected field for the records being browsed. Place this Summary field in a sub-summary part if you want to calculate group averages.

Example: If bowling scores of 112, 142, and 175 were being summarized, the average displayed would be 143 — the sum of the scores (429) divided by the number of scores (3).

If you select the Weighted average option, the statistic is weighted by another field of your choice (instead of being calculated as a simple average).

Example: In a Want List database, imagine that one Calculation field displays the percentage of the catalog value at which each collectible item was purchased. If you were to use the Average summary function to compute the average percentage, the result would have little meaning because (from a monetary standpoint) purchases for hundreds of dollars would be treated the same as purchases for pennies. Weighting the average by the purchase price, on the other hand, gives greater importance to the more expensive purchases.

✦ ***Count/Running Count:*** Placed in any part other than a sub-summary, the Count function shows the number of records that contain *any* value in the selected field across the records that are currently being browsed. This function is considerably more useful when placed in a sub-summary part, however, where it shows how many qualifying records are in each group (after being sorted by the appropriate field).

Example: To determine how many records have an entry in an Address field, place a Count Summary field in any layout part other than a sub-summary. The Count Summary field then shows the number of records from which you can create usable mailing labels. If you create a Count Summary field based on a field that is always filled in, place it in a sub-summary part, and then sort by the appropriate field, you can get an accurate count of the number of members in each subgroup. For example, if you summarized a list of DVDs by genre, the Count Summary field would tell you how many comedies, dramas, cartoons, and so forth were in your inventory.

The Running Count function is also more informative when placed in a sub-summary part, where it shows the cumulative number of records in each group (after being sorted by the appropriate field). When you place a Running Count Summary field in another layout part, it simply matches the record numbers — as in 1, 2, 3, 4, and so on.

✦ *Minimum:* When placed in any part other than a sub-summary, the Minimum function shows the smallest value for the chosen field across all records being browsed. When you place it in a sub-summary part, Minimum shows the smallest value for the chosen field for each group of records being browsed.

Example: In a software inventory database, a Minimum Summary field can show you the cheapest program in the lot. If you perform a Find based on a particular software category, the field displays the least expensive program of that type. Placed in a sub-summary part and then sorted by software category, the Summary field shows the least expensive program for each type of software, on a category-by-category basis.

✦ *Maximum:* When placed in any part other than a sub-summary, the Maximum function shows the largest value for the chosen field across all records being browsed. When placed in a sub-summary part, Maximum shows the largest value for the chosen field for each group of records being browsed.

Example: In a software inventory database, a Maximum Summary field can show you the most expensive program in the lot. If you perform a Find based on a particular software category, the field displays the most expensive program of that type. Placed in a sub-summary part and then sorted by software category, the Summary field shows the most expensive program for each type of software, on a category-by-category basis.

✦ *Standard Deviation/By Population*: This function computes a statistic (a standard deviation) for the chosen field across all records being browsed. The Standard Deviation function shows how widely the values summarized vary from one another.

If you select By population, the formula used to compute the standard deviation is a population — rather than a sample — statistic.

Example: You can use a Standard Deviation function in a student database to see how much the students' grades vary. Place the same field in a sub-summary part and then sort by age, grade level, or teacher name, for example, to get the same information separately for each group.

✦ *Fraction of Total/Subtotaled:* When placed in any part other than a sub-summary, this function shows how great a portion of the total each record comprises. When placed in a sub-summary part, the function shows the portion of the total for a field that can be accounted for by each group rather than by each record. If you check the Subtotaled option and sort the database by the selected field, the Fraction of Total figures are fractions of each group rather than of all visible records; that is, the Fraction of Total figures within each group will add up to 1.0 (or 100 percent).

Example: In a household expense database, place this field in any layout part other than a sub-summary to determine the fraction of total expenses that each transaction accounted for. Place the same field in a sub-summary part and then sort by Expense Category to see the fraction of the category that can be attributed to each expense item.

More help with Summary functions

If you're having trouble making sense of Summary fields, how the different functions work, and when you should use them, the quickest path to understanding is to create a test file and try out the various options. A database called Summary Field Tester was created for this purpose in an earlier edition and it is still useful today. You'll find the Summary Field Tester on this book's companion CD-ROM.

Summary File Tester contains only six records and consists of the following four fields:

✦ City: A Text field

✦ Age: A Number field

✦ Salary [in thousands]: A Number field

✦ Summary: A Summary field

The same Summary field appears in two places in the database — in the body and in a trailing sub-summary part (at the bottom of each record). That way, you can determine the correct layout part in which to place your own Summary fields. The following figure shows a record from Summary Field Tester in which City is the Sort field.

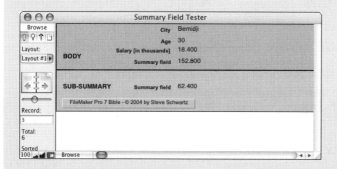

To see how each summary function and option works:

1. Choose File ➪ Define ➪ Database and select the Fields tab.

The Fields pane appears.

Continued

Continued

2. Select Summary field in the list of defined fields and click Options.

The Options for Summary Field "Summary field" dialog appears.

3. Choose a different option from the summary function list or alter the status of the check box, if one appears at the bottom of the dialog.

Make sure that Salary [In Thousands] remains selected.

4. To dismiss the dialogs, click OK and then click Done.

If the status area shows that the records are Unsorted or Semi-Sorted, choose the Records ➪ Sort command. The Sort dialog should show that the database will be sorted by City, which is the Sort field set for the sub-summary part. Click Sort to execute the sort.

Repeat these steps as often as you like, testing a different summary function or option each time. After each definition has been completed, flip through the records to see what the Summary field is summarizing, both in the body and in the sub-summary part.

Finally, to employ a field as a GlobalStorage field, you select the field in the Define Database dialog's Fields pane, click the Options button, and select the Storage tab. On the Storage pane, select the Use global storage (one value for all records) check box.

Changing the field order

A field list appears in the Define Database dialog's Fields pane. By default, the fields are listed in the order in which you created them. Working with this list can often be easier if you establish a new order for the fields. To change the order, choose one of the following options in the View by pop-up menu/drop-down list in the upper-right corner of the Fields pane (see the accompanying figure):

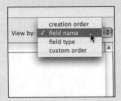

✦ **creation order:** Fields are listed in the order in which they were defined.

✦ **field name:** Fields names are sorted alphabetically.

✦ **field type:** Fields are grouped by type (Text, Number, and so on). Within each type, the fields are presented in alphabetical order.

✦ **custom order:** You can manually drag fields to new positions in the list. This process is described below in the step-by-step instructions.

You can also sort the Fields pane by field name or field type by clicking the Field Name or Type column headings, respectively.

Follow these steps to create a custom field order:

1. In the Fields pane, move the pointer over the name of the field you want to move. When the pointer moves over the symbol preceding a field name, it changes to a two-headed arrow.

2. With the two-headed arrow pointer visible, click and drag the field up or down in the list, and release the mouse button when the field is where you want it to be.

As soon as you move a single field, the View by pop-up menu/drop-down list automatically shows that the custom order setting has been selected.

3. Repeat these steps for any additional fields you want to move. Note that even if you switch among several different field order views, when you next choose the custom order view, all the manual modifications you made to the field order are restored.

Setting Field Options

The types of options you can set for a field vary with the field type. Options for Global, Calculation, and Summary fields have already been discussed in the "Defining Calculation, Summary, and Global fields" section. The options you can set for Text, Number, Date, Time, and Container fields are as follows:

✦ *Data auto-entry:* When you create a new record or modify an existing record, you can have FileMaker Pro automatically enter into the chosen field the creation or modification date, time, or timestamp for each record; the name of the user who created or last modified the record; a serial number; the value from the previous record; a default value; a calculated value; or a value looked up in another database.

✦ *Data validation:* Depending on the options you choose, you can require that a field must have strict type-checking (no alphabetic characters in a number field, for example), not be left blank, the value entered must be unique, the value already exists in another record, the data must be of a particular type, the data is restricted to entries in a value list, the entered value match the result of a calculation, the field has a maximum character length, or entries fall within a specific range.

✦ *Look up data values in another file:* When data is entered into a lookup field, FileMaker Pro automatically looks up information in another file and then copies selected data into one or more fields in the current file. Using this option in an inventory database, you could enter a part number into a field. FileMaker Pro would then open the second database file that you specified; find the part name, description, color, and unit cost for the part; and then transfer a copy of that information to the first database. Because of the complexity of this concept, lookups — along with relationships — are discussed separately in Chapter 18.

✦ *Repeating values:* This option enables you to enter multiple values in what normally would be considered a single field. In an invoice database, for example, you can define Quantity, Item Description, Price, and Extended Price fields as repeating, each of which can receive up to ten values to allow up to ten line items on the invoice. (You specify an arbitrary maximum number of values.)

You can use the Furigana option to auto-enter a phonetic rendition of the current field's Japanese text contents into another, specified, field.

The following steps describe the general procedure for setting options for a Text, Number, Date, Time, Timestamp, or Container field. Instructions for setting specific kinds of field options are explained in the sections that follow.

STEPS: Setting Options for a Text, Number, Date, Time, Timestamp, or Container field

1. Choose File ⇨ Define ⇨ Database and select the Fields tab (or press Shift+⌘+D/Shift+Ctrl+D).

   The Fields pane appears (refer to Figure 5-1).

2. In the field list, select the Text, Number, Date, Time, Timestamp, or Container field for which you want to set options.

   or

   If the field doesn't already exist, define the field by following the instructions presented earlier in this chapter.

3. Click Options (or double-click the name of the field in the field list).

   The Options for Field *Field Name* dialog appears, as shown in Figure 5-10. Note that the title of the Options dialog changes to reflect the name of the selected field. The specific options you can set vary with the field's data type. For example, the only validation options available for a Container field are Not empty and Validated by calculation.

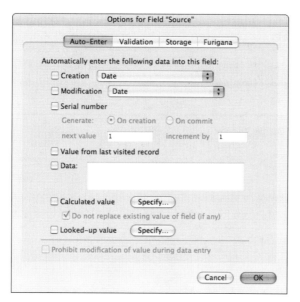

Figure 5-10: The Options dialog displays auto-enter, validation, storage, or Furigana options.

4. Click a tab at the top of the dialog and set options as desired.

5. If you want to set other options for the same field, click another tab at the top of the dialog.

6. Click OK to return to the Define Database dialog's Fields pane.

7. To set options for additional fields, repeat Steps 2–5. Click OK when you are through setting options.

Auto-enter options

When you click the Auto-Enter tab at the top of the Options dialog, you see options that provide for the automatic entry of several types of information in a field when you create or modify a record. The various auto-entry options are discussed in the following sections.

Creation Date, Creation Time, Modification Date, Modification Time, Creator Name, and Modifier Name

Select the first check box on the Auto-Enter screen, and choose an option from the pop-up menu to the right (see Figure 5-11). The specific choices you can select in the pop-up menu depend on the type of field for which you are setting options. If you are defining options for a Date field, for example, you can select only the Creation date and Modification date options. Other options are grayed out (dimmed).

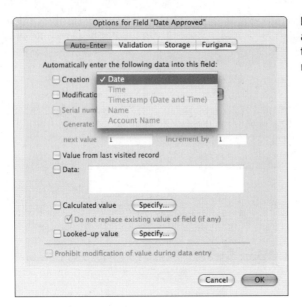

Figure 5-11: Setting an automatic date, time, timestamp, creator name, or modifier name for a field.

Problems with setting field options after the fact

You should note that setting entry options for a field after the field contains data for some records can cause problems. FileMaker Pro does not warn you about existing records that, as a result of the new field options, might now contain invalid data. You have to find and correct them yourself. The following table lists Find request symbols that are helpful in performing this task.

Find Symbol or Operation	Action
=	Find empty fields
!	Find duplicate values
value1 . . . value2	Find values that fall outside of the range (and select the Omit check box)

You can also search for invalid dates and times by entering a question mark (?) in a Date, Time, or Timestamp field. However, because the contents of these fields are automatically restricted to valid dates and times, this type of search is necessary only if you have converted a field to a Date or Time field from some other field type (a Text field, for example).

Selecting Creation date or Creation time causes FileMaker Pro to enter the appropriate data automatically as each new record is created. When these options are set, you can tell how old each record is, so you have an idea of whether the record is up to date.

Note

If you define a Creation Date, Creation Time, or Creator Name field after the database already contains records, the field will be blank in existing records. You might want to enter this information manually for the old records.

Modification date, Modification time, and Modification timestamp show the date and/or time that *any* field in a record was last changed. FileMaker Pro automatically enters the appropriate value when you finish editing a record (by pressing Enter or switching to a different record). If you're interested only in how current a record is — as opposed to when it was originally created — use the Modification date option. When a new record is created, the modification date is the same as the creation date.

Creation name and Modification name show the name of the person who created or last modified the record, respectively. These field options are extremely helpful in a multi-user environment to determine who is creating or modifying records.

Performing automatic time calculations

If you do time billing, you can use the Creation time and Modification time auto-entry options to track time spent on the phone with a client or time spent working on a project. For example, you can create a simple database like Time Billing (shown in the accompanying figure). When a client calls, you immediately create a new record. The Creation Date (Date), Creation Time (Start Time), and Modification Time (End Time) values are automatically filled in for you. The Total Time is calculated by subtracting the Start Time from the End Time. When you create the record, the result of this formula is initially zero (0).

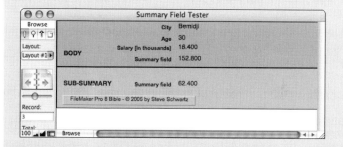

Enter the client's name. When the call ends, press Enter (Macintosh) or Ctrl+Enter (Windows) to complete the record. The Modification Time is then automatically updated to reflect the current time, and the Total Time is recalculated to show the actual length of the call.

To select the name that FileMaker Pro will use for the Creation Name and the Modification Name, choose Edit ➪ Preferences. Click the General tab at the top of the Preferences dialog. Enter the name you want to use in the User name box and then click OK.

To select the name FileMaker Pro will use for the Creation Name and the Modification Name, choose FileMaker Pro ➪ Preferences. Click the General tab at the top of the application Preferences dialog. Near the bottom of the dialog is the User Name section, as shown in Figure 5-12. Select the System radio button to use the Owner Name that you set up in Accounts System Preferences. To enter a different name, select the Other radio button and type a name. After choosing the option you want to use, click OK.

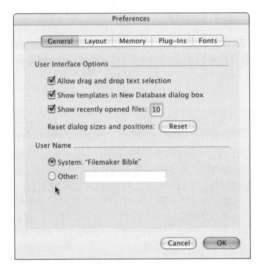

Figure 5-12: Setting application preferences for User Name.

Account Name shows the name you used to log into a shared database, tied to FileMaker Pro 8's privileges implementation. Privileges and accounts are covered in more detail in Chapter 19.

Serial number

You use this option to enter a number that automatically increases by a set amount for each new record. For example, you can use this option to create invoice and statement numbers.

The following steps describe how to create a field in which FileMaker Pro automatically enters serial numbers using the increment that you specify.

STEPS: Creating a Field for Incremental Serial Numbers

1. In the Define Database dialog's Fields pane (refer to Figure 5-1), select or create a Number or Text field, and click the Options button.

2. Click the Auto-Enter tab at the top of the Options dialog and then select the Serial number check box.

3. In the Next Value text box, enter the starting serial number.

   This number will be assigned to the next new record you create.

4. In the Increment By text box, enter a number for the amount that you want each new serial number to increase over the previous serial number.

5. Click OK to return to the Define Database dialog.

 Tip   You should note that a serial number does not have to be a simple number. For example, you can set the starting serial number (Next Value) as A27B-1000. In a mixed text-and-number entry such as this one, FileMaker increments the serial number by using the right-most numeric string, ignoring other numbers in the string. In this example, assuming that the increment was 1, the next serial numbers would be A27B-1001, A27B-1002, and so on.

FileMaker Pro 8 allows you to specify when the serial number is generated, a capability introduced with FileMaker Pro 7. If you select the On creation radio button, the field's value will be established when you choose Records ⇨ New Record (⌘+N/ Ctrl+N). Alternatively, you can select the On commit radio button to defer the serial number generation until you leave the record or press Enter, thereby committing it to the database. This latter capability is particularly useful if your data entry is controlled via a script employing the Commit Records script step.

Protecting auto-entered values

To protect auto-entered values, you might want to select the Prohibit modification of value during data entry check box near the bottom of the Options dialog. Setting this option prevents you and other users of the database from inadvertently altering the contents of an auto-entry field. You need to set this option for *each* field you want to protect (a serial number field, for instance).

If you later discover that you need to edit one or more of the auto-entered values for a particular field, return to this screen, remove the check mark from the Prohibit modification of value during data entry check box, edit the field contents as necessary, and then restore the check mark.

Value from last visited record

If you enter data in presorted batches, this auto-entry option can be very helpful. Selecting the Value from last visited record option instructs FileMaker Pro to use the most recently entered data for this field as the default entry in each new record.

For example, suppose you need to enter warranty card information. If the cards are already sorted by city and you set the Value from last visited record auto-entry option for the City field, you'll have to type only the city name when you encounter a different city in the card stack.

Data

The Data option enables you to specify a piece of data that you want to have automatically entered for every record. As such, this option creates a default entry for a field. For example, in an employee database, employees often live in the same city. By using the name of this city as auto-entry data, you can save some typing. If you create a record for an employee who lives in a different city, you can edit the name of the city in that record and know that subsequent new records will default to your preselected value.

Calculated value

This auto-entry option enables you to use a formula to set a default value for any Text, Number, Date, Time, Timestamp, or Container field. Unlike formulas entered for Calculation fields, the results of auto-entered formulas *can* be edited.

When you select the Calculated value check box (or click its Specify button), a version of the Specify Calculation dialog appears (refer to Figure 5-7). Create the formula and click OK. Note that the formula's result type must match the field's data type. Optionally, you can remove the check mark from the Do not evaluate if all referenced fields are empty check box at the bottom of the dialog.

Looked-up value

This auto-entry option instructs FileMaker Pro to look up information in a second table (or in the same table) and copy it into the current table. When you create several databases or tables sharing some common element, such as address information, you can minimize the data entry duplication required by instructing each of these databases to extract the address information from a separate Address table, for example.

A *lookup* is a one-way function in which data is (physically) copied into the current file (much like importing field information but affecting only the current record rather than the entire database).

Cross-Reference   To learn more about lookups and the relational capabilities of FileMaker Pro 8, see Chapter 18.

STEPS: Creating a Lookup Field

1. Choose File ⇨ Define ⇨ Database (or press Shift+⌘+D/Shift+Ctrl+D) and select the Fields tab.

   The Fields pane appears.

2. Select or create a field to receive the copied (lookup) data and then click Options or double-click the field name in the field list.

   The field type of the selected field must be Text, Number, Date, Time, Timestamp, or Container.

3. Click the Auto-Enter tab at the top of the Options dialog and then select the Looked-up value check box.

   The Lookup for Field *Field Name* dialog appears, as shown in Figure 5-13.

Figure 5-13: The Lookup for Field dialog.

4. From the pop-up menus/drop-down lists, choose the relationship from which you intend to extract the lookup information.

   If a relationship that links the two tables doesn't already exist, choose Define Relationships from the pop-up menu and then define the relationship.

Note Whenever a lookup accessing a table in another file is executed, the second file is automatically opened as part of the lookup process.

5. In the Copy Value from Field section of the dialog, select the name of the field whose data you want to copy into the current field.

Choose the match field wisely

When selecting a field on which to base a lookup, you'll be much happier if you choose one whose contents will be unique for each record, such as a customer ID number or Social Security number. For example, if you use the Last Name field, you will run into problems if you have people in the database who share the same last name. No matter how many times you execute the lookup, you'll find only the *first* person who has that particular last name. That's the way lookups work.

When the lookup is executed, the contents of the selected field are copied into the current field, whose name is shown in the title of the dialog. (In the example shown in Figure 5-13, Product ID will be copied from the lookup file into the Product ID field in the current file.)

Note   After a lookup executes, you can still edit the contents of the field into which data was copied. However, if you ever edit the *trigger field* (the field in the current database that initiates the lookup), the lookup will be executed anew. If a match is found, your edited data will be replaced.

6. In the section of the dialog labeled If no exact match, then, select from the following options to tell FileMaker Pro what to do if it doesn't find an exact match:

   • *do not copy:* This option is the default (and, in most cases, is what you want). Rather than copying erroneous data, the field is left as is.

   • *copy next lower value:* Choose this option to copy the next-lower value (numerically or alphabetically, depending on the type of data stored in the field).

   • *copy next higher value:* Choose this option to copy the next-higher value (numerically or alphabetically, depending on the type of data stored in the field).

   • *use:* This option enables you to specify a string that will be used if no match is found. For example, if the lookup is based on a phone number and the search comes up empty, you can have *Not a current customer* inserted into the field.

7. *Optional:* Select the Don't copy contents if empty check box to avoid copying information from a blank field into the current table.

   In the example shown in Figure 5-13, if you had hand-entered a Product ID in the Product ID field, selecting this option would prevent the number from being replaced by a blank one from the Product Catalog table.

8. Click OK to accept the options you have just set, or click Cancel to ignore the new settings. Click OK again to dismiss the Options dialog.

9. Repeat Steps 2–8 to define additional lookup fields, as desired. Click OK when you're ready to close the Define Database dialog and return to the database.

Here are some other important factors to keep in mind when you are creating and using lookups:

✦ To determine whether a match has been found, FileMaker Pro compares only the first 110 characters (or until the first carriage return) in the match fields. It ignores word order, punctuation, and capitalization, as well as any text that is contained in a Number field.

✦ You can select any FileMaker Pro file in which to do a lookup, including the current file. This technique can be extremely useful with any database that contains multiple records for the same customer, client, or subject. As an example, an invoice database can look for a customer ID among the existing records and then, if a match is found, fill in the fields of the mailing address for you.

✦ If the data in the looked up table changes, a lookup that you previously performed might now contain incorrect data. To correct this situation, you can instruct FileMaker Pro to perform the lookup again by tabbing into or clicking in the field that is used to trigger the lookup and choosing the Records ➪ Relookup Field Contents command.

Tip

Unlike a regular lookup, which is performed for only the current record, a relookup is performed for all records being browsed. To perform a relookup for only the current record, the easiest method is to cut the data from the trigger field, paste it back into the field, and then tab to the next field. Editing the data in the trigger field automatically causes the lookup to be executed.

Using lookups to fill in multiple fields

At first glance, you might not think you can trigger a lookup that will copy multiple fields to the original database. As the example in the instructions for creating a lookup field shows, when a match is located, the lookup copies the contents of only one field from the source table into one field in the current table.

The solution is to define a lookup individually for *every* field you want to copy, using the same trigger field for each lookup. For example, to copy an entire address, begin by identifying a unique field, such as a customer ID number field. Then create a separate lookup for each field in the address (First Name, Last Name, Address, City, State, and ZIP) using the same trigger and match fields in each lookup definition (the Customer ID number). When you enter the information in the trigger field during data entry, FileMaker Pro will perform all the lookups simultaneously. Although FileMaker Pro will appear to be performing only one lookup, it will, in fact, perform half a dozen of them — pulling all the data from the same record in the lookup table.

Data validation options

Click the Validation tab at the top of the Options dialog to set or view data validation options. These options govern the types of information that must be entered, may be entered, or may not be entered in a chosen field (see Figure 5-14).

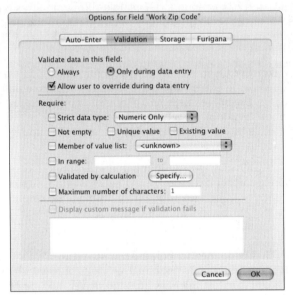

Figure 5-14: Data validation options.

You need to keep two things in mind when you set validation options for a field. First, you can set validation options only for Text, Number, Date, Time, Timestamp, and Container fields. Second, even with a validation option set, unless you also deselect the Allow user to override during data entry check box, FileMaker Pro gives you (or any other person having write access who might be using the database) the option of overriding the validation requirements. If you leave a required field blank, for example, you see a dialog like the ones shown in Figure 5-15.

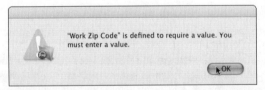

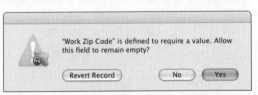

Figure 5-15: The top alert box appears if only Not empty is selected; the bottom one appears if both Not empty is selected and the user is allowed to override.

The following sections describe the validation options.

The Strict data type option

Use this option to indicate that only a number, a date with a four-digit year, or a time of day (00:00:00 to 23:59:59) is an acceptable entry for the field. Setting this option ensures that only numbers are entered in Number fields, for example. (A number can include a decimal separator, thousands separator, sign, and parentheses.)

As with the other data validation options, the user can still override the warning dialog that appears when the wrong data type is entered unless you also clear the Allow user to override during data entry option.

In versions before FileMaker Pro 7, FileMaker Pro defaulted to not allowing override and labeled the option as "Strict" Do not allow user to override data validation. FileMaker Pro 7 and 8's default behavior is the exact opposite, and the option's wording has been reversed to reflect the new behavior.

The Not empty option

Select this check box to create a *required field* (one that must not be empty). In many databases, you will have essential fields that render a record worthless if their data is left blank. In a customer database, for example, you cannot send out bills if the Name, Address, or City field for a customer is blank. If you attempt to switch to another record or press Enter to complete the record without filling in a required field, FileMaker Pro displays a warning. (Refer to Figure 5-15.)

The Unique value option

This option requires that every record in the database have a different value for the field. FileMaker Pro warns you if you enter a value that already exists in another record. For example, Social Security numbers, customer IDs, or record ID numbers generally must be unique.

When determining whether an entry is unique, FileMaker Pro ignores punctuation, capitalization, and word order. Thus, it considers **Steve Schwartz** and **schwartz, steve** to be identical.

The Existing value option

Use this option to ensure that every value entered in a particular field matches a value in that field in another record. Essentially, this is the opposite of the Unique value option and exists primarily for historical purposes from the days before Value Lists were introduced. When determining whether one entry matches another, FileMaker Pro ignores punctuation, capitalization, and word order.

Note   The Unique value and Existing value entry options are mutually exclusive. For any given field, you can set at most one of these options.

The Member of value list option

Select this option to restrict data to the items in a value list. For example, you might have a Payment Method field that includes all allowable forms of payment in a value list (such as cash, VISA, MasterCard, American Express, and Discover). Linking the validation options to this value list prevents your salespeople from entering (and presumably accepting) other forms of payment, such as personal checks or other credit cards.

If a suitable value list hasn't already been created for the database, choose Define Value Lists from the pop-up menu/drop-down list and create the value list. (See the section, "Value lists," later in this chapter, for instructions.)

Note   Value lists in FileMaker Pro 4 and higher are not treated as though they are linked to a specific field. Any value list that you define for a database can be associated with any field in the database — or with several fields, if you like. For example, you could create a single value list that contained the choices *Yes, No,* and *Don't know,* and use this value list with every Yes/No question in a survey database.

The In range option

Select this option to specify an allowable range for a Text, Number, Date, Time, or Timestamp field. Enter the lowest acceptable value in the first text box and the highest acceptable value in the second text box. Because text is handled alphabetically (subject to the sorting sequence determined by your default language), you can enter the letters A and E to restrict acceptable entries to text strings that begin with the letters A, B, C, and D, as well as the single character E, for example.

Tip   This example points out why it is important to think through your design. Choosing A and E as the bounding values means that no values greater than E, such as Eager, would be permitted. Although it is not necessarily intuitive (except to programmers), you probably want some value like Ezzzz as your upper-bound.

Tip   For numeric ranges, you may want to set Numeric Only as the Strict data type, as well as setting the In range option. This ensures not only that the value will be in range but also that it will be the proper data type: that is, a number. In order to get precisely the type of validation you need, it's not uncommon to select two or more validation options working in concert.

The Validated by calculation option

To set the Validated by calculation option, select its check box. A slightly modified version of the Specify Calculation dialog appears. Enter a *Boolean* formula (one that returns a true or false result), check or remove the check mark from the Validate only if field has been modified check box, and click OK.

Note If necessary, any Text, Number, Date, Time, Timestamp, or Container field can be validated by a Boolean (true/false) formula. As an example, the formula Age ≥18 could be used to determine whether the entry in Age is a legitimate one (≥18) or should be flagged (<18).

Tip It is not strictly necessary for the result to be Boolean. Any non-zero result is treated as true, and an empty or zero result is treated as false.

The Allow user to override during data entry option

When set in combination with one or more other validation options, this option prevents you or other users from overriding validation warnings (refer to Figure 5-15). Thus, if you specify Strict data type: Numeric only for a field and also deselect the Allow users to override option, users will be prevented from entering anything other than a legitimate number in the field rather than simply being warned of their error and allowed to override the warning.

The Display custom message if validation fails option

This option enables you to present a dialog with a custom message if the validation fails (see Figure 5-16). (This option can be selected only if you have also chosen at least one other validation option.) Rather than rely on FileMaker Pro's standard validation error messages, you might prefer to display a detailed explanation of what you expect from the user.

Figure 5-16: An example of a custom message.

Repeating fields

Although most fields are intended to handle only one piece of data, you might sometimes want to use a single field to collect multiple bits of information. This type of field is a *repeating field.*

In older, less-capable database programs (or database programs without relational capabilities), you often had to handle repeating fields the hard way. For example, to create an eight-line invoice, you had to define eight separate Quantity, Item Description, Unit Price, and Extended Price fields. Calculations based on these fields were cumbersome to create, as in ExtPrice1 + ExtPrice2 + ExtPrice3. . . . The FileMaker Pro invoice shown in Figure 5-17, on the other hand, was created by defining a single field for each of the following: Quantity, Item Description, Unit

Price, and Extended Price. Then the Repeating field option was assigned to each field. You can set any type of field to repeat except for Summary fields.

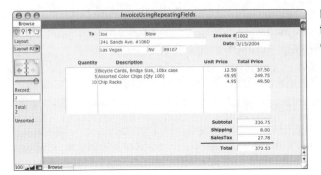

Figure 5-17: Repeating fields in an invoice database.

STEPS: Setting the Repeating Field Option for a Field

1. Choose File ➪ Define ➪ Database (or press Shift+⌘+D/Shift+Ctrl+D) and select the Fields tab.

   The Fields pane appears. Refer to Figure 5-1.

2. From the scrolling field list, select the Text, Number, Date, Time, Timestamp, Container, or Calculation field that you want to define as a repeating field.

3. Click the Options button.

   An Options for *field type "field name"* or Specify Calculation dialog appears. (The specific dialog that appears depends on the type of field you chose in Step 2.)

4. Locate the Repetitions option.

   If this is a Text, Number, Date, Time, Timestamp, or Container field, click the Storage tab at the top of the dialog. If this is a Calculation field, the option is at the bottom of the displayed dialog.

5. Enter the maximum number of repetitions.

   This number is simply the upper limit of repetitions that the field can store. You set the number of repetitions that are displayed, on the other hand, by switching to Layout mode, selecting the field on the layout, and choosing the Format ➪ Field Format command (described in Chapter 6).

6. Click OK to return to the Define Database dialog.

7. Repeat Steps 2–6 for additional fields you want to define as repeating fields.

8. Click Done to record the changes and return to the database.

Note Several built-in functions are provided expressly for the purpose of performing computations on repeating fields. You're already familiar with many of them, such as
Total and Average, from the discussion in this chapter concerning summary functions (see "Defining Calculation, Summary, and Global fields"). For calculation purposes, you can use the Extend built-in function to treat a non-repeating field as
though it repeats. Use the GetRepetition function to reference a specific repetition,
and use the Last function to find the last valid, non-empty repetition.

You need to be aware of some important facts about repeating fields:

✦ Regardless of the number of repetitions that are visible on the current layout,
FileMaker Pro uses *all* repetitions in calculations.

For example, if you alter an invoice layout that was originally designed to show
eight line items so that it now shows only five, FileMaker Pro will also consider
the other three line items when it calculates the Sum function. If you really want
to stop the additional entries from being included in the calculation, you must
delete them or add the results of separate GetRepetition calls.

✦ When you conduct a sort that is based on a repeating field, only the first repetition is used in the sort.

✦ Other database programs almost certainly will not correctly handle a
FileMaker Pro export that contains repeating fields.

Value lists

If you have been impressed by the pop-up menus and drop-down lists used in many
programs, you will be equally impressed to learn that FileMaker Pro enables you to
create the same type of choice lists for your database fields.

You determine the values that appear in the list. Depending on the format you select
for a field, the list can be presented as a pop-up menu, a pop-up list, a set of check
boxes, or a set of radio buttons. When you tab into a field that is formatted as a
pop-up list, the list automatically appears. When you click a field that is formatted
as a pop-up list or a pop-up menu, the list or menu appears. Even if a field has an
associated value list, you can still type different information in the field (unless you
also set the Member of value list validation option, as described previously in this
chapter).

Just as you can define relationships on the fly, you can also create value lists in various FileMaker Pro dialogs. However, regardless of how you initiate their creation,
you will always be shown the same Define Value Lists dialog. After you create a
value list, you can associate it with one or more fields by using the Format ➪ Field
Format command.

STEPS: Creating a Value List

1. Choose File ➪ Define ➪ Value Lists.

The Define Value Lists dialog appears, as shown in Figure 5-18.

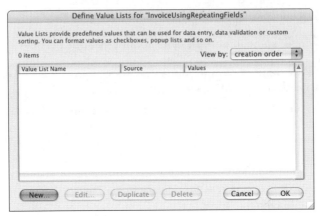

Figure 5-18: The Define Value Lists dialog.

2. Click the New button.

The Edit Value List dialog appears.

3. Type a name for the list in the Value List Name text box.

The name can be anything you like. Because it never appears anywhere on a layout, make it something descriptive.

4. Choose one of the following options:

- *Use custom values:* Type entries for the value list, pressing Return/Enter after each entry except the last one. (If you press Return/Enter after the final entry, you will end up with an extra blank line at the end of the list.) Note that FileMaker Pro doesn't have an option to alphabetize values in a value list. If you want them in a particular order, you have to type them in that order. However, you can change the order by cutting and pasting.

  This is the most common type of value list. If you wanted to create a Days of the Week or a Charge Cards value list, for instance, this is the method you'd use (see Figure 5-19).

Tip   You can type a hyphen (–) on any line by itself to create a dashed line in pop-up menus and pop-up lists or an empty space between radio buttons and check boxes.

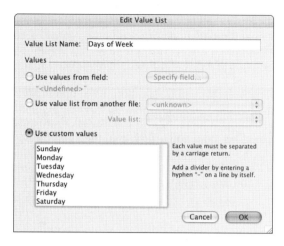

Figure 5-19: Create or edit value lists in the Edit Value List dialog.

- *Use values from field:* When you select this radio button, the Specify Fields for Value List dialog appears (see Figure 5-20). Choosing this option instructs FileMaker Pro to create a value list based on the contents of a field — in this or another database. By default, FileMaker Pro lists all fields in the current table. Choose a field on which to base the value list from the scrolling list on the left. (Optionally, you can select a second field from the list on the right.) To view fields in a different table, click the Specify button.

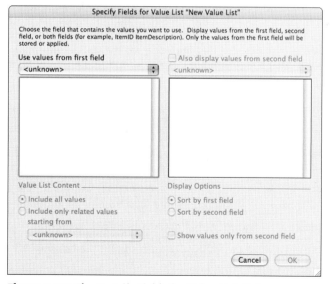

Figure 5-20: The Specify Fields for Value List dialog.

To restrict field choices to those in a related file, select the Include only related values radio button and choose a relationship from the pop-up menu/drop-down list. This option creates a value list in which only a subset of data in a given field (based on a relationship) is presented as the values. For instance, you might have a Main database that was related by Customer ID to a Contact Information database. The Contact Information database has a Phone Number repeating field that is designed to store up to five phone numbers. You could create a value list from that Phone Number field and attach it to the Phone field in the Main database. Then when you enter a Customer ID in the Main database and tab into the Phone field, only *that* particular customer's phone numbers will appear in the pop-up list.

Note that you can also display the values from a second field. This can help you determine which of the values in a value list to choose. For example, if you have a list of customer IDs (constructed from the Customer ID field), the corresponding customer's name would be helpful in deciding which ID to pick from the list.

Tip   Although you can display a second field, such as a customer's last name, you cannot display more additional fields. In the example above, it might be more helpful if you could display the last name, first name, and city together—which is what you'd probably need to figure out if the chosen ID belonged to the customer you wanted. One solution is to create a Calculation field that combines all the fields you want to see, and then use that Calculation field as the second field in the value list.

Tip   You can also base a value list on the *current* field. If you get tired of typing customer names, companies, cities, product names/IDs, and the like, create a value list from the current field, attach it to the field, and display it as a pop-up menu/drop-down list. After the database has sufficient records, you can just choose the item from the list. This also helps ensure that the value will be spelled identically each time—no more instances of Apple, Apple Computer, and Apple Computer Inc in the same field!

- *Use value list from another file:* Choose this option if you want to use a value list that you've created in a different database. Choose Add File Reference from the top pop-up menu/drop-down list, and then select the database from the file dialog that appears. Choose a value list from the second pop-up menu/drop-down list and then click OK.

  As you can see, FileMaker makes it extremely easy to reuse value lists — even allowing you to use value lists from other databases.

5. When you have finished defining the value list, click OK.

The Define Value Lists dialog is now front and center and includes the new value list.

6. You can do any of the following:

- To create additional value lists, repeat Steps 2–5.

- To edit an existing value list, double-click it (or select it and click Edit).

- To base a new value list on an existing one, select a value list and click Duplicate. Edit the duplicate (named "*value list* Copy"). In the Edit Value List dialog, rename the duplicate and make any other desired changes.

- To eliminate an unnecessary value list, select it and click Delete.

- If you're through working with value lists, click OK.

Of course, defining value lists is only the first step. As mentioned previously, FileMaker Pro doesn't consider a value list to be part of a field. Instead, a value list is merely associated with one or more fields and is considered part of a field's Validation settings. Follow the steps below to associate a value list with a field.

STEPS: Associating a Value List with a Field

1. Switch to Layout mode by choosing View ➪ Layout (⌘+L/Ctrl+L), choosing Layout from the Mode pop-up menu, or clicking the Layout button in the Tools sidebar. Then select the field to which you want to attach a value list and choose Format ➪ Field/Control ➪ Setup (Option+⌘+F/Alt+Ctrl+F).

The Field/Control Setup dialog appears, as shown in Figure 5-21.

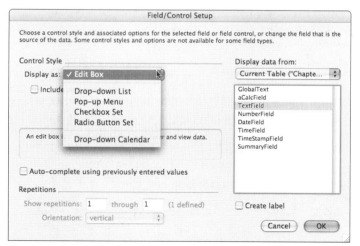

Figure 5-21: Choose a format for the value list in the Field/Control Setup dialog.

Selecting multiple radio buttons or check boxes

If you format a value list field as a set of check boxes (in the Field/Control Setup dialog), you can select multiple options when you enter data in the field. And although radio button options are mutually exclusive in most programs (you can normally choose only one radio button from a set), you can select multiple radio buttons on a FileMaker Pro layout by holding down the Shift key as you click each one.

2. To attach a value list to this field, choose anything other than Edit Box or Drop-down Calendar from the Display as pop-up menu/drop-down list in the dialog's Control Style section, as shown in Figure 5-21. Select one of the following options: Drop-down List, Pop-up Menu, Checkbox Set, or Radio Button Set.

3. Choose the name of a value list from the Display values from pop-up menu/ drop-down list that appears.

4. Click OK to record the changes.

New Feature

As a matter of nomenclature, what FileMaker Pro used to call a *pop-up list* is what Windows and Mac users are accustomed to seeing called a *drop-down list*. In FileMaker Pro 8, the term is now named consonant with our expectation.

When formatting a field with a value list (in the Field/Control Setup dialog), if you select any format other than Drop-down List, you can select the check box for Include other item to allow entry of other values. This adds a choice marked Other to the pop-up menu, check boxes, or radio buttons. An Other choice facilitates the entry of data that is not present in the field's value list.

If you've created a custom value list by typing its entries and selected either a drop-down list or pop-up menu, you can select the check box for Include Edit item to allow editing of value list. This adds an Edit choice to the pop-up list or pop-up menu. If you choose this option during data entry, you'll be allowed to edit the contents of the value list—adding, editing, deleting, or reordering the items. When you next click or tab into a field that uses this value list, the edited value list will be presented.

Indexing and storage options

In FileMaker Pro 4 or higher, you must decide whether any or all fields are indexed, as well as whether calculation results are stored with the data file or are calculated only as needed.

Indexing improves the speed with which Find and sort operations are performed. Any fields that you regularly sort the database by or use as the basis of Find commands are good candidates for indexing.

Indexing options can be set for any Text, Number, Date, Time, Timestamp, or Calculation field that isn't stored as a Global field. (Indexing cannot be set for Container or Summary fields.) In addition to indexing options, you can also set storage options for Calculation fields.

STEPS: Setting Indexing Options for a Text, Number, Date, or Time Field

1. Choose File ➪ Define ➪ Database (or press Shift+⌘+D/Shift+Ctrl+D) and click the Fields tab in the Define Database dialog that appears.

The Fields pane appears. (Refer to Figure 5-1.)

2. Select the field and click Options. (If the field has not yet been created, create it first and then click Options.)

An Options dialog appears.

3. Click the Storage tab at the top of the Options dialog (see Figure 5-22).

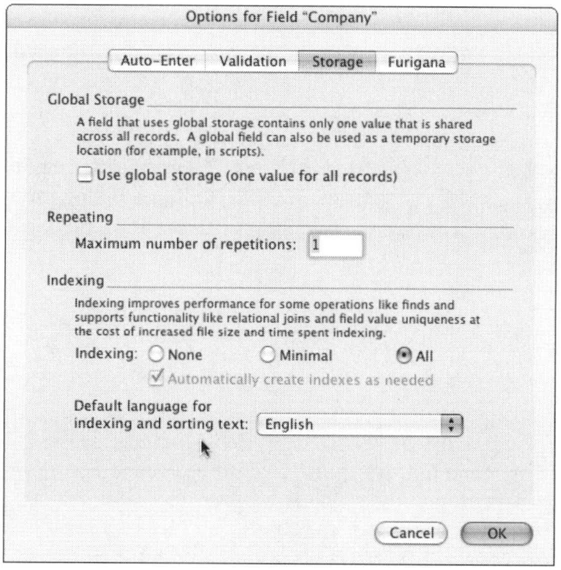

Figure 5-22: Storage options for a non-Global Text, Number, Date, Time, or Timestamp field.

> Options for Field "Company"
>
> | Auto–Enter | Validation | Storage | Furigana |
>
> **Global Storage**
> A field that uses global storage contains only one value that is shared across all records. A global field can also be used as a temporary storage location (for example, in scripts).
> ☐ Use global storage (one value for all records)
>
> **Repeating**
> Maximum number of repetitions: [1]
>
> **Indexing**
> Indexing improves performance for some operations like finds and supports functionality like relational joins and field value uniqueness at the cost of increased file size and time spent indexing.
> Indexing: ○ None   ○ Minimal   ⦿ All
>   ☑ Automatically create indexes as needed
> **Default language for indexing and sorting text:** [English ⬍]
>
> (Cancel) (OK)

Note If the Use global storage check box is selected, the Indexing section will be dimmed (unavailable).

4. To turn on indexing for a field, select the All radio button. Or, for a Text field, you can select Minimal, which only indexes the first 100 characters (or up to the first carriage return) in what FileMaker refers to as a *value index*.

If you decide to leave off indexing, you can still instruct FileMaker Pro to index the field if it becomes necessary by selecting the Automatically create indexes as needed check box.

5. *Optional (for Text fields only):* You can select a particular language to be used in determining sort and index orders from the pop-up menu/drop-down list at the bottom of the dialog.

6. Click OK in Storage Options dialog to return to the Define Database dialog.

STEPS: Setting Indexing Options for a Calculation Field

1. Choose File ➪ Define ➪ Database (or press Shift+⌘+D/Shift+Ctrl+D) and click the Fields tab in the Define Database dialog that appears.

   The Fields pane appears. (Refer to Figure 5-1.)

2. Select the Calculation field for which you'd like to set storage options and click Options.

   The Specify Calculation dialog appears. (Refer to Figure 5-7.)

3. Click the Storage Options button.

   The Storage Options for Field *Field Name* dialog appears, as shown in Figure 5-23.

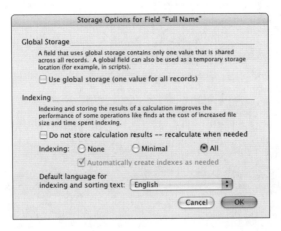

Figure 5-23: The Storage Options dialog for a Calculation field.

4. To turn on indexing for a Calculation field, select the All radio button.

   If you decide to leave indexing off, you can still enable FileMaker Pro to index the field if it becomes necessary by selecting the Automatically create indexes as needed check box.

5. To instruct FileMaker Pro to store calculated results for this field as part of the file's data, leave the Do not store calculation results check box clear. (This is the default setting.) If you want to reduce storage requirements for the database (at the expense of increased time to perform recalculations), mark its check box.

6. *Optional (for Calculation fields that return a Text result only):* You can select a particular language to be used in determining sort and index orders from the pop-up menu at the bottom of the dialog. You can also select Minimal indexing, which tells FileMaker Pro to index only the field and not each word in the field.

7. Click OK to return to the Define Database dialog.

 Tip

If a Calculation field needs to be frequently recalculated (such as one that computes the number of days until a project is due), select the Do not store calculation results check box.

Modifying Field Definitions, Names, and Options

A few capabilities of the Fields pane remain unexplored (and unexplained). As previously mentioned, FileMaker Pro enables you to add, change, or delete field definitions and options whenever you like. You can also rename fields. And to speed the process of creating fields, FileMaker Pro enables you to duplicate existing field definitions. The step-by-step instructions in the following sections explain how to perform these tasks.

Changing field names

Unless you give a lot of thought to field names when you design databases, you'll find that some of the names can stand a little improvement. Feel free to change them to names that are more appropriate. FileMaker Pro automatically corrects field labels, sort instructions, and other references to the field (in formulas, scripts, and across relationships, for example).

STEPS: Renaming a Field

1. Choose File ⇨ Define ⇨ Database (or press Shift+⌘+D/Shift+Ctrl+D) and click the Fields tab in the Define Database dialog that appears.

   The Fields pane appears. (Refer to Figure 5-1.)

2. Select the field you wish to rename.

   The field name appears in the Field Name text box.

3. Type a new name in the Field Name box and click Change.

FileMaker Pro renames the field and automatically adjusts any references to the field in Calculation field formulas, Summary fields, and scripts to reflect the new field name. If, when you originally created the field, you accepted and placed the default label for the field in a layout, FileMaker Pro also changes the label to match the new field name. Field labels that you've manually edited or typed from scratch, on the other hand, are unaffected.

4. To rename additional fields, repeat Steps 2 and 3. Click Done when you're through renaming fields.

Actually, field names aren't that important. As long as the field name clearly indicates to you what each field is meant to hold, it doesn't matter whether you name a field Sale Amount, Sale, Amount, Amt, or S1. However, because each field's default label is identical to the field name, you might well want to edit the label to something more descriptive. Remember, a field label is just a piece of static text and can be changed as you like, whenever you like.

Tip   Developers sometimes use a simple naming trick that enables them to quickly tell the field type of any field. Begin every field name with a lower-case letter that indicates its type. You could use **t** for Text, **n** for Number, **d** for Date, **i** for Time, **m** for TimeStamp, **o** for Container, **c** for Calculation, **s** for Summary, and **g** for Global, for example (the same character that is used with ⌘/Ctrl to select the field type in the Define Database dialog's Fields pane). Follow the letter with the remainder of the field name, such as **nSales** or **tAddress**.

Deleting a field and its data

The more you work with a particular database, the more familiar you become with the data it was designed to collect. If you decide that you no longer need a particular field (or perhaps that you should never have created it in the first place), follow these steps to delete the field and the data it contains.

STEPS: Deleting a Field

1. Choose File ➪ Define ➪ Database (or press Shift+⌘+D/Shift+Ctrl+D) and click the Fields tab in the Define Database dialog that appears.

The Fields pane appears. (Refer to Figure 5-1.)

2. Select the field you want to delete and then click the Delete button.

One of two sequences occurs:

• The normal dialog simply asks whether you're sure you want to delete the field and its contents. (See Figure 5-24, top.)

• If the field is referenced in a Calculation or Summary field or in a relationship with another table in the same file, another dialog will now appear (see Figure 5-24, bottom), explaining that you cannot delete the field. To delete such a field, you first have to edit the appropriate Calculation and Summary field formulas and options or the relationship so they no longer reference the field that you want to delete.

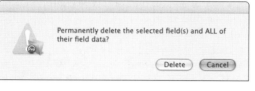

Figure 5-24: The top dialog appears when you attempt to delete a field. The bottom appears if the field is referenced in another field (Calculation, Summary, or Relation).

3. Click the Delete button in the dialog to delete the field, or click Cancel if you change your mind.

4. To delete additional fields, repeat Steps 2 and 3. Click Done when you are ready to return to the database.

Caution

As the topmost dialog in Figure 5-24 warns, deleting a field eliminates the field and all data for the field. You cannot undo a field deletion. If there is a chance that you might later need the data, you should make a backup copy of the file by choosing the File ➪ Save a Copy As command before deleting the field.

An alternative to deleting fields

Instead of deleting a field, you can simply remove it from all layouts. Removing a field in this manner does not delete it. All data previously entered in the field remains intact. To be able to see the data, all you have to do is put the field back onto a layout. This approach makes the database larger than necessary, however, because it is still storing information you might never use again. If you're certain that you no longer need to continue collecting the data for a field, the best approach is to make a backup copy of the original database, delete the field in the current version of the file, and then move on.

If a layout includes a field from a related table and you delete that field definition or the related table, a placeholder containing the text `<Field Missing>` or `<Table Missing>` remains on the layout, respectively.

Duplicating fields

To save time, you might want to duplicate some existing fields, particularly fields that have complex options that you don't want to re-create. After you duplicate a field, editing and renaming the new field is a simple matter. (See the instructions for renaming a field, earlier in this section.)

For example, in an invoice or statement database, you might have a series of repeating fields that you use to record each line item (such as Quantity, Description, Unit Cost, and Extended Cost). You would use separate Calculation fields to compute the total for each of the cost fields. After defining a formula for the first Calculation field as Sum (Unit Cost), you could duplicate the field definition and, in the formula, simply replace **Unit Cost** with **Extended Cost**.

STEPS: Duplicating a Field

1. Choose File ⇨ Define ⇨ Database (or press Shift+⌘+D/Shift+Ctrl+D) and click the Fields tab in the Define Database dialog that appears.

   The Fields pane appears. (Refer to Figure 5-1.)

2. Select the field you want to duplicate and click the Duplicate button.

   FileMaker Pro creates an exact duplicate of the field and appends the word Copy to its name. For example, if the field to be duplicated is named Comments, the duplicate is named Comments Copy. Additional duplicates of the same field are named Comments Copy2, Comments Copy3, and so on.

3. To rename the duplicate field, select the field in the Fields pane's scrolling field list, type a new name in the Field Name box, and click Change.

4. *Optional:* To change any of the options for the duplicate field, select the field and click Options.

5. To duplicate additional fields, repeat Steps 2– 4. Click OK when you are through duplicating fields.

Setting options for existing fields

You don't have to set field options when you initially define a field. You can set or change them later as the need arises. (However, if you enter data before setting options for a field, you might need to go back and correct some of the earlier entries for the field.)

STEPS: Setting Options for Previously Defined Fields

1. Choose File ➪ Define ➪ Database (or press Shift+⌘+D/Shift+Ctrl+D) and click the Fields tab in the Define Database dialog that appears.

   The Fields pane appears. (Refer to Figure 5-1.)

2. Select the field for which you want to set options and click the Options button. (You can also double-click any field in the list to move directly to the Options dialog for that field.)

3. In the dialog that appears, set options as described in "Setting Field Options," earlier in this chapter.

4. To accept the new options, click OK. To ignore the options you have selected, click Cancel.

5. To set options for other fields, repeat Steps 2–4. Click OK when you are through setting options.

Changing a field's type

The following steps describe how to change a field's type.

STEPS: Changing a Field's Type

1. Choose File ➪ Define ➪ Database (or press Shift+⌘+D/Shift+Ctrl+D) and click the Fields tab in the Define Database dialog that appears.

   The Fields pane appears. (Refer to Figure 5-1.)

2. Select the field you want to change.

Replacing one field with another

Has this ever happened to you? After carefully selecting, placing, resizing, and setting attributes for fields on a layout, you discover that one of the fields wasn't the right one. Rather than deleting the errant field and then adding the correct one, you can use the following trick to redefine the field as a different field:

1. Switch to Layout mode, and double-click the field you want to redefine.

   The Specify Field dialog appears, listing the fields for this database, as well as the fields available in any defined relationships.

2. Select a replacement field and click OK.

Redefining a field preserves its original placement on the layout as well as its dimensions and formatting.

3. To change the field's type, select a new type and click Change.

If switching to the new field type has any potential problems, FileMaker Pro presents a warning alert, such as the ones shown in Figure 5-25. (The particular dialog displayed is related to the type of change you want to make.) This warning contains information that you should consider before proceeding with the conversion. If such an alert appears, you might want to use the Save a Copy As command to make a backup copy of the database before you proceed.

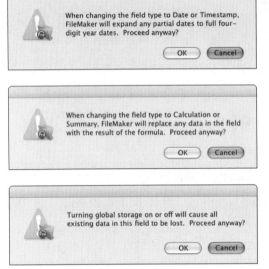

Figure 5-25: Warnings like these might appear when you are changing a field's type or converting it to a GlobalStorage field.

4. If you are changing the field to a Summary or Calculation field, a dialog will appear. Select a summary function or create the formula for the Calculation field, and click OK to accept the changes or Cancel to revert to the original settings.

5. To change additional field definitions, repeat Steps 2– 4 for each field. When you are through, click Done to leave the Define Fields dialog.

Changing or deleting options for a field

To modify or delete options for a field, follow these steps.

STEPS: Modifying a Field's Options

1. Choose File ➪ Define ➪ Database (or press Shift+⌘+D/Shift+Ctrl+D) and click the Fields tab in the Define Database dialog that appears.

The Fields pane appears. (Refer to Figure 5-1.)

2. Select the field whose options you want to change and then click the Options button or double-click the field name in the field list.

   An Options dialog appears, appropriate to the data type of the selected field.

3. Change the options you want to modify and then click OK to return to the Define Fields dialog.

   The means of changing options is always obvious. You can add or remove options by selecting check boxes, clicking buttons, making selections from pop-up menus/drop-down lists, and using normal editing techniques (to change formulas, for example).

4. To change options for other fields, repeat Steps 2 and 3. Click Done when you are through changing field options.

Summary

✦ FileMaker Pro 8 includes eight field types: Text, Number, Date, Time, Timestamp, Container, Calculation, and Summary. The type you choose for a field determines the kinds of information you can enter in the field.

✦ You can specify any field as a GlobalStorage field, enabling you to record a single value that is used for every record in the table. A GlobalStorage value is stored only once in the entire table (rather than storing a separate copy of the value for every record).

✦ You can set auto-entry options for a field to instruct FileMaker Pro to enter a value for a field whenever you create a new record or, in some cases, when you edit a record. By selecting the Prohibit modification of value during data entry option, you can protect the auto-entered data from inadvertent (or deliberate) modification.

✦ Any value list that has been defined for a database can be associated with many fields in the database. You can also associate value lists from other databases with fields in the current database.

✦ You can store multiple values in a single field using repetitions. This is very handy for fields that normally have multiple values, such as line items on an invoice when you don't want to set up multiple tables. By using calculation functions, you can easily sum the multiple values that appear in a repeating value field.

✦ Data validation options help ensure that only acceptable values are entered for a field. By deselecting the Allow user to override during data entry option, you can protect the integrity of the field's data and ensure that only the right kind of information is accepted.

✦ You can alter the fields for a database at any time by changing their names, definitions, or options. You can also add new fields or delete existing fields.

✦ ✦ ✦

Layouts

If you've used other database programs — particularly
any of the simpler ones, such as Microsoft Works or
AppleWorks — before you switched to FileMaker Pro, you
might have become used to creating every field that was
needed for a database and then dutifully arranging all the
fields on a single form. That, however, is not how FileMaker
Pro works.

Although you can create dozens or even hundreds of fields
for a FileMaker Pro database, it's unlikely you'd ever want or
need to display them all on the same form. To print envelopes
or mailing labels, for example, you need only the name and
address fields for each client in your database. You don't need
information about the products that each client has ordered.
If you're preparing a summary of recent sales figures, client
address information is of little importance. Similarly, you will
seldom want calculation fields on a form used solely for data
entry. Even though all this data could be collected in the same
database, you need to display it only where it's appropriate.
The FileMaker Pro feature making this possible is the *layout*.

A *layout* is a particular arrangement of some of — or all — the
fields that have been defined for a database. You choose the
fields that are included in each layout — as many or as few
fields as you like. You can arrange the fields in each layout to
address a specific need, such as printing labels, entering data,
or presenting a report. You can add layout parts (for example,
a header and footer to make some information repeat on
every page). And you can include special items to help identify your layouts or make them more attractive, such as titles,
3-D field borders, graphics, and buttons. You can have as
many layouts for a given database as you like — one to suit
every need (subject to having enough disk space).

**Cross-
Reference**

For a quick introduction to creating and modifying layouts,
see Chapter 4.

Layout Basics

A FileMaker Pro layout comprises layout parts (the sections of the layout, such as the body, header, and footer), fields (in which data is entered and displayed), and static objects (such as graphics, titles, and field labels).

When you design a new database and define its initial table and set of fields, FileMaker Pro automatically creates a default layout for you named to match the table on which it is based. The default layout is a one-column arrangement of all fields that have been defined for the database in the order they were defined.

STEPS: Creating the Initial Layout for a New Database

1. To create a new database when launching FileMaker Pro, select the Create a new empty file radio button from the New Database dialog that automatically appears.

   or

   If FileMaker Pro is already running, choose File ⇨ New Database. Then select the Create a new empty file radio button from the New Database dialog that appears.

   The Define Database dialog appears, showing the Fields pane.

2. Define the initial fields for the database by following the procedures outlined in Chapter 5. Click OK when you're finished.

   A default layout named the same as your table appears (see Figure 6-1), ready for you to begin entering data. The first record is automatically created for you, and the database switches to Browse mode.

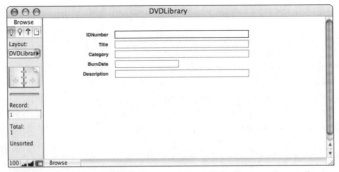

Figure 6-1: A new default layout automatically arranges all defined fields in a column.

Note

In versions prior to FileMaker Pro 7, the default initial layout was named (some-what unimaginatively) Layout #1. Accompanying the change to support multiple tables in a single database was the logical change of naming the default layout to match the table from which it is generated. After all, if you have five tables in the database, you really don't want to have five Layout #1s.

For many data collection purposes, the initial layout is all you'll need. If you have other layout requirements, such as printing labels or generating reports, you will want to create additional layouts that present the data in other ways.

Note

You aren't locked into using the default layout as is — or at all, for that matter. You might find that it can serve as the basis for a custom layout. Simply change the formatting and arrangement of its fields. On the other hand, if you don't even want to use it as the starting point for a custom layout, you can delete it as long as you've created at least one more layout. The Layouts ⇨ Delete Layout command isn't available if you have only a single layout in your database. Modifying and deleting layouts are explained later in this chapter.

You create new layouts and modify existing ones in Layout mode, which is one of FileMaker Pro's four operational modes. (The others are Browse, Find, and Preview.) Switch to Layout mode by choosing View ⇨ Layout Mode (⌘+L/Ctrl+L), and you'll see a screen similar to Figure 6-2, which displays the Inventory template's Form View layout.

A pop-up menu listing the layouts that have been defined resides in the status area, just below the mode buttons. This menu enables you to choose an existing layout to edit. Below the pop-up menu is a book icon and associated text, also giving you access to available layouts by name. You click the book icon or type a layout number (and then press Return/Enter) to switch between the available layouts in creation order. Beneath the book icon are the tools that you use to add or modify elements on a layout. You use the field and part icons to create new layout parts and to add fields to the layout.

You'll find important Layout mode features and options in the View, Insert, Format, Layouts, and Arrange menus. These menus contain commands enabling you to add items to layouts, arrange items, and specify how the items should display.

STEPS: Switching to Layout Mode

1. Launch FileMaker Pro if it isn't already running.

2. Open the database in which you want to add, modify, or view layouts.

3. Choose View ⇨ Layout Mode, press ⌘+L/Ctrl+L, click the Layout button at the top of the sidebar (the T-square), or choose Layout from the mode selector pop-up menu at the bottom of the document window (refer to Figure 6-2).

4. From the layout pop-up menu beneath the mode buttons at the top of the sidebar, choose the layout you want to view.

or

Click the book icon to page through the available layouts until the one you want appears.

Note   You can also type a number in the Layout text box and press Return/Enter to go to a specific layout. These numbers are sequential and indicate the order in which the layouts were created.

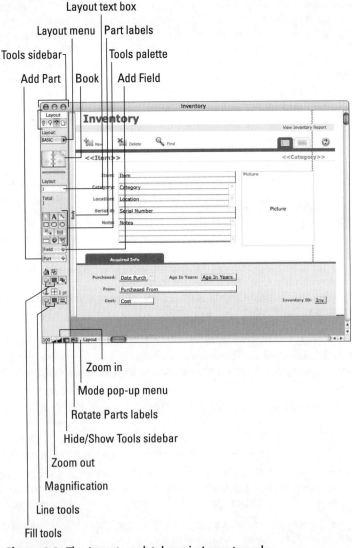

Figure 6-2: The Inventory database in Layout mode.

Creating New Layouts

After you define fields for a new database, FileMaker Pro creates your first layout for you. You can immediately use this layout for data entry and browsing if you like.

To view data in other ways, you must create more layouts. FileMaker Pro 8 includes seven predefined layout styles — see Table 6-1 — that you can use as starting points.

Table 6-1
FileMaker Pro Predefined Layout Styles

Layout Name	Purpose
Standard Form	Shows one record per screen, with all fields displayed in the order in which they were defined; similar to the default layout used when creating a new database.
Columnar List/Report	Fields are displayed left to right in columns. Fields that don't fit the current page width are either wrapped to the next line or extend beyond the page break (depending on the option you choose).
Table View	Data is displayed in spreadsheet fashion in which each record is a row, and each column is a field.
Labels	Fields are formatted for use with mailing and other types of labels.
Vertical Labels	Primarily useful with Asian languages. Text characters are rotated so the labels can be used vertically.
Envelope	Fields are formatted for use with business (No. 10) envelopes.
Blank Layout	Used to create custom layouts.

To make it simpler to create layouts, FileMaker Pro 8 steps you through the process with its New Layout/Report Assistant. All new layouts (beyond the initial one) are created via this assistant.

STEPS: Creating a New Layout from a Predefined Style

1. Determine what sort of layout you want and the fields you need to display.

2. Switch to Layout mode by choosing View ⇨ Layout Mode (or by pressing ⌘+L/Ctrl+L).

3. Choose Layouts ⇨ New Layout/Report (or press ⌘+N/Ctrl+N).

   The New Layout/Report Assistant appears, as shown in Figure 6-3.

4. Type a name for the new layout.

Table selection pop-up (Mac)/drop-down (Windows)

Sample thumbnail

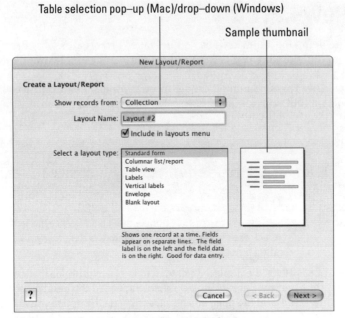

Figure 6-3: The New Layout/Report Assistant.

5. Choose the layout style you want to use by selecting one from the list. (Do not choose the Blank Layout type unless you want to create a layout from scratch, as described later in this chapter.)

6. Decide whether the layout should appear in the layout pop-up menu by leaving or removing the check mark in the Include in layouts menu check box.

7. Click Next. (Or, if you choose Blank layout, click Finish.)

If you choose the Blank layout, FileMaker Pro creates your layout immediately. The Blank layout contains no fields (just a blank page).

Additional steps follow, depending on the layout style chosen.

The remaining layout types (other than the default and Blank) use a limited set of the fields. Additional dialogs appear in which you select fields and set options, as explained in the following layout-specific sections.

Note   Regardless of the type of layout you choose, the sections included in the layout, called *layout parts,* are restricted to a body (where the fields are generally placed) and (in some cases) a header and a footer. Read all about adding, removing, and modifying layout parts in "Understanding layout parts," later in this chapter.

Hiding layouts

The ability to display or hide the name of a layout in the layout pop-up menu/drop-down list can be very useful. For example, if you're distributing a shareware template, you might want to reveal certain layouts only after users have paid the shareware fee. Similarly, there might be some layouts that you never want users to see. Hiding a layout by removing the check mark from the Include in layouts menu check box (refer to Figure 6-3) makes it impossible to select the layout in Browse mode. (It can still be seen in Layout mode, however, or displayed in Browse mode via a script.) Hiding the layout in this manner and setting appropriate access options can make it completely invisible to users or to a subset of the user base, depending upon the access level that you (or their database administrator) grant them.

You can also hide any layout to which you don't want users to be able to switch. In a database that is entirely script controlled, for example, you might list only the layout for the main menu or the data entry screen, leaving the layout-switching task to navigation buttons and their attached scripts. This way, you can keep users from inadvertently messing up the database by directly selecting layouts that should normally be reached only as part of a script.

Standard form layouts

A Standard form layout is similar to the one FileMaker Pro creates as the default data entry layout when you define fields for a new table. That is, the fields are automatically placed on the layout, one above the other, and each has a label matching the field name. Note these two differences from the initial default layout. First, rather than using all the fields in your database, only the ones you choose are added to the layout. Second, you can choose a layout *theme* (a set of coordinated colors applied to the layout parts and fields).

Tip

For those of you conversant with XML (eXtensible Markup Language), the various themes are XML files and are easily duplicated and modified if you wish to create your own. On the Mac, they are buried within the application package (Contents ⇨ Resources ⇨ English.lproj ⇨ Themes, for example). On Windows, you can find them in `C:\Program Files\FileMaker\FileMaker Pro 8\Extensions\ English\Themes`. (Actually, in both cases, replace *English* with the language of your system if you are not using an English-based environment.) Themes have an `.fth` filename extension. Whenever you modify distribution files in this way, be sure to work on a copy.

In a Standard form layout, one record is displayed at a time. In addition to the body area, where the fields are displayed, the layout includes blank header and footer parts.

STEPS: Creating a Standard Form Layout

1. Switch to Layout mode by choosing View ⇨ Layout Mode (or by pressing ⌘+L/Ctrl+L).

2. Choose Layouts ➪ New Layout/Report (or press ⌘+N/Ctrl+N).

   The New Layout/Report Assistant appears (refer to Figure 6-3).

3. Choose a table from the Show records from pop-up menu/drop-down list and type a name for the new layout.

4. Choose Standard Form.

5. Determine whether the layout should appear in the layouts menu by leaving or removing the check mark in the Include in layouts menu check box. Click Next to continue.

   The Specify Fields screen appears (see Figure 6-4).

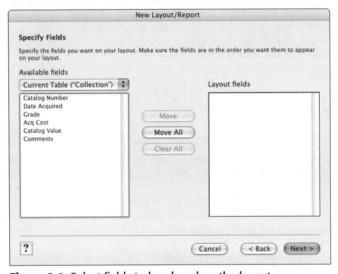

Figure 6-4: Select fields to be placed on the layout.

6. Select fields to be included in the layout by clicking the Move or Move All button. The Move button is available only (undimmed) when one or more fields are selected. Note that you can select multiple contiguous fields by Shift+clicking them or select noncontiguous fields by ⌘/Ctrl+clicking them. Click Next to continue.

Tip   You can also move a field by double-clicking it in the Available Fields list. Additionally, you can move a field multiple times. (You might wish to use it in more than one layout part.) If you decide that you don't really want to include a field in the layout, select it in the Layout Fields list and click the Clear button. (Move toggles to Clear when you're working in the Layout fields list.)

Note   The order in which fields appear in the Layout Fields list is the order in which they will appear (initially) in the layout. You can rearrange the fields by dragging them up or down in the Layout Fields list.

7. Choose a layout theme. Note that every theme (other than Default and Standard) is available in two versions: one for onscreen viewing and another for printed output. Click Finish.

Note

> This is the *only* time you can assign a theme to a layout. After the layout exists, themes may not be applied. Further, themes specify only an initial appearance. Any changes made subsequent to the layout's creation become part of the layout and override whatever the theme might have specified as an initial appearance.

The new layout is created and displayed (see Figure 6-5). Make any necessary changes (changing fonts and adding static text to the header and footer parts, for example) as you learned to do in Chapter 4.

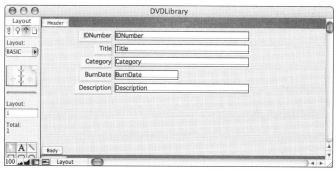

Figure 6-5: A Standard form layout.

Columnar list/report layouts

Early versions of FileMaker Pro (prior to FileMaker Pro 7) offered two kinds of *columnar layouts* (in which fields are displayed in columns across the page). In the Columnar report layout, FileMaker attempted to fit all fields on a single line but wrapped excess fields to the next line. In the Extended columnar layout, all fields were displayed on a single line, no matter how wide the line was. In FileMaker Pro 8, you can create either type of report layout by choosing Columnar List/Report. A columnar list/report can be a simple columnar arrangement of fields or a complex report (with record groups, subtotals, and totals).

STEPS: Creating a Simple Columnar Layout or Report

1. Switch to Layout mode by choosing View ➪ Layout Mode (or by pressing ⌘+L/Ctrl+L).

2. Choose Layouts ➪ New Layout/Report (or press ⌘+N/Ctrl+N).

The New Layout/Report Assistant appears (refer to Figure 6-3).

3. From the Show records from pop-up menu/drop-down list, choose a base table from which to select the layout's fields.

4. Type a name for the new layout.

5. Choose Columnar list/report.

6. Specify whether the layout should appear in the layout pop-up menu/ drop-down list by leaving or removing the check mark in the Include in layouts menu check box. Click Next to continue.

The Choose Report Layout screen appears (see Figure 6-6).

Make all columns fit within page, wrapping if necessary.

Simple column report   Sample page thumbnail

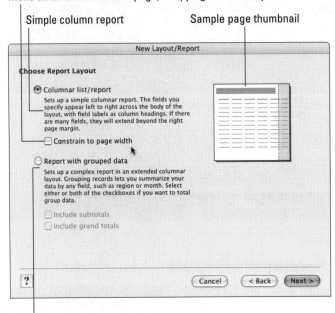

Complex report with grouping and summaries

Figure 6-6: The Choose Report Layout screen.

7. Select the Columnar list/report radio button to create a simple columnar report.

If all columns of your report are meant to fit the width of a normal page, select the Constrain to page width check box. (Note that if the fields don't initially fit, some will be placed in a row beneath the other fields.) This corresponds to the Columnar report layout in earlier versions of FileMaker Pro.

or

If you don't want to restrict the initial width of the layout, don't mark the Constrain to page width check box. (Note that you can always resize fields later to fit within a normal page, if you like.) This corresponds to the Extended columnar report layout in earlier versions of FileMaker Pro.

8. Click Next to continue.

9. In the Specify Fields screen, select the fields you want to include in the report and click Move to add them (one at a time) to the Layout fields list. (You can also double-click a field to move it.) To select multiple fields simultaneously, Shift+click to select contiguous fields or ⌘/Ctrl+click to select noncontiguous fields. Note that the order that fields appear in the Layout fields list is the order in which they will appear in the report layout. To change a field's position in the list, you can click and drag it to a new position. Click Next to continue.

Note Because FileMaker Pro is a relational database program, you can also add fields from related tables to layouts. To choose fields from any currently defined relationship, choose the name of the relationship from the pop-up menu/drop-down list located above the Available Fields list in the Specify Fields screen. If necessary, you can also define a new relationship at this time by choosing Define Database from the pop-up menu/drop-down list. (For information about relationships, see Chapter 18.)

The Sort Records screen appears. (See Figure 6-7.)

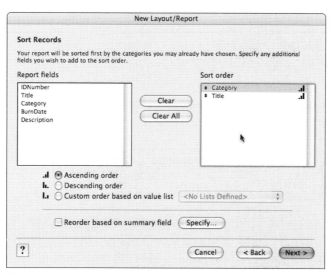

Figure 6-7: Specify sort fields for your report on the Sort Records screen.

10. If the report requires that records be arranged in a particular order, select the appropriate sort field or fields and click Move (remember that this toggles from Clear) to add them to the Sort order list. Click Next to continue. (For additional information on sorting records, see Chapter 10.)

Note If you don't intend to use the New Layout/Report Assistant to create a script that you can use to generate the report as shown in Step 12 of this list, the choices you make for sort fields are irrelevant.

The Select a Theme screen appears.

11. Depending on whether you want the current layout to be used for onscreen or printed reports, select a screen or print theme (based on the examples that appear in the right side of the screen). Click Next to continue.

The Header and Footer Information screen appears. (See Figure 6-8.)

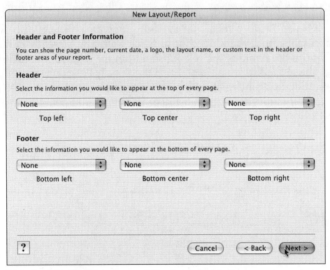

Figure 6-8: The Header and Footer Information screen.

12. Using the Header and Footer pop-up menus/drop-down lists, select header and footer elements and their positions. Click Next to continue.

The Create a Script for this Report screen appears.

13. If you want to automate the report-generation process, click Create a script and enter a name for the script (or accept the default name). Click Next to continue.

For additional information on creating and editing scripts, see Chapter 15. To learn what this specific script does, see the paragraph immediately following these steps.

Note   If you create a script, it is automatically added to the Scripts menu.

14. You can either view the report layout in Preview mode or go to Layout mode to make any necessary changes. Select an option and click Finish.

After cleaning up the layout (changing field widths and placements, for example), if you created a script in Step 12 to generate the report, you'll want to examine it in ScriptMaker. You'll see that this basic script makes the report layout active, performs a sort (if specified in Step 9), enters Preview mode, and pauses until you click the

Continue button. Then it switches to Browse mode and displays whichever layout was active when you executed the script. You might want to modify this script so that it includes appropriate Find instructions, maximizes the database to the full size of your screen, and prints, for example (as demonstrated in Chapter 4). See Chapter 15 for detailed instructions concerning scripting.

Creating a complex columnar report

You can also create more complex reports that are grouped according to some criterion, such as city, job classification, month, or the like. This is referred to as a *complex columnar report.*

STEPS: Creating a Complex Columnar Report

1. Switch to Layout mode by choosing View ➪ Layout Mode (or by pressing ⌘+L/Ctrl+L).

2. Choose Layouts ➪ New Layout/Report (or press ⌘+N/Ctrl+N).

   The New Layout/Report Assistant appears (refer to Figure 6-3).

3. Name the report and choose Columnar list/report as the layout style.

4. Indicate whether the layout should appear in the layouts menu by leaving or removing the check mark in the Include in layouts menu check box. Click Next to continue.

   The Choose Report Layout screen appears (refer to Figure 6-6).

5. Select the Report with grouped data radio button. If you want to compute totals for the groups, mark one or both of the check boxes (Include subtotals and Include grand totals). If you elect to include subtotals or grand totals, you will specify the summary fields to use to generate these totals in Steps 9 and 10. Click Next to continue.

   The Specify Fields screen appears (refer to Figure 6-4).

6. Select the fields that you want to include in the report, and click Move to add them to the Layout fields list. Be sure to include any fields by which the database will be sorted. (If you've elected to create subtotals or grand totals in Step 5, don't include the summary fields at this time. The summary fields will be specified in Step 9.) Click Next to continue.

   The order that fields appear in the Layout fields list is the order in which they will appear in the report layout. To change a field's position in the list, simply click and drag it to a new position.

Note

Because FileMaker Pro is a relational database program, you can also add fields from related tables to your layouts. To choose fields from any currently defined relationship, choose the name of the relationship from the pop-up menu/drop-down list located above the Available Fields list in the Specify Fields screen. If necessary, you can also define a new relationship at this time by choosing Define Database from the pop-up menu/drop-down list. (For information about relationships, see Chapter 18.)

The Organize Records by Category screen appears.

7. Select one or more grouping fields and move them to the Report categories list, as shown in Figure 6-9. Click Next to continue.

Tip   Be sure to examine the sample report layout thumbnail on the right side of the dialog. It shows how the selected field(s) will be grouped. As in the other parts of the New Layout/Report Assistant, you can change the order of the grouping fields by dragging them up or down.

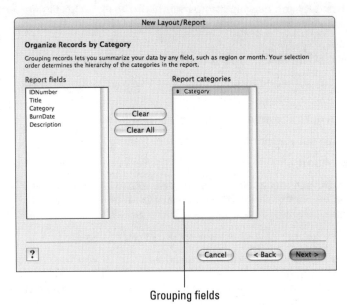

Grouping fields

Figure 6-9: Choose grouping fields. In this example, records are grouped by Category.

The Sort Records screen appears (refer to Figure 6-7).

8. By default, the database will be sorted by the grouping fields selected in Step 7. These grouping fields are often called *break fields* because there is a break for other information when their value changes. If you want to sort by additional fields, select and move them to the Sort Order list. Click Next to continue.

Note   The grouping fields have a small padlock icon preceding them in the Sort Order list, indicating that you can neither remove nor change their order in the list. The database is always sorted by them first, in the order specified in Step 7. Any additional sort fields must appear lower in the Sort Order list. To change the grouping fields or their order in the list, click the Back button to return to the Organize Records by Category screen.

The Specify Subtotals screen appears (see Figure 6-10) unless you elected not to generate subtotals in Step 5.

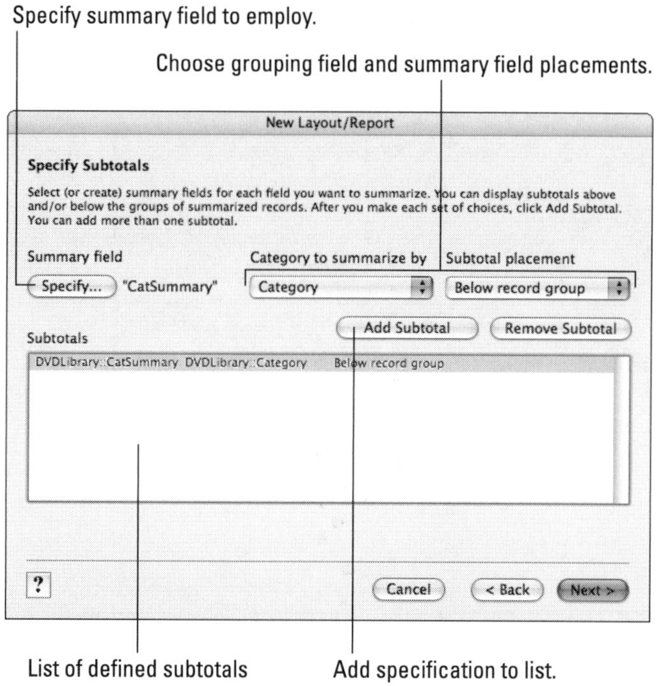

Specify summary field to employ.

Choose grouping field and summary field placements.

New Layout/Report

Specify Subtotals

Select (or create) summary fields for each field you want to summarize. You can display subtotals above and/or below the groups of summarized records. After you make each set of choices, click Add Subtotal. You can add more than one subtotal.

Summary field   Category to summarize by   Subtotal placement

(Specify...) "CatSummary"   [Category ▼]   [Below record group ▼]

Subtotals   (Add Subtotal) (Remove Subtotal)

DVDLibrary::CatSummary   DVDLibrary::Category   Below record group

[?]   (Cancel) (< Back) (Next >)

List of defined subtotals   Add specification to list.

Figure 6-10: To designate a subtotal, select a summary field, choose a category field by which to summarize, indicate where the subtotal will appear, and click the Add Subtotal button.

9. Choose one or more Summary fields to calculate the subtotals for each record group. For each Summary field, specify the grouping field to be subtotaled and the location of the subtotal (above the break field, below it, or both above *and* below it). Click Next to continue.

The Specify Grand Totals screen appears (see Figure 6-11) unless you elected not to generate grand totals in Step 5.

Tip In either Step 8 or Step 9, if you have not yet created the Summary field, you can do so by clicking the Specify button. In the Specify Fields dialog that appears, choose Define Database from the pop-up menu/drop-down list.

10. Choose one or more Summary fields to calculate a grand total across all records in the report, and choose a location for each grand total. Click Next to continue.

The Select a Theme screen appears.

11. Depending on whether you intend the current layout to be used for onscreen or printed reports, select a screen or print theme (based on the examples that appear in the right side of the screen). Click Next to continue.

The Header and Footer Information screen appears (refer to Figure 6-8).

Choose placement of summary information.

Specify summary field to display.

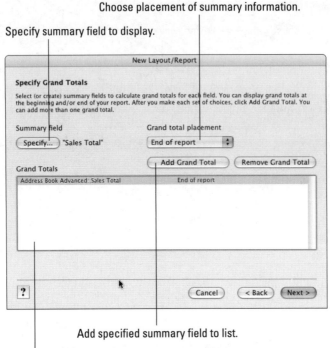

Add specified summary field to list.

List of defined summary fields and placements

Figure 6-11: To designate a grand total, select a summary field, indicate where you want the total to appear, and click the Add Grand Total button.

12. Select header and footer elements (such as page number or date) and the locations in which each element will appear. Click Next to continue.

    The Create a Script for this Report screen appears.

13. If you want to automate the report-generation process, click Create a Script and enter a name for the script (or accept the default name). Click Next to continue.

Note   If you create a script, it is automatically added to the Scripts menu. (For information on creating and editing scripts, see Chapter 15.)

14. You can either view the report layout in Preview mode or go to Layout mode to make any necessary changes. Select an option and click Finish.

Table View layouts

A Table View layout displays selected fields in a spreadsheet-style table. Each row is a record and each column is a field.

STEPS: Creating a Table View Layout

1. Switch to Layout mode by choosing View ⇨ Layout Mode (or by pressing ⌘+L/Ctrl+L).

2. Choose Layouts ⇨ New Layout/Report (or press ⌘+N/Ctrl+N).

The New Layout/Report Assistant appears (refer to Figure 6-3).

3. Type a name for the new layout, and choose Table View as the layout type.

4. Determine whether the layout should appear in the layout menu by leaving or removing the check mark in the Include in layouts menu check box. Click Next to continue.

The Specify Fields screen appears (refer to Figure 6-4).

5. Select the fields you want to include in the report and click Move to add them to the Layout Fields list. Click Next to continue.

> **Note**
>
> The order that fields appear in the Layout Fields list is the order in which they will appear in the report layout. To change a field's position in the list, simply click and drag it to a new position.

The Select a Theme screen appears.

6. Depending on whether you want the current layout to be used for onscreen or printed reports, select a screen or print theme (based on the examples that appear in the right side of the screen). Click Next to continue.

7. You can either go directly to Browse mode or switch to Layout mode to make any necessary changes. Select an option and click Finish.

If you examine a Table View layout in Layout mode, you'll note that it looks nothing like a table. In fact, the field arrangement is exactly what you'd see if you'd created a Standard form layout. The chosen fields are displayed one above the other. However, when a Table View layout is displayed in Browse mode, the View ⇨ View as Table command is automatically selected, thus causing the layout to take on its expected spreadsheet-style appearance.

You can rearrange the fields (columns) of a Table View layout in Browse mode by selecting any column heading and dragging it to a new position. You can also change the width of any column. Move the pointer over the column heading's right edge until it turns into a double-headed arrow. Then click and drag to the left or right to change the column's width.

Because you're working in a table, it's not uncommon to want to rearrange the data so that it's sorted by one of the fields or columns. To quickly accomplish this, Control+click/right-click the column heading by which you want to sort and choose a Sort command from the contextual menu that appears (see Figure 6-12). If you prefer to sort by merely clicking a column heading in Table View, you can set this Table View property by switching to Layout mode, choosing Layouts ⇨ Layout Setup, clicking the Views tab, marking the Table view check box, clicking the Properties button, and then selecting Sort data when selecting column.

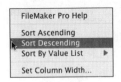

Figure 6-12: This menu appears when you Control+click/ right-click a column heading in a Table View.

Tip   Strictly speaking, it isn't necessary to create a separate layout for viewing records as a table. You can view any existing layout (a data entry layout, for example) as a table whenever you want by choosing View ➪ View as Table. The main advantages to creating separate table layouts is that you can specify the fields to use and set a permanent display order for them.

Label layouts

The Labels layout style is designed specifically for printing labels. As such, it has only a Body part. You can specify any of the supported Avery or DYMO label formats, or you can create your own label format.

STEPS: Creating a Label Layout

1. Switch to Layout mode by choosing View ➪ Layout Mode (or by pressing ⌘+L/Ctrl+L).

2. Choose Layouts ➪ New Layout/Report (or press ⌘+N/Ctrl+N).

   The New Layout/Report Assistant appears (refer to Figure 6-3).

3. Type a name for the new layout, and choose Labels as the layout type.

4. Determine whether the layout should appear in the layout menu by leaving or removing the check mark in the Include in layouts menu check box. Click Next to continue.

   The screen shown in Figure 6-13 appears.

5. If you will be printing on an Avery label (or its equivalent) or on a supported DYMO label, select the Use label measurement for radio button, and choose the Avery (or DYMO) part number from the pop-up menu/drop-down list. Click Next to continue.

   or

   Select the Use custom measurements radio button. The dimmed area at the bottom of the dialog becomes active. Enter the height and width for a single label, as well as the number of labels across the sheet. If required for your printer, select the Fixed page margins option to specify the offsets (in inches) from the edges of the label sheet to the printable area of the sheet. Click Next to continue.

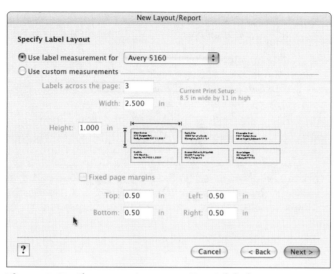

Figure 6-13: Choose an Avery or a DYMO label or create a custom label layout.

The Specify Label Contents screen appears, as shown in Figure 6-14.

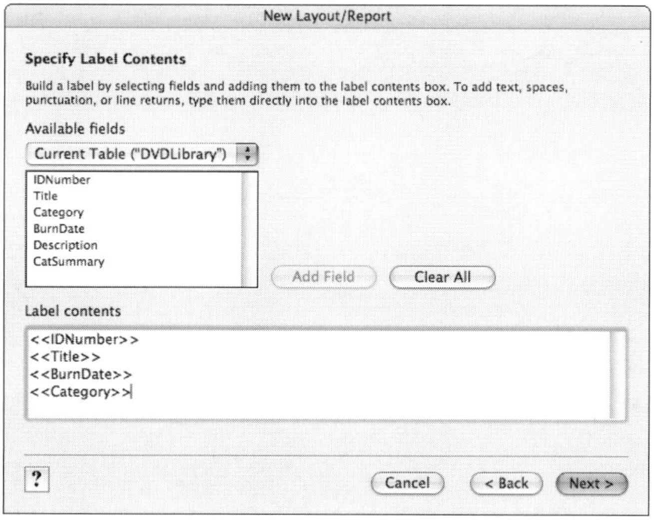

Figure 6-14: Select fields and design the label layout in the Specify Label Contents screen.

6. Add fields to the layout by double-clicking them or by selecting them and clicking the Add Field button. Add spaces between fields and punctuation marks as necessary. Be sure to press Return/Enter to end each label line (except the last one). Click Next to continue.

Previewing and printing layouts in columns

If you merely want to print data in a multicolumn format (similar to the column formatting in advanced word processing programs), you don't need to create a separate columnar layout. Using the Layouts ➪ Layout Setup command, you can instruct FileMaker Pro to print or preview any layout in two or more columns. The columns are visible only in Preview mode or when you print the database; Browse mode still shows the original layout.

To view the Layout Setup dialog shown in the following figure, choose Layouts ➪ Layout Setup.

To display columns, click the Printing tab, select the Print in check box, and then indicate how many columns you want by typing a number in the text box. Finally, specify how records will fill the columns by selecting the radio button that corresponds to the desired option:

✦ **Across first:** Fills each column across the page before proceeding to the next row. This option is good for printing labels, and it helps you conserve paper.

✦ **Down first:** Fills an entire column on a page and then moves to the top of the next column. This option is appropriate for phone directory listings and sheets of mailing labels (3-Up, for example).

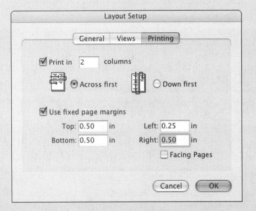

You can also specify page margins, as in a word processing application, by selecting the Use fixed page margins check box and indicating the desired margins. Additionally, you can mark the Facing pages check box to cause left and right (odd and even) pages to mirror their margins—Left and Right change to Inside and Outside when the Facing pages check box is selected.

Note   Because FileMaker Pro is a relational database program, you can also add fields from related tables to your layouts. To choose fields from any currently defined relationship, choose the name of the relationship from the pop-up menu/drop-down list located above the Available Fields list in the Specify Fields screen. If necessary, you can also define a new relationship at this time by choosing Define Database from the pop-up menu/drop-down list. (For information about relationships, see Chapter 18.)

7. You can either view the label layout in Preview mode or go to Layout mode (see Figure 6-15) to make any necessary changes. Select an option and click Finish.

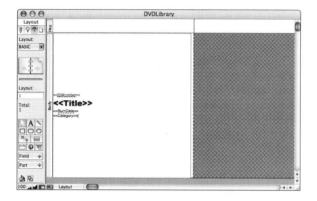

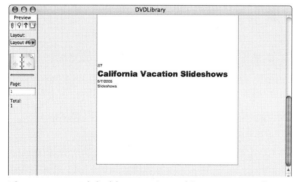

Figure 6-15: A label layout viewed in Layout mode (top) and Preview mode (bottom).

Note

FileMaker Pro 8 will wrap your fields to the next line in Layout mode to keep them within the label's borders; however, the previewed and printed labels will not wrap. In fact, if you click with the Text tool within the text element, the wrapping disappears.

Note

If your database contains no records, viewing this layout in Preview mode — as well as any other layout that doesn't have a theme — will present a blank page.

As you can see, when defining a Labels layout, the choice and placement of fields is all handled in the Specify Label Contents screen rather than on the layout itself. And the entire label is placed as a block of *merge fields*. (Merge fields are surrounded by angle brackets, as shown in Figure 6-15.) Unlike a normal field, a merge field doesn't have to be resized; it automatically expands as needed to handle the data it must contain. In fact, when you finally see the layout that has been generated, the only thing you might want to change is the formatting (selecting a different font or size, for instance).

To format a merge field, select the Text tool (the capital A) from the status area and use it to select both a field name and its surrounding brackets as we did to create the presentation seen in Figure 6-15. You can then apply formatting commands to the field, such as choosing a different font, style, color, or size. If you want to apply the same formatting to all merge fields, use the Pointer tool to select the entire block of fields and then choose formatting commands.

Caution   When you apply styles and fonts to merge fields, be careful to select the entire field, including the brackets (<< and >>). If you select just part of a merge field when making a style change, FileMaker Pro will ignore it.

An essential detail that isn't covered by the New Layout/Report Assistant is the handling of blank fields within labels. When printing address labels, for example, it's not uncommon for some records to include a company name while others don't have this information. Similarly, if you provide two address lines for each label, some records might have only a single address line. To keep such records from printing with blank lines, you must tell FileMaker Pro how to handle this situation by using the Sliding/Printing command.

STEPS: Using Sliding/Printing to Eliminate Blanks

1. Change to Layout mode and use the Pointer tool to select the block of merge fields.

2. Choose Format ➪ Sliding/Printing (Option+⌘+T/Ctrl+Alt+T).

   The Set Sliding/Printing dialog appears (see Figure 6-16).

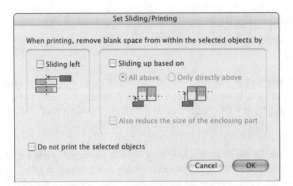

Figure 6-16: The Set Sliding/Printing dialog.

3. If at least one line of the label layout contains multiple fields and one or more of the fields could be missing in some records, mark the Sliding left check box.

and/or

If one or more entire label lines might be blank for some records, mark both the Sliding up based on check box and the All above radio button.

4. Click OK to dismiss the dialog.

Tip

Sliding/Printing doesn't always work the way you'd first expect. For example, the second line of a label layout might contain two merge fields, separated by a space:

```
<<Work Address>> <Mail Stop>>
```

Even though you might have set the Sliding left option, the space between the merge fields will force the second line to print in records that contain neither a work address nor a mail stop. You will either have to change the label layout (by putting the two fields on separate lines, for instance), or you can consider replacing the multifield line with a Calculation field:

```
If(IsEmpty(Work Address) and IsEmpty(Mail Stop) ,"", Work
    Address & ", " & Mail Stop)
```

Tips for creating custom label formats

If you buy labels from a company other than Avery and don't know which (if any) Avery label is compatible, you can choose the Use custom measurements option to create your own label format.

If you know a couple of fairly simple rules, you can design labels from scratch. First, the height of the header in your layout should equal the distance from the top of the label sheet to the top of the first row of labels. Second, when entering the dimensions, set the height to match the label's *vertical pitch* (the distance from the top of the first row of labels to the top of the second row). Set the width to match the label's *horizontal pitch* (the distance from the left edge of one label to the left edge of the next label).

After dismissing the New Layout/Report Assistant, switch to Layout mode. Click the Header part label to select it. Then, in the Size palette (choose View ➪ Object Size), click the bottom text box and enter the distance from the top of the label sheet to the top of the first row of labels.

Label descriptions (like Themes) are stored on your disk as an XML file. On the Mac, you can find the file containing the Avery and DYMO descriptions (LabelsUS.flb) in /Applications/FileMaker Pro 8/Extensions/Labels and, on a Windows system, in C:\Program Files\FileMaker\FileMaker Pro 8\Extensions\Labels. Following the schema demonstrated with the supplied labels, you can create your own FLB file(s), containing descriptions of customized labels or labels from other vendors you might use so that it is unnecessary to re-enter custom specifications each time you want to use one of the unrecognized label formats. As usual, work on a copy of the file rather than the original.

In English, this formula checks whether both Work Address and Mail Stop are blank. If so, they are replaced with nothing (" "). Otherwise, the two fields are combined and separated by a comma and a space, as in "Apple Computer, MS 27B." (Note that even this formula isn't perfect. If a record contains *only* a work address or *only* a mail stop, the result would be "Apple Computer" or "MS 27B.") Getting all the little details like this ironed out is *programming* and illustrates why software contains bugs. There are literally thousands upon thousands of little details and special cases that have to be handled, and sometimes human beings will miss one or two of them. Computers are fast, and they are (extremely) literal. That is, whatever you (as a programmer or user) leave out, computers will leave out as well. They do *exactly* what you tell them — no more and no less.

Vertical Label layouts

In reality, Vertical Label layouts are identical to Label layouts as described in the preceding section, but they implement rotated text display for Japanese characters (Format ➪ Orientation ➪ Sideways). Unless your system is configured for Japanese text entry, this discussion is moot. If you do have Japanese text entry support, see the Label layout discussion above and recognize that the characters will be rotated in a Vertical Label layout.

Envelope layouts

The process of creating an Envelope layout is very similar to that of creating a Label layout. Unlike Label layouts, FileMaker Pro creates a Header part and a Body part.

Note   The initial Envelope layout reflects what is known as a No. 10 business envelope. If your envelopes have different dimensions, you will need to resize the layout parts accordingly.

STEPS: Creating an Envelope Layout

1. Switch to Layout mode and choose Layouts ➪ New Layout/Report (or press ⌘+N/Ctrl+N).

   The New Layout/Report Assistant appears (refer to Figure 6-3).

2. Enter a name for the layout and select the Envelope layout type.

3. Determine whether the layout should appear in the layout menu by leaving or removing the check mark in the Include in layouts menu check box. Click Next to continue.

   The Specify Envelope Contents screen appears. (See Figure 6-17.)

4. Add fields to the Envelope layout by double-clicking them or by selecting them and clicking the Add Field button.

   Add space between fields and punctuation marks, as necessary. Press Return/ Enter to end each address line (except the last one). Click Next to continue.

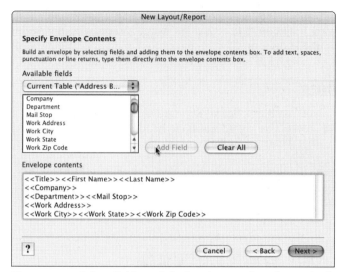

Figure 6-17: Select fields and design the Envelope layout in the Specify Envelope Contents screen.

5. You can either view the Envelope layout in Preview mode or go to Layout mode to make any necessary changes. Select an option and click Finish.

FileMaker uses merge fields to format the body of an Envelope layout, just as it does with a Label layout. Rather than place normal, resizable fields on the layout, the entire envelope address is a single text object with the field names embedded in it. If you attempt to click any of the address information, you'll see that four *handles* (black dots) surround the field. If you want to change the formatting of the address, you can use the Text tool to select individual field names and their surrounding brackets (<< >>) and then choose commands from the Format menu.

As with any other type of layout, you can add static graphic and text items (such as your logo or the return address). These operations are detailed in the later section, "Designing Your Own Layouts."

An essential detail that isn't covered by the New Layout/Report Assistant is the handling of blank fields within addresses. When printing envelopes, it's not uncommon for some records to include a company name while others don't have this information. Similarly, if you provide two address lines, some records might have only a single address line. To keep such records from printing with blank lines, you must tell FileMaker Pro how to handle this situation by using the Sliding/Printing command, as explained previously in "Label layouts."

Note

When printing an Envelope layout, be sure to see your printer manual for instructions on envelope feeding procedures. You might need to set Page Setup/Print Setup for landscape mode printing. Refer to Chapters 2 and 13 for additional information on printing within FileMaker Pro. As an additional note for Mac users, you might want to see which side is the *leading edge* when doing a landscape envelope print. Windows users might need to rotate the layout 180 degrees, depending on how their printer feeds envelopes.

Blank layouts

As its name suggests, the Blank layout style presents you with a blank form, devoid of fields and field labels. The layout contains header, body, and footer parts. Choose the Blank layout style when you want to create a layout entirely from scratch.

 Tip As an alternative, you might sometimes find it easier to edit an existing layout (a Standard form layout, for example) or to duplicate an existing layout and then edit the duplicate.

Designing Your Own Layouts

There's often more to creating layouts than just choosing a layout style and tossing in a few fields. For example, you might want to put fields in different positions in the layout; or you might want certain fields to print only at the top or bottom of a page or only after a group of sorted records. You also might want to apply formatting to different fields and add extra objects, such as field labels and graphics. Layout mode has tools and commands enabling you to do all these things and more.

Understanding layout parts

All FileMaker Pro layouts are divided into parts that control how and when data appears. When you change to Layout mode, each layout part is labeled. Figure 6-18 shows many of the available layout parts as they appear when you're in Layout mode and Preview mode. The various layout parts are described in the following sections.

Body

In general, every layout has a body. The layout body is displayed once for each record. If you have fields that you want to see in every record you view, you should place those fields in the layout body. The majority of the fields usually appear in the body.

 Tip If you don't want to see detailed data for each record, you can remove the body from the layout as long as you leave some other part, such as a sub-summary or summary part. One example where you might want to eliminate the body is when generating a report of sales by department and don't want to clutter it with the data for each salesperson — leave the summary part and the sub-summary part totaling a department's sales.

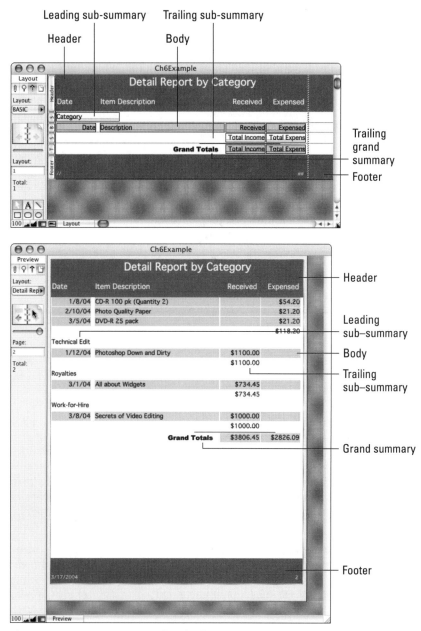

Leading sub-summary   Trailing sub-summary

Header   Body

Trailing grand summary

Footer

Header

Leading sub–summary

Body

Trailing sub–summary

Grand summary

Footer

Figure 6-18: Layout parts as they look in Layout mode (top) and in Preview mode or when printed (bottom).

Specifying layout views

Any FileMaker Pro 8 layout can be displayed in three views: Form, List, and Table. In addition, you can specify *which* of the views are enabled for a given layout. Switch to Layout mode, choose Layouts ➪ Layout Setup, and click the Views tab in the Layout Setup dialog. Add or remove check marks, as desired, to enable or disable the views. (See the accompanying figure.) When you later examine the layout in Browse or Find mode, you can switch between all enabled views by choosing View menu commands.

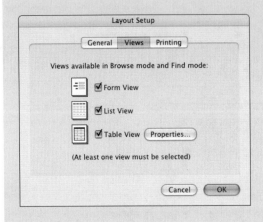

Header

FileMaker Pro displays the header at the top of every page. The header is visible in all modes. At printing time (or in Preview mode), the header is printed (or shown) at the top of each page. You can use headers for column headings, report titles, logos, and so on. Layout navigation buttons are often placed in the header area. You can also create a title header part that is visible only on the first page of a printed or previewed report. On subsequent pages, the normal header part appears.

Footer

FileMaker Pro displays the footer at the bottom of every page. The footer is visible in all modes. At printing time (or in Preview mode), the footer is printed (or shown) at the bottom of each page. You can also create a special title footer part that prints only on the first page of a report. On subsequent pages, the normal footer part appears.

Sub-summary and grand summary parts

Sub-summary and grand summary parts are used to print information that summarizes the *found set* of records (the current subset of records you're browsing). You use these parts to display information calculated by Summary fields that have been placed in these parts. A Summary field, in effect, computes a statistic (such as a total or average) across all records in the found set.

Note The found set can also be all records in the database. To include all records, choose Records ➪ Show All Records (⌘+J/Ctrl+J). The entire database becomes the current found set.

Sub-summary parts are used to display or print a summary of values for records sorted by a specific field. A sub-summary of total sales by salesperson, for example, would show the sales subtotal for each salesperson in the current found set. In this example, you must first sort the database by the Salesperson field. The field on which the database is sorted is also referred to as a *break field* because it breaks the database into groups. You must select a break field when you create the sub-summary part.

 Note You must sort the data before previewing or printing if you want the report to break accurately. This is usually performed via a script step attached to your report layout but can be performed manually if you haven't attached a script.

A *grand summary* part is used to display or print summary figures for the entire found set (rather than for each subgroup in the found set, as is done in a sub-summary part). For example, you could display the grand total of sales for all salespeople in a database.

You can place a sub-summary or grand summary part before or after the body. The former is called a *leading sub-summary* or *leading grand summary,* and the latter is called a *trailing sub-summary* or *trailing grand summary.* To learn more about using summary fields and summary parts, see Chapter 5.

Adding a layout part

You use the Layouts ➪ Part Setup command to add a part to a layout. The Part Setup dialog appears, as shown in Figure 6-19.

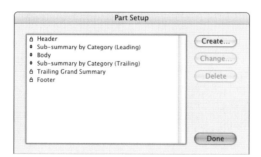

Figure 6-19: The Part Setup dialog.

This dialog shows all parts currently used in the layout. To add a new part, click the Create button. The Part Definition dialog appears, as shown in Figure 6-20.

Tip   You can go directly to the Part Definition dialog—without seeing the Part Setup dialog first—by clicking the Part icon in the status area and dragging it onto the layout. You can also open the Part Definition dialog by double-clicking any existing part label (the Body label, for example).

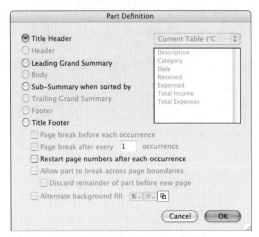

Figure 6-20: The Part Definition dialog.

To specify the type of part you're creating, select the appropriate radio button. (Buttons are dimmed for parts that already exist or that aren't appropriate for the type of layout you're modifying.) Below the radio buttons are check box options for page numbering and page break options. The specific options that can be set vary with the type of part you're creating.

STEPS: Adding a New Part to a Layout

1. In Layout mode, choose the appropriate layout from the layout pop-up menu/drop-down list.

2. Do one of the following:

   • Choose Layouts ➪ Part Setup. When the Part Setup dialog appears (as previously shown in Figure 6-19), click Create.

   • Drag the Part tool onto the layout.

   • Choose Insert ➪ Part, and the Part Definition dialog appears (as shown previously in Figure 6-20).

3. Select the radio button for the part you want to add.

   If the button is dimmed, the part already exists or isn't appropriate for the layout you're modifying.

4. *Optional:* Set page numbering and page-break options and/or set the graphic fill (color, pattern, or none).

5. If the part is a sub-summary, choose the sort field from the field list on the right side of the dialog.

The sort field can also be selected from any file that is related to the current database. To display these fields, choose the name of the relationship from the pop-up menu.

6. Click OK.

If you began this process by dragging a part onto the layout, you're immediately returned to Layout mode.

If you began this process by choosing the Part Setup command, you return to the Part Setup dialog. Click Done to return to Layout mode.

Modifying layout parts

You can change existing parts in several ways. For example, you can do any of the following:

✦ Change a part's size.

✦ Change the order in which parts appear on a page — within limits. (You can't place a header below the body or a footer above it, for instance.)

✦ Change the part types and options.

✦ Move the part labels out of your way.

✦ Delete a part.

These procedures are explained in the following sections.

Resizing layout parts

To change the height of a part, drag its label. Part labels appear on the left side of the layout area or horizontally in the part's bottom-left corner. The name of the part appears in its label, although it might be truncated if displayed vertically.

Part labels can be dragged only when they are displayed horizontally. If they're currently vertical, click the part label control (the right-most icon at the bottom of the document window). The part label control icon governs the orientation of all part labels. (You can still alter part sizes when the part labels are vertical, but you don't drag the label. Instead, move the cursor over the bottom of the part you want to resize, click, and hold down the mouse button. The cursor should change to a double-headed arrow/spreader bar, indicating that you can now resize the part.)

STEPS: Making a Layout Part Larger or Smaller

1. Switch to Layout mode and choose the appropriate layout from the layout pop-up menu/drop-down list.

2. Locate the label for the part you want to resize. (The label contains the part's name.)

3. Click and drag the part label in the appropriate direction: up to make the part shorter or down to make it taller.

4. Release the mouse button when the part is the size you want.

 Note

FileMaker Pro enables you to drag a part until you come to some other object — a field in another part, for example. To drag past an object (text, a graphic, or a field), hold down the Option/Alt key while you drag.

You can also set the height of a part by choosing the View ⇨ Object Size command. This command enables you to set the part's height precisely. Choosing the Object Size command brings up the Size palette, as shown in Figure 6-21.

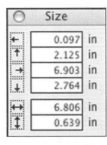

Figure 6-21: The Size palette.

The Size palette displays the part's distance from the left, top, right, and bottom margins, as well as the part's width and height. The Size palette is discussed in more detail in Chapter 4.

STEPS: Using the Size Palette to Set a Part's Height

1. In Layout mode, choose the appropriate layout from the layout pop-up menu/ drop-down list.

2. Choose the View ⇨ Object Size command.

The Size palette appears. (Refer to Figure 6-21.)

3. Click the label of the part that you want to resize.

The part label turns dark to show that it is selected.

4. Enter the desired height for the selected part in the bottom text box. Press Tab or Enter to put the new height into effect.

 Tip

You can also color any layout part, if you like. In Layout mode, click to select the part label (Body, for instance) and choose a color from the Fill Color palette. Similarly, you can apply a fill pattern by using the Fill Pattern palette. Use the two palettes in conjunction to create colored pattern fills.

Multipage layouts

If you like, you can extend the body over two or more pages. To do so, simply make the body very long, changing its height by dragging its part name (Body) downward on the layout. FileMaker Pro displays a dashed line to show a page break. Place the fields that you want to appear on the first page above the dashed line; place fields for the second page below the dashed line. Of course, pages can be broken left to right (the wide way) as well.

Reordering layout parts

Within certain logical limitations, you can change the order in which parts appear in a layout. Headers always go at the top and footers at the bottom, for example.

Tip   You can change part order in two ways: by using the Part Setup dialog (as described in the following steps) or by holding down the Shift key while you drag a part's label.

STEPS: Changing the Order of Parts

1. In Layout mode, switch to the appropriate layout.

2. Choose Layouts ➪ Part Setup.

   The Part Setup dialog appears. (Refer to Figure 6-19.)

3. Drag part names up or down in the part list to set their new order by grabbing and dragging the double-headed arrow to the left of the part name.

Note   A part name with a lock icon next to it (such as a trailing grand summary) cannot be moved.

4. Click Done.

Changing part types and options

You can change a part's type, and you can reset certain options for parts. (For example, you might want to choose a different break field for a sub-summary part.) You do both of these in the Part Definition dialog.

STEPS: Changing a Part's Type or Options

1. In Layout mode, switch to the layout that contains the part you want to modify.

2. Double-click the label for the part you want to change.

   or

   Choose Layouts ➪ Part Setup, select the part name, and click the Change button.

   In either case, the Part Definition dialog appears for the chosen part. (Refer to Figure 6-20.)

3. Select options to make the necessary changes. (Options that are dimmed are unavailable or are not allowed for this part type.)

4. Click OK.

If you began this process by double-clicking a part label on the layout, you immediately return to Layout mode.

If you began this process by choosing the Part Setup command, the Part Setup dialog is again frontmost. Click Done to return to Layout mode.

Deleting layout parts

The method that you use to delete a layout part depends on whether the part contains objects (fields, labels, or graphics). If the part is empty, you can drag it upward on the layout until it disappears. Or you can select the part's label and press the Delete/Backspace key. You can also delete a part from the Part Setup dialog in Layout mode by choosing Layouts ➪ Part Setup, selecting the name of the part, and clicking the Delete button.

> **Note**   Every layout must contain at least one part. If you attempt to delete that last part, an alert appears, informing you that you cannot delete it.

If a part contains objects, you'll see an alert when you try to delete it because any objects in the part will be deleted with the part. Any fields that are removed in this manner can be added back to the layout by using the Field tool or the Insert ➪ Field command. However, other objects, such as graphics or static text, will have to be re-created if you find that you still want or need them.

> **Caution**   To recover a part that you deleted with the Delete/Backspace key, choose Edit ➪ Undo Delete (or press ⌘+Z/Ctrl+Z) *immediately* after deleting it. You cannot, however, use the Undo command to recover Part deletions accomplished within the Part Setup dialog.

Adding items to a layout part

You now know enough about layout parts to create well-ordered, appropriately sized blank layout parts. However, the purpose of a layout part is to display information rather than blank space. You must add objects to the parts. Objects include fields, field labels, text, graphics, portals, and buttons. To add objects, you use the tools in the Tools sidebar on the left side of the document window. Additional options for placing, arranging, and formatting objects are available in the View, Insert, Format, and Arrange menus.

> **Tip**   You can also insert a field by choosing the Insert ➪ Field command. If you'd like to indicate the approximate spot on the layout where the new field should be added, click that spot prior to choosing the command. Other Insert commands that work similarly include Portal and Button, as well as all of the items in the Insert ➪ Graphic Object submenu (Text, Line, Rectangle, Rounded Rectangle, and Oval).

Adding and removing fields

Fields are generally the most important objects in any layout. You've seen how to add fields at layout creation time. The initial default layout automatically places every field you've defined for the database. When you design a new layout with the New Layout/Report Assistant, you specify which fields to place as well as the order in which they are placed. You can also add a field to any layout at any time, even if the field didn't exist when you created the layout.

You add fields to an existing layout by selecting the Field tool, by choosing Insert ⇨ Field, or by clicking the Insert Field button on the Tools toolbar (if you have the Tools toolbar visible). The Field tool is in the center of the Tools sidebar.

STEPS: Adding Fields to a Layout

1. In Layout mode, choose the layout to which you want to add fields.

2. Click the Field tool and drag the field object to the spot where you want to place the field.

   The Specify Field dialog appears, as shown in Figure 6-22.

Figure 6-22: The Specify Field dialog.

3. Click the name of the field you want to add.

   You can choose any field that has been defined for the database as well as any field in a related file. To view fields in related files, choose the name of the relationship from the pop-up menu/drop-down list at the top of the Specify Field dialog.

   Tip If you need to create a new field, you can choose Define Database from the pop-up menu/drop-down list at the top of the Specify Field dialog.

4. If you want a matching field label to be created, make sure that a check mark appears in the Create field label check box. (If you don't want a label, remove the check mark.)

5. Click OK.

The field appears in the layout part in which it was placed.

6. Move and resize the field as necessary.

To move a field within a layout, select the Pointer tool, click once within the field to select it, and then drag the field to a new location, or nudge it by pressing the arrow keys. To resize a field, select the Pointer tool, click once within the field to select it, and then drag any of the field's *handles* (the black dots in the four corners of a field).

To delete a field from a layout, click to select it and then press the Delete/Backspace key. Note that this action merely removes the field from the layout. Its field definition still exists, and the field can still be placed on this or any other layout for the current database.

Tip

If you find that you've simply added the wrong field to a layout, here's a better approach to correcting this problem than deleting the errant field and then adding the correct one: You can swap one field for another. In Layout mode, double-click the field. The Specify Field dialog appears and presents a list of all fields that have been defined for the database. Choose the replacement field from the field list. All formatting options that were set for the old field are automatically applied to the new field.

You can use a similar technique to duplicate the formatting of an existing field. Just quickly press Option/Ctrl as you drag the field. When you release the mouse button, the Specify Field dialog appears. Choose a field from the field list.

Adding merge fields

In most database programs, the process of performing a mail merge involves two steps: exporting the merge data from a database program and then merging it with a word processing document that includes field placeholders (to show where the merge data should be inserted). Although you can also do it this way with FileMaker Pro, you can perform a merge without leaving FileMaker by embedding one or more merge fields in any text block.

STEPS: Adding Merge Fields to a Layout

1. In Layout mode, switch to the layout to which you want to add the merge fields.

2. Create or select an existing text element in the layout, and then set the text insertion point by clicking or pressing the arrow keys.

Note

To create a block of merge text from scratch, it's sufficient to just click the desired spot by using the Text tool and then immediately choosing the Insert ➪ Merge Field command.

3. Choose Insert ➪ Merge Field (or press Option+⌘+M/Ctrl+M).

A variant of the Specify Field dialog (it lacks the Create field label check box) appears. (Refer to Figure 6-22.)

4. Choose a field to insert by selecting it and clicking OK.

The merge field is added at the current text insertion point. A merge field is always surrounded by bracket symbols, as in <<Last Name>>. Figure 6-23 shows a form letter containing four merge fields. Merge fields can also be selected from any related table as well as from the current table. To view the fields in a related table, choose the name of the relationship from the pop-up menu/drop-down list at the top of the Specify Field dialog.

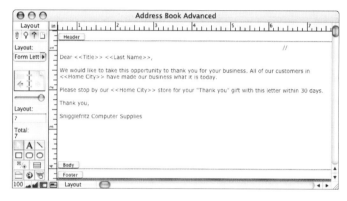

Figure 6-23: A layout with four merge fields in Layout mode (top) and Browse mode (bottom).

Note

Like any other text, you can format merge fields by changing the font, style, size, color, and so on. When formatting a merge field, you must also apply the formatting to the surrounding brackets.

Adding graphics

FileMaker Pro provides several ways for you to add graphic elements to layouts. You can create simple graphics — including ellipses, rectangles, and lines — directly in the program by using the Line, Rectangle, Rounded Rectangle, and Oval tools in the status area. (See Figure 6-24.)

Tab Control tool

Checkbox/Radio button tool

Rectangle tool

Pointer/Selection tool

Text tool

Rounded Rectangle tool

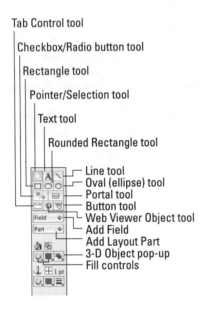

Line tool
Oval (ellipse) tool
Portal tool
Button tool
Web Viewer Object tool
Add Field
Add Layout Part
3-D Object pop-up
Fill controls

Figure 6-24: The Tools palette in Layout mode.

Note   The Oval tool creates ellipses and circles. However, it cannot (regardless of its name) create a generic oval.

STEPS: Adding a Simple Graphic Element to a Layout

1. In Layout mode, choose the layout to which you want to add the element.

2. Use the Fill, Border, Effects, and Line Width palettes to select the appropriate formatting for the new element. As an alternative, you can set the object's properties after you create it, if you want.

Tip   If you preselect options in any of these palettes when no element is currently selected in the layout, they become the new default settings and are automatically applied to the next layout element you create.

3. Click the tool that represents the type of graphic element you want to add (Line, Rectangle, Rounded Rectangle, or ellipse).

4. Position the tool over the spot where you want to add the graphic, and then click and drag until you create an element of the desired size.

You can constrain object shapes such as rectangles and ellipses by holding down the Option/Ctrl key while you drag with any of the tools. When Option/Ctrl is pressed, the Rectangle and Rounded Rectangle tools create squares and rounded-corner squares; the Oval (really an ellipse) tool creates circles; and the Line tool is restricted to straight horizontal, vertical, or 45-degree lines.

If you don't feel like using the graphic tools, FileMaker Pro 8 provides a quicker way to create basic objects. Simply choose the type of object you want to create from the Insert ➪ Graphic Object submenu. Then, with the new object still selected, apply any necessary formatting to it or drag a handle to change its size and/or shape.

To change the formatting for an existing object, click the object to select it and then choose options in the Fill, Border, Effects, and Line Width palettes. You can also drag an object to change its position and drag its handles to change its size.

Complex graphics, such as logos or elaborate illustrations, are better created in a dedicated graphics program. To bring graphics in from other programs, you can use the Insert ➪ Picture command.

STEPS: Inserting a Graphic from a File

1. In Layout mode, switch to the layout to which you want to add the graphic.

2. Choose Insert ➪ Picture.

A modified file dialog appears, as shown in Figure 6-25. The specific dialog displayed depends on your computing platform, operating system, and any operating system theme you might have applied.

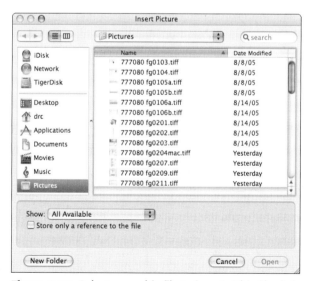

Figure 6-25: Select a graphic file to insert. (This file dialog is from Mac OS X, v. 10.4.)

3. *Optional:* To limit the file list only to graphic images saved in a particular format, choose a format from the Show pop-up menu /Files of type drop-down list.

4. Find the graphic's name in the list and click to select it.

5. *Optional:* To store a reference to the graphic file in the database (rather than the actual graphic), mark the Store only a reference to the file check box.

6. Click Open.

The graphic appears in the current layout.

7. Drag the graphic to the appropriate position in the layout. Drag the graphic's handles to change its size, if necessary.

Graphics can also be added to a layout via copy-and-paste. Simply open the graphic file in its original program, select it, issue the Edit ⇨ Copy command, and then — in FileMaker Pro — issue the Edit ⇨ Paste command.

To remove any graphic on a layout, select it with the Pointer tool and press the Delete/Backspace key.

Tip

FileMaker Pro 8 supports drag-and-drop. When using drag-and-drop, you can move a graphic or text object from one program to another by simply selecting it in the original program's document and then dragging it to the other program's document. If you have a graphics program that supports drag-and-drop, such as AppleWorks (formerly known as ClarisWorks and ClarisWorks Office), for example, you can drag a graphic directly onto a FileMaker Pro layout. You cannot, however, drag the icon of a graphic from the Mac Finder (except for clipping files) or Windows desktop into a layout.

Adding OLE objects to a layout (Windows only)

FileMaker Pro enables you to add OLE (Object Linking and Embedding) objects directly to a layout. You can create these OLE objects with any application that can behave as an OLE Server. The kinds of objects you can add depend on the applications you have installed on your Windows PC.

STEPS: Adding an OLE Object to a Layout

1. Switch to Layout mode by choosing View ⇨ Layout Mode or pressing Ctrl+L.

2. Choose the layout into which you want to insert an OLE object.

3. Choose Insert ⇨ Object.

The Insert Object dialog appears. (See Figure 6-26.)

4. Select the Create New radio button to create a new OLE object.

or

To create an OLE object from an existing file, go to Step 7.

5. Select the *object type* (the application for creating the OLE object) from the Object Type list and click OK.

FileMaker Pro opens the selected application.

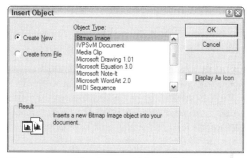

Figure 6-26: The Insert Object dialog.

6. Create the OLE object in the application and then close the application.

   The new OLE object appears in the layout as text (for textual objects), graphics (for graphic documents), or an icon (for nondisplayable objects, such as sounds).

   Note

   An OLE object created in this way is *embedded* in the database—you can access the object only through FileMaker Pro—and the object is included with the database if you give the database to someone else. (See Chapter 8 for more information on embedding, linking, and editing OLE objects.)

7. Select the Create from File radio button to create the OLE object from an existing file. The dialog changes to display new options. (See Figure 6-27.)

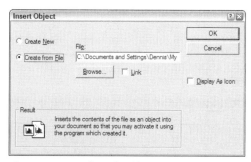

Figure 6-27: Select the filename of the OLE object that you want to embed.

8. Type the full pathname of the file in the File text box, or click the Browse button and select the filename from the dialog that appears.

9. If you want to link the file as an OLE object rather than embedding it, mark the Link check box.

   The new OLE object is displayed in the layout as text (for textual objects), graphics (for graphic documents), or an icon (for nondisplayable objects like sounds).

Mac users can view, cut, copy, and paste OLE objects found on layouts, but they cannot create nor edit them.

After you add an OLE object to a layout (as opposed to adding it to a Container field in a record, as discussed in Chapter 8), you can modify the OLE object — either edit or play it — only when you're in Layout mode. In Browse mode, you can see the object, but you can't access it. Also, you can modify links for OLE objects (choose Edit ⇨ Object ⇨ Links) only in Layout mode. For additional information on working with OLE objects, see "About working with OLE objects" in FileMaker Help.

An OLE object created as a link can be accessed from the original application just like any other file. If you change the file from outside FileMaker Pro, you have the option to configure the link so that the OLE object in the layout is automatically updated to show the latest version. However, this flexibility comes with a price: If you give your database to someone else (or even move it to another computer or a different disk), you must move the linked file as well and reestablish the link.

Adding buttons to a layout

Ever since scripting was introduced in FileMaker Pro, you could make the program perform special tasks for you in response to a button click. In addition to buttons you draw in FileMaker, any object — text or graphic — can be made to function as a button.

STEPS: Creating a New Button with the Button Tool

1. In Layout mode, choose the layout to which you want to add the button.

2. Click the Button tool in the status area to select it. (The Button tool looks like a finger pushing a button.)

3. On the layout, click and drag to set the height and width of the button, and then release the mouse button.

   The new button becomes visible, and the Button Setup dialog appears, as shown in Figure 6-28.

4. Select the script step to be assigned to the button, set any necessary options, and choose a button shape (rectangular or rounded). Mark the Change to hand cursor over button check box in the Button Style section at the bottom of dialog if you'd like to make the cursor behave as it does in a browser (changing to a pointing finger when it passes over the button).

If you want to associate an existing script with the button (rather than just a single script step), choose the Perform Script step in the list of script steps. For more information about scripting, see Chapter 15.

5. Click OK.

   The Specify Button dialog is removed, and a text insertion point appears in the center of the blank button.

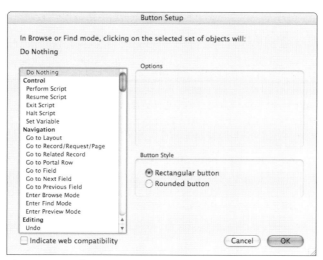

Figure 6-28: The Button Setup dialog.

6. Type a name for the button.

7. Press Enter/Return or click anywhere outside the button to end the button definition process.

8. If you'd like to resize the button, click to select it and drag one of its handles (or select it and use the Size palette to specify precise coordinates and dimensions).

Note

When marked, the Indicate web compatibility check box beneath the Script Step list in Figure 6-28 dims any script steps that are not applicable/available for databases that you host on the Web. One example of an inapplicable action is Enter Preview Mode. If you intend to host your database on the Web (or an intranet), you should mark this check box before specifying your button actions. As you will see in Chapters 15 and 20, ScriptMaker includes the same check box to help you avoid pitfalls when creating scripts for a Web-hosted database.

To remove a button from a layout, select it with the Pointer tool and press the Delete/Backspace key. If you simply want to move the button to a different layout in the same database, select it, choose the Edit ➪ Cut command (or press ⌘+X/ Ctrl+X), switch to the target layout, and then choose Edit ➪ Paste (or press ⌘+V/Ctrl+V).

Tip

To make another kind of object (such as a text string or graphic image) function as a button, switch to Layout mode, select the object, and then choose Format ➪ Button Setup.

Adding check boxes and radio button fields to a layout

When you add a field to the layout, you'll often find it necessary to display the Field/Control Setup dialog and specify how the field is to be displayed (Edit Box,

Drop-down List, Pop-up Menu, Checkbox Set, Radio Button Set, Drop-down Calendar).

New Feature

If you select the new Checkbox/Radio button tool and drag an outline on the layout, FileMaker Pro 8 will automatically present the Field/Control Setup dialog, allowing you to specify the field's style. You can also use this method to specify that a date field object be displayed as a Drop-down Calendar.

Adding tabs to a layout

A long time ago — at least in terms of computer years — both Apple and Microsoft introduced tabbed dialogs in an attempt to control ever-expanding sets of options, particularly in Preferences and Settings dialogs. In the past few years, tabbed windows have become increasingly popular in Web browsers, reducing window proliferation and clutter.

New Feature

Now, FileMaker Pro 8 introduces layout tabs, allowing you to reduce the number and size of your databases' layouts. For example, if you keep a consolidated database of your video collection, you might have both videotapes and DVDs, each with fields specific to a video on that medium. You can create tabs for videotape- and DVD-specific fields, only one set of which is visible at a time because they both occupy the same region on your layout. Figure 6-29 displays the Home and Work tabs for the Address Book Advanced example described in detail in Chapter 4.

STEPS: Creating a Tab Control

1. In Layout mode, choose the layout to which you want to add the tab control.

2. Click the Tab Control tool in the status area to select it. (The Tab Control tool looks like a tabbed file folder. It's located directly beneath the Button tool.)

3. On the layout, drag to indicate the height and width of the tab area, and then release the mouse button.

   The tab becomes visible, and the Tab Control Setup dialog appears, as shown in Figure 6-30.

More about buttons

When choosing an action for a button (Step 4 in the button creation procedure), you can select Do nothing for any button for which a final script doesn't yet exist. To later assign a permanent action to the button, simply select the button and choose Format ⇨ Button Setup.

Also, because a button is like any other object in a FileMaker layout, you can change its formatting. Features that you might want to alter include the button label (changing its font, size, style, or color); the button's fill color, pattern, or border; and the size of the button.

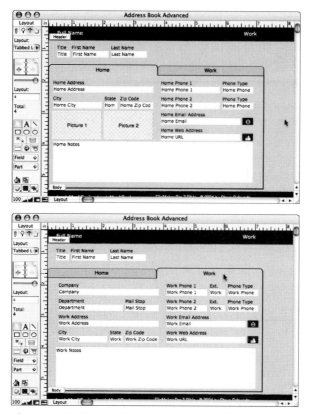

Figure 6-29: The Address Book Advanced Home (top) and Work (bottom) tabs.

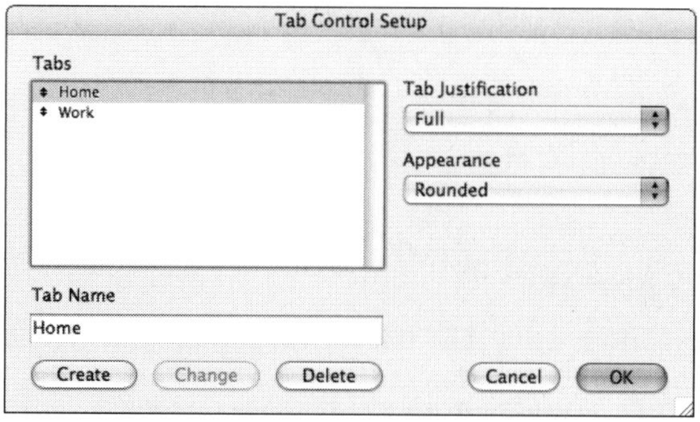

Figure 6-30: The Tab Control Setup dialog.

4. Choose how the tabs should be justified — left, right, center, or fully — from the Tab Justification pop-up menu/drop-down list.

5. Choose whether the tabs should have rounded or squared edges from the Appearance pop-up menu/drop-down list.

6. Enter names for the tabs you wish created in the Tab Name text box, clicking Create (or pressing Return/Enter) after each name. The tab names will appear in the Tabs list. You can reorder the tabs by dragging the double-headed arrow, just as in other FileMaker Pro list boxes.

7. Click OK to dismiss the Tab Control Setup dialog.

8. Add fields and other objects (such as labels or images) by using the status area's tools panel or by choosing the desired item type from the Insert menu.

Caution   Any object that you want to be part of a tab's display must lie completely within the tab's boundary. If even one edge lies outside the tab, the object will not be "on" the tab.

9. Click other tabs and repeat Step 8 for items that are to appear on that tab pane.

Adding portals to a layout

Fields from related tables can be placed directly onto a layout (as described previously in "Adding and removing fields"). However, related fields placed in this manner can show only the value from a single matching record. If you want to display values from multiple matching records, you place the related fields in a portal.

Think of a *portal* as a window into a related table. All fields placed within a portal must be from a previously defined relationship. Any record that meets the requirements of that defined relationship will display its data in the portal.

For example, Figure 6-31 shows a portal listing the items checked out from a fictitious lending library, using the Lending Library template that comes with FileMaker Pro 8.

Current Checked Out: 2				Duration		Extensions		
Asset	Check Out Date/Time		Due Date/Time		Reminder Date		Check In Date/Time	
iLife Bible	3/17/2004	1:13:52 PM	3/20/2004			0		X
Kodak EasyShare	3/17/2004	1:12:39 PM	3/20/2004	12:00 pm	3/19/2004	0		X

Figure 6-31: A portal displaying fields from a related table.

STEPS: Creating a Portal

1. If you haven't already done so, define the relationship that will be used for the portal's data by choosing File ⇨ Define ⇨ Database and then click the Relations tab. (See Chapter 18 for information about defining relationships.)

2. In Layout mode, choose the layout to which you want to add the portal.

3. Click the Portal tool in the status area to select it. (The Portal tool looks like a light rectangle stacked atop two darker rectangles. It's located just to the right of the Tab Control tool.)

4. On the layout, drag to indicate the height and width of the portal, and then release the mouse button.

The portal becomes visible, and the Portal Setup dialog appears, as shown in Figure 6-32.

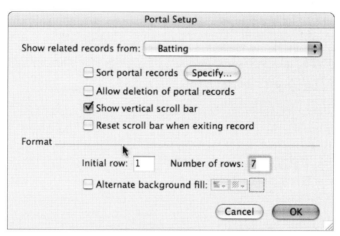

Figure 6-32: The Portal Setup dialog.

5. Choose a relationship from the pop-up menu/drop-down list at the top of the dialog.

6. Enter the number of rows that the portal will display in the Number of rows text box, and the item (row) you wish displayed at the top of the portal in the Initial row text box.

7. Change any of the other options you want, as follows:

- Select the Sort portal records check box and click the Specify button to define your sorting criteria if you wish the portal record display sorted.

- Select the Allow deletion of portal records check box if you want to be able to delete records in the related table by selecting them in the portal.

- If you think the number of records will sometimes exceed the number of portal rows set in Step 6, select the Show vertical scroll bar check box. Doing this enables you to scroll through all related records in the portal.

- If you opted to show the vertical scroll bar (previous option), you may also specify that the scroll bar be reset when exiting the record. Resetting the scroll bar means that the first related record will appear at the top and not resetting the scroll bar means that the portal will remain scrolled when the next record's related entries are retrieved. Since you don't know how many related items will appear for the next record, you should probably opt to reset the scroll bar as a matter of course.

- To make it easier to distinguish each portal record from the next, select the Alternate background fill check box and then choose a fill color and/or pattern. (The button with two overlapping squares indicates no fill or pattern.) When you switch to Browse mode, you'll see that the portal row colors alternate between white and the selected color/pattern combination (much like green-bar printer paper or some types of ledger paper).

8. Click OK to dismiss the Portal Setup dialog.

9. Click the Field tool in the status area and drag a field into the portal.

   When you release the mouse button, the Specify Field dialog appears. (Refer to Figure 6-22.)

10. Choose a related field and then click OK. (Names of related fields are preceded by a pair of colons, as in ::Last Name.)

    The field and its label appear in the portal.

11. Drag the field into the top row of the portal. Move the field's label so that it's above the field's position (outside the portal) or, if you prefer, you can delete the field label.

12. Repeat Steps 9–11 for additional related fields that you want displayed in the portal.

Note   Fields inside the portal, as well as the portal itself, can be resized as needed. If you later need to modify the portal settings, you can select the portal and choose the Format ➪ Portal Setup command or simply double-click the portal. In either case, the Portal Setup dialog appears.

For more information about portals and relationships, see Chapter 18.

Formatting Fields and Other Objects

Newly placed fields are seldom exactly as you want them. A field might be too small or too large, or it might be in the wrong position. The field's formatting—text attributes, borders, color, and so on—might not display the field in the manner you had intended. Other objects, such as buttons and graphics, might also be in the wrong place, be the wrong size, or need additional formatting. Fortunately, you can easily correct these problems. FileMaker Pro includes a variety of tools that make the placement and formatting of fields and other objects as simple as possible.

Note   Although this section concentrates on the size, placement, and formatting of fields, the majority of the commands and procedures apply to any object on a layout, such as buttons, field labels, graphics, and static text.

Using the measurement and alignment tools

The View menu in Layout mode (as shown in Figure 6-33) includes many commands that make it easy to place or arrange fields, labels, graphics, and other objects accurately on the layout — even when you're doing it manually by dragging them.

Figure 6-33: Layout mode's View menu.

The alignment, placement, and measurement tools listed in the View menu provide the following functions:

✦ *Page Margins:* Choose the Page Margins command to see where layout objects will appear in printouts in relation to the page margins.

✦ *Graphic Rulers:* Graphic rulers can be shown at the top and left edges of the layout area. Choose the Graphic Rulers command to toggle these rulers on and off. When you select and drag any object, its dimensions and location are indicated on the rulers.

✦ *Text Ruler:* FileMaker Pro has a text ruler and an associated ruler bar that can be displayed at the top of the document window. Although the main purpose of the text ruler is for formatting fields and text objects (such as field labels), it is also useful for showing and checking an object's horizontal location on the layout. Choose the Text Ruler command to toggle this ruler on and off.

✦ *Ruler Lines:* You can display dotted lines that correspond to major divisions on the rulers. You can use these lines to check layout spacing and positioning of objects. Choose the Ruler Lines command to toggle the lines on and off.

✦ *T-Squares:* These are solid vertical and horizontal lines. You use T-square lines to precisely position an object relative to the rulers. (You can move the lines by dragging them.) Choose View ➪ T-Squares or press ⌘+T/Ctrl+T to toggle the T-square lines on and off.

✦ *Object Size:* As described earlier in this chapter and in Chapter 4, you can type entries in any of the Size palette's six text boxes to change the location and dimensions of the currently selected object in a layout. To display the Size palette (illustrated previously in Figure 6-21), choose View ➪ Object Size.

FileMaker Pro maintains an invisible grid corresponding to current ruler settings. If the grid is on, objects being moved or resized move in grid increments, snapping to the nearest grid intersection. Choose Arrange ➪ Object Grids (⌘+Y/Ctrl+Y) to toggle the grid on and off.

To change the spacing and units for the grid and rulers, choose Layouts ➪ Set Rulers and select new settings in the Set Rulers dialog, as shown in Figure 6-34.

Figure 6-34: The Set Rulers dialog.

Tip

If the graphic rulers are enabled, you can quickly change ruler and grid measurement units by clicking the Units box in the upper-left corner of the document window. Each time you click it, the box switches to a different measurement unit, such as inches or centimeters. (You can also Control+click/right-click a ruler and choose a measurement unit from the contextual menu that appears.)

The View ➪ Show submenu contains additional options to make objects visible or stand out while in Layout mode. You can choose any of the following helpful options:

✦ *Buttons:* Surrounds all buttons in the layout with a patterned border.

✦ *Sample Data:* Displays sample data of the correct type in each field, rather than the field name. Note that there must be at least one record in the database containing data in that field.

✦ *Text Boundaries:* Surrounds all static text in the layout (such as field labels and title text) with a gray border.

✦ *Field Boundaries:* Surrounds each field in the layout with a black border.

✦ *Sliding Objects:* Shifts the remaining objects (if any of the objects originally defined in the layout are missing). Sliding objects — commonly found in label and envelope layouts, as well as merge forms — are indicated by tiny left-pointing and upward-pointing arrows to indicate the direction that they will be shifted. In an address label, for example, you normally want fields to move up to remove blank lines if an entire record line (such as a company name or department) is missing.

✦ *Non-Printing Objects:* Surrounds all objects that have been designated as non-printing with a gray border. These objects are visible only onscreen and will not appear in printouts or in Preview mode.

In order to be Microsoft Office-compliant, FileMaker Pro 8 also includes a series of toolbars providing quick access to common commands and procedures. In Layout mode, you can display up to four toolbars: Standard (not relevant to formatting), Text Formatting (for choosing font, size, style, color, and alignment options), Arrange (for issuing Arrange menu commands), and Tools (duplicates many commands in the Tools sidebar). To enable or disable any of the four toolbars, choose its name from the View ➪ Toolbars submenu. (The names of enabled toolbars are preceded by a check mark.)

Moving and resizing fields and objects

It is simple to change a field's or object's position on a layout. Click the field or object to select it, and then drag it to a new location. (The tools described in "Using the measurement and alignment tools" can be very helpful in this task.)

Altering a field's size is often necessary, too. If a Text field is too small, part of the text might be hidden until you click or tab into the field. A Number field that is too small to show its contents displays only a question mark. On the other hand, the default width for some fields, such as a State field that is designed to hold a two-letter abbreviation, might be much too wide.

STEPS: Changing a Field's Size or Position

1. In Layout mode, choose the layout containing the field you want to modify.

2. Click the Pointer tool in the status area.

3. To move the field, click-and-drag the field to the desired location.

   To restrict the movement of the field to straight horizontal or vertical, hold down Shift while you drag.

4. To change the field's size, click to select the field, and then click-and-drag a *handle* (any of the four black dots) until the field is the desired size.

   You can press Shift as you resize any field to restrict changes to only the field's vertical or horizontal dimension.

Setting field formatting

When you define fields for a database in the Define Fields dialog, you must specify a type for each field, such as Text, Date, Time, or Number. Although the field type determines the kind of data the field will store, it doesn't determine how that field's data will be displayed in a layout. To set a display format for a field, switch to Layout mode, select the field, and do any of the following:

✦ Choose formatting options from the Format menu.

   ✦ Choose settings from the Fill, Pen, Effects, or Line palettes in the Tools palette.

   ✦ Choose options from the Text Formatting toolbar.

Any formatting options that you set for a field while in Layout mode will be applied to the field and its data when viewed in Browse mode, as described in the following sections.

Using the Format menu

To set formatting options for a field, switch to Layout mode, select a field, and then choose commands from the Format menu. (See Figure 6-35.) Regardless of the type of the selected field, these commands at the top of the Format menu can be chosen: Font, Size, Style, Align Text, Line Spacing, and Text Color. (These same commands can also be issued from the Text Formatting toolbar. If you Control+click/right-click a field, a variety of formatting commands appear, as shown in Figure 6-36.)

Figure 6-35: The Format menu (in Layout mode on a Mac).

Figure 6-36: Control+clicking/right-clicking a field displays this pop-up menu.

The commands available in the second and third sections of the Format menu depend on what type of object is currently selected: a graphic object, a field of a particular type, a field label, and so on. For example, if a Date field is selected, the Text, Date, and Button Setup formatting commands are available in the Format menu. Text can be chosen because the field contains alphanumeric characters, as do most field types (everything but Container); Date can be chosen because the field is a Date field; and Button Setup can be chosen because virtually any object on a layout can be made into a button.

The Format ⇨ Text command

As shown in Figure 6-37, choosing the Format ⇨ Text command is an easy way to assign multiple text formatting commands to a field, field label, or piece of static text. Rather than having to select multiple commands from the Format menu or the Text Formatting toolbar, you're able to set all text formatting options in the Text Format dialog. (The Paragraph button is grayed out unless you're currently formatting a Text field.)

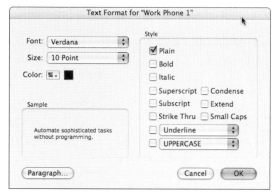

Figure 6-37: The Text Format dialog.

The Date and Time commands

When formatting a Date, Time, or Timestamp field, choose Format ⇨ Date or Format ⇨ Time. The Date Format or Time Format dialog appears, as appropriate. (See Figure 6-38.) Rather than enabling you to set text attributes for the fields — as the Text Format dialog does — these dialogs let you assign a particular date or time display format for the field. You can either display the dates and times as they were typed into the field (by selecting the Leave data formatted as entered radio button), or format them by setting options for the field (such as leading characters and separators). The Sample box at the bottom of the dialog shows your choices' effects. (Note that if you also want to set general text-formatting options for a Date or Time field, you can click the Text Format button at the bottom of the Date Format or Time Format dialog.)

Date format

Time format

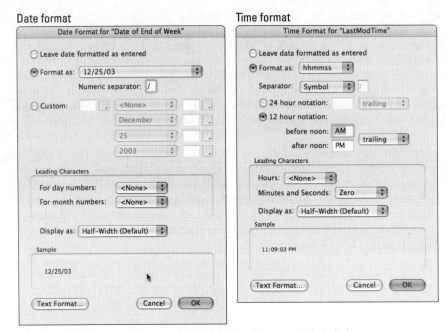

Figure 6-38: The Date Format (left) and Time Format (right) dialogs.

The Graphic command

When you select a graphic or a Container field on a layout, you can choose the Format ➪ Graphic command. The Graphic Format dialog appears, as shown in Figure 6-39. By choosing options in the dialog, you can change the size of the graphic (scaling horizontally, vertically, both, or neither) or its alignment.

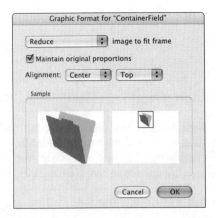

Figure 6-39: The Graphic Format dialog.

The most important options are contained in the pop-up menu/drop-down list at the top of the Graphic Format dialog. These options determine how the image will be sized to fit the frame in the layout. The options are

✦ *Crop:* If the image is larger than the frame, it will be *cropped* (edges removed) to fit. If the image is smaller than the frame, no modifications will be made. (Note that the Crop option interacts with the Alignment setting for the graphic or Container field. When the item is centered, cropping is done symmetrically. However, when top-left aligned, for example, cropping is performed from the bottom and/or right.)

✦ *Reduce:* If the image is too large to fit the frame, FileMaker Pro will reduce the size of the image to fit within the frame. If the image is already smaller than the frame, FileMaker Pro will not modify the image.

✦ *Enlarge:* If the image is smaller than the frame, FileMaker Pro will enlarge the image to fit the frame. However, if the image is already larger than the frame, FileMaker Pro will not modify the image.

✦ *Reduce or Enlarge:* This is a combination of the previous two options. If the image is smaller than the frame, it will be enlarged. Alternatively, if the image is larger than the frame, it will be shrunk to fit.

Note

The Maintain original proportions check box tells FileMaker whether to reduce or enlarge symmetrically. If left unchecked, FileMaker stretches or compresses each dimension independently rather than scaling the object/picture as an entity.

Be sure to also choose Alignment options from the remaining two pop-up menus. Check the images in the Sample box to see the effects your choices will have.

The Portal Setup command

If you select a *portal* (a rectangular area that holds a group of related fields) and choose Format ⇨ Portal Setup, the Portal Setup dialog appears (as previously shown in Figure 6-32). In the Format portion of the dialog, you can specify the number of rows displayed, which item/row is initially displayed, whether a vertical scroll bar appears on the right side of the portal (so that you can scroll through all related records in the portal), and whether every other row of the portal should be colored and/or patterned (to distinguish records from one another). Formatting portals is discussed in "Adding portals to a layout," earlier in this chapter.

The Tab Control Setup command

You can select the Format ⇨ Tab Control Setup command if the current object is a tab control. The Tab Control Setup dialog allows you to add, rename, or delete tabs, as well as specify how tabs will be justified and whether the tabs will be displayed as rounded or rectangular.

The Button Setup command

You can select the Format ⇨ Button Setup command if the current object could conceivably be defined as a button. Because every element on a layout can be made into a button — including normal fields — the Button Setup command is always available.

When you choose Format ⇨ Button Setup, the Button Setup dialog appears (refer to Figure 6-28). To define the object as a button, simply choose the script or script step that will execute whenever the button is clicked. Options (when available) are set in the right side of the dialog.

Tip   If you hold down the Option/Alt key while you double-click fields and other objects on a layout, an appropriate Format dialog is automatically presented.

Adding borders

Although fields are frequently displayed in Layout mode with boxes around them, these boxes appear only for your convenience in moving and resizing the fields. If you want borders to appear around a field when you browse or print (that is, when you are actually *using* the database), you must create the borders by issuing the Field Borders command.

STEPS: Adding Borders to a Field

1. In Layout mode, switch to the layout that contains the field to which you want to add borders.

2. Click to select the appropriate field.

   If there are additional fields to which you'd like to apply the same border options, you can Shift+click or drag a selection rectangle around them.

3. Choose Format ⇨ Field/Control ⇨ Borders (Option+⌘+B/Ctrl+Alt+B).

   The Field Borders dialog appears, as shown in Figure 6-40.

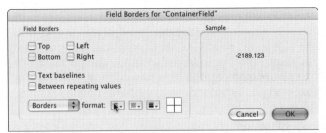

Figure 6-40: The Field Borders dialog.

4. Mark the appropriate check boxes for the borders you want to add.

5. Choose Borders from the pop-up menu/drop-down list.

6. Choose the desired color, pattern, and line width for the borders from the pop-up palettes.

The effects of your choices appear in the Sample box on the right side of the dialog.

7. Click OK.

Adding baselines

You might want the contents of a field to appear as though you were writing on lined paper. FileMaker Pro refers to this line as a *baseline*. As with borders, you add baselines by using the Field Borders dialog (previously shown in Figure 6-40).

Click the Text Baselines check box and choose Baselines from the Field Borders dialog's pop-up menu/drop-down list. Then choose the desired color, pattern, and line width for the baselines from the pop-up palettes. The effects of your choices appear in the Sample box on the right side of the dialog.

Setting fill colors and patterns

You can add a fill color and/or pattern to a field regardless of whether the field has a border or not. In Browse mode, the color and/or pattern appears behind the field's data.

You can specify fill colors and patterns in two ways. The first way is to use the Fill tools (the first two pop-up palettes below the bucket icon in the Tools sidebar; refer to Figure 6-24). If a field is currently selected, its fill color and/or pattern take on the new settings. If no field is currently selected when you choose a color or pattern with these tools, the color and pattern become the default fill color and pattern for new fields. If you now add a field, it is automatically formatted with the selected fill pattern and color.

Tip   You can also set default formatting options by simply pressing ⌘/Ctrl and clicking any field or object. Then, whenever you create a new field or text object, the clicked field or object's format settings will automatically be applied.

As an alternative, you can use the Field Borders command to select a fill for a field. Choose Fill from the dialog's pop-up menu/drop-down list and then choose the desired color and pattern for the fill from the pop-up palettes. The effects of your choices appear in the Sample box on the right side of the dialog.

Adding 3-D effects

You can quickly add 3-D effects to fields (or any other object) by choosing commands from the 3-D Object pop-up palette in the Tools sidebar. (Refer to Figure 6-24.) Choose Embossed to make the field or object look like it's raised from the page. Choose Engraved to make the field or object appear sunken into the page. Choose Drop Shadow to make the field or object appear engraved with a drop shadow on its bottom and right edges.

Note   The thickness of the line chosen for the object's border determines the intensity of the 3-D effect.

Adding scroll bars

If you don't make a Text field large enough initially, the entire contents of the field might not always be visible. Although you could simply make the field larger, this method might not produce the effect you want, especially if the available space in your layout is limited or if it forces you to relocate other layout objects. To make viewing the additional contents of a Text field possible, you can add vertical scroll bars to the field. These scroll bars enable you to scroll the field and view its additional contents, just as you can with many document windows.

STEPS: Adding Vertical Scroll Bars to a Text Field

1. In Layout mode, choose the layout containing the Text field to which you want to add scroll bars.

2. Click to select the field.

3. Choose Format ⇨ Field/Control ⇨ Setup (⌘+Option+F/Alt+Ctrl+F).

   The Field/Control Setup dialog appears.

4. In the Control Style section of the dialog (see Figure 6-41), select the Include vertical scroll bar check box.

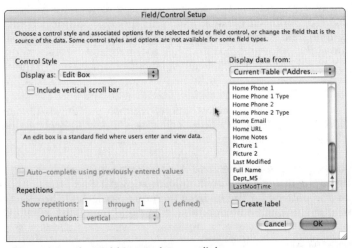

Figure 6-41: The Field/Control Setup dialog.

5. Click OK.

Rotating text and objects

You can rotate any layout object in 90-degree increments. Rotating comes in handy when you need to add a label that runs up or down the side of a portal, for example. You can also label a block of fields with vertical text, taking up less of the valuable room in your layout.

STEPS: Rotating an Object

1. In Layout mode, choose the layout containing the object you want to rotate.

2. Click to select the object.

3. Choose Arrange ⇨ Rotate (or press Option+⌘+R/Alt+Ctrl+R).

Each time you issue the Rotate command, the selected object rotates 90 degrees clockwise.

Note

When editing static, rotated text in Layout mode, the text is temporarily displayed in its unrotated form, thus enabling you to edit it. When you finish editing, the text resumes its rotated form.

You can also rotate fields. When you click or tab into a rotated field in Browse mode, the field is temporarily displayed in its unrotated form. After you tab out of the field or click elsewhere in the layout, the field resumes its rotated form. However, unless you have an exceptional reason for rotating a field, you should avoid doing so; users will find it at least as obnoxious as flashing text on a Web page.

Caution

Be aware that rotating an object four times might not return it to its original position. FileMaker strives to keep the object completely within the layout with each rotation, which can cause its center point to move.

Formatting repeating fields

As you learned in Chapter 5, some fields can contain more than one entry. These fields are *repeating fields*. (You designate a field as repeating in the Options for Field *Field Name* dialog's Storage pane.) In an invoice database, for example, you might have a repeating field named Price containing a series of prices — one for each item in an order.

STEPS: Setting Options for Repeating Fields

1. In Layout mode, select the repeating field you want to format.

2. Choose Format ⇨ Field/Control ⇨ Setup.

The Field/Control Setup dialog appears. (See Figure 6-42.)

3. Enter the repetition range to display for the field. (You can optionally display fewer repetitions than were defined for the field.)

4. Choose an orientation from the pop-up menu/drop-down list as follows:

- Choose Vertical to display repetitions in a single column.

- Choose Horizontal to display repetitions in a row.

5. Click OK.

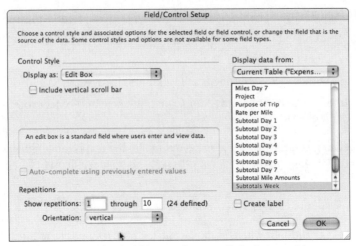

Figure 6-42: Use the Field/Control Setup dialog's Repetitions section to set display options for repeating fields.

Adding and modifying text

To make identifying items in a layout easy, you can add extra text. For example, you can add a title to a report layout and place it in the header, place an automatic page number and a date stamp in the footer, and create custom labels for fields.

You add text by using the Text tool (the letter A in the Tools palette). When you click this tool, the mouse pointer changes to an insertion I-beam. Click to position the bracket where you want the text to appear and then type the text. Text appears with the current settings for font, size, color, and so on, but you can change these attributes at any time.

To change the formatting of an existing text block (such as a field label or a title), switch to Layout mode, use the Pointer tool to select the text object you want to change, and then select the desired Font, Size, Style, Align Text, Line Spacing, and Text Color options from the Format menu or the Text Formatting toolbar.

To edit existing text, use the Text tool to select the text, position the insertion point inside the text box, and use the standard editing commands to modify the text. You can mix and match fonts, colors, and styles within a text block by applying formatting options to selected text within a block.

Besides adding standard text items, you can paste special items onto a layout, such as the current time and date, an automatic page number, or your user name.

STEPS: Inserting Special Text Items

1. In Layout mode, click the Text tool.

2. Click to position the insertion point where you want the special text to appear.

3. Choose one of the following options from the Insert menu: Current Date, Current Time, Current User Name, Date Symbol, Time Symbol, User Name Symbol, Page Number Symbol, or Record Number Symbol.

Tip You can also insert these elements *without* setting the insertion point or even selecting the Text tool. Simply choose the appropriate Insert command and the element will appear on the layout as a new, selected text block.

Duplicating formats

FileMaker Pro 8 provides a means of duplicating object formatting (without having to duplicate the object itself, like you do when duplicating a field). The Format Painter works in the same manner as the Microsoft Office tool of the same name, enabling you to copy the formatting from a selected object and apply it to another object.

STEPS: Duplicating Formats with the Format Painter

1. Switch to Layout mode and click to select the object whose attributes you want to duplicate.

   If you select multiple objects, only the attributes that they have in common will be copied.

2. Click the Format Painter icon (the paintbrush) on the Standard toolbar or choose Format ⇨ Format Painter.

3. To apply the formatting of the selected object(s) to one object, click that object. The formatting is applied, and the Pointer tool is reselected.

   or

   To apply the formatting to multiple objects, drag a selection rectangle around the objects. When you complete the selection rectangle by releasing the mouse button, the formatting is applied to all selected objects.

Tip Wanting to apply the same format to multiple objects isn't uncommon. To make this easier to do, lock the Format Painter in the on position by double-clicking its toolbar icon. When you're done applying the formatting, press Esc to unlock the Format Painter. (To accomplish the same thing when using the menu command, you must set the Always lock layout tools option on the Layout tab of the Preferences dialog.)

Applying the finishing touches

Even after you add all the desired elements to a layout, the layout might still need minor adjustments. If object alignment is a problem, you can easily correct it. You can also group objects so that you can move or format them as a unit. You can even set the order in which fields are filled during data entry.

Aligning objects

The Align submenu commands in the Arrange menu enable you to align objects with other objects on the layout. If you have a vertical stack of fields, you can use these commands to align one edge of each of the fields and field labels, for example.

STEPS: Aligning Two or More Objects

1. In Layout mode, select the objects you want to align. (You can hold down the Shift key to select additional objects after the first object or simply drag a selection rectangle around all the objects.)

Tip   If you hold down the ⌘/Ctrl key while you drag, touching or passing through the objects is sufficient to select them. It isn't necessary for the selection rectangle to surround them as it normally must do. Note, though, that if you initiate the click within a tab control, you have selected the tab control — when you want to select multiple objects on a tab, this tip doesn't help since the tab control is, itself, one of the objects selected.

2. Choose Arrange ⇨ Align ⇨ Left Edges (or Centers, Right Edges, Top Edges, Middles, or Bottom Edges as desired).

   The alignment setting is applied to the selected objects. If you find that you have made an error, you can correct it by immediately choosing the Edit ⇨ Undo Align command.

Note   In earlier versions of FileMaker Pro, it was necessary to invoke a Set Alignment dialog. Because the new method dispenses with the dialog, you should find aligning objects much faster and you can see the effect immediately.

You can also have FileMaker Pro automatically snap objects to a grid by enabling Object Grids (choose Arrange ⇨ Object Grids or press ⌘+Y/Ctrl+Y). This option makes field and label placement extraordinarily simple because each placed or moved object snaps to the nearest grid intersection. (Grid increments are based on the current ruler settings, as described earlier in this chapter.)

Grouping objects

To make it easier to move several aligned objects to a new position without messing up their alignment, you can group the objects. FileMaker Pro treats grouped objects on the layout as though they were a single object. Formatting attributes applied to the group are applied to every object in the group.

STEPS: Grouping Selected Objects

1. In Layout mode, select the objects you want to group. (Hold down the Shift key to select additional objects after the first object or simply drag a selection rectangle around all the objects.)

2. Choose Arrange ⇨ Group (or press ⌘+R/Ctrl+R).

   FileMaker Pro groups the objects, displaying them with a single set of handles.

To ungroup objects, select the group and then choose Arrange ➪ Ungroup (or press Shift+⌘+R/Shift+Ctrl+R).

Other object commands

You can also change the layering order in which objects are displayed (back to front) with the Bring to Front (Option+⌘+[/Alt+Ctrl+[), Send to Back (Option+ ⌘+]/Alt+Ctrl+]), Bring Forward (Shift+⌘+[/Shift+Ctrl+[), and Send Backward (Shift+ ⌘+]/Shift+Ctrl+]) commands in the Arrange menu. These commands are particularly useful for placing background graphics behind fields or other graphics.

If you want to make sure a particular object isn't moved by mistake, you can lock it in place by choosing the Arrange ➪ Lock command (or by pressing Option+⌘+L/ Alt+Ctrl+L). To unlock an object (so that you can change its size, position, or attributes, for example), choose Arrange ➪ Unlock (or press Shift+Option+⌘+L/ Shift+Alt+Ctrl+L).

Tip   If you frequently use the Arrange commands, you might find it beneficial to enable the Arrange toolbar. Choose View ➪ Toolbars ➪ Arrange to enable or disable this toolbar, as shown in Figure 6-43. One reason to do so is the Select objects by type button, which has no Arrange menu equivalent and allows you to select all labels by clicking one label.

Figure 6-43: To avoid having to choose menu commands or memorize keyboard shortcuts, you might want to enable the Arrange toolbar (Mac).

Setting the tab order for data entry

You can set the order in which you move from field to field on a layout when you press the Tab key. Although this has no effect on the appearance of the layout, it can often be the difference between an easy-to-use layout and one that the user finds annoying. The default tab order is from left to right and top to bottom. You can change this order and even omit fields from the tab order, if you want. To change the tab order, you use the Set Tab Order command.

STEPS: Changing the Tab Order for a Layout

1. In Layout mode, choose Layouts ➪ Set Tab Order.

   The Set Tab Order dialog appears. A numbered arrow marks each field in the layout. (See Figure 6-44.)

2. If you wish to add Objects (fields, tab controls, and buttons), only fields, or only buttons to the tab order — or if you want to remove fields or buttons from the existing tab order — choose from the Add Remaining and Remove pop-up menus/drop-down lists, respectively.

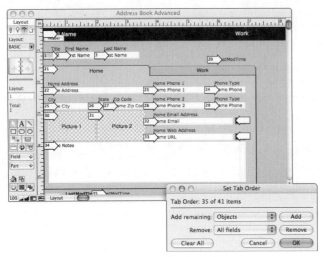

Figure 6-44: Setting the tab order for a layout.

3. To edit the tab order for fields, change the numbers in the arrows that appear next to each field in the layout. Enter **1** in the arrow for the field that you want first, click and type **2** for the field that you want second, and so on.

Note When you renumber an arrow, the numbers on other objects will automatically change to avoid conflicts.

Note To omit a field from the tab order, leave its arrow blank. When the user presses the Tab key, omitted fields are skipped.

4. Click OK to save the new tab order, or click Cancel if you change your mind.

Duplicating, Renaming, Reordering, and Deleting Layouts

There are several additional operations you can perform on layouts. You can use an existing layout as the basis for a new one, preserving the old while modifying the new. You can change the display order for layouts, and you can give any layout a new name. You can also get rid of layouts that are no longer needed. These layout operations are discussed in the following sections.

Duplicating a layout

To create a new layout that differs only slightly from an existing one, the easiest method is to duplicate the existing layout and make small changes to the copy. As an example, when you write letters, you might at times use preprinted envelopes that include your return address and at other times use plain, unprinted envelopes. If you already have a layout for printing on one type of envelope, you can duplicate the layout, make a couple of small changes, and handle the other type of envelope as well.

To duplicate a layout, switch to Layout mode, choose the layout you want to duplicate from the layout pop-up menu/drop-down list, and choose Layouts ➪ Duplicate Layout. By default, the layout is named *layout name Copy*. You can change its name by following the instructions in the section, "Renaming a layout," later in this chapter.

Reordering layouts

In the layout pop-up menu/drop-down list, layouts are displayed in the order in which you created them. However, this order might not be what you want. For example, you might want to display the layouts you use most frequently at the top of the list or arrange them in order of importance or organize them by function.

STEPS: Changing the Order in Which Layouts Are Listed in the Layout Pop-up Menu

1. In the appropriate FileMaker Pro database, switch to Layout mode.

2. Choose Layouts ➪ Set Layout Order.

The Set Layout Order dialog appears, as shown in Figure 6-45.

Figure 6-45: The Set Layout Order dialog.

3. Drag layout names into the desired order.

To make a layout first in the list, for example, click-and-drag its name to the top of the list.

4. Click OK to put the new order into effect.

As Figure 6-45 shows, you can also change whether a layout's name appears in the layout menu. A check mark in front of a layout name signifies that it will be listed in the layout pop-up menu. The check mark works as a toggle: You can click in front of any layout name to add or remove the check mark. You can also select multiple layouts in the list and mark the Include in layouts menu check box beneath the list to toggle them all on or off. Also, when multiple layouts are selected, toggling the check box for any one of them causes the check boxes for all other selected layouts to match.

Tip   If you like, you can add separator lines to the layout menu. Simply create a new blank layout and name it "-" (hyphen).

Renaming a layout

The default names assigned to new and duplicated layouts (such as Layout #2 and Data Entry Copy) aren't very useful. You can use the Layout Setup dialog to give any layout a new name.

STEPS: Renaming a Layout

1. Switch to Layout mode.

2. From the layout pop-up menu/drop-down list, choose the layout you want to rename.

3. Choose Layouts ⇨ Layout Setup.

   The Layout Setup dialog appears, as shown earlier in this chapter in the "Previewing and printing layouts in columns" sidebar, but this time with the General pane selected.

4. Type a new name for the layout in the Layout Name text box.

5. Click OK.

Deleting a layout

A layout might no longer be useful for several reasons. For example, the layout might not have been exactly what you wanted; you might have created it just to test certain FileMaker Pro layout features with no real intention of putting the layout to use, or you might no longer require the kind of report for which the layout was designed.

STEPS: Deleting a Layout

1. Switch to Layout mode.

2. Choose the layout you want to delete from the layout pop-up menu/ drop-down list.

3. Choose Layouts ⇨ Delete Layout (or press ⌘+E/Ctrl+E).

   An alert appears, asking you to confirm the deletion.

4. Click the Delete button.

FileMaker Pro removes the layout from your database. Keep in mind that at least one layout must remain in every database.

Summary

✦ FileMaker Pro databases can have multiple layouts. The particular fields placed in each layout and their formatting are up to you.

✦ Layouts can be based on any of seven predefined layout styles, including columnar lists/reports, Avery/DYMO labels, and business envelopes. All new ayouts (after the initial one) are designed with the help of the New Layout/Report Assistant.

✦ Layouts can have multiple sections *(parts),* including headers, footers, a body, sub-summaries, and a grand summary.

✦ Layout parts can include fields, text, and graphics. Objects of any type can be aligned and moved as a group.

✦ FileMaker Pro includes many tools enabling you to precisely size and place fields and objects on a layout. You can apply powerful formatting commands to fields and objects to make them look as you want.

✦ To quickly duplicate a selected FileMaker Pro object's formatting, you can choose the Format Painter tool and click the target object.

✦ If you're a Microsoft Office or AppleWorks user, you might want to enable one or more of the FileMaker Pro 8 toolbars. If you're comfortable with toolbars, you can choose common formatting commands from the icons and pop-up menus on the toolbars.

✦   ✦   ✦

Setting Preferences

✦ ✦ ✦ ✦

In This Chapter

Setting application preferences and file options

Setting memory preferences for a portable computer

Enabling FileMaker Pro plug-ins

Setting database start-up and closing actions

✦ ✦ ✦ ✦

Not everyone likes to work the same way. Some of us are morning people while others are night owls, for example. The same holds true for using FileMaker Pro. The way you prefer to create database layouts, enter data, and work with a database might differ significantly from the way your co-workers perform the same tasks. Fortunately, you can set preferences customizing how you work with the program as well as how you work with specific databases.

Knowing what the available preferences are, how to set them, and how to change them are important when you find yourself working on someone else's computer or with a database another person created. If the other person's computer or setup behaves differently from yours, you benefit from knowing that the differences are likely because of alternate preferences and that you can easily change them to match your way of working. (Be considerate, though: If you change the preferences on someone else's computer, put them back the way you found them when you're through.)

The two types of FileMaker Pro preferences are

✦ *Application preferences:* These are global settings that affect the way FileMaker Pro always operates, regardless of what database you are using.

✦ *Document preferences:* These are specific to a particular database. Every database can have its own set of document preferences.

Setting FileMaker Pro 8 Preferences

You set all application-wide preferences from the Preferences dialog (shown in Figure 7-1). To access this dialog from

Windows, choose Edit ➪ Preferences. From Mac OS X, choose FileMaker Pro ➪ Preferences.

Macintosh   Windows

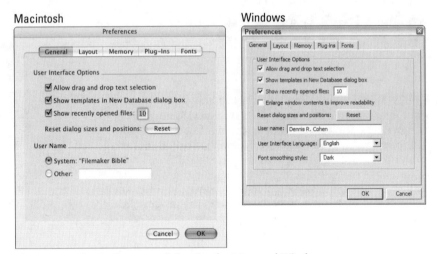

Figure 7-1: The Preferences dialog for the Mac and Windows.

The five Preferences categories are as follows:

✦ *General preferences* govern how FileMaker Pro behaves as a whole.

✦ *Layout preferences* affect only actions performed and items seen in Layout mode.

✦ *Memory preferences* enable you to adjust the frequency with which FileMaker Pro saves data to disk and to optionally adjust the size of FileMaker's memory cache.

✦ *Plug-Ins preferences* are used to enable or disable FileMaker Pro *plug-ins* — add-ins that increase FileMaker Pro's functionality. For example, FileMaker Pro 8 comes with an Auto Update plug-in enabling live updates from a FileMaker Server 8.0 installation. (FileMaker Server 8 is not covered in this book. It is, however, a solution for corporate installations of shared FileMaker databases.)

See Chapter 22 for information on other commercially available plug-ins.

✦ *Fonts preferences* enable you to specify the default font to use for each input type, such as Roman (for most Western languages), Kanji (Japanese), Cyrillic (Russian), or Hangul (Korean). If you're working only in American English, for example, you need to worry only about setting a default font for Roman; the defaults are Helvetica on the Mac and Arial on Windows.

Note

Mac and Windows provide different input systems, so your choices will differ significantly from one platform to the other.

STEPS: Setting Application Preferences

1. Open the Preferences dialog (refer to Figure 7-1).

   • *Mac:* Choose FileMaker Pro ➪ Preferences (⌘+, [comma]).

   • *Windows:* Choose Edit ➪ Preferences.

2. Click the tab at the top of the dialog corresponding to the Preferences category you want to view or change.

3. Make the desired changes.

4. Choose another category by clicking the appropriate tab.

   or

   Click OK to put your changes into effect and dismiss the Preferences dialog.

Note The Preferences dialog in FileMaker Pro 8 also has a Cancel button. Clicking Cancel discards all changes and dismisses the dialog.

The following sections discuss the specific options that you can set in each category.

Setting General preferences

The General preferences (refer to Figure 7-1) govern overall program behavior. The General preference options are as follows:

✦ *Allow drag and drop text selection:* FileMaker Pro supports the drag-and-drop feature found in Macintosh and Windows operating systems. When this option is enabled, you can select and drag information from one field to another, from one FileMaker Pro database to another, and between FileMaker Pro databases and documents created in other programs (such as word processing, spreadsheet, and graphics programs). This option is on by default.

Note To drag text or objects between FileMaker Pro and another application, the other application must also support drag-and-drop.

✦ *Show templates in New Database dialog box:* FileMaker Pro 8 includes a variety of business, home, and educational templates you can use to create ready-to-use databases. Select this option if you want these templates to be listed and selectable in the New Database dialog that appears when you launch FileMaker Pro or choose the File ➪ New Database command. This option is on by default.

✦ *Show recently opened files:* You can have FileMaker Pro display the most recently opened databases in an Open Recent submenu of the File menu, making it simple to reopen them. Select this check box and type the number of files you want to list. This option is on by default and is set to 10; the maximum is 16.

✦ *Enlarge window contents to improve readability* (Windows only): Select this check box if you want FileMaker Pro to increase the size of all layout objects, thus making text more legible. When this preference is in effect, the magnification level in the lower-left corner of the window's status bar is accompanied by an asterisk (*).

✦ *Reset dialog sizes and positions:* FileMaker Pro 8 remembers the last screen position of each dialog as well as each one's size. If you've resized or moved any of them from their normal positions, you can click the Reset button to restore them all to their defaults.

✦ *User Name* (Macintosh): This option governs whether FileMaker Pro uses the system user name or a name you supply here. The default is to use the system name (System), which is set in the OS X Accounts System Preferences panel. Select the System radio button to use the name that appears in quote marks, or select the Other radio button and enter another name in the text box.

After you specify a user name, you can enter it into a field with the Insert ⇨ Current User Name command, automatically enter it in a field by setting an appropriate auto-entry option, or use it in scripts. In a networked database, for example, you could automatically enter the current user's name as the person who created or most recently modified each record.

✦ *User Name* (Windows): In the Windows version of FileMaker Pro, you only have the option to enter a User Name.

After you specify a user name, you can enter it into a field with the Insert ⇨ Current User Name command, automatically enter it in a field by setting an appropriate auto-entry option, or use it in scripts. In a networked database, for example, you could automatically enter the current user's name as the person who created or most recently modified each record.

Tip

You can also create scripts that employ the custom user name. For example, you might want to create a script that finds data specific to a given individual, such as all telephone orders taken by a particular telemarketer. Instead of creating a separate script for every user, you can have FileMaker Pro use the custom user name. To find information for a different person (another telemarketer, for instance), you merely change the custom user name in the Preferences dialog before running the script. (See Chapter 15 for more information about scripts.)

✦ *User Interface Language* (Windows only): This establishes which language FileMaker Pro employs for menus, dialogs, and alerts. Mac users specify this in the International System Preferences pane.

✦ *Font smoothing style* (Windows only): This sets the font-smoothing style employed for text display. Mac users set this attribute in their Appearance System Preferences, and FileMaker Pro uses this system-wide setting.

Setting Layout preferences

Layout preferences (see Figure 7-2) apply to actions that can take place while you're in Layout mode — either designing a new layout or editing an existing one.

Settings chosen in the Layout section of the Preferences dialog affect *all* databases, not merely the database that is active when the Preferences command is chosen.

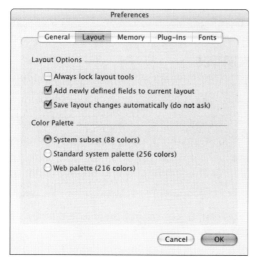

Figure 7-2: Layout preferences.

The Layout preferences govern the following functions:

✦ *Always lock layout tools:* This option determines how tools behave when you're designing or modifying layouts. By default, FileMaker Pro automatically switches back to the Pointer tool after you perform an operation with any other tool. Although this way of operating enables you to quickly select an item after you modify it, it can be annoying if you routinely perform several operations in a row with the same tool. When Always lock layout tools is selected, FileMaker Pro keeps the same tool selected until you choose a different tool or press the Enter key.

Note If this option is not selected, you can still lock a tool by double-clicking it.

✦ *Add newly defined fields to current layout:* This option determines whether new fields that you define will automatically be added to the current layout. By default, FileMaker Pro is set to add them. If you want to define new fields without automatically placing them on the current layout, remove the check mark from this option. You will then have to add newly defined fields manually (by dragging them onto the layout).

✦ *Save layout changes automatically (do not ask):* This option tells FileMaker Pro 8 to save changes to the current layout whenever you exit Layout mode or switch to a different layout while in Layout mode.

✦ *Color Palette:* When adding colors to objects, you can now specify one of three color palettes to use. (If you are creating cross-platform databases or ones you intend to publish with the Web Companion and believe that some of your visitors will be using either older machines or older Web browser versions, select the Web palette.)

Setting Memory preferences

Memory preferences control the manner in which FileMaker Pro saves data to disk. (See Figure 7-3.) As you work, FileMaker Pro saves data in two ways: by using the memory cache (which defaults to 8MB) and by copying new data to the disk that contains the original database document. The *cache* is a special part of RAM that FileMaker Pro sets aside. Changes are accumulated in the cache until a specific time since the last disk save was performed, until it is full, or until an opportune moment arises (that is, when the system is idle). At this point, changes are flushed from the cache and saved to disk.

Note   ScriptMaker includes a step that you can use to control the cache directly: Flush Cache to Disk. To learn about this step, see Chapter 15.

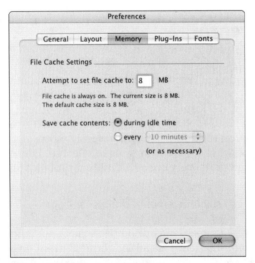

Figure 7-3: Memory preferences.

Saving the cache when the system is idle is fine for desktop computers. On laptops, however, it can waste battery power. One of the most energy-consuming aspects of laptop operation is powering up and spinning the disk drives. For this reason, the drives on a laptop are frequently powered down when data isn't being read from or written to them. If FileMaker Pro is set to save all changes to disk during idle time, however, it can keep the drives running more often and longer than normal, decreasing the amount of work time you get from a battery charge. To prevent such power waste, you can alternatively specify that FileMaker Pro save only after a given interval — perhaps once every 30 minutes.

Setting a save interval involves a significant trade-off. The longer the interval you choose, the less battery power is consumed, but the more data you put at risk. If you suffer a crash between saves, you will normally lose everything in the cache. This problem is not significant if you're using the database only to look up information or if you're making only limited changes. Note, however, that even if you set a relatively long save interval, FileMaker Pro will still save if the cache fills before the interval is reached.

Tip   You can change the cache size by entering a new number in the Attempt to set file cache to *x* MB text box. By increasing the size of the cache, you will fill it less frequently — or at least less quickly — thereby reducing the number of disk accesses.

To set a save interval in the Memory section of the Preferences dialog, use the setting under Save cache contents. Select the Every *x* (or as necessary) radio button and choose the desired interval from the pop-up menu/drop-down list. Remember that longer intervals are riskier to data, but they save more power. If you decide that you'd rather save new data as soon as possible, select the During idle time radio button (the default).

Setting Plug-Ins preferences

FileMaker Pro versions 4.0 and higher support *plug-ins* — small applications that add functionality to FileMaker Pro. FileMaker Pro 8 includes an auto-update plug-in enabling a networked copy of FileMaker Pro to automatically download newer versions of installed plug-ins from FileMaker Server. You use the Plug-Ins preferences (see Figure 7-4) to enable and disable plug-ins or to configure enabled plug-ins.

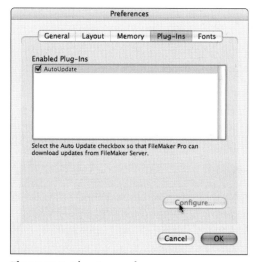

Figure 7-4: Plug-Ins preferences.

To enable a plug-in, select that plug-in's check box. After you enable particular plug-ins, you can click the Configure button to set options specific to the plug-in, if any options exist.

Tip　To learn what a particular plug-in does, select its name from the list—refer to Figure 7-4—and a brief description of the plug-in appears below the list in the dialog.

Note　FileMaker, Inc. (www.filemaker.com) is not the sole source of plug-ins. Some FileMaker Pro developers—such as Troi Automatisering (www.troi.com)—offer plug-ins that extend FileMaker Pro's functionality. (See Chapter 22 for some examples.)

Setting Fonts preferences

FileMaker Pro 8 allows setting default fonts for use with any *input type* (a method matching languages and writing systems). For example, the Roman (Mac)/Western (Windows) method is employed for English, Spanish, Italian, French, and a number of other languages, and the default font is Helvetica on a Mac and Arial on Windows. Cyrillic is employed for Russian, with a default font of Geneva CY on the Mac and Arial CYR on Windows. Hangul is used for Korean (Mac) with a default font of Seoul or AppleGothic, depending upon your version of Mac OS X. The input types available are dependent upon what your particular operating system provides. The Mac Fonts Preferences pane appears in Figure 7-5.

Figure 7-5: Mac fonts preferences.

Select the input type from the list (scrolling if necessary) and choose the font you prefer as a default from the Specify font pop-up menu/drop-down list. If you want your system to automatically switch input methods to one matching the field's font, select the Synchronize input method with font on field entry check box. The Use Font Locking check box tells FileMaker Pro to apply font changes only to characters that exist in the new font.

Tip   Font locking is on by default, but FileMaker Pro is a little faster with it turned off. If you aren't going to be mixing input methods within a field, you might wish to turn off this option.

Setting Document-Specific Options

In addition to setting preferences for FileMaker Pro as a whole, you can set preferences specific to each database. For instance, you can set a start-up action for a given database by setting a preference directing it to open to a particular layout or automatically run a script.

Open/Close file options

Every database can have different document preferences. To view or change document preferences, choose File ➪ File Options. The File Options dialog appears, as shown in Figure 7-6.

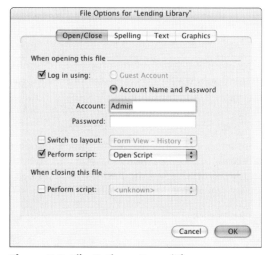

Figure 7-6: File Options: Open/Close.

Click the Open/Close tab to set the following document preferences:

✦ *When opening this file, Log in using:* In addition to normal and blank passwords (which are discussed in Chapter 19), FileMaker Pro enables you to specify accounts with associated passwords that are automatically tried when a user opens a particular database. You can associate specific privileges with the default account (such as allowing the user to only browse through records but not edit, create, or delete them). One advantage of establishing user accounts rather than using a simple password system is that the user is never confronted with a request to enter a password. The database opens automatically (just like most other databases), and only the FileMaker Pro features specified by the person who developed or administers the database are enabled. Accounts and privilege sets are covered in Chapter 19.

You set the default account option by selecting the Log in using check box and then typing the default account name and password in the text boxes.

Tip   If this option has been set for a database and you want to force the password dialog to appear (so that you can enter a different account and password), hold down the Option key (Mac) or Shift key (Windows) when you open the database.

✦ *When opening this file, Switch to layout:* This option specifies a particular layout to display whenever the database is opened. If you do not set this option, the database opens to whatever layout was active when the database was last closed.

This option is especially helpful in two situations. First, many databases are menu-driven. A database might contain a menu of buttons enabling the user to select which portion of the database or function he/she wants to perform (data entry, report printing, or label generation, for example). By selecting the menu layout as the opening layout, you can ensure that users aren't confused by starting in a different (possibly foreign) section of the database each time.

Second, many databases are designed so that they revolve around one basic layout. For example, the Address Book Advanced database presented in Chapter 4 has a data-entry layout as the central layout. Because most of the work a user will do is on that layout, having FileMaker Pro open automatically to it makes sense.

✦ *When opening this database, Perform script:* This option automatically performs a selected script when the database opens. For instance, you can specify a script that opens to the last record (rather than the first one), sorts the database, or sets a particular display option (such as a 150% zoom).

Spelling file options

You can also set document options for the spell checker, as shown in Figure 7-7. Click the Spelling tab at the top of the File Options dialog.

Macintosh   Windows

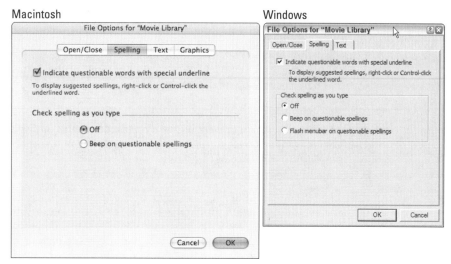

Figure 7-7: File Options: Spelling (Mac and Windows).

You can set these options:

✦ *Indicate questionable words with special underline*: This check box, new in FileMaker Pro 8, is yet another method for checking spelling as you type (see the following bullet). When FileMaker Pro encounters an unrecognized word, it underlines that word (a dotted underline is employed), and you can Control+ click (right-click) the word for a shortcut menu of suggested corrections.

The underline spell-check method is new to FileMaker Pro 8.

This is more in the nature of a mild rant, but this option is automatically enabled for all new documents. Would it have been so difficult to provide a global preference as to whether this new, live spell-checking should be enabled by default? Many people (these authors vociferously among them) believe that spell-checking should be performed only when requested and that beeping, flashing, or underlining distracts the user and detracts from productivity — your mileage may vary, but that's why preference settings exist.

✦ *Check spelling as you type:* Select the appropriate radio button to make your selection. If you enable this feature, FileMaker Pro will either beep or flash the menu bar when you type a word that it isn't in its spelling dictionary. If you select the Off radio button, FileMaker Pro doesn't spell check as you type. However, you can still perform manual spell checks by choosing commands from the Edit ➪ Spelling submenu. If you select the Beep on questionable spellings radio button and enter a word that FileMaker Pro's dictionaries do not recognize, FileMaker will beep.

✦ *Flash menubar on questionable spellings* (Windows only): When encountering an unrecognized word, FileMaker Pro makes the menu bar blink.

The power user's guide to preferences

Setting a start-up or closing script with the Perform Script option is a great way to exert control over a database. Scripts can instruct FileMaker Pro to perform any of the following actions automatically when a database is opened or closed:

✦ Make sure the database is sorted in a particular order.

✦ Select a subset of records with which to work or make certain all records are visible.

✦ Perform a relookup procedure so that all lookup fields contain current data.

✦ Open a report layout and automatically print a current copy of the report.

✦ *When closing this file, Perform script:* This option automatically performs a selected script when the database closes—when you click the database's close button/box, choose File ➩ Close, press ⌘+W/Ctrl+W, or quit FileMaker Pro while the database is still open. For example, you might want to execute a script that prints a daily report. Setting this script as a closing action—rather than as an opening action—enables you to avoid a lengthy delay at the beginning of your work session.

Text file options

The two sets of text options on this pane, as shown in Figure 7-8, are Text Handling and Data Entry.

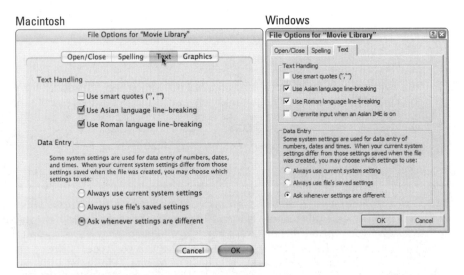

Figure 7-8: File Options: Text.

Manually entering curly quotes (Mac only)

In some databases (ones that contain measurements in feet and inches, for example), using smart quotes might not be to your advantage. If the Use smart quotes option is selected, you cannot type straight quotation marks (' and "). If you find that you frequently need to use straight quotes in a particular database, the best approach is to remove the check mark from the Use smart quotes setting. When you need curly quotes, you can enter them manually in the Mac version, as we explain in the following table. (As a bonus, you can also use the instructions in the table to produce curly quote characters in other programs that don't provide a smart quotes option.)

Type This	To Produce This Curly Quote Character
Option+[	" (double left quote)
Shift+Option+[	" (double right quote)
Option+]	' (single left quote)
Shift+Option+]	' (single right quote)

The three (Mac)/four (Windows) Text Handling options are

✦ *Use smart quotes:* This option instructs FileMaker to use curved open and closed quotation marks and apostrophes (' ' and " ") rather than the foot and inch marks (' and ") used for quotation marks as an artifact of the typewriter era. The former characters are commonly referred to as *curly* or *smart* quotes and are generally favored because they look more professional.

Note

Another time you will want to use straight quote symbols is when entering Global Positioning System (GPS) coordinates as ' to designate minutes of longitude or latitude and " to indicate seconds.

FileMaker Pro contains a set of rules determining when it uses a left quote and when it uses a right quote. When the Use smart quotes option is selected, the appropriate curly quote character is typed each time you press the single or double quotation mark key. Note that this preference option has no effect if the font you're using doesn't contain symbols for the curved quotes; straight quotes are used instead.

✦ *Use Asian language line-breaking:* This option tells FileMaker to use Asian language rules determining which characters are permitted to begin or end a text line. This option is on by default.

✦ *Use Roman language line-breaking:* On by default, this option enables such expected features as word-wrapping. If turned off, lines could break in the middle of a word.

✦ *Overwrite input when an Asian IME is on* (Windows only): Off by default, this option tells FileMaker Pro to overwrite rather than insert characters when the insertion point is in the middle of text and new characters are entered.

The Data Entry section has three mutually exclusive options, establishing how to handle inconsistencies between current OS settings for numbers, dates, times, and those formats in effect when the database was created. You can opt to select Always use current system settings, Always use file's saved settings, or Ask whenever settings are different. The default is to prompt the user when a mismatch is detected.

Graphics file options (Mac only)

The only option in this pane is Auto-initiate photo import when camera is plugged in, as shown in Figure 7-9: This option supports FileMaker Pro's ability to import photographs (JPEG and TIFF only) as well as their EXIF (EXchangeable Image File) information, directly from a connected digital camera into a Container field. See Chapter 16 for additional information, including instructions for making FileMaker Pro 8 your preferred application for photo importing.

Note   FileMaker Pro will extract EXIF information only from directly connected cameras and memory card readers. If the file is already on disk (for example, in your iPhoto Library), FileMaker Pro will not import the EXIF information, even when present.

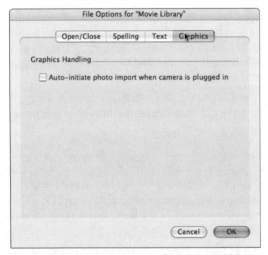

Figure 7-9: File Options: Graphics (Mac only).

Summary

✦ You can customize FileMaker Pro's operation, as well as the start-up and closing actions of individual databases, by choosing the FileMaker Pro/Edit ➪ Preferences and File ➪ File Options, respectively.

✦ Selecting the Use smart quotes option instructs FileMaker Pro to substitute curved left and right quotation marks for straight quotation marks. However, using this option makes entering foot and inch symbols (straight quotation marks) difficult.

✦ You can save battery power on a portable Macintosh (a PowerBook or iBook) or portable PC by specifying the frequency with which FileMaker Pro saves data to disk, as well as setting a larger or smaller memory cache.

✦ FileMaker Pro plug-ins can be enabled, disabled, or configured in the Preferences dialog's Plug-Ins pane.

✦   ✦   ✦

Working with Databases

◆   ◆   ◆   ◆

◆   ◆   ◆   ◆

Working with Records

As a FileMaker Pro user, you will spend most of your time in Browse mode, one of the four FileMaker Pro operational modes discussed in Chapter 1. Whenever you want to view, enter, or edit data; add new records; or delete records, you must first switch to Browse mode.

Browse Mode Basics

As its name suggests, you can use Browse mode to flip through a database record by record, examining, creating, and modifying records as you go. You also have to be in Browse mode to omit records (temporarily hide them) or to sort records. Because you usually omit records in conjunction with a Find request, this topic is discussed in Chapter 9. Sorting is covered in Chapter 10.

You can be in only one mode at a time. Determining which mode you are in is easy. As Figure 8-1 illustrates, the current mode has a check mark next to it in the View menu (left figure). The name appears above the mode selector buttons at the top of the Tools sidebar (top-right figure) and also in the mode selector pop-up menu near the bottom-left corner of the database window (bottom-right figure).

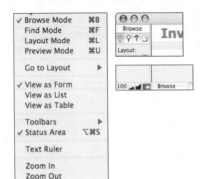

Figure 8-1: The current mode is indicated in (left) the View menu, (top right) the mode selector buttons, and (bottom right) the mode selector pop-up menu.

Switching to Browse mode

Regardless of the mode you're in, you can switch to Browse mode in four ways:

✦ Choosing the View ➪ Browse Mode command (or pressing ⌘+B/Ctrl+B) — we're counting this as two ways.

✦ Clicking the Browse mode button (the pencil) at the top of the Tools sidebar.

✦ Choosing Browse from the mode selector pop-up menu at the bottom of the database window.

You can also switch to other modes (Find, Layout, and Preview) in the same four ways.

Note   When you first open a database, FileMaker Pro automatically displays it in Browse mode. This is convenient because browsing is what you do most.

Using Browse mode controls

As shown in Figure 8-2, fewer status area controls are available in Browse mode than in *Layout mode* — the mode in which database layouts (arrangements of fields, graphics, and static text) are designed. The available Browse mode controls are all related to record navigation and data viewing.

Using the Layout pop-up menu/drop-down list to switch layouts

As we emphasize throughout this book, layouts are extremely important in FileMaker Pro. A *layout* is a particular arrangement of database fields. Because no single way of displaying fields is equally useful for all tasks, many databases have multiple layouts. For example, a layout that makes it easy to enter data might not be the best one for displaying a report. You can change layouts in Browse mode at any time.

Figure 8-2: Browse mode controls.

In the upper-left corner of the window, just below the mode selector buttons, is the Layout pop-up menu/drop-down list (shown in Figure 8-2).

Note

FileMaker Pro's dialogs and Help refer to this pop-up menu/drop-down list as simply the *Layouts menu.* We'll follow that convention for the remainder of this chapter.

You use this menu to determine which layout is currently displayed and to switch between available database layouts. For example, follow these steps to switch the Inventory database provided with FileMaker Pro 8 from one layout to another and then back again.

STEPS: Switching Databases Example

1. With the Inventory database displayed, choose the List View layout from the Layouts menu. (See Figure 8-3.)

   The display changes to show the List View layout. The Layouts menu shows that you have changed to a new layout.

2. Choose the Form View layout from the Layouts menu to switch back again.

Keep in mind that different layouts might require different amounts of screen space. When changing from one layout to another, you might sometimes need to resize the database window.

Tip

If you want, you can specify an opening layout for each database. Instead of opening to the layout that was displayed when you last closed the database (which is the default), FileMaker Pro displays the opening layout that you set in the File Options dialog. For instructions on setting an opening layout, see Chapter 7.

Using the book icon to navigate among records

Below the Layouts menu is the book icon. (See Figure 8-4.) In Browse mode, you use the book to navigate among records and select the next one you want to work with or view.

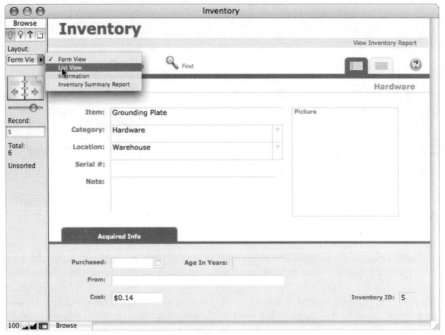

Figure 8-3: Switching to the List View layout in the Inventory database.

Note

The book has different functions in other modes. In Find mode, you use it to switch among multiple Find requests. In Layout mode, each book page represents a different layout. In Preview mode, you click the book to view different report pages.

Figure 8-4: The book icon.

In Browse mode, the navigation operations that you can perform using the book include the following:

✦ Flipping from one record to the next or the previous record (by clicking the right or left pages of the book, respectively)

✦ Quickly moving to the first or last record (by dragging the slider beneath the book to the extreme left or right)

✦ Moving to an approximate position in the database (by dragging the slider)

✦ Moving to a specific record (by typing a record number in the record number indicator area located below the slider)

The slider beneath the book shows the approximate position in the database of the currently displayed record. The number in the text box beneath the slider shows the exact position of the current record. The first record in the database is record #1, the second is record #2, and so on (in the current sort order). FileMaker Pro displays the total number of records that are currently in the database, the number of records that are being browsed (if all records aren't presently visible), and whether the database has been sorted (arranged in a particular order) beneath the text box. In the example shown in Figure 8-4, the fifth record out of five is currently displayed, and the database has not been sorted.

The following sections explain the various methods of navigating through the database. If you want to experiment with the different methods, you can use the example Address Book Advanced database (as shown in Chapter 4) or any other database that's handy.

Moving to the next or previous record in a database

You can use the book icon or keyboard shortcuts to move forward and backward in a database one record at a time.

STEPS: Moving One Record Forward or Backward

1. To move forward in a database, click the right-hand book page.

   Each click switches to the next record in the current sort order, making it the current record. The book slider moves right slightly, and the new record displays.

   or

   To move backward through a database, click the left-hand book page. Each click switches to the previous record in the current sort order, making it the current record. The slider moves left slightly, and the new record displays.

2. Continue clicking until the desired record appears.

Tip

FileMaker Pro 8 also provides keyboard shortcuts that you can use to move to the next or previous record. To go to the next record, press Ctrl+↓. To go to the previous record, press Ctrl+↑.

Browsing suggestions

Looking up individual records is a common database activity. After all, the purpose of a database is to store information for retrieval. Although you can locate and examine records in several ways (many of which are discussed in later chapters), frequently you'll just flip through records one at a time until you find the one you want.

However, flipping through records can be time-consuming when you are working with a large database. (See Chapter 9 for quicker, more efficient search methods.) One thing you can do to simplify this process is to employ a layout displaying more than one record at a time (such as the Address Book Advanced database's Phone Directory layout) or displaying the current layout's records as a list or table. (See the section, "Navigating without using the book," later in this chapter.)

Moving to the first record in a database

Follow these steps to move to the first record in a database's current found set.

STEPS: Moving to the First Record

1. Click the slider knob and drag left until it reaches the slider's left end.

2. Release the mouse button.

   or

1. Click the record number indicator directly below the book to select it.

2. Type **1** and then press Return/Enter.

   You can type any number to move directly to a particular record. Although you normally won't know specific record numbers, you will always know the first one.

   The first record in the database becomes the current record.

You can tell when you are at the first record of a database because the left page of the book icon is dimmed. As usual, the record number (1, in this case) is displayed beneath the book.

Tip   If you want to go to a specific record, you can select the record number indicator (beneath the book icon) by pressing the Esc key. You might find this faster than clicking to select the record number indicator. Note that this works only if no record or field is currently selected.

If the current layout displays one record per screen (such as the Address Book Advanced database's Data Entry layout), only the first record is visible. If you have chosen View as List or View as Table from the View menu, as is often done in reports, a thin vertical bar on the left side of the record marks the current record in the list.

Who's on first?

The particular database record that is displayed as first and the one that is last depends on whether the database has been sorted — and if so, by which field or fields. For example, the first record originally entered in Address Book Advanced might have been the one for Don Smith.

If you sort the database by the Last Name field, the new first record might be that of Adam Aarons. (See Chapter 10 for more information on sorting and how it affects a database.)

Moving to the last record in a database

Follow these steps to move to the last record in a database's current found set.

STEPS: Moving to the Last Record

1. Click the slider knob and drag right until it reaches the slider's right end.

2. Release the mouse button.

   The last record in the database becomes the current record.

   or

1. Click the record number indicator directly below the book to select it.

2. Type a number greater than or equal to the number of records in the database (displayed below the book area) and press Return/Enter.

   As long as the number is greater than or equal to the number of records that are currently being browsed, the last record is displayed, and it becomes the current record.

When the last record is selected, the book's right page is dimmed, signifying that no records follow the current one. As always, the record number is displayed immediately below the slider.

Note Regardless of the record navigation method you use, if you attempt to move up past the first record or down past the last record, nothing happens.

Moving to a specific record in a database

You can also move to a specific record number if you happen to know, for example, that the desired record is the fourth one in the current found set's sort order.

STEPS: Moving to a Specific Record

1. Click the record number indicator below the book to select it.

   or

   If no record or field is currently selected, press Esc.

In either case, the record number indicator highlights to show that it is selected.

2. Type the number of the record you want to examine, and press Return/Enter.

The corresponding record appears on the screen and becomes the current record.

Note   When you are browsing a database, you usually have all its records at your disposal. Sometimes, however, you might want to view only a subset of the records. To view a subset, you can issue a Find request. A Find request restricts visible records to those that match the find criteria (Salary < 50000, for example). For more information about searching for record subsets, see Chapter 9.

Navigating without using the book icon

By choosing View ➪ View as List, you can bypass the book icon when browsing records. In list view, all records are displayed as a continuous, scrolling list. You use the scroll bar at the side of the database window to change which records are currently visible. Reports and data-entry screens that have few fields are often worked with in list or table view. If you have an appropriate keyboard, you can also use the keys in Table 8-1 to move through the database in list view.

Note   If all the records are currently visible, none of the keystrokes in Table 8-1 have any effect. However, if it is necessary to scroll the list/table, the selected record will change to match the action taken.

Table 8-1
Navigational Shortcuts for View as List and View Table Modes

Key	Effect
Home	Scroll, if necessary, to display the first record
End	Scroll, if necessary, to display the last record
Page Up	Scroll up one screen
Page Down	Scroll down one screen

Note that these keys are purely for viewing and navigating through records. If you want to add data to or edit the current data in a record, you must select the record by clicking somewhere inside it.

In addition to form and list views, FileMaker Pro 8 offers a third way to view records: table view. Choose View ➪ View as Table to display the fields from the current layout in a spreadsheet-style grid. (See Figure 8-5.) The navigation commands available in list view can also be used in table view.

If list view or table view are not the views you normally use for the current layout, choose View ➪ View as Form. The display reverts to one record per screen.

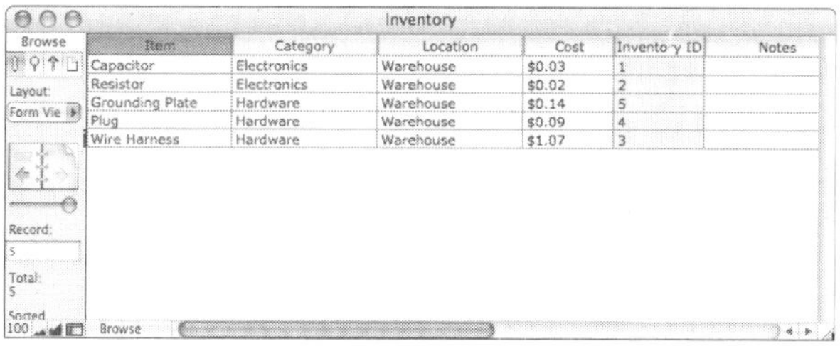

Figure 8-5: View as Table.

Changing the magnification level

Below the status area (at the bottom of the database window) are three tools that enable you to change your view of the database: the *magnification level, zoom out,* and *zoom in controls.* For example, you can decrease the magnification (or zoom out) to get a bird's-eye view of a layout or report (as shown in Figure 8-6). You can also increase the magnification (or zoom in) to concentrate on a particular section of a record. Although these tools are more useful in Layout or Preview mode, you can also use them in Browse mode.

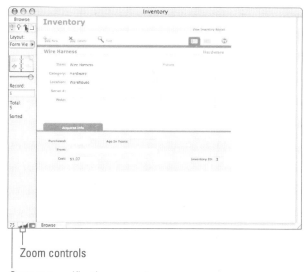

Zoom controls

Current magnification percentage

Figure 8-6: Inventory's form view zoomed to 75 percent.

The current magnification is shown as a percentage: 100 means that the database is shown actual size, 200 means that it's twice the actual size, and so on. Clicking the number toggles the display between 100 percent and the most recently selected zoom level. You use the pair of buttons to the right of the magnification percentage to zoom out (decrease magnification) and zoom in (increase magnification), respectively. Each time you click one of the buttons, the magnification is increased or decreased, to a maximum of 400 percent and a minimum of 25 percent.

Showing and hiding the status area

To the right of the zoom controls is the *status area control*. This button works as a toggle, enabling you to hide or show the status area. Hiding the status area gives you more room in which to display the database but hides all your tools. When you click the status area control to hide the status area, the current layout fills the entire window. Click the status area control again to display the status area and regain access to the tools.

Finally, to the right of the status area control button is the *mode selector pop-up menu*. As mentioned earlier in this chapter, you can use this menu to switch from one operational mode to another.

Working in different views

When browsing, you can display records in any of three views: form view (one record per screen), list view (all records displayed in a scrolling list using the current layout), or table view (all fields from the current layout displayed as a spreadsheet-style grid). You can switch freely among the different views — depending on your current needs — by choosing a View As command from the View menu.

Form view is frequently used for entering data. List view is commonly used for onscreen and printed reports. Table view is useful for examining the entire database or all records of a found set. Optionally, you can specify which of the three views are available for a given layout — enabling one view and disabling the other two, for example.

STEPS: Specifying Available Views for a Layout

1. Choose a layout from the Layouts menu in the status area.

2. Switch to Layout mode (press ⌘+L/Ctrl+L, choose View ➪ Layout Mode, click the Layout button at the top of the status area, or choose Layout from the mode pop-up menu at the bottom of the database window).

3. Choose Layouts ➪ Layout Setup.

    The Layout Setup dialog appears.

4. Click the Views tab. (See Figure 8-7.)

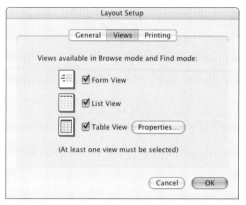

Figure 8-7: Specify the enabled views for the current layout.

5. Add and remove check marks to enable and disable views for this layout, as desired.

6. *Optional:* If the Table View check box is enabled, click the Properties button to set table view options. Otherwise, go to Step 11.

   The Table View Properties dialog appears. (See Figure 8-8.)

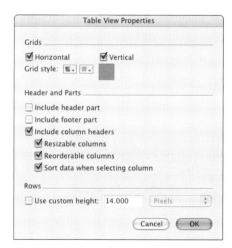

Figure 8-8: The Table View Properties dialog.

7. Set grid display options in the Table View Properties dialog's Grids section:

   • The Horizontal and Vertical options determine whether the table is shown with horizontal and/or vertical gridlines between records and fields, respectively.

- If you want to display the gridlines in a different color or pattern than solid black, select a color and/or a pattern from the Grid style pop-up palettes.

8. Specify the layout parts that will be displayed in table view, as well as the behavior of column (field) headings (if present), in the Table View Properties dialog's Header and Parts section:

    - Select the check boxes to Include header part and/or Include footer part if you have text or other information that you want displayed in these parts. It is common to have a header and/or footer part in a report layout or when you want to display a layout title, for example.

    - Select the Include column headers check box to display the field names at the top of the columns.

    - Select the Resizable columns check box if you want to be able to manually resize columns by clicking and dragging the right edge of any column heading.

    - Select the Reorderable columns check box if you want to be able to change the column order by clicking and dragging column headings to new positions.

    - Select the Sort data when selecting column check box if you want to be able to sort the browsed set by the contents of a clicked column. (This can be extremely useful. Note that this is enabled by default, which is a behavioral change from FileMaker Pro 6 and its predecessors.)

9. To set a custom height for rows (records), select the Use custom height check box and enter a row height in pixels, centimeters, or inches.

10. Click OK to dismiss the Table View Properties dialog.

11. Click OK to dismiss the Layout Setup dialog.

Data Entry and Editing

Perhaps Browse mode's most important uses are entering and editing data. As you work with FileMaker Pro, you'll discover that a wealth of commands and techniques have been provided to make data entry and editing as simple as possible.

Creating new records

Few databases are static entities that you just browse through now and then. (There are some, such as dictionaries.) Whether you've just finished designing a database or are working with one that you've had around for years, you'll want to add new records to it at some point. For example, a new contact requires a new record in your Address Book Advanced database. After you create the new record, you can enter the appropriate information in each of the record's fields.

The exact way in which you add a record to the database can depend on how the database was designed. For example, in some databases, you might be able to click a New Record button to activate a script that adds a new record to the database. Most database layouts, however, do not have such a button. Instead, you switch to Browse mode and choose the Records ⇨ New Record command (or press ⌘+N/Ctrl+N).

The new record appears onscreen, and it is added in the database immediately after the current record. Unless you have set auto-entry options for some fields (see Chapter 5), the record is blank.

Note   If adding the new record disrupts an existing sort order (the indicator below the book and slider reads Semi-sorted), you can restore order to the database by sorting again, as discussed in Chapter 10.

Entering data

A blank record isn't very useful. After adding a record, you need to enter appropriate information into it. First, however, you need to select the field in which you want to enter data, either by clicking in the field or tabbing into it.

You enter information one field at a time. The *current field* is the one in which you can immediately enter and edit data. A solid border surrounds the current field; borders around all other fields are dotted. The current field also contains the *insertion point,* a blinking vertical line that is sometimes called the *cursor.* Figure 8-9 shows a new record's current field and insertion point.

Current field

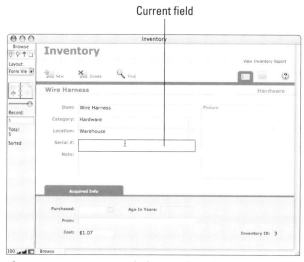

Figure 8-9: A new record about to be filled out.

Note   A field's alignment (chosen from the Format ⇨ Align Text submenu) determines the insertion point's position in a blank field. For example, when a field is left aligned, the insertion point appears on the left side of the field. When a field is right aligned — as Number fields frequently are — the insertion point is on the right side of the field.

To enter data in another field, you first need to make it the current field. You can either click the field with the mouse or tab into the field by pressing the Tab key. Pressing Tab moves you forward through a record one field at a time. Pressing Shift+Tab moves you back to the previous field.

Starting with FileMaker Pro 7, you can specify that any or all of the Tab, Return, and Enter keys advance to the next field. In Layout mode, choose Format ⇨ Field/ Control ⇨ Behavior (Option+⌘+K/Alt+Ctrl+K) to display the Default Field Behavior dialog shown in Figure 8-10. Note that it is inadvisable to allow Return/Enter to advance from one field to the next if the field you're advancing to might contain multiple lines of text, such as the Notes fields in Chapter 4's Address Book Advanced database. If one or more fields are selected when choosing this command, any options you set apply only to the selected fields. If no fields are selected, you are setting a default behavior.

You cannot tab into a Summary or Calculation field because you cannot edit or manually enter data in these types of fields. (The only permissible action in these fields is copying the contents.) To select a Summary or Calculation field for copying, you must click the field with the mouse.

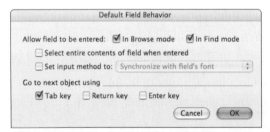

Figure 8-10: Specify which key(s) advance to the next field in the Default Field Behavior dialog.

You can disallow entry into any field, even by clicking. Select the fields for which you want to disallow entry, choose Format ⇨ Field/Control ⇨ Behavior, and in the Default Field Behavior for "<*fieldname*>" dialog (refer to Figure 8-10), clear the Allow field to be entered In Browse mode check box. Now, even clicking in the field will not allow entry. Similarly, if you disallow the field to be entered in Find mode (see Chapter 9 for details), you will disallow searches involving that field's contents.

Note   By default, when you press the Tab key, the insertion point moves through the fields from left to right and top to bottom. However, you can create a custom tab order by changing to Layout mode and choosing the Layouts ⇨ Set Tab Order command. (See Chapter 6 for details.)

When you are finished entering data in the record, press Return/Enter, choose New Record again, or use the book icon to switch to a different record. The record is immediately evaluated by FileMaker Pro and examined for data validation failures, such as leaving a required field blank. If you've committed any errors, FileMaker Pro will inform you.

Keep in mind that you can enter data in any layout in which fields (other than Calculation and Summary fields) are displayed—including report or mailing label layouts, for example. Of course, because some layouts show different sets of fields, arranged in different orders, some layouts make data entry more convenient than others. Regardless of which layout you use when entering or editing data, a field's new data is recorded in all layouts in which that same field appears. For example, the Address Book Advanced database had two data entry layouts: Work and Home, in previous editions (and you can find that version on the CD-ROM that accompanies this book). The Title, First Name, and Last Name fields are in both layouts. Adding or changing the text in these fields, in either layout, simultaneously changes the text in the other layout. (**Remember:** Every layout is simply a different arrangement or presentation of the data contained in the database.)

Using the data-entry and cursor-control keys

As you're entering data, some keys actually enter data *(data-entry keys)* and others merely move the insertion point *(cursor-control keys)*, either within a field or between fields. The differences between the data-entry and cursor-control keys are explained in the following sections.

The data-entry keys

Data-entry keys do what their name suggests. When you press a data-entry key, a corresponding character is entered in a field at the insertion point. The data-entry keys consist of the letters a–z, the numerals 0–9, and the punctuation keys, as well as these same keys pressed in combination with Shift (Mac/Windows), Option (Mac only), and Shift+Option (Mac only). Return/Enter also acts as a data-entry key. Pressing Return/Enter ends the current line and adds a new line to the field unless you specify in the Default Field Behavior dialog that pressing Return or Enter advances to the next field.

Note

A Windows system's keyboard has two keys named Enter — one on the numeric keypad and one on the main keyboard (to the right of the quote/apostrophe key). On a Mac, these keys are Enter and Return, respectively, and send different codes to the system. When we cite Return/Enter, we are referring to the key on the main keyboard.

Note

Number fields do not accept a Return. You need to enter all numbers on a single line within the field.

You can embed a Tab character within any Text field by pressing Option+Tab/ Ctrl+Tab. By default, tab stops are set every half-inch. To insert a new tab stop for a Text field, click or tab into the field, choose View ➪ Text Ruler, and then click the appropriate position on the ruler. A left tab appears at the spot you clicked, as shown in Figure 8-11. To change the new tab to a right, center, or decimal-aligned tab, double-click the tab stop. The Tabs dialog appears (see Figure 8-12), in which you modify or change the current field's tab stops. To remove a tab stop, click the tab stop indicator and drag it down off the ruler.

Note   When setting a tab stop in Browse mode, you are setting it only for the active field in the current record. If you want to set tabs for another field in the same record or for the same field in a different record, you must set them again. To permanently set tab stops for a field and have it affect all records, switch to Layout mode, select the field, choose Format ➪ Text, click the Paragraph button, and then click the Paragraph dialog's Tabs button to display the Tabs dialog.

Tab stops   Text rules

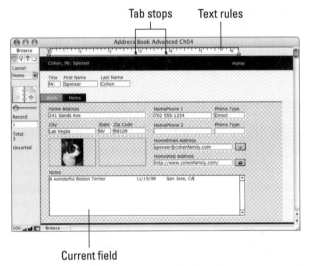

Current field

Figure 8-11: With the text ruler displayed, you can set tab stops for the current field.

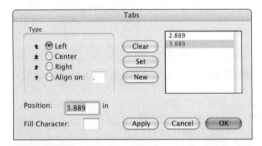

Figure 8-12: The Tabs dialog.

The cursor-control keys

You use the cursor-control keys to move within and between fields. As the name suggests, a cursor-control key merely moves the cursor. Table 8-2 lists the cursor-control keys and their functions.

After you master the cursor-control keys, entering data is relatively straightforward. FileMaker Pro supports the text-entry, cursor-control, and editing functions that you have already learned in other programs (such as pressing Delete/Backspace to remove the previous character and using the Cut, Copy, and Paste commands). Keep in mind, however, that some field types and definitions may restrict the range of acceptable data that you can enter, as described in the next section.

Table 8-2	
Cursor-Control Keys	
Key or Key Combination	*Function*
Tab	Moves to the next field
Shift+Tab	Moves to the previous field
↑	Moves up one line in the current multiline field or to the beginning of a single-line field or one where you're already on the first line
↓	Moves down to the next line in the current multiline field or to the end of a single-line field or one where you're already on the last line
←	Moves one character position left in the current field, if possible; otherwise, does nothing
→	Moves one character position right in the current field, if possible; otherwise, does nothing

Entering different types of data

In FileMaker Pro, each defined field is one of eight different data types: Text, Number, Time, Date, Timestamp, Container, Calculation, and Summary. You cannot enter or edit data in Calculation and Summary fields. The following sections describe data entry and editing procedures that you can use with the other six types of fields. (If you need additional help in determining what kinds of information can and cannot go into the different field types, see Chapter 5.)

Note   Any formatting (other than text attributes such as bolding or underlining) that you set for a field is applied after you enter the data and move to another field.

Typing special characters

On a Mac

On a Mac, you use the Option and Shift+Option key combinations to type special characters, such as symbols and foreign language characters. For example, to type a bullet (•) in most fonts, you press Option+8. If you want to find out where those special characters are hiding—the ones that aren't visible on the keyboard—you can use the Keyboard Viewer, available on the International System Preferences Input Menu tab.

As you hold down Shift, Option, or Shift+Option, Keyboard Viewer shows the characters you can type by pressing a particular letter, number, or punctuation key in combination with the modifier key or keys that you're holding down. A *modifier key* is any key that changes the meaning of a normal key. In regular typing, the modifier keys are Shift and Option. The Ctrl and ⌘ modifier keys—if supported—are under program control and are usually reserved for issuing commands from the keyboard and similar functions. Keyboard Viewer passes the clicked keys directly to the frontmost application.

In Windows

In Windows, you can use an accessory included with every copy of Windows called Character Map. Like the Mac's Keyboard Viewer, this accessory shows all the characters available in all your installed fonts.

Beware: If you need to move a database between the Macintosh and Windows versions of FileMaker Pro, or if you are using a database on a mixed PC and Mac network, be sparing with your use of special characters, especially those dependent upon a specific font. In most cases, these characters will not translate appropriately from one platform to the other unless you have the same font from the same vendor installed on both platforms. See Chapter 16 for details.

Text fields

Text fields can contain any kind of character data, including text, numbers, and other characters. A single Text field can accept up to 2 billion characters of text (over 1,000 times the contents of this book).

If you exceed the dimensions of a Text field (as designed in Layout mode) when entering information into it, the field automatically expands downward to accommodate the excess text. When you leave the field, it reverts to its original dimensions, and the extra text is hidden from view. To see all the information that's stored in the field, you must click or tab into the field (see Figure 8-13). If you want to use the field's contents in a printed report, be aware that whatever you normally see onscreen is also what will appear in the report. If the contents of the entire field are not visible in Preview mode, you should expand the field in Layout mode or edit the field's contents before printing.

Tip   If you have a valid Web address in a Text field (such as http://www.filemaker.com), you can view the referenced Web page in your default browser. Ctrl+click/right-click the field and choose Open *address* from the contextual menu that appears. You must have an active Internet connection for this feature to work.

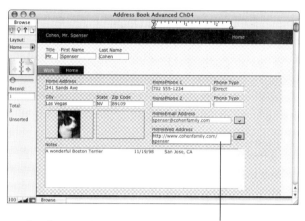

Overflow text is displayed only when the field is selected.

Figure 8-13: Text overflow in a field.

Number fields

FileMaker ignores nonnumeric data in a Number field when performing calculations based on the field, when executing Find requests based on the field, and when recording index entries for the field. Number values can consist of up to 400 characters, combined, on either side of the decimal separator, typed on a single line; no Returns are allowed. Any numeric formatting you have set for the field (with the Format ⇨ Number command in Layout mode) is applied only to the numeric parts of data within the field.

If a number exceeds the width of its field, it displays as a question mark. You can see the entire number by clicking the field or tabbing into it. A question mark also appears in a Calculation or Summary field if the formula cannot be evaluated or if it results in a divide-by-zero error

Tip   Although you can enter any kind of character in a Number field, restricting the field to numeric data might be helpful, particularly if someone else will be doing the data entry. To restrict the field to numeric data, choose the Strict data type: Numeric only validation option when you are defining the Number field. See Chapter 5 for instructions on how to set field validation options.

You use the Format ⇨ Number command (in Layout mode) to set a display format for the field.

Creating multiword index entries

As part of its record-keeping routine, FileMaker Pro creates a separate index for each database field for which the indexing storage option has been turned on. The index consists of every word or value entered in each Text, Time, Date, Timestamp, Number, and Calculation field. If you want an entire phrase from a Text field to serve as an index entry (such as **Jim Knowles**), press Option+spacebar/Ctrl+spacebar between each word in the phrase. This unseen character is called a **non-breaking space** and can be used to visually separate words with a space but still treat the entire phrase as a single word for spell checking, indexing, line wraps, and so on. See Chapter 5 to learn more about field indexing.

Time fields

When entering data in a Time field, you can use either the standard 12-hour format or the 24-hour military time format or enter a specific number of seconds. When you type values, you must use colons to separate the hours, minutes, and seconds (for example, 1:00 PM or 13:00:00). In 12-hour format, if you leave off the AM or PM designation, FileMaker assumes that you mean AM. If you simply enter the number **7**, for example, it is interpreted as 7:00 AM.

Unlike with Number fields, you must leave any extraneous, non-time-related data out of a Time field. FileMaker Pro accepts only legitimate times.

You use the Format ⇨ Time command (in Layout mode) to set a different display format for the time. Note that this formatting command affects only how the time is displayed in the record, not how you enter it.

Date fields

Date fields are similar to Time fields. The maximum length of a Date field is ten characters — up to eight characters for the month (two), day (two), and year (four), plus two separators. You can separate the parts of the date with any non-alphanumeric character, such as a slash or dash (but not a space).

Although four digits should be entered to prevent ambiguity in the year portion of dates, you can also enter two digits to represent most current years. FileMaker Pro 8 will convert two-year digit values to the corresponding four-digit year, up to 70 years prior or 30 years subsequent to the date it was entered. For example, if you enter 3/20/50 in the year 2005, FileMaker Pro will enter that as March 20, 1950; however, if you enter 7/30/28 in the year 2005, FileMaker Pro treats that as July 30, 2028. If you omit the year altogether, FileMaker assumes that you mean the current year (per the system clock).

Caution

The above conversion of two-digit year numbers is not employed when converting databases created in previous FileMaker Pro versions. When performing the conversion, FileMaker Pro assumes that two-digit years fell between 1900 and 1999 and converts the data accordingly. If you plan to convert an older database containing two-digit years, we (and FileMaker, Inc.) recommend that you manually clean up any date data by using the old version before performing the conversion.

You use the Format ⇨ Date command (in Layout mode) to set a different display format for the date. This command affects only how the date is displayed in the record, not how you enter it. Regardless of the date format, leading zeros (as in 04/07/98) are optional. As with Time fields, you must leave any extraneous, non-date-related data out of a Date field. Only legitimate dates are accepted.

In Time and Date fields, you can edit auto-entry times or dates (information that's taken from the system clock) unless the Prohibit modification of value option is set as part of the field's definition. See Chapter 5 for details on setting auto-entry options for fields.

Note If the database was created on a computer that uses U.S. date formats, you enter dates in month-day-year format (11/19/98, for example). If the database was created on a system that uses a non-U.S. format for dates (day-month-year, for example), you have to use that same format when you enter dates. You can use the Mac's International System Preferences (Formats pane) or the Windows Date and Time control panel (Windows 2000)/Regional and Language Options control panel (Windows XP) to set an international date or time format for programs such as FileMaker Pro. If the system date formats on the current computer are different from those where the database was created, the first time you open the file, FileMaker Pro 8 will ask which system formats to employ.

Timestamp fields

Timestamp fields require a date followed by a space and a time, as described above. The date must be entered in the system date format employed when the file was created, and the time must be hours followed by minutes (optionally followed by seconds), in either 12- or 24-hour format. For example, 11/19/1998 07:20 would be a valid Timestamp entry, but 11/19/1998 7 PM would not (no minute portion).

Container fields

Container fields can contain still images, sounds, QuickTime movies, QuickTime audio clips, Object Linking and Embedding (OLE) objects (created on a Windows PC), or any file.

Cross-Reference See Chapter 5 for instructions on working with OLE objects.

Working with Container fields is a little more complicated than working with Text or Number fields. In the case of movies, audio clips, and sounds, the Macintosh or PC needs to have special capabilities that are provided in software, hardware, or a combination of the two (described later in this section).

FileMaker Pro 8 relies on Apple's QuickTime technology to support the inclusion of graphic, audio, and movie data within Container fields. Table 8-3 lists many of the most popular supported graphics and sound file formats. (A *format* is a specific method for storing a particular kind of data.) For a complete list of supported formats, see "Working with data in Container fields" in FileMaker Pro Help.

Table 8-3
Supported Video, Graphics, and Sound Formats

Format	Description
AAC (Advanced Audio Codec)	An audio format based on the MPEG-4 audio specification, most commonly encountered with iTunes and the iTunes Music Store.
AIFF (Audio Interchange File Format)	An audio format commonly used on Macintosh and SGI computers.
AVI (Audio Video Interleave)	A popular container specification for Windows-based video clips (requires that the appropriate codec [compressor/decompressor] for the format employed be present).
BMP (Windows Bitmap)	The default graphics format for Windows; extremely wasteful of space.
EPSF or EPS (Encapsulated PostScript)	A graphics format for detailed drawings; favored by illustrators. The quality of the graphic depends on the output device.
GIF (Graphics Interchange Format)	A compressed image format popular for storing Web graphics and graphics downloaded from online services. Limited to 8-bit (256-color) images.
JPEG (Joint Photographic Experts Group)	Another compressed image format used for Web graphics. Some image information might be lost during compression.
MIDI (Musical Instrument Digital Interface)	A musical description language used to control various electronic musical instruments. MIDI files are instrument-only sound files.
MP3 (MPEG-1 Layer 3 audio)	A widely used format for compressing and distributing songs.
MPEG-1 (Motion Pictures Expert Group)	A common format for distributing video clips.
MPEG-2 (Motion Pictures Expert Group)	A common format for distributing higher-quality video clips (used for SVCD and DVD video). Requires an MPEG-2 codec to be installed.
MPEG-4 (Motion Pictures Expert Group)	A common format for distributing highly compressed video, such as DivX, xvid, and the content for the video iPod.

Format	Description
Photoshop PSD	The native file format of Adobe Photoshop. Unlike many bitmap images, PSD images can have multiple layers.
PICT	A widely used Macintosh-specific graphics format.
QuickTime Movie	QuickTime movie container specification.
TIFF (Tagged Image File Format)	A common multiplatform graphics format. Images can be color or grayscale. Compressed versions are supported but might not be compatible with all programs. Between the Mac and PC, there are many varieties of TIFF, but not all are supported.
WAV	The most common sound format for Windows.
WMF (Windows Metafile)	Windows metafiles are often used in conjunction with Microsoft Office. The clip art supplied by Microsoft and other vendors is in WMF format.

You can use a variety of methods to insert pictures, sounds, and movies into a Container field:

✦ You can insert picture and movie files by using commands in the Insert menu.

✦ If you have an appropriate program or system utility that can open a picture, movie, or sound, you can copy or cut the picture, movie, or sound to the Clipboard and then paste it into the Container field.

✦ If your Mac or PC has a microphone, you can record sounds directly into the field.

FileMaker Pro can import an entire folder of pictures at one time (all operating systems), as well as import pictures directly from any supported digital camera or similar device. Because these are both Import procedures, they are discussed in Chapter 16.

The remainder of this section describes how to use each of these methods to insert data into a Container field.

Note

Most PCs, unlike Macs, do not come with QuickTime preinstalled. If you do not have QuickTime installed, FileMaker Pro dims the Insert ➪ QuickTime menu item, and you will not be able to insert movies into Container fields as described in the following steps. QuickTime for Windows is freely available as a download from www.apple.com/quicktime/download. You can also download the Windows version of iTunes from the same location.

About QuickTime

QuickTime is an Apple technology providing a set of tools and standards for creating, editing, storing, and playing time-based data (such as movies or audio) on Macs and PCs. An important facet of QuickTime is its ability to play movies on any Mac and most PCs. QuickTime movies can require a great deal of disk space, depending upon the compressors used, the frame size, the frame rate, and a variety of other factors. For example, a one-minute movie created using the DV (digital video) compressor employed with most digital camcorders occupies over 200MB!

Getting video data into a Macintosh or PC often requires special hardware (such as a video capture card) or special software (such as iMovie). Although you can use simple utility programs to capture and edit movies, serious QuickTime work requires serious software, such as iMovie, Adobe Premiere, or Final Cut Express (or Pro). If you do not want to create your own movies, many prerecorded QuickTime movies are available as commercial products or can be downloaded from the Web.

STEPS: Inserting a Picture or a Movie into a Container Field

1. Switch to Browse mode by choosing View ➪ Browse Mode (or by pressing ⌘+B/Ctrl+B).

2. Make the Container field the current field by clicking or tabbing into it.

3. To insert a still picture, choose Insert ➪ Picture.

4. To insert a movie or QuickTime audio clip, choose Insert ➪ QuickTime.

   A file dialog appears.

5. If the desired picture or movie isn't shown in the file list, use normal navigation techniques to move to the appropriate disk and folder. For help with file navigation, see Chapter 2.

6. Select the picture or movie that you want to insert.

7. Click Open to place the picture or movie in the field.

Caution

When a movie is inserted into a Container field, only a reference to the movie file is actually stored in the database (rather than the movie itself). This means that if you move the database or the movie (for example, by giving it to someone else or by copying it onto a removable medium such as a disk cartridge), the references to the movies become unresolved. Such unresolved references will result in a prompt to the user saying that the file could not be found. When importing a picture, on the other hand, the actual picture is stored in the database unless you mark the Store only a reference to the file check box.

You can also copy a picture, movie, or sound and paste it into a Container field.

FileMaker Pro 7 added the feature of storing any disk file in your database. Thus, you can store a font, a Microsoft Word document, an Excel spreadsheet, or any other file in a FileMaker Pro database.

STEPS: Inserting a File into a Container Field

1. Switch to Browse mode by choosing View ➪ Browse Mode (or by pressing ⌘+B/Ctrl+B).

2. Make the Container field the current field by clicking or tabbing into it.

3. To insert a file, choose Insert ➪ File.

   A file dialog appears.

4. If the desired file isn't shown in the file list, use normal navigation techniques to move to the appropriate disk and folder. For help with file navigation, see Chapter 2.

5. Select the file that you want inserted.

6. Click Open to place the file in the field.

Caution

Like movies, inserting a file into a Container field stores only a reference to the file rather than the actual file contents. Therefore, if you move the database to another disk, the file references become unresolved. Unresolved references will cause FileMaker Pro to prompt the user for the location of the associated file(s). Thus, it is critical to copy the associated files as well if you copy the database to another machine.

Note

Storing a file is different from OLE Linking (a Windows-only feature) in that double-clicking the Container field will launch the application that created the associated file and open (a copy of) the file, but the changes that you make won't be stored in the database's copy.

STEPS: Pasting a Picture, Movie, or Sound into a Container Field

1. Open the file containing the picture, sound, or movie that you want to copy, using whatever program is appropriate for that media type (QuickTime Player, for example).

2. Within the program, select the item you want copied, and then choose Edit ➪ Copy (or press ⌘+C/Ctrl+C) to copy the item to the Clipboard.

3. Open the FileMaker Pro database into which you want to copy the picture, sound, or movie.

4. Select the Container field into which you want to copy the picture, sound, or movie (making that field the current field).

5. Choose Edit ➪ Paste (or press ⌘+V/Ctrl+V).

Dealing with lost movies or files

When you copy or insert a QuickTime movie or a file into a FileMaker Pro 8 Container field, a link is created to the original movie or file. The actual movie or file data is not copied into the database. Using this method saves disk space but also has important consequences. If you delete the original movie or file or move the database to another computer without also supplying a copy of the movie or file, the link will be broken, and FileMaker Pro won't be able to play the movie or locate the file. However, you will be given an opportunity to insert the disk that contains the data.

If you think that the movie or file is on an already mounted disk (displayed in the Finder or Windows Explorer), you can tell FileMaker Pro where to find the file or ask the program to search for the file. If the file is nowhere to be found, the contents of the Container field are changed to a still picture or a message that the file is missing. If you eventually locate the movie or transfer a new copy of it to your hard disk, the next time you open the database referencing the file, the link will be reestablished

You can record sounds directly into a Container field if you have a Macintosh or PC that is equipped with a microphone, audio CD, TV/radio tuner card, or other audio-capable devices.

STEPS: Recording a Sound Directly into a Container Field

1. Double-click an empty Container field into which you want to record, or select a Container field and choose Insert ⇨ Sound.

   A Record or Sound Record dialog appears, as shown in Figure 8-14.

   Click the control buttons at the top of the dialog to record, stop recording, pause the recording, and play back the recording, respectively. A bar below the buttons indicates the length of the recording. The icon that looks like a speaker indicates the sound level.

Figure 8-14: Recording a sound on a Mac (left) or a Windows PC (right).

2. When you are ready to record, click Record (the first button).

3. Speak or otherwise direct sound into the microphone.

4. When you are done recording, click Stop (the second button).

5. Click Play (the fourth button) to listen to the sound that you recorded.

Playing back stored sounds or movies is simple. To play a sound, simply double-click the field in which it is stored. To play a movie, click the Play/Stop button on the movie's frame (see Figure 8-15) or double-click the movie itself. To stop playback, click the movie once or click the Play/Stop button again. Other movie controls enable you to change the playback volume and step forward or backward through the movie one frame at a time.

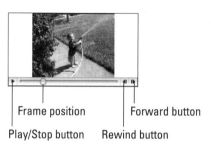

Frame position   Forward button

Play/Stop button   Rewind button

Figure 8-15: A movie and its control bar.

Caution

Some sounds recorded on a Mac might not be playable on a Windows-based computer, depending upon the compression format employed and the decompressors available on the Windows computer.

Working with value lists

Not all data has to be typed or imported. Using the Format ➪ Field/Control ➪ Setup command (in Layout mode), you can format fields to display as drop-down lists, pop-up menus, radio buttons, or check boxes (see Figure 8-16). These formats help speed data entry by providing a set of predefined choices from which you can select. The list of choices is a *value list.* Any of these formats (except drop-down lists) can also have an Other choice appended to it. (For information on creating value lists and attaching them to fields, see Chapter 5.)

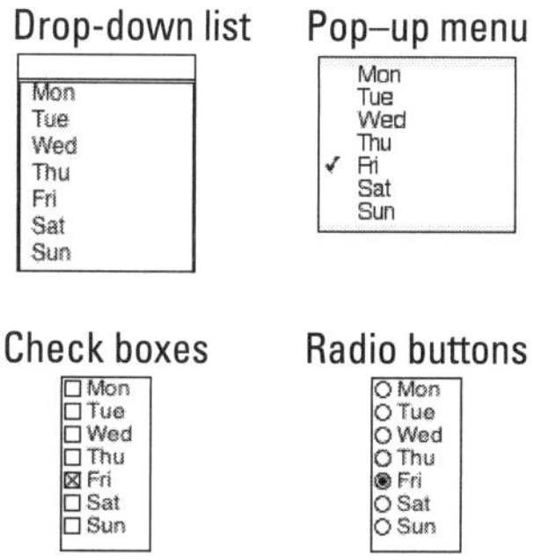

Drop-down list   Pop–up menu

Mon	Mon
Tue	Tue
Wed	Wed
Thu	Thu
	✓ Fri
Fri	Sat
Sat	Sun
Sun	

Check boxes   Radio buttons

☐ Mon	○ Mon
☐ Tue	○ Tue
☐ Wed	○ Wed
☐ Thu	○ Thu
☒ Fri	◉ Fri
☐ Sat	○ Sat
☐ Sun	○ Sun

Figure 8-16: Examples of fields formatted as a drop-down list, a pop-up menu, check boxes, and radio buttons.

The following sections describe how to make a choice from different kinds of value lists.

Choosing an item from a drop-down list

When you click or tab into a field formatted as a drop-down list, a scrolling list of values appears, similar in appearance to a list you often find in Windows dialogs.

STEPS: Choosing an Item from a Drop-down List

1. Click or tab into the field that contains the drop-down list.

   The list automatically expands.

2. Select the item of interest by clicking it once.

   The choice is registered, and the insertion point moves to the next field.

   or

   If you want to enter a response that is not included in the value list, ignore the list and click once in the field, type a different response, and then press the Tab key to move to the next field. (This is the reason drop-down lists don't provide an "other" choice.)

You can also use the arrow keys to choose a particular item. The up arrow and left arrow move up in the list; the down arrow and right arrow move down in the list. In addition, you can type the first letter or two of a value to quickly select that item. Complete your selection by pressing Return/Enter.

A drop-down list can also have an Edit choice. Include such a choice when you want the user to be able to edit the value list on which the field choices are based. (See Chapter 5 for instructions.)

Choosing an item from a pop-up menu

When you click a field formatted as a pop-up menu, a traditional pop-up menu appears. Unlike using a drop-down list, you cannot manually enter a value that is not in the menu unless you have included an Other menu choice.

STEPS: Choosing an Item from a Pop-up Menu

1. Click or tab into the field that contains the pop-up menu.

   Initially, the field is blank.

2. Click the blank box to expose the pop-up menu and then drag to select your choice.

   or

   If an Other value was included in the original field format, you can record a choice that is not listed in the menu by choosing Other from the pop-up menu. Type your choice in the Other dialog that appears (see Figure 8-17) and click OK.

Figure 8-17: The Other dialog.

To clear a record's Other choice, choose Other again and then delete the text you previously entered in the Other dialog.

Note   A pop-up menu can also have an Edit choice. Include such a choice when you want the user to be able to edit the value list on which the field choices are based. (See Chapter 5 for instructions.)

Choosing an item from a group of check boxes

Check boxes can be used to enable users to choose multiple value list options.

STEPS: Choosing an Item from a Group of Check Boxes

1. Click or tab into the field containing the check boxes.

2. To select a particular check box, do one of the following:

   • Click the check box once.

   • Select the check box by using the arrow keys and then pressing Return/Enter or the spacebar.

   • Select the check box by typing the first letter or two of the check box label and then pressing Return/Enter or the spacebar.

   When selected, a check box is marked with an X.

   or

   If an Other value was included in the original field format, you can record a choice that is not listed as an option by clicking or otherwise selecting the Other check box. Type your choice in the Other dialog (refer to Figure 8-17) and click OK. To clear an Other choice from a record, click the Other check box again and then delete the text that you previously entered in the Other dialog.

   Although an alternate choice is recorded, you cannot see it on the layout. You just see that Other has been selected. To determine the exact wording of the choice, click the Other check box again. The Other dialog appears, showing what you originally typed.

Caution   Multiple choices are frequently found in market research surveys. You often see a set of check boxes preceded by the statement Check all that apply. No special procedure is necessary to check several check boxes; simply click all the ones that you want. Note, however, that sorts, calculations, and summaries that are based on a field with multiple choices can produce unexpected results.

Choosing an item from a group of radio buttons

Radio buttons are employed when you want the user to be allowed to choose only one option from among the listed choices.

STEPS: Choosing an Item from a Group of Radio Buttons

1. Click or tab into the field that contains the radio buttons.

2. To select a particular button, click the button once or select the radio button by using the arrow keys, and then press Return/Enter or the spacebar. Or, you can select the radio button by typing the first letter or two of the button's label and then pressing Return/Enter or the spacebar.

   When selected, the radio button blackens.

   or

   If an Other value was included in the original field format, you can record a choice that is not listed as an option by clicking or otherwise selecting the Other radio button. Type your choice in the Other dialog (refer to Figure 8-17) and click OK. To clear an Other choice from a record, mark the Other radio button again and then delete the text that you previously entered in the Other dialog.

   Although an alternate choice is recorded, you cannot see it on the layout. You just see that Other has been selected. To determine the exact wording of the choice, select the Other radio button again. The Other dialog appears, showing what you originally typed.

Note   Although radio buttons are normally used in most programs to present mutually exclusive choices, FileMaker Pro enables you to select multiple radio buttons if you want. Just press Shift as you make your selections. Note, however, that sorts, calculations, and summaries that are based on a field with multiple choices can produce unexpected results.

Changing a value in a value list

To change a value that you have previously selected from a value list, use the following procedures:

✦ *Drop-down lists* and *pop-up menus:* Select a different item from the drop-down list or pop-up menu.

✦ *Radio buttons:* Select a different radio button. The previously selected button or buttons become deselected.

✦ *Check boxes:* Each check box works as a toggle. Select to reverse the state of any given check box.

To change a value that you have manually typed in a drop-down list field or an Other choice that you've selected in a pop-up menu, radio button, or check box field, use normal editing techniques.

Copying and reusing data

If you have already typed a particular piece of data somewhere else — either within or outside the current database — you can use it again without retyping it. The simplest method is to select the data that you want to use from another record, another field, or another program (such as a word processor or graphics program), copy it to the Clipboard, and then paste it into the database field where you want it. (If you'd rather move data from one field or record to another, use the Edit ➪ Cut command rather than the Copy command.)

You can also copy the contents of a field formatted as a value list (a drop-down list, a pop-up menu, radio buttons, or check boxes). Simply select the field and choose Edit ➪ Copy (or press ⌘+C/Ctrl+C). Then, in the field where you want the value to appear, choose Edit ➪ Paste (or press ⌘+V/Ctrl+V). The appropriate information will appear in the field.

Copying data from a field index

You can reuse data that you previously typed in the database by selecting it from the index that FileMaker Pro maintains for the field (assuming, of course, that you have turned on the indexing storage option as part of the field's definition, as explained in Chapter 5). Each index consists of all the words and numbers you've entered in that field. You can use the index to make sure a particular value is always entered in the same form in every record in which it appears. In a customer database, for example, you can use this technique to ensure that you don't have half a dozen different entries for the same company name (such as Apple, Apple Inc., Apple Computer, and Apple Computer Inc.).

STEPS: Entering Data from a Field Index

1. Select the field into which you want to enter data, making it the current field.

   If the field is currently empty, skip to Step 3.

2. If the field currently contains data, you can either replace all or part of that data or append the new information to the existing data as follows:

   • To replace the existing data, select the data.

   • To append the new information to the existing data, click in the field to position the insertion point where you want the new data to be pasted.

3. Choose the Insert ➪ From Index command (or press ⌘+I/Ctrl+I).

   The View Index dialog appears, as shown in Figure 8-18.

Figure 8-18: The View Index dialog.

4. Select the item that you want to insert by typing the first few characters of the item's name, using the arrows and other navigation keys (Home, End, Page Up, Page Down), or using the mouse to select the item directly.

5. Click the Paste button to insert the item in the current field.

The View Index dialog has a check box at the bottom that specifies whether individual indexed words are listed or multiword text strings are displayed as they were originally typed. Showing multiword strings is preferable when working with certain types of fields, such as a company name field, for example. Note that when an individual indexed word is selected, punctuation is not recorded in the index and every indexed word is capitalized, so you might still have to do some minor editing after pasting from the index.

Duplicating a field from the previous record

If data in the current field will be exactly the same as in the corresponding field in the last record you entered or edited, you do not have to retype it. You can copy the data directly into the new field by using the Insert ➪ From Last Visited Record command. (Think of this as a *ditto* command.)

STEPS: Duplicating a Field from a Previous Record

1. Make sure the last record that you entered or changed has the data you want to duplicate.

2. Select the field in the new record into which you want to copy the data.

3. Choose Insert ➪ From Last Visited Record (or press ⌘+' [apostrophe]/ Ctrl+' [apostrophe]).

    The data from the corresponding field in the last record you viewed is immediately entered in the current record.

Creating a duplicate record

Sometimes working with a duplicate record is preferable to creating a whole new record and copying fields, especially if you want to enter a new record that is very similar to an existing one. In the Address Book Advanced database, for example, you might have a new contact at a company that is already in the database. Your previous contact still works there, so you don't want to modify that person's record. Instead, you can duplicate the record and then edit the duplicate.

STEPS: Duplicating a Record

1. Select the record that you want to duplicate.

2. Choose Records ⇨ Duplicate Record (or press ⌘+D/Ctrl+D).

A duplicate record is added to the database and becomes the current record. You can now edit the duplicate.

Entering the current date, time, or user name

You can insert the current date, current time, or the current user's name into a field by choosing the appropriate menu command.

STEPS: Inserting the Current Date, Time, or User Name

1. Select the field into which you want to insert data, making it the current field.

2. Choose one of the following commands from the Insert menu:

- *Current Date* (⌘+– [hyphen]/Ctrl+– [hyphen]) inserts the current system date.

- *Current Time* (⌘+; [semicolon]/Ctrl+; [semicolon]) inserts the current system time.

- *Current User Name* (Shift+⌘+N/Ctrl+Shift+N) inserts the current user name. (See Chapter 7 for information on setting the user name in Application Preferences.)

Editing records

Data is seldom static; information needs to be updated from time to time. In the case of the Address Book Advanced database, for example, people might move, change jobs, and get new titles or phone numbers. You can edit the records for these individuals to keep them current. You can also eliminate records if you no longer require their data.

In a nutshell, editing an existing record involves locating the record, moving into the first field that you want to edit, changing the data in it, and then repeating this process until you have made all desired changes. The procedures discussed previously in this chapter, as well as the way the data-entry and cursor-control keys work, apply to the process of editing data, too.

Note   You can also edit data that is entered automatically, such as the date, time, or a default value, unless you have set the option for Prohibit modification of auto-entered values as part of the field's definition. See Chapter 5 for details.

The usual editing keys that are supported in most programs are also supported in FileMaker Pro. In addition to the data-entry keys discussed previously, you can use the keys, commands, and procedures listed in Table 8-4 while entering and editing data.

Table 8-4 Editing Techniques	
Key, Command, or Procedure	**Function**
Delete (Mac); Backspace (PC)	Deletes the character to the left of the insertion point; or if text is selected, deletes the selection; also deletes contents of Container fields
Del (Apple extended keyboards); Del or Delete (PC)	Deletes the character to the right of the insertion point; or if text is selected, deletes the selection; also deletes contents of Container fields
⌘+X/Ctrl+X or Edit ⇨ Cut	Deletes the current selection within a field and places a copy of it on the Clipboard
Clear (Mac) or Edit ⇨ Clear	Deletes the current selection within a field without placing a copy of it on the Clipboard
⌘+C/Ctrl+C or Edit ⇨ Copy	Copies the current selection within a field and places it on the Clipboard
⌘+V/Ctrl+V or Edit ⇨ Paste	Pastes the contents of the Clipboard into a field at the current insertion point
⌘+A/Ctrl+A or Edit ⇨ Select All	Selects the entire contents of the current field
Double-click	Selects the current word within a field
Triple-click	Selects the current line within a field
Quadruple-click	Selects the current paragraph within a field
Quintuple-click	Selects all text within the current field

STEPS: Modifying a Record

1. With the database open, find the record that you want to modify and make it the current record.

2. Tab into or click to select the first field you want to modify.

3. Edit the data by using normal editing procedures.

4. Tab into or click the next field you want to modify, and edit the data. Continue editing in this manner until you have made all changes you want to make.

As you edit and move from field to field, FileMaker Pro evaluates the changes. FileMaker will notify you if it discovers an error.

5. When you have finished editing the current record, press Enter or switch to another record.

If you make an inadvertent change to a field, you can often correct it by choosing the Edit ➪ Undo command (or by pressing ⌘+Z/Ctrl+Z). The wording of the Undo command changes to reflect the most recent undoable action, such as Undo Typing. Note that Undo is available only for the most recent action you performed. For example, if you type some text and then press the Delete/Backspace key to remove a character, you can only undo the single character deletion — *not* the typing.

Tip
FileMaker Pro has a powerful form of Undo. To undo all changes made to the record since you made it the current record, choose Records ➪ Revert Record.

Tip
Changing the format of a field is also editing (applying italics or boldface to a word for emphasis, for instance). If you can't remember the keyboard shortcuts or don't feel like dragging the mouse pointer all the way to the top of the screen to choose the appropriate command, you can use the contextual menu.

Within any field, select the characters of interest, press the Mac's Control key, and click the mouse button or, if you're running Windows or have a multibutton mouse on a Mac, right-click. A context-sensitive menu appears from which you can choose character formatting commands and standard editing commands. Note that other commands, such as the Insert commands, are also available from these contextual menus.

Deleting records

Unneeded records are best deleted, rather than allowing them to take up space and distract you from your important data.

STEPS: Deleting the Current Record

1. Locate the record that you want to delete and make it the current record.

2. Choose Record ➪ Delete Record (or press ⌘+E/Ctrl+E).

   An alert appears, asking you to confirm that you want to delete the record.

3. Click Delete to remove the record or click Cancel to dismiss the alert without deleting the record.

Caution
Before you delete a record, think carefully about whether you need the information it contains. After you delete the record, it is gone for good. You cannot get it back by using Undo.

Replacing data in multiple records

You can replace data in several records at the same time with the Records ⇨ Replace Contents command. One handy use of this command is to reorder and renumber serialized records that have been mixed up after records were imported from other sources. Because the Replace Contents command is best used on a limited group of records (rather than on a whole database), coverage of this topic is postponed until the next chapter, where finding and selecting groups of records are discussed.

Mass deletions are often performed on *found sets* (groups of records that are identified by one or more Find requests). For example, in a client database, you might want to delete records for any person or company that hasn't done any business with your firm in the last several years. After performing the appropriate Find operation, you can choose Records ⇨ Delete Found Records to eliminate those records. If the found set consists of all records in the database, the command is worded as Records ⇨ Delete All Records. The Delete Found Records and Delete All Records commands are also discussed in Chapter 9.

Caution As is the case with deleting individual records, deleting the found set or all records are not undoable actions. If you plan on wholesale deletions (via the Delete All Records or Delete Found Records command), making a backup copy of the database before you delete the records is a good idea. Old data is sometimes useful, so erring on the conservative side is often best.

Using the spell checker

Depending on the type of database with which you are working, FileMaker Pro's spell checker might be helpful. You can instruct the program to check spelling as you type or to check it on command (to examine a particular layout, record, group of records, or a text selection). You access the spell checker and spelling options by choosing commands from the Edit ⇨ Spelling submenu. Or you can avail yourself of FileMaker Pro 8's new automatic underlining of unrecognized words (with the accompanying shortcut menu of suggested changes). The spell checker is discussed in Chapter 11.

Summary

✦ You use Browse mode to view records within an existing database, to enter new records, and to modify or delete existing records.

✦ Databases can have multiple layouts, serving different purposes, such as data entry and reports. You select layouts in Browse mode from the Layouts menu.

✦ You can display the records within a database one per screen, as a scrolling list, or as a spreadsheet-style table.

✦ The book icon enables you to move from one record to another, to an approximate position within the database, or to a specific record number. When a database is displayed in list form (View as List) or table form (View as Table), the scroll bar functions in much the same way as the book icon.

✦ FileMaker Pro databases can store still-picture, sound, and moving-picture data in many file formats as well as (references to) any desired file of any type of (on Windows) OLE objects. Only one copy of a given sound or picture is stored in the particular database's library, no matter how many records contain that sound or picture. You can specify whether each sound or picture is stored within the database or whether only a pointer to the element's location on disk is recorded.

✦ FileMaker Pro maintains an index for each database field in which the indexing storage option has been turned on. The index contains every word and number that has been entered in the field. To improve consistency, entries can be made into fields directly from the index. Container, Calculation, and Summary fields cannot be indexed.

✦   ✦   ✦

Searching for and Selecting Records

I n Chapter 8, you learned about browsing database records by using the book icon. Although this method works well when browsing a small database, using it to deal with larger databases is both tedious and cumbersome. And Browse mode is no help at all when you want to identify *groups* (subsets) of your records. In working with the Address Book Advanced database, for example, you might want to see all your business contacts, excluding friends and relatives.

New Feature FileMaker Pro 8 introduces a Quick Find capability to Browse mode so that you can find all records matching the selected text. Thus, you need to have located at least one record already containing the desired value.

Find mode provides a way to locate individual records and to group records that share some characteristics. Within Find mode, you can quickly search all records in a database for information matching the contents of a field (such as a particular last name or a known telephone number). You can also create groups of records that share a characteristic (such as all your business contacts or everyone within a certain ZIP code). Going well beyond simple searches, Find mode provides powerful tools for locating and working with individual records and groups.

Find Mode Basics

Find mode does much more than make record browsing easier. The immediate effect of a Find request is to change the set of records that you're currently browsing — that is, the ones that are visible. After performing a Find, the remaining visible records are referred to as the *found set*. When you want to see only one particular record, you can search by using a field that contains unique data, such as a Social Security number, phone number, inventory code, or customer ID number. Performing a Find is often an important part of preparing reports. For example, in a prospective customer database, you might want to see only your successes or clients for whom you've scheduled a follow-up. To produce such a list, you execute a Find request prior to printing the report.

Switching to Find mode

You can switch to Find mode in three ways, regardless of the mode you're currently in:

✦ Choose the View ➪ Find Mode command or press ⌘+F/Ctrl+F.

✦ Click the Find (magnifying glass) mode button at the top of the status area.

✦ Choose Find from the mode pop-up menu at the bottom of the database window.

Using Find mode tools and functions

Figure 9-1 shows the Inventory database (one of the templates provided in FileMaker Pro 8) in Find mode. As you can see, Find mode has more status area controls than Browse mode but fewer than are present in Layout mode.

The Browse mode tools are also available in Find mode. You can switch to a different layout by clicking the Layouts menu below the mode buttons in the status area. You can change the current magnification at which the database is displayed by clicking the zoom in and zoom out buttons below the status area. You can also toggle the status area display by clicking the hide/show status area button at the bottom of the document window. All these controls work as they do in Browse mode (described in Chapter 8).

The Symbols pop-up menu (see Figure 9-2) plays an important role in Find mode. This menu contains special symbols that you can use to specify search criteria. With these symbols, you can search for values that are less than, equal to, or greater than a specified value; fall within a range of values; and so on. For instance, you can search for all records that have an entry in the Last Name field that begins with the letter *H* or later in the alphabet. You can also look for invalid values. Read more about using these symbols in the section, "Matching all criteria: AND searches," later in this chapter.

Book

Layouts menu

Mode buttons   Enter search criteria in corresponding layout fields

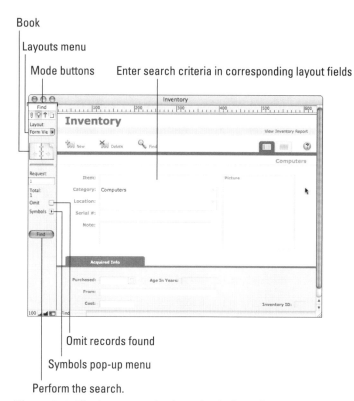

Omit records found

Symbols pop-up menu

Perform the search.

Figure 9-1: The Inventory database in Find mode.

Figure 9-2: The Symbols pop-up menu.

Finding Records

Suppose you work in the marketing department of a small company. While you were at lunch, your receptionist took a message for you and then left for lunch, too. Unfortunately, you can't make out anything other than that the caller's last name is Thompson and the call was urgent. You don't want to wait until the receptionist returns from lunch to find out who called and what the phone number is. What do you do?

Using your Address Book Advanced database, you can search through all your contacts for a Thompson. An examination of the found records ought to give you an idea about who this eager person might be. The following steps show you how to do it.

STEPS: Searching for a Particular Contact

1. Launch FileMaker Pro and open the Address Book Advanced database that we created in Chapter 4 (and which is on the companion CD).

   The Form layout appears, showing names and phone numbers. (If the database opens to a different layout, use the Layouts menu to switch to the correct layout.)

2. Switch to Find mode by using the mode pop-up menu, the Find mode button, choosing View ➪ Find Mode, or pressing ⌘+F/Ctrl+F.

   A blank Find request appears (refer to Figure 9-1). You enter search criteria into the Find request.

3. Type **Thompson** in the Last Name field.

4. Click the Find button.

   FileMaker Pro searches for all records that contain the last name *Thompson* and displays one record with that name. Because only one record was found that matches your criteria, you call Mr. Thompson to discover that he needs to place a large rush order and would have called a competitor if you hadn't responded so quickly.

This example of using Find mode shows the basic steps involved in locating specific database records. With the database open, you switch to Find mode and choose a layout showing the fields containing the information you seek. You then enter search criteria into the layout's fields and click the Find button. Finally, you examine the *found set* — the set of all records resulting from a Find operation. (Records that don't match your search criteria are automatically hidden from view; that is, they are *not* part of the found set.)

Searches are performed on the contents of one or more fields in every record in the database. You can look for an exact match in a given field, such as all records that contain *Thompson* in the Last Name field. You can also look for records that contain only partial matches (matching one set of criteria or another), as well as for records that contain specific pieces of information in two or more fields.

As soon as you click the Find button, FileMaker Pro locates any matching records and switches to Browse mode, displaying only the found set. The number of records in the found set is shown beneath the book icon. The rest of the records in the database are temporarily hidden from view. You can then browse — as well as sort or print — the found set as you would normally browse the entire database. To make all the records visible again when in Browse mode, choose Records ➪ Show All Records or press ⌘+J/Ctrl+J. To make all records visible from Find mode, choose Requests ➪ Show All Records (or press ⌘+J/Ctrl+J).

Note   The search operations described here are called *filters* in some other database products and database-related literature. If you're familiar with Excel, for example, you will see similar search constraints referenced as filters.

When performing a standard Find, FileMaker Pro searches *all* records in the database, regardless of which records are in the current found set. You can, however, conduct additional Finds based on the current found set — rather than on the entire database — by *extending* or *constraining* the found set. These search capabilities are discussed later in this chapter.

Matching all criteria: AND searches

The simplest Find operation consists of searching for records that match all of one or more specific criterion/criteria. The preceding scenario — in which you combine a single-field search with manual browsing of the found set — is an example of using a single search criterion. You can also conduct multiple-field searches; all you need to do is enter information in each field on which you want to search.

For example, to locate all Thompsons in the state of Washington, you would use two criteria. You would enter **Thompson** in the Last Name field and **WA** in the State field. To further narrow the search, you can enter information in as many additional fields as you like. This type of multifield search is called an *AND search*. When you type search instructions in multiple fields, you're asking to identify only those records that match *all* the criteria (Last Name = Thompson AND State = WA, for example).

When you enter search criteria by simply typing some text or numbers into a field, FileMaker Pro not only locates records that exactly match the specified information, but also finds records that contain the search string at the beginning of any word within the field. Thus, if you enter *Smith,* FileMaker Pro finds not only Smith but also Smithy, Smithers, and Bobby Joe Smith. You can restrict searches to exact matches if you want (only a real Smith, for example). Refer to the section on "Matching text exactly," later in this chapter.

If no records are found that satisfy all your search criteria, a dialog appears telling you that. (See Figure 9-3.) You can either click the Modify Find button to return to the Find request and change the criteria or click Cancel to return to Browse mode.

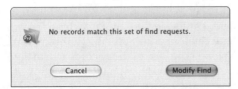

Figure 9-3: No matches were found.

Using symbols in search criteria

To narrow a search, you can include special symbols in any or all of the search criteria. You can select symbols from the Symbols pop-up menu (in the status area), or you can type them directly into the appropriate fields on a Find layout. As shown in Table 9-1, some symbols must precede the search string, others must surround it, and still others must be embedded within it. In the section, "Matching Special Items" (later in this chapter), the proper use of each kind of search symbol is discussed.

	Table 9-1 **Find Symbols**	
Symbol	**Meaning**	**Example**
<	Less than	<50000 (Find persons who make less than $50,000 per year.)
≤	Less than or equal to	≤5 (Find cities with annual rainfall less than or equal to 5 inches.)
>	Greater than	>7/4/94 (Find any date after July 4, 1994.)
≥	Greater than or equal to	≥10:43 (Find any time that is equal to or later than 10:43 a.m.)
=	An exact word match	Match exactly a whole word portion of the field's contents. (For example, =Toys will find Toys "R" Us but won't find Tolstoy.)
...	Data within a range	80210...80218 (Find ZIP codes that fall within that range.)
!	Duplicate values	! (Entered in an ID field, selects all records with duplicate ID numbers.)
//	Current date	// (Selects all records with today's date in the chosen Date field.)

Symbol	Meaning	Example
?	Invalid dates or times	? (Entered in a Date or Time field, finds all records with invalid dates or times.)
@	Wildcard for a single character	B@ (Finds Band, Bend, Bind, and Bond.)
#	Wildcard for a single numeric digit	1#3 (Finds 103, 113, 123, 133, 143, 153, 163, 173, 183, 193.)
*	Wildcard for zero or more characters	B*S (Finds BS, bus, bats, and business.)
" "	Literal text	"Homer" (Finds Homer Simpson, Homer's Iliad, and Hi there, Homer!.)
~	Relaxed search	For Japanese text. (Finds matches that don't differentiate between Hiragana/Katakana and various other input differences. Field must be Japanese-indexed.)
==	A Field content match	Match the entire contents of the field. (For example, == Toys will only match Toys, not Toys "R" Us.)

Matching one criterion or another: OR searches

At times, you might want to search for all records that match any of two or more criteria sets. This kind of search is known as an OR search — as in, "Find all records that match this set of criteria OR that set." For example, you might want to find all Smiths who live in either California or New York. The manner in which you specify an OR search is quite different from trying to match all of several criteria (that is, an AND search). To create an OR search, you must fill out a separate Find request for each criterion by choosing Requests ➪ Add New Request. FileMaker Pro combines the results of the Find requests into a single found set. This found set combines all records that match *any* set of search criteria.

STEPS: Performing an OR Search

1. Open the database in which you want to search, and then switch to a layout that shows the fields you want to use for criteria and the fields you want to view.

2. Switch to Find mode by clicking the mode pop-up menu, choosing View ➪ Find Mode, clicking the Find mode button, or pressing ⌘+F/Ctrl+F.

   A blank Find request appears.

3. Enter the first criterion into the appropriate field.

4. *Optional:* If you want to use additional criteria for this Find request (Last Name = Jones *and* Salary < 25000, for example), tab to the appropriate fields and enter the criteria.

5. Choose Requests ➪ Add New Request or press ⌘+N/Ctrl+N.

The database window is cleared, and a new blank Find request form appears.

6. Enter the criteria for this Find request into the appropriate field or fields.

7. Repeat Steps 5 and 6 until you have created all necessary Find requests.

8. Click the Find button.

All Find requests are evaluated. The found set is presented, consisting of all records that satisfied the criteria in at least one Find request.

Whenever you click Find, all previous searches are cleared. If you want to repeat the most recent search, choose Records ➪ Modify Last Find (or press ⌘+R/Ctrl+R) in Browse mode. To find out more about performing multiple Find requests, see "Creating additional Find requests," later in this chapter.

Matching different kinds of text

By using one of the special Find symbols (refer to Table 9-1), you can make FileMaker Pro do more than locate matches for single words. You can look for a specific text string, accepting no substitutes (*Smith,* but not *Smithers,* for example). You can also look for text that contains certain words or phrases. As an example, you can search a Notes field for all instances of the word *email* — regardless of where the word falls within the field. You can also use this technique to look for text fragments that aren't in a field's index, such as consecutive groups of letters (*mith,* for example). However, such non-index searches can take longer to perform, especially in large databases.

Matching text exactly

In a Find request, using the equal sign (=) in a field tells FileMaker Pro to look only for an exact full word match (case-insensitive) to the text that you have entered some-where within the contents of the field. A *word* in this context refers to a sequence of characters delimited by spaces or punctuation. For example, to find all customers whose last name is Schwartz, you enter **=Schwartz** in the Last Name field. This search will also find customers with the last name of Schwartz-Brown but won't find cus-tomers whose last name is Schwartzkopf.

Using the double-equal sign (==) in a field tells FileMaker Pro to look for only those records where the search criteria you have entered exactly matches the contents of the field. To find all customers whose last name is Schwartz but *not* those with a last name of Schwartz-Brown (or any other variation), you enter **==Schwartz** in the Last Name field.

To locate an exact match to a phrase, enter the phrase but precede each word with an equal sign (for example, **=Sinbad =Schwartz**).

Individual Finds aren't the same as multiple Find requests

Each time you switch to Find mode and issue one or more Find requests, two important things happen. First, regardless of which records are currently visible, FileMaker Pro considers all records in the search. Second, if you have created multiple Find requests (to conduct an OR search), all requests are carried out at the same time.

Every Find request starts from square one; the effects are not cumulative. For example, if you conduct two separate Find operations — the first searching for Smiths from California and the second searching for Smiths from New York — when you execute the second search, only the Smiths from New York appear in the found set. On the other hand, if you conduct a single Find operation that contains two Find requests — one for California Smiths and another for New York Smiths — the found set shows you all Smiths who are either from California *or* from New York.

Note that unlike versions prior to FileMaker Pro 7, FileMaker Pro 8 will allow you to conduct additional searches that begin from the current found set rather than reexamining the entire database. See "Working with Found Records," later in this chapter, for instructions on extending or constraining the found set.

Finding text alphabetically above or below a value

You can also look for records that contain values that are less than, less than or equal to, greater than, or greater than or equal to a given value by using the appropriate mathematical symbols. For example, entering ≥**Schwartz** in a Last Name field searches for all last names that are either Schwartz or come alphabetically after Schwartz. To identify only those records for persons with a last name greater than but not including Schwartz (that is, those that come after Schwartz), use the greater-than symbol instead — as in >**Schwartz.**

Using wildcard characters for partial matches

You can search for records containing a specific group of letters. To do so, use wildcard characters to represent the missing letters. FileMaker Pro supports @, #, and * as wildcards. The @ symbol stands for a single character, the # symbol stands for a single numeric digit (0–9), and the * symbol represents a group of characters of any length, including zero characters.

If, for example, you want to find all seven-letter names that begin with John, use three @ signs in the last three positions of the search criterion (=**John@@@**). Searching for this string of letters finds Johnson and Johnley but not Johnston (because it contains eight letters rather than seven). To find all values that start with a particular group of letters (such as John), you merely need to enter the exact group without any wildcards following it. Searching by using **John** will find John, Johnson, Johnley, and Johnston. (You can also include the asterisk wildcard, if you like — such as **John*** — although it isn't necessary.)

You can also use wildcard characters in the middle of a word. For example, to find all last names that begin with Smith and end with the letter *n*, enter **Smith*n** in the Last Name field. FileMaker Pro finds Smithson, Smithsonian, and so on. To find words that differ only by a single character, use the @ sign. For example, searching for **Sm@th** finds both Smith and Smyth.

Searching for non-indexed (literal) text

The preceding text search methods find only indexed text items. You will recall that FileMaker Pro can create an index for any Text, Number, Date, Time, Timestamp, or Calculation field (read Chapter 5), keeping a record of each word or value in the field for all records in the database. (To enable indexing for a given field, choose File ➪ Define ➪ Database, select the Fields tab, double-click the field's name, click the Storage tab in the dialog that appears, shown in Figure 9-4, and set Indexing to either All or Minimal.)

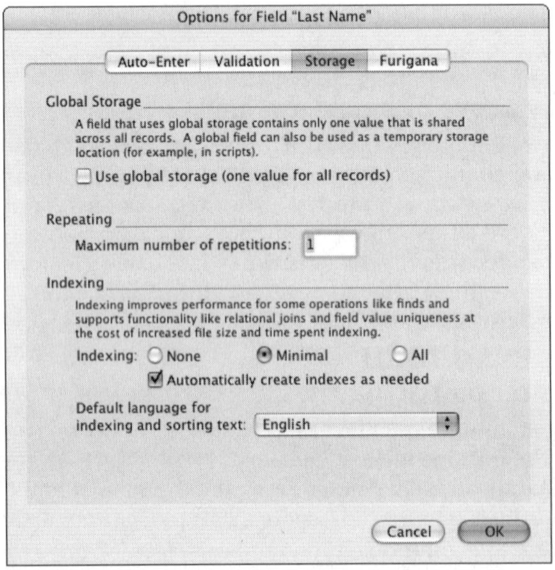

Figure 9-4: Enabling indexing for a field.

If you want to look for information that isn't part of a field's index (including phrases whose component words aren't separated by Option+space/Ctrl+space characters), you have to enclose the search text in double quote marks. (When entering data, you can press Option+spacebar/Ctrl+spacebar between words to force FileMaker Pro to index a phrase rather than the individual words that make up the phrase.) If you need to include punctuation marks in your search string, you *must* use this method to search for them, as in **"Johnson, Jr."**

FileMaker Pro 7 introduced a new indexing option for Text fields (or Calculation fields returning Text values): Minimal vs. All. Selecting Minimal results in an index similar to a numeric field's index, using up to the first 100 characters of each *paragraph* (sequence of characters terminated by end-of-field or carriage return) value in the Unicode Collation Algorithm. Selecting All results in indexing every word of the field (similar to the indexing in previous versions). Word indexes of large fields can take up a great deal of disk space, and FileMaker, Inc. recommends Minimal be selected for most fields. However, if you expect to do frequent searches for specific words in one or more fields, those fields might benefit from the All option.

You can type the quotation marks directly if you want, but FileMaker Pro provides an alternate method. Choose " " *literal text* from the Symbols pop-up menu (refer to Figure 9-2). Doing so immediately enters both a pair of quotation marks and places the insertion point between them.

More about Find Requests

Whenever you switch to Find mode and enter information on the blank form that appears, you're creating a Find request. FileMaker Pro lets you manipulate Find requests in several ways. You can delete requests or repeat requests, perhaps editing them slightly to alter the search criteria. For example, if you looked for all Smiths from California one time, you could repeat the request and change **CA** to **NY** to find all Smiths from New York.

Creating additional Find requests

Creating a new Find request is easy. FileMaker Pro creates the first Find request automatically when you switch to Find mode. You might want to create additional requests, however, when searching for information that matches one of several criteria: that is, an OR search.

You have two options when creating additional Find requests. You can create an entirely new Find request (by choosing Requests ➪ Add New Request or pressing ⌘+N/Ctrl+N), or you can duplicate the current Find request and edit its contents (by choosing Requests ➪ Duplicate Request or pressing ⌘+D/Ctrl+D). Until you click the Find button to execute the Find requests, you can use the book icon to page through all current Find requests, just as you use it in Browse mode to flip through records or in Layout mode to flip through layouts.

Repeating and editing Find requests

When you finish entering all the search criteria and click the Find button, FileMaker locates all matching records and displays them in Browse mode as the found set. If FileMaker Pro does not find any matches, you'll see the alert shown in Figure 9-3, and you can either modify and repeat the search, or you can cancel the search and return to Browse mode.

When you again switch to Find mode, FileMaker Pro presents you with a new (blank) Find request form. In some cases, however, you might want to use your previous Find requests as the basis for a new search. For example, if a search for Smiths in California doesn't yield results, you might want to go back and look for Smiths in Oregon. By using the Records ⇨ Modify Last Find command, you can return to the last search, preserving all Find requests that you defined within it. You can then edit any or all of these Find requests to match any new search requirements that you have.

STEPS: Repeating or Modifying the Previous Set of Find Requests

1. From Browse mode, choose Records ⇨ Modify Last Find (or press ⌘+R/Ctrl+R).

   FileMaker Pro displays the previous set of Find requests.

2. Choose the previous Find request you want to use.

   • To simply repeat the last Find request(s), go directly to Step 4.

   • If multiple Find requests appear, use the book icon to move to the request(s) you want to edit.

3. Use normal editing procedures to change the search criteria.

   You can also add more requests to the set, duplicate any of the requests, or delete requests (as long as at least one still remains) by choosing the appropriate command from the Requests menu (Add New Request, Duplicate Request, or Delete Request, respectively).

4. Click the Find button.

   The Find request or requests are executed.

Tip

If you find that you've made a mistake when entering search criteria (particularly while modifying the most recent request), you can choose Requests ⇨ Revert Request to restore the request to its state when you entered Find mode.

Deleting Find requests

If one or more requests within the current set of Find requests don't meet your needs, you can get rid of them.

To delete Find requests, use one of the following methods:

✦ To specify search criteria from scratch (effectively deleting all current Find requests), choose View ⇨ Find Mode again (or press ⌘+F/Ctrl+F).

✦ To delete a specific Find request, use the book icon to move to the request that you want to delete and choose Requests ⇨ Delete Request (or press ⌘+E/Ctrl+E). Repeat this procedure for each request you want to delete.

Note that you can only delete Find requests when you have created more than one. If a Find consists of only a single request, the Delete Request command is disabled (dimmed). Rather than delete the request, you can simply alter it, employing the correct criteria.

Tip   If you think you'll be using a particular Find request over and over again, you can create a script that remembers your Find request and performs the Find automatically. Scripts are excellent for Finds with multiple requests or complex criteria. (See Chapter 15 for more details on writing scripts.)

Matching Special Items

As mentioned earlier in the chapter (in the section, "Using symbols in search criteria"), you can employ special symbols in your search criteria by choosing them from the Symbols pop-up menu (refer to Figure 9-2 and Table 9-1). By using these symbols, you can find all records that have values between two extremes, such as two dates, times, ZIP codes, or salaries. You can also use symbols to perform database maintenance by searching for erroneous or duplicate values, and then editing or eliminating the records containing them.

Matching values in a range

You use the ellipsis symbol (...) to indicate values within a range. You can look for alphabetic values between two text strings, numeric values between two calculated or numeric items, or chronological values between two times or dates (note that the boundary values are included within the range). For example, you can search for all records that have last names between Smith and Zane or for all records created between January 1 and December 31, 2002. In the former case, you enter **Smith...Zane** in the Last Name field; in the latter case, you type **1/1/2002...12/31/2002** in the Date field.

To enter a range in a search field, separate the two values by typing three periods or by choosing the ... symbol from the Symbols pop-up menu. On a Mac, you can also press Option+; (semicolon) to create an ellipsis.

Matching the current date

Assuming the system clock in your Macintosh or PC is set correctly, you can easily search for records that match the current date, even if you don't happen to know it yourself. This feature is especially useful in scripts because you don't need to enter specific information. Instead of having to re-create the script each time (changing the date from 8/5/05 to 8/18/05, for example), you can just instruct the script to find today's date — whatever that date happens to be. (See Chapter 15 for more information on scripts and their uses.)

Note   To check or set your computer's system clock, open the Date & Time System Preferences item (Mac) or Date and Time Control Panel (Windows).

STEPS: Finding All Values That Contain the Current Date

1. In Find mode, move the cursor to the Date field in which you want to search.

2. Choose the Today's Date option from the Symbols pop-up menu or type a pair of slashes (//), as shown in Figure 9-5.

Symbol for Today's Date

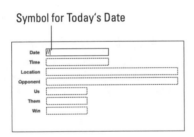

Figure 9-5: Searching for today's date.

3. Click Find to execute the search.

Searching for empty fields

Occasionally, errors creep into a database. For example, you might create extra records and forget to fill them in, or you might get interrupted and neglect to complete the current record. FileMaker Pro provides a way for you to look for all records that have no information in one or more fields. You simply enter only an equal sign (=) in that field. You can then correct or delete the erroneous records.

If you want to find all records that contain one or more blank fields, you need to create a separate Find request for each potentially blank field and then click Find. If you enter all potentially blank fields in a single Find request, FileMaker Pro will find only records in which *all* of these fields are blank. (Remember, when you specify multiple criteria in one Find request, you are conducting an AND search. All criteria must be satisfied in order for a match to be found.) Thus, records that have some fields blank and other fields filled in will not be identified.

The correct procedure is to create multiple Find requests — one for each field that you want to check for blanks. Although this procedure might sound as if it requires a great deal of work, it usually doesn't. In most cases, you want to search for blanks in a small set of critical fields — those that if left blank, would render the record useless (at best) or misleading (at worst).

Searching for values greater or less than a given value

In the "Finding text alphabetically above or below a value" section (earlier in this chapter), you saw that you can use the <, ≤, >, and ≥ symbols to find text that is alphabetically greater or less than a particular value. You can also use these symbols to find numeric, date, time, or timestamp values. For example, to find all records dated on or after January 1, 2000, you would enter ≥**1/1/2000**.

STEPS: Finding Values That Exceed or Are Less Than a Given Value

1. Switch to Find mode.

2. Click the field that you want to use in the search.

3. Choose the appropriate symbol from the Symbols pop-up menu (or type it directly into the field):

    - \> (greater than): Find all items that exceed the value entered.

    - ≥ (greater than or equal to): Find all items that exceed or are exactly equal to the value entered.

    - < (less than): Find all items that are smaller than the value entered.

    - ≤ (less than or equal to): Find all items that are smaller than or exactly equal to the value entered.

To type the ≤ or ≥ symbols, press Option+, (comma) or Option+. (period), respectively. If you don't wish to remember the keystrokes, you can also type <= and >= respectively, and FileMaker Pro will still understand.

4. Type the search value after the symbol that you entered in Step 3.

5. Click Find to execute the search.

The greater than or equal to symbol (≥) and the less than or equal to symbol (≤) are not enterable characters in Windows. If you want to manually enter either symbol rather than using the Symbols pop-up menu, you should type >= or <=, respectively.

Searching for duplicate records

You can use Find mode to help you perform another form of database maintenance: identifying records that have the same information in several fields. Although some people do have the same last names, for example, some of these records might be duplicates. If you've checked your mail recently, you probably noticed that some direct mail firms are sending you multiple copies of their catalog. They have a problem with duplicate database records — the ones that contain *your* name. FileMaker Pro has a special symbol enabling you to find all records having duplicate information in the specified field. After identifying these records, you can browse them to eliminate any exact duplicates.

STEPS: Searching for Duplicates

1. Switch to Find mode.

2. Move to the field whose contents you suspect is shared by two or more records.

3. Choose Duplicates from the Symbols pop-up menu or type a single exclamation point (!).

4. Click Find to execute the Find.

As when looking for empty fields (discussed previously), if you want to find all records that have duplicate values in one or more of several different fields, you need to create a separate Find request for each of these fields. Otherwise, you will find only records that match in *all* potential fields. (Check those catalog mailing labels again. In most cases, you'll note that the labels aren't *exactly* the same. Your name or address might be slightly different, for example.) As a rule, you should include only one Duplicates criterion in each Find request.

Note

Three restrictions apply when searching for duplicates. First, when determining whether data in Text fields is duplicated, FileMaker Pro examines only the first 100 alphanumeric characters of each word in the field. A maximum of 100 characters, including spaces, is examined per field. Second, for two records to be considered duplicates, the word order in the chosen field must be identical. Third, you can search for duplicates only in indexed fields.

Searching for invalid information

Sometimes, you might find that time or date calculations don't yield valid results, particularly when working with data imported from another database or program. To search for records that have invalid dates, times, or timestamps, enter a question mark (?) into a Date, Time, or Timestamp field (or choose Invalid Date or Time from the Symbols pop-up menu).

Finding records that don't match the criteria

When you're trying to narrow a search for very specific kinds of records, you might find that a little "negative logic" is easier to apply than the conventional kind. For example, suppose you want to find all your contacts in every state except California. You can create a separate Find request for each of the other 49 states, but doing so is a lot of work. As an alternative, you can enter **California** in the State field and then elect to *omit* from the found set all records containing California in the State field. FileMaker Pro makes this task easy. Find mode has an Omit check box in the status area (refer to Figure 9-1). Select this check box to turn a conventional Find request into one that hides the found records and shows only the records that are left.

In a series of Find requests, if you use the Omit option in some but not in others, you should put all Find requests that include the Omit option at the end of your list. FileMaker Pro works through all Find requests in the order that you specify. If you put Omit requests first, subsequent Find requests will tend to wipe out their results. For example, if you want to find all records of employees who are older than 25, or have a salary greater than $27,000, or are not from Houston, you create the following three Find requests, making sure that you create the request that uses the Omit option last:

- ✦ >25 (in Age field)
- ✦ >27000 (in Salary field)
- ✦ =Houston (in City field) and Omit check box checked

Remember that whenever you issue multiple Find requests, you are conducting an OR search — looking for records that satisfy any one or more of the Find requests.

If you later want to look at just the records that the Find request(s) omitted, choose Records ➪ Show Omitted Only. Essentially, this command instructs FileMaker Pro to show all records *except* those that are currently being browsed; that is, it reveals all the hidden records while hiding those that are currently visible. Choosing it again toggles back to the original set.

You can also omit records after conducting a Find request, as described in the upcoming section, "Omitting records from a found set."

Working with Found Records

A found set provides more options than just browsing through the records. Many operations you can perform directly relate to the reason you searched for the records. For example, if you search for duplicate records, you probably do so because you want to delete the duplicates. Another thing that you can do with found records is copy them to the Clipboard and then paste them into another database or another program.

Omitting records from a found set

When working with a found set, you might want to temporarily hide some of the found records. For example, if you conduct a search to locate duplicate records, the found set contains both the records you want to keep and the duplicates. Before you can delete the duplicate records, you need to omit the originals from the found set by using the Omit Record or Omit Multiple commands. (Omitting records merely hides them from view, removing them from the found set. The records still remain in the database, however, and can be revealed with the Records ⇨ Show All Records command.) After omitting the originals from the found set, you can delete the duplicates with the Delete All command (discussed in "Deleting found sets," later in this chapter).

STEPS: Omitting a Record from the Found Set

1. Select the record that you want to omit.

   If you're in form view (View ⇨ View as Form), use the book icon to select the record. If you're in list view or table view (View ⇨ View as List or View ⇨ View as Table), you can click in any field to select the record.

2. Choose Records ⇨ Omit Record (or press ⌘+T/Ctrl+T).

   The current record is removed from the found set; that is, it is hidden.

3. Repeat Steps 1 and 2 for each additional record that you want to omit from the found set.

If a found set contains several consecutive records that you want to omit from the found set, you can omit all of them with a single command — Omit Multiple — as described in the following steps.

STEPS: Omitting Consecutive Records from the Found Set

1. *Optional:* If the records to be omitted are not grouped consecutively, you might be able to use a Sort command (⌘+S/Ctrl+S) to group them in the desired manner. See Chapter 10 for information on sorting.

2. Use the book icon to select the first record you want to omit from the found set.

   If the layout is displayed in list view (View ⇨ View as List), you can click in any record to select it.

3. Choose Records ⇨ Omit Multiple or press Shift+⌘+T/Shift+Ctrl+T.

   The Omit Multiple dialog appears, as shown in Figure 9-6.

4. Enter the number of consecutive records to omit.

5. Click the Omit button.

   The records are omitted; that is, they are hidden from view.

Figure 9-6: The Omit Multiple dialog.

If you want to restore all records omitted from a found set, simply choose Records ➪ Modify Last Find (⌘+R/Ctrl+R) to repeat the last Find request. You cannot restore omitted records directly (there's no Reveal or "Un-omit" command), but you can use other methods to view those records again, as you will see in the next section.

Swapping found sets with omitted records

In the stamp want list example presented in the sidebar, "Omit Record can be used with or without a found set," you learned that you could use the Omit Record command to handpick records you want to remove from a found set. On the other hand, those omitted records might be the ones that really interest you at the moment. Suppose, for example, that you want to prepare a list of all stamps that you have no interest in buying. Perhaps you want to take the list to stamp shows and to meetings with dealers to prevent yourself from buying something that you don't want or need. By choosing Records ➪ Show Omitted Only, you can make the omitted records the new found set. Show Omitted Only swaps the remaining records in the found set with all omitted ones. The omitted records then become the new found set.

STEPS: Swapping a Found Set with Records Omitted from It

1. Use the Records menu's Omit Record or Omit Multiple commands to mark those records that you actually want to keep.

2. Choose Records ➪ Show Omitted Only.

   Omitted records become the new found set, and the remaining records are omitted in their place.

Omit Record can be used with or without a found set

Although Records ➪ Omit Record is most frequently used with a found set (following a Find request), you can use it at any time to temporarily hide records. In effect, such use of the Omit Record command manually creates the equivalent of a found set. Suppose, for example, that you're using a database to prepare a list of stamps that you want to purchase from a mail-order dealer. After preparing the want list, you can use the Omit Record command to eliminate several stamps selectively — either because buying them will put you in the poorhouse or because you think they're currently overpriced.

Tip   You can also use Show Omitted Only after issuing a normal Find request. For instance, after examining the records of all club members with delinquent dues payments, you can use Records ⇨ Show Omitted Only to display the records of the members whose dues are current.

Extending and constraining the found set

Prior to FileMaker Pro 6, all Find requests automatically searched the entire database, regardless of whether you were currently browsing all records or a smaller subset. To perform an AND search, you had to enter multiple criteria in the same Find request form. To perform an OR search, you had to create multiple Find requests. You can now perform after-the-fact OR or AND searches by choosing Requests ⇨ Extend Found Set and Requests ⇨ Constrain Found Set, respectively.

For example, suppose you're anticipating a targeted mass mailing to your customers. You start by performing a Find for all clients in the 01775 ZIP code, and you discover 127 matching customers. Because you were prepared to pay for as many as 300 brochures, you *extend* the found set by searching for customers in the 01776 ZIP code. On the other hand, if the results of the initial Find had yielded too many customers, you might *constrain* the found set by performing a second search that eliminated all customers whose last name didn't begin with the letters A–M.

STEPS: Extending or Constraining the Found Set

1. Perform a normal Find. (Switch to the desired layout, enter Find mode, specify search criteria, and click the Find button.)

   FileMaker Pro performs the Find, switches to Browse mode, and displays the found set.

2. Choose View ⇨ Find Mode again.

3. Enter the additional search criteria.

4. Do one of the following:

   • To extend the found set (performing an OR search), choose Requests ⇨ Extend Found Set.

   • To constrain the found set (performing an AND search), choose Requests ⇨ Constrain Found Set.

   FileMaker Pro performs the Find, switches to Browse mode, and then displays the modified found set.

5. If you want to further modify the found set, repeat Steps 2–4.

Copying found sets

You can copy an entire found set of records to the Clipboard. From there, you can paste the data elsewhere — into documents from other applications, for example. Each field is separated from the next by a Tab character, and each record ends with a Return character. (This is commonly known as a *tab-delimited text file*.) To copy a found set to the Clipboard, press Option+⌘+C/Shift+Ctrl+C.

When you press the Option key with the Edit menu open, the Copy command changes to Copy All Records.

Note

This procedure is a quick-and-dirty version of the Export command with tab-delimited as the selected format. The main difference is that you have less control over the particular fields that are copied and the order in which they are copied. Whatever layout is in effect when you issue the command determines the selected fields and their order.

Deleting found sets

One major use for Find mode is to locate records you want to delete from a database. After you have omitted records that you want to save from a found set, removing the remainder of the records from the database is simple.

STEPS: Deleting All Records in the Found Set

1. Enter Find mode and create the Find requests needed to identify the records you want to delete.

2. *Optional:* Examine the found set and use Records ➪ Omit Record to leave out records that you do not want deleted from the database.

3. Choose Records ➪ Delete Found Records.

    An alert appears, asking you to confirm that you want to delete the records in question. (See Figure 9-7.)

Figure 9-7: Record deletions must be confirmed.

Note   The Delete Found Records command you employ in this procedure affects only the visible (browsed) records, not all records in the database. When the found set consists of *all* records in the database, the command is worded Delete All Records.

4. Click the Delete All button to proceed or click Cancel to dismiss the alert without deleting the records.

Caution   As with other Delete commands in FileMaker Pro, you cannot use the Undo command to undo the Delete Found Records or Delete All Records commands. Because you risk significant data loss if you make a mistake when using this command, you might want to make a backup copy of the database using the File ➪ Save a Copy As command (as described in Chapter 2) before issuing either of these irreversible Delete commands.

Replacing values in a found set

Another thing you can do with a found set is simultaneously replace the contents of a single field in all found records (in much the same way as you use a word processor's Replace All command). After using Find requests to locate the particular records in which you want to make the replacement, you can use the Replace command to replace the contents of any single field with data that you specify.

This global replacement procedure is often useful. For example, either of the following situations would be prime candidates for the Replace command:

✦ A company in one of your databases has recently changed its name or moved. Search for the original name of the company, and then use Replace to enter the new name or new address in all found records. If the company has changed both its name and address, use two Replace procedures on the same found set: first the company name and then the address. (You can use this same procedure to ensure consistent wording for text in selected fields. By identifying all records containing Apple in the Company field, for instance, you can use Replace to change all entries to read *Apple Computer, Inc.*)

✦ A major kennel association reclassifies a particular breed of pooch from a non-sporting breed to a working dog. Search for all instances of that breed and then use Replace to change the classification for each of the found dogs.

STEPS: Replacing the Contents of a Field in All Records in the Found Set

1. Switch to Find mode and use one or more Find requests to select the group of records whose contents you want to replace.

This creates the found set. (In this example, we'll search for and replace every instance of *Phillies* with *Pirates.*)

2. In Browse mode, select the field you want to replace by tabbing into or clicking in the field.

   It doesn't matter what record is currently displayed; any record in the found set will suffice.

3. Type the replacement text or value in the field.

4. Choose Records ➪ Replace Field Contents (or press ⌘+=/Ctrl+=).

   The Replace Field Contents dialog appears (see Figure 9-8).

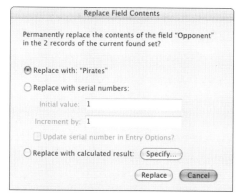

Figure 9-8: Use this dialog to replace the contents of a field with a single text string or value.

5. Select the Replace with option.

   The replacement text or value is shown within quotes. (The quoted replacement string in Figure 9-8 is "Pirates".)

6. Click Replace.

   The specified text string or value replaces the contents of the current field in all the found set's records.

Replacing the contents of a field with a serial number

As you can see in Figure 9-8, you can also use the Replace command to replace the contents of a field in the found set with serial numbers. This option is useful when, for example, you've imported records into a database and have left gaps or otherwise thrown off the existing numbering scheme.

STEPS: Replacing the Contents of a Field in a Found Set with Serial Numbers

1. Switch to Find mode and use one or more Find requests to select the group of records that you want to renumber.

   This creates the found set.

2. In Browse mode, select the field you want to reserialize by tabbing into or clicking the field.

3. *Optional:* Sort the database.

   When the records are reserialized, numbers are assigned according to each record's position within the found set. The first record gets the first new serial number, the second record gets the second number, and so on. By using the Sort command, you can change the order of the records to a more meaningful arrangement. (See Chapter 10 for more information on sorting records.)

4. Choose Records ⇨ Replace Field Contents (or press ⌘+=/Ctrl+=).

   The Replace Field Contents dialog appears (refer to Figure 9-8).

5. Select the Replace with serial numbers radio button.

6. In the Initial value text box, enter the value for the new first serial number to be issued. In the Increment by text box, enter the value by which each successive serial number should increase over the previous number.

7. Click Replace.

Remember that a serial number can contain characters other than numbers. If your serial number is a mix of numbers and text, only the numeric portion of the field will change when the field is reserialized. Also, if the selected field was initially defined as an auto-entry field that would receive a serial number, you may want to select the Replace Field Contents dialog's Update serial number in Entry Options? check box. When reserializing the found set, this option instructs FileMaker Pro to note the last serial number used and to make sure that the next new record created continues the serialization sequence. (It updates the Next Value figure in the Entry Options dialog for the serial number field.)

Some live examples

We realize that after you move beyond a simple one-field search, you can easily get confused. Remembering how to do AND and OR searches, how to look for duplicates, and so on might be difficult for you. Reading about Find mode isn't necessarily the best way to learn about it. You might find it easier to understand if you just create a series of Find requests and see what happens. To make the learning process simpler, we've created a Find Examples database included on the CD accompanying this book, showing examples of many typical Find requests, each prepared as a script that you can execute via a button click.

To use the Find Examples database, click any of the text buttons on the menu screen. FileMaker Pro enters Find mode and displays another screen showing the appropriate Find request. Because the requests are displayed in list view (each line represents a separate Find request), you can see all the necessary requests on this single screen. After examining the requests, click the status area's Continue button. The Find requests execute, and the results display. To return to the menu screen, click the Return to Menu button at the bottom of the screen.

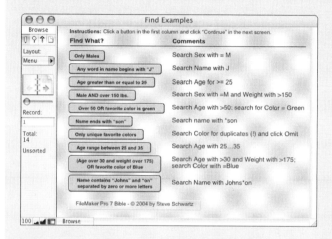

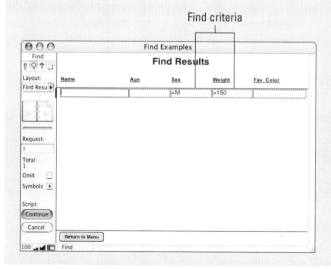

Find criteria

Tip   You can also use the Replace command to create a record-numbering system where none existed before. Simply define a new field to hold the serial numbers, add it to a layout, issue a Records ➩ Show All Records command (⌘+J/Ctrl+J), sort the records (if necessary), select the field, and then issue the Replace command.

Replacing the contents of a field with a calculated result

You can also use the Replace command to replace the contents of a field with a calculated result. Suppose, for example, that you want to increase the salary of a group of employees by 5 percent. After using a Find request to select the set of employees, you would choose the Replace command; select the Replace with calculated result radio button; and in the Specify Calculation dialog that appears (see Figure 9-9), enter either of these formulas:

```
Salary + (Salary * .05)
```

or

```
Salary * 1.05
```

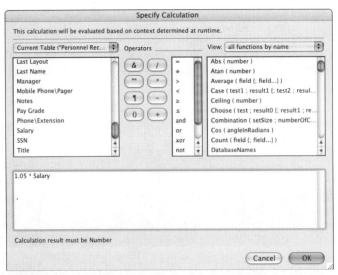

Figure 9-9: Enter the formula that will calculate the new value to be used in the found set.

The result type for the Replace formula must be the same as the replaced field's type (as set in the Define Fields dialog when the field was created). If the field is a Text field, for instance, only a formula that returns a text string is allowed. (To learn about defining fields, refer to Chapter 5.)

Note

When defining a replacement formula, the Specify Calculation dialog that appears works exactly the same as when you're defining a formula for a Calculation field. (See Chapter 5 for more information.)

Working with all records again

When all is said and done, you will probably want to go back to working with all the records in the database. To do so, switch to Browse mode and choose Records ⇨ Show All Records (or press ⌘+J/Ctrl+J). All records that you previously omitted instantly become visible again. (If you're currently in Find mode, the equivalent command is Requests ⇨ Show All Records.)

Finding Matches in Browse Mode

 New Feature

Probably the most common Find operation is to locate all the records matching a specific value — for example, locating all the invoices where a DVD was sold, or finding all the address records in the 89109 ZIP code. In previous versions of FileMaker Pro, as described earlier in this chapter, you had to enter Find mode and create a Find request. Then you would be back in Browse mode with the new found set. FileMaker Pro 8 eliminates the mode shift and manual entry when only one value is in question. As shown in Figure 9-10, you can now select a value (or field) in Browse mode by Control-clicking/right-clicking and choosing Find Matching Records from the shortcut menu that appears.

Figure 9-10: Select from the shortcut menu to do a Find without leaving Browse mode.

As you can also see in Figure 9-10, extending and constraining the found set is also accessible without having to leave Browse mode.

Note   Thank you, FileMaker, for making this very common operation more convenient.

Summary

✦ In Find mode, you can locate records matching specific criteria.

✦ FileMaker Pro performs Find operations on one or more fields in a database. Such operations compare the contents of the fields in each record in order with find matches to the search criteria. Each set of criteria is known as a Find request.

✦ You can use any layout when creating a Find request. Before creating a Find request, you can select the layout you'd like to use by choosing it from the Layouts menu.

✦ All records matching the search criteria are grouped into a found set, which you can then browse in the same manner you would normally browse the entire database. Records that don't match the criteria are temporarily hidden.

✦ You can have multiple Find requests, each of which is evaluated in order.

✦ To conduct an AND search (in which all criteria must be matched), you specify the criteria on a single Find request form. To conduct an OR search (in which any of multiple criteria must be satisfied), you create a series of Find requests.

✦ Find mode supports the use of special symbols, enabling you to search for records within a range of values, for invalid or blank values, for duplicate values, and so on.

✦ You can change a request to find records matching specific criteria to a request omitting these records from the found set. To do so, select the Omit check box on the appropriate Find request.

✦ Other useful activities that you can perform with a found set include manually omitting certain records, swapping the omitted records for those that remain in the found set (creating a found set from the previously omitted records), and deleting the found set. You're also able to copy a found set to the Clipboard for use outside the original database.

✦ If there is only one search criterion and it is an exact match, you can perform your Find request without ever leaving Browse mode.

✦ Normally, every Find operation examines the entire database for records that meet the specified criteria. You can, however, operate on the found set by choosing the Requests menu's Extend Found Set and Constrain Found Set commands.

✦   ✦   ✦

Sorting Records

Issuing Find requests (discussed in Chapter 9) is one way to locate information in a FileMaker Pro database, but Find requests aren't always the most convenient method. Although you can simply flip through records to find information, it can be very time-consuming when working with a large database. The primary reason flipping through records can take so long is because of how FileMaker stores records. Records are stored in the order in which they are entered. Unless you're importing or hand-entering data from an existing database (as described in Chapter 16), your records might not be in any recognizable order.

About Sorting

Consider the Address Book Advanced database you created in Chapter 4. On the first day, you recorded the information for James Johnson when he sent you a letter. Your next several contacts were with Susan Brown, Tom Ziegler, and Paula Short. If you create new records for every person in the order the contacts were made, the records are stored in that order. What you need is a way to change the order of the records so browsing through them is easier, and you don't need to issue a Find request every time you want to locate a specific record. You can change the display order of the records by *sorting* the database.

In life, we're used to seeing information in a particular order. Phone books are organized alphabetically, entries in check registers are arranged by the date of transaction, and so on. In FileMaker Pro, sorting is the process of ordering the records that are being browsed according to the values contained in one or more of the database fields. Both the fields used and the type of sort order imposed on each field (ascending or descending, for example) are up to you. For instance, you can

◆ ◆ ◆ ◆

In This Chapter

Sorting by one or several database fields

Specifying a sort order for a field

Choosing an alternate language for a sort field

Modifying sort specifications

Restoring records to their original order

◆ ◆ ◆ ◆

sort the Address Book Advanced database in ascending order by the Last Name field. After FileMaker Pro completes the sort, the database is arranged so records with last names beginning with A appear first in the database, those beginning with H are near the middle, and records with last names beginning with Z are at the end. Conversely, if you choose descending order, last names beginning with Z appear first, and so on.

Even if you have never performed a sort in a database program before, you have probably done so in Finder windows. Open any folder from the Desktop and choose View ➪ As List (⌘+2). You can sort the folder's contents by any column heading, as explained in Figure 10-1.

More about sorting

All computer systems contain data that has to be located from time to time. The rapidity with which this information can be found is of critical importance to the system's speed and efficiency. Because searching through ordered information is easier than searching through random information (both for the computer and for the computer's users), the process of sorting persists as an important topic in computer science research.

One of the simplest sorting methods — frequently taught to beginning computer science students — is the *bubble sort.* In this sort method (or algorithm), the first record is compared with each subsequent record. If the two records are out of order, they are swapped; causing the record that was being compared with the first record to become the new first record.

After all subsequent records have been compared with the first record (which can change during the comparison process), the sort moves to the second record and repeats the process. Every subsequent record is then compared with the second record. Swapping occurs if the two records are found to be out of order. The procedure continues for the third and every record subsequent to it down to the next-to-last record. Records are said to *bubble up* into the correct order — hence, the name of the algorithm.

The bubble sort works, but it consumes copious amounts of computing power and is very slow, especially when used with a large database. A more efficient method is the *binary sort,* which makes comparisons within increasingly smaller subdivisions of the list being sorted. The binary sort uses far fewer steps than does the bubble sort. Other sort methods also exist. You can view demonstrations of many common sorting algorithms at www. cs.ubc.ca/spider/harrison/Java/sorting-demo.html.

You should note that the true storage order for a FileMaker Pro database is rarely (if ever) changed by a sort operation. Physically moving records to reflect a new database order is inefficient and unnecessary. Instead, the current sorted order of the database is often maintained within a separate (internal) list. This list indicates which record is currently first, second, and so on. Normally, only this list (or *index*) is physically changed when a database is sorted.

Figure 10-1: To sort a folder in list view in Mac OS X, click any column heading. A second click will reverse the sort order.

Even if you have never performed a sort in a database program before, you have probably done so in Windows Explorer or in a folder — with Active Desktop enabled. The View ➪ Arrange Icons By submenu (Figure 10-2) provides a number of commands that enable you to sort files and folders in any window by name, type, size, and modification date. If you choose to View ➪ Details, you can click the column headings to sort the files and folders by that column's attribute.

FileMaker Pro's sorting works in much the same way sorting in the Finder or Windows Explorer works. Depending on your needs at the moment, you might decide to sort by last name and then later re-sort by ZIP code. Just as you can sort a Finder or Windows folder in any way that you like, you can sort a FileMaker Pro database as often as you want and by any field or fields that currently interest you.

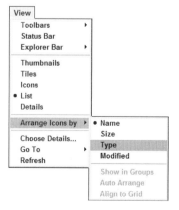

Figure 10-2: The View ➪ Arrange Icons By submenu in Windows XP.

When people first use sorting, they usually keep it simple, restricting each sort to a single field. They might sort an employee list by last name only, for example. Unfortunately, an important limitation of single-field sorts is that *ties* (cases in which more than one record has the same value for the sort field) aren't broken. If you sort only by last name, all the people who share the same last name are listed in whatever order their records were originally entered into the database, perhaps as follows:

```
Jones, Evan
Jones, Marcia
Jones, Bobby
Jones, Abbie
```

FileMaker Pro, however, can sort by more than one field, solving the problem of what to do when at least two records contain identical information in the primary sort field. In this example, you could have FileMaker Pro sort the database by the Last Name *and* First Name fields. Records with identical last names would then be arranged in order according to their first name. Thus, performing an ascending sort on the Last Name and First Name fields would arrange the Jones records like this:

```
Jones, Abbie
Jones, Bobby
Jones, Evan
Jones, Marcia
```

As you can see, adding First Name as the second sort field re-sorts all records that have the same last name although ties could still exist when two (or more) individuals share a given name and surname (multiple *John Smith* entries in a motel register database, for example).

After you apply the proper sorting options, browsing the database can be much easier, just as the alphabetical ordering of entries makes finding words in a dictionary or names in a phone book easier. In this chapter, you learn how to sort a database, set sorting options, and — if need be — restore the records to their original order.

Improving sorts by indexing

In FileMaker Pro 8, indexing is optional. In fact, the default is to index nothing. If you want to index a particular field, you must specifically set that option for the field. Choose a field in the Define Database dialog's Fields pane, click the Options button, click the Storage tab, select the All (or the Minimal) radio button, and then click OK (as described in Chapter 5). The best candidates for indexing are fields on which sorts or Finds will be based, as well as those for which you intend to use the Insert ➪ From Index command to fill the field.

However, the default indexing option for every new field (other than container and summary fields) is Automatically create indexes as needed. Thus, if you don't routinely intend to sort or base Finds on a given field, you can rest assured that FileMaker will take care of the indexing, if it's required. You might see a progress dialog the first time you sort on a field.

Note   Sorting not only makes your browsing more convenient but also makes possible grouping and sub-summary breakdowns in your reports, as shown in Chapter 6.

Creating a Sort Order

When sorting a database, you must make three basic decisions:

✦ *Whether to sort the entire database or only part of it:* By using Find requests or the Records menu's Omit Record, Omit Multiple, or Show Omitted Only commands (see Chapter 9), you can restrict the visible portion of any database to a selected set of records (referred to as the *found set*). As with many FileMaker Pro commands, sorting affects only currently visible records, and expanding the found set (for example, by choosing Find ➪ Show All Records) ignores previously applied sorting.

✦ *The field or fields on which to sort:* Which fields you sort on depends on how you want to use the database. Use the field or fields that are presently of greatest importance to you as the sort fields. For example, in a customer database, you might be concerned with sales totals. Sorting on the Total field enables you to see which customers are big buyers and which ones have recently bought little or nothing from you.

Note   You can also sort on fields from a *related database:* that is, one for which a relationship with the current database has been defined. Related fields can appear anywhere within the list of sort fields. Note, however, that if several records in the related file match a record in the current file, the sort will use the first matching record found in the related file. We discuss relations in much greater detail in Chapter 16.

✦ *Whether records should be arranged in ascending, descending, or a custom order:* Text data is usually more useful when sorted in ascending order. That is, you normally want to see the A entries first rather than the Z entries. Numeric information, on the other hand, is frequently more useful when you view it in descending order (largest number to smallest). When you examine cost figures, for example, your primary interest will often be in the greatest dollar amounts.

If you've defined value lists for the database, you can sort according to the order established in any of these value lists. This is a great way to organize records in a specific order that is neither alphabetical nor numerical. For example, you might have a value list that consists of the department names of your company organized in a specific order. For example, you can sort according to this value list (rather than alphabetically, as you normally might), ensuring that people in Administration will be listed before those in Accounting. See the section, "Additional Sort Options," at the end of this chapter for details.

You sort by choosing the Records ⇨ Sort command (or by pressing ⌘+S/Ctrl+S). The Sort Records dialog appears, in which you specify sort options, as shown in Figure 10-3. You've seen this dialog before, in Chapter 4, when creating the Address Book Advanced database's Summary report.

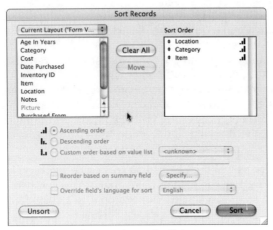

Figure 10-3: The Sort Records dialog.

The list area on the left side of the dialog enumerates the fields by which you can sort the database. Eligible sort fields include all fields you've defined for the database — not just the ones that appear on the current layout or in the current table. By choosing a previously defined relationship from the pop-up menu/ drop-down list above the field list, you can also sort the database by any field in a related file. (If the current database has no defined relationships, you can create them by choosing Define Database from the same pop-up menu/drop-down list.)

New Feature

As an added convenience, FileMaker Pro 8 makes the default list contain only those fields on the current layout — an option that did not exist in previous versions. If you wish to sort based on a field not present on the current layout, choose Current Table (or a related table) from the pop-up menu/drop-down list.

Cross-Reference

For information about relationships, see Chapter 18.

You can also use Summary fields as sort fields if you select the Reorder based on summary field check box. For details, see the "Sorting by Summary fields" section, near the end of this chapter. You cannot, however, sort on Container fields.

A list of the currently chosen sort fields is on the right side of the dialog in the Sort Order area. The fields appear in an order corresponding to the order in which the database will be sorted. In Figure 10-3, for example, the database will first be sorted by the Location field. Within each location, records will be re-sorted by each item's category and then by the item's name. An icon following each field name in the Sort Order list indicates the sort order (ascending, descending, or custom) for that field. The icons' meanings are shown at the bottom of the dialog. To rearrange the sort fields, click the double-headed arrow preceding a field name and drag the field name to its new place in the Sort Order list.

The two buttons in the center of the dialog enable you to manage the Sort Order list's contents. At the bottom of the dialog are three radio buttons you can use to specify, for each sort field, whether you want an ascending sort, a descending sort, or a sort based on a value list.

Following are brief explanations of the Sort Records dialog's components:

✦ *Move:* Click this button to copy the selected field from the field list to the Sort Order list. Use Move to choose each field by which you intend to sort.

   Move toggles with Clear.

✦ *Clear:* When you select a field in the Sort Order list (the Sort Order list is shown in Figure 10-3), this button replaces the Move button. Click Clear when you want to remove the selected field from the Sort Order list. (Clear enables you to selectively remove fields from the Sort Order list. Use Clear All to remove all fields from the Sort Order list.)

Tip

You can also double-click an item in the Sort Order list to remove it from the list.

✦ *Clear All:* Click this button to remove all fields from the Sort Order list. Use Clear All when you want to define a sort order from scratch and ignore any fields that were previously selected.

✦ *Ascending order:* Select this radio button to sort the selected field from the lowest value to the highest value (from A–Z, for example).

✦ *Descending order:* Select this radio button to sort the selected field from the highest value to the lowest value.

✦ *Custom order based on value list:* If you have prepared any value lists for the database (see Chapter 5), select this radio button and choose the name of the value list from the pop-up menu. This action instructs FileMaker Pro to use the order of the value list as the sort order for the field. (If an appropriate value list doesn't already exist, you can choose Define Value Lists from the pop-up menu.)

As an example, the days of the week in chronological order might constitute a value list. Using this value list, records would appear in the order Sunday, Monday, Tuesday, and so on, rather than in ascending or descending alphabetical order.

✦ *Reorder based on summary field:* This check box (or its accompanying Specify button) presents the Specify Field dialog, allowing you to select a grouping field for the report. That field will be moved into the Sort Order list, above the normal sort fields.

✦ *Override field's language for sort:* This check box and associated pop-up menu/drop-down list enable you to specify an international sorting convention for any selected sort field. (See "Setting an international sort order," later in this chapter.)

✦ *Unsort:* This command undoes any current sort order and restores the records to the order in which you entered them into the database. You seldom need to restore records to the original order — unless, of course, you created or imported the records in some meaningful order that you cannot duplicate by using a Sort command.

✦ *Cancel:* This command dismisses the Sort Records dialog without sorting.

✦ *Sort:* Click this button to sort the database according to the current settings.

Sorting on one field

The simplest and most common kind of sort is one based on a single field — sorting only by the ZIP Code, Invoice Total, Age, or Grade Point Average field, for example. Depending on the complexity of your databases, you might find that the majority of your sorts use only a single sort field.

STEPS: Sorting on One Field

1. Decide whether you want to sort the entire database or only selected records. FileMaker sorts only the current found set of records (those being browsed).

2. Use the Quick Find feature or the Find, Omit Record, Omit Multiple, and related commands to select the records of interest. (See Chapter 9 for instructions.)

   or

   If you're currently browsing only a subset of records and want to sort the entire database, choose Records ⇨ Show All Records (or press ⌘+J/Ctrl+J).

3. Choose Records ⇨ Sort (or press ⌘+S/Ctrl+S).

   The Sort Records dialog appears. (Refer to Figure 10-3.)

4. If the Sort Order list includes fields you don't want to use in this sort operation, click Clear All to remove them all or individually select each field and click Clear.

Note If you haven't sorted the database before, the Sort Order list will already be clear. Otherwise, it will contain the fields used in the most recent sort.

5. In the scrolling field list on the left side of the dialog, click the name of the field by which you want to sort.

6. Select the radio button corresponding to the sort order you want to use for the field:

- Select the Ascending order radio button to start with the smallest numeric value and end with the largest, to sort words alphabetically (from A–Z), or to arrange times and dates chronologically.

- Select the Descending order radio button to start with the largest numeric value and end with the smallest, to sort words in reverse alphabetical order (from Z–A), or to arrange times and dates from the most recent to the oldest.

- Select the Custom order based on value list radio button to use a value list you've defined, and then choose the value list from the pop-up menu/ drop-down list.

7. Click Move to transfer the field to the Sort Order list.

or

Double-click the field name to select it in the field list and simultaneously move it to the Sort Order list.

8. Click Sort to sort the database in the specified order by the selected field.

When the sort is finished, the status area changes to show that the database has been sorted, as shown in Figure 10-4.

Figure 10-4: The status area for a sorted database.

Canceling a sort operation

Sometimes in the middle of a sort operation, you might decide that you want to sort on fields other than the ones you've chosen. Instead of waiting for FileMaker Pro to finish sorting the database, you can cancel the sort by pressing ⌘+. (period)/Esc. This feature is especially helpful when the database is large and the sort operation is time-consuming. For small databases, you are unlikely to be quick enough to cancel the operation before it completes.

Tip   FileMaker Pro 8 eliminates the need for most single-field sorts to visit the Sort dialog. Control-click/right-click a field in the layout and choose Sort Ascending or Sort Descending from the contextual menu to immediately sort the layout's found set on that field. If you wish to sort by a value list, choose the value list from the Sort by Value List item's submenu, as shown in Figure 10-5.

Figure 10-5: Choosing a value list for a quick single-field sort.

Sorting on multiple fields

Sorting by a single field isn't always sufficient, particularly in a database where the sort field in several records might have the same value. In such cases, you might want to further organize the records by specifying additional sort fields.

As an example, you might have several records for people having the same last name. Sorting only by the Last Name field will leave the first names in whatever order the records were in when you created them. (Can you imagine what a mess a metropolitan phone directory would be if it were sorted only by last name? Try finding Jake Johnson in a 20-page listing of Johnsons where there was no secondary sort based on the first name!) Selecting First Name as the second sort field is often a smart move. And if you believe (or know) that some people have the same last names and the same first names, you can consider adding a third sort field, such as Middle Initial, Phone Number, Address, or Age.

When specifying multiple sort fields, select them in the order of their importance. Fields further down in the Sort Order list are merely tiebreakers, as shown in Figure 10-6. Working with the Address Book Advanced database, you might decide that your main interest is in companies, rather than in people, and choose Company as the first sort field. If you have multiple contacts at various companies, you can use Last Name or Department as the second sort field. If the companies are very large, you might also want to select a third sort field, such as First Name.

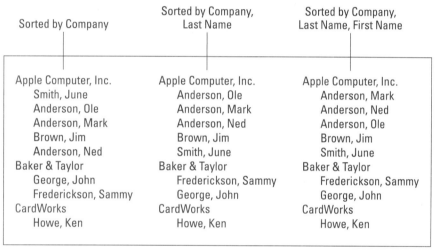

Figure 10-6: As additional sort fields are added, the ordering of records becomes progressively more useful.

The only difference between sorting by one field and sorting by multiple fields is the presence of the additional fields in the Sort Order list. (For instructions, refer to the "Sorting on One Field" steps in the preceding section.)

Tip   If you discover that the fields in the Sort Order list are in the wrong order, you don't have to clear them and start over. You can rearrange the fields by simply dragging them to new positions in the list. To do this, place the pointer over the double arrow to the field's left in the Sort Order list that you want to move. When the pointer changes to a double-headed arrow, click and drag the field to its new position in the list, and then release the mouse button.

Sorting on multiple fields versus performing multiple sorts

Performing a sort that includes multiple sort fields is not the same as performing several successive sorts that use those same fields. Every sort always starts from the original record order — not from the order that's currently appearing onscreen.

For example, if you sort a database by the Company and Last Name fields, the records are arranged in order according to company. Within every company, records are further arranged alphabetically by the employees' last names. A sort that includes multiple sort fields is sometimes called a **compound sort.** On the other hand, if you perform two sorts — the first by the Company field and the second by the Last Name field — each sort works independently of the other; the effects aren't cumulative. The first sort arranges records in company order. The second merely arranges the records according to last names, completely ignoring the results of the first sort.

Modifying Sort Specifications

After you've defined a sort for a database and set options, you might later decide that you want to change some of the options or sort on different fields. Although you can click Clear All in the Sort Records dialog and specify new sorting instructions from scratch, changing the options is often easier. For example, you can do any of the following:

✦ *Clear unnecessary fields from the Sort Order list:* Click Clear All; select individual fields in the Sort Order list, and then click Clear; or, double-click individual fields in the Sort Order list to clear them.

✦ *Add new sort fields:* Select them in the field list and click Move.

✦ *Change the order of fields in the Sort Order list:* Drag them to new positions.

✦ *Change to an ascending, descending, or value list sort order for a field:* Select the field in the Sort Order list and then click a different sort order radio button.

Sorting Data in Portals

In FileMaker Pro 4.0 and higher, related data displayed in a *portal* (a layout element providing a viewport into a related table) can be sorted. In the absence of a sort order specification in the Portal Setup dialog or in the Relationship definition, FileMaker Pro displays the records in a portal in the order in which they were entered. For example, if you have a database of video rental invoices, each customer invoice record could have a portal showing video rental details: the movie ID, category, title/description, and price. The video rentals in the portal are displayed in whatever order they were entered.

To change the sort order for records in a portal, set the sort order as part of defining the relationship between the main file (Invoices, in this example) and the related table (Customer Rentals, in this example).

Note

FileMaker Pro 8 requires that all tables involved in a relationship be specified in the Define Database dialog's Tables pane and that the relationship be specified in the Define Database dialog's Relationships pane. This material will be covered in much greater detail, with explanations, in Chapter 18. For the time being, if you're following along, don't worry about why we're doing what we're doing.

STEPS: Establishing a Sort Order for Portal Records

1. Choose File ➪ Define ➪ Database. (You can also choose Define Database from any dialog where it is available, such as the Portal Setup dialog and the Specify Field dialog.)

   The Define Database dialog appears.

2. Click the Relationships tab to bring up the Relationships pane, as shown in Figure 10-7.

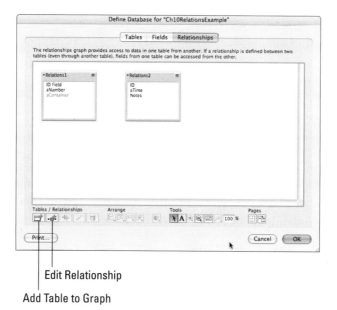

Edit Relationship

Add Table to Graph

Figure 10-7: The Define Database dialog's Relationships pane.

3. Create a new relationship by clicking the Edit Relationship button to open the Edit Relationship dialog. (See Figure 10-8.)

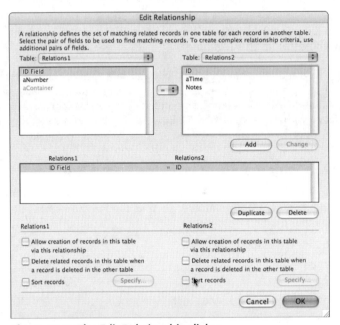

Figure 10-8: The Edit Relationship dialog.

4. Choose the tables between which you want to specify a relationship from the Table pop-up menus/drop-down lists.

5. Select the fields you wish to correlate in the two lists and click the Add button below the right-hand list.

   For this example, we're going to leave the type of relationship set to an *equi-join* (where the comparison of the fields is for equality). Commencing with FileMaker Pro 7, *comparative joins* (less-than, greater-than, inequality, and so on) are specifiable by choosing from the pop-up menu/drop-down list of symbols between the two field lists. We cover this more deeply in Chapter 18.

6. Select the Sort records check box below the table that will appear in the portal.

   The Sort Records dialog appears.

7. As with any other sort, select the fields in the file on which you want to sort and click the Move button to add them to the Sort Order list. For each sort field, select the Ascending order, Descending order, or Custom order based on a value list radio button.

8. Click OK in the Sort Records dialog, and then click OK in the Edit Relationship dialog. Finally, click OK to close the Define Database dialog.

The need for re-sorting

FileMaker Pro tries to maintain the current sort order for a database, even when you add new records to a previously sorted database. Because it doesn't do a perfect job, however, you sometimes see *Semi-sorted* (rather than *Sorted*) in the status area. To ensure that all records are correctly sorted, you must use the Sort command again whenever you add new records. FileMaker Pro remembers the last set of sort criteria you used for that layout, so re-sorting the database is as simple as choosing the Sort command and then immediately pressing Return/Enter (or clicking the Sort button).

Executing a Find request, on the other hand, has a more profound effect on the current sort order. The Find obliterates the sort order. (Swapping the found set with the Omitted set also obliterates the sort order.) The layout's status area reports the database as Unsorted. (This follows logically from the fact that a sort operates only on the found set, rather than on the entire database. A new Find results in a new found set.) Thus, you will usually want to re-sort the database following a Find.

FileMaker Pro will display the records in the portal in the specified sort order. For example, if you chose to sort the portal records in order of Rental charge (descending), the most expensive item in the video invoice would be listed at the top of the portal.

Additional Sort Options

You can sort a database in more than one way. The Sort command offers additional capabilities, many of which are useful for tasks such as preparing reports. You can sort a database in the order defined by a value list, sort by Summary fields, sort in a way that makes the organization of records more useful for individuals in a different country, and restore the records to the order in which they were entered in the database.

Using a value list to set a sort order

Ascending and descending sorts aren't always appropriate. For example, if you sorted the months of the year in ascending order, you would end up with an alphabetized list that started with April and August and ended with September — probably not what you had in mind. Sorting according to a value list-defined order offers a way around such problems.

A *value list* displays the acceptable values for a field in a preset order. You can sort the database by any value list that has been defined for the database, substituting the order defined in the value list for the normal alphabetical, numerical, and chronological orders used by ascending and descending sorts.

To sort according to a value list, select a field in the Sort Order list and select the Custom order based on value list radio button (refer to Figure 10-3). Then select a value list from the pop-up menu/drop-down list — in most cases, a value list that has been associated with the chosen sort field. (FileMaker Pro 4.0 and higher, however, doesn't impose this restriction. For example, you could use a value list composed of day-of-the-week names, even if that value list has never been associated with the chosen sort field.)

Note You can also choose Define Value List from the pop-up menu/drop-down list to create a value list on the fly. In fact, you can create value lists for use solely as sort criteria if you wish, never associating them with any particular field.

When you select the value list sort option, the order used for the sort matches the order in which the various values appear in the value list. As shown in the example in Figure 10-9, a value list for the Category field contains IRS Schedule C expense categories, which have been arranged in a manner that closely approximates the order in which they're listed on Schedule C rather than in a strict alphabetical order.

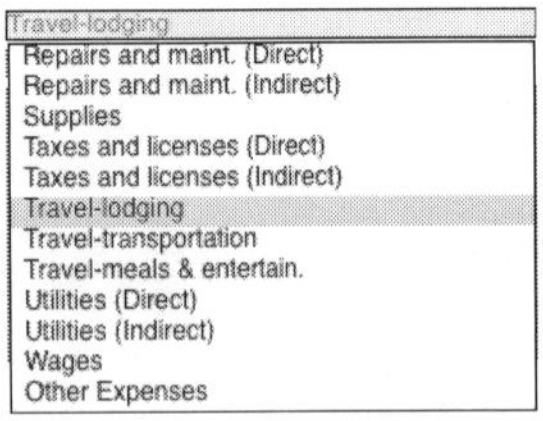

Travel-lodging
Repairs and maint. (Direct)
Repairs and maint. (Indirect)
Supplies
Taxes and licenses (Direct)
Taxes and licenses (Indirect)
Travel-lodging
Travel-transportation
Travel-meals & entertain.
Utilities (Direct)
Utilities (Indirect)
Wages
Other Expenses

Figure 10-9: Sorting by a value list is appropriate when you want records sorted in a special, predetermined order rather than alphabetically, numerically, or chronologically.

Setting an international sort order

Different countries follow different conventions for sorting information. Many languages use a non-Roman alphabet, for example, and some differences also exist among languages employing the Roman alphabet. FileMaker Pro enables you to select an international sorting convention for any field by choosing a language.

To choose a sorting convention for a field, select the field in the Sort Order list, select the check box for Override field's language for sort, and choose a language from the pop-up menu/drop-down list (see Figure 10-10). The sort language affects only the selected field. To sort additional fields by the same or a different language, repeat this procedure for those fields.

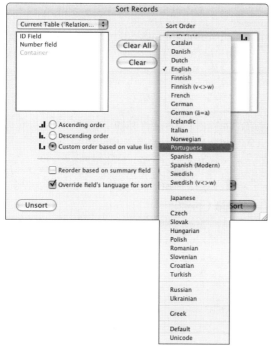

Figure 10-10: Setting an international sort order for a field.

Sorting by Summary fields

As you might recall from Chapter 5, Summary fields summarize information from a single field across a series of records. For example, a Sales Total field might combine individual orders into one sales figure for all records that you're currently browsing.

When placed in a data entry layout, the data in many Summary fields is the same, no matter which record you're viewing. For example, any Total or Average Summary field always shows the same total or average, regardless of which record is currently visible. For this reason, sorting by a Summary field makes more sense in a layout designed for reporting than in one designed for data entry.

Here's an example: Suppose you want to create a report that shows total sales for each member of your company's sales force. To accomplish this task, all you must do is create a layout that contains a sub-summary part, define the part as "Sub-summary when sorted by Salesperson," and then place the Sales Total Summary field in the sub-summary part. When you want to see the summary figures, sort by the Salesperson field and then print or preview the report. (As explained in Chapters 5 and 6, you must sort before printing or switching to Preview mode if you want the information in the sub-summary part to display correctly. This is frequently accomplished by attaching a script to the layout.)

This accomplishes two things:

✦ The sort settings group sales by salesperson. All of Bob's sales are listed together, for example, instead of being scattered throughout the database.

✦ Adding the Summary field enables you to see a separate sales total for each salesperson. The report is shown in Figure 10-11.

The handling of "other" choices

When you create a value list, providing an Other choice as a catchall is often helpful. In a value list to be used with a Shipping Method field, for example, you might list choices for Federal Express, UPS, and USPS. Because your company occasionally uses other carriers, you can add an Other choice to the value list so that they, too, can be recorded.

In performing an ascending or descending sort on such a field, FileMaker Pro arranges the records in which the Other choice was selected according to the actual contents of the field (Yellow Cab, Jimmy's Messenger Service, and so on). That is, it doesn't group all the records together as though they all contained the same value (that is, Other). On the other hand, when FileMaker Pro performs a custom sort based on a value list (rather than a simple ascending or descending sort), all Other choices are grouped together at the end of the database, followed only by records in which nothing at all was chosen or entered for the field. (The procedure for adding an Other choice to a value list is described in Chapter 5.)

An ascending sort based on a value list.

A custom sort based on a value list.

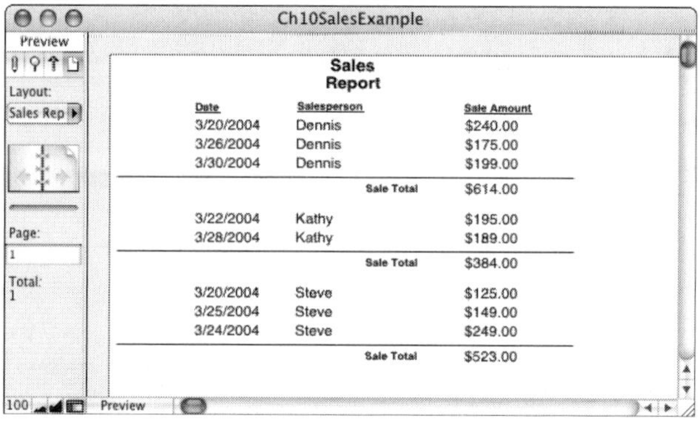

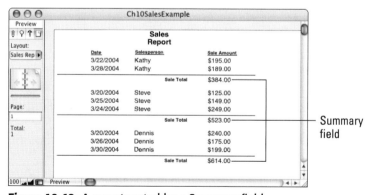

Figure 10-11: This report is generated when the database is sorted by the Salesperson field.

Note, however, that what you have accomplished so far has been done without sorting by the Summary field. Although the salespeople are effectively grouped (for example, all of Kathy's sales are listed together), arranging the groups in alphabetical order isn't necessarily the most informative manner of presenting the data. If you select the Salesperson field in the Sort Order list of the Sort Records dialog and after selecting the Reorder based on summary field check box (or click its adjoining Specify button), select the Total Sales summary field in the Specify Field dialog that appears, you can make the report even more useful. As Figure 10-12 shows, not only are the records still grouped by salesperson, but they're also arranged in order of increasing sales (Kathy, Steve, and Dennis).

Figure 10-12: A report sorted by a Summary field.

Special sorting tips and considerations

Although the examples in this chapter concentrate on sorting the contents of Text and Number fields, you can sort records based on the contents of any field other than a Container field. For example, sorting by date is frequently useful (when you're organizing a check register, for example). And if you were recording harness racing results, you might want to sort by finish time. Calculation fields, such as sales totals, are also often useful as sort fields.

Here are some additional sorting tips you might find helpful:

✦ When a Number field is selected as a sort field, any non-numeric data in that field is ignored.

✦ Some Text fields routinely include numbers. For instance, a ZIP code field is frequently defined as a Text field because it is the only way to easily include leading zeros (as in 01764); leading zeros would automatically be stripped out if it were a Number field. When sorting on a Text field that stores numbers, the numbers sort according to character position rather than numerically. Thus, all numbers that start with 1 will appear before any number that begins with 2 (as in 1, 123, 1745, 2, 222, and so on). Text data will appear after all numeric data or data that begins with a number, such as 167 Oak Street.

✦ If a record contains nothing in the sort field (that is, the field is blank) and you perform an ascending sort, it will appear at the beginning of the set of sorted records.

✦ If you want to sort on a Container field, create an additional field (normally a Text field) describing or naming the picture, movie, audio clip, file, or sound in the Container field and then sort on that Text field instead.

✦ Repeating fields will sort by the value in the first repetition.

✦ You can set options for the Sort page in any Web-published FileMaker Pro database. See Chapter 20 for instructions.

As with other sort fields, you can sort a Summary field in ascending or descending order. However, because you cannot associate a value list with a Summary field, you cannot select the value list option for such a field. Similarly, you cannot select a different language for a Summary field.

In versions prior to FileMaker Pro 7, you added the summary field directly to the Sort Order list. (This was made possible by an Include Summary Fields option in the Sort dialog.) FileMaker Pro 7 increased the flexibility of the summary field sorts by letting you associate different summary fields with different fields in the Sort Order list. You will see a sort field's ascending or descending sort symbol enclosed within a document icon when a summary field is associated.

Unsort: Restoring the original record order

If you want to restore the layout's record display order to the order in which you entered them into the table, click the Unsort button in the Sort Records dialog. The records are then displayed in the order in which you entered them. (This is the actual order in which records are stored, even after you sort them.)

Tip

You don't need to issue an Unsort command before issuing a new Sort command. Every sort operates on the records in their original order (as you entered them in the database), not on the currently visible order.

Summary

✦ Sorting is the process of arranging a group of records into a specific display order. The mechanics of sorting is an important topic in computer science.

✦ A sort operation is based on the value of one or more fields in the records to be sorted.

✦ You can use any field type other than a Container field as the basis for a sort.

✦ Sorting doesn't change the physical location of records in a table. It merely changes the order in which records are displayed in that layout. Records are always stored in the order in which you entered them. As a result, you can easily restore the display order of records to the order in which you entered them by clicking the Unsort button in the Sort Records dialog. (As an added bonus, this means that you can easily display different sort orders in different layouts because the initial order never really changes.)

✦   ✦   ✦

Reports

O ne of the main reasons why you enter data into and maintain a database is so that you can later view and present the data in an organized and informative fashion: that is, a report. In earlier chapters, you learned how to locate and filter information in a database by using Find mode and Quick Find and how to organize that information with the Sort command. You also learned about using layouts to view different arrangements of your data. Now, you'll learn how to put these procedures together to produce reports you can keep and share.

Report Design Essentials

A *report* is a summary of the data entered into a database, or an organized, collated view of the data. You don't necessarily have to print a report (you can use Preview mode to view it onscreen or create a PDF file to share with others), but the process of creating a report is much the same whether you choose to print it or not. (You can read more about printing in Chapter 13.)

Preparing a report involves four considerations:

1. *Designing a report layout:* Create a layout displaying only the fields you want to see. Make sure that the layout takes advantage of available page space and that the data is clearly presented. You use Layout mode to create and modify layouts (as explained in Chapter 6).

2. *Selecting records to include in the report:* You don't always want to see the entire database in a report. Your needs for the report will dictate the particular records selected. You might want to include only records in a given time frame, records associated with certain individuals or organizations, or records with some other specific property, such as overdue invoices. Records are selected in Find mode by creating Find requests or by using related procedures, such as the Omit Record command. (Find requests are covered in Chapter 9.)

In This Chapter

Designing a
typical report

Creating reports with
the New Layout/
Report Assistant

Tips for designing
attractive, useful
reports

3. *Sorting the records:* If they've not been sorted, records are displayed in the order in which they were entered into the database. For report purposes, records usually need to be arranged in some other order so that readers can easily locate particular records and make sense of the information. You arrange records in a FileMaker Pro report using the Sort command. (Sorting is covered in Chapter 10.)

4. *Printing:* When designing a report layout, keeping your printing requirements and capabilities in mind (unless you intend to view the report only onscreen) is important. The type of printer you have can affect the layout you use and how information must be arranged within that layout. Finally, certain kinds of information (such as Summary fields) appear only when you display a print preview or print the report (either on paper or as a PDF file).

The following sections provide more information about these four essential facets of the report preparation process.

Designing a report layout

When designing a report layout, you should ask yourself these questions:

✦ *What is this report's purpose?* This is the key to determining what information the report layout should display. To begin, you should exclude any fields that aren't needed. In a phone directory created from an employee database, for example, you wouldn't want to display information about employees' ages or Social Security numbers even though that data is routinely collected for the database. If currently existing layouts include extraneous information, you must either

  • Edit a duplicate of the most appropriate layout.

  • Design a new layout especially for the report.

✦ *How much information can — and should — I put on a page?* You should make optimal use of the print area but not at the expense of the report's clarity. Provide an adequate amount of white space between records as well as between fields in each record. It's also important to recognize that when printing or displaying records, FileMaker Pro truncates data that doesn't fit within a field. This isn't a problem in Browse mode because the field expands the moment you click in it or tab to it. In Preview mode or when printing, on the other hand, you aren't able to click within fields. You might have to resize some fields in the report layout to completely display the data.

✦ *Is the report layout clear?* A report should be self-explanatory. Report recipients should be able to recognize its purpose without having to ask for explanations. Fields and summary sections should be clearly labeled and possibly separated from the next record by white space or dividing lines. Furthermore, don't underestimate the utility of headers and footers for labeling and numbering report pages. The report's purpose can be further reflected in its title, which is normally printed in the header.

After you create an appropriate report layout, you can switch to that layout at any time by selecting its name from the status area's Layouts menu. Because creating a report is a multistep process (described previously), you might want to design a FileMaker Pro script that does the necessary preparatory work, changes to your report layout, and then prints the report for you. (Scripts are discussed in detail in Chapter 15.)

Note   In versions of FileMaker Pro prior to 5.0, all layout design was done manually. When you chose the New Layout command, the only part of the design that you could automate was to select an appropriate layout style (such as Standard or Columnar Report) and choose the fields to be included. What inevitably followed was extensive *tweaking* (rearranging and moving fields, changing fonts and sizes, and so on). In FileMaker Pro 5.0 and higher, on the other hand, you use an assistant to create all new layouts. When you choose Layouts ⇨ New Layout/Report, you're presented with a series of dialogs enabling you to design an attractive report with minimal tweaking. (Of course, you can still modify any assistant-generated layout, if needed or desired.) To learn how to use the New Layout/Report Assistant to design reports, see "Creating New Layouts" in Chapter 6.

Selecting records to include in the report

Selecting records is perhaps the subtlest step in creating a report. What records do you need to display? Your choice will likely be based on the content of one or more database fields. You might want to choose all records that have a certain value or range of values in a field — for example, all invoice records prepared during the third quarter of this calendar year.

After you decide which records to include in the report, you can create one or more Find requests locating those particular records — and *only* those records. After performing a Find or using other related commands (such as Omit Record and Omit Multiple), the remaining visible records are referred to as the *found set,* as described in Chapter 9. Whether you intend to print your report or just preview it onscreen, the records included in the report are always drawn exclusively from the found set.

Cross-Reference   Refer to Chapter 9 for more information on finding records and working with found sets.

Tip   Many reports must display every record in the database. To include all records in a report, simply choose the Records ⇨ Show All Records command (or press ⌘+J/ Ctrl+J). Show All Records instantly places every record in the found set.

Sorting the found set

Unless the found set has previously been sorted, the records appear in the order in which they were entered into the database. To create a more meaningful order for the data, you can sort the found set.

You might want to sort on the same fields you used to create the found set. If a field contains names, it is usually best to sort alphabetically (from A–Z). For a sales report in which you want to highlight the performances of your best salespeople, you might want to sort a Sales field numerically in a descending order (showing highest sales first and lowest ones last).

Keep in mind that you can sort by more than one field. In the sales report example, you could sort records first by salesperson name and then by the amount of each sale. This produces a report in which each salesperson's sales are grouped with the most prominent sale appearing at the top of the group. (Refer to Chapter 10 for more information on sorting records.)

If you're using a layout that includes a sub-summary part, you must sort by the field that you designated when you created the sub-summary; otherwise, the summary information won't appear in the report. Sorting by the specified field has the result of splitting the records into groups based on that field. For example, if a City field were the designated sort field, the report would have separate sections for each city.

Keeping selected objects from printing

Occasionally, there will be items (buttons, static text, and so on) that are part of your report layout that aren't meant to be printed. To keep one or more items from printing, change to Layout mode, select the item(s), and choose Format ➪ Set Sliding/Printing (Option+⌘+T on a Mac). The Set Sliding/Printing dialog appears (see the accompanying figure). Select the Do not print the selected objects check box, and then click OK.

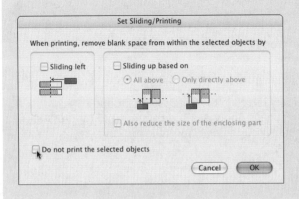

For more information on sorting and summary fields, refer to Chapters 5, 6, and 10.

Printing or previewing the report

After preparing the report, you can view your work onscreen by switching to Preview mode. (Choose View ➭ Preview Mode, press ⌘+U/Ctrl+U, click the status area's Preview button, or choose Preview from the mode pop-up menu at the bottom of the document window.)

Note

When previewing a report onscreen, FileMaker uses the currently chosen printer, paper size, and paper orientation (as specified in Page Setup/Print Setup information stored in the database). If the report doesn't look the way you intended it, be sure that you've selected the right printer and Page Setup/Print Setup options. For example, different printers will often have different printable areas for the same paper size, resulting in changes to where lines and pages break. After verifying that your settings are correct, try Preview mode again.

To produce a report that can be shared with others, however, you will usually print it. When designing a report you intend to print, you should consider the following issues:

✦ *What type of paper will I be using?* This consideration is especially important when you're working with odd paper sizes or with special stock, such as mailing labels. You want your layout to fit and to print properly on that paper. The paper you use can dictate the size of the layout body, the distribution of fields in the layout, and whether you will include headers and footers.

✦ *How much information will the report contain?* Short reports can use large type sizes while smaller type sizes help conserve paper in longer reports as well as increase the number of fields that can fit across the page. Don't choose type so small that it's difficult to read, though.

✦ *Do I have all the fields I need?* If you want to summarize information in certain fields across records or within individual records, you might need to define Summary and/or Calculation fields. You can also use a Calculation field to convert data from one format to another format that is more appropriate for your report. (See Chapter 14.)

✦ *Which orientation should I use: portrait or landscape?* Because many columnar reports require multiple fields, it's sometimes better to print the report in *landscape* mode (that is, sideways) than it is to reorganize and resize the fields so that they'll fit in portrait mode. To set the display and printing of the report to landscape or portrait, choose the appropriate orientation icon from the Page Setup/Print Setup dialog.

✦ *Is data being fully displayed?* The amount of data that can be displayed in any field in a printed report or in Preview mode is limited to the size of the field on the layout. Before printing, switch to Preview mode and flip through the report pages. That way, you can quickly determine whether some of the fields are too small to display the information they hold. You can then change their sizes on the layout, as necessary.

Refer to Chapter 13 for instructions on printing from FileMaker Pro.

New Feature

Although Mac-based FileMaker Pro users have been able to easily produce PDF output of their reports through the OS X Print dialog's Save as PDF option, Windows users were left in the lurch unless they purchased additional software (Adobe Acrobat). FileMaker, Inc. addressed that platform disparity by incorporating the DataLogics PDF Library, thus providing PDF output capability to all FileMaker Pro 8 users. You create your PDF files via the File ➪ Save/Send Records As ➪ PDF menu choice, as shown in Figure 11-1. A standard Save dialog appears, as appropriate for your operating system, with a Save pop-up menu/drop-down list where you choose whether all Records being browsed, the Current record, or a Blank record should be output, as shown in Figure 11-2. (That latter option is handy when you want to create an empty form for manual entry.) Adjacent to the pop-up menu/drop-down list is an Options button that, when clicked, presents the PDF Options dialog shown in Figure 11-3.

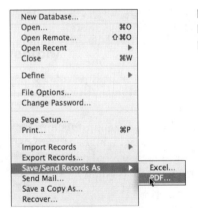

Figure 11-1: You can create a PDF file from a FileMaker report by choosing File ➪ Save/Send Records As ➪ PDF.

The three tabs in the PDF Options dialog are as follows:

✦ The Document tab is where you specify a title for your document, include header information (subject, author, and keywords), the minimum level of Acrobat backward-compatibility desired, and (as in a Print dialog) which pages you want saved.

✦ The Security tab is where you determine security and privacy levels. You can require a password simply to open the document or limit printing and editing capabilities to those with the assigned password, or you can assign no password at all (the default).

✦ The Initial View tab controls how Adobe Reader (or, in earlier versions, Acrobat Reader) presents the PDF file when the PDF is first opened.

Note

Although the File ➪ Save/Send Records As submenu groups Excel and PDF together, formatting is not retained on an Excel save of this type. Thus, it does not qualify as a "report." Saving as Excel is covered in Chapter 16, along with other data exchange possibilities.

Figure 11-2: Indicate whether you want to save the current found set, the current record, or a blank form to the PDF file.

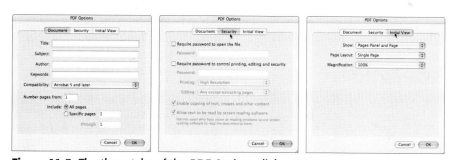

Figure 11-3: The three tabs of the PDF Options dialog.

Modifying and Reusing Layouts

Even with the New Layout/Report Assistant's capable help, there's inevitably some clean-up that remains to be done. You might find, for example, that some layout parts (such as a footer) are unnecessary or that you wish to add other parts. Or you might have already designed a similar layout that with minor changes would meet your needs for a particular report.

Working with layout parts

Some of the major parts of a report layout are shown in Figure 11-4. Every layout part that you've defined for your report appears in a particular place when the layout is printed or viewed in Preview mode.

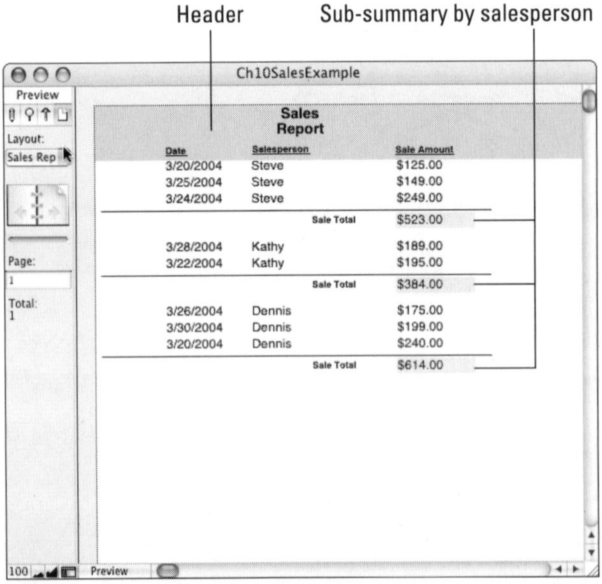

Figure 11-4: An example of a report layout, as viewed in Preview mode.

Keep the following facts in mind when choosing parts for a report layout:

✦ *A title header* (if any) is printed once at the top of the first page. If you make the title header a full page long, you have effectively created a cover sheet. A field placed in the title header displays data from the first record in the found set.

✦ *A regular header* (if any) prints at the top of every page. If you also included a title header, the title header takes the place of the regular header on the first page. A field placed in the header displays data from the first record on that page.

✦ If a *leading grand summary* is part of the report, it prints above the body, before the contents of any records are printed. (For more information on grand summaries and sub-summaries, see Chapter 5.)

✦ All the found and sorted records are printed in the report's *body*. You can exclude the body part from a report if you want to print only summary information. This method is useful for getting total sales information from an invoice database, for example, when you have no interest in seeing the data from individual invoices.

✦ If you have placed *sub-summary parts* above or below the body, each sub-summary prints once for each group of records. You must sort the database with the Sort By field for a sub-summary part to appear. If you like, you can specify a page break before or after a sub-summary in Layout mode's Part Definition dialog (Layouts ⇨ Part Setup, followed by selecting a part from the list and clicking Change), forcing a break after each new group has been printed, for example.

✦ If the report contains a *trailing grand summary,* the summary prints below the body once, after the contents of all records are printed.

✦ A *title footer* (if any) is printed once at the bottom of the first page. A field placed in the title footer displays data from the last record in the found set.

✦ The regular *footer* (if any) prints at the bottom of every page. If you also included a title footer, the title footer takes the place of the regular footer on the first page of the report. A field placed in the footer displays data from the last record on that page.

Duplicating a report layout

When you design a report's layout, you can begin in either of two ways:

✦ Start from scratch by choosing an appropriate predefined layout, such as the Standard form or Columnar list/report.

✦ Duplicate and then modify an existing layout.

The method you choose will depend on whether you already have a layout that's close to the final report that you envision. For example, a collector's want list database might reuse a report layout to present two different arrangements of the same data: purchases sorted by catalog number and purchases sorted by purchase date. After creating the first report layout, these steps could be used to create the second report layout:

1. Create a duplicate of the layout by switching to Layout mode and choosing Layouts ⇨ Duplicate Layout.

2. Edit the title in the header part of the duplicate layout to reflect the new sort order that will be used (Purchases By Date, for example).

3. Create a duplicate copy of the script that produces the original report, and then modify the duplicate script so that it uses the correct sort instructions. (Scripting is covered in Chapter 15.)

Because many reports are often only a minor variation of another report, you'll find that using this approach enables you to generate informative reports with minimal effort.

Transferring layouts between databases

You might already have a perfect report layout, but that layout might reside in a different FileMaker Pro database. If you used the same field names in both databases, you can transfer layout elements from the first database to the second.

STEPS: Moving Layout Elements from One Database to Another

1. Open the database containing the layout elements you want to copy.

2. Choose View ➪ Layout Mode (or press ⌘+L/Ctrl+L).

3. Choose the layout you want to duplicate from the status area's Layouts menu.

4. Open the database in which you want to use the layout.

5. Switch to Layout mode.

6. Choose Layouts ➪ New Layout/Report (or press ⌘+N/Ctrl+N).

   The New Layout/Report Assistant appears, as shown in Figure 11-5.

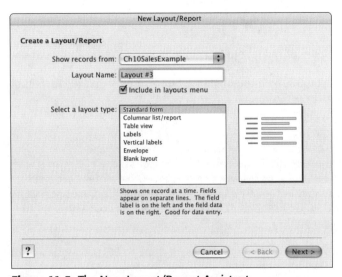

Figure 11-5: The New Layout/Report Assistant.

7. Enter a name for the layout, choose Blank layout from the layout type list, and click Finish.

Next changes to Finish when you choose Blank layout.

8. Drag the Body label so that the body is either the same length or longer than the body of the original layout.

9. In the original database, select the objects that you wish to include in the layout in the new database.

10. Drag the objects into the new, blank layout.

11. Adjust layout parts and objects to the correct positions and sizes.

Any fields from the first (source) database that don't already exist in the second database are added but are undefined. Because they don't represent real fields, data cannot be entered into them. To assign actual fields to the undefined fields, double-click each one. The Field/Control Setup dialog appears, as shown in Figure 11-6, enabling you to assign an existing field (in this table or a related one) to the undefined field. You can eliminate the fields you don't care to define by selecting them and pressing the Delete/Backspace key. (See Chapter 6 for more information on editing layouts.)

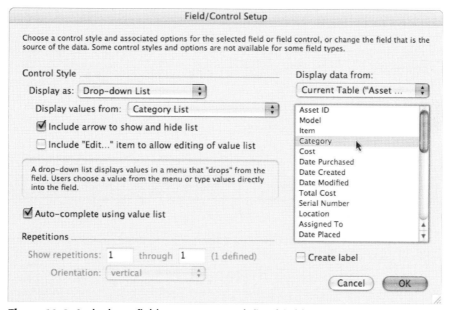

Figure 11-6: Assigning a field name to an undefined field.

Note that buttons can also be dragged between layouts, but you must redefine the attached scripts.

Note   If you'd rather not use *drag-and-drop* (the system software feature explained in the preceding set of steps) to move objects between the layouts, you can also transfer them by using the Edit ⇨ Copy (⌘+C/Ctrl+C) and Edit ⇨ Paste (⌘+V/Ctrl+V) commands. To simultaneously select *all* objects in the initial layout, choose Edit ⇨ Select All (⌘+A/Ctrl+A).

Summary

✦ A report is a printed, a PDF, or an onscreen copy of a selected group of records sorted in a specific order, arranged in a way that provides information that viewing individual records does not (and cannot).

✦ The process of preparing a report typically includes selecting or designing an appropriate layout, selecting records to include by using Find mode commands, arranging the records in a meaningful fashion with the Sort command, and then displaying the report onscreen with Preview mode or printing it with the Print command.

✦ Before committing a lengthy report to paper, examining it in Preview mode is a good idea. Because Preview mode shows exactly what a report will look like when printed, you can quickly identify problems — such as field data that's being truncated, header information that's improperly aligned, and so forth.

✦ Many reports can be created almost entirely with the New Layout/Report Assistant.

✦   ✦   ✦

Using the Spelling Checker

The spelling checker provided with FileMaker Pro 8
includes Main Dictionary files for a number of languages.
You can find these dictionaries in the Dictionaries folder within
the FileMaker Pro 8 application's Extensions folder on either
Mac or Windows. These files contain spellings of more than
100,000 words for each of the languages to which they apply.
Each Main Dictionary file's name has the extension .mpr.

Of course, no dictionary designed for general use will contain
the spellings of all words that are relevant to your business
or your life. For example, you aren't likely to find company
names, people's names, or esoteric technical terms in the
Main Dictionary. Similarly, many common acronyms and
abbreviations are also likely to be absent. Rather than having
the spelling checker flag each of these items as a *questionable
spelling* (the checker's term for a word not found in its dictionary), you can create user dictionaries containing additional
words that are important to you. When you install FileMaker
Pro, it creates the first User Dictionary for you, which is called
User.upr.

We don't know how to emphasize this strongly enough, but
here goes: *A spelling checker is not a panacea for your typing
and spelling woes.* Although it can be a useful tool, you should
not depend upon it too heavily. Spelling checkers only check
to make certain that the words exist in their dictionaries, not
whether they are the correct word, a typo forming another
real word, or a homonym for the intended word. For example,
a spelling checker would find no fault with the sentence, "Two
many people fined it hare too spell write." (Too many people
find it hard to spell right.) As long as the individual words are
in the dictionary, the spell checker blithely continues on, possibly leaving you with the misconception that your prose is
correct. After you've run the spelling checker, proofread your
typing visually. You'll likely find spellings to correct as well as
other problems (repeated words, missing words, split infini-
tives, and so on).

You can also employ Mac OS X's Speech capability (FileMaker Pro ⇨ Services ⇨ Speech ⇨ Start Speaking Text) to read selected passages. Some people find the audio feedback helpful although Dennis isn't one of them.

Setting Spell-Checking Options

FileMaker Pro provides two ways for you to check spelling:

✦ *On request:* FileMaker Pro examines the current record, set of found records, text selection, or layout only when you choose the appropriate command from the Edit ⇨ Spelling submenu.

✦ *On the fly:* As you type, FileMaker Pro automatically checks each word against the words in the current Main Dictionary and User Dictionary. By default, this feature is disabled.

Note

The manner in which spell checking is performed is document-specific. That is, you must set spell-checking preferences individually for each database.

STEPS: Setting Spell-Checking Options for a Database

1. Launch FileMaker Pro and open the database for which you want to set spell-checking preferences.

2. Choose File ⇨ File Options.

   The File Options dialog appears.

3. Click the Spelling tab.

   The Spelling preferences pane appears. (See Figure 12-1.)

4. To initiate on-the-fly spell checking, select either of these radio buttons in the Check spelling as you type section:

   • Beep on questionable spellings

   • Flash menu bar on questionable spellings (Windows only)

   The advantage of this type of spell checking is that you can react immediately and correct errors as the spelling checker discovers them. And you're still free to ignore the beeps (or flashes) if you prefer to continue typing and make corrections later.

   If FileMaker Pro is currently set to check spelling as you type, you can switch to have FileMaker check spelling on request by selecting the Off radio button. (Note that even if you've enabled on-the-fly spell checking, you can still manually request a spelling check whenever you want.)

Mac

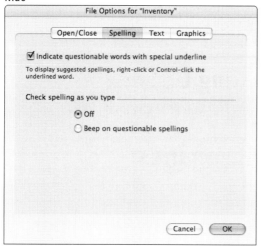

Windows

Figure 12-1: The File Options dialog's Spelling pane for Mac (top) and Windows (bottom).

New
Feature

Even though it seems to be yet another manifestation of on-the-fly spell checking, the new Indicate questionable words with special underline capability is handled separately. Even with the Check spelling as you type option turned off (the default), the underlining of questionable spelling is turned on by default — you need to clear it unless you wish to see little red dots appearing under words the dictionaries don't recognize, as shown in Figure 12-2. When you encounter one of these special underlines, you can Control+click/right-click the offending "word" and choose an alternate or an action from the Suggested Spellings submenu of the shortcut menu that appears.

Figure 12-2: The Mac's idea of a special underline for unrecognized spellings.

5. When you have finished making changes to the Spelling options, click OK.

Specifying Your Dictionaries

When you run a spelling check, you can have only one Main and one User Dictionary active. However, you can create as many additional User Dictionaries as you like.

The Select Dictionaries command enables you to specify which Main and User Dictionaries you wish to be referenced. You can also use this command to let FileMaker Pro know that you've moved any dictionaries to a new location on your hard disk.

STEPS: Selecting a New Dictionary

1. Launch FileMaker Pro and open a database.

   Unless a database is open, the Spelling commands are disabled.

2. Switch to Browse or Layout mode.

   The Spelling commands are available only in these modes.

3. Choose Edit ➪ Spelling ➪ Select Dictionaries.

   The Select Dictionaries dialog appears, as shown in Figure 12-3.

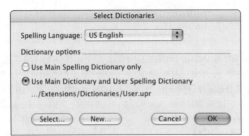

Figure 12-3: The Select Dictionaries dialog lets you specify which dictionaries (and language) you want used.

4. If you do not wish to employ a User Dictionary, choose a language from the Spelling language pop-up menu/drop-down list and select the Use Main Spelling Dictionary only radio button. FileMaker Pro will use the presupplied dictionary for that language.

Note
Most users leave the Main Dictionary supplied with FileMaker Pro that matches your System's language setting as the selected one. The only times you might have to select a Main Dictionary are after you've moved it to a different location on disk or when you want to use a different dictionary supplied by FileMaker, such as the UK English dictionary or the US English (Medical).

5. To specify a User Dictionary, select the Use Main Dictionary and User Spelling Dictionary radio button. The currently selected User Dictionary and location, if any, is indicated below the radio button's text label. If you wish to change to a different User Dictionary, click the Select button and navigate to the dictionary you desire in the file dialog that appears.

Any User Dictionary or Main Dictionary that you specify is now used rather than the previous one. To return to the Main Dictionary or User Dictionary that you previously used, repeat these steps and select the old dictionary (or dictionaries).

The steps to create a new User Dictionary are presented in "Creating a User Dictionary," later in this chapter.

After it's chosen, the Main Dictionary is used for all databases until explicitly changed. User Dictionaries, however, do not work the same way. Every database can have a different User Dictionary. When you specify a User Dictionary, it affects only the current database. Whenever you close a database, FileMaker Pro notes the last User Dictionary chosen for the file and automatically makes it available the next time you open the same database.

Checking Your Spelling

Spell checking on request is more commonly used than spell checking on-the-fly although FileMaker, Inc. obviously believes that the new underlining feedback (described earlier in this chapter) will satisfy those who have avoided the more intrusive on-the-fly notification methods previously available. (FileMaker, Inc. touts it as a *major new feature*.) If you prefer to use the on-the-fly method, you can skip ahead to the "On-the-fly spell checking" section.

Spell checking on request

By selecting the appropriate command from the Edit ⇨ Spelling submenu (see Figure 12-4), you can request that spelling be checked for any of the following:

✦ Currently selected text

✦ The current record

♦ The current set of found (visible) records

♦ Labels in the current layout (available only in Layout mode)

Note   The Spelling submenu is available only when in Browse or Layout mode. Further, its contents are dependent upon whether you're in Browse or Layout mode, as shown in Figure 12-4.

In preparation for a spell-checking session, you must decide what you want to check, as follows:

♦ *To check selected text:* In Browse mode, use normal text-selection techniques to select text within a field. The amount of text can be as little as a single word or a field's entire contents. To begin the spelling check, choose Edit ➪ Spelling ➪ Check Selection. The Check Selection command is particularly useful when you want to restrict a spell check to a single field rather than examine the entire record.

Layout mode

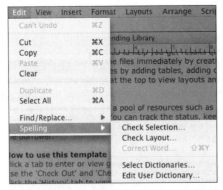

Browse mode

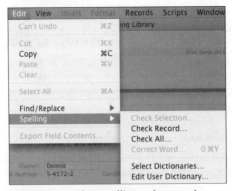

Figure 12-4: The Spelling submenu in Layout mode and Browse mode.

✦ *To check the current record:* In Browse mode, choose Edit ➪ Spelling ➪ Check Record. The spelling of all text in all fields on the current record is checked.

✦ *To check a subset of records or all visible records:* Issue a Find, Omit, Omit Multiple, or a related command to select a group of records. Or, if you prefer to check all records in the database, choose Records ➪ Show All Records (or press ⌘+J/Ctrl+J). Following the Find request, the database automatically switches to Browse mode; at that time, you can choose Edit ➪ Spelling ➪ Check All. FileMaker Pro checks the spelling of all text in all displayed fields of the visible (found) records. (For more information on using Find mode and omitting or selecting records, refer to Chapter 9.)

✦ *To check the current layout:* Select the layout of interest by choosing it from the status area's Layouts menu, change to Layout mode, and then choose Edit ➪ Spelling ➪ Check Layout. (The Check Layout command appears in the menu only when you're in Layout mode whereas Check Record and Check All do not appear.) Check Layout is useful after you've designed a new layout or altered an existing one. Using it enables you to make certain that all the layout's field labels and other static text are correctly spelled words.

STEPS: Performing a Manual Spell Check

1. Decide what you want to check (selected text in a field, the entire current record, all records in the found set, or static text on the current layout), as described previously.

2. Choose the appropriate command from the Edit ➪ Spelling submenu (Check Selection, Check Record/Check Layout, or Check All).

The Spelling dialog appears. (See Figure 12-5.) The spelling checker identifies the first questionable spelling it finds and displays it in the Spelling dialog's Word text box.

The questionable word appears in context (within the sentence or phrase in which it is embedded) in a rectangle at the bottom of the dialog.

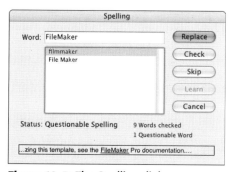

Figure 12-5: The Spelling dialog.

3. For each questionable spelling found, click one of these buttons:

- *Replace:* Click Replace to use a replacement word from the list of words that is provided. Highlight the appropriate word and click Replace or double-click the replacement. The questionable word is replaced by the selected word, and the spelling check continues. (As an alternative, if you know the correct spelling of the questionable word, you can edit it within the Word box. Make the necessary edits and then click Replace.)

  Note that in some cases, the spelling checker offers more replacement words than can fit on a single screen. You can use the scroll bar to see the additional word choices.

- *Check:* If you've manually edited the word in the Word box (to correct an obvious typo, for instance), you can check the edited word against the current dictionaries before clicking Replace. To check the word, finish your editing and click Check. Most people edit questionable words manually when they're in a rush or when the spelling checker doesn't suggest the correct replacement word.

- *Skip:* Click the Skip button to ignore the questionable word here and throughout the rest of text to be examined. You usually use Skip when you know that a word is spelled correctly but don't want to add it to the current User Dictionary. For example, the street name Cyrian isn't in the Main Dictionary file, but unless it's a word that will be used frequently in this or your other databases, you probably have no reason to add it to a User Dictionary.

- *Learn:* Click Learn to accept the word's spelling and add it to the current User Dictionary. If you're certain that a word is spelled correctly and you want it to be known in future spell-checking sessions, click the Learn button. (A User Dictionary records the spellings that you've added with the Learn command. By supporting user dictionaries, the spelling checker isn't limited to just those words that are included in its Main Dictionary. Main and User Dictionaries are discussed in more detail elsewhere in this chapter.)

4. Repeat Step 3 for each additional questionable spelling in the selected text, record, group of records, or layout.

5. After all words have been examined, click Done to conclude the spelling check.

Note that you can click Cancel at any time during a spelling check to halt the process immediately.

If you're working in a password-protected file or in a file in which you don't have access privileges for all fields, you might not be allowed to replace some questionable words. In those cases, the Replace button is labeled Next. Click Next to continue.

On-the-fly spell checking

If you have set the spell-checking options to notify you of suspected spelling errors as you type, FileMaker Pro automatically checks each word the moment you press the spacebar, Option/Ctrl+Tab, or Return/Enter, or type a punctuation mark. (These actions signify the completion of a word.) You can quickly check the most recent questionable spelling by doing one of the following:

✦ Choose Edit ➪ Spelling ➪ Correct Word.

✦ Press Shift+⌘+Y/Shift+Ctrl+Y.

If you're using Mac OS X, and you don't have a "most recent questionable spelling," you're going to be in for a surprise when you press Shift+⌘+Y, and Mac OS creates a new Stickie note and pastes the selection into it.

The normal Spelling dialog appears (as previously shown in Figure 12-5), providing a list of possible replacements for the questionable word. Respond to the dialog as you would in on-request, spell-checking mode. After you deal with the word, the dialog disappears, and you can continue typing.

If you're sure that a flagged word is correct and you have no desire to add it to the current User Dictionary (by clicking the Learn button), you're free to ignore the spelling checker's beep (or flash). Similarly, if you know the correct spelling of a word, making the correction directly in the field is much faster than summoning the Spelling dialog.

New Feature

Far less intrusive is the new facility where FileMaker Pro underlines unrecognized words. You don't have to deal with beeping or flashing and you can immediately see the word over which FileMaker Pro is stumbling — just Control+click/right-click the word and either choose a replacement or otherwise resolve the matter via the shortcut menu's Suggested Spellings submenu, as shown in Figure 12-6.

Note that you cannot rely on on-the-fly spell checking to catch *all* errors. For example, if you move the mouse back into a word that has already been checked and edit it but make a spelling error in the process, FileMaker will not notice the error. Thus, if you're unsure of your spelling skills, using both checking methods is a good idea. Check as you type and then recheck the entire record by choosing the Check Record command.

Tip

Always be aware that a spelling checker — even one as good as the one provided with FileMaker Pro — is only a small first step. All a spelling checker can do is verify that the words are present in the dictionaries it references, not that they are the correct words. For example, *filed* would be considered correct even if *field* were the appropriate word. Similarly, using the incorrect homonym (*to* instead of *too*, or *bow* instead of *bough*) won't result in an error. Always read your data for a visual check and, if possible, have someone whose spelling and grammar skills you trust make a pass through the data.

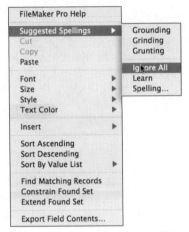

Figure 12-6: Resolve your spelling issues via this shortcut menu.

Working with User Dictionaries

User Dictionaries contain words/character sequences you want FileMaker Pro to recognize as correctly spelled. Although only one User Dictionary at a time can be active, you can create as many User Dictionaries as you like. In this section, we discuss working with User Dictionaries: creating, adding, and merging the contents of User Dictionaries.

Creating a User Dictionary

FileMaker Pro automatically creates the first User Dictionary for you during the installation process. For many of you, this initial dictionary—named User.upr—will be the only User Dictionary you'll ever need. Every new learned word (see the earlier step list, "STEPS: Performing a Manual Spell Check" to read how to train your dictionary to learn a word) can automatically be added to that User Dictionary, and the same word will be recognized when encountered in other databases.

However, you might prefer to create several, special-purpose User Dictionaries instead of simply jamming all your unique words into a single User Dictionary. If you dedicate a User Dictionary to a special purpose or type of terminology, you might find maintaining it easier. For example, you could create separate User Dictionaries for medical, legal, and insurance terms, and another containing the names of companies with which you regularly do business. This approach works best when a single User Dictionary (just the legal one for database A, just the medical one for database

B, and so on) can serve for each of your databases. If you find that many databases must be checked with more than one User Dictionary, you're better off combining them into one large dictionary.

STEPS: Creating a New User Dictionary

1. Launch FileMaker Pro and open a database.

   Unless a database is open, the Spelling commands are disabled.

2. Switch to Browse or Layout mode.

   The Spelling commands are available only in these modes.

3. Choose Edit ➪ Spelling ➪ Select Dictionaries.

   The Select Dictionaries dialog appears. (Refer to Figure 12-3.)

4. Click New to create a new User Dictionary. In the file dialog that appears, enter a name and navigate to a location for the dictionary and click Save. (Be sure to save the dictionary in the FileMaker Extensions folder's Dictionaries subfolder if you wish the dictionary to be accessible to other users of your Mac or Windows machine.)

   The new dictionary is created and becomes the current User Dictionary.

Whenever you want to use one of your User Dictionaries with a particular database, follow the instructions in the section, "Specifying Your Dictionaries," earlier in this chapter, to make the dictionary of your choice the current User Dictionary. In the next section, you'll learn to add words to the new dictionary.

Adding words to a User Dictionary

You can add words to a User Dictionary in several ways:

✦ *Adding words as you go:* As you work with a database and perform on-the-fly or on-request spelling checks, you can click Learn whenever FileMaker Pro finds an important word that it doesn't know. (This includes choosing it from the shortcut menu's Suggested Spellings submenu when using the new on-the-fly spell checking.) The advantage of this approach is that you add only words that are essential because, by definition, they have already been encountered at least once in a spell-checking session. The disadvantage is that until you have used FileMaker Pro for a fair amount of time, you might be adding words quite frequently, interrupting the flow of the spelling checks — and, more intrusively, your actual work.

✦ *Manually adding words:* You can use the Edit ➪ Spelling ➪ Edit User Dictionary command to add new words. This option enables you to add key terms to a User Dictionary without waiting for them to be encountered in a spell-checking session.

✦ *Importing a word list:* You can also use the Edit ⇨ Spelling ⇨ Edit User Dictionary command to import a list of words (in Text-Only format) that you want to add to a User Dictionary *en masse.* This approach makes the most sense when you already have a list of terms prepared, perhaps as a User Dictionary that you created in another program. Because such a list can contain many words, this is easily the fastest way to build a User Dictionary. To be useful, however, you should carefully screen the contents of the word list beforehand to avoid having to delete unnecessary terms later.

Manual editing

You already know how to use the Learn button to add words to a User Dictionary. The following steps show you how to manually add or remove words from the current User Dictionary.

STEPS: Editing a User Dictionary

1. Launch FileMaker Pro and open a database.

   Unless a database is open, the Spelling commands are disabled.

2. Switch to Browse or Layout mode.

   The Spelling commands are available only in these modes.

3. Choose Edit ⇨ Spelling ⇨ Edit User Dictionary.

   The User Dictionary dialog appears and presents a list of the words that the dictionary contains (initially, it's empty), as shown in Figure 12-7.

Note   If a User Dictionary isn't currently installed or chosen, the Edit User Dictionary command cannot be selected. See "Creating a User Dictionary," earlier in this chapter, for instructions on installing a User Dictionary.

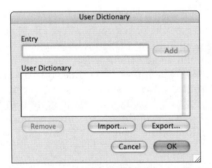

Figure 12-7: The User Dictionary dialog.

4. To add a word to the User Dictionary, type the word in the Entry box and click Add.

   If the word already exists in the User or Main Dictionary, FileMaker Pro informs you. Otherwise, the word is added to the User Dictionary.

5. To remove a word from the User Dictionary, select the word in the word list and click Remove.

   You cannot edit words in the User Dictionary. You must remove the old word and then add the replacement (spelled correctly, of course).

6. Repeat Steps 4 and 5 as desired.

7. To accept the additions and deletions, click OK. Or, to ignore all changes, click Cancel.

Importing or exporting a word list

Importing a word list is another way to add words to a User Dictionary. FileMaker Pro can also export the contents of a User Dictionary so that it can be used in other programs. Whether you're importing or exporting a word list, the files are always in Text-Only format. On import, FileMaker Pro doesn't require that the words be set up in any particular way. As long as a space, Tab, or Return character separates every word from the next word, FileMaker will consider the word for inclusion in the User Dictionary. On export, a User Dictionary is written as a text file, with every word separated from the next word by a line feed and carriage return (also known as a *DOS Text File*).

Importing and exporting work hand-in-hand. You export data from one program so that it can be imported into and used by another program. (To find out about other FileMaker Pro import and export capabilities, check out Chapter 16.)

STEPS: Importing or Exporting a Word List

1. Launch FileMaker Pro and open a database.

   Unless a database is open, the Spelling commands are disabled.

2. Switch to Browse or Layout mode.

   The Spelling commands are available only in these modes.

3. Choose Edit ➪ Spelling ➪ Edit User Dictionary.

   The User Dictionary dialog appears and presents a list of the words that the dictionary contains.

4. *To import a word list,* click Import, select a text file to import from the file dialog that appears, and click Open.

Importing word processing documents into a dictionary

During an import, FileMaker Pro ignores words already present in its Main Dictionary or in the current User Dictionary. Other than requiring Text-Only format, FileMaker isn't picky about the setup of the word list. You can use this fact to your advantage. You can take *any* word processing document, save a copy of it in Text-Only format, and then import the entire new document into the User Dictionary. Any new terms that are encountered will be added to the dictionary; words that are already in the Main or User Dictionary (the bulk of them, in most cases) will be ignored.

The words in the text file are compared with those in the Main and User Dictionaries. Any words that aren't found are added to the current User Dictionary; words that already exist in either of the dictionaries are ignored. An alert notifies you when the import is complete.

or

To export a word list, click Export. In the file dialog that appears, type a name for the file (or accept the one that is suggested), select a destination disk and folder, and click Save.

The User Dictionary's entire contents are saved as a text file. Each word is separated from the next word by a carriage return and line feed. An alert notifies you when the export is complete.

5. Click OK to dismiss the notification alert and click OK a second time to dismiss the User Dictionary dialog.

Merging User Dictionaries

Although it's nice to be able to create as many special-purpose User Dictionaries as you like, switching from one dictionary to another can be a pain. And if you aren't keeping careful track of which one you used last, chances are better than average that the wrong User Dictionary might be currently active.

If your User Dictionaries aren't gigantic, you can make life simpler by merging them into a single User Dictionary that you can use for most spell-checking sessions.

Note   In the following procedure, the new dictionary is referred to as the *primary User Dictionary.*

STEPS: Merging Dictionaries

1. Begin by creating a new User Dictionary to hold the merged User Dictionaries. Follow the steps listed in the section, "Creating a User Dictionary," earlier in the chapter and go to Step 4.

or

To merge dictionaries into an already existing User Dictionary, go to Step 2.

2. Choose Edit ⇨ Spelling ⇨ Select Dictionaries.

The Select Dictionaries dialog appears, as previously shown in Figure 12-3.

3. Click the Select button and navigate to the User Dictionary into which you wish to merge. Click Select to dismiss the Select a User Dictionary dialog and then click OK to close the Select Dictionaries dialog.

The selected User Dictionary becomes the current one.

4. Choose Edit ⇨ Spelling ⇨ Edit User Dictionary.

The User Dictionary dialog appears. (Refer to Figure 12-7.)

5. Click Export.

A standard file dialog appears.

6. Select an output location, and enter a name for the export file (or accept the proposed filename).

Tip

After you merge the export file with the primary User Dictionary (after completing Step 13), you'll have no further use for the export file. Although you can save it here to any disk and folder that you choose, you might want to save it to a location where it's easy to find and delete, such as the root (top) level of the start-up hard disk or to the Desktop/desktop.

7. Click Save.

The export commences. An alert notifies you when the export process is complete.

8. Click OK to dismiss that alert, and then click OK again to dismiss the User Dictionary dialog as well.

9. Choose Edit ⇨ Spelling ⇨ Select Dictionaries, and then select the primary User Dictionary. (See Step 1.)

10. Choose Edit ⇨ Spelling ⇨ Edit User Dictionary.

The User Dictionary dialog appears once again.

11. Click Import.

A standard file dialog appears.

12. Navigate to the disk and folder in which you saved the export file in Step 7, select the exported file, and click Import.

The import commences. After FileMaker Pro has successfully merged the two User Dictionaries, an alert will notify you.

13. Click OK to dismiss the alert, and then click OK again to dismiss the User Dictionary dialog as well.

If you want to merge additional User Dictionaries with the primary User Dictionary, repeat Steps 4–13.

Spelling Tips and Tricks

This section examines several easily mastered tricks for creating useful User Dictionaries and working with the spelling checker.

Creating a spelling list from an existing database

Having a spelling checker that questions most company names, unusual last names, and technical terms wastes time. Worse still, it encourages you not to use the spelling checker at all! (This is precisely why most people go, "Huh?" when they discover that a database program has a spelling checker. Because databases are often filled with proper nouns, spell-checking sessions can take forever.)

If you've been using FileMaker Pro for a while, you might have already completed the first step toward creating useful User Dictionaries. In an address database (Address Book Advanced, for example), you might have collected dozens of company names and people's last names. In an inventory database, you might already have entered the precise spellings of most of the important items that your company sells. A medical records database might contain the names of the majority of diseases that you treat. By using FileMaker Pro's Import/Export command, you can export the contents of these fields and create a text file that you can then import into a User Dictionary.

STEPS: Creating a Word List from an Existing Database

1. Open the database from which you intend to extract the word list.

2. Choose File ➪ Export Records.

   A file dialog appears, as shown in Figure 12-8.

3. Select a location for the export file, enter a filename for it, set the type to Tab-Separated Text (if it isn't already chosen), and click Save.

   The Specify Field Order for Export dialog appears, as shown in Figure 12-9. This dialog works much like the Sort dialog. The left side contains a list of all fields that have been defined for the database; the right side contains a list of the fields that are currently chosen to be exported (in the order in which they will be exported).

4. Add fields to be exported to the Field export order list by selecting them in the left-hand list and clicking Move. Remove unnecessary fields from the Field Order list (on the right) by clicking Clear All or by selecting individual fields and clicking Clear.

Mac

Windows

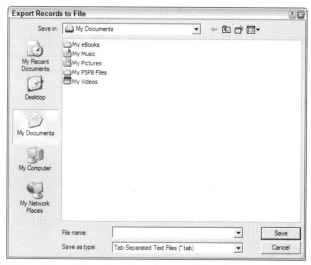

Figure 12-8: Exporting data from a FileMaker Pro database.

FileMaker Pro 7 added the option of exporting your data grouped by whatever grouping fields are specified for the current layout. You won't need that option here, but we mention it because you can see it in Figure 12-9.

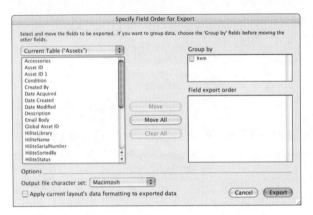

Figure 12-9: The Specify Field Order for Export dialog.

Note   Because FileMaker Pro databases can be relational, you might have defined one or more relationships between the current table and other tables. You can export fields from a related table by choosing the name of the relationship from the pop-up menu/drop-down list above the field list.

5. Make sure the Apply current layout's data formatting to exported data check box is not selected, and then click Export.

   The export file is created.

6. Choose Edit ➪ Spelling ➪ Select Dictionaries. The Select Dictionaries dialog appears, as previously shown in Figure 12-3. Click Select, navigate to and select the appropriate User Dictionary from the file list, and click Select/Open.

   These actions make the selected User Dictionary the one to receive the word list.

7. Choose Edit ➪ Spelling ➪ Edit User Dictionary.

   The User Dictionary dialog appears.

8. Click Import.

   A standard file dialog appears.

9. Navigate to the disk and folder in which you saved the export file in Step 3, select the export file, and click Open.

   The import commences. When FileMaker Pro has successfully imported the word list, an alert will notify you. Click OK to dismiss that dialog.

10. Scan the new word list, deleting any unnecessary entries by selecting each one and clicking Remove.

11. Click OK again to dismiss the User Dictionary dialog, saving the changes.

Restricting spelling checks to a subset of fields

Depending on the types of database fields you have created, you might have no desire to check the spelling in every field (using the Check Record command). Unfortunately, the only other option is to select and check one field at a time. Performing this task manually is time-consuming. However, you can simplify the process by creating a script that selects and checks only the desired fields one by one.

Figure 12-10 shows a sample script that checks the contents of a series of fields in a database. When the script executes, it selects the entire contents of the first field (Company) and executes the Check Selection command. After the first field is checked, the second field (Department) is selected, and the same procedure is used to check that field, and so on. Note that this script performs the spelling check for only the current record, and you must click the Done button to move from one field to the next.

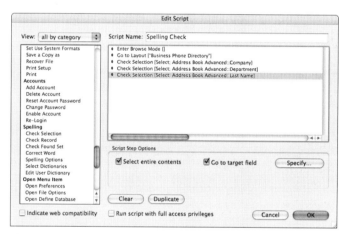

Figure 12-10: Steps for the Spelling Check script.

Note This is just an example showing how such a script might be created. In general, surnames and company names won't be in a dictionary (unless you imported your Address Book to avoid misspelling contact names).

To add fields to such a script, simply include additional Check Selection script steps. Be sure that the Select entire contents check box is selected for each Check Selection script step.

Summary

✦ You can have spelling checked as you type, on request, or both. You can check the spelling of any record, group of records, text selection, or set of field labels and static text on a given layout.

✦ You can employ a new alternative to as-you-type spell checking, where suspect words are underlined onscreen, allowing you to go back and (via a shortcut menu) resolve them on a case-by-case basis without the intrusion of traditional spell checking as you type.

✦ Only one Main Dictionary and one User Dictionary can be active at any given moment, but you can have more than one of each stored on disk and switch among them as needed.

✦ Each database remembers the last User Dictionary that was used. The next time you open the database, the same User Dictionary will be active again.

✦ User Dictionaries contain the special or unusual words you've added to them. You add words by clicking the Learn button during a spelling check, by editing the User Dictionary and typing the words, or by importing words from a standard text file.

✦ When FileMaker Pro imports a word list into a User Dictionary, it checks each word against the contents of the current Main Dictionary and User Dictionary, ignoring words that are already included.

✦ You can script a database to automate the spell checking of specific fields.

✦ You can import a User Dictionary that was created in another program if the dictionary can be saved as a text file.

✦   ✦   ✦

Printing

Having mastered the theory of designing and producing database reports, you're no doubt eager to see your work on paper. This chapter takes you step by step through the printing process — from setting up your computer to work with a particular printer to resolving problems that might arise as you print.

Although you'll usually want to print a report, FileMaker also allows you to print individual records, blank records (showing field placement in the current layout), script definitions, and field definitions. Many of the general printing procedures discussed in this chapter can be applied to printing documents in other programs, too.

The Steps in Printing

Printing from within FileMaker Pro involves three or four basic steps:

1. *Decide what to print.* After opening the appropriate database, you must decide what you want to print: a database report, only the current record, a blank record (no data) showing the current layout, one or all script definitions, or the field definitions.

    To print a report, you select the desired layout, select the records you want to include in the report, and sort the records. To print the current record, you must switch to the record that you want to print. To print a blank record, all you have to do is switch to the appropriate layout. To print script or field definitions, no preparatory work is needed. You specify what you want to print in the Print dialog.

2. *Specify a printer and print settings.* To select the printer you want to use, use the Printer Setup Utility or the Print dialog (Mac OS X); or the Print Setup or Print dialog (Windows).

In This Chapter

Specifying a printer to use

Setting page options for various printers

Preparing and previewing reports

Using the FileMaker Pro Print command

Avoiding and correcting printing problems

After you select a printer, you set print options in the Page Setup/Print Setup and Print dialogs within FileMaker Pro. (You can omit the process of selecting a printer if you always use the same printer. You can often omit choosing print options as well.)

After selecting a printer and Page Setup options, you can then preview the output in FileMaker Pro to make sure that it will print correctly. Previewing before printing is a good way to save paper.

3. *Print.* In the Print dialog (resulting from the File ➪ Print command), you specify what you want to print and then route it to a printer. If all goes well, the result of this process is a printout that contains just the information you need.

4. *Troubleshoot.* If you don't get the results you want, adopt a systematic approach to isolate and correct the problem.

Note   The Page Setup and Print dialogs shown in this chapter are from Mac OS X (version 10.4.3, a.k.a. "Tiger") and Windows XP Home, unless otherwise stated. If you have a different system software version or a different printer from the ones discussed here, the dialogs you see might appear slightly different.

Step 1: Decide what to print

The Print dialog (see Figure 13-1) offers FileMaker-specific print options. What you decide to print determines the necessary preparatory steps, if any. Here are the options:

✦ *Records being browsed:* Use this option when printing a report consisting of all or a selected subset of records.

✦ *Current record:* This option prints only the currently displayed record, as shown in the current layout.

✦ *Blank record, showing fields:* This option prints a blank record for the current layout. Fields can be displayed as formatted on the layout, with boxes around them, or underlined.

In versions prior to FileMaker Pro 7, you chose to print scripts from the Print dialog's FileMaker options/Print drop-down list. In FileMaker Pro 8, you select the script(s) you want printed in the ScriptMaker dialog and click the dialog's Print button. A standard Print dialog appears.

Similarly, printing field definitions has been moved to a Print button in the Define Database dialog (File ➪ Define ➪ Database or Shift+⌘+D/Ctrl+Shift+D) when the Fields pane is visible. When the Tables pane is visible, the Print button will cause the field definitions for any selected tables to print. However, when the Relationships pane is visible, the Print button prints the Relationships graph (after asking whether you want it on one or multiple pages). A standard Print dialog then appears.

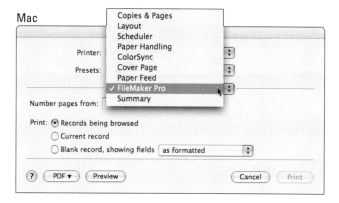

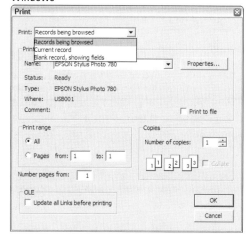

Figure 13-1: In the Print dialog, use the FileMaker options (Mac) or Print drop-down list (Windows) to specify what you want to print.

Records being browsed

When printing a report, this is the option you'll use. Because reports can be complex, you might have to take several preparatory steps prior to printing.

First, there's the matter of record selection. When printing using this option, File-Maker includes only the visible records: that is, the records that are contained in the current found set. To print the entire database, choose Records ➪ Show All Records. On the other hand, if you're interested in only a subset of the records, you can issue Find requests and/or manually hide irrelevant records by using the Omit Record command. The nature of your report determines which records you'll opt to print.

Consider this example. Susan is head of sales at a small company, and she has a FileMaker database containing records of every sales transaction. Susan wants to see how her West Coast salespeople have been doing.

All Susan needs to do is open the database and issue a Find request (Find requests are covered in Chapter 9) to locate all records in which West appears in the Region field. She switches to Find mode and enters **=West** into the Region field on the Find request. She also enters ≥**1/1/2005** in the Date of Sale field to limit the search to sales from the current calendar year.

Note To further restrict or expand the found set, Susan could use the Requests menu's Constrain Found Set or Extend Found Set commands, respectively. She might want to include the Alaska and Hawaii sales reps or eliminate California sales from the report, for example.

Next, there's the matter of data order. Rather than view records in the order in which they were created, you'll generally want to arrange them in an order that's appropriate for your report. You accomplish this by choosing the Records ➪ Sort command, selecting sort fields, and specifying a sort order for each selected field (ascending, descending, or custom — based on the order of a value list). In our example, Susan uses the Sort command to arrange the records alphabetically according to the salesperson's name (in ascending order) and, within each salesperson, the records are further sorted according to the amount of each sale (in descending order). You can refresh your memory about how Sorting works by reviewing Chapter 10.

Note When specifying sort fields for a report that relies on one or more sub-summary fields, be sure to specify, for each field affected, by which summary field it should be reordered.

Finally, you choose a layout and view. Both are used to format the data in the print-out. Susan switches to a previously created layout she designed for this report. The layout includes a Summary field — one that shows each salesperson's total sales this year — so that she won't have to add them manually. The layout is already in list view, which is often used in reports. After viewing this lengthy report (after all, it *does* include every sale made by every West Coast salesperson), Susan might want to generate a second report that omits the individual sales and only shows each person's total, sorted by state and salesperson.

STEPS: Preparing to Generate a Report

1. Open the database containing the information from which you want to prepare a report.
2. From the status area's Layouts menu, choose an appropriate layout from which to generate the report.

3. Switch to Find mode and issue one or more Find requests to locate the records you want to use in the report. (Or, in the case of a report that will use all records, choose Records ➪ Show All Records.)

4. Choose Records ➪ Sort to arrange the found set in a meaningful order.

5. Be sure that the records are displayed in the view that you want to print by choosing the appropriate View ➪ View As command (Form, List, or Table).

Current record

Prior to printing using this option, all you have to do is display the desired record. Switch to the appropriate layout; locate the record by clicking the book icon, moving the slider, or issuing a Find request; and then make certain the correct view (form, list, or table) is used by choosing the View ➪ View As command.

Blank record, showing fields

Two reasons why you might want to use this Print option follow:

✦ Printing a blank record is an excellent way to document each of the database layouts you've designed.

✦ A blank record can serve as a paper-and-pencil form for gathering the data.

When selecting this option, open the pop-up menu or drop-down list in the Print dialog (see Figure 13-2) to specify how the fields will be displayed in the printout: *as formatted* (as they appear on your layout), *with boxes* (surrounded by boxes that coincide with each field's width and height), or *with underlines* (underlines matching each field's placement on the layout and its width).

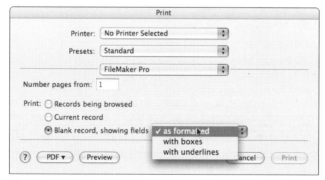

Figure 13-2: When printing a blank record, you can specify how the fields will be formatted.

Tip   Even though it *is* the default, printing by using the *as formatted* option is often the least appropriate choice. Many databases are designed so that the fields have no visible boxes around them or lines beneath them. Printing such a layout using this option will not give a clear indication of where the field boundaries are supposed to be.

Script

You might want to print a script when troubleshooting or documenting a database's scripts. The only decision you have to make is how many scripts you wish to print. Choose Scripts ➪ ScriptMaker, select one or more scripts in the list (as shown in Figure 13-3), and click the Print button. A standard Print dialog appears.

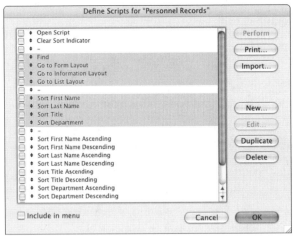

Figure 13-3: You can print any scripts you select in ScriptMaker.

Field definitions

Printing field definitions is another way to document a database's design. All information in the Define Database dialog's Fields pane is printed in an easy-to-read format. It doesn't matter whether a given field is used in *any* layout: Its field definition will still be included in the printout.

Tip   You can print field definitions from the Tables pane as well. In fact, you can select multiple tables and click the Print button to print field definitions for all the selected tables at one time.

Relationships Graph

The FileMaker Pro 8 Relationships Graph is a great step forward in graphically illustrating the structure and relationships between a database's tables, as shown in Figure 13-4.

Use the buttons in the View section to zoom or fit the graph into the visible area. The buttons in the Pages area show/hide page breaks and present the Page Setup/Print Setup dialog, respectively. Click Print when you're ready to use the standard Print dialog.

Step 2: Specify a printer and print settings

Before printing, you must choose a printer and use the Page Setup command (Mac) or Print Setup command (Windows) to enable FileMaker to print correctly. This is where you can specify the paper size or that the report should print in landscape orientation, for example.

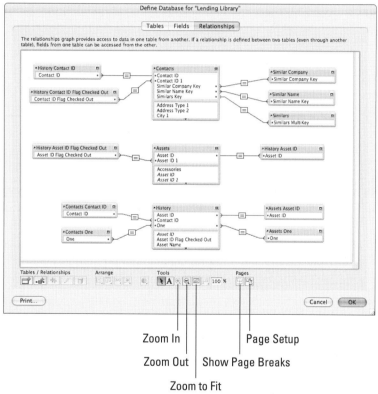

Zoom In   Page Setup

Zoom Out   Show Page Breaks

Zoom to Fit

Figure 13-4: You can also print the Relationships Graph.

Selecting a printer for a Macintosh

In Mac OS X, documents are automatically routed to your default printer unless you select a different printer during a given print job. To set a printer as your default printer, open Printer Setup Utility (found in the Applications ➪ Utilities folder), select the printer's name in the Printer List window, and choose Printers ➪ Make Default. (If you have only one installed printer, you can skip this procedure. When you installed the printer, it was automatically set as the default. If you later add another printer, it will become the default. Return to Printer Setup Utility as necessary to specify a different default printer.)

Note   If you are using Mac OS X, 10.4.x (Tiger), you can also set the default printer in the Print & Fax System Preferences pane.

You can specify a different (nondefault) printer for any print job. Choose File ➪ Print. The Print dialog appears. Select the printer's name from the Printer pop-up menu. (Refer to Figure 13-1.)

Selecting a printer for a Windows PC

Each time you print from a program running under Windows, you can send the print job to any installed printer. You can choose a printer from the Print dialog (refer to Figure 13-1) or the Print Setup dialog. (See Figure 13-5.)

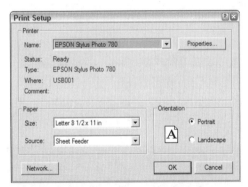

Figure 13-5: To specify a printer for the current print job, you can also choose it from the Name drop-down list in the Print Setup dialog.

Note   Under Windows, there is no standard name for the dialog in which you specify printer and page settings. It might be called Print Setup, Printer Setup, or Page Setup, depending on the program you're running. In FileMaker Pro, it's called Print Setup.

If you don't see your printer listed (perhaps you recently purchased a new printer, for example), you can add a printer driver for it by opening the Printers control panel and double-clicking the Add Printer icon.

Note When you install FileMaker Pro 8 for Windows, it initially uses the default Windows printer. If you later choose a different printer in the FileMaker Pro Print Setup dialog, the chosen printer becomes the new default but only for that FileMaker Pro database. The default Windows printer and the default FileMaker Pro printer are independent.

Using the Page Setup dialog on a Macintosh

When you choose File ⇨ Page Setup, the Page Setup dialog appears. It contains controls and options you use to adapt your printer settings for the kind of output you want to produce. Different printers and different versions of the Macintosh system software present different versions of the Page Setup dialog. Options that are listed depend on the printer's capabilities and on the types of paper the printer supports.

Page Setup options are document-specific rather than global. Even if you always want to print in landscape mode, for example, you must set that option individually for each document. (Thus, the time to normally use Page Setup in FileMaker Pro is just before you print a report from the currently open database.) Luckily, however, the most recent Page Setup settings used with a given document are stored along with the document when it is saved.

Although the printer you use is probably different from ours, in order to help you understand what the various Page Setup options mean, the paragraphs that follow explain how Page Setup works with an NEC SuperScript 4200N color laser printer. Refer to your printer's documentation or Help file for information concerning your particular printer.

Begin by opening the Format for pop-up menu and selecting the name of the printer you're going to use, as shown in Figure 13-6. Doing so enables you to print to printer-specific sizes of paper. (If you don't mind restricting your paper choices to ones that are generally available to all printers, such as US Letter and US Legal, you can select Any Printer.)

The three Page Setup options are Paper Size, Orientation, and Scale. Click the Paper size pop-up menu to choose the size you wish to use for the current print job.

Next, you'll see three orientation icons. Click the icon on the left for portrait mode, in which text prints in the usual way. Click either of the other two icons for *landscape mode,* in which text prints across the long dimension of the paper (sideways). The landscape choices are good for fitting wide records or reports onto a single sheet of paper. Note that the landscape choices differ in the direction in which text will be printed. The center icon indicates that when a sheet comes out of the printer, the top-most text on each page will be positioned on the right edge of the paper. To cause the text to appear on the left edge of the page (as it comes out of the printer), click the third icon.

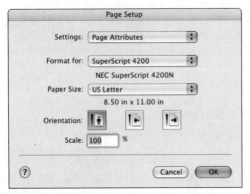

Figure 13-6: The Page Setup dialog in Macintosh OS X.

 Note

If you're wondering why there are two landscape settings, it's to facilitate printing of two-sided documents or on paper that is prepunched or has a preprinted header. This allows you to match the print orientation with the paper characteristics as loaded in the printer. As an example, viewgraph transparencies frequently have a white edge along one side. You'll typically want that to be the top of your landscape print, and you can tell Page Setup whether that top edge is on the right or the left. (Summary Reports often make good slides for a corporate presentation.) The two landscape printing choices are sometimes called *short-edge binding* and *long-edge binding*, from left to right.

Finally, the Scale text box at the bottom of the dialog is where you set scaling or magnification. Type a number directly into the text box to set the scaling percentage. To print a document at its normal size, leave Scale set at 100 (the default setting).

Setting page options on a Macintosh

No matter what printer you're using — whether it's the latest model or an old standby — you set page options for your printer in the same way. The following procedure describes in general terms how to use the Page Setup dialog for almost any printer:

1. Open the document you want to print (a FileMaker Pro database, for example).

2. Choose File ➪ Page Setup.

   A Page Setup dialog appears.

3. Select the size of paper you will be using.

   The standard choice in the United States is US Letter.

4. Choose a paper orientation.

   Click the left icon, which has an image of an upright torso, to choose portrait mode. Click the center or right icon to choose landscape mode.

5. Select a magnification/scaling level or leave this option at 100% to print at the standard size.

6. Click OK.

If you always intend to print information from this document or database on the same kind of paper, in the same orientation, and at the same size, you need to configure Page Setup only once — these settings are saved when you save the document. Remember, however, that the Page Setup options you just selected are specific to this document or database; they have no effect on how any *other* document or database will print.

Using the Print Setup dialog on a PC

When you choose Print Setup, Printer Setup, or Page Setup from the File menu of any Windows program, a dialog similar to the one shown in Figure 13-5 appears. At a minimum, the primary dialog has four options:

✦ *Name:* The printer you intend to use to print the current document. (All printers for which you have installed printer drivers are listed in the Name drop-down list.)

✦ *Size:* The size and type of the paper that will be used.

✦ *Source:* Where the paper will be fed from, such as the default paper tray.

✦ *Orientation:* Whether the document will be printed right-side up (portrait) or sideways (landscape).

To view and set additional printer-specific options, click the Properties button. Depending on the capabilities of the printer, the dialog's Properties section might contain one or several pages of options, such as Paper and Graphics. To view different classes of printer properties, click a tab at the top of the dialog.

Tip

Although the options that you will always want to check are presented on the first page of the Print Setup/Page Setup dialog, you should also familiarize yourself with the options in the Properties section of the dialog.

Previewing before printing

More paper has been wasted because of minor problems with a document's appearance than any other problem. Paper waste can often be avoided by previewing documents onscreen prior to printing them. Admittedly, checking them isn't always easy (or even possible) in all Macintosh and Windows applications. FileMaker Pro, however, has a Preview mode enabling you to see how a job will print.

To switch to Preview mode, choose it from the mode selector pop-up menu at the bottom of the database window, via the Preview mode button at top of the status area, or from the View menu (or press ⌘+U/Ctrl+U). You'll see a view similar to that shown in Figure 13-7.

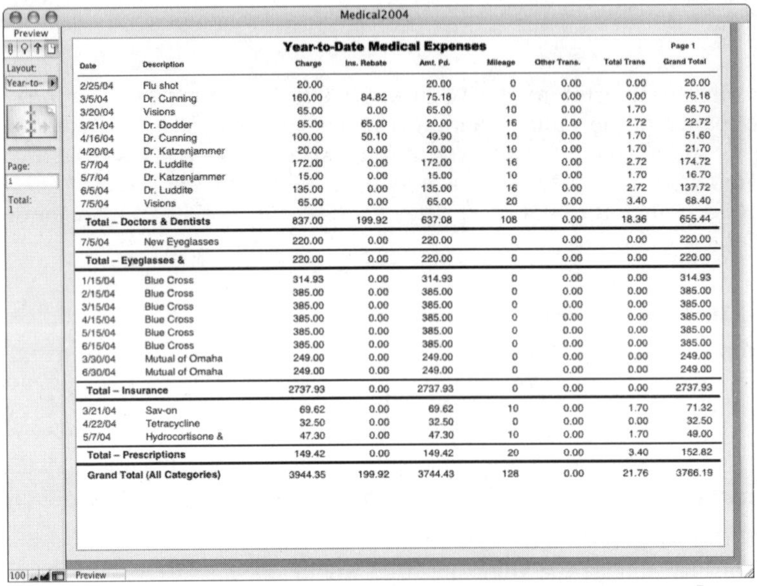

Figure 13-7: A database report in Preview mode.

Preview mode's output is divided into pages, navigable by clicking the book icon. Use the scroll bars to move around in the view and check its contents. If you want to determine the total number of pages in the report, drag the slider under the book icon all the way to the right. (FileMaker Pro doesn't know how many pages the report contains until you perform this action or click through all the book pages unless there is only one page.)

If your report looks satisfactory and you want a permanent copy of it, you can print it by choosing File ➪ Print (⌘+P/Ctrl+P).

If problems are detected in Preview mode, you have several options. If the problem is just a case of getting everything to fit, you might be able to correct it by adjusting the scaling in the Page Setup dialog or by switching from portrait to landscape printing (although the latter will also affect the number of pages in the report). This might not be the best solution if you're preparing presentation copies of reports, however.

For more serious Preview problems, you might need to go back to Layout mode and make adjustments. Omitting unnecessary fields is often a good idea to provide more room for relevant data. Preview mode can also show you which fields are being truncated, giving you an opportunity to go to Layout mode and expand them to accommodate the data. (Consult Chapter 11 for more information on the art of preparing reports, including tweaking the layout and creating new, report-specific layouts.)

STEPS: Previewing a Report and Correcting Errors

1. Prepare a report according to the steps presented earlier in this chapter.

2. Switch to Preview mode.

3. If the screen isn't large enough to display the entire page, use the scroll bars to move around on each page, use the Zoom controls, or resize the database window.

4. Click the book icon or move the slider to view any additional pages of the report.

5. Carefully review each page to ensure that all data fits without running off the edge. Also check for other problems, such as data that's truncated within fields.

6. Correct errors in Layout mode or by setting different options in the Page Setup/Print Setup dialog.

When the report appears satisfactory, you're ready to print.

Step 3: Print

Printing should seem like a breeze after all this preparatory work. To print records, reports, field definitions, or scripts in FileMaker Pro, choose the File ➪ Print command (or press ⌘+P/Ctrl+P) and then set options in the Print dialog that appears.

Printing on a Macintosh

Choosing the Print command presents a Print dialog. The contents and appearance of the dialog vary, depending on the printer you've chosen and the version of the system software you're using. The following section explains how to use the Print dialog in OS X (Panther) for one fairly capable printer.

The Print command: NEC SuperScript 4200N

The Macintosh Print dialog is divided into categories; you select a category from the pop-up menu near the dialog's center. We'll start with the Copies & Pages category. (See Figure 13-8.)

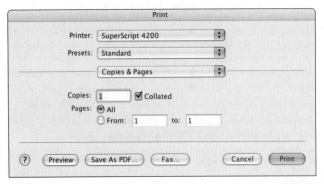

Figure 13-8: The Print dialog for a NEC SuperScript 4200N.

In the Copies text box, enter the number of copies you want to print. Select the Collated check box if you wish the report to print straight through for each copy. If Collated is unchecked, you will get *n* copies of the first page, followed by *n* copies of the second page, and so forth.

Next, specify the particular pages to print. Select the All radio button to print the entire report. On the other hand, if you want to print a range of pages, enter the appropriate page numbers in the From and to text boxes. For example, enter **2** in the From box and **4** in the to box to print pages 2–4.

You can view and set additional print options by choosing another category from the pop-up menu in the Print dialog. Here are some of the other important print options you might find, depending upon your printer:

✦ *Layout (Layout category):* This option enables you to print multiple report pages on each piece of paper, as well as optionally print a border around each page. See "Using the Page Setup dialog on a Macintosh," earlier in this chapter.

✦ *Destination (Output Options category):* Select the File check box to create a PDF or PostScript file into which the print job is spooled. You can send such a file to a service bureau for printing on a high-end image-setter. (Note, however, that this is seldom done with a database. Generating print files is more commonly done with illustrations and desktop publishing files.)

Note   You can also create a PDF file without going through this step by clicking the Save As PDF button at the bottom of the Print dialog. (With Mac OS X 10.4 – Tiger – it is simply the PDF button with some additional options if you click, turning it into a pop-up menu of choices.)

✦ *Scheduled Printing (Scheduler category):* In the Print dialog's Scheduler pane, you can tell your Mac to print the job now, to print at a specific time, or to save it in the print queue for later printing. You can also set a priority for the job, which moves it higher or lower in the printer's job queue.

Note On Hold is a handy option for those occasions when you're traveling and not connected to the printer or to the network with the printer. You can have the print job all set to go when you get back to the office and use Printer Setup Utility to print the saved job.

✦ *Paper Handling (Paper Handling category):* In the Print dialog's Paper Handling pane, you can tell your Mac to print the pages in reverse order. You can also specify whether all pages, just the odd-numbered pages, or just the even numbered pages should print. The latter two choices are useful if you wish to print two-sided because most printers don't directly support *duplex* (two-sided) printing.

✦ *Print Color (ColorSync category):* Choose whether the color matching should be done on your Mac or in the printer from the Color Conversion pop-up menu. Choose any Black & White or tone filter from the Quartz Filter pop-up menu.

✦ *Cover Page (Cover Page category):* You use this option to designate whether to include a cover page as part of the print job and whether to place the cover page at the report's beginning (Before) or end (After). A cover page is useful if you're printing on a network printer and you want to make sure your print job is properly identified. You can modify the cover page with various stamps such as Confidential or Secret, depending upon the printer type.

✦ *PostScript Errors (Error Handling category):* You can select one of the following notification methods to be used if an error occurs during a print job: No special reporting (nothing happens) or Print detailed report (an error report is sent to the printer). Some printers, such as the SuperScript 4200N, also allow you to specify that the printer should switch to a different paper tray when encountering an error.

✦ *Paper Source (Paper Feed category):* You can specify which paper tray (if the printer has multiple trays) supplies the paper and whether the printer should print the first page from one tray and subsequent pages from a different tray (handy when dealing with letterhead). Additionally, if the printer supports manual feed, you can specify that here.

✦ *FileMaker Pro (FileMaker category):* Be sure to choose this category to set options that are specific to FileMaker Pro. (See Figure 13-9.) The Number pages from text box is where you to enter the number to use for the first page of the printout. For example, you would enter a number other than 1 if you were preparing several smaller reports that will eventually be assembled into one grand document. In that example, you would let FileMaker Pro know to begin numbering each report section where the previous section left off.

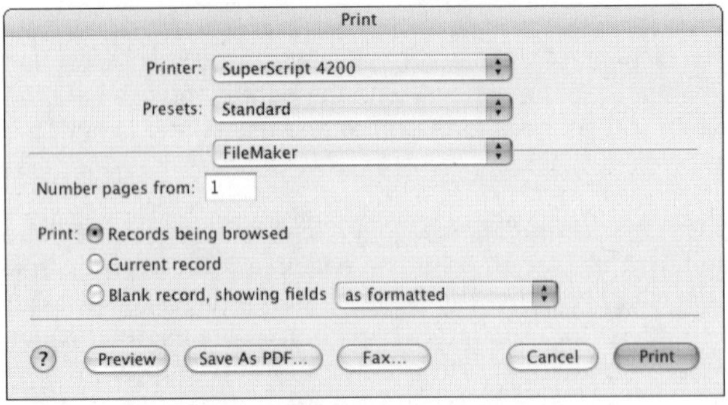

	Print
Printer:	SuperScript 4200 ⬍
Presets:	Standard ⬍
	FileMaker ⬍

Number pages from: 1

Print: ⦿ Records being browsed
⃝ Current record
⃝ Blank record, showing fields as formatted ⬍

? Preview Save As PDF... Fax... Cancel Print

Figure 13-9: FileMaker-specific print options.

Tip If you have a group of settings that you will be using frequently, choose Save As from the Presets pop-up menu and name your settings group in the dialog that appears. In future print sessions (in FileMaker Pro or other programs), you can choose that settings group from the Presets pop-up menu without having to go through each pane. Further, you can make one-time, minor modifications to a Preset if you have one relatively close to what you want.

When you have finished setting options in the Print dialog, click Print to print the material or click Cancel if you change your mind.

Tip OS X applications can create an Adobe Acrobat (PDF) file during a print job instead of routing the output to a printer. The advantage of such a file is that it can be viewed and printed by virtually anyone, using a free copy of Acrobat Reader or the free Preview application that comes with OS X. Just click the Print dialog's Save As PDF pop-up menu in OS X 10.4 (at the bottom). Of course, if you are printing a report, you have even more versatility employing FileMaker Pro 8's new File ➪ Save/Send Records As ➪ PDF menu option. However, for a PDF of (for example) the Relationships Graph, the Save As PDF button (PDF button in OS X 10.4) is your route to success.

Printing on a PC

Choosing the File ➪ Print command (or pressing Ctrl+P) presents a Print dialog. (See Figure 13-10.)

Regardless of the printer chosen from the Name list, the options remain the same. The most important ones are as follows:

✦ *Name:* Selects the printer that will receive the print job. (If you want to change some of the print options for the current print job only, click the Properties button. After printing, the properties will revert to their previous settings.)

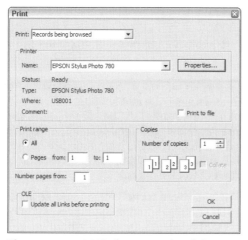

Figure 13-10: A Windows XP Print dialog.

✦ *Print range:* Specifies the pages to print. Select the All radio button to print the entire report. On the other hand, if you want to print a range of pages, enter the appropriate page numbers in the from and to text boxes. For example, enter **2** in the from box and **4** in the to box to print pages 2–4.

✦ *Copies:* Specifies the number of copies you want to print. If you're making multiple printouts, select the Collate check box to request that each copy be printed separately.

✦ *Number pages from:* Sets the page number to be used on the first page of the printout. For example, you would enter a number other than **1** if you were preparing one grand document from several smaller reports. In this case, you would let FileMaker Pro know to begin numbering each report section where the previous section left off.

✦ *OLE:* If the current database contains OLE (embedded) objects, you can elect to print them in their current state (unchecked) or only after they have all been updated (checked). Note that updating OLE links can be time-consuming.

The most important FileMaker-specific print option is chosen from the Print drop-down list at the top of the dialog, where you specify what you want printed: Records being browsed, Current record, or Blank record showing fields. For a detailed explanation of these options, refer to "Step 1: Decide what to print," earlier in this chapter.

After you've set all options, click OK to begin printing or Cancel if you change your mind.

Step 4: Troubleshoot

Things occasionally go wrong. Here are some common printing problems and what to do if you encounter them:

✦ *My printer doesn't do anything.* Is it turned off (the #1 cause of missed print jobs), or is it offline? Are cable connections snug and secure? On a Mac, if you're using a printer that doesn't require AppleTalk, be sure that the correct connection type is selected in the Printer Setup Utility. On a PC, make certain that your chosen printer is indeed connected to the port specified in the Where line of the Print or Print Setup dialog. (Serial printers connect to COM or USB ports; parallel printers connect to LPT ports.)

✦ *The printer isn't ready.* If your printer has been turned off, be sure to allow enough time for it to warm up. If you try to print immediately after you turn on the printer, you will likely see a message telling you the printer isn't responding. Give it a minute or so before you try again. (Other issues, such as a paper jam or being out of toner, ink, or paper, can also cause the printer to be "not ready.")

✦ *No printers are listed in the Print dialog or in Printer Setup Utility (Mac).* If you've recently installed OS X and have an older printer, there's a chance that you won't be able to print directly from FileMaker Pro (or anything else). Support for many older printers — especially those over four years old — is spotty although you might find that they still work when printing in Classic (OS 9). You have several options:

  • Open Printer Setup Utility and attempt to add your printer. (Choose File ⇨ Print from FileMaker or any other application, choose Edit Printer List from the Printer pop-up menu in the Print dialog, and then click the Add Printer button in Printer Setup Utility.) If this fails, check Apple or the printer manufacturer's Web site for OS X-compatible printer drivers.

  • Buy an OS X-supported printer.

  • In the Print dialog, set options and then click the Save As PDF button to generate an Adobe Acrobat (PDF) file rather than a printout. Open the PDF file with an OS 9 copy of Acrobat Reader in Classic and print the file.

✦ *Print quality seems poor.* Does your laser printer need more toner; does your inkjet need more ink or to have its nozzles cleaned; or does your dot-matrix printer need a new ribbon? Failure to print dense, even, black tones can be caused by any of these situations. You can temporarily correct this problem on a laser printer by gently rotating the toner cartridge a few times or by increasing the print density setting (if the printer has one).

✦ *Laser printing is taking too long.* Occasionally, some print jobs might simply be too complex for your laser printer to handle, especially older PostScript printers with limited memory. Try reprinting them with different print options, printing a smaller set of pages, or turning off background printing. This might help you isolate the cause of the problem.

✦ *Script-driven reports are printing incorrectly.* In order to make it simple to create routine reports, it's common practice to create a ScriptMaker script to automate the process. Unfortunately, the process of changing printers or computers can occasionally cause the script to produce some unusual results. For example, landscape reports can revert to portrait mode. To correct such a problem, use the appropriate procedure for your computer and operating system to select the desired printer, switch to the report layout, choose File ➪ Page SetUp/Print Setup, and set the correct orientation. Finally, choose Scripts ➪ ScriptMaker, edit the report script, and immediately click OK when the Script Definition dialog appears. In the dialog that appears next, choose to Replace the Page Setup settings.

Effective Printing Tips

Every type of printer has some quirks. Understanding the more common idiosyncrasies and knowing how to deal with them cannot only save you some grief but can also help you achieve better results. The following basic hints apply to the most common types of printers.

Laser printers

✦ *Right side up:* Not many people are aware that most laser paper and copier paper has a good side and a so-so side. (The same holds true for inkjet papers.) The paper's manufacturer intends for the paper to be printed only on the good side. You can achieve the best results by making sure you print on the correct side.

Sometimes, you cannot easily determine which side is the good side by just looking. Although the good side might be shinier, looking at the paper package is a better way to tell. In most cases, you'll see an arrow or a similar indicator that shows which side is meant to be printed on. When inserting the paper into your printer, be sure that the correct side is up. (Some printers expect paper to be inserted face up, and others print on the side of the paper that is face down. If you aren't sure which way you should insert paper into your printer, refer to the printer manual.)

✦ *Paper jams:* Everybody hates paper jams and misfeeds. You can't avoid them all, but you can cut down on their number and frequency. When you load a printer, grasp the paper firmly and *riffle* the edges with your thumb. (Draw your thumb down the edges.) This action loosens the sheets from each other, lessening the chance that multiple sheets will be drawn into the printer together.

✦ *Font issues:* A PostScript printer takes a long time to do two things: construct a font for use in a document and prepare a graphic. You can save time by using only fonts that are built into the printer or are available on a printer's dedicated hard disk. (The printer doesn't have to construct these fonts.) Also, try to limit the number of different text styles you use. Using too many fonts makes documents print slowly and can, in extreme cases, crash the system or the printer.

✦ *Printing labels:* Several companies (such as Avery) make special labels for use in laser printers. Resist the temptation to use only a few labels from one sheet and then reuse the sheet later. After a few passes, the heat of the printing process can cause the remaining labels to peel off during printing, resulting in expensive trouble. Try to do label printing jobs in large batches and throw away the unused labels from each batch (or find another use for them).

Inkjet printers

✦ *Be careful what you print.* Avoid printing long reports that have a large number of graphics. Graphics consume a great deal of expensive ink and take longer to print. You can also conserve ink by carefully choosing or formatting your layouts. Avoid creating or choosing layouts that include large areas or bands of solid color, for example.

✦ *Lower quality equals faster printing.* To speed up printing, limit the number of fonts in the report. You might also want to select a lower print quality for jobs that will not be used for presentations.

✦ *Match your paper and quality settings.* Most reports are printed on standard laser or inkjet paper. Choosing a high-quality setting (or dots per inch) when using low-quality paper wastes ink and often produces a soggy print job. If you need high-quality printouts, invest in appropriate paper.

Dot-matrix printers

✦ *Set the proper tension.* When you're using tractor-fed computer paper, make sure the tension is adjusted correctly between the two feed mechanisms. Too little tension can cause the paper to jam and misfeed; too much tension can tear off the perforated edges and cause another kind of misfeed. Getting the tension exactly right is an art.

✦ *Use fresh or well-inked ribbons.* Use only new ribbons and keep them well inked. Old ribbons can fray, resulting in ugly printouts and potential damage to the print head.

Summary

✦ In Mac OS X, you can print to any printer that has been installed under Mac OS X. Specify the printer to use by running Printer Setup Utility or by selecting the printer's name in the Print dialog's Printer pop-up menu.

✦ On a PC, you can print to any printer that has been installed under Windows. You can select a printer to use for the current print job from either the Print Setup or the Print dialog.

✦ In the Page Setup/Print Setup dialog, you set page options for the document you're about to print. On a Mac, these options include the size of paper you want to use, the amount of scaling/magnification (if any), and the page orientation. Page Setup settings are document-specific and are saved along with the other information contained in the document. On a PC, options include the printer to be used, the size and type of paper, the source of the paper, and the page orientation.

✦ Prior to printing a FileMaker Pro report, you should select the records you want to include, sort them in an appropriate order, and choose a layout and view in which to display them.

✦ You can use Preview mode to view a report onscreen. Preview mode shows *exactly* how the report will look when you print it. You can correct problems at this stage before you waste time, paper, and toner (or ink).

✦ Printing is accomplished via the Print dialog. You can use it to set the number of copies to print; which pages to print; whether to use color or grays (if your printer can handle them); and exactly what database content to print, including the current record or the found set.

✦ You can avoid many potential printing problems by configuring your printer correctly before you print. Checking the integrity of all cable connections, loading paper the right way, and restricting the use of fonts and graphics can ensure better results.

✦   ✦   ✦

Putting FileMaker Pro to Work

Calculations and Computations

One key advantage FileMaker Pro (and other database management systems) has over traditional file cabinets of forms is its ability to quickly and accurately generate derived data. You've seen this already with Summary fields, which derive information for a collection of records. Calculation fields are similar in many ways, but they derive their contents from other fields within the same or related records. For example, in an invoice database where each record is an order, you can total all the item prices and compute the sales tax. If the cost of shipping varies according to distance, you can determine how much to charge each order, based on the destination ZIP code. FileMaker Pro has a variety of computational capabilities to make these and similar tasks easy.

You use a Calculation field to perform an operation or a series of operations on fields within a record (and in related records). The operations you can perform include the standard arithmetic functions, logical operations, and even special operations (called *functions*) that perform complex calculations on numbers, dates, times, timestamps, and text.

About Calculation Fields

The data in a given Calculation field consists of whatever result is obtained when the field's definition is evaluated for that particular record. The definition specifies, in mathematical form, what manipulations to perform on the contents of one or more other fields in the current record and/or related records. The results of these manipulations (or operations) are then displayed as the field's contents.

Here's an example: Suppose you have an invoice database containing a field named Merchandise Total. You want to compute the sales tax on this total and display the bill's grand total (the merchandise total plus the sales tax). You could use Calculation fields for both the sales tax and the grand total. The field definitions might look like this:

```
Sales Tax = Merchandise Total * .06 [Multiply total by tax rate]
Grand Total = Merchandise Total + Sales Tax [Add tax to total]
```

If the current record shows a Merchandise Total of $23.75, the Sales Tax field would display $1.425, and the Grand Total would display $25.175. Of course, you would want to round this figure off to the nearest cent before presenting a bill. FileMaker Pro enables you to round numbers easily, as you will see shortly.

As noted at the beginning of this chapter, Calculation fields are similar to Summary fields. There is one significant difference, however. Summary formulas are calculated across all browsed records, whereas the Calculation field formulas apply only to data in that individual record (and related records). For example, if you want to compute the total sales for all the invoices issued over a certain span of time, you define a Summary field, but to calculate the merchandise total *within* an invoice, you use a Calculation field.

Calculation fields can do much more than just add or multiply the contents of other fields. Calculation fields can also manipulate the contents of Text fields and can perform tests on the contents of fields to determine which alternative course of action to take.

A formula in a Calculation field can contain several components: field references, operators, constants, and built-in functions. You should have a basic understanding of these components before you begin creating Calculation fields.

Note   FileMaker Pro doesn't restrict the use of formulas to Calculation fields. Formulas can also be used to validate field data as it is entered or edited, as information to be auto-entered into fields and as components of scripts. For information on using formulas for data validation or auto-entry, see Chapter 5. For details on using formulas in ScriptMaker scripts, refer to Chapter 15.

FileMaker Pro uses *operators* to specify how to manipulate data items. Operators fall into four categories:

✦ *Arithmetic:* Perform computations on numbers.

✦ *Logical:* Test whether specified conditions are true or false; this information can then be used to determine a course of action.

✦ *Comparison:* Compare its operands and return a true or false value.

✦ *Text:* Work with text, extracting information from it or converting it to another form.

Arithmetic operators

The arithmetic operators in Table 14-1 perform the basic functions of arithmetic.

<table>
<tr><td colspan="2" align="center">Table 14-1
Arithmetic Operators</td></tr>
<tr><td>*Operator*</td><td>*What It Means*</td></tr>
<tr><td>( )</td><td>Parentheses override the natural evaluation precedence. FileMaker Pro evaluates expressions from left to right, performing exponentiation first, followed by multiplication and division, followed (finally) by addition and subtraction.</td></tr>
<tr><td>+</td><td>The plus sign performs addition (for example, 2 + 3 yields 5).</td></tr>
<tr><td>−</td><td>The minus sign performs subtraction (for example, 3 − 2 yields 1).</td></tr>
<tr><td>*</td><td>The asterisk indicates multiplication (for example, 2 * 3 yields 6).</td></tr>
<tr><td>/</td><td>The slash indicates division (for example, 3 / 2 yields 1.5).</td></tr>
<tr><td>^</td><td>The caret indicates exponentiation, raising a number to a power (for example, 3 ^ 2 is three to the second power, or 9).</td></tr>
</table>

Logical operators

Logical operators combine *Boolean* (true and false) values to test for the truth of a more complex expression. Here's an example:

```
From California AND FEMALE [the individual is a woman from California]
```

This statement is true when both conditions are true, and false if either is false *or* if both are false.

Why should you care? Because you can have a Calculation field perform additional steps that are based on whether a statement is true or false. For example, you might use the following formula in the Calculation field to determine the magnitude of a salesperson's bonus:

```
If ((Salary > 50000) AND (Sales >= 10000), Salary * 0.03, If
((Salary <= 50000) AND (Sales >= 10000), Salary * 0.035, If
(Sales >= 7500), Salary * 0.02, 0), 0)
```

If the salesperson has a base salary over $50,000, his bonus is 3% of his salary when his sales hit or surpass $10,000; however, if his salary is $50,000 or less, he receives a 3.5% bonus when sales exceed $10,000 or a 2% bonus when sales reach $7,500 but don't reach $10,000. You will learn more about using logical operators to perform tasks such as this as the chapter progresses. (Pay particular attention to the section on the If function.)

Table 14-2 lists the logical operators and their meanings.

Table 14-2
Logical Operators

Operator	What It Means
AND	Used to combine the results of two separate tests. The result is true *if and only if* the results of both tests are true. For example, 3 > 2 AND 2 < 3 is true.
OR	Used to combine the results of two separate tests. The result is true if either or both of the tests are true. For example, 3 > 2 OR 2 > 3 is true.
XOR	Used to combine the results of two separate tests. The result is true only when just one of the tests is true. If both tests are true or both are false, the result is false. For example, 3 > 2 XOR 2 > 3 is true. (In computer parlance, this is known as an *exclusive OR*.)
NOT	Used to switch a test's result to its opposite. For example, NOT 2 > 3 is true.

Comparison operators

Comparison operators evaluate how two values compare and, like logical operators, return a TRUE or FALSE value (1 and 0, respectively). Table 14-3 enumerates the comparison operators.

Table 14-3
Comparison Operators

Operator	What It Means
=	Means *equal*. The test is true if the items on both sides of the sign are exactly equal in value. For example, the statement 1 + 1 = 2 is true.
<> or @@ (Mac); <> (PC)	Means *not equal to*. The test is true if the items on both sides of the sign are not equal in value. For example, "Apple" <> "Banana" is true.
>	Means *greater than*. The test is true if the value of the item at the left of the sign exceeds the value of item to the right. For example, 3 > 2 is true. For text arguments, *greater than* means later in the standard collating sequence (for example, alphabetic order).

<	Means *less than.* The test is true if the value of the item at the left of the sign is smaller than the value of the item to the right. For example, $2 < 3$ is true. For text arguments, *less than* means earlier in the standard collating sequence (for example, alphabetic order).
≤ <= (Mac); <= (PC)	Means *less than or equal to.* For example, $2.9 + 0.1 \le 3$ is true.
≥ or >= (Mac); >= (PC)	Means *greater than or equal to.* For example, $2.9 + 1.5 \ge 3$ is true.

You can type the less-than-or-equal-to (≤), greater-than-or-equal-to (≥), and not-equal (≠) symbols by pressing Option+, [comma], Option+. [period], and Option+= [equal], respectively. These symbols don't exist on a PC, as noted in Table 14-3.

Text operators

Table 14-4 lists the three basic text operators.

Table 14-4
Basic Text Operators

Operator	What It Means
&	Used to combine *(concatenate)* two Text fields (or expressions) into one. For example, "market" & "place" yields marketplace.
" "	Used to indicate a text constant. If you enter a text item without quotes, FileMaker assumes that you mean the name of a field. "Jennifer" + Last Name returns Jennifer Simpson, if the Last Name field contains Simpson.

¶	Used to indicate a paragraph break within a text constant. If you want a constant to have more than one line, use this operator to separate the lines. (The symbol must be enclosed within the quotation marks of the text constant.) For example, "Jennifer¶Simpson" yields the following:
	
	`Jennifer`
	`Simpson`
	
	To type the ¶ symbol on a Mac, press Option+7. On a Windows PC, you can select this character from the Character Map utility (choose Start ⇨ All Programs ⇨ Accessories ⇨ System Tools ⇨ Character Map). Additionally, you will find a button for this symbol with the other operators (+, -, *, and so forth) in Calculation dialogs.

Creating an expression

Operators are combined with numeric or text constants and field names to create expressions. Think of an expression as a mathematical statement. From an earlier example, both of the following are statements:

```
Sales Tax = .06 * Merchandise Total
Grand Total = Merchandise Total + Sales Tax
```

The sales tax rate (.06) is a numeric *constant;* that is, its value doesn't change. Merchandise Total represents the contents of that field in the current record; it can change from record to record. If you recall your junior/middle/high school algebra, you will recognize Merchandise Total (or any valid field name) as a *variable.* Expressions consist of constants and variables separated by operators.

You can build complicated expressions in FileMaker Pro. For example, consider the following expression:

```
1 + 2 * 3
```

FileMaker Pro evaluates expressions according to the standard algebraic order of operations, which specifies that all multiplication is done before any addition. The result for the preceding expression is 7 (2 * 3 = 6; 6 + 1 = 7) and not 9 (1+ 2 = 3; 3 * 3 = 9), which you might expect if all operations were performed strictly in left-to-right order.

To force FileMaker Pro to perform operations in the order you want, you can use parentheses. Operations within parentheses are performed first, from innermost to outermost. You can nest operations within parentheses to gain further control. For example, the following expression yields 18:

```
((( 1 + 2 ) * 3 ) * 2 )
```

Without parentheses, it would equal 13.

The standard order of operations is as follows:

1. Exponentiation

2. Multiplication and division

3. Addition and subtraction

You can also use parentheses with logical and comparison expressions. For example, the following expression is true:

```
(3 > 2 OR 2 > 3) AND 2 > 1
```

Creating a Calculation Field

To create a Calculation field, you decide what type of results you want, determine the necessary expression, and then define the field. After you create the Calculation field in the Define Database dialog's Fields pane, the Specify Calculation dialog appears. (See Figure 14-1.)

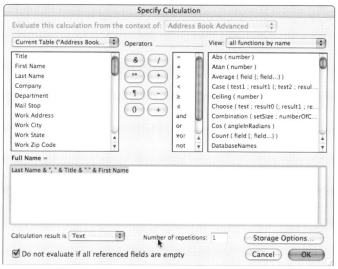

Figure 14-1: Defining a Calculation field.

The current table's fields appear in a scrolling list at the left. If you want to use a related table's fields in this equation, choose the relationship from the pop-up menu/drop-down list above the field list.

The available operators are in the center of the dialog. To the right are the FileMaker Pro functions. You'll learn more about functions in the next section. For now, you need only to know that a function is a predefined set of operations that operate on specific kinds of data. A function operates on the data, known as the function's *arguments,* and then returns a *result.*

Beneath these sections is a large blank area. As you create the formula for the Calculation field, it appears in this area. You can type the formula directly or simply choose the appropriate field names, operators, and functions (by clicking or double-clicking them). Below this area, a pop-up menu/drop-down list indicates what type of data the field's result should be. You must select the correct result type. The check boxes and buttons in this section of the dialog enable you to set storage options for the field, designate it as a repeating field (used in invoice line items, for example), and tell FileMaker Pro what to do if all fields referenced in the formula are empty.

As an example, suppose that you have a database for entering sales information. The following steps show how to define a new Calculation field named Sales Tax that calculates a 7 percent tax. (To keep things simple, assume that *all* items sold are taxable.)

1. Choose File ⇨ Define ⇨ Database and select the Fields tab in the Define Database dialog that appears.

   The Fields pane appears.

2. Type **Sales Tax** as the field name, choose Calculation (⌘+L/Ctrl+L) from the Field Type pop-up menu/drop-down list, and then click Create (or press Return/Enter).

   The Specify Calculation dialog appears. (Refer to Figure 14-1.)

3. Double-click Subtotal in the field list (or type it) and then type * .07 to complete the formula.

4. Using the Calculation result is pop-up menu/drop-down list, set the result type to Number.

5. Click OK.

   You return to the Define Database dialog, and the new Calculation field appears in the list of defined fields.

In addition to these two required procedures (specifying a formula and setting a result type), there are several options you can set (shown at the bottom of the Specify Calculation dialog in Figure 14-1):

✦ *Number of repetitions [x]:* You can define the Calculation field as a repeating field by entering a number greater than 1 in this text box. An Extended Price field that multiplies the Item Price by the Quantity Ordered for each line item in an invoice (where Item Price and Quantity are repeating fields) is one example of a repeating Calculation field. You define a field as repeating by specifying the maximum number of times it can repeat within each record.

✦ *Storage Options:* Click the Storage Options button to display the Storage Options for Field *Field Name* dialog. (See Figure 14-2.) This dialog enables you to turn indexing on or off for the field, as well as specify whether FileMaker Pro will store the results of the calculations as part of the database.

   If you intend to sort by the results of this field frequently or perform Find requests using this field as a search criterion, you might want to turn on indexing by selecting the All radio button. If disk space is at a premium or this field must be recalculated often, select the Do not store calculation results — recalculate when needed check box.

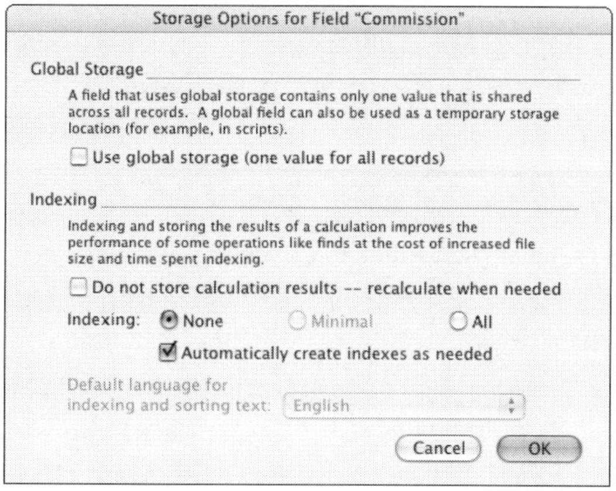

Figure 14-2: Setting storage options for a Calculation field.

You can also specify that the calculation field be a Global field, rather than a field existing in each record, by selecting the Use global storage (one value for all records) check box.

✦ *Do not evaluate if all referenced fields are empty:* When checked, this option prevents the calculation of a result for the current record when all fields referenced in the formula are blank or have no values.

Note

You can examine Calculation fields in any database by displaying the Define Database dialog's Fields pane. If you can't see a Calculation field's entire formula, you can resize the dialog by clicking and dragging the bottom-right corner. To view especially lengthy formulas, simply select the Calculation field and click the Options button or double-click the Calculation field to display the Specify Calculation dialog for that field.

Using FileMaker Pro's Built-In Functions

FileMaker Pro includes dozens of predefined functions you can use to define formulas for Calculation fields. The purpose of each of these functions is described in Table 14-5. Names of new functions that were introduced in FileMaker Pro 8 are shown in bold. For a detailed explanation of each function and example formulas, see Appendix C.

Table 14-5
FileMaker Pro's Built-In Functions

Function Name	Purpose
Abs	Calculates the absolute value of an expression.
Atan	Calculates the arc tangent of an expression, in radians.
Average	Computes the average value (the arithmetic mean) of all values in one or more fields.
Case	Performs a series of tests and selects one answer (or the default answer, if no test is found to be true).
Ceiling	Returns the smallest integer value greater than or equal to its argument.
Choose	Selects one answer from a series.
Combination	Calculates the number of unique ways to select n items from a group of m items.
Cos	Calculates the cosine of an argument expressed in radians, returning a value between −1 and 1.
Count	Counts the number of valid, nonempty entries in one or more fields.
DatabaseNames	Returns the filenames of all currently open FileMaker Pro databases.
Date	Converts month, day, and year values into a valid date.
Day	Returns the day of the month, 1–31, for a given date.
DayName	Returns the weekday name for a given date.
DayNameJ	Returns the Japanese (Kanji) text string for the weekday name for the date passed as the argument.
DayofWeek	Displays the number of the day within a week, 1–7, for a given date.
DayofYear	Displays the number of the day within a year, 1–366, for a given date.
Degrees	Converts a value in radians into degrees.
Div	Calculates the result of integer division (no fractional part).
Evaluate	Calculates the result of treating a text argument as an expression.
EvaluationError	Returns the (numeric) error code, if any, from attempting to calculate the expression passed as an argument.
Exact	Returns a 1 (true) if two text expressions match exactly (including case); 0 (false) otherwise.
Exp	Returns the antilog (base e) of an expression.
Extend	Makes a nonrepeating field into a repeating field (with the identical value in each place) for use in calculations with other repeating fields.

Function Name	Purpose
External	Used to pass data to and from an external function (plug-in).
Factorial	Returns the numeric result of multiplying the sequence of integers from 1 to the argument. Supports a second argument (i), saying to use only the last i factors.
FieldBounds	Returns the location and rotation angle of a given field in a particular database layout.
FieldComments	Returns the specified field's comment (part of the definition).
FieldIDs	Returns a list of all unique (FileMaker-internal) field ID numbers (including related fields) in the specified database and layout.
FieldNames	Returns the names, separated by carriage returns, of all fields used in a particular layout (or in all layouts) of a specified database.
FieldRepetitions	Returns the number of repetitions of a given repeating field as it is formatted on a particular database layout.
FieldStyle	Returns information about how a field in a particular layout is formatted, as well as any value list associated with it.
FieldType	Returns the field definition for a specified field in a particular database.
Filter	Returns the characters in the first argument existing in the sequence passed as the second argument.
FilterValues	Returns the characters of the second argument in the order they appear in the first argument.
Floor	Returns the largest integer less than or equal to the argument passed.
FV	Computes an investment's future value for a given payment amount, interest rate, and number of periods.
Get	Returns a value based upon the parameter (called a state variable) passed. See Appendix C for a list of all the parameters available to the Get() function. These both replace and augment the arguments from earlier FileMaker Pro versions State function.
GetAsBoolean	Returns 0 (false) if the argument is empty or zero, 1 (true) otherwise.
GetAsCSS	Returns as a Cascading Style Sheet (CSS) formatted string, the textual argument passed.
GetAsDate	Returns the text argument converted to Date format.
GetAsNumber	Returns the text argument's numeric characters as a number.
GetAsSVG	Returns the text argument in Scalable Vector Graphics (SVG) format.

(continued)

Table 14-5 (continued)

Function Name	Purpose
GetAsText	Returns the argument as a text string.
GetAsTime	Returns the text argument converted to Time format.
GetAsTimeStamp	Returns the text argument converted to Timestamp format.
GetField	Returns the contents of the specified field.
GetNextSerialValue	Returns the next serial number for the specified field in the specified database.
GetNthRecord	Returns the value of the specified field in the specified record.
GetRepetition	Returns the contents of a particular repetition in a repeating field.
GetSummary	Calculates the value of a particular Summary field when the database has been sorted by the specified break field.
GetValue	Returns the entry indicated by the ordinal parameter from a list of values.
Hiragana	Converts Katakana characters in the argument to Hiragana.
Hour	Displays the number of hours in a time expression.
If	Performs a logical test and returns one value if it is true; another if it is false.
Int	Returns the integer portion of a numeric value.
IsEmpty	Determines whether a value or field is blank.
IsValid	Determines whether a related field can be found and contains valid data, and whether a related file can be found.
IsValidexpression	Returns 1 if the argument forms a syntactically correct expression; 0 otherwise.
KanaHankaku	Converts Hankaku Katakana to Zenkaku Katakana
KanaZenkaku	Converts Zenkaku Katakana to Hankaku Katakana.
KanjiNumeral	Converts Arabic numerals to Kanji numerals.
Katakana	Converts from Hiragana to Zenkaku Katakana.
Last	Returns the last valid, non-empty entry in a repeating field or the last related record's field value.
LayoutIDs	Returns a list of all layout ID numbers for the specified database.
LayoutNames	Returns the names of all layouts in a specified database.

Function Name	Purpose
Left	Returns the specified number of characters of a text string, counting from the left.
LeftValues	Returns the number of items specified by the second argument from the list specified as the first argument.
LeftWords	Returns the specified number of words from a text string, counting from the left.
Length	Returns the number of characters in a given text string or the size of a container field's content.
Let	Assigns a specified value to a specified variable (analogous to the BASIC Let command).
Lg	Returns the binary (base 2) logarithm of the argument.
Ln	Computes the natural (base e) logarithm of an expression.
Log	Computes the common (base 10) logarithm of an expression.
Lookup	Looks up the referenced value in a related table.
LookupNext	Looks up the referenced value in a related table. If not found, returns the next higher/lower value, as specified by the second parameter.
Lower	Converts a text string to all lowercase.
Max	Returns the greatest value among those in specified fields.
Middle	Returns the middle portion of a supplied text string, starting at a given position and extending a specified number of characters.
MiddleValues	Returns the number of items specified by the third parameter from the list in the first parameter, starting with the item specified by the second parameter.
MiddleWords	Returns the specified number of words from a text string, counting from the specified starting word.
Min	Returns the smallest value among those in specified fields.
Minute	Returns the minute portion of a time expression.
Mod	Returns the remainder when an expression is divided by a given number.
Month	Returns the number of the month in a date expression, within the range 1–12.
MonthName	Returns the name of the month in a date expression.
MonthNameJ	Returns the Kanji month name for the specified value.

(continued)

Table 14-5 (continued)

Function Name	Purpose
NPV	Finds the net present value of an investment, using values in repeating fields as unequal payment values and a given interest rate.
NumToJText	Converts a numeric expression to Kanji (or Zenkaku or Hankaku) text.
PatternCount	Returns the number of instances of a specified text string found within another text string or field.
Pi	Returns the value of the mathematical constant pi.
PMT	Calculates a loan payment, using a given principal, interest rate, and term.
Position	Scans text for the specified string starting at the given position; returns the location of the specified occurrence of the string.
Proper	Converts the first letter of each word in the text string to uppercase (used to capitalize names, for example).
PV	Calculates the present value of an investment, using a given payment amount, interest rate, and periods.
Quote	Returns the argument to a quoted text string with any special characters escaped, appropriately.
Radians	Converts a degree value to radians (for use with trigonometric functions).
Random	Generates a random number between 0 and 1.
RelationInfo	Returns information about relationships that have been defined for the current database.
Replace	In a text string, starts at the given position, removes the specified number of characters, starting at the specified position with the specified new text string.
RGB	Returns an integer corresponding to the color specified by the red/green/blue (RGB) components passed.
Right	Counting from the right, returns a given number of characters in a text expression.
RightValues	Returns a list containing the last numberOfValues from the list specified in the first parameter.
RightWords	Returns the specified number of words from a text string, counting from the right.
RomanHankaku	Converts from Zenkaku characters to Hankaku characters.
RomanZenkaku	Converts from Hankaku characters to Zenkaku characters.

Function Name	Purpose
Round	Rounds off a numeric expression to the specified number of decimal places.
ScriptIDs	Returns a list of all script ID numbers for the specified database.
ScriptNames	Returns the names of all scripts that have been created for a given database, separated by Returns.
Seconds	Displays the seconds portion of a time expression.
SerialIncrement	Increments the first argument as a serial number by the amount specified in the second argument without affecting non-numeric characters.
SetPrecision	Computes the expression passed as the first argument to the number of decimal places specified by the second argument.
Sign	Examines a numeric expression and returns 1 for positive, −1 for negative, or 0 for 0.
Sin	Computes the sine of an angle expressed in radians.
Sqrt	Computes the square root of a numeric expression (the same as expression ^ 0.5).
StDev	Examines all values in any repeating or nonrepeating field or fields in related records and gives the sample standard deviation.
StDevP	Examines all values in any repeating or nonrepeating field or fields in related records and gives the population standard deviation.
Substitute	Substitutes one set of characters in a text string for another.
Sum	Totals all values in specified fields.
TableIDs	Returns a list of all table IDs in the database file passed as the argument.
TableNames	Returns a list of all Relationship Graph occurrences for the argument passed.
Tan	Computes the tangent for a given angle expressed in radians.
TextColor	Changes the color of the text to the RGB value specified as the second parameter.
TextColorRemove	Reverts text to the default text color for the field.
TextFont	Changes the font of the text to that specified by the second parameter.
TextFontRemove	Reverts text to the default font for the field.
TextFormatRemove	Reverts text to the default text style for the field.

(continued)

Table 14-5 (continued)

Function Name	Purpose
TextSize	Changes the font size of the specified text as specified.
TextSizeRemove	Reverts text to the default font size for the field.
TextStyleAdd	Adds the specified basic styles to the text.
TextStyleRemove	Removes the specified basic styles from the text.
Time	Converts three given numeric values into a time equivalent.
Timestamp	Converts the date and time passed as arguments to Timestamp data format.
Trim	Strips the specified text expression of leading and trailing spaces.
TrimAll	Removes trailing and leading spaces, as well as some embedded spaces from both Roman and non-Roman text, based upon the parameters passed.
Truncate	Truncates a number to the specified number of decimal places.
Upper	Converts a text expression to all uppercase.
ValueCount	Returns the number of *paragraphs* (blocks of text separated by carriage returns).
ValueListIDs	Returns a list of all value list ID numbers for the specified database file.
ValueListItems	Returns the items in a particular value list for a given database file.
ValueListNames	Returns the names of all value lists that have been defined for a given database file.
Variance	Returns the statistical variance of the specified series of nonblank values.
VarianceP	Returns the statistical population variance of the specified series of nonblank values.
WeekofYear	Determines the number of the week in the year, 1–54, for the specified date expression.
WeekofYearFiscal	Determines the number of the week in the year, 1–53, for the specified date expression (in accordance with the particular day that is considered the first day of the week).
WindowNames	Returns a list of currently open windows' names.
WordCount	Returns the total number of words found in a text expression or field.
Year	Returns the year part of the specified date expression.
YearName	Returns the Japanese (Kanji) year name.

All functions work the same way. A function performs operations on data (the arguments to the function) and then returns a result. The arguments are enclosed in parentheses directly after the function name. For example, in the following expression

```
Round(Sales Tax, 2)
```

Round is the function name, and Sales Tax and 2 are the arguments. (This formula rounds the data in the Sales Tax field to two decimal places.)

> **Note** Round can also accept a *negative* number for the second argument. For example, Round (71527.394, -2) would result in 71,500 or the rounding of the 27.394 portion of the number.

A function expects certain types of data for each argument: numbers, text, expressions, or logical tests. Failure to provide the correct types of arguments will result in errors. For example, although you can choose a Text field as an argument to the Round function, the calculation doesn't make any sense and results in a blank field. The kinds of data expected for each argument appear to the right of the function's name in the Specify Calculation dialog. (Refer to Figure 14-1.)

Functions don't have to be the only component in an expression. They can be combined with constants or references to fields, as shown in the following example:

```
Product Total + Round(Sales Tax Amount, 2)
```

This example shows an expression to define a Grand Total field, obtained by adding the Product Total to the results of rounding off the Sales Tax Amount field's contents to two decimal places.

The following example demonstrates that an expression can also be used as the argument to a function:

```
Round(Product Total * .07, 2)
```

In this example, the Sales Tax Amount field is replaced by an expression that yields the same result. The result of this expression is Sales Tax Amount rounded to two decimal places.

The functions are divided into 16 categories: text, number, date, time, timestamp, text formatting, aggregate, summary, repeating, financial, trigonometric, logical, get, design, custom, and external.

> **Cross-Reference** Appendix C provides a detailed explanation for each of FileMaker Pro's built-in functions. The functions are listed alphabetically within the category to which they belong. In addition to an explanation of each function's purpose and an example

of how the function is used, the sections include a statement that shows how to phrase the function and its arguments. (The order for arranging the function and its arguments is called the *syntax* of the function.) Special notes and cautions, as well as references to other related functions, are included in the explanations of some of the functions.

To use a function in a Calculation field definition, double-click its name in the function list in the upper-right section of the Specify Calculation dialog. (Refer to Figure 14-1.) Then replace the function's arguments with the appropriate field names or expressions.

If you don't know the specific name of the function you need, click the View pop-up menu/drop-down list above the Specify Calculation dialog's rightmost list. (See Figure 14-3.) Depending on your selection from this menu, you can view an alphabetical list of all functions (by selecting All functions by name), an alphabetical list of all functions grouped by category (by selecting All functions by type), or just a particular category of functions (by selecting Text functions, Logical functions, and so on).

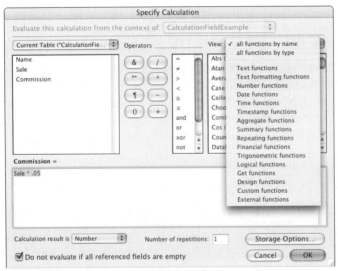

Figure 14-3: Choose an option from the View pop-up menu/drop-down list to specify how the functions are listed.

Tip　Viewing the function list with the All functions by name option selected does *not* display all the functions. Get and External are each a group of functions but only the general format for each group is listed. To see *all* the functions — including all the variations of the Get and External functions — choose All functions by type from the View pop-up menu/drop-down list. As an alternative, you can view *only* the Get or External functions by choosing Get functions or External functions from the View pop-up menu/drop-down list.

Validation by Calculation

Another place that calculations come up in FileMaker Pro is the Validated by Calculation validation field option. This option, which is discussed in Chapter 5, enables you to specify a formula with a Boolean (true/false) result that will determine whether the data in the current field should be allowed (a true result) or rejected (a false result).

For example, suppose your store or Web site sells some products that have age restrictions. An Age field could record the customer's current age (or it could be calculated based on the person's birth date). A Sell field with a yes and no value list attached to it could be validated with the following simple Boolean equation:

```
Age ≥ 18
```

If the customer's age fell short of 18 and you select the Yes radio button, the validation test would fail and automatically present a warning alert.

Calculation Logic

Although calculation logic is often simple and straightforward, what initially appears to be a no-brainer can sometimes turn into a serious head-scratcher. Suppose, for example, that you want to know the elapsed time for an event, such as a phone call. Your database contains two Time fields (Start and End) and a Calculation field (Elapsed Time). On first glance, you might think that the formula End – Start will yield the correct result. And it will — *so long as both times are in the same day!* If a phone call starts at 11:45 p.m. and ends at 12:15 a.m., the result would be –23:30 rather than the expected 00:30:00 (that is, 0 hours, 30 minutes, 0 seconds).

So how do you get the correct computation when a call runs past midnight? Here's a solution:

```
If (End ≥ Start, End - Start, End - Start + 86400)
```

This formula performs a test to see whether the ending time is larger than or equal to the starting time. If this is true (that is, both times occur in the same calendar day), the formula calculates End – Start. If the test is false (the End time occurs in the following day), the formula calculates the second condition: End – Start + 86400. (The 86400 is the number of seconds in a day: that is, 60 * 60 * 24.) Note that this formula still isn't perfect. In the (hopefully) unlikely event that a phone call spans an entire 24-hour period, the result will be incorrect.

When you come up with a real stumper and have exhausted your personal resources at coming up with a working formula, there are two other sources to which you can turn. First, the TechInfo Knowledge Base section of the FileMaker, Inc. Web site has solutions for many of the most common, but complex, calculation problems. Visit `www.filemaker.com/support/techinfo.html` and search for *calculation*. Second, you can become a member of the FileMaker Pro Talk mailing list. (Refer to Appendix D for subscription instructions.) Because many major FileMaker developers subscribe to the list and delight in showing off their database prowess, it's likely that someone on the list can come up with — or already has — a solution for you.

Summary

✦ FileMaker Pro supports the use of Calculation fields. These fields can perform operations on data in other fields in the current record or related records in another file.

✦ A Calculation field's definition consists of a formula made up of mathematical expressions and functions. Calculation fields can combine data from other fields and can also contain literal or constant values.

✦ An expression consists of one or more operators that combine fields or literal values. Database fields are similar to algebraic variables.

✦ An expression for a Calculation field can include arithmetic, logical, comparison, and text operators.

✦ FileMaker Pro 8 includes more than 150 built-in functions. These functions perform data conversion and also perform date, logical, mathematical, financial, statistical, summary, text, time, and trigonometric calculations. They can also be used to determine the status of important system and database properties.

✦   ✦   ✦

Automating FileMaker Pro

When most people — particularly new computer owners — see the terms *script* or *scripting,* they think of programming. And when they think of programming, they quickly skip to the next section of the manual, assuming that this feature is not meant for them. Unfortunately, in many cases, they're right. But FileMaker Pro provides an easier, kinder, and gentler way to create scripts:

+ Rather than type scripts in a word processing program or text editor, you design scripts in FileMaker Pro by choosing script steps from a list. Step options are set by clicking buttons and selecting check boxes.

+ You can create many scripts simply by executing sort instructions, Find requests, and similar commands and then telling FileMaker Pro that you want to use the identical procedures in a script.

In FileMaker Pro 5.5 and earlier, when you performed these important steps just before creating a script, FileMaker Pro included them for you as part of the default script. Starting in FileMaker Pro 6, there is no default script; it is initially blank. (However, FileMaker still notes and uses the current settings for the most recent Find, sort, Page/Print Setup, Import, and Export command — but it no longer automatically uses them as part of a default script.)

To make it easy to design scripts, FileMaker Pro provides a built-in script-creation utility called *ScriptMaker.* Using ScriptMaker, you can automate almost any FileMaker Pro function that you usually execute manually by choosing menu commands. After it's defined, a script can be added to the Scripts menu and/or attached to a button in any layout, making it simple to execute the script any time you like. To make it simple to reuse existing scripts, FileMaker Pro even allows you to import scripts from other FileMaker databases.

Although this chapter is primarily devoted to explaining how you create and use scripts, you can automate FileMaker Pro functions in other ways as well, such as

✦ Creating auto-entry fields that are filled in for you whenever a new record is created or a record is edited. (Refer to Chapter 5.)

✦ Setting a start-up or shut-down script for a database (discussed in Chapter 7).

✦ Using AppleEvents and AppleScript (Mac only) or DDE (Dynamic Data Exchange; Windows only) to enable FileMaker Pro to interact with other programs.

✦ Controlling FileMaker Pro for Windows using ActiveX components. (See "About ActiveX Automation" in the FileMaker Pro Help file.)

Using ScriptMaker

FileMaker Pro scripts are created in ScriptMaker. The commands used in the script are called *steps* or *script steps*. In many cases, the steps duplicate FileMaker Pro menu commands. (See the "Script Step Reference" section, later in this chapter, for information about specific steps.) As you read through this chapter, however, you will learn that script steps are often more powerful than the menu commands they represent. For example, you can use a Clear script step that makes a particular field the active one, selects the entire contents of that field, and then clears its contents. To clear a field without such a script, you must click the field and then manually select its contents (or use the Select All command) before choosing the Clear menu command. Thus, multiple steps can frequently be combined into one.

The real power of FileMaker Pro scripts becomes apparent when you design a sequence of steps to carry out a complex function. With a script, you can be sure that the steps are executed in precisely the same manner each time. If you prefer, the same script can be designed so that the user can select different options each time it runs. For example, you could create a Find script that selects a particular group of records (such as all people in the database who are younger than 30) and then displays information about those records in a different layout. With only a minor modification, the same script can be designed so that the Find criteria can be changed by the user each time the script is performed. Similarly, a script designed to act on a specific field can be modified so it simply acts on whatever field happens to be current. In that way, the script can be used with any field in the database.

Cross-Reference   Scripts are still available when you publish a database on the Internet or an intranet using Instant Web Publishing. See Chapter 20 for details.

Creating a script is not a complex process, as you'll see in the following steps.

STEPS: Creating a Script

1. Open the database for which you want to define a script.

Scripts are stored with the database in which they are created.

2. Choose the Scripts ⇨ ScriptMaker command.

The Define Scripts dialog appears, as shown in Figure 15-1.

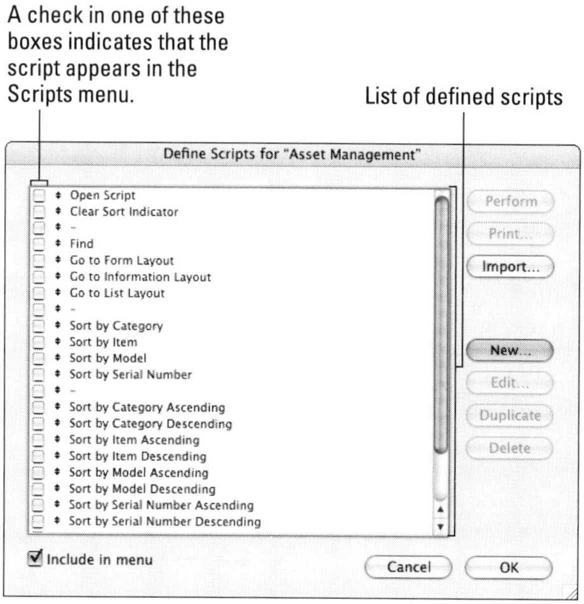

A check in one of these
boxes indicates that the
script appears in the
Scripts menu.   List of defined scripts

Figure 15-1: The Define Scripts dialog.

3. Click the New button.

The Edit Script dialog appears, as shown in Figure 15-2. The script is initially blank; that is, it contains no steps.

4. In the Script Name text box, type a name for the script.

5. Create the script by performing the following actions:

- *To add a step to the script,* select it in the steps list (on the left side of the dialog) and then either click Move or double-click the step.

- *To set options for a script step,* begin by selecting the step in the script. Options that can be set for the step appear below the list of script steps.

- *To rearrange the order of steps in the script,* click the double-headed arrow to the left of the step you want to relocate and drag it to the desired position.

- *To remove individual unwanted steps,* select them in the current script (in the right side of the dialog) and then click Clear. (The Clear button replaces the Move button when a step is selected.)

- *To remove all steps from the script,* click Clear All.

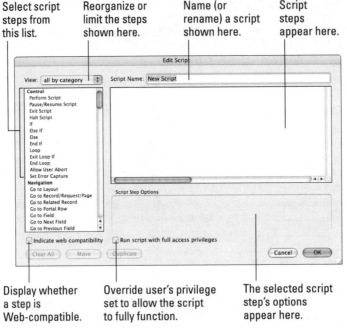

Select script steps from this list.

Reorganize or limit the steps shown here.

Name (or rename) a script shown here.

Script steps appear here.

Display whether a step is Web-compatible.

Override user's privilege set to allow the script to fully function.

The selected script step's options appear here.

Figure 15-2: The Edit Script dialog.

6. To accept the script definition, click OK. To ignore the changes you've made, click Cancel.

You return to the Define Scripts dialog.

7. If you do not want to list the script in the Scripts menu, remove the check mark from the Include in menu check box. (If you *do* want to list the script in the Scripts menu, be sure that Include in menu is checked.)

You can change the status of this check box at any time during the script creation or editing process. For additional information about this option, see "Listing scripts in the Scripts menu," later in this chapter.

Tip   If a script consists of only one step, you might be able to avoid the script-definition process by assigning the step to a button. (See "Attaching a Script to a Button," later in this chapter.)

Listing scripts in the Scripts menu

As mentioned earlier, if the Include in menu check box is selected for a defined script, the script is assigned a place in the Scripts menu. The first ten such scripts shown in the Define Scripts dialog with a check mark in front of their names are special in that they are assigned keyboard shortcuts (⌘+1 through ⌘+0 for the Mac or Ctrl+1 through Ctrl+0 for Windows) so you can also execute them from the keyboard. You can position the scripts that you need to use most often among the first ten to make them easily accessible.

To change the position of a script in the Define Scripts dialog, click the double-headed arrow that precedes its name in the script list. The pointer changes to a larger version of the double-headed arrow. Then, while continuing to hold down the mouse button, drag the script up or down in the script list. When the script is in the correct position in the list, release the mouse button. Repeat this process for other scripts that you want to move.

Note   You can assign a script to the Scripts menu, attach the script to a button, make the script the start-up script, or set none of these options. The decision is entirely yours. You can also change a script or button assignment at any time by following the procedures outlined in this chapter. Note that the Define Scripts dialog's Perform button can be used with any script, regardless of the other ways in which the script can be accessed.

Running a script

After you finish defining a script, you can run it in any of several ways:

✦ Select the name of the script in the Define Scripts dialog and click the Perform button.

✦ Choose the script name from the Scripts menu (only if the Include in menu check box was selected when you defined the script).

✦ Press the ⌘+key/Ctrl+key combination assigned to the script (only if the script is one of the first ten Include in menu scripts defined for the database).

✦ Click a button to which you've attached the script (if you've assigned the script to a button).

✦ Open the database file (if you defined the script as a start-up script that runs automatically each time you open the database) or close the database (if you defined the script as a closing script that runs automatically each time you close the database). See Chapter 7 for more information on this option.

Learning by example

Learning to create scripts can be facilitated by looking at examples. In this and other chapters in this book, you'll find plenty of scripts that you can use as starting points. Want to understand an interesting action that you've seen in someone else's database? Choose Scripts ➪ ScriptMaker, select the script you want to examine, and click Edit. You'll see the list of steps that the author of the database selected for the script. (Be aware, however, that some databases—including some that you can buy and those that are available for download from popular online services—are protected. Unless you know the necessary account name and password, you might not be allowed to see or modify the scripts.) You could use the ScriptMaker window's Duplicate button to make a copy of the script to modify, while keeping the original script intact.

If you need to stop a script in progress, press ⌘+. (period)/Esc. If a script is paused by using a Pause step option or the Pause/Resume Script step (described later in this chapter), you can stop the script by clicking the Cancel button (instead of the Continue button, as you normally would).

Modifying a script

FileMaker Pro provides several methods for altering scripts, including renaming, duplicating, deleting, editing, and changing their order. These important script-editing techniques are discussed in the following sections.

Renaming a script

If you add a script to the Scripts menu by marking the Include in menu check box in the Define Scripts dialog (previously shown in Figure 15-1), whatever name you give the script is what appears in the Scripts menu. (Otherwise, script names are visible only when you are editing scripts, assigning scripts to buttons, or setting a start-up action. In such cases, the specific script names aren't nearly as important because they are normally hidden from the user's view.)

If you decide to change the name, select the script in the Define Scripts dialog, click the Edit button, rename the script in the Edit Script dialog's Script Name text box, and then click the OK buttons for both the Edit Script and Define Scripts dialogs.

Duplicating a script

Rather than create every new script from scratch, you will sometimes find it easier to edit a copy of an existing script. For example, you might have already created a script that prints a report for you. If you want a similar script that displays the report onscreen, just create a duplicate of the script and change the Print step to an Enter Preview Mode step in the duplicate script.

Choosing script names

When you name or rename a script, it's always best to choose a descriptive name. Although you could follow the same naming conventions that FileMaker Pro uses for layouts (instead of Layout #1, Layout #2, and so on, you could use Script #1, Script #2, and so on), you'll have a miserable time later trying to determine what each script does. On the other hand, there will be little possible confusion if you name your scripts descriptively—for example, Sort by State, Find Recent Purchases, and Print Aging Report.

Note, too, that the length of each script name is limited to 100 characters. However, before going overboard and naming a script something lengthy like "Aging Report (designed for a LaserWriter in landscape mode)—to be printed only on the last day of the month," keep two things in mind:

✦ The Define Scripts dialog doesn't expand to show all characters in an extremely long script name. FileMaker Pro displays only as much text as fits in the script list; the remainder is shown as ellipses.

✦ If a long script name is included in the Scripts menu, the width of the Scripts menu will expand as much as possible to display the longest script name—an arrangement that can result in a ridiculous-looking pull-down menu. (Steve used to have two monitors attached to his Mac. When he assigned the long script name described earlier to the Scripts menu, the resulting pull-down menu extended off his main monitor and halfway onto a nearby two-page display!)

STEPS: Duplicating a Script

1. From the script list in the Define Scripts dialog (previously shown in Figure 15-1), select the name of the script that you want to duplicate.

2. Click the Duplicate button.

   A copy of the script is created and is listed as *script name* Copy (for example, Print Sales Report Copy).

3. Click the Edit button to access the Edit Script dialog and then edit the new script as desired.

4. *Optional:* Change the name of the duplicate script to something more descriptive by editing its name in the Script Name box of the Edit Script dialog.

5. Click OK when you finish working with the script.

Deleting a script

If you no longer need a script, you can delete scripts or stop them from showing in the Scripts menu. (You can still activate a script that doesn't appear in the menu from a button on the layout.)

Make your own keyboard shortcuts

The first ten scripts you create having the Include in menu check box selected are automatically assigned a Command-key equivalent (⌘+1 through ⌘+0) on the Mac or a Control-key equivalent (Ctrl+1 through Ctrl+0) in Windows. You can also use any of these first ten script slots to create Command-key equivalent (Mac) or Control-key equivalent (Windows) menu commands for which FileMaker Pro doesn't provide keyboard shortcuts.

For example, you might want to create a one-step script that simply executes the normal Page Setup command (Page Setup [ ] or Page Setup [Restore]). As long as this script is one of the first ten scripts added to the Scripts menu, you can issue its command by pressing its new Command-key or Control-key equivalent (⌘+3/Ctrl+3, for example). You can use this trick to add all your frequently used menu commands to the Scripts menu, such as Save a Copy As (to make a backup copy of the current database) and Check Record (to check the spelling of the current record)

STEPS: Deleting a Script

1. In the Define Scripts dialog, select the name of the script that you want to delete.

2. Click Delete.

3. In the confirmation dialog that appears, click Delete to remove the script or click Cancel if you change your mind.

To remove a script from the Scripts menu without deleting it, select the script name and remove the check mark from the Include in menu check box. As an alternative, you can remove the check mark from the check box in front of the script's name.

Editing a script

Other editing actions that you can perform on a script include adding, removing, or changing the order of steps and altering the options for steps. To change a script's listing in the database's Scripts menu, you can either select the script name and select the Include in menu check box in the Define Scripts dialog or select the check box in front of the script's name. This acts as a toggle; each click reverses the state of the option.

Note   If any steps relevant to the Page Setup/Print Setup, Sort, Find, Import, and Export commands are used in a script, their settings are saved as part of the script.

In versions prior to FileMaker Pro 7, editing a script containing Print Setup, Sort, Find, Import, or Export commands presented a dialog inquiring whether you wished to retain the previous settings or establish new settings. Starting with FileMaker Pro 7, the old settings are retained as a default, and you must remember to use the Edit Script dialog's Specify button for the steps in question when you want different settings in place.

Printing scripts

If you want a permanent record of a script, you can print it by selecting its name in the Define Scripts dialog (refer to Figure 15-1) and clicking the Print button. You can also print selected scripts by selecting multiple script names and clicking the Print button. If you want to print every script for a database, select all the script names. A standard Print dialog for your platform and operating system appears.

Importing scripts from other databases

If you regularly use ScriptMaker, you'll probably create some general-purpose scripts that you'd like to reuse in other databases. Rather than re-creating them from scratch, you can use the Define Scripts dialog's Import button to copy a script from one database to another.

STEPS: Importing a Script

1. Open the database that will receive the imported script(s).

2. Choose Scripts ➪ ScriptMaker.

   The Define Scripts dialog appears.

3. Click the Import button.

   A standard file dialog appears.

4. Select the database containing the script(s) you want to import and then click Open.

   The Import Scripts dialog appears (see Figure 15-3).

Figure 15-3: Select scripts to import from the Import Scripts dialog.

5. Check each script that you want to import and then click OK.

   You return to the Define Scripts dialog.

   FileMaker processes each of the scripts, mapping them as closely as possible to the field names, relationships, and so on present in the receiving database.

6. Select each imported script in the Define Scripts dialog, click Edit, and make any necessary changes.

   During the import process, when matches aren't found for referenced fields, relationships, layouts, script names, and so on, the script step will include the word *<unknown>*. Be sure to correct all such incorrect references.

Tip   Rather than trying to keep track of where your general-purpose scripts are stored, you might want to create a special database that serves as a repository for such scripts. Dennis keeps a few such databases, named (not-so-creatively) *Utility Scripts*, *Sorting Scripts*, *Report Scripts*, and *Find Scripts*.

Script Step Reference

Each script element is called a *step*. In this section, the step explanations are presented in the same order in which you'll encounter them in the left side of the Edit Script dialog.

Note   The Windows version of FileMaker Pro 8 includes several script steps that are not supported by the Macintosh version of the program, and vice versa. These steps are related to support for system software features, such as AppleEvents and AppleScript (on the Macintosh) and OLE, DDE, and messaging capabilities (Windows). If any of your scripts rely on platform-specific steps, users on the other platform will not be able to run them. (If the scripts are examined on the other platform, these steps are shown in italic.)

Tip   Although FileMaker Pro makes scripting very simple, scripting is still programming, and there are a few basic rules to remember. Computers are stupid, literal, and unquestioningly obedient. They do *exactly* what you tell them to do, no more and no less, and they do it amazingly quickly. If you leave out a step in your instructions, the computer will omit that step when following the instructions. There is no thought process about *what does this mean?* If you mistakenly tell FileMaker Pro to sort on the ZIP code field in your Sort by Name script, you'll get a ZIP code sort — there is no awareness of context. Scripting (programming) is at least as much about making a set of instructions idiot-proof as it is anything else — and the computer is the idiot!

Script step options

As you examine the different script steps in ScriptMaker, you'll notice that many of them include options that you can set. The options are individually explained within each step definition (as presented in "Script step definitions" later in this chapter), but here's a rundown of the effects of the most common step options:

✦ *Perform without dialog:* Many script steps that are normally performed with an accompanying dialog can in fact be performed without displaying the dialog. A script step allowing you to select a particular file would be one example of such a dialog-less action. Set the Perform without dialog option when as part of the script step, you have already specified the file to be opened or other options to be performed, and there is no need for the user to examine or change those options.

✦ *Specify:* Many script steps include a Specify pop-up menu/drop-down list or button where, depending upon the type of script step you're creating, you might want to specify a particular file, record, field, and so on. If you see a Specify button, clicking it presents a context-appropriate dialog. If you see a Specify pop-up menu/drop-down list, the available choices allow you to select alternative actions.

Note For field-related Specify choices, you can choose an appropriate field from the current file or from any related file.

✦ *Select entire contents:* In script steps that deal with field contents (particularly the editing steps, such as Copy, Paste, and Clear), this option causes the entire contents of the chosen field to be selected. Otherwise, only the portion of the field that has been preselected by the user before executing the script will be affected.

✦ *Restore (import order, sort order, setup options, find requests, and so on):* The wording of the Restore option varies depending on the step to which it is attached. For example, in conjunction with a Sort step, it reads Restore Sort Order. Set this option when you want FileMaker Pro to execute whatever settings were in effect for this procedure at the time the script was created. If neither Restore nor Perform without dialog is chosen, FileMaker Pro displays the appropriate dialog when the script step is executed (enabling you to set options as you like).

✦ *Refresh window:* This option causes the screen to be redrawn when the step is reached.

✦ *Pause:* This option adds Continue and Cancel buttons to the associated script step. The purpose of this option is to give the user an opportunity to perform an action (entering criteria in a Find request or browsing through the report information that is currently displayed, for example) before continuing the current script.

✦ *Exit after last:* This option is available for relative record navigation steps (Go to Record/Request/Page). When this option is selected and the script tries to select a record that is outside the range of record numbers (choosing a record before the first record or after the last record in the current browsed set), the step is not performed, and either the script ends (if the record navigation command is executing outside a loop structure), or the loop is exited and the rest of the script is executed (if the record navigation command is executing inside a loop structure). When this option is not selected and the script tries to select a record that is outside the range of record numbers, the step is performed on a record that it *can* reach (either the first or last record in the database) and keeps on operating. This is one way a script can go off into an infinite loop — something you really want to avoid.

✦ *On/Off:* Use the On or Off options to toggle a script feature on or off. In many cases, such a script step is used in pairs: The first instance turns on a feature (such as error capture) and a second instance turns it off.

Script step definitions

FileMaker Pro 8 provides over 125 steps (we count 132) you can use individually or in combination with other steps to form a script. The following sections provide detailed explanations of each step, including the ways in which the available options affect the step. For additional information on a menu-related script step, refer to the chapter in which the equivalent menu command is discussed.

Debugging a script

When a script doesn't do what you intended it to do, you should check several things:

✦ Are the steps in the proper order?

A script is not executed *en masse.* This is, its steps run in the order in which they're listed. If you need to set a printout for landscape mode, for example, you would place a Print Setup step before the Print step.

✦ Should you have performed a preparatory action before executing the script?

If a step acts on a field, for example, you must somehow make the field the current one. If no field is selected, the step does nothing. Use a Specify Field option as part of the step (if one is allowed); include a Go to Field, Go to Next Field, or Go to Previous Field step; or manually select the desired field before running the script.

✦ Have scripts, layouts, or fields been renamed or deleted?

Reexamine your scripts in ScriptMaker. If any Perform Script, Go to Layout, or Go to Field step now reads *unknown,* it means the database doesn't know what script or sub-script it is supposed to perform, the layout to which it is supposed to switch, or the field it is supposed to select. This is often the case when you copy buttons from one database and paste them into another.

✦ Are you in the proper FileMaker Pro mode?

Although a script can be run from any mode, it cannot operate in Layout mode. For example, a Delete Record/Request step cannot be used to delete a layout. If you're in Layout mode when you execute a script, the script will switch to the mode that the step requires (Browse, Find, or Preview) before continuing.

Control script steps

The following script steps are used to execute sub-scripts and external scripts, control script execution, provide conditional branching and looping, and enable or disable FileMaker Pro's normal error handling mechanism.

Note If the step is new in FileMaker Pro 8, we will list it as *New in FileMaker Pro 8* between the step's name and its Purpose description. Similarly, we will note new Options or changed names.

Perform Script

Purpose: Use Perform Script to execute another script from within the current script. When the execution of the other script concludes, the original script resumes automatically.

Options: Specify

Use the Specify button to select the script you want to perform from the Specify Script Options dialog that appears. The name of every currently defined database script is listed in this dialog. Additionally, the penultimate option in the pop-up menu/drop-down list above the list of scripts is Add File Reference. Choose Add File Reference if you want to execute a script that's in another FileMaker Pro database. When an external script is executed, its database is automatically opened in FileMaker Pro and then the script runs. You can also choose Define File References to include multiple files that the script might reference (for fields, scripts, value lists, and so on).

Tip To quote the FileMaker 8 Script Steps reference (available from www.filemaker. com): "If you've performed an external script and you want to return to the original file, add an Enter Browse Mode step or Go to Layout step right after the Perform Script step in the original file, so that the script returns to the original file."

Example: Suppose you have two databases: Invoices and Addresses. You could create a script in Invoices — using the Perform Script command — that executes a Find request in Addresses (enabling you, for example, to locate a particular customer address or all addresses that include *San Francisco* in the City field).

Pause/Resume Script

Purpose: Use this script step to pause a script, enabling the user to perform some nonscript action during the execution of a script.

Options: Specify

A script can be paused indefinitely, for a duration specified by a calculation, or for a specific amount of time (see Figure 15-4). When a Pause/Resume Script step is executed, the status area of the document window changes to show Continue and Cancel buttons, indicating that the script has been paused. If Indefinitely (the default choice) is selected, the script will remain paused until the user clicks

Continue. If a pause duration is specified (either by the contents of a specific field or by entering a particular pause time), the script will continue when the user clicks Continue or when the specified time period has elapsed, whichever occurs first.

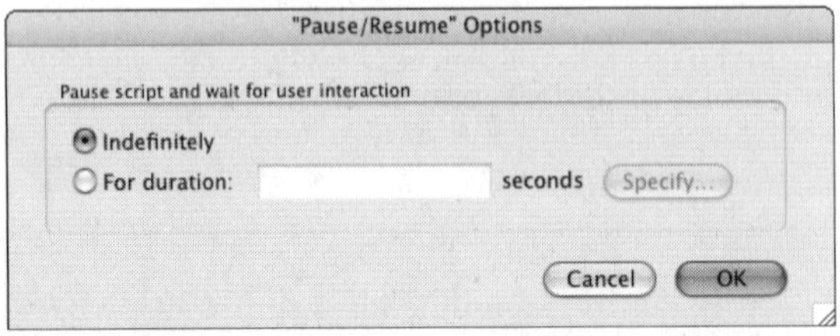

Figure 15-4: The Pause/Resume Options dialog.

Example: You can alternate Go to Field steps with Pause/Resume Script steps to walk a novice user through a data-entry routine.

Exit Script

Purpose: The Exit Script step is used to immediately end the execution of any sub-scripts or external scripts and then resume executing the main script.

Options: None

This script step is particularly useful when executed in conjunction with the If step to test for error conditions or another reason to end a sub-script or external script prematurely.

See also: Halt Script

Halt Script

Purpose: When encountered in a script, the Halt Script step immediately ends the execution of the current script as well as any sub-scripts or external scripts. Like the Exit Script step, a conditional test (an If step) is often used to determine when it is necessary to end the script.

Options: None

See also: Exit Script

If

Purpose: Use the If step to evaluate a calculation (set with the Specify option) and perform a conditional action based on the result. If the calculation evaluates as true (a nonzero result), the additional steps are performed. If the calculation evaluates as false (zero), the remaining steps associated with the If script structure (until an Else If, Else, or End If is encountered) are skipped.

Note Every If structure must end with an End If step (added automatically by FileMaker Pro when you add an If step). You can specify alternate conditions by including Else If steps and/or an Else step.

Options: Specify

See also: Else, Else If, End If, Loop

Else If

Purpose: Use the Else If step to evaluate a calculation (set with the Specify option) and perform an alternative conditional action based on the result. If the calculation evaluates as true (a nonzero result), the steps up to the next Else If, Else, or End If step are performed. If the calculation evaluates as false (zero), those steps are skipped.

Options: Specify

See also: If, Else, End If, Exit Loop If

Else

Purpose: The Else step is used in conjunction with the If step (and Else If steps) to perform an alternate course of action.

Options: None

Example: The following script moves to Field 1 if the current record contains *Redmond* in the City field (true); otherwise, it moves to Field 2 (false):

```
If ["City = "Redmond""]
    Go to Field ["Field 1"]
Else
    Go to Field ["Field 2"]
```

See also: If, Else If, End If, Exit Loop If

End If

Purpose: The End If step ends every If script structure. When you insert an If statement into a script, an End If is automatically added by FileMaker Pro.

Options: None

See also: If, Else, Else If

Loop

Purpose: The Loop step is used to repeat a series of script steps. (In most BASIC programming language dialects, loops are performed by combining For/Next,

Do/Until, and Repeat/While statements.) An End Loop statement must be the final step in the loop, and FileMaker Pro automatically adds it.

The loop repeats as directed or until the condition specified in an enclosed Exit Loop If step option within the loop is fulfilled.

Options: None

Examples: Here are two ways to exit from a loop. In the first example, the loop is exited after the first ten records in the database have been processed. (The Global field Count is used to keep track of the number of passes made through the loop — one pass per record.)

```
Go to Record/Request/Page [First]
Set Field ["Count","0"]
Loop
  ...
statements to be executed go here
  ...
  Set Field ["Count", "Count + 1"]
  Exit Loop If ["Count = 10"]
End Loop
```

In the second example, the loop automatically ends when the last record in the file is encountered. (An Exit Loop If step is unnecessary.) The first record to be processed as part of the loop is specified in the first script step. Rather than using a Global field as a counter, the [Next] option (near the bottom of the loop) is used to step through the records. The loop is exited after reaching the end of the found set, as instructed by the Go to Record/Request/Page step's [Exit after last] option:

```
Go to Record/Request/Page [First]
Loop
  ...
statements to be executed go here
  ...
Go to Record/Request/Page [Next; Exit after last]
End Loop
```

See also: Exit Loop If, End Loop

Exit Loop If

Purpose: This step specifies the condition that, when tested, determines whether a loop has been completed. The calculation is evaluated on each pass through the loop. If the result of the calculation is true (nonzero), the loop is exited; otherwise, the loop continues.

Tip   If you place the Exit Loop If step at the top of the loop, you can simulate a Repeat While loop. Placing the Exit Loop If step at the bottom of the loop simulates a Repeat Until loop.

Example: For an example of how the Exit Loop If step works, see the Loop step (described earlier).

Options: Specify the calculation

See also: Loop, End Loop

End Loop
Purpose: The End Loop step is the final step in every Loop structure. When you insert a Loop step into a script, FileMaker Pro automatically adds an End Loop step.

Options: None

See also: Loop, Exit Loop If

Allow User Abort
Purpose: This script step either enables or prevents the user from halting the script to which it is attached. When Allow User Abort is on, scripts can be stopped by pressing ⌘+. (period; Mac) or Esc (Mac/Windows). The default setting is On.

Options: On or Off

Examples: In continuously running demos, it is a good practice to set Allow User Abort to Off and make it the first step in the script. When Allow User Abort is set to Off for such a script, not only do you prevent the script from being halted, but you effectively prevent the user from quitting the program, too.

As another example, if a script contains a critical section that must never be interrupted, you can precede the section by Allow User Abort [Off] and then conclude the section with Allow User Abort [On], thus restoring the ability to halt the remainder of the script.

Tip   You should not disable user aborts until you have finished testing (debugging) your script, lest you lock yourself out while testing.

Set Error Capture
Purpose: By default, FileMaker Pro presents alerts when encountering an error it is designed to handle. (This is the equivalent of Set Error Capture [Off].) By adding this step and setting its option to On, you tell FileMaker Pro to suppress all error messages while the script is running, usually because you intend to do the error trapping yourself by using the Get (LastError) function.

Options: On or Off

Note   A list of the error codes that Get (LastError) generates can be found in the FileMaker Pro Help listing for that function.

Set Variable
New in FileMaker 8

Purpose: This long-requested step allows you to create and assign values to variables, either local to the script or global in scope. Variable names have the same restrictions as field names with local variable names beginning with a single dollar sign ($) and global variable names beginning with a double dollar sign ($$). Local variables cease to exist when the script completes; however, global variables can be referenced and altered in calculations or other scripts and persist until the file is closed. Variables can be arrays and are referenced as repeating fields.

Options: None

Navigation script steps

The navigation script steps enable FileMaker Pro to switch to or select a particular layout, record, field, and so on, as well as change to a specific mode (Browse, Find, or Preview).

Note   There are no script steps that change to Layout mode because scripts can't be executed when FileMaker Pro is in Layout mode.

Go to Layout

Purpose: Use this step to switch to a particular layout that has been created for the current database (which is the same as choosing a specific layout name from the status area's Layouts menu).

Options: Specify

Use the Specify pop-up menu/drop-down to select the layout that you want to display. In most cases, you will want to change to a particular layout; to do so, choose its name (Menu or Data Entry, for example) from the Specify menu/list.

You can also switch to a layout based on a calculated name or number. If you choose to switch to the layout given by the contents of a chosen field, the specified field must contain a number. The number corresponds to the order of the layouts in the file. For example, if you use the field Layout Number and that field contains 1, the script will switch to the first layout in the file (as specified in the Set Layout Order dialog).

The Specify pop-up menu/drop-down list also has an original layout option that is useful for ending a script. This option tells FileMaker Pro to switch back to whatever layout was current when the script was executed. For example, a Print Report script could be invoked from a layout named Data Entry. The script might switch to a report layout, print a copy of the report, and then—using the Original Layout option—end by switching back to the Data Entry layout. The advantage of using original layout rather than specifying the exact layout name (Data Entry, in this case) is that the script could conceivably be invoked from any layout and still return the user to the layout he or she was using.

Tip

Go to Layout is one of the most frequently used script steps. It's not unusual to begin a script with this step (to ensure that the correct layout is displayed, for example). In many databases, this step is attached to navigation buttons that display a help or report layout.

Go to Record/Request/Page

Purpose: This step is used to display a particular record in the current found set or to enable the user to select one of these records to display. Go to Record/Request/Page is frequently used to move directly to the first or last record in the database. (Specify First to go to the first record; specify Last to go to the last record.) When executed from Find mode, Go to Record/Request/Page displays a Find request page instead of a record. When run from Preview mode, Go to Record/Request/Page displays the specified report page.

Options: Specify First, Last, Previous, Next, By Calculation; Exit after last (when Previous, or Next is chosen); Perform without dialog (when by Calculation is chosen)

Depending on the Specify option you select, this step can display the previous, next, first, or last record, (Find) request, or (Preview) page. It can also display a particular record, request, or page (if you choose By Calculation).

Records can be selected only from the current found set. If you are using the by Calculation option to select a specific record and it is conceivable that the record could be hidden, you will usually want to precede this script step with a Find request to ensure that the record of interest will indeed be available. If the record to be displayed could be different for each execution of the script, leave the Perform without dialog check box unchecked.

When Perform without dialog is checked, no dialog appears, and the script immediately displays the specified record, Find request, or report page.

In FileMaker Pro versions prior to FileMaker Pro 7, you could ask the user to specify a record/request/page number choosing By Number. This usually isn't too useful because users seldom know which record number corresponds to which record. By Number is gone, but the capability still exists. When the By Calculation option is chosen, no Calculation is defined, and Perform without dialog is unchecked, the dialog in Figure 15-5 appears. By Field Value and By Number have been consolidated into By Calculation.

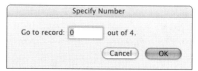

Figure 15-5: The Specify Number dialog.

Tip   The contents of the referenced field can be a calculation's result. For example, you could use a particular customer's customer number to reference another record based on a calculation including the customer number.

The Exit after Last option can be used in conjunction with the Previous, or Next choices. When selected, Exit after Last keeps the script or loop from wrapping around when the last or first record, request, or page is encountered (when Next or Previous is chosen, respectively). This is of special concern when you are using a script to step through the records of a database, for example.

See also: Go to Related Record

Go to Related Record

Purpose: This script step is used to display a record from a related table, based on the current relationship and the presently active field. If the selected field is either a field in a portal or a related field that has been placed directly on the layout, executing the Go to Related Record step displays the matching record from the related table. If the field defining the relationship is selected, the first matching record from the related table is displayed.

Options: Specify

Use the Specify button to select a relationship (or define one, if none currently exists) and specify which layout should be used to show the record(s), as shown in Figure 15-6. The Show only related records option can be very useful. Choose it to limit the visible records (the found set) in the related file to those that meet the criteria of the relationship. Select the Show in new window check box if you want FileMaker Pro to display the found record(s) in a separate window, so as to maintain your original context.

> **"Go to Related Record" Options**
>
> This script step will show a related record using a layout based on the same table. If the table is defined in an external file, you can choose to show the record using a layout in the external file.
>
> Get related record from: [Address Book Advanced   ⬍]
>
>   ☐ Use external table's layouts
>
> Show record using layout: [<Current Layout>   ⬍]
>
>   ☐ Show in new window   (Specify...)
>   ☐ Show only related records
>
>   (Cancel) (OK)

Figure 15-6: The Go to Related Record Options dialog.

When you select the Show in new window check box, a New Window Options dialog appears where you can specify the new window's name, dimensions, and location from the screen's top-left corner. These values can all be literal, field references, or calculation results, at your discretion.

If you wish to display the found records using layouts associated with the related table from a different file, select the Use external table's layouts check box.

See also: Go to Record/Request/Page, Go to Portal Row

Go to Portal Row

Purpose: This step enables you to move to a particular row in the active portal. If a portal isn't active, the step is applied to the first portal encountered in the layout's stacking order (that is, the frontmost, highest one).

When changing portal rows, this step attempts to keep the same field active (if one is currently active). If no field in the portal is active, the step activates the first field that it can enter.

Options: Select entire contents; Specify First, Last, Next, Previous, or By Calculation; Exit after last (if Previous or Next is chosen); Perform without dialog (if By Calculation is chosen)

Choose Select Entire Contents if you want the entire portal row to be selected, rather than just making a single field active. You must use the Specify pop-up menu/drop-down list to choose a target portal row (First, Last, Next, Previous, or By Calculation).

The Next and Previous options include an Exit after last option enabling this script step to end if you attempt to select a portal row that is before the first or after the last row. If you don't include this option, the step simply wraps around and goes to the last or first portal row, respectively.

Choose the By Calculation option to specify a particular portal row by its number or by a particular field's value. When executed, this step can present a dialog in which you choose a row number, or it can go directly to a particular row when Perform without dialog is checked.

See also: Go to Related Record, Go to Field

Go to Field

Purpose: Use this step to go to a particular field in the current layout or in a layout for a related table.

Options: Select/perform, Go to target field, Specify

Note

Both the Go to target field check box and the Specify button present the Specify Field dialog so that you can designate the target field. Their use is interchangeable.

When a script includes steps that copy, cut, or paste information, you can use Go to Field to specify the appropriate field for each editing operation. You can also use this step to move to a particular field in preparation for data entry. Use the Specify option to tell FileMaker Pro the field to which you want to go. (You must specify a field; otherwise, the script fails at this step.)

Set the Select/perform option if you want to select the contents of a field (usually as a prelude to editing). If you set Select/perform and choose a Container field that contains a sound or a movie, the sound or movie plays.

 If you choose a field that contains an OLE object, FileMaker Pro activates the application that created the object and loads the OLE object into the application, ready for editing. When you exit the creating application, you will have the option to update the contents of the OLE object in the FileMaker Pro field to reflect the editing changes you made.

See also: Go to Next Field, Go to Previous Field

Go to Next Field

Purpose: Use this step to move to the next field in the current layout. If no field is selected when a Go to Next Field step executes, you move to the first field in the current layout. FileMaker Pro uses the tab order that is set for the layout to determine what the "next" field is.

Options: None

Example: After starting a script with a Go to Field step to set the first field, you could use a series of Go to Next Field steps — each followed by a Pause/Resume Script step — to walk a new user through a data-entry layout. The beginning of the script might look like this:

```
Go to Field ["Last Name"]
Pause/Resume Script
Go to Next Field
Pause/Resume Script
Go to Next Field
```

See also: Go to Previous Field, Go to Field

Go to Previous Field

Purpose: Use this step to move to the preceding field in the current layout. If no field is selected when a Go to Previous Field step executes, you move to the last field in the current layout. FileMaker Pro uses the tab order that is set for the layout to determine what the "previous" field is.

Options: None

See also: Go to Next Field, Go to Field

Enter Browse Mode

Purpose: Regardless of the active mode of the current database, this step switches to Browse mode (which is the same as choosing View ➪ Browse Mode or pressing ⌘+B/Ctrl+B). You use Browse mode to enter and edit data.

Options: Pause

Select the Pause option if you want to pause the script temporarily to enable the user to enter or edit data.

See also: Enter Find Mode, Enter Preview Mode

Enter Find Mode

Purpose: This script step switches the current layout to Find mode, enabling you to execute Find requests (which is the same as choosing View ➪ Find Mode or pressing ⌘+F/Ctrl+F).

Options: Specify Find requests, Pause

Select Specify Find requests to start each Find request with the criteria that were in effect when the script was created. If you prefer to start the Find request from scratch, leave this option unchecked. If additional steps follow Enter Find Mode, you should also select the Pause option — assuming you want users to have an opportunity to modify the Find requests.

See also: Perform Find, Enter Browse Mode, Enter Preview Mode

Enter Preview Mode

Purpose: This step switches the current layout to Preview mode (which is the same as choosing View ➪ Preview Mode or pressing ⌘+U/Ctrl+U).

Options: Pause

Preview mode is often used to display onscreen reports or to examine a layout before printing (commonly called a *print preview* in many programs). When other steps follow the Enter Preview Mode step, you might want to use the Pause option so users of the database will have an adequate opportunity to examine the preview.

See also: Print, Enter Find Mode, Enter Browse Mode

Found Sets script steps

The Found Sets script steps enable you to execute Sort and Find commands in scripts, as well as set options for these procedures.

Sort Records

Purpose: Use the Sort Records step to sort the browsed records in a particular order (which is the same as choosing Records ➪ Sort Records or pressing ⌘+S/Ctrl+S).

Options: Specify sort order, Perform without dialog

Note   The Specify button and the Specify sort order check box are synonymous.

If Specify sort order is checked, the sort order defaults to the sort instructions that were in effect at the time the script was created. If Specify sort order is not selected, the sort order defaults to the most recently executed sort instructions for the database.

If you want to be able to set different sort instructions each time the step executes, make sure you leave the Perform without dialog option unmarked. If, on the other hand, the sort instructions will not change from one execution of the script to another, or if you want to keep users from modifying the instructions, select Perform without dialog.

Note   Prior to FileMaker Pro 7, this step was named Sort.

See also: Unsort Records

Unsort Records

Purpose: Use Unsort Records to restore records to the order in which they were entered into the database (which is the same as clicking the Unsort button in the Sort Records dialog).

Options: None

Example: This script step is most useful when you have a database with records that were created in a purposeful order but now are sorted in some other order. Records in a checkbook database, for example, are normally created in date order; records in an invoice database are entered in order of invoice number. Unsort Records restores the records to their original order.

Note   Prior to FileMaker Pro 7, this step was named Unsort.

See also: Sort Records

Show All Records

Purpose: This step makes all records visible (which is the same as choosing Records ➪ Show All Records or pressing ⌘+J/Ctrl+J). Use Show All Records when you want to work with all records in the database rather than with just the current found set.

Note   Prior to FileMaker Pro 5.0, this step was named Find All.

Options: None

See also: Enter Find Mode, Perform Find, Modify Last Find, Omit Record, Omit Multiple Records, Show Omitted Only

Show Omitted Only

Purpose: This step swaps any records that aren't currently in the found set for those that are in the found set (which is the same as choosing Records ➭ Show Omitted Only). The omitted records become visible, and the previously browsed records are hidden. Note that if all records are currently being browsed, this step has no effect.

Note   Prior to FileMaker Pro 5.0, this step was named Find Omitted; in FileMaker Pro 5 through 6, this step was named Show Omitted.

Options: None

See also: Enter Find Mode, Perform Find, Show All Records, Modify Last Find, Omit Record, Omit Multiple Records

Omit Record

Purpose: This step omits (hides) the current record from the found set (which is the same as choosing Records ➭ Omit Record or pressing ⌘+T/Ctrl+T). If the script step is performed in Find mode, the Find request becomes an Omit request.

Note   Prior to FileMaker Pro 5.0, this step was named Omit.

Options: None

See also: Enter Find Mode, Perform Find, Show All Records, Modify Last Find, Omit Multiple Records, Show Omitted Only

Omit Multiple Records

Purpose: This step omits (hides) the next x consecutive records from the found set (which is the same as choosing Records ➭ Omit Multiple or pressing ⌘+Shift+T/ Ctrl+Shift+M).

Options: Specify records, Perform without dialog

Note   The Specify button and the Specify records check box are synonymous. The number specified can be literal or the result of a calculation.

When an Omit Multiple Records step executes, a dialog normally appears asking for the number of records you want to omit, beginning with the current record.

The Specify records option enables you to set the number of records that you want to omit (as always, beginning with the record that is current at the time the step is performed). If Perform without dialog is also selected, the specified number of records is automatically omitted. Otherwise, the normal dialog appears, and it uses the number of records that you specified as the default entry.

 Note   Prior to FileMaker Pro 7, this step was named Show Omitted.

 Note   If the Perform without dialog option is selected and Specify records is not, the step defaults to omitting only the current record (such as, the number of records is 1), just as though you had used the Omit Record step.

See also: Enter Find Mode, Perform Find, Show All Records, Modify Last Find, Omit Record, Show Omitted Only

Perform Find

Purpose: Use this step to execute the current Find request or requests (which is the same as clicking the Find button on a Find request screen).

Options: Specify Find requests

The Specify Find requests option was introduced in FileMaker Pro 7. Selecting Specify Find requests (or clicking the Specify button) presents the Specify Find Requests dialog shown in Figure 15-7. Clicking the New button presents the Edit Find Request dialog shown in Figure 15-8. Select a request in the list and then click the corresponding button to edit/duplicate/delete it.

Figure 15-7: The Specify Find Requests dialog.

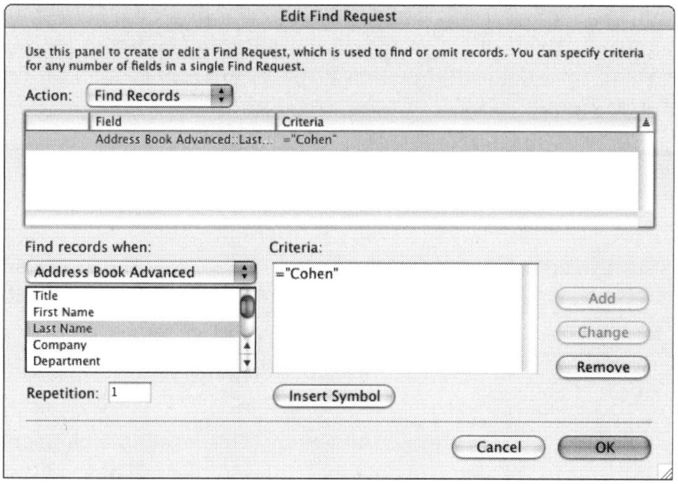

Figure 15-8: The Edit Find Request dialog.

In the Edit Find Request dialog, use the Find Records When field list and the Criteria text box to create your Find (or Omit) conditions, just as you would in a layout's field. Click Add to add that action to your conditions in the top list. Select a condition in the top list and click Change to edit it or Remove to delete that condition.

See also: Show All Records, Modify Last Find, Enter Find Mode

Modify Last Find
Purpose: This step presents the most recently executed Find request, which you can reexecute or use as the basis for a new Find request (which is the same as choosing Records ➪ Modify Last Find or pressing ⌘+R/Ctrl+R).

This script step is always performed by displaying a normal Find request onscreen.

Options: None

See also: Enter Find Mode, Perform Find, Show All Records, Omit Record, Omit Multiple Records, Show Omitted Only

Constrain Found Set
Purpose: This step, introduced in FileMaker Pro 7, lets you reduce the found set (which is the same as choosing Requests ➪ Constrain Found Set). This is equivalent to an AND search.

Options: Specify Find requests

Like the Perform Find script step, you select the Specify Find requests check box (or click the Specify button) to display the Specify Find Requests dialog (shown earlier in Figure 15-7). Create the constraining condition(s) here and in the Edit Find Request dialog. (Refer to Figure 15-8.)

See also: Perform Find, Extend Found Set

Extend Found Set

Purpose: This step, introduced in FileMaker Pro 7, lets you enlarge the found set (which is the same as choosing Requests ➪ Extend Found Set). This is equivalent to an OR search.

Options: Specify Find requests

Like the Perform Find script step, you select the Specify Find requests check box (or click the Specify button) to display the Specify Find Requests dialog (shown earlier in Figure 15-7). Create the extending condition(s) here and in the Edit Find Request dialog. (Refer to Figure 15-8.)

See also: Perform Find, Constrain Found Set

Editing script steps

The editing script steps enable you to execute standard editing commands (cut, copy, paste, clear, or make a selection) within scripts and apply them to specified fields.

Undo

Purpose: This step reverses the most recent action performed in the database (which is the same as choosing Edit ➪ Undo or pressing ⌘+Z/Ctrl+Z). The "most recent action" could also have been another script step.

Options: None

Not all actions can be undone. Any command associated with deleting records, for example, cannot be reversed. When a command cannot be undone, the Undo command reads Can't Undo, and the Undo script step has no effect.

Cut

Purpose: This step cuts the selected contents of a field to the Clipboard (which is the same as choosing Edit ➪ Cut or pressing ⌘+X/Ctrl+X). Information that is cut with this step is available for pasting elsewhere in the record, in a different record (enabling you to move existing information from one record to another), or in another program.

Cutting removes the selected text from the field. If your intent is merely to duplicate the information, use the Copy step instead.

Options: Select entire contents, Go to target field

Using the options alone or in combination, you can cut the entire contents of the current field (Select entire contents), cut the selected contents of a particular field (Go to target field), or cut the entire contents of a particular field (Select entire contents; Go to target field). The Specify button is synonymous with the Go to target field check box.

> **Note**
>
> Like the other editing script steps, Cut must be directed to a specific field in order for it to work. You can use a Go to Field script step to move to a particular field or use the Go to target field option. If you want this step to apply to *any* field on a layout, you must tab into or click the field before executing the step.

See also: Clear, Copy, Paste

Copy

Purpose: This step copies the selected contents of a field to the Clipboard (which is the same as choosing Edit ➪ Copy or pressing ⌘+C/Ctrl+C). Information that is copied with this step is available for pasting elsewhere in the record, in a different record (enabling you to duplicate existing information), or in another program.

Options: Select entire contents, Go to target field

Using the options alone or in combination, you can copy the entire contents of a field (Select entire contents), copy the selected contents of a particular field (Go to target field), or copy the entire contents of a particular field (Select entire contents; Go to target field). The Specify button is synonymous with the Go to target field check box. If no field is active and no options are specified, this step copies the current record's field contents to the Clipboard (just like choosing Copy from the Edit menu).

See also: Cut, Paste

Paste

Purpose: This script step pastes the current contents of the Clipboard into the current field (which is the same as choosing Edit ➪ Paste or pressing ⌘+V/Ctrl+V) or into a specified field.

Options: Select entire contents, Paste without style, Go to target field, Link if available (Windows only)

Data can be pasted into a field that is specified as a script step option or into the current field, depending on whether the Go to target field option is used. Pasted data can replace the entire contents of the field (with Select entire contents checked) or can be added to the field at the insertion point (with Select entire contents unchecked). If Paste without style is selected, any style formatting applied to the text (bold or italic, for example) is ignored. Otherwise, the pasted text includes whatever styles were originally applied to the text. The Specify button and the Go to target field check box are synonymous.

You should be aware of several common-sense restrictions when you use the Paste step. First, if the Clipboard is empty, nothing is pasted. Second, if the Clipboard contains data that is inappropriate for the selected field (such as a sound, picture, or movie that you are attempting to paste into a Text field), a validation error will appear when you exit the field. Third, if no field is selected in the current layout and a field is not specified as an option for the script step, nothing is pasted.

Because the Clipboard is shared among all programs, the material pasted can come from a program other than FileMaker Pro. For example, you could use a macro utility such as QuicKeys to copy some text in a word processing program and then use the Paste step to transfer a copy of the text to a database field.

 The Link if available option is for Windows users only. It is dimmed in the Macintosh version of FileMaker Pro. When you paste a link in Windows, the contents of the field are then linked to the original material (such as word processing file, graphic, sound, and so on). If the original material is modified by the creating program, the contents of the field can be updated in the FileMaker Pro field either automatically or manually, depending on how the link was set up.

See also: Insert Text, Insert from Last Visited, Insert from Index, Insert Current Time, Insert Current Date, Insert Current User Name, Cut, Copy

Clear

Purpose: The Clear step removes data from the current field (which is the same as choosing Edit ⇨ Clear) or removes it from the particular field specified in the script step. Depending on the option selected, this step can delete all the data from a field or only the data that is currently selected.

Options: Select entire contents, Go to target field

Clear can be used either on the currently selected field (by leaving the Go to target field option unmarked) or on a particular field (by clicking Go to target field and then choosing a field in the current table or in a related table). To clear all data from a field, select the Select entire contents check box. To clear only the currently selected data from the field, leave Select entire contents unchecked. If the script step doesn't use the Select entire contents option, you must preselect text in the field before executing the script; otherwise, the step has no effect. The Specify button is synonymous with the Go to target field check box.

 Unlike Cut, the Clear step doesn't save a copy of the data that has been removed to the Clipboard; that is, the data isn't available for pasting. If you make a mistake, however, you can correct the Clear operation by immediately choosing the Edit ⇨ Undo Clear command.

See also: Cut

Select All

Purpose: The Select All step selects the entire contents of the current field (which is the same as choosing Edit ⇨ Select All, pressing ⌘+A/Ctrl+A, or quadruple-clicking a field). If no field is currently selected, nothing happens.

Options: None

Perform Find/Replace

Purpose: The Perform Find/Replace step enables you to perform a word processing-style Find or Find/Replace in the current record/request or across all records/requests in the current field or in all fields. The step can be executed in Browse or Find mode, performing on records or Find requests, respectively.

Options: Specify; Perform without dialog

Click Specify to set step options. The Specify Find/Replace Options dialog appears, as shown in Figure 15-9. You'll note that it contains all the options of the Find/Replace dialog that appears when you choose Edit ⇨ Find/Replace ⇨ Find/Replace.

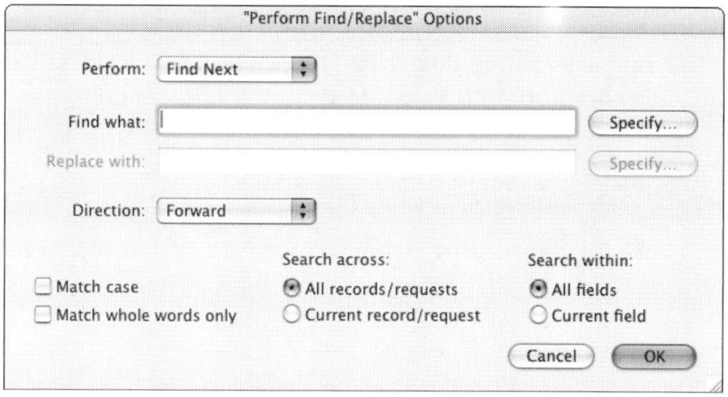

Figure 15-9: The Specify Find/Replace Options dialog.

You can set the following Find/Replace options:

✦ *Perform:* You can perform a Find Next, Replace & Find, Replace, or Replace All. (Choose the Find Next option to perform a Find without replacing data.)

✦ *Find what* and *Replace with:* For each of these options, enter a specific text string or click Specify to specify a field containing text string. (If you've chosen the Find Next option, the setting for Replace with is irrelevant; it isn't used.)

✦ *Direction:* Set the direction of the Find/Replace operation as Forward, Backward, or All. This option works in conjunction with the settings of the Search across and Search within options.

✦ *Match case:* When searching with this option checked, only strings that match the lettercase of the Find what string will be considered matches. (*Apple* will not match *apple,* for example.) If case is irrelevant, do not select this check box.

✦ *Match whole words only:* When this option is checked, only whole words that match the text string will be considered matches. The string *son* will treat only other instances of *son* as matches, while ignoring John*son,* for example.

✦ *Search across:* Restrict the chosen operation to the current record/request or apply it to all records/requests.

✦ *Search within:* Restrict the chosen operation to the current field or apply it to all fields.

Note   If you don't set Find/Replace options by clicking the Specify button (or by entering text in the Find what field), this step does nothing. If your intent is to let the user specify Find/Replace actions at the time the step executes, you must use the Open Find/Replace script step.

See also: Open Find/Replace (in Open Menu Item category)

Set Selection

Purpose: The Set Selection script step lets you specify a portion of a field as the current selection (just like using the mouse to select text). If no field is selected, no selection is made.

Fields script steps

These steps are used to paste or place information of various types into a selected field.

Set Field

Purpose: Use the Set Field step to set the contents of a particular field, based on the result of a calculation or entered as a literal value. The result of the calculation must be of a type that is appropriate for the target field.

Options: Specify target field, Specify calculated result

If the Specify target field option is not used to select a field, the currently active field (if any) is set. The Calculated result Specify button is used to create the formula used by the step.

Example: The Set Field step can be used to set the value for a Global field. For example, when using a loop to move through all records in a database and calculate a value, you can create the following Set Field step to initialize the value (held in a Global field named Total):

```
Set Field ["Total", "0"]
```

Then you can use the Set Field step again within a loop to update the value in Total, as follows:

```
Go to Record/Request/Page [First]
Loop
    If ["Insurance = "Yes""]
        Set Field ["Total", "Total + Insurance Amount"]
    End If
    Go to Record/Request/Page [Exit after last, Next]
End Loop
```

Thus, if there is a Yes entry in the Insurance field for a record, the value of Total is updated by adding the amount in the record's Insurance Amount field.

See also: Insert Calculated Result, Set Next Serial Value

Set Next Serial Value

Purpose: Use the Set Next Serial Value step to set the next value to be used for an auto-entry serial number field. You can specify a literal value or a calculated result.

Options: Specify target field, Specify calculated result

If the Specify target field option is not used to select a field, the currently active field (if any) is set. This field must be an auto-entry serial number field; otherwise, this script step has no effect. The Calculated result Specify button is used to specify the literal value or create the formula used by the step.

See also: Set Field, Insert Calculated Result

Insert Text

Purpose: Use this step to paste a specific string (text or number) at the insertion point within the current field or another specified field. Click Specify to indicate the string that you want to paste. If you don't specify a field (by selecting the Specify Field check box), this script step assumes that you have selected a field and positioned the insertion point before the step is executed — either manually or by adding a script step that moves to a field (Go to Field, for example).

 Note   In versions of FileMaker Pro prior to FileMaker Pro 6, this step was named Paste Literal.

Options: Select entire contents, Go to target field, Specify

Insert Text can be used either on the currently selected field (by leaving the Go to target field option unchecked) or on a particular field (by clicking Go to target field and then choosing a field in the current table or in a related table). To replace all data in the field, select the Select entire contents check box. To replace only the currently selected data from the field or paste at the insertion point (if no text is selected), leave Select entire contents unmarked.

See also: Paste

Insert Calculated Result

Purpose: This step pastes the result of a calculation (specified as part of the Insert Calculated Result step) into a particular field on the current layout in the current record.

Note   Prior to FileMaker Pro 5.0, this step was named Paste Result.

Options: Select entire contents, Go to target field, Specify calculated result

Select Go to target field (or click its associated Specify button) to choose a field in which to paste the result. If no field is specified, the result is pasted into the active field (if any) on the current layout. If no field is active, or if the target field is not available on the current layout, this step has no effect.

Click Calculated result's Specify button to create the calculation.

Click Select entire contents to replace the entire contents of the target field. If this option is not chosen, only the selected contents of the field are replaced, or a paste is performed at the current insertion point. (If there is no current insertion point, the result is pasted at the end of the target field's contents.)

Both the Insert Calculated Result and Set Field steps take the result of a calculation and use it to change the contents of a field. However, there are two notable differences, as follows:

✦ Insert Calculated Result can only change fields that are on the currently selected layout. Set Field doesn't care what layout is active or even whether the field has been placed on a layout.

✦ Set Field automatically replaces the entire contents of the selected field. Insert Calculated Result can be directed to replace just the currently selected portion of the target field, or it can insert the result at the current text insertion point.

See also: Set Field

Insert from Index

Purpose: This step enables you to paste information into a field by selecting the data to be pasted from the index for that field (which is the same as choosing the Insert ➭ From Index command or pressing ⌘+I/Ctrl+I). When this script step is executed, FileMaker displays the index for the current field (see Figure 15-10) and allows you to select the index entry that you want to paste. This step is very helpful for ensuring the correct spelling and consistent wording of field entries.

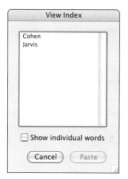

Figure 15-10: The Last Name field's index is presented in the View Index dialog.

 Note   Prior to FileMaker Pro 5.0, this step was named Paste from Index.

Options: Select entire contents, Go to target field

If you don't set the Go to target field option, FileMaker assumes that you will preselect a field before executing this script step.

 Caution   The Insert from Index step sets an error code that can be obtained with the Get(LastError) function but performs no action if the chosen field doesn't exist in the current layout. The same is true if no index has been created for the field and "automatically turn indexing on if needed" is not part of the field's definition.

See also: Paste

Insert from Last Visited

Purpose: This step pastes information from the same field in the most recently modified record into the selected field of the current record (which is the same as choosing Insert ➪ From Last Record or pressing ⌘+' (apostrophe)/Ctrl+').

 Note   Prior to FileMaker Pro 5.0, this step was named Paste from Last Record. In FileMaker Pro 6, its name changed to Insert from Last Record. The current name was changed to Insert from Last Visited in FileMaker Pro 7.

Options: Select entire contents, Go to target field

If the field to be used is not set with the Go to target field option, FileMaker Pro assumes that you will select the field manually or as a previous script step before executing the Insert from Last Visited step. Because you will generally want to replace whatever is in the chosen field with the entire contents of that field from the last modified record, the Select entire contents option is the one you will most often need to use with this step.

See also: Duplicate Record/Request

Insert Current Date

Purpose: This step places the current date (according to your system clock) into the active field (which is the same as choosing Insert ⇨ Current Date or pressing ⌘+– (dash)/Ctrl+–) or in a field specified as a step option.

Note The insertion action functions identically to a Paste action except that the information is not on the Clipboard, subject to subsequent Paste actions.

Note Prior to FileMaker Pro 5.0, this step was named Paste Current Date.

Options: Select entire contents, Go to target field

The date can be placed into a field specified as a step option or into the current field, depending on whether the Go to target field option is used. The inserted date can replace the entire contents of the field (with Select entire contents selected) or can be added to the field at the insertion point (with Select entire contents unchecked). For the step to work, the chosen field must be of a proper type to accept a date.

Example: If you do not already have an auto-entry field that automatically receives the current date when a new record is created or edited, you can use this script step to add a date-stamp, such as a step in a data-entry or report-preparation script.

See also: Paste, Insert Current Time

Insert Current Time

Purpose: This step places the current time (according to your system clock) into the current field (which is the same as choosing Insert ⇨ Current Time or pressing ⌘+; (semicolon)/Ctrl+;) or in a field specified as a step option.

Note Prior to FileMaker Pro 5.0, this step was named Paste Current Time.

Options: Select entire contents, Go to target field

The time can be placed into a field specified as a step option or into the current field, depending on whether the Go to target field option is used. The inserted time can replace the entire contents of the field (with Select entire contents selected) or can be added to the field at the insertion point (with Select entire contents unmarked). For the step to work, the chosen field must be of a proper type to accept a time.

Example: If you don't already have an auto-entry field that automatically receives the current time when a new record is created or edited, you can use this script step to add a timestamp, such as a step in a data-entry or report-preparation script.

See also: Paste, Insert Current Date

Insert Current User Name

Purpose: This step places the name of the current user — according to the setting in the Preferences dialog's General section — into the current field or in a field specified as a step option. This is the same as choosing Insert ⇨ Current User Name or pressing Shift+⌘+N/Ctrl+Shift+N. (See Chapter 7 for instructions on setting or changing the current user name.)

Note   Prior to FileMaker Pro 5.0, this step was named Paste Current User Name.

Options: Select entire contents, Go to target field

The user name can be placed into a field specified as a step option or into the current field, depending on whether the Go to target field option is used. The pasted name can replace the entire contents of the field (with Select entire contents selected) or can be added to the field at the insertion point (with Select entire contents unmarked).

See also: Paste

Insert Picture

Purpose: Use this script step to insert a graphic from a disk file into a Container field (which is the same as choosing Insert ⇨ Picture).

Note   Prior to FileMaker Pro 5.0, this step was named Import Picture.

Options: Store only a reference to the file, Specify source file

For Insert Picture to work, a Container field must be selected before the step is executed — by clicking or tabbing into the field before executing the script or by adding a Go to Field step to the script specifying the Container field.

Select Specify source file if you always want the script step to insert the same picture. If you don't specify a file as a step option, a standard file dialog appears when the step executes. Use normal navigation techniques to select the drive and/or folder in which the image file is stored. By clicking the dialog's Show pop-up menu Files of Type drop-down list, you can restrict the files displayed to those of a specific graphic type, such as JPEG or TIFF.

Note   This script step is not Web-compatible.

See also: Go to Field, Insert QuickTime, Insert Object (Windows), Insert File

Insert QuickTime

Purpose: This script step is used to insert a QuickTime movie, QuickTime VR clip, or a QuickTime audio clip into a Container field in the current record (which is the same as choosing Insert ➪ QuickTime). When executed, this step displays a dialog in which you can select a movie file to be imported.

Note   Prior to FileMaker Pro 5.0, this step was named Import Movie. In FileMaker Pro 5, 5.5, and 6, it was named Insert Movie.

Options: Specify source file

Select Specify source file if you always want the script step to insert the same QuickTime item at every invocation. If you do not specify a file as a step option, a standard file dialog appears when the step executes. Use normal navigation techniques to select the drive and/or folder in which the QuickTime item is stored.

For Insert QuickTime to work, a Container field must be selected before the step is executed — by clicking or tabbing into the field before executing the script or by adding a Go to Field script step specifying the Container field. The QuickTime software must also be installed and enabled.

See also: Go to Field, Insert Picture, Insert Object (Windows), Insert File

Insert Object
Windows

Purpose: This step enables you to insert an OLE object into a Container field. This is the same as choosing Insert ➪ Object. This step does nothing if the selected field is not a Container field.

Options: Specify object

To specify the OLE object to insert into the Container field, select either the Specify Object check box or click the Specify button. FileMaker Pro opens the Insert Object dialog (see Figure 15-11).

In the Insert Object dialog, you can create a new OLE object or create an OLE object from a file.

STEPS: Creating a New OLE Object

1. Select the Create new radio button.

2. Select the OLE object type from the Object Type list. The options available in the list depend on the OLE server applications you have installed on your PC.

3. If you want the final result displayed as an icon (rather than the actual contents of the OLE object), select the Display as icon check box. Showing the contents as an icon speeds up the FileMaker Pro layout display.

4. Click OK.

    When the script step executes, FileMaker Pro opens the application that can create the selected object type. For example, if you selected Adobe Photoshop Image, Adobe Photoshop (or Adobe Photoshop Elements) opens.

5. Create the OLE object in the selected application.

6. When you have finished creating the OLE object, exit the application and choose to update FileMaker Pro. If you change your mind, you can select the option in the other application to not update FileMaker Pro.

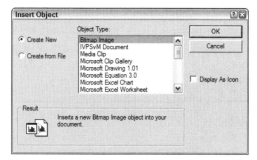

Figure 15-11: The Insert Object dialog enables you to create a new object type or use an existing object type as the contents of a Container field.

STEPS: Creating an OLE Object from a File

1. Select the Create from file radio button.

    A File text box replaces the Object Type list.

2. Type the full path to the file you want used as the OLE object into the File text box or click the Browse button to choose the file from the Browse dialog.

3. If you want to create a link to the file rather than embed the file in the Container field, select the Link check box.

    If you elect to link, any changes you later make to the file using the original application can be automatically updated in the Container field. However, if the linked file is not available (for example, if you delete it or open FileMaker Pro on another computer that doesn't have the file), the Container field will be empty.

See also: Update Link

Insert File

Purpose: Use this script step (introduced in FileMaker Pro 7) to import a disk file (or reference to a disk file) into a Container field (which is the same as choosing Insert ➪ File).

Options: Store only a reference to the file, Go to target field, Specify source file

For Insert File to work, a Container field must be selected before the step is executed — by clicking or tabbing into the field before executing the script, using the Go to target field option (or clicking Specify), or by adding a Go to Field step to the script specifying the Container field.

Select Specify source file if you always want the script step to insert the same file. If you don't specify a file as a step option, a standard file dialog appears when the step executes. Use normal navigation techniques to select the drive and/or folder in which the file is stored.

Selecting Store only a reference tells FileMaker Pro to store only a link to the file (similar to a Mac alias or Windows shortcut) and can significantly reduce the size of your FileMaker Pro database file. However, if the referenced file is not available, the Container field displays no data.

Note This script step is not Web-compatible.

See also: Go to Field, Insert QuickTime, Insert Object (Windows), Insert Picture

Replace Field Contents

Purpose: Use this script step to replace a field's value in every record in the current found set.

Options: Perform without dialog, Go to target field, Specify

When this script executes, FileMaker Pro will present the Replace Field Contents dialog unless you select the Perform without dialog check box.

The active field will be assumed as the target unless you select the Go to target field check box (or click its associated Specify button) to designate the field whose contents are to be replaced or employ a Go to Field script step.

Click the Specify button to designate the value (or calculation) to employ as the replacement value.

Note Prior to FileMaker Pro 7, this step was named Replace Contents.

See also: Relookup Field Contents

Relookup Field Contents

Purpose: This script step forces FileMaker Pro to verify that the data in a match field contains the current contents of the lookup source field. The action is performed for all records in the current found set.

Options: Perform without dialog, Go to target field

The active field will be assumed as the target unless you select the Go to target field check box (or click its associated Specify button) or employ a Go to Field script step to designate the field whose contents are to be replaced.

If you want the user to confirm each replacement, leave Perform without dialog unchecked; otherwise, the replacements will occur without user interaction.

 Note   Prior to FileMaker Pro 7, this step was named Relookup Contents.

See also: Replace Field Contents

Export Field Contents

Purpose: This script step, introduced in FileMaker Pro 7, writes the contents of a specified field in the active record to a new disk file.

Options: Specify output file, Specify target field

The active field will be assumed as the target field unless you select the Specify target field check box (or click its associated Specify button) or employ a Go to Field script step to designate the field whose contents you wish exported.

If you want the user to specify the output file, leave Specify output file unchecked. If you select Specify output file (or click its associated Specify button), FileMaker Pro presents you with a standard file dialog where you can designate the output file.

Update Link
Windows

Purpose: Updates the link to an OLE object in a Container field. Updating a link displays the most recent version of the OLE object in the FileMaker Pro layout.

Options: Go to target field, Specify

To specify the field for which you want to update the link, select the Go to target field check box or click the Specify button. Although the field list includes all fields in the table (with access to related tables as well), this script step performs no visible action if

- ✦ You choose a field that is not a Container field.
- ✦ You choose a Container field that doesn't contain an OLE object.
- ✦ You choose a Container field that contains an OLE object that is not linked (in other words, one that is embedded).

See also: Insert Object

Records script steps

These steps enable you to create, delete, and duplicate records as well as issue other record-related commands.

New Record/Request

Purpose: Use this script step to create a new blank record or Find request. When used in Browse mode, this step has the same effect as choosing Records ➪ New Record (or pressing ⌘+N/Ctrl+N). When used in Find mode, this step has the same effect as choosing Requests ➪ Add New Request (or pressing ⌘+N/Ctrl+N).

Options: None

Example: When scripting a data-entry routine to be used by people unfamiliar with your database, you might begin the script with a New Record/Request. You could also attach this single-step script to a New Record button so users could create additional records without having to know the Command/Control key sequence or the menu in which the command is located.

Duplicate Record/Request

Purpose: When executed in Browse mode, this step makes a duplicate of the current record (which is the same as choosing Records ➪ Duplicate Record or pressing ⌘+D/Ctrl+D). When executed from Find mode, the step makes a duplicate of the current Find request (which is the same as choosing Requests ➪ Duplicate Request or pressing ⌘+D/Ctrl+D).

Options: None

Example: Making a duplicate record and then editing the duplicate is a common data-entry shortcut for working with records that contain similar information. In a home-expenses database, for example, you undoubtedly would record expenses to some companies over and over. If the only items that change are the amount and/or payment date, you can save time by finding a previous record for the same company, duplicating the old record, and then editing the record by typing the new dollar amount and transaction date.

See also: Insert from Last Visited

Delete Record/Request

Purpose: This step is used to delete the current record (which is the same as choosing Records ➪ Delete Record or pressing ⌘+E/Ctrl+E) or the current Find request (which is the same as choosing Requests ➪ Delete Request or pressing ⌘+E/Ctrl+E).

Options: Perform without dialog

Select Perform without dialog if you don't want to give the user the opportunity to confirm or reject the Permanently delete this ENTIRE record? query that normally appears. Keep in mind, however, that — as with other Delete commands — you cannot undo a record deletion.

See also: Delete All Records, Delete Portal Row

Delete Portal Row

Purpose: This step is used to delete the selected portal row (and the associated data in the related record).

Options: Perform without dialog

Select Perform without dialog if you do not want to give the user the opportunity to confirm or reject the deletion. Keep in mind, however, that as with other Delete commands, you cannot undo a record deletion. If a portal record is not selected when this script step executes, nothing happens.

See also: Delete All Records, Delete Record/Request

Delete All Records

Purpose: Use the Delete All Records step to delete all records in the current found set. This is the same as choosing Records ➪ Delete All Records (when all records are being browsed) or Records ➪ Delete Found Records (when only a subset of records is being browsed).

Options: Perform without dialog

To make sure that this step is performed on the correct set of records, you should first issue appropriate Find commands or use a Find step, such as Perform Find, to select the group of records to be deleted.

Caution   As with other Delete commands, you cannot undo a Delete All Records step.

See also: Delete Record/Request, Show All Records, Perform Find, Enter Find Mode, Modify Last Find, Omit Record, Omit Multiple Records, Show Omitted Only

Open Record/Request

Purpose: This step is used to make an existing record or Find request available for editing. Assuming that the current user has adequate access privileges to edit the record or request, FileMaker Pro will lock the record to prevent other users from attempting to simultaneously modify it.

Options: Perform without dialog

Revert Record/Request

Purpose: This step is used to restore the current record or the current Find request to its state before you began editing the record (which is the same as choosing Records ⇨ Revert Record) or the Find request (which is the same as choosing Requests ⇨ Revert Request).

Options: Perform without dialog

Commit Records/Requests

Purpose: This step is equivalent to clicking outside of the active record or pressing Enter to complete a record or clicking the Find button to invoke a request. Following a Commit Record/Request, field data for the record is updated and no field is currently active.

Options: Skip data entry validation, Perform without dialog

The Skip data entry validation option is ignored for fields whose options are set to Always Validate. Select the Perform without dialog check box when you don't want the user prompted to accept the record commitment action.

Note   Prior to FileMaker Pro 7, this step was named Exit Record/Request.

Copy Record/Request

Purpose: This step copies the contents of all eligible fields for the current record to the Clipboard in tab-delimited format. Graphics and sounds are not copied. Similarly, all fields of a Find request are written to the Clipboard in tab-delimited format.

Options: None

Note   When copying a record that contains repeating fields, ASCII 29 (a nonprinting character known as *GS,* for *Group Separator*) separates the repetitions.

See also: Copy All Records/Requests

Note   Prior to FileMaker Pro 7, this step was named Copy Record.

Copy All Records/Requests

Purpose: This step copies the contents of all eligible fields for all browsed records or all Find requests to the Clipboard in tab-delimited format (which is the same as pressing Option/Shift while choosing Edit ➪ Copy with no active field). Graphics and sounds are not copied.

Options: None

> **Note**
>
> When copying a record that contains repeating fields, ASCII 29 (a nonprinting Group Separator character code) separates the repetitions.

See also: Copy Record/Request

> **Note**
>
> Prior to FileMaker Pro 7, this step was named Copy All Records.

Import Records

Purpose: Use the Import Records step to import data into the current database from another FileMaker Pro database or from a compatible data file. (This is the same as choosing a command from the File ➪ Import submenu.)

Options: Specify import order, Perform without dialog, Specify data source

Leave all options unchecked to perform an import operation from scratch. When the step executes, FileMaker Pro displays a dialog from which you select the source of the data to be imported. When it is from a file, you can select a particular file type from the dialog's Show pop-up menu/Files of type drop-down list to make the file list more manageable.

The Import Records script step was greatly expanded in FileMaker Pro 6. It governs *all* types of importing rather than just data files. It can import several types of files, including pictures from a connected digital camera (Mac only), XML (eXtensible Markup Language) source data, Open Database Connectivity (ODBC) source data, or an entire folder of images or text. The item you select from the Show pop-up menu/Files of type drop-down list determines what you will see when the script step executes. If you choose XML source, for example, the Specify XML and XSL Options dialog appears. (See Figure 15-12.)

Like a normal record import, you can automate the entire process of importing from a camera (Mac only), XML file, ODBC source, or folder by selecting the Specify data source check box (or clicking the associated Specify button), selecting the desired type of item from the Show pop-up menu/Files of type drop-down list, and then responding to the dialogs that appear.

If you are performing a standard record import, the Import Field Mapping dialog appears when the step executes. (See Figure 15-13.) To execute the import operation, match the fields in the two tables (as explained in Chapter 16), and select a radio button to indicate that you want to Add new records, Update existing records in found set, or Update matching records in found set. If the last option is chosen, you can optionally Add remaining data as new records (that is, new records in the target database will be created from all non-matching records). Click OK to perform the import procedure.

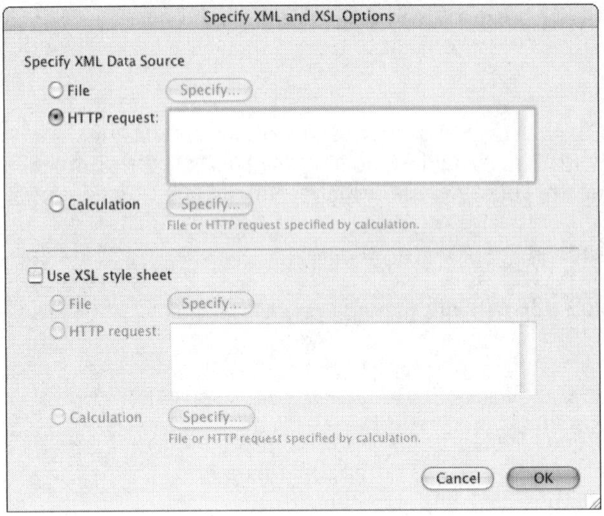

Figure 15-12: When importing XML data, this dialog appears.

Note In versions prior to FileMaker 7 Pro, Update existing records in found set was called Restore import order, but most users found that description confusing, leading to the more descriptive option name now employed.

Figure 15-13: The Import Field Mapping dialog.

If you previously selected the import file and the matching fields, you can select the Update existing records in found set option to repeat the same import operation each time.

Note
Some data sources, such as spreadsheets and various tab-delimited text files, include a first record specifying the data set's fieldnames. When such a possibility exists (it's not a FileMaker Pro database or some other rigidly defined format like dBASE III), the Don't import first record (contains field names) check box will be undimmed for you to set appropriately.

Example: Suppose that you periodically export new address records to a tab-separated text file called New Addresses. After importing these records into the Address Book Advanced database once (see Chapter 4), you can create a script using the Import Records step to import the new records automatically by using the same data file (choose File in the Script Definition dialog's Specify data source pop-up menu/drop-down list to select the New Addresses file) and the same import order (Update existing records in found set) each time. In this case, you could also add the Perform without dialog option because nothing would change that might require user intervention.

See also: Export Records

Export Records

Purpose: Use the Export Records step (which is the same as choosing File ⇨ Export Records) to export data from the current FileMaker Pro database so the data can be imported (read) into another FileMaker Pro database or another program.

Note
Export Records automatically exports data from all records in the current found set. If you want to limit exports to a subset of records, use Find requests or related commands (or script steps) to select those records beforehand. If you want to ensure that all records in the database are exported, choose Records ⇨ Show All Records or use the Show All Records script step before the Export Records script step. See Chapter 9 for details on finding and selecting records.

Options: Specify export order, Perform without dialog, Specify output file

Leave all options unmarked to perform an export from scratch. When the step executes, FileMaker displays the Export Records to File dialog in which you name the new export data file and select a file type for the export file (Tab-Separated Text, for example). Next, the Specify Field Order for Export dialog appears. (See Figure 15-14.) To execute the export, choose the fields that you want to export, set options (as explained in Chapter 16), and then click OK.

New Feature
New in FileMaker Pro 8 is the option to automatically attach the exported file to an e-mail message.

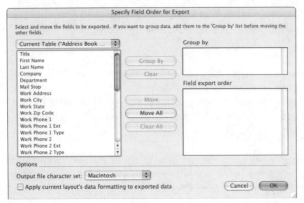

Figure 15-14: The Specify Field Order for Export dialog.

The Specify export order option tells FileMaker Pro to use the export order in effect at the time you created the script. That order will be displayed for you to edit. In previous versions, this option was called Restore export order. You can export data as XML in either of two grammars (FMPXMLRESULT or FMPDSORESULT) with an optional XSL (eXtensible Stylesheet Language) style sheet. To export as XML, choose XML from the File Type pop-up menu/drop-down list in the Specify Output File dialog. When you click OK, the Specify XML and XSL Options dialog appears (see Figure 15-15), in which you can choose the output grammar and optionally specify an XSL style sheet.

Caution   When using the FMPDSORESULT grammar, do not export fields whose names are single-byte Kana characters or whose names are purely numeric (12, for example).

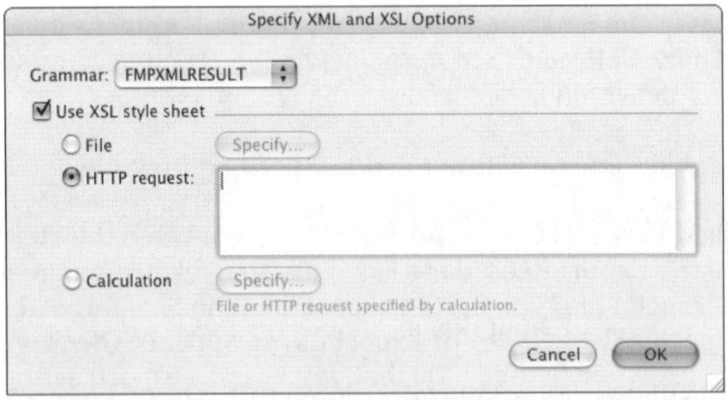

Figure 15-15: The Specify XML and XSL Options dialog.

Example: Suppose that you periodically export new address records to a tab-separated text file called Addresses. After performing this export operation once, you can create a script that uses the Export Records step to export the new records to the same output file automatically. In this case, you could also add the Perform without dialog option because nothing would change that might require user intervention.

See also: Import Records

Save Records as Excel
New in FileMaker Pro 8

Purpose: Use the Save Records as Excel script step (which is the same as choosing File ➪ Save/Send Records As ➪ Excel) to export data from the current FileMaker Pro database as an Excel worksheet.

Note Your privilege set must include Allow exporting to employ this script step.

Options: Specify options, Perform without dialog, Specify output file

The Specify options option displays the Save Records as Excel dialog, where you can specify saving either the current record or all records in the current found set, specify whether the values in the first row should be field names or data, and designate values for worksheet, title, subject, and author. Perform without dialog tells FileMaker Pro not to display the Excel Options dialog. If you have not designated a file, the Save Records as Excel dialog appears; otherwise, no dialog appears. You can specify the output file by selecting Specify output file, and you can also opt to Automatically open file or Create email with file as attachment in the Specify dialog.

Save Records as PDF
New in FileMaker Pro 8

Purpose: Use the Save Records as PDF script step (which is the same as choosing File ➪ Save/Send Records As ➪ PDF) to export data from the current FileMaker Pro database as an Acrobat (PDF) file.

Note Your privilege set must include Allow printing to employ this script step.

Options: Specify options, Perform without dialog, Specify output file

The Specify options option displays the Save Records as PDF dialog; clicking the Options button in that dialog displays the PDF Options dialog, as shown in Figure 15-16. Perform without dialog tells FileMaker Pro not to display any dialogs (Print or PDF-specific) when executing this step. You can specify the output file by selecting Specify output file and can also opt to Automatically open file or Create email with file as attachment in the Specify dialog.

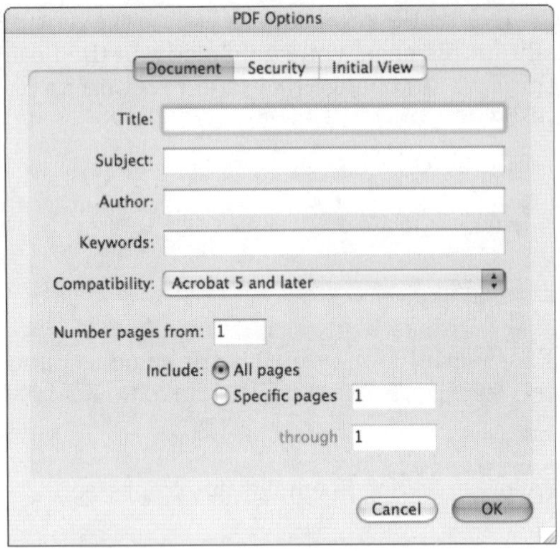

PDF Options

Document   Security   Initial View

Title:

Subject:

Author:

Keywords:

Compatibility: Acrobat 5 and later

Number pages from: 1

Include: ⦿ All pages
○ Specific pages 1
through 1

Cancel   OK

Figure 15-16: The PDF Options dialog.

In the Document pane, you can designate descriptive information either via manual entry or as the result of a calculation. In the Security pane, you can specify PDF security settings, such as passwords, print limitations, or editing limitations. The Initial View pane is where you can specify the default layout and magnification Adobe Reader should employ when opening the PDF file.

Windows script steps

The windows script steps enable you to create and control the appearance of document windows.

New Window

Purpose: This step creates a new window containing the same layout, table, found set, and active record/field as the current frontmost window. It is equivalent to choosing Window ➪ New Window.

Options: Specify

Click Specify to name, size, and position your new window.

Caution   The Distance from top and Distance from left positioning choices have different effects on Mac and Windows. On the Mac, they determine the distance from the top and left edge of the (main) screen; however, on Windows, they specify the distance from the top and left edges of the FileMaker Pro application window.

FileMaker Pro will not allow you to specify dimensions less than the minimum width or height, nor greater than the maximum allowable width and height for your current screen resolution. If you specify too small or too large of a window, FileMaker Pro will size it to the minimum permissible or maximum permissible, respectively.

See also: Move/Resize Window

Select Window

Purpose: This script step sets the designated window as the active (frontmost) window.

Options: Specify

Click Specify to present the Select Window Options dialog shown in Figure 15-17.

Figure 15-17: The Select Window Options dialog.

You can designate the Current window (default) or another window, either literally or as the result of a calculation.

See also: Close Window

Close Window

Purpose: This step tells FileMaker Pro to close a window.

Options: Specify

By default, the current window (the one from which the script is running) will be closed. However, you can click the Specify button to display the Select Window Options dialog shown previously in Figure 15-17, at which point you can enter a (non-case-sensitive) window name or Specify a calculation (Specify button) returning a window name.

Adjust Window

Purpose: This step resizes or hides a FileMaker Pro window.

Options: Specify

Click the Specify button to select an adjustment option from the following list:

✦ *Resize to fit* shrinks the window to the smallest size that will still display the entire layout. If the window cannot be made large enough to display the entire layout without exceeding the screen resolution, this will be equivalent to the Maximize option.

✦ *Maximize* resizes the window to the largest size possible to fit within the screen boundaries (Mac) or application window (Windows).

✦ *Minimize* is equivalent to clicking the Minimize (yellow/–) button in the window's title bar, placing it on the Dock/in the status bar.

✦ *Restore* returns the window to its most recent, previous size.

✦ *Hide* is equivalent to the Window ⇨ Hide Window command, leaving it open but moving it offscreen.

See also: Move/Resize Window

Move/Resize Window

Purpose: This step resizes a FileMaker Pro window and/or moves it to a new location.

Options: Specify

Click the Specify button to select an adjustment option from the following list:

✦ *Current window or name* selects the active window or the window with the specified name as the target.

✦ *Height* resizes the window to the specified vertical dimension.

✦ *Width* resizes the window to the specified horizontal dimension.

✦ *Distance from top* places the top of the window the specified number of pixels from the top of the main screen (Mac) or the top of the application window (Windows).

✦ *Distance from left* places the window's left edge the specified number of pixels from the left edge of the main screen (Mac) or the left edge of the application window (Windows).

Note

The relocated or resized window's layout, root table, found set, and active record and field are unchanged.

See also: New Window, Adjust Window

Arrange All Windows

Purpose: This step resizes and repositions all open FileMaker Pro windows.

Options: Specify

Choose an arrangement option from the Specify pop-up menu/drop-down list, as follows:

✦ *Tile horizontally* resizes windows and positions them into a non-overlapping side-by-side (left-to-right) arrangement.

✦ *Tile vertically* resizes windows and repositions them into a non-overlapping stack of windows.

✦ *Cascade window* resizes windows and overlaps them with a slight horizontal and vertical offset. The bottom-most window will be resized to fill the screen/ application window, and each subsequent window will be reduced in size by the offset times its position in the stack both horizontally and vertically.

✦ *Bring all to front* (Mac only) brings all FileMaker Pro windows to the front of the (interleaved) stack of windows from all open applications.

Freeze Window

Purpose: The Freeze Window step instructs FileMaker Pro to perform the current script without updating information in the document window until either the script ends or a Refresh Window script step is executed.

Options: None

Note　Using Freeze Window can save a great deal of screen flashing, as well as the time required to draw the updated information when the script performs a sequence of operations to achieve a specific goal (such as a complex Find, followed by a Sort).

See also: Refresh Window

Refresh Window

Purpose: This step causes FileMaker Pro to redraw (or refresh) the document window. A Refresh Window step is often used following a Freeze Window step to force a screen refresh to occur. Select the Bring to front option if you want to make sure that the document window is the frontmost database window.

Tip　It is unnecessary to include this step as the last step of a script because FileMaker Pro automatically refreshes the display when a script ends.

See also: Freeze Window

Scroll Window

Purpose: This step scrolls the document window to the desired position or in the indicated direction.

Options: Specify

Choose one of the following options from the Specify pop-up menu/drop-down list: Home, End, Page Up, Page Down, To Selection.

Home scrolls the document to the top of the window, End scrolls to the bottom of the window, Page Up scrolls up one page, and Page Down scrolls down one page. If you have a keyboard including these keys, choosing any of these options has the same effect as pressing the key of the same name.

Choose To selection to scroll the window so that the current field is visible.

Example: In a very tall data entry layout (one that extends beyond the height of most screens), you could attach a Scroll Window [Page Down] step to a button to make it easier for data entry personnel to reach the second screen. Another button at the bottom of the layout could use the Scroll Window [Home] step to return immediately to the top of the screen.

> **Note** Unlike most other script step options, you *must* choose one of the scrolling options.

Show/Hide Status Area

Purpose: This step enables you to toggle the state of the *status area* (the section of the document window that contains FileMaker Pro controls, such as the book icon and the Tools panel) between visible and hidden.

Options: Specify (Toggle, Show, or Hide), Lock

To toggle the state of the status area (switching from Hide to Show or from Show to Hide), choose Toggle from the Specify pop-up menu/drop-down list. Choosing Toggle has the same effect as clicking the document window's status area control. To switch to a specific state, whether the status area is currently shown or hidden, choose either Hide or Show from the Specify pop-up menu/drop-down list.

Select the Lock check box if you want to prevent the user from changing the status area display from the way you've set it.

> **Note** Prior to FileMaker Pro 7, this step was named Toggle Status Area.

See also: Set Zoom Level

Show/Hide Text Ruler

Purpose: This step hides or shows the text ruler.

Options: Specify (Toggle, Show, or Hide)

Choose Toggle from the Specify pop-up menu/drop-down list to switch the state of the text ruler from Hide to Show and vice versa. Choose Show or Hide to set the text ruler to a specific state (regardless of its current state).

Note Prior to FileMaker Pro 7, this step was named Toggle Text Ruler.

Set Window Title

Purpose: Changes the window name of any open FileMaker Pro window.

Options: Specify

Click the Specify button to present the Set Window Title Options dialog, as shown in Figure 15-18. In this dialog, you can designate which window is to be renamed, either the Current window (the default) or a window whose name you provide, either literally or as the result of a calculation. You also indicate the name the new window is to receive, again either literally or as the result of a calculation.

Figure 15-18: The Set Window Title Options dialog.

Set Zoom Level

Purpose: This step sets the zoom level of the frontmost database document window.

Options: Lock, Specify

Selecting the Lock check box disables (dims) the zoom controls in the document window, freezing the display at the chosen zoom level. Choose any of the normally supported magnification percentages (between 25 and 400 percent) from the Specify pop-up menu/drop-down list or choose the Zoom In and Zoom Out step options to achieve the same effect as choosing the View ⇨ Zoom In and View ⇨ Zoom Out commands.

Tip   In many cases, Set Zoom Level steps are used in pairs — one step (or script) to zoom the screen to a particular level and a second step (or a second script) restoring the window to the original zoom level. Similarly, after locking the zoom level (to prevent the user from changing what you want to show), you must also execute a script step to unlock the zoom level. Otherwise, it will continue to be frozen for the window.

By using the Set Zoom Level step in combination with the Scroll Window step, you can display a particular section of a database window at a specific magnification. You can also use this step as part of a start-up script to set a preferred magnification for a given database.

See also: Show/Hide Staus Area

View As
Purpose: This step can be used to specify the way records are displayed (as one record per screen, as a continuous scrolling list, or in spreadsheet form) or to switch from the current display mode to another display mode.

Options: Specify (Cycle, View as form, View as list, View as table choices)

Choose Cycle from the Specify pop-up menu/drop-down list to cycle through the three display modes. Each time a script is executed (or a button clicked) that contains the View as [cycle] step, the view changes to the next viewing method. The order in which the views cycle is form, list, and table.

To set the display mode to a specific state, regardless of the current display mode, choose View as Form, View as List, or View as Table from the Specify pop-up menu/drop-down list.

Files script steps
These steps are used to open, close, and save database files; create new files; and set file-related options.

New File
Purpose: This step displays the New Database dialog (which is the same as choosing File ⇨ New Database), enabling the user to create a new empty file or one based on any of the installed templates if the Show templates in New Database dialog preference is on; otherwise, FileMaker Pro displays the Create a New File Named standard file dialog.

Note Prior to FileMaker Pro 7, this step was named, simply, New.

Options: None

Open File

Purpose: This step enables the user to select a FileMaker Pro database to open (which is the same as choosing File ➪ Open or pressing ⌘+O/Ctrl+O) or to open a specific database file automatically.

Options: Specify, Open hidden

If a file is specified, that file is opened when the step executes. If no file is specified, a standard file dialog appears, enabling the user to select a database to open. In either case, a database opened with this script step becomes the current database.

If you set the Open hidden option, the database opens but is not displayed onscreen. To view open but hidden databases, look in the Window menu's Show submenu.

Note that if you intend to perform a script in another database, you don't have to open the other database first. Simply use the Perform Script step, specify that an external script is to be used, and then select the database to open and the particular script you want to perform.

Note Prior to FileMaker Pro 7, this step was named, simply, Open.

See also: Close File

Close File

Purpose: This step closes the current file (which is the same as choosing File ➪ Close or pressing ⌘+W/Ctrl+W) or closes another specific FileMaker Pro file.

Note If the Close File step closes the current file, the script terminates, and no subsequent steps will be performed. Thus, it is advisable to employ only a script step that closes the current file as the terminal step in a script's logic.

Options: Specify

Note Prior to FileMaker Pro 7, this step was named, simply, Close.

If no option is set, the Close File step simply closes the current file (same as File ➪ Close or ⌘+W/Ctrl+W). You can choose a particular file to close (Sales.fp7 or Sales, for example) from the Specify pop-up menu/drop-down list.

Example: The Close File step is useful for ending a script that performs a final action for a database. You could, for example, create a script that sorts the database in a specific way (to be sure that the database is ready for use the next day) and then closes the file. If you have a database that works in conjunction with other databases, you can use the Close File step to close the other file or files when they're no longer needed. (Closing unnecessary files frees memory for other FileMaker Pro activities.)

See also: Open File, Quit Application

Convert File

Purpose: This step converts a file, XML data, or ODBC data into a FileMaker Pro database.

Options: Specify data source, Perform without dialog

This step is very similar to the Import Records script step except that it creates the FileMaker Pro file and imports the data from only one file (no folder option).

See also: Import Records

Set Multi-User

Purpose: This step turns the multi-user status for a database on or off (allowing or disallowing network or Internet access to the data).

Options: On, On (Hidden), Off

Choosing the On option is equivalent to choosing FileMaker Pro/Edit ➪ Sharing ➪ FileMaker Network and selecting the FileMaker Network Settings dialog's Network sharing on radio button; choosing Off is equivalent to selecting the Network sharing off radio button. Choosing On (Hidden) sets the database for multi-user status but doesn't list the database in the Open Remote dialog. This is the equivalent to choosing the FileMaker Network Settings dialog's Don't display in Open Remote File dialog check box.

Set Use System Formats

Purpose: Macintoshes and PCs have Preference panes and control panels where you set default formats for displaying dates, times, and numbers. On a Macintosh, the Formats tab of the International System Preferences is used. On a PC, the Regional Settings (or Regional and Language Options) control panel (with Number, Time, and Date tabs) is used. FileMaker Pro, however, saves its own default settings for displaying dates, times, and numbers as part of each database file. The Set Use System Formats step enables you to choose between using the normal system formats for these entities or the formats that are stored with the database.

Options: On, Off

Select the On option to use the current system formats that were set in the control panels or System Preferences. Select the Off option to use the formats that were saved with the file.

Save a Copy As

Purpose: This step is the same as choosing the File ⇨ Save a Copy As command. If no options are set for the Save a Copy As step, the Create a Copy Named/Create Copy file dialog appears when the script executes the step. (See Figure 15-19.) The dialog enables you or the current user to name the copy, determine where on disk the file will be saved, and select the type of copy that is made (a duplicate, a compacted copy, or a clone).

Figure 15-19: Saving a copy of a database (Mac).

Options: Specify, Specify output file

Click the Specify Output File button if you always want the file to be saved in a particular location, using the same filename and type. You'll be presented with a standard file dialog where you establish the name and location for the saved file.

Choose the type of save desired (copy of current file, compacted copy [smaller], or clone (no records) from the Specify pop-up menu/drop-down list.

Example: An example of using the Save a Copy As script step appears in the section in Chapter 2 on automatic backups.

Recover File

Purpose: The Recover File script step performs the same action as choosing the File ⇨ Recover command. Its purpose is to repair damaged database files.

There must be enough free space on the disk to recover the file successfully.

Options: Perform without dialog, Specify source file

Prior to FileMaker Pro 7, this step was named Recover.

If you want to specify the file to recover, select Specify source file. FileMaker Pro opens a dialog displaying a list of files. Choose the file you want to recover. Choose Perform without dialog if you don't want the user to have the choice of which file to recover or to see the summary alert at the end of the recovery process. However, if you select Perform without dialog but do not specify a file, the Open Damaged File dialog will still open when this script step is executed because FileMaker Pro won't know which file to recover.

Most FileMaker developers agree that a recovered file isn't safe to continue using. It is recommended that you export the data from the recovered file and then import it into a backup clone of the database. (You do keep backups of your critical databases, right?)

Print Setup

Purpose: Use this script step to specify Page/Print Setup options, such as paper size and orientation, for a print job. This is the same as choosing File ➪ Page Setup or File ➪ Print Setup.

Options: Perform without dialog, Specify page setup

Prior to FileMaker Pro 7, this step was named Page Setup (in Mac versions).

Select Specify page setup to display the Page Setup/Print Setup dialog so that you can establish settings to be stored with the script. If you don't select Perform without dialog, the user will be presented with a Page Setup/Print Setup dialog when the script step executes, allowing him or her to establish settings.

See also: Print

Print

Purpose: Use this step to send data to a printer or other output device (such as a fax/modem) according to the options set in the Print dialog (which is the same as choosing File ➪ Print or pressing ⌘+P/Ctrl+P).

Options: Perform without dialog, Specify print options

By default, FileMaker Pro assumes you want to use the Print options that were in effect when you last printed the database or that you stored with the script via the

Specify print options option. If you want to give the user the capability to specify different Print options each time the script runs, leave Perform without dialog unchecked. When the script runs, the user sees the normal FileMaker Pro Print dialog. We recommend this option because if the user has a different printer or printer driver than you, the output could be rendered useless. On the other hand, if you always want to print with the same set of Print options (or you don't want to give users an opportunity to select other Print options — inappropriate ones that might ruin the print job, for example), use Specify print options and then select Perform without dialog.

Tip

If special Page/Print Setup options are necessary for a print job to print correctly (such as printing labels on a dot-matrix printer or printing in landscape mode), you will want to include Print Setup as an earlier script step. Before creating the script, start by printing the job correctly. Then when you enter the Print and Page/Print Setup steps in the script, FileMaker Pro will note the options that are set for these two steps and use those options whenever the script executes.

See also: Print Setup, Enter Preview Mode

Accounts script steps

The Accounts script steps let you manage user accounts.

With the exception of the Change Password script step, all these script steps were new to FileMaker Pro 7.

Add Account

Purpose: Use this step to add a new user account (including password and privilege settings).

Options: Specify

The Specify button displays the Add Account Options dialog, shown in Figure 15-20. The Account Name and Password can be literals or calculation results (associated Specify buttons). Choose access levels from the Privilege Set pop-up menu/drop-down list. If you select the User must change password on next login check box, you prevent the user from continuing to use the initial password assigned.

Note

You cannot assign Full Access via this script step. Full Access privileges can only be assigned manually.

Caution

If you wish this script step to execute regardless of the logged-in user's privileges, select the Edit Script dialog's Run script with full access privileges check box.

Delete Account

Purpose: Use this script step to delete the specified account without displaying any feedback.

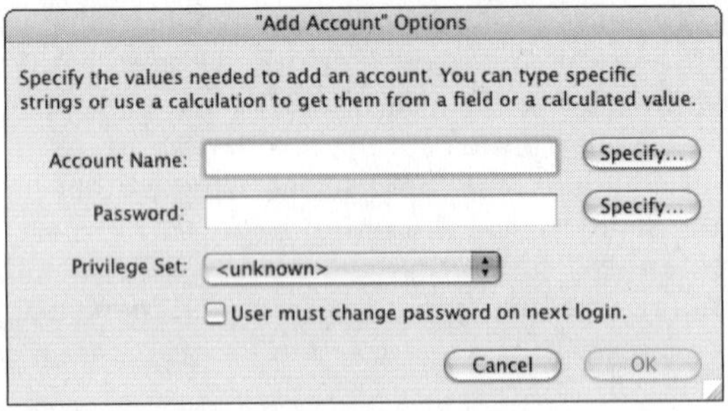

Figure 15-20: The Add Account Options dialog.

Options: Specify

Use the Specify button to designate the account to be deleted. Like the Add Account script step, Full Access privileges are required to execute this step. Thus, you should select the Edit Script dialog's Run script with full access privileges check box if you want to guarantee that it is performed.

Note   This script step cannot be used to delete a Full Access account. Such a deletion must be done manually.

Reset Account Password
Purpose: This step resets the specified account's password.

Options: Specify

Click Specify to display the Reset Account Password Options dialog. You can enter literal strings or specify calculations for both the Account Name and the New Password. There is also a User must change password at next login check box, identical to the one in the Add Account Options dialog, shown earlier in Figure 15-20.

See also: Add Account, Change Password

Change Password
Purpose: This step enables the user to change his or her FileMaker account password.

Options: Perform without dialog, Specify

When executed, this script step presents the Change Password dialog shown in Figure 15-21 unless the Perform without dialog option is selected.

Note   If the user does not have change password privileges, the script must run with full access privileges for this step to execute.

Figure 15-21: The Change Password dialog.

See also: Reset Account Password, Add Account

Enable Account

Purpose: This step allows you to enable or disable a specified account.

Options: Specify

Click Specify to display the Enable Account Options dialog. You can enter literal strings or specify a calculation for Account Name. Select either the Activate account or Deactivate account radio button, depending upon the action you want taken.

Note   The script must run with full access privileges or the user must have sufficient privileges for this step to execute.

Re-Login

Purpose: This step lets the user specify a different account (and its access privileges) for the current session without having to close and reopen the database.

Options: Perform without dialog, Specify

Click Specify to display the Re-Login Options dialog. You can enter literal strings or specify calculations for the Account Name and/or the Password. If you select the Perform without dialog check box, you must specify these settings for the script step to succeed.

Spelling script steps

The spelling script steps enable you to check the spelling of a field, an entire record, or the found set, as well as to correct words and select and edit dictionaries.

Check Selection

Purpose: This step uses the spelling checker to examine the selected text in the current field (which is the same as choosing Edit ➪ Spelling ➪ Check Selection).

Options: Select entire contents, Go to target field (Specify)

With no options set, this step can be used to check the spelling of selected text in any field of any layout. However, if no text is selected when the script executes, nothing happens: That is, no spell check is performed.

When only the Select entire contents option is set, this step causes a spell-check to be executed for the entire contents of the current field (the one that contains the cursor). If no field is current, the spell-check is skipped.

If only the Go to target field option is selected, the spell-check is restricted to selected text within the specified field.

When both options are set, the entire contents of the specified field are checked. This method can be particularly useful for ensuring that the spelling is correct in a long text field (a Comments or Notes field, for example).

See also: Check Record, Check Found Set

Check Record
Purpose: This step instructs the spelling checker to examine every field in the current record (which is the same as choosing Edit ⇨ Spelling ⇨ Check Record).

Options: None

See also: Check Selection, Check Found Set

Check Found Set
Purpose: This step performs a spelling check for every field in all records in the current found set — that is, the records that are currently being browsed. This step is the same as performing a Find and then choosing Edit ⇨ Spelling ⇨ Check All. When all records are in the found set (following a Records ⇨ Show All Records command, for example), all records will be checked.

Options: None

See also: Check Selection, Check Record

Correct Word
Purpose: This step opens the Spelling dialog so you can correct a word that FileMaker has identified as misspelled. This is the same as choosing Edit ⇨ Spelling ⇨ Correct Word after performing a spell check (for a selection, record, or all current records).

To work correctly, Check spelling as you type must be enabled in the File Options dialog's Spelling tab (File ⇨ File Options), and the spelling checker must have identified a misspelled word. If there are no misspellings, nothing happens when this script step is executed.

Options: None

See also: Check Record, Check Found Set, Check Selection

Spelling Options

Purpose: This step opens the File Options dialog to the Spelling tab, enabling the user to set spelling options for the current database. This is the same as choosing File ➪ File Options and then clicking the File Options dialog's Spelling tab.

Options: None

> **Tip** This step is particularly useful for situations where you've restricted the user's access to menus.

See also: Open File Options

Select Dictionaries

Purpose: This step opens the Select Dictionaries dialog so the user can choose either a User Dictionary or a Main Dictionary. This is the same as choosing Edit ➪ Spelling ➪ Select Dictionaries.

Options: None

Edit User Dictionary

Purpose: This step opens the User Dictionary dialog, enabling the user to edit the User Dictionary's contents. This is the same as choosing Edit ➪ Spelling ➪ Edit User Dictionary.

Options: None

Open Menu Item script steps

This category contains script steps to open the appropriate dialogs for modifying preferences, creating database definitions (field and relationships), getting Help, accessing ScriptMaker, and changing the network/Internet sharing.

Open Preferences

Purpose: This step opens the Preferences dialog. The user can modify different preferences classes by clicking tabs at the top of the dialog. This is the same as choosing FileMaker Pro ➪ Preferences/Edit ➪ Preferences ➪ Application.

Options: None

Note   Prior to FileMaker Pro 7, this step was named Open Application Preferences.

See also: Open File Options

Open File Options

Purpose: This step opens the File Options dialog. The user can modify the File Options by clicking tabs at the top of the dialog. This is the same as choosing File ➪ File Options.

Options: None

Note   Prior to FileMaker Pro 7, this step was named Open Document Preferences.

See also: Open Preferences, Spelling Options

Open Define Database

Purpose: This step displays the Define Database dialog, enabling you to create and edit tables, fields, and relationships. This is the same as choosing File ➪ Define ➪ Database or pressing Shift+⌘+D/Shift+Ctrl+D. See Chapter 5 for more information about defining fields and Chapter 17 for more information concerning tables and relationships.

Options: None

Note   FileMaker Pro 7 consolidated two script steps (Open Define Fields and Open Define Relationships) into this step.

Note   You must have full access privileges for this script step to work. If you want this step to execute regardless of the current user's access privileges, select the Edit Script dialog's Run script with full access privileges check box.

Open Define File References

Purpose: This step displays the Define File References dialog, enabling you to create and edit references to files used throughout the database. This is the same as choosing File ➪ Define ➪ File References.

Options: None

Note   You must have full access privileges for this script step to work. If you want this step to execute regardless of the current user's access privileges, select the Edit Script dialog's Run script with full access privileges check box.

Open Define Value Lists

Purpose: This step opens the Define Value Lists dialog so the user can define new value lists or edit existing value lists. This is the same as choosing File ➪ Define ➪ Value Lists.

Note You must have full access privileges for this script step to work. If you want this step to execute regardless of the current user's access privileges, select the Edit Script dialog's Run script with full access privileges check box.

Options: None

Open Find/Replace

Purpose: This step opens the Find/Replace dialog, enabling you or another user to perform a word processing-style Find/Replace in the current record or across all records within the current field or in all fields. This is the same as choosing Edit ➪ Find/Replace ➪ Find/Replace (or pressing Shift+⌘+F/Shift+Ctrl+F).

Options: None

See also: Perform Find/Replace

Open Help

Purpose: This step opens FileMaker Pro Help. This is the same as choosing Help ➪ FileMaker Pro Help.

Options: None

Open Remote

Purpose: This step opens the Open Remote dialog, enabling the user to open any database that is currently being shared via a network connection. Within FileMaker Pro, the Open Remote dialog can be opened by choosing the new File ➪ Open Remote command (Option+⌘+O/Shift+Ctrl+O) or by clicking the Remote button in the Open dialog (File ➪ Open).

Options: None

Note Prior to FileMaker Pro 7, this step was named Open Hosts.

Open ScriptMaker

Purpose: This step presents the Define Scripts dialog (the opening screen that normally appears when ScriptMaker is chosen from the Scripts menu). Any steps that appear after the Open ScriptMaker step are not performed.

Options: None

Example: The Open ScriptMaker step is useful when you are modifying or debugging scripts. In addition, if you find yourself frequently popping in and out of ScriptMaker, you can attach this step to a button or add it as one of the first ten scripts to the Scripts menu, giving it a ⌘+key/Ctrl+key equivalent.

Open Sharing

Purpose: This step opens the FileMaker Network Settings dialog, where you can set up network database sharing. This is the same as choosing the FileMaker Pro/ Edit ➪ Sharing ➪ Network Settings command.

Options: None

Note

The user's access privileges must include changing sharing settings for this script step to work. If you want this step to execute regardless of the current user's access privileges, select the Edit Script dialog's Run script with full access privileges check box.

Miscellaneous script steps

This catch-all category includes steps that perform special, less-frequently needed script actions, such as dialing a phone, beeping, displaying messages, and executing AppleScripts.

Show Custom Dialog

Purpose: This step displays a custom dialog that can prompt a user to enter data for up to three fields. Fields for user input must be of type Text, Number, Date, Time, Timestamp, or Container. To determine which button the user pressed, use the Get (LastMessageChoice) function. From right to left in the dialog created by this step, the buttons correspond to 1, 2, and 3; button 1 is treated as the default and can be selected by pressing Return/Enter.

Caution

Data obtained via the Show Custom Dialog step overrides any existing validation settings for the input fields—including the Strict option. As such, it might not be a good idea to use Show Custom Dialog to input data into fields for which critical validation criteria have been set. Similarly, this step also overrides the Allow Entry into Field field formatting option. That is, even if Allow Entry is disabled, the Show Custom Dialog step will still be allowed to receive and record input for the field.

Options: Specify

Note

In previous versions of FileMaker Pro, there was also a Show Message script step. That script step no longer exists, but you can emulate it with a Show Custom Dialog step where no input fields are specified.

Click the Specify button to enter options for the custom dialog. On the General tab of the Show Custom Dialog Options dialog (see Figure 15-22), specify a title for the dialog (by taking its name from a value contained in field, constructing it via a calculation, or by typing a name in the Title text box), specify a text message to be displayed in the dialog (in the same manner), and enter labels for up to three buttons that will appear at the bottom of the dialog. (If you do not want to display one or more buttons, leave their labels blank.)

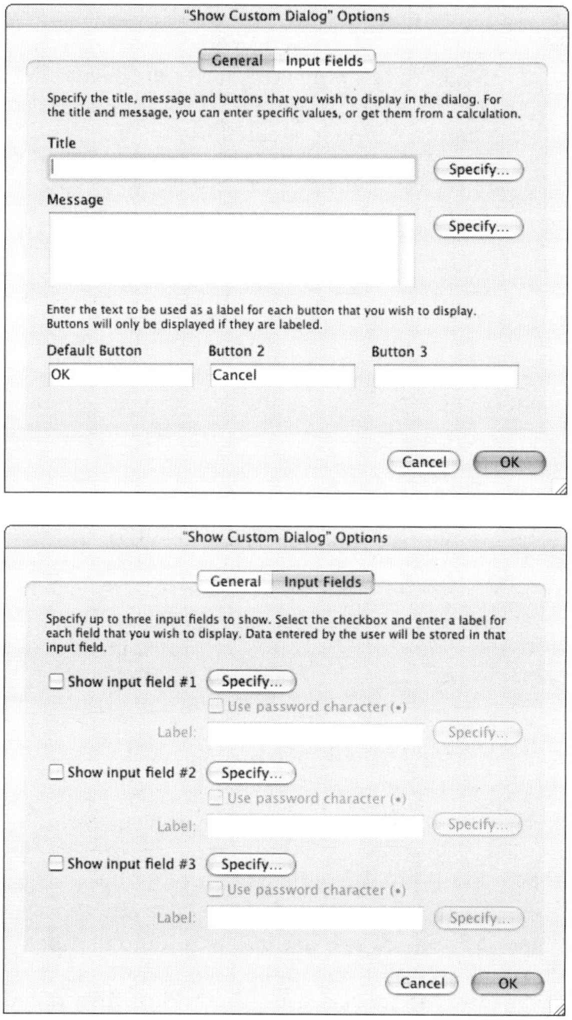

Figure 15-22: The General (top) and Input Fields (bottom) tabs of the Show Custom Dialog Options dialog.

Click the Input Fields tab to choose up to three fields for which you want to gather data (one field per Input tab). Click the Specify button to select a field. (Note that the field does *not* have to be present on the current layout.) To assign a label for the input field, type the label text. If you'd like the label text to be based on the contents of field, on the other hand, click the associated Specify button. Be sure that the Show input field check box is selected.

As you'll note in Figure 15-22, you can gather sensitive data in a custom dialog. Select the Use password character check box to automatically have whatever the user types be shown as bullet (•) characters.

Example: To transfer up to three fields of data to the current record, leave the Button labels on the General tab as (1) OK and (2) Cancel. Specify the fields and labels on the Input tabs. When the custom dialog is presented (see Figure 15-23), the user enters as many of the requested fields' input as he or she likes, and then clicks OK. The data becomes a part of the current record. (If Cancel is clicked, on the other hand, anything entered in the dialog is ignored.)

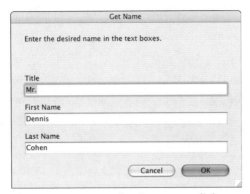

Figure 15-23: Example of a custom dialog.

 Note   If the specified input fields in the current record already contain data, those values are displayed in the custom dialog. If Use password character is enabled, the values are displayed as a series of bullet characters.

Allow Toolbars

Purpose: This script step is used to enable or disable the display of toolbars and the related commands in the View ➪ Toolbars submenu. The toolbar settings are affected only while the database that activated the script step is running.

 Note   The script step has no effect on standalone databases (created with FileMaker Developer) that are running in kiosk mode.

Options: On or off

Beep

Purpose: This step plays the current sound for the system alert. You can alter the sound that is played by selecting a different alert sound in the Sound System Preferences (Mac), or the Sounds (or Sounds and Audio Devices) control panel (Windows). The Beep step is useful for signaling user errors, script errors, and the conclusion of lengthy scripts.

Options: None

Speak (Mac-only)

Options: Specify (Text to speak, Use voice, Wait for speech completion before continuing)

Click the Specify button to set speech options. The Speak Options dialog appears. (See Figure 15-24.) To speak a string based on a calculation (could be just a field's contents), click the Specify button and define the calculation. To make the step speak a particular text string, type the text string in the text box.

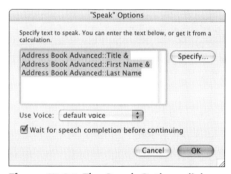

Figure 15-24: The Speak Options dialog.

If you don't want to use the default voice for the speech, choose a voice from the Use Voice pop-up menu. (If you intend to combine several Speak steps in a script, you must select a voice for each step. For all Speak steps in which no voice is chosen, the default voice is used.)

The Wait for speech completion before continuing option enables you to control the timing of the speech segment. When this option is unchecked, the script continues regardless of whether the speech has completed; however, when it is checked, the next step doesn't execute until the speech has completed.

Dial Phone (Windows only)

Purpose: This step is used to dial phone numbers through an attached modem or the computer's speaker.

Options: Perform without dialog, Specify

Click Specify to set dialing options. The phone number can be taken from a specific field in the current record, the result of a calculation, or can be a constant that always dials the same number, regardless of the record that is currently displayed. Select Use Dialing Preferences if you want this step to take user-defined dialing preferences from their operating system location settings into account

The Dial Phone step is not supported on Macintoshes. You can still create the script steps; however, you will be alerted each time you click the Specify button that the step is not supported on this operating system.

Install Menu Set
New in FileMaker Pro 8

Purpose: This step is used to install a specified set of displayed menus based upon conditions set in the script.

Options: Use as File Default, Specify

The Use as File Default option overrides any default menu set in the file's Define Custom Menus dialog with the menu set specified in this step; however, the override is effective only until the file is closed, at which point the default again will hold sway. Click the Specify button to designate the overriding menu set.

Open URL
Purpose: This step enables you to handle different types of Internet URL (Uniform Resource Locator) protocols. The text value for the URL can be specified as part of the script step, or a calculation's result can be used.

Options: Specify, Perform without dialog

Exactly what happens when the script step executes depends on the contents of the URL (specified as either text or calculation). The five types of URLs that FileMaker Pro can handle are

✦ *http:* If the text or field contents begin with `http://`, FileMaker Pro will launch your preferred Web browser and navigate to the Web location specified by the rest of the URL. For example, if the URL reads `http://www.filemaker.com`, your Web browser will display the FileMaker, Inc. home page.

✦ *ftp:* If the text or field contents begin with `ftp://`, FileMaker Pro will launch your preferred FTP (File Transfer Protocol) helper application and retrieve the file specified by the balance of the URL. For example, if the URL reads `ftp://ftp.webnet.com/example.txt`, FileMaker Pro will retrieve the file `example.txt` from the Webnet FTP site. If the URL doesn't specify a particular file, the FTP helper application opens to the designated directory.

✦ *fmp7:* This URL is used to open FileMaker Pro databases on your local network.

✦ *file:* If the text or field contents begin with `file:`, FileMaker Pro will launch the application that is associated with the file specified by the balance of the URL. For example, if the URL reads `file://C:/Example.txt` or `file://MacintoshHD:Example.txt`, FileMaker Pro will launch the application that is associated with `Example.txt` (which might be Notepad in Windows or TextEdit on a Mac) and load the file for viewing.

✦ *mailto:* If the text or field contents begin with `mailto:`, FileMaker Pro will launch your preferred e-mail program and create a new e-mail message addressed to the address specified by the balance of the URL. For example, if the URL reads `mailto:spenserpup@mac.com`, your preferred e-mail program will open with a new e-mail message addressed to the e-mail account for Dennis' Boston terrier.

If you specify that the script step should perform without a dialog, you must specify a calculation resulting in a URL or supply the text of the URL in the Open URL Options dialog. (See Figure 15-25.) If you do not select the Perform without dialog check box, the user will have the opportunity to supply a field, calculation, or the URL text when the script step executes.

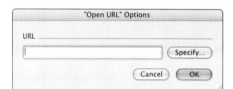

Figure 15-25: Specifying the URL to use with the Open URL script step.

Send Mail

Purpose: This script step sends an e-mail message (Internet or intranet) to specified recipients using your preferred e-mail program. You can specify that the recipients (both To: and CC:), subject, and message contents come from either a text box or from a calculation.

Options: Specify, Perform without dialog

For this script step to work, you must have an e-mail application properly installed on your Macintosh or PC, and it must be one supported by FileMaker Pro 8. (For a list of supported mail clients, see "Send Mail Script Step" in FileMaker Pro Help.) If you choose the Specify option, FileMaker Pro opens the Specify Mail dialog. (See Figure 15-26.)

Fill out the Specify Mail dialog as follows:

✦ To address the e-mail message, choose Specify Field Name or Specify Calculation from the pop-up button to the right of the To text box. If you choose Specify Field Name, the Specify Field dialog appears, where you choose the field containing the address information for the primary recipients. If the field is a repeating field, you can specify which repetition contains the addressee information by entering a number in the Specify Field dialog's Repetition text box. You can also choose whether to use only the field value in the current record (for a single addressee) or the field values in all records in the found set (for multiple addressees). If you choose Specify Calculation, the Specify Calculation dialog appears where you can define your calculation. Alternatively, you can type in the addresses.

✦ To add *CCs* (carbon copies; addressees who are copied on the e-mail message), make the same decisions in the CC: row as you did in the To: row.

✦ To add *BCCs* (blind carbon copies; addressees who are copied on the e-mail message but whose addresses don't display on recipient's e-mail), make the same decisions in the BCC: row as you did in the To: and CC: rows.

✦ To add a subject to the e-mail message, make a choice from the Subject row's pop-up arrow as above. Alternatively, you can type a subject in the text box.

✦ To create the message contents, choose as above from the Message row's pop-up arrow.

✦ To attach a file to the message, select the Attach file check box; in the Specify File dialog that appears, designate the file to attach.

If you select Perform without dialog, FileMaker Pro places the composed e-mail message directly into your e-mail program's Outbox. If you do not select this option, the composed message is left open in the e-mail application or stored in the Drafts folder (depending on which e-mail application you use) so you can review and change it before sending it.

Note   If the user's mail client is Microsoft Entourage on the Mac or Outlook Express on Windows, the message will be left in that application's Drafts folder.

The Specify Mail dialog's pop-up arrows contain an extra option marked Specify Email Addresses in the To:, CC:, and BCC: rows. Choosing this option opens the address book for your e-mail package, enabling you to choose addressees.

See also: Open URL

Send Event
Mac

Purpose: You use the Send Event step to facilitate interaction between FileMaker Pro and other programs — or even instruct FileMaker Pro to send messages to itself via AppleEvents.

Options: Specify

AppleEvents — a system software feature — enable you to send messages (commands and data) between programs. Although most users will never personally create a script that uses AppleEvents, anyone can easily use this script step to launch other programs and documents from FileMaker Pro (discussed in "Using AppleEvents," later in this chapter). The collection of AppleEvents that an application will understand varies from one application to another.

Click the Specify button to set options for this script step.

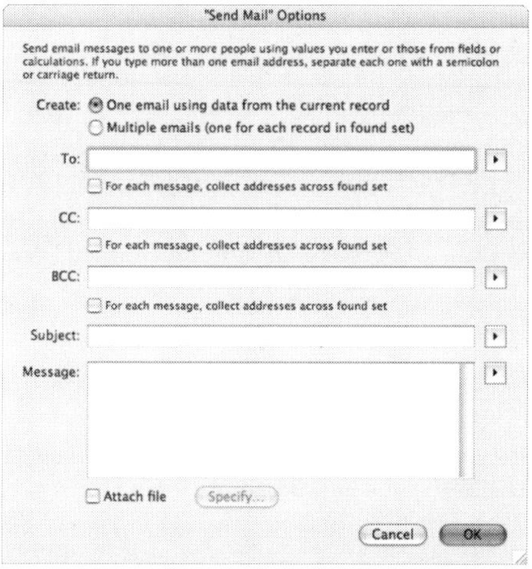

Figure 15-26: Use the Specify Mail dialog to specify the addressees, subject, message, and optional attachments for your e-mail.

Send Event
Windows

Purpose: Use this step to start another application, open a document in another application, or print a document in another application.

Options: Specify

Click the Specify button to set options for this script step.

Send DDE Execute
Windows

Purpose: This script step sends a Dynamic Data Exchange (DDE) command to another application, telling it to execute a series of commands available in that application. The exact commands that can be sent depend on the receiving application.

Options: Specify

For each Send DDE Execute step, you can specify the following items:

✦ *Service Name:* This is the name of the application that executes the DDE commands. You must check the documentation for the receiving application to find out its service name. You can type the service name into the text box or use the contents of a field to specify a value for it. If the field is a repeating field, you can choose which repetition contains the service name by typing a value in the Repetition text box.

✦ *Topic:* A topic is used by the receiving application to group a set of commands. Check the documentation of the receiving application for the valid topics. You can choose to specify the topic by typing text in the text box, selecting a filename, or choosing a field value and specifying the field that contains the topic name. If the field is a repeating field, you can choose which repetition contains the topic by typing a value in the Repetition text box.

✦ *Commands:* Specify the actual commands that instruct the receiving application to perform the tasks you want. Check the documentation of the receiving application for valid commands. You can choose to specify the commands by typing them in the text box or specifying the field that contains the commands.

Tip   If you use the script step Send DDE Execute following a Send Event step to open another application, you might need to insert a Pause step after the Send Event step to allow the application to open.

See also: Send Event

Perform AppleScript
Mac

Purpose: This step is used to send AppleScript commands to another program. The AppleScript commands must be contained in a designated field on the layout, or they can be typed into the Specify AppleScript text box when you add this step to a script. To use this script step, the target application must be scriptable.

 When a Perform AppleScript step is encountered while running on Windows, it is ignored, but an error code is set, retrievable by the Get(LastError) function.

Options: Specify

When you click the Specify button, the Perform AppleScript Options dialog appears. Select the Calculated AppleScript radio button to choose the field containing the text of the AppleScript or construct a formula resulting in the text of the AppleScript to be performed. If the script is not stored in a field or constructible from a calculation, select the Native AppleScript radio button and enter or paste the AppleScript in the text box.

FileMaker must recompile scripts stored in text fields or calculated at runtime whenever the script runs. Scripts entered in the text box, on the other hand, are compiled immediately and saved in compiled format. FileMaker always checks for script errors during the compilation process.

Tip

If the AppleScript has already been created elsewhere (as will often be the case), you don't have to retype it in FileMaker Pro. Instead, simply open the script in Apple's Script Editor application, copy it, and then paste it into the appropriate field or the text box in the Perform AppleScript Options dialog.

Execute SQL
Purpose: This step enables you to send SQL queries from within FileMaker Pro to any supported ODBC data source for which you have an installed ODBC driver. The query text can be entered in the Specify SQL dialog (see Figure 15-27) or be the result of a calculation. A script can optionally contain multiple Execute SQL steps.

Options: Specify, Perform without dialog

To completely automate a query, select the Perform without dialog check box and click the Specify button. Enter the information requested — the ODBC data source, the password, and the Structured Query Language (SQL) query text, which could be literal text (SQL text radio button and text box) or a calculated result (Calculated SQL text radio button). Be careful to select the Save user name and password check box in the dialog where you specify your ODBC data source; otherwise, users will (usually) be unable to access your data source. If Perform without dialog is *not* selected, the step will present the necessary dialogs to conduct the query: Specify SQL, Select ODBC Data Source, and Password.

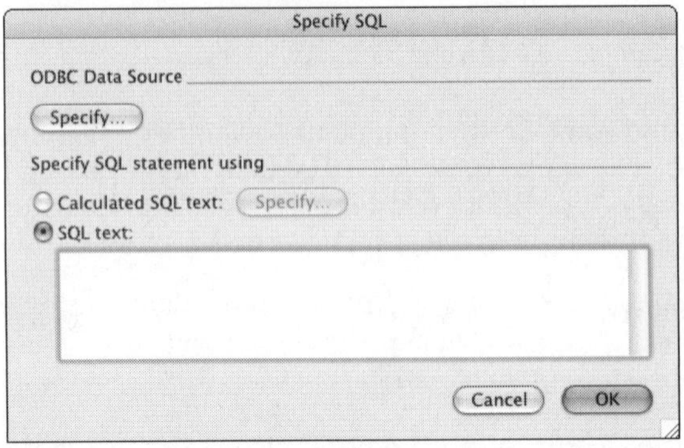

Figure 15-27: Specify an ODBC data source and the SQL query in the Specify SQL dialog.

Comment

Purpose: Use the Comment step to insert nonexecuting comments in your scripts. Comment steps make it easy to explain script logic and assumptions both for your own records and to inform others.

Options: Specify

Click the Specify button to enter the text for the comment. Comments are preceded by a pound sign (#) and are displayed in boldface.

Flush Cache to Disk

Purpose: With this step, you can force the contents of FileMaker Pro's internal cache to be written to disk (rather than waiting for this action to be performed automatically at the designated time).

Options: None

Exit Application
Name changed from Quit Application

Purpose: This step quits FileMaker Pro and returns the user to the Desktop/desktop. This is the same as choosing FileMaker Pro ➪ Quit FileMaker Pro, pressing ⌘+Q (Mac), or choosing File ➪ Exit or pressing Ctrl+Q/Alt+F4 (Windows). Any files that are currently open are saved automatically, if necessary.

Options: None

Example: The Exit Application step can be useful as a final command in a cleanup script. If you always print a report from a particular database as the final activity for the day, for example, you could define a script that performs the printing and then ends by quitting FileMaker Pro.

See also: Close File

Attaching a Script to a Button

As mentioned previously, you can attach scripts to buttons. When a button is clicked, the script or script step attached to that button executes instantly, exactly as if you'd chosen the script name from the Scripts menu or selected the script in the Define Scripts dialog and clicked Perform.

Buttons are frequently added to layouts to make it easy and convenient for users to perform a simple or complex series of commands. By assigning the Go to Layout step to a button, for example, you can quickly navigate to a particular layout, such as a Help screen or a report layout. You can also attach a multistep script that executes a Find request, performs a sort, prints a report, returns to the data-entry screen, and then restores the database to its state before the button was clicked.

Although FileMaker-drawn buttons and graphic icons are frequently used as buttons, you can use any layout object as a button, including static text strings.

STEPS: Attaching a Script Step or a Script to a Button

1. Switch to Layout mode. (Choose View ➪ Layout Mode, press ⌘+L/Ctrl+L, click the status area's Layout button, or choose Layout from the mode pop-up menu at the bottom of the database window.)

2. Select the object that you want to make into a button.

   When selected, an object has a handle (black dot) in each of its corners.

3. Choose Format ➪ Button.

   The Specify Button dialog appears, as shown in Figure 15-28.

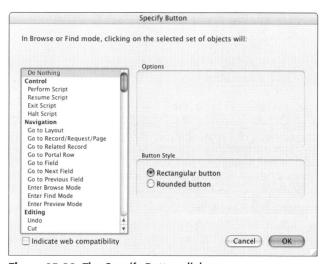

Figure 15-28: The Specify Button dialog.

4. To assign a single script step to the button, select the script step, set any options that appear for that step, and then click OK.

or

To assign a particular script to the button, select Perform Script, click the Specify button in the dialog's Options section, select the script (either from the Current File or another in the Specify Script Options dialog), click OK to return to the Specify Button dialog, and click OK to close the Specify Button dialog.

Here are a few more things you should know about working with buttons:

✦ If you're having trouble identifying which particular objects in a layout are buttons (as opposed to ordinary graphics, static text, and other objects), change to Layout mode and choose View ➪ Show ➪ Buttons. Each button will be surrounded by a gray outline.

✦ When you copy a button, that button's definition is also copied — that is, any script or script step attached to the button is attached to the copy. If you paste the button into another layout in the same database or a different one, the pasted button will attempt to perform the same function as the original button. You might need to edit the script or script step so the duplicate now refers to the proper layout, field names, and so on.

✦ To delete a button you no longer need, switch to Layout mode, select the button, and then choose Cut or Clear from the Edit menu. Or you can press the Delete/Backspace key.

✦ To remove a script or script step from a button (undefine it), perform Steps 1–3 in "STEPS: Attaching a Script Step or a Script to a Button," select Do Nothing, and click OK.

In versions prior to FileMaker Pro 7, you could attach only a relatively small subset of script steps to a button. You can now assign any script step that does not involve *branching* — no If or Loop steps, in other words. This means that you no longer have to create a separate script for these actions and then attach them to the button via Perform Script: They can now be attached directly.

What does this button do?

If you're curious about a script step or script that has been assigned to a button, here's a simple way to determine what the step or script does. Just switch to Layout mode, select the button, and choose the Format ➪ Button Setup command. In the Specify Button dialog that appears, the step or script that is assigned to the button will be highlighted.

Advanced Scripting Procedures

You can create many perfectly functional scripts by selecting single steps and by combining steps for commands with which you are familiar, such as Go to Layout, Sort, Find, and Print. However, some of the steps, step options, and system software features supported by ScriptMaker can add extraordinary flexibility and power to FileMaker Pro. Although you might not immediately be interested in pursuing these power-scripting features, the following sections discuss them.

Decision-making in scripts

In versions of FileMaker Pro prior to 3.0, the If script step enabled you to perform limited decision-making: That is, "If the conditional test x is true, perform this step. Otherwise, do nothing." FileMaker Pro 3.0 extended the decision-making capabilities of scripts by adding Else and End If steps. The End If step marks the end of every If structure. When embedded within an If structure, the Else step enables you to select a second alternative in response to a conditional test, as in the following script:

```
If [x]
    Do this if test x is true
Else
    Do this if test x is false
End If
```

Note

Multiple statements can be included in both the true and false sections of an If structure, and Ifs can be nested within other Ifs.

FileMaker Pro 7 extended the conditional evaluation even further by adding the Else If script step, eliminating some of the more convoluted nesting previously required.

Using loops in scripts

Support for looping enables you to repeat a sequence of commands a set number of times or until a particular condition has been fulfilled. The three loop commands are Loop, End Loop, and Exit Loop If.

One interesting use for loops is to step through the records in a database or the current found set. For example, in a bookkeeping database, we created a layout by scanning an IRS Schedule C. Each line item is represented by a Global field, such as Advertising or Legal Expense. To calculate these year-to-date expenses and income, we used a loop to step though the records in the database, one by one. The income/expense category for each record is examined, and then the total for the appropriate Global field is adjusted by that record's income or expense amount. When the loop is exited (after examining the last record in the database), the Global field amounts are displayed on the scanned Schedule C.

Environment considerations

Using a Get function in an If step enables you to determine information about the current state of the database, as well as the environment in which it is being run. Based on the results of the various Get tests, you can use other script steps to change the appearance of the display, branch to appropriate sub-scripts and external scripts (disabling Windows-related steps if the database is being run on a Mac or vice versa, for example), or display relevant messages. The Get functions are a boon to any developer who intends to offer cross-platform databases. Get replaced the Status functions of previous versions and significantly increased the number of state variables that can be tested—from 47 in FileMaker 6 to 70 in FileMaker Pro 7 and 8.

Executing other scripts from within a script

A script can be instructed to perform other scripts, known as *sub-scripts*. (In programming parlance, sub-scripts are called *subroutines*.) To allow one script to perform another script, you simply choose the Perform Script step. After running a sub-script, the original (or *calling*) script continues from where it left off.

Tip   Sub-scripts can be extremely helpful in restoring the state of a database at the conclusion of a script. For example, a report script might switch to landscape mode, establish a particular sort order that is needed to produce the report, and then return you to the layout you were in when the script was executed.

Any script that is executed as part of a Perform Script step—whether it is the object of the step or a sub-script—can be an internal or external script. An *internal script* is a script that is defined within the current database. An *external script* is a script in another database. When you run an external script, FileMaker Pro automatically opens the external database and executes the script. When the external script is completed, control returns to the original script and database, just as it does when a sub-script is performed.

STEPS: Running an External Script

1. When you define the script, choose Perform Script as one of the steps.

2. With the Perform Script step selected in the script, click the Specify button and choose Add File Reference from the Specify Script Options dialog's pop-up menu/drop-down list.

    The referenced file's scripts appear, as shown in Figure 15-29.

3. Select the script that you want to perform.

4. Click OK to record your choice.

Figure 15-29: The Specify Script Options dialog with an external file's scripts listed.

Using AppleEvents

Mac

The Send Event script step enables you to send messages from FileMaker Pro to itself and to other programs. Although not all programs support the required events and do-script events, most programs should be able to respond to a request to launch or to open a document. This section describes how to perform these simple actions from within a FileMaker Pro database.

STEPS: Creating a Program or Document Launcher Using AppleEvents

1. Create a new script, choose the Send Event step, and click Specify.

   The Send Event Options dialog appears, as shown in Figure 15-30.

2. From the Send the pop-up menu at the top of the dialog, choose Open Application.

   A standard file dialog appears, in which you select the program that you want the script to launch.

   or

   From the Send the pop-up menu, choose Open Document. Select the Document radio button and click its accompanying Specify button to choose a document.

3. At the bottom of the Send Event Options dialog, set any desired options.

   In most cases, you will want to choose Bring Target Application to foreground. Otherwise, when the program or document is launched, it might be hidden behind your database window.

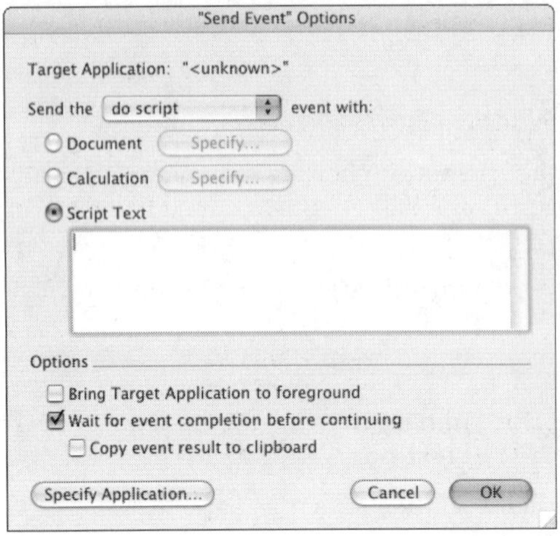

Figure 15-30: The Send Event Options dialog.

4. To save the script step settings, click OK.

To learn more about how FileMaker uses Apple Events, check out the FileMaker database named AppleEvents Reference and the many examples in that database.

Tip   After defining a program- or document-launcher script, you can pretty things up by using a screen-capture utility to capture a picture of the program's or document's icon, paste the icon into your FileMaker Pro layout, and then use the Format ⇨ Button command to make the icon into a button that launches the AppleEvents script. If you frequently use several utilities while running FileMaker Pro (such as a calculator, clock, and address book, for instance), you can employ this technique to create a string of buttons. Because these button definitions are not specific to one database, you can copy and paste them into any database. As long as the databases are run on your machine and you do not change the locations of the programs or documents to be launched, the buttons should work fine.

Using AppleScript

Mac

Available as part of the Mac system software, *AppleScript* is a native language-based programming language you can use to integrate Macintosh programs and customize the way your Mac works. Unlike using the scripting feature in FileMaker Pro, using AppleScript really *is* programming.

STEPS: Executing an AppleScript from within FileMaker

1. In ScriptMaker's Define Scripts dialog, specify whether you are creating a new script or editing an existing one. To edit an existing script, select its name in the list box and click Edit.

2. In the Script Definition dialog, select the Perform AppleScript step.

3. Click the Specify button.

   The Perform AppleScript Options dialog appears.

4. Select the Calculated AppleScript radio button and define your calculation. The calculation could be a simple field reference, if you have the AppleScript stored in a field.

   The calculated AppleScript commands are compiled each time FileMaker Pro runs the script.

   or

   Select the Native AppleScript radio button, and then type or paste the AppleScript commands into the text box.

   The commands are compiled and then stored as part of the database.

5. Finish defining the script and then click OK.

Scripting tips

The following are some useful script-making tips passed on by Max Pruden of FileMaker Technical Support:

✦ The Insert Text step works only if you first specify a target field for the paste by using the Go to Field step or by having an active field on the layout.

✦ When you exit a Find step, you automatically switch to Browse mode, and the first record in the found set is displayed. Thus, you do not need to include an Enter Browse Mode step or a Go to Record/Request/Page step to go to the first record.

✦ Two types of scripts can be executed by the Perform Script step: *internal scripts* (scripts in the current file) and *external scripts* (scripts in other files). When you use Perform Script to execute an external script, you don't need to use the Open step to open the other database.

✦ If you use the Copy step without setting any options, the step copies the contents of all fields in the layout for the current record (which is the same as the Copy Record step).

✦ A script executes in its own database. To perform procedures that affect two files, such as a Copy from one database and a Paste into another, you need two scripts: one in each database. For this example, you would create a script that copies the contents of a field in the current file and include a step to perform an external script (defined in the other database) that selects the appropriate field and then pastes. Note that because you can now have multiple tables and relations in a single file/database, this tip is far less necessary

Summary

✦ FileMaker Pro provides a built-in, script-creation utility called ScriptMaker. Using ScriptMaker, you can automate almost any FileMaker Pro function that you usually execute manually by selecting commands from menus. After it's defined, a script can be added to the Scripts menu and/or attached to a button in any layout, making it simple to execute the script any time you like.

✦ Rather than type scripts in a word processing program or text editor, you design scripts in FileMaker Pro by choosing script steps from a list. Step options are set by choosing from pop-up menus/drop-down lists, clicking buttons, and selecting check boxes.

✦ You can create many scripts simply by executing sort instructions, Find requests, and similar commands and then telling FileMaker Pro that you want to use the same procedures in a script.

✦ FileMaker Pro 8 provides 132 script steps (both platforms, combined) you can use individually or in combination with other steps to form a script.

✦ Scripts can be imported from other FileMaker databases.

✦ You can attach scripts to buttons you include on a layout. When you click a button, the script or script step attached to that button executes instantly, as though you had chosen the script name from the Scripts menu or clicked Perform in the Define Scripts dialog.

✦   ✦   ✦

Exchanging Data

As nice as it might be, you probably won't spend your computing life using only one application (such as FileMaker Pro). You likely work with many applications, and perhaps you've even stored database information in some other programs before you became a FileMaker Pro user. Wouldn't it be great to be able to move all that data into FileMaker Pro? For example, you might want to transfer your address and phone number data directly to FileMaker. Similarly, you might want to move data from a FileMaker Pro Invoices database to a spreadsheet program so you can see how you're doing and make predictions.

There are many reasons why you might want to move data around. The good news is that you can do so without much trouble, as this chapter explains.

Cross-Reference

This chapter covers the most common formats and techniques used with FileMaker Pro to import and export data. The material covered in this chapter is easily accessible and usable by any FileMaker Pro user, regardless of your level of computer proficiency. The more advanced formats and techniques of data exchange (ODBC, JDBC, and XML) are discussed in Chapter 21.

Moving Data between Programs

FileMaker Pro can work with data produced by many other programs. If a program can save or export its data in one of several common formats (such as tab-delimited text), FileMaker Pro can read and use the data. This data exchange is a two-way street: FileMaker can produce data files other applications can use *(exporting)*, and it can take data from other applications for use in a FileMaker Pro database *(importing)*.

♦   ♦   ♦   ♦

In This Chapter

Understanding file formats

Importing from other sources: programs, digital cameras, and folders

Creating a new database from a foreign file

Exporting data from FileMaker Pro

Moving data using drag and drop

Working with the Windows version of FileMaker Pro

Exchanging data with Microsoft Office

♦   ♦   ♦   ♦

About importing and exporting

When you import data into FileMaker Pro, you bring that data in from another program's data files. FileMaker Pro can import data from many popular Mac and PC programs' data file formats, such as dBASE, FoxBASE/FoxPro, AppleWorks, and Microsoft Excel. You can also import data from another FileMaker Pro database — even one created on a different type of computer.

You can import data into FileMaker Pro in four ways:

✦ You can open a non-FileMaker file by using the File ➪ Open command, automatically converting it *en masse* to a new FileMaker Pro database. (Data files from certain applications, such as Microsoft Excel, can also be opened by being dropped onto the FileMaker Pro 8 application icon.)

✦ If you already have a FileMaker Pro database, you can use the File ➪ Import Records submenu command to import records from another FileMaker Pro database or from a file created in a different program. Better yet, starting with FileMaker Pro 8 Advanced (sorry, not available in the base product), you can import tables directly from another FileMaker Pro database, obviating the need to manually create the table into which you want to import records.

✦ FileMaker Pro can also import pictures directly from a connected digital camera or similar device (Mac only) as well as import an entire folder of image or text files.

✦ You can take advantage of FileMaker's Open Database Connectivity (ODBC), Java Database Connectivity (JDBC), or XML (eXtensible Markup Language) support to import data from any compliant application, such as Microsoft Access, into an existing FileMaker Pro database. (See Chapter 21 for more information.)

Note   When you import records, you can choose to append the new records to your existing file, use the new data to replace existing records, or update only the changed records. (The third capability was introduced in FileMaker Pro 5.) When you import, FileMaker Pro copies data but does not copy layouts or field definitions. In addition, you cannot import data into Calculation or Summary fields.

You can also make a FileMaker Pro database's information available for use in other applications. For example, you might export the current found set of records to a spreadsheet program for further analysis.

New Feature   FileMaker Pro 8 introduces a new capability to save a record or found set directly to an Excel worksheet, as described later in this chapter, making spreadsheet interactivity even easier.

Another common use of exporting is to prepare for a mail merge in a word processing program. In FileMaker Pro, however, you can perform a mail merge completely within FileMaker. See Chapter 6 for details.

FileMaker Pro cannot export to remote sources nor can it export data directly into an existing FileMaker Pro file. Instead of exporting directly into the target application file, you simply export the data to a temporary file and then import it using the target application's procedures to import data. The net effect is the same.

Understanding file formats

Although FileMaker Pro can work with data from many different applications, its capability is limited by the ways in which these applications store their data. The way that data is stored in an application is the application's *file format.*

A file format specifies how an application's data is organized and interpreted. You can think of a file format as being a recipe for creating the finished file from its raw data (from the text that you type, for example). The instructions for interpreting a file format must be stored within the program in which you want to use the data; otherwise, very strange and unsatisfactory results generally occur.

FileMaker Pro supports the file formats discussed in the following sections. Note that some formats are for importing data only and others are solely for exporting data.

Tab-separated text

This format is sometimes called ASCII (pronounced *ASK-ee*), but a few differences exist between tab-separated text and ASCII text. ASCII (American Standard Code for Information Interchange) refers to plain, unformatted text arranged according to an industry-standard coding scheme. In tab-separated text, Tab characters separate fields in a record, and Return/Enter characters separate records. Virtually all computer applications can interpret files that are in this format.

Comma-separated text

This format is used for BASIC programming and in some applications. Commas separate field values, and Return/Enter characters separate records. All field values except unformatted numbers are surrounded by quotation marks. Many Windows applications use this format, referred to as *CSV (comma-separated values),* as a standard interchange format.

SYLK

SYLK stands for *symbolic link format,* a spreadsheet format in which data is stored in rows and columns. Each field is a column, and each record is a row. Returns are output as spaces, and dates and times are output as text within quotation marks. Non-numeric data in a number field is suppressed, and fields are limited to a maximum of 245 characters.

DBF

DBF is the dBASE III and dBASE IV (also known as *xBASE*) database format. Field names can be no more than 10 characters long, with a maximum of 254 characters per field and 128 fields per record, with a maximum record size of 4,000 characters. (FoxBASE and FoxPro can also generate DBF files.)

DIF

DIF (Data Interchange Format) is another spreadsheet format, used by older applications such as VisiCalc (the great-granddaddy of spreadsheet programs) and the original AppleWorks (the program for the old Apple II computer). Each field is a column, and each record is a row. Further, all fields are treated as Text fields when importing from DIF.

WKS

WKS (worksheet format) is a spreadsheet format used by Lotus 1-2-3. Each field is a column (with a maximum of 240 characters), and each record is a row. Date and Time fields are exported as functions.

BASIC

This format is similar to comma-separated text but is designed for use with Microsoft's standard BASIC language. Each field is limited to 255 characters.

Merge

Merge is an export format that you use to create special documents for the data portion of mail merges. Commas separate field values on U.S. systems (some systems might use a semicolon to separate fields), Return/Enter characters separate records, and the ASCII character 29 (Group Separator character code) separates repeating fields. Embedded carriage returns in fields are exported as ASCII character 11 (Vertical Tab). In this format, the first record is the header. The header lists the field names contained in the file. Quotation marks surround field data. FileMaker can both export and import merge data.

Microsoft Excel

This import-only format enables you to import Microsoft Excel worksheets into FileMaker Pro databases. Mac worksheets created with Excel 8, 98, 2001, v. X, and 2004 can be imported. In Windows, Excel 95, 97, 2000, 2002, and 2003 are supported. (Note that data, but not named ranges, can be imported from Excel 4.)

HTML table

This export-only format is used to translate a FileMaker Pro database into a table that can be published as a page on the Web. Field names become column headings. Each record is a row in the table; each field is a column, and repeating fields are exported as nested tables. After creating an HTML table, you can open the resulting text file in any text editor or word processing program, copy it, and paste it into the source code for your Web page. Figure 16-1 shows the code as it appears when exporting to an HTML table. Figure 16-2 shows the table that this HTML code produces when viewed in a Web browser.

Tip

Field names are not always appropriate as column heads. Instead of *Qty*, you might prefer *Quantity*, for example. You can change any of the field names by editing the HTML lines that begin with <TH>, as shown in Figure 16-1.

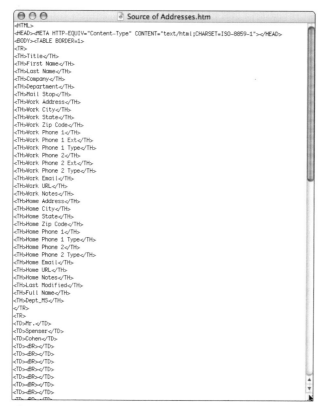

Figure 16-1: Code produced when exporting to an HTML table.

FileMaker Pro

FileMaker Pro 8.0 can import data from any FileMaker Pro database between versions 3.0 and 8.0. Exported FileMaker Pro 7 and 8 data cannot be read by earlier versions of FileMaker Pro.

Note

FileMaker Pro 8.0 can read FileMaker 5.0, 5.5, 6.0, and 7.0 files directly. When opening earlier versions of FileMaker databases than 7.0, FileMaker Pro 8.0 asks permission to convert them to 7.0 format, which is the format shared by both FileMaker Pro 7 and 8.

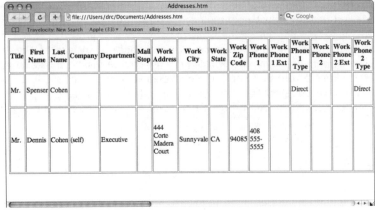

Figure 16-2: When viewed in a Web browser, the HTML code produces this table.

Tip   Check out the `FM8 Converting Databases.pdf` electronic document found in the FileMaker Pro application folder's English Extras ⇨ Electronic Documentation subfolder.

XML

FileMaker Pro 8 can export and import data in XML format, so long as it employs either the FMPXMLRESULT grammar (FileMaker's preferred grammar) or the FMPDSORESULT grammar (Microsoft's Data Source Object grammar). It can use an optional XSLT (eXtensible Stylesheet Language Transformation) style sheet to format the data when importing or exporting.

Importing Data from Other Sources

You have several options when you import data from another source. For example, you can combine information stored in several places into one master file (which might contain only selected fields from several similar files). You can also change the order in which records are stored. Although FileMaker Pro normally stores records in the order in which they are entered, it imports records in their sorted order — if the source file is sorted. If you import data that includes repeating fields, you can split the latter values into separate records.

Format selection

When importing data, FileMaker Pro makes it easy to determine whether the import file is in an appropriate format. When you choose the File ⇨ Import Records ⇨ File command, the Open File dialog lists only the file types that FileMaker Pro understands (based in part on the files that were copied into the FileMaker Extensions folder as part of FileMaker Pro's installation procedure). If the file that you want to import appears dimmed in the Open File dialog's list of files, you might need to check the relevant application's documentation to determine the file format it uses. If FileMaker Pro doesn't support the native file format of your source application, you'll need to use the application to output a new data file in a format that FileMaker Pro can use. Many applications can output tab- or comma-separated text, for example.

FileMaker Pro can import data from the following types of files:

✦ FileMaker Pro

✦ Tab-separated text

✦ Comma-separated text

✦ SYLK

✦ DIF

✦ WKS

✦ BASIC

✦ Merge

✦ DBF (dBASE)

✦ Excel

Data clean-up prior to importing

Data that you want to import might not be in perfect shape. You might find, for example, that the match between fields in your source and target files isn't as clean as you had hoped or that you don't have access to a supported file format. The procedures outlined in the following sections show you how to solve some of these problems.

Cleaning up data in a spreadsheet

If you had your computer for a while before you bought FileMaker Pro, you probably also had one or more address or contacts files that you created in other programs — address data recorded in an included contact manager such as the Mac OS X Address Book or Microsoft Outlook Express (Windows), for example. Rather than keep this information spread across a handful of programs, it's usually preferable to put all the data into one database or program. Unfortunately, most of us don't plan for (or count on) the difficulties encountered when trying to create one composite file from two or more separate address files. In particular, the various files are likely to contain different fields. This section discusses some simpleprocedures you can use to clean up your disparate data before importing it into, or exporting it from, FileMaker Pro.

> The Apple Address Book application doesn't export data in any of the formats supported by FileMaker Pro; however, both FileMaker Pro 8 and Address Book have excellent AppleScript support. Freely available AppleScripts, such as AB2FM (http://econtact.slade.de/en), will do the job for you.

Following are two of the most common problems in importing address data:

✦ Address, phone number, and name fields in the file you want to import are split into two fields (address line 1 and address line 2, area code and phone number, and first name and last name), but the FileMaker Pro database contains only one field for the corresponding items, or vice versa.

✦ When exported, some ZIP codes might lose their leading zero (for example, 1276 rather than 01276).

Rather than import the data as it is and clean it up in the database afterward, using a spreadsheet application (such as Excel or the one included in AppleWorks) to make the necessary transformations to the data is more efficient.

STEPS: Transforming Data in a Spreadsheet

1. Export the data from your database or address book program as a tab-delimited ASCII text file.

2. Open the text file in a spreadsheet program, make the transformations to the data (creating new fields as necessary), and save the revised file as a text file.

3. Open the FileMaker Pro database into which you intend to import the data.

4. Use the Import Records command to import the tab-separated text file into the database.

The simplest way to make the spreadsheet transformations is to create additional columns on the right-hand side of the spreadsheet. The following text explains how to accomplish this task within the Microsoft Excel spreadsheet environment. The procedure will be similar in other spreadsheet applications, such as the one in AppleWorks.

Each new column must contain a formula combining or converting one or more columns of the original data. Create the appropriate formula and then use the Fill Down command to copy the formula into the remaining cells in the column.

The simple spreadsheet shown in Figure 16-3 illustrates the formula needed to convert First Name and Last Name fields into a single Name field. Column A contains first names, column B contains last names, and column C contains the combined first and last names. The formula shown in the entry bar (=A1 & " "& B1) takes the first name in cell A1 (George), adds a space (" "), and then adds the last name from cell B1 (Washington) to the end of the text string. As mentioned previously, you use the Fill Down command to copy the formula to all the rest of the cells in column C.

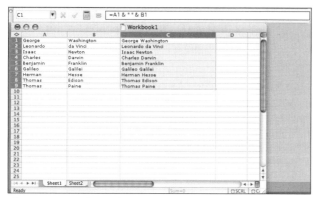

Figure 16-3: A formula to combine first and last names into a single name.

Extracting first and last names from a Name field is more complex, but with a little spreadsheet wizardry, it can be accomplished. Figure 16-4 shows a spreadsheet in which column A contains a list of names, each having a single first and last name, with no honorifics or generational suffixes. To extract the first name George from the combined name George Washington in cell A1, you use this formula in cell B1:

```
LEFT(A1,FIND(" ",A1,1)-1)
```

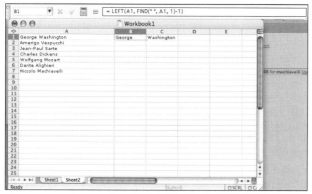

Figure 16-4: Extracting the first name from a Name field.

The FIND function searches for the first occurrence of a space in the name in cell A1, and then subtracts one from the character position where the space was found. For George Washington, the FIND returns a result of 7, which is then decremented to 6. The LEFT function operates on this result, extracting the first six characters from the name in cell A1 — or George, in this case. (You could extract all seven characters, but that would include the trailing space.)

To extract the last name, this complex formula is entered in cell C1:

```
RIGHT(A1,LEN(A1)-FIND(" ",A1,1))
```

The LEN function returns the length of the text string in cell A1; for the name George Washington, it returns a result of 17. The result of the same FIND function used previously (searching for the first space in the name in cell A1) is subtracted from the LEN result — in this case, 17 – 7 for a result of 10. The RIGHT function then extracts the 10 rightmost characters from the name in cell A1 — Washington, in this case. To complete the spreadsheet, all you need to do is select the formulas in cells B1 and C1, highlight the blank cells beneath them, and choose Fill Down.

Suppose you have a database or other address file in which address information is split into two lines or fields, and you want to import that data into a file in which Address is only a single line or field. However, some addresses in the original file have only one line while others in the file have two. The equation

```
=IF (B2 <> "", A2 & ", " & B2, A2)
```

checks whether the address has a second line (B2 <> ""). If the address has a second line, the formula combines the two portions, separating them with a comma followed by a blank, as in

```
251 Rock Road, P.O. Box 116
```

If the address has no second line, the formula simply copies the first address part (A2) into the cell.

Because ZIP codes are often treated as numbers, the leading zero might disappear when the data is exported, resulting in an improper four-digit code. The lengthy formula shown in Figure 16-5 checks whether the ZIP code is less than five digits long (LEN(A1)<5). If the ZIP code contains fewer digits, leading zeroes are prepended to the ZIP code, bringing it to up to 5 digits, which is then converted to text. If the ZIP code contains five digits, the ZIP code is converted to text and passed through unaltered (NUMTOTEXT(A1)).

Converting ZIP codes to text is necessary to display leading zeros and to handle blank ZIP code fields. If the formula ended simply with A2 rather than NUMTOTEXT(A1), a blank ZIP code would translate as 0 (zero). The preceding doesn't handle the case of an empty ZIP code field — we'll leave that as an exercise to the reader.

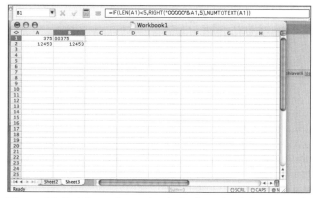

Figure 16-5: A formula to check the length of the ZIP code.

Tip   The general technique of prepending a string of zeros and extracting the rightmost characters is also useful for converting sequence numbers into textual serial numbers, where you want all serial numbers to be of the same length.

Converting Return-delimited text

Another clean-up problem you might encounter is data that has been exported in Return-delimited format. In this format, Return characters separate fields, and records are separated by two Returns. You can convert this format to tab-delimited format if you have access to a word processing program that can search for and replace hidden characters, such as the ASCII Return and Tab characters. Microsoft Word and AppleWorks can perform this task, as can many other applications.

STEPS: Converting Return-Delimited Text

1. Open the Return-delimited file in your word processing program.

2. Choose the application's Find/Change command.

   In Microsoft Word, for example, you would choose Edit ⇨ Replace from the main menu.

3. Perform the following change operations:

   • Find all occurrences of two Returns (^p^p in Word, for example) and change these characters to something else, such as *xxxx* or some other character sequence that doesn't appear in your file.

   • Find all occurrences of a single Return (^p in Word) and change these characters to tabs (^t in Word, for example).

   • Find all occurrences of *xxxx* and change these characters to single Returns.

4. Save the result as a text file.

The file is now in tab-delimited format.

Importing records

When your data is cleaned up (if clean-up was needed), you're ready to import. To add new records to a FileMaker Pro database or to replace the current found set with imported records, follow these steps.

In addition to any FileMaker Pro-imposed access privilege requirements, you must have write-access to the database files in order to perform an Import operation. If the File ➪ Import Records menu item is dimmed (disabled), you should close the database and arrange to modify your System-level access privileges for the file.

STEPS: Importing Records from a File

1. Open the destination database file in FileMaker Pro and switch to Browse mode.

2. *Optional:* If you intend to replace or update records in the current database with imported records, you can use Find commands to select the records to be replaced or updated. (This assumes that you do not wish to replace or update *all* records in the database.)

3. Choose File ➪ Import Records ➪ File.

The Open File dialog, as shown in Figure 16-6, appears. At the bottom of the dialog is a Show pop-up menu /Files of type drop-down list where you can select the format of the file that you want to import.

The default option in the pop-up menu/drop-down list is All Available. This tells FileMaker to list every file that it can read. In most cases, this is fine. However, if you're having a hard time finding the particular file you want to import, you can choose its specific type from the Show pop-up menu/Files of type drop-down list.

4. Select the name of the file you want to import.

5. Click Open. (If the chosen database is password-protected, you will be asked to enter a password.)

The Import Field Mapping dialog appears. (See Figure 16-7.) This dialog's purpose is twofold:

- Match fields in the source file with those in the destination file.

- Pick the fields you want imported and the ones you want to ignore.

For some file types, such as Excel worksheets, you will see field names (or column headers) in the first record displayed. Because you (almost surely) do not want to import this as data, select the Don't import first record (contains field names) check box at the bottom left of the dialog.

Mac

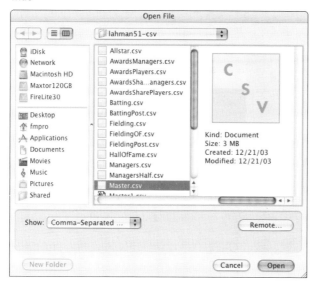

Windows

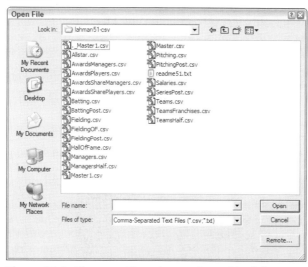

Figure 16-6: Choose a file to import from this dialog.

6. *Optional:* To import fields for which there are currently no matching fields, click the Define Database button.

   The Define Database dialog appears, enabling you to create the additional fields in the current database (in the Fields pane). See Chapter 5 for details.

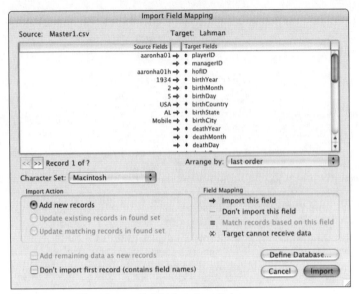

Figure 16-7: The Import Field Mapping dialog.

7. Select the radio button specifying whether you want to add new records or
replace data in the current found set. The Add new records option simply
appends the imported records to the destination file. The Update existing
records in found set option replaces as many records from the current found
set in the current sort order as you import — if there are more records in the
import set, it either ignores or adds them as specified by the state of the Add
remaining data as new records check box.

or

Select the radio button labeled Update matching records in found set if you
want to synchronize the two databases. This option is described in the next
set of steps ("Updating the Records in a Database").

Caution   The Import Records command cannot be undone, so a mistake can have serious
consequences for your data. Note, too, that if the destination file has fewer records
in it than the imported file, the leftover records will not be imported if you use
Update existing records option unless you also specify the Add remaining data as
new records option.

8. Match the fields that you want to import.

An arrow following a field name in the center column indicates that the field
will be imported into the field in the destination file. If you don't want to
import a particular field, click its arrow. The indicator changes to a dash,
indicating that the field will not be imported.

Because fields in the two files can be in any order, you might need to rearrange them manually so that they match. You can drag field names in the destination file (on the right side of the dialog) to change their order.

9. *Optional:* Click the Record *x* of *y* buttons to review the matching fields in several records.

   This is mainly a sanity check. By scanning several records, you can assure yourself that the fields do indeed match properly and that you have not omitted an important field.

10. Click the Import button.

Note

When importing data, you should understand these restrictions. First, you cannot import data into Calculation, Summary, or related fields, nor into any field with the Global Storage attribute set. To import data into related fields, open the database in which they are stored and then perform the import. Second, you can import data only into Container fields if you're importing from a FileMaker Pro database. (FileMaker Pro 8, however, can import a *folder* of images into a Container field as a batch procedure. See "Importing data from a folder," later in this chapter, for an explanation of this feature.)

As seen in Figure 16-7 and mentioned in Step 7, you can update changed records, merging two databases. This option enables you to synchronize two copies of a database. For example, you might have a master copy of a Contacts database on your desktop computer (or on a network) and periodically need to update it with changes you made to a copy on your laptop.

STEPS: Updating the Records in a Database

1. Perform Steps 1–6 from the previously described import procedure.

2. In the Import Action area of the Import Field Mapping dialog, select the Update matching records in the found set radio button.

3. *Optional:* Select the Add remaining data as new records check box.

   All records for which no match is found will be added as new records in the destination database.

4. In the center column of the Import Field Mapping dialog (see Figure 16-8), click to select match fields.

   Match fields are used by FileMaker Pro to determine which records from the two databases are matches and, hence, should be updated during the import procedure. You can specify one or several match fields. (If possible, match fields should be unique, such as a Social Security number or client ID.) An equal sign (=) designates a match field. (Match fields can be specified *only* when you select the Update options.)

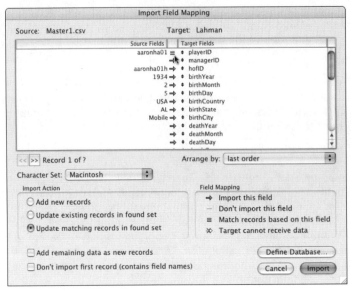

Figure 16-8: Specifying match fields.

5. *Optional:* Click the Record *x* of *y* buttons to review the matching fields in several records.

6. Click the Import button.

   FileMaker examines the two databases and determines which pairs of records are matches, based on the match fields chosen in Step 4. All fields that you have marked for importing overwrite the designated fields in the destination database.

Opening a foreign data file to create a new database

If you want to change an existing file from some other program directly into a new FileMaker database, you can do so without first creating the database fields and layouts in FileMaker Pro. That is, you don't need to have a FileMaker Pro database to receive the new data — one can be created for you automatically.

Tip   FileMaker Pro 8 can also convert supported file types by using drag and drop. That is, you can drag an Excel worksheet file onto the FileMaker Pro 8 icon to create a new FileMaker database. If you take this approach, jump to Step 4 in the following step list. (Note that FileMaker will also attempt to convert many types of unsupported files using drag-and-drop, such as AppleWorks/ClarisWorks worksheets. The results, however, are frequently unsatisfactory. In such instances, the preferred method is to export the unsupported file as one of the FileMaker-supported file types, such as tab-delimited text.)

Changing the field order when importing data

The Import Field Mapping dialog (refer to Figures 16-7 and 16-8) includes an Arrange by pop-up menu/drop-down list you can use to facilitate matching fields between the two databases. The option that you choose from this menu/list determines the field display order in the destination database (on the right side of the dialog). The Arrange by field names option is particularly useful for quickly locating all matching field names in the two files. Note, however, that the matching fields option is available only when the file to be imported contains a header record or other information specifying the file's field names. FileMaker Pro files and dBASE files, for example, include field specification information.

STEPS: Creating a New Database from a File in Another Program

1. Choose the File ➪ Open command.

   A standard file dialog appears.

2. From the Show pop-up menu /Files of type drop-down list, choose All Available or the specific type of file you want to open.

   The list of file types is identical to the list displayed when you import data using the Import Records command.

3. Select the file and click Open.

4. When opening a worksheet, you might see the First Row Option dialog, as shown in Figure 16-9, asking whether the first row contains field names or data. Select a radio button to signify your choice and then click OK.

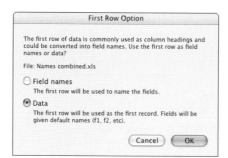

Figure 16-9: The First Row Option dialog.

5. A new file dialog appears in which you are asked to save the converted file, as shown in Figure 16-10.

Mac

Windows

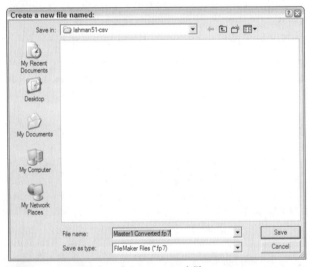

Figure 16-10: Saving the converted file.

6. Accept the proposed name for the converted file or type a new name in the Save As/File name text box. Click Save.

The new database is converted to FileMaker Pro format and then opens in a new window. Fields are presented in the default vertical format or in Table view (depending on the type of file opened — for example, tab-delimited imports result in a tabular layout) and are named using the convention f1, f2, f3, and so on. You can now clean up the database by using the File ⇨ Define ⇨ Database command to rename and define additional fields, and you can change the layout as necessary by switching to Layout mode. FileMaker Pro 8 creates both the standard form and columnar layouts for all non-FileMaker files imported.

Tip

Field names and definitions carry over to FileMaker if the opened file was an Excel, DIF, DBF (dBASE/xBASE), or Merge file. FileMaker Pro correctly translates field types when opening the following file types: Excel and DBF (dBASE/xBASE). When importing a dBASE/xBASE database, two FileMaker Pro layouts are automatically created — a standard layout and a columnar layout in Table view — but here, the correct field names and types are in place.

Importing data from a digital camera (Mac only)

If you have a Mac OS X-supported digital camera or similar device (such as a memory card reader), you can import images directly from your camera or device into an open FileMaker Pro 8 database. This feature is available for Mac only.

Note

By default, connecting a camera or inserting a camera memory card will launch iPhoto for importing the pictures. You can set a different default application, such as FileMaker Pro 8 (or Photoshop CS2, for example) via the Image Capture utility, found in the Applications folder.

STEPS: Importing Pictures from a Digital Camera or Other Device

1. Open the database into which you want to import the pictures.

2. If you're replacing or updating records in the current database, perform the necessary Find requests to select only the records you intend to replace or update.

3. Connect the camera to your Mac, turn on the camera, and set it for the mode in which it can transmit pictures to the Mac.

   or

   Insert the camera's memory card into the connected card reader.

   A disk icon for your camera or memory card appears on the Desktop. If another camera-related program automatically launches, click the FileMaker Pro icon on the Dock to make it the active application.

4. Switch to Browse mode and choose File ⇨ Import Records ⇨ Digital Camera.

   The FileMaker Pro Photo Import Options dialog appears. (See Figure 16-11.)

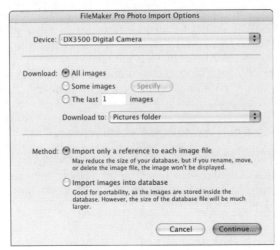

Figure 16-11: The FileMaker Pro Photo Import Options dialog.

5. Choose your camera or other connected device from the Device pop-up menu.

6. In the Download section of the dialog, select a radio button to indicate whether you wish to download which of the following:

   • *All images:* Download all images from the connected camera or memory card.

   • *Some images:* Click the Specify button and select the images you want to download from the Specify Images to Import dialog. (See Figure 16-12.)

   • *The Last x images:* Enter a number in the text box to download the most recent *x* images in the camera or on the memory card.

7. *Optional:* Select a Download to folder into which the images will be downloaded.

8. Select a radio button to specify a storage option: import/store a reference to each file or import/store the actual images in the database.

Tip   In addition to the dialog's caveats concerning moving, renaming, or deleting the image files, you should be aware that if you wish to move the database to another computer, you have to remember to move the pictures as well and then manually reestablish the links between the database and the pictures. In other words, Import images into database is usually the preferable option.

9. Click OK.

   The Import Field Mappings dialog appears. (Refer to Figure 16-8.)

10. Match the fields that you want to import.

   An arrow following a field name in the Source Fields column indicates that the camera/memory card data will be imported into the field in the destination file. If you don't want to import a particular item, click its arrow. The indicator changes to a dash (—), showing that the item will not be imported.

You might need to rearrange the fields manually so that they match. You can drag field names in the destination database (on the right side of the list) to change their order.

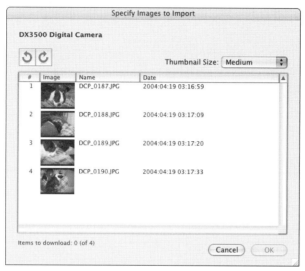

Figure 16-12: When you select the Some Images option, you can pick the images that will be imported. Click OK to continue.

11. *Optional:* If necessary, you can create additional fields in the target database to store the image data by clicking the Define Database button. (Note that both the Image and Image Thumbnail must be matched with Container fields if you wish to import them. File Name and File Path must be imported to Text fields.)

12. Specify an Import Action by selecting the appropriate radio button (as explained previously in this chapter).

13. Click the Import button.

FileMaker Pro Help offers some excellent tips for importing photos. Here are the highlights:

✦ If you want to import EXIF (EXchangeable Image File) information about your photos, such as the date, time, and shutter speed, you must import directly from the camera or a card reader. That is, if you've already transferred the images to your hard disk and then imported them using FileMaker Pro 8's Folder import option, the EXIF information won't be available.

✦ Only JPEG and TIFF files can be imported with this procedure. If your camera also makes movies or can record sound, use the Mac OS X Image Capture application to move these items to your hard disk. Then use the Insert ⇨ QuickTime or Insert ⇨ Sound command to insert the material into a Container field in your database.

✦ You can set a File Options item for any FileMaker Pro 8 database instructing it to automatically open the FileMaker Pro Photo Import Options dialog whenever it senses a connected camera or memory card reader. (See Figure 16-13.)

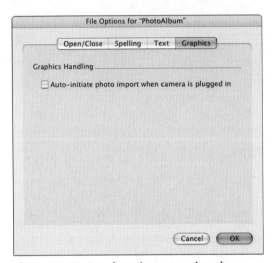

Figure 16-13: Set photo import options here.

To automatically start a photo import for the current database whenever a camera is sensed, select the Auto-initiate photo import when camera is plugged in check box (in the File Options dialog's Graphics pane).

✦ You can make FileMaker Pro 8 your preferred application for initiating photo imports if you wish (as mentioned in the earlier Tip). Open the Image Capture application (see Figure 16-14), choose Preferences, click the General tab (Camera tab if using OS X 10.3), choose Other from the When a camera is connected, open the pop-up menu, navigate to FileMaker Pro in the sheet that appears, click Open, and then click OK.

Importing data from a folder

Using the File ⇨ Import Records ⇨ Folder command, you can import an entire folder of image files, QuickTime movies, or text files into the current database. (You can specify that all enclosed subfolders be imported as well.) Like other Import procedures, the imported material can create new records, update records in the found set, or replace the records in the found set. Unlike importing files from a digital camera, *all* FileMaker 8-supported platforms can use the Folder import procedure.

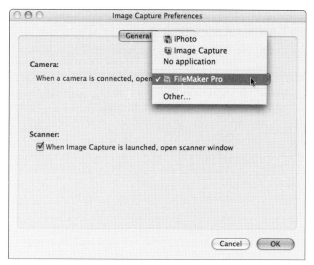

Figure 16-14: To make FileMaker Pro the application that opens when a camera is connected, set it in the Image Capture Preferences dialog's General pane.

STEPS: Importing Data from a Folder

1. Open the database into which you want to import data.

2. *Optional:* If you intend to replace or update records in the current database with imported data, you can use Find commands to select the records to be replaced or updated. (This assumes that you do not wish to replace or update all records in the database.)

3. Choose File ➪ Import Records ➪ Folder.

   The Folder of Files Import Options dialog appears. (See Figure 16-15.)

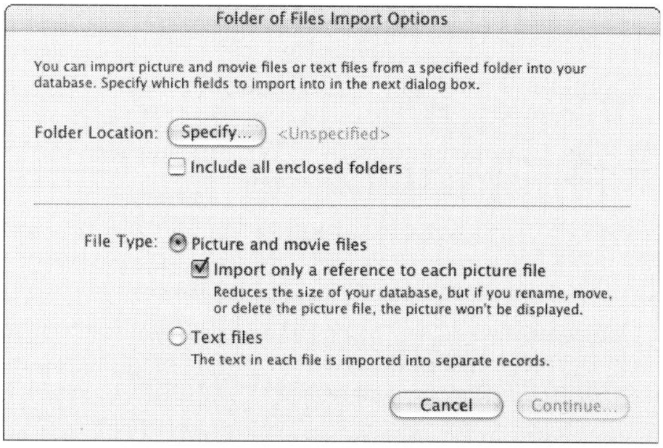

Figure 16-15: Set options for the folder import.

4. In the bottom half of the dialog, select a radio button to select the type of file you wish to import: Picture and movie files or Text files.

Under Mac OS X, you can use this technique to import a folder of Adobe Acrobat (PDF) files into a Container field. When viewed in Browse mode, each PDF file appears in a QuickTime movie frame that you page through using the controls at the bottom of the frame (as shown in Figure 16-16). To manually insert a complete PDF file into a Container field, use the Insert QuickTime command.

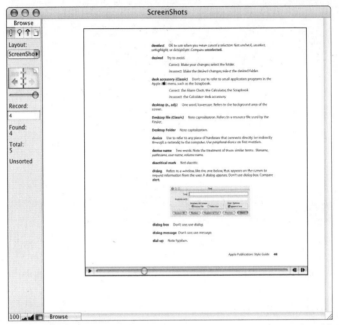

Figure 16-16: If you're using Mac OS X, you can insert "playable" PDF files into Container fields.

5. If importing pictures, you can import the actual pictures or just references to where they are stored on your computer. (Using references will keep the database smaller but sacrifice portability. That is, the database won't contain the actual pictures if you transfer a copy of it to someone else, nor will it find pictures that have been moved, deleted, or renamed.)

6. To select a folder to import, click the Specify button.

The Choose a Folder/Browse for Folder dialog appears.

7. Select the folder you wish to import and click Choose/OK.

8. In the Folder of Files Import Options dialog, click Continue.

The Import Field Mapping dialog appears. (Refer to Figure 16-8.)

9. Specify an Import Action by selecting the appropriate radio button (as described previously in this chapter).

10. Click the Import button.

   The folder import is conducted, per your instructions.

Note   If the selected folder contains aliases (Mac) or shortcuts (Windows) to documents, FileMaker will locate and import the original files. Files of an incorrect type are ignored during the import. For example, if you elect to import image files, images in an unsupported format will not be imported. On the other hand, QuickTime (used by FileMaker Pro to scan for importable images) will convert text files into movies with one paragraph per frame and then import those movies when you import a text file as an image. (It's really subtitling an otherwise empty movie.)

Tip   If you imported the file paths, you can open the original file in its creating application. Select the path text in the FileMaker Pro field, Control+click (Mac) or right-click (Windows) the selected text, and choose Open *filename* from the shortcut menu that appears.

Exporting Data

When you export records from FileMaker Pro, you change FileMaker Pro data to a format another program can use. The process is virtually the same as importing except that it operates in reverse.

Format selection

When you export records, you don't save directly into a document in another application — you simply create a new document that the target application can open. As you do when importing records, you need to determine the file formats supported by the destination program before you export the FileMaker data. You might need to check the relevant application's documentation to determine what file formats it can use. If FileMaker Pro doesn't support the application's native file format, you'll have to instruct FileMaker to export a new data file in a format that the destination application *can* use. Many programs can read tab- or comma-delimited text files, for example.

FileMaker Pro supports the following formats for export purposes:

   ◆ FileMaker Pro

   ◆ Tab-separated text

   ◆ Comma-separated text

   ◆ SYLK

   ◆ DBF (dBASE III)

✦ XLS (Excel)

✦ DIF

✦ WKS

✦ BASIC

✦ Merge

✦ HTML table

✦ XML

Data clean-up

Just as you do when importing, you might need to clean up your data, either before exporting it or prior to opening it in the destination program. In particular, you might find unnecessary Returns and spaces at the end of some records. These unneeded characters are usually the result of careless data entry and can cause trouble in your target file when you export data to it.

As a solution, you can define a new Calculation field for each field to be exported. The definition of this field is a procedure that strips spaces and returns. Use the following definition:

```
If(Position(FieldName,"¶",1,1), Trim (Left(FieldName,
Position(FieldName,"¶",1,1)-1)),Trim(FieldName))
```

Replace *FieldName* with the name of the field that you want to strip. (To insert the ¶ symbol into the formula, click its button to the left of the Operators list in the Specify Calculation dialog.) You must define a separate Calculation field for each potential source field. Then export the Calculation fields rather than the originals.

Caution

If you use this formula on a field containing intentional Returns (for example, in a Comments field containing multiple paragraphs), the formula truncates the field contents at the end of the first paragraph, thus effectively deleting all paragraphs that follow. If you really need to retain all the text, try to determine a character that isn't used (perhaps a tilde or an accent grave) and use Find/Replace to convert the paragraph breaks to that character.

Exporting records

With data clean-up behind you (in the event that clean-up was necessary), you are ready to export the data.

STEPS: Exporting FileMaker Pro Data for Use in Another Application

1. Open your source FileMaker Pro database.

2. Use Find mode to locate the records you want to export.

An export always consists only of records in the current found set. You can also use the Sort command to sort these records, if desired.

3. Switch back to Browse mode and choose File ⇨ Export Records.

A standard file dialog appears, similar in appearance to the dialog previously shown in Figure 16-10.

4. Type a name for the destination file.

5. Choose a file format for the destination file from the Type pop-up menu/Save as type drop-down list.

6. Click Save.

The Specify Field Order for Export dialog appears, as shown in Figure 16-17.

Note If you choose Excel from the Type pop-up menu/Files of type drop-down list, an Excel options dialog will appear first, and then the Specify Field Order for Export dialog appears.

Figure 16-17: The Specify Field Order for Export dialog.

7. In the left side of the dialog, select the fields that you want to export.

As each field is selected, click the Move button to transfer it to the Field Order list.

8. Drag field names up or down to change the export order, if necessary.

Click to select the name of the field you want to move and then drag it to a new position in the Field Export Order list. In most cases, you will want the order of the fields to match the order in which they appear in the destination file (assuming the destination file already exists).

9. Select the appropriate radio button specifying whether you want to format the output.

Select the Apply current layout's data formatting to exported data check box if you want the data to be formatted to match the number, date, and time formats you've applied to the current layout's fields. Additionally, ensure that you have the Character set pop-up menu/drop-down list set appropriately; otherwise, you might export 16-bit (Unicode) text to an application that can't handle it.

Note   Excel mandates 16-bit (Unicode) text as the character set.

10. Click Export.

The target data file is created in the chosen format.

Note   If you've defined one or more relationships for the current database, you can also export fields from any of the related files. To view the field names in any related file, just choose the name of the relationship from the pop-up menu/drop-down list above the Field list. In the Field export order list, fields from the current file and from related files can be mixed.

You can also to export (sub)summary data from a FileMaker Pro database.

STEPS: Exporting Summary Data

1. Open your source FileMaker Pro document.

2. Repeat Steps 2–6 as described previously in the export procedure.

3. Sort the file on the break field that groups the records.

4. In the Specify Field Order for Export dialog, select the summary field's check box in the Group by list.

5. Click Export.

Moving Data Using Drag-and-Drop

FileMaker Pro 8 can import and export selected text strings using a system function called *drag-and-drop*. With drag-and-drop enabled, you can copy data by selecting and then dragging it from one field to another, from one database to another, or from a database to any other drag-and-drop–enabled application—such as a spreadsheet or word processing program—or vice versa.

To enable drag-and-drop in FileMaker Pro, choose FileMaker Pro/Edit ➪ Preferences. Click the General tab at the top of the Preferences dialog and then select the check box for Allow drag and drop text selection, as shown in Figure 16-18.

You can also use drag-and-drop to convert foreign data files into FileMaker Pro databases, as described previously. For example, if you drag the file icon for a

Microsoft Excel worksheet onto the FileMaker Pro 8 icon, FileMaker launches (if it isn't already running) and immediately initiates the procedure to convert the worksheet into a database. For details, refer to "Exchanging Data with Microsoft Office," later in this chapter.

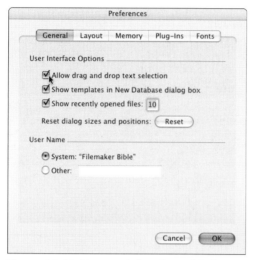

Figure 16-18: Drag-and-drop is enabled or disabled in the Preferences dialog.

Exchanging Data between Macs and PCs

Because FileMaker Pro 8 runs under various Mac operating systems (10.3.x and 10.4.x) and under Microsoft Windows 2000 and XP with the appropriate service packs installed, you can move data between platforms as well. Keep two things in mind when you transfer data between a Mac and a PC. First, you actually have to get the data from your Mac to a PC and vice versa. Second, you need to understand the differences between the Macintosh and PC versions of FileMaker Pro. The following sections explain both of these activities.

Moving data to and from FileMaker Pro for Windows

You can share files between a Mac and a PC in several ways. You can use a network (which provides direct access to files), you can use the time-honored *sneaker net* (physically moving files — on floppy disks or another removable medium, such as a CD, keychain drive, or Zip disk — between machines), and you can transfer files electronically (using a modem, serial ports on both computers, or the Internet). Here's how these methods work:

✦ *Network:* Setting up a mixed network of Macs and PCs is a task outside this book's scope. You'll seldom find it covered in Windows books, but you can find excellent instructions in *Mac OS X Bible (Tiger Edition),* by Samuel A. Litt et al (Wiley). FileMaker Pro 8 supports TCP/IP (Transmission Control Protocol/Internet Protocol) networking for multi-user file sharing. (See Chapter 20 for more information about using FileMaker Pro on a network.)

✦ *Removable media:* The Mac and PC must be equipped with the same type of drive, whether it be floppy, flash memory drive, CD-ROM, or Zip. If both computers have floppy drives, for example, you can use PC-formatted floppies to exchange databases between the two types of computers. (A Mac can read PC floppies, but a PC can't read Mac floppies unless it's outfitted with special software.) If your source computer has a CD burner, you might well be able to use the included CD-mastering software to create a CD that can be read by the other platform.

A Mac equipped with a USB-connected floppy drive, however, might be able to read only high-density floppies, treating others as unformatted (and unreadable).

✦ *Serial communications:* You can transfer files by using a modem and the appropriate communications software.

✦ *E-mail:* When you don't feel up to messing with a network or cables, one of the simplest ways to exchange files is by sending them as e-mail attachments. Even if both computers are yours, all you have to do is e-mail the database to your normal e-mail address, quickly turn off the e-mail program, fire up the e-mail program on the other platform, and then just receive the file. (Ain't technology grand?)

Microsoft Internet Explorer (PC) and Apache (included with Mac OS X) can enable your computer to act as a personal Web server. You can use this software to make files on your hard disk available over the Internet or a local intranet. Similarly, by creating and posting ordinary Web pages with file links, you can use the Internet or an intranet as a repository for files you wish to make available to others, regardless of their computer platforms.

After you've transferred the files, both the Mac and PC versions of FileMaker Pro can work with the databases without any further ado; importing and exporting are unnecessary. You might, however, run into some problems caused by the differences between Macs and PCs, as well as minor differences between the two versions of FileMaker Pro (as explained in the following section).

When running on a mixed PC/Mac network, it isn't necessary for each user to have a separate copy of a FileMaker database. Any FileMaker Pro user can host a database on the network, making it available to other network users.

Understanding the compatibility issues

In general, you should watch out for eight potential problem areas when you move a Macintosh FileMaker Pro document to Microsoft Windows (or vice versa):

✦ Character sets

✦ Fonts

✦ Filenames

✦ Colors

✦ Graphics formats

✦ Printing

✦ OLE (Object Linking and Embedding) support

✦ Platform-specific capabilities

Character sets

Characters with ASCII values 0–127 (low ASCII) are the same in both systems. Characters with ASCII values greater than 127 (high or extended ASCII) might be different, depending on the Windows font you're using. Some Macintosh high-ASCII characters — such as the bullet character (Option+8) — do not translate properly in Windows. Thus, if you enter text with special characters (the *é* characters in *résumé,* for example) on your Mac, you might get unexpected results that require cleaning up on the PC.

Fonts

TrueType, PostScript, and OpenType fonts are available for both systems. However, you should use the same technology on both computer systems if you can. Otherwise, you're likely to encounter text-alignment problems in your layouts. You might find, for example, that the comparable font on the other platform is too large, causing text to spill into adjacent areas in your otherwise attractive layout. As a result, it might be necessary to tweak the layout when moving a database between platforms.

Tip   Mac OS X recognizes PC TrueType and PostScript fonts as well as OpenType fonts, so you could conceivably use the same font files on both platforms.

Tip   Your Mac includes a set of core Windows fonts, such as Arial and Verdana. If you restrict yourself to these fonts, you will go a long way to eliminating cross-platform font problems.

Filenames

Filenames in FileMaker Pro 8 for Windows end with an `.fp7` extension (as in `SALES.fp7`) rather than no extension, as is still a common practice when naming files on a Mac. Thus, databases that you want users to be able to run on either platform should include the `.fp7` extension (which, fortunately, FileMaker Pro 8 offers as a default even on the Mac).

Colors

Colors are organized into palettes. Colors are not necessarily mapped the same way on the two systems, so you might see strange color effects on your PC when you open a Mac document. However, you can avoid color-related incompatibilities by choosing the 216-color Web palette in Preferences' Layout section.

Printing

Depending on the print driver you use on your PC, your PC results might differ from your Mac results, even when using the same printer. It is not uncommon for printer manufacturers to create printer drivers supporting different features on different platforms. Additionally, *font metrics* (size, spacing, kerning, and so forth) can vary between the platforms, even for the same font from the same type foundry. You might have to create two versions of each report layout: one tailored to the PC and the other for your Macintosh.

OLE support

Only Windows users can insert or edit OLE objects in a FileMaker Pro database. Although Mac users can view, cut, copy, and paste OLE objects, they cannot insert or modify them in any way.

Platform-specific capabilities

Several capabilities of the two operating systems are platform-specific; that is, they are available only in Windows or only on the Mac. If such features are used in designing a script, the script will not run on the other platform. Some examples of platform-specific capabilities are listed here.

Mac-specific features

✦ Ability to play Macintosh `.snd` (sound) files

✦ Importing from a digital camera

✦ AppleScript and AppleEvents support

Windows-specific features

✦ IPX/SPX (Internetwork Packet eXchange/Sequenced Packet eXchange) networking support

✦ Microsoft Registry support

✦ DDE (Dynamic Data Exchange) messaging

Note   TCP/IP is the only network protocol supported by FileMaker Pro 8 across all platforms.

Exchanging Data with Microsoft Office

FileMaker Pro 8 lets you automatically create new FileMaker Pro databases from Excel files simply by opening them.

Note Because of the file format changes between FileMaker Pro 6 and FileMaker Pro 7 (and 8), Excel and Word versions current at the writing of this book cannot open or directly read FileMaker Pro 7 or 8 files as the Macintosh versions of Word and Excel (Microsoft Office X) can read FileMaker Pro 5 and 6 files. Microsoft Office 2004 does not include such support for .fp7 files, either.

Using Excel Data in FileMaker Pro

FileMaker Pro is well equipped to quickly turn many of your Excel spreadsheets into FileMaker databases. You can accomplish the conversion via drag-and-drop or by opening the spreadsheet in FileMaker Pro. Note, however, that spreadsheets that are simple lists convert best. Macros are ignored during the conversion and only the *results* of formulas — rather than the formulas themselves — are transferred to the new database.

Tip FileMaker can treat the contents of the first spreadsheet row as field names. If the spreadsheet has column labels but there are blank rows above them, you might want to rearrange the spreadsheet so that the column labels are in row 1. An alternative tactic — creating a named range from only the portion of the spreadsheet that you wish to transfer to FileMaker Pro — also works well. Finally, if the spreadsheet's active area contains blank rows, you might want to eliminate them (to avoid creating blank records).

STEPS: Creating a New Database from an Excel Worksheet

1. To create the database by using drag-and-drop, drag the worksheet file icon onto FileMaker Pro 8's icon.

   or

   In FileMaker Pro, choose File ➪ Open. In the Open File dialog that appears (see Figure 16-19), choose Excel from the Show pop-up menu /Files of type drop-down list, and then open the desired worksheet file.

2. If the worksheet contains multiple sheets or named ranges, a Specify Excel Data dialog appears in which you must select a sheet to open. (See Figure 16-20.)

3. To select one of multiple sheets, select the Display Worksheets radio button, select a sheet from the list presented, and click OK.

   or

To select from one or more named ranges within the worksheet, select the Display named ranges radio button, select a named range from the list presented, and click Continue.

Mac

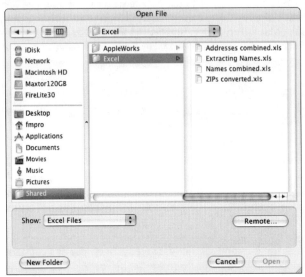

Windows

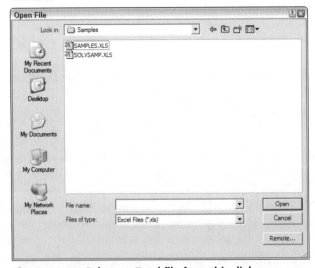

Figure 16-19: Select an Excel file from this dialog.

Figure 16-20: Select a sheet or named range from the open worksheet.

The First Row Option dialog appears. (See Figure 16-21.)

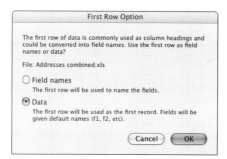

Figure 16-21: Indicate whether the first spreadsheet row contains field names or data.

4. Select a radio button to indicate whether the first row of the worksheet or named range should be treated by FileMaker as field names or as merely another data record.

5. Click OK to create the new database.

   The Create a New File Named dialog appears.

6. Navigate to the drive and folder in which you want to save the converted spreadsheet, enter/edit the proposed filename, and click Save.

   The database is saved with two layouts and opens with the columnar layout displayed in Table view.

Saving FileMaker Pro Data to Excel

One of the most common external uses (arguably *the* most common) of FileMaker Pro data has taken place in Microsoft Excel—utilizing the data in an assortment of data analysis tasks. Until FileMaker Pro 8, you needed to export the data, as described earlier in this chapter, choosing Excel (WKS) as the destination format. Although this method works and is still available, FileMaker Pro 8 makes the common task even simpler—just have a layout that presents the data you want exported (in other words, a report), with all the filtering and sorting already performed. Then, choose File ⇨ Save/Send Records As ⇨ Excel. You'll be presented with the dialog shown in Figure 16-22 (or its Windows equivalent), allowing you to specify a filename and whether to save just the current record or all the records in the current found set (Records being browsed). Clicking the Options button displays the dialog shown in Figure 16-23, where you can establish Excel metadata—the worksheet name within the workbook, a title, a subject, or an author—and specify whether the FileMaker Pro field names should be used as column headers in the worksheet's first row.

Figure 16-22: Name and select a destination for your Excel file.

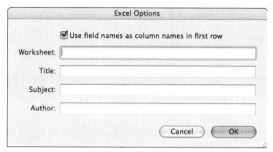

Figure 16-23: Specify your Excel worksheet options.

Although PDF shares the File ⇨ Save/Send Records As submenu with Excel, a PDF save doesn't give you (easily) manipulated data. PDF is, in reality, another form of printing, and this option is discussed in Chapter 13.

Summary

✦ You can exchange FileMaker Pro data with other applications and with FileMaker Pro for another platform (Windows or Macintosh). FileMaker Pro supports a variety of popular import and export file formats.

✦ FileMaker Pro can import data created in other programs, such as spreadsheets and other database applications.

✦ When importing FileMaker Pro data into an existing FileMaker database, you can merge (or synchronize) the files by using the Update matching records in found set option.

✦ You can save the current record or found set as an Excel worksheet, with all filtering and sorting imposed in the current layout applied to the saved data.

✦ Macintosh users can directly share databases with users of the Windows version of FileMaker Pro, but layouts might differ, especially in terms of fonts and colors.

✦ ✦ ✦

Creating and Using Templates

You've already learned a lot about designing and using databases. However, it isn't always necessary to reinvent the wheel. You might find a template developed by someone else that you can use as-is or modify simply to meet your needs. A *template,* in the case of FileMaker Pro, is a ready-to-use database into which you can enter your own data. More specifically, a template is a database without any records.

The FileMaker Pro 8 Templates

When you install FileMaker Pro 8, a collection of FileMaker Pro templates is copied to your hard disk. You can use any of them by choosing File ⇨ New Database, selecting the Create a new file using a template radio button (in the New Database dialog), choosing a template category (Business, Home, or Education) from the pop-up menu/drop-down list, and selecting a template from the category's list (see Figures 17-1 and 17-2), and clicking OK.

To find out more about any of the templates that are included with FileMaker Pro 8, click the Template Info button.

These templates serve two purposes: First, they give you some databases with which you can safely experiment. Second, they're full-featured databases that you might be able to use for your business, home, organization, or school record keeping.

This chapter discusses the techniques and commands you must know in order to work with any FileMaker Pro template, regardless of whether you receive it with FileMaker Pro 8, from an online information service or off the Internet, from a friend or a colleague, or purchase it as a commercial product from a member of the FileMaker Solutions Alliance (see Appendix E). For details on creating your own templates with the intent of giving or selling them to others, see Chapter 23.

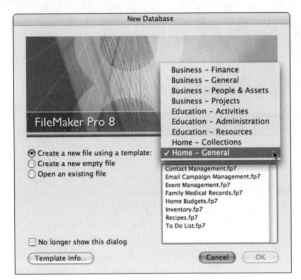

Figure 17-1: In the New Database dialog, you can create a database from templates in any of the provided categories.

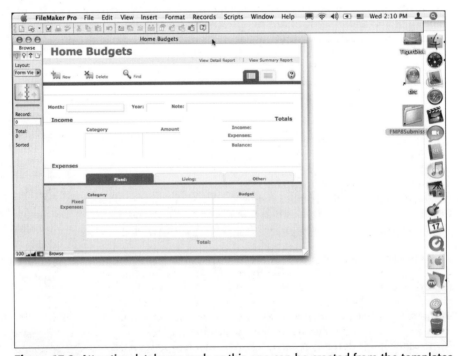

Figure 17-2: Attractive databases such as this one can be created from the templates provided with FileMaker Pro 8.

Installing a Template

When you obtain a FileMaker Pro template, the database designers provide several different methods to help you install their templates. Here are some of the most common procedures used to install templates or databases:

✦ *Run a special installer program.* This method is often associated with commercial packages, such as FileMaker Pro. When you run the installer program, you might be given an option to install all or selected parts of the software — usually to any disk and folder you choose.

✦ *Double-click a self-extracting archive.* To save disk space, templates (and other software) are frequently compressed into self-extracting archives. A *self-extracting archive* contains a compressed copy of the template, thus conserving disk space and reducing download time (for templates that are distributed through online information services or the Internet). A self-extracting archive is so-named because it includes a built-in file extraction program. When you double-click a self-extracting archive, a dialog appears asking where you want to install the files. After you select a destination, the files are extracted from the archive, expanded to their normal sizes, and copied to the destination disk and folder.

✦ *Extract the templates from a normal archive.* This is a variation of the preceding distribution method. Instead of creating self-extracting archives, normal archives are sometimes created. The only difference is that you might need a separate file-extraction utility (such as StuffIt Expander or StuffIt Deluxe on the Mac; WinZip or WinRAR on the PC) in order to extract the files. This distribution method (as well as the preceding one) is commonly used with templates, programs, and other materials that you'll find on the Internet and online services, such as America Online. Zip extraction (and creation) is built into both Mac OS X (10.3 and later) and Windows XP.

✦ *(Mac) Drag the templates from a mounted disk image.* A common form of Mac distribution is to create a disk image file that you mount by double-clicking. The disk image files are also compressed, saving download time and storage disk space.

Tip　Because either Macintosh or Windows users can use FileMaker Pro template and database files, Windows users must occasionally "unstuff" Macintosh StuffIt archives. To handle this situation, you can download a free copy of StuffIt Expander for Windows (Allume Systems) from www.allume.com.

　　 If you don't have file extraction utilities, you can download many of the most popular ones from www.allume.com (StuffIt Expander) and www.winzip.com (WinZip).

✦ *Use the Finder or Windows to make a copy of the template.* Many database templates are distributed as normal, uncompressed files. To install these templates, all you must do is copy them to your hard disk, just as you would any other file or program. When making the copy, however, be sure to respect any folder organization that exists in the original. Multifile solutions might work correctly only if the necessary files are together in the proper folder(s) on your hard disk.

When copying a Windows template from a CD to your hard disk, Windows might consider the resulting copy to be locked. (Because a CD is a locked media, Windows treats all the files on it as locked, too.) If the template doesn't work correctly when opened in FileMaker Pro, quit FileMaker Pro, locate the template on your hard disk, right-click its file icon, and then choose Properties from the shortcut menu that appears. On the Properties dialog's General tab (see Figure 17-3), remove the check mark from Read-only and then click OK.

Figure 17-3: To unlock a Windows file, remove the check mark from Read-only.

Reinstalling a Fresh Copy of a Template

Like any other FileMaker Pro database, any changes you make to a template (entering or editing data, changing field definitions, rearranging fields on a layout, and so on) are instantly saved and become a permanent part of the file. Thus, when you are finished experimenting with a new template and are ready to begin entering your own data, you might want to start with a fresh copy of the template. Here are two safe ways you can accomplish this:

✦ Rerun the installation program, double-click the self-extracting archive, or run the necessary file-extraction utility.

✦ For templates that are distributed as normal uncompressed files, drag a fresh copy of the template from the distribution disk to your hard disk.

As an alternative, it might be simpler to just think ahead. Whenever you receive a template, make a backup copy of the uncompressed templates. When you're through trying it out and are ready to commit your own data to the template, you can use the Finder or Windows to make a new copy of the template from your backup copy.

Tip   If you want to preserve the field definition and layout changes you've made but want to eliminate any sample or test data that's present, you can choose File ➪ Save a Copy As and choose Clone (no records) as the type of file you wish saved.

Saving a Database as a Template

FileMaker Pro templates are also referred to as clones. (The terms *template* and *clone* are interchangeable.) A *clone* is an exact copy of a database but without any records. The clone contains the same tables, relationships, field definitions, layouts, buttons, and scripts as the original database. Because all the records have been removed, however, it is in the perfect state to receive fresh data.

In several instances, you might want to create a clone of an existing database:

✦ *To create an archival copy of the structure of an important database — just in case:* Many of us tend to tweak a database as we use it: moving fields around, trying out new layouts, and testing scripts, for example. Because FileMaker Pro automatically saves any change that you make to a database, these little experiments can sometimes wreak havoc — like causing scripts to stop functioning, Calculation fields to present the wrong results, and so on. If you've created a clone of the original database, you can get back to square one by simply importing the data from your current database into the clone.

Tip   An even simpler method of protecting the structure of a database and its data is to make an exact copy of the database. Choose File ➪ Save a Copy As and then choose Copy of Current File from the Type pop-up menu/Save as drop-down list.

✦ *To begin a new weekly, quarterly, or other time-based database:* Many databases are designed to be used only for a certain period of time and then started over with new records. For example, suppose you create a database in which you do your bookkeeping. The IRS expects you to turn in an annual Form 1040 and Schedule C, so you need a fresh copy of this database at the beginning of each fiscal year. Another example would be if you were to make a call-tracking database that your department's receptionist will use to make a permanent record of incoming calls. You might want to start a fresh copy on a more frequent basis (monthly, weekly, or even daily, depending on the call volume).

✦ *To remove sample records and prepare a commercial or shareware database for your own data:* Some templates contain a small set of sample records, enabling you to get a feel for how the database works without having to enter (or risk) your own data. As long as you restrict your experimentation to adding, deleting, and editing records, you can strip out all the sample records by simply making a clone of the database; then you're ready to begin entering your own data.

✦ *To enable you to give a template away or sell it:* Unless your records are meant to be used as a sample, you probably don't want to include your personal or business data in a template. Making a clone strips out that data in one easy step.

STEPS: Making a Template or Clone from an Existing Database

1. Open the database in FileMaker Pro.

2. Choose File ➪ Save a Copy As.

   A standard file dialog appears. (See Figure 17-4.)

3. Choose Clone (no records) from the Type pop-up menu/Save a drop-down list.

4. Select a destination disk and folder by using normal file navigation procedures.

5. Type a name for the clone in the Save as (Mac OS X) or File name (Windows) text box.

   If you're saving the file in a different folder and/or disk than the one where the current database is stored, you can use the same name as that of the original database. If you're storing it in the same folder and/or disk, you'll want to use a new name or the default name proposed by FileMaker Pro (`filename Clone.fp7`).

Caution

Under no circumstances should you use the same name as the original database when saving the template in the same folder and/or disk location! Doing so replaces your original database with an empty template. FileMaker Pro will warn you if you attempt this particular faux pas.

6. Click Save.

   The clone is created but not opened. The original template file remains open. If you want to immediately begin working with the clone, close the original database (choose File ➪ Close or press ⌘+W/Ctrl+W) and then open the clone (choose File ➪ Open or press ⌘+O/Ctrl+O).

The other two Save a Copy As options presented in the pop-up menu are

✦ *Copy of Current File:* Creates a backup copy of the current database with all records intact

✦ *Compressed Copy (smaller):* Creates a compressed backup copy of the current database with all records intact

Note

Although they aren't used to create clones, these two additional Save options are very useful in their own right. For more information about these options, see Chapter 2.

Mac

Windows

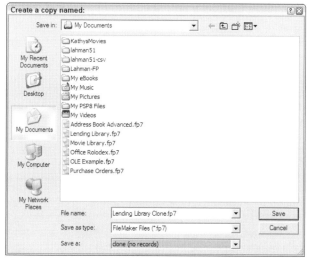

Figure 17-4: Saving a clone of the current database.

Avoiding that blank look (in your templates and on users' faces)

There's nothing so potentially confusing to a new user as a blank screen. To avoid causing a panic, you can make one small modification to your template before handing or selling it to a user: Add a single new record and then close the file. When users open the file, they will see whatever you originally intended them to see, such as a blank data-entry form for record #1 or an opening menu.

Working with a New Template

The only difference between a database and a template (or clone) is that the latter contains no records. This presents one immediate problem for many users: When a template is first opened, the database window's fields might be blank. Because a template initially contains no records, FileMaker Pro might have nothing to display other than an empty database window.

To begin working with the template, choose Records ➪ New Record (or press ⌘+N/Ctrl+N). The opening layout immediately appears, and you can get down to business.

Summary

✦ By using any of a number of methods, you can install FileMaker Pro templates and databases that you obtain from others. The most common methods include running a special installation or file-extraction program, running a separate file-extraction utility, and making a copy from the Finder or Windows Explorer.

✦ To adapt a database for use as a template, you clone it by using the Save a Copy As command. The file dialog has a Clone (no records) option that omits records from the new copy. In FileMaker Pro, the terms *template* and *clone* are used interchangeably.

✦ When working with a clone or template, you might have to create the first record in order to make the various layouts appear.

✦   ✦   ✦

Mastering
FileMaker Pro

Linking Tables: Relationships and Lookups

Since version 3.0, FileMaker Pro has been fully relational. This means that any database can draw information from any *related tables* (ones with matching data in a key field, such as a customer identification number, a part number, or a Social Security number). This has some important implications for how you create databases. From FileMaker Pro 3 through FileMaker Pro 6, though, each FileMaker Pro file contained precisely one table, and there were few tools (and no good ones) to document the relationships between different tables. FileMaker Pro 7 introduced a massive simplification to the process of maintaining a relational database.

First, related tables are smaller and easier to maintain than the monolithic single-table database required in the early versions of FileMaker Pro. Rather than stuffing every possible field into each table, you can divide the information among several smaller tables. For example, address information for your customers, clients, or suppliers can be kept in an Address table that is separate from an Invoices table. In that way, a person's address need only be entered once (in the Address table) and then simply referenced in an Invoices database or Accounting database. Related data stays in the table in which it is entered, regardless of how many different related tables reference it. When you request data that is in a related table, it is displayed only onscreen rather than copied into the target table.

As with previous versions of FileMaker Pro, lookups are still supported as an alternative to relationships. A lookup works similarly to a relationship, but instead of merely displaying the related data, the data is actually copied into the target table. Because lookups are actually preferable in some (increasingly rare) cases, you should be sure to read the following section so you understand the differences between lookups and relationships.

Lookups versus Relationships

Here's how a lookup works: When you make an entry in a key field in the primary table, a search is done in a secondary table. FileMaker Pro locates the first record containing a match for the key field, and data is then copied from a selected field in the secondary table into a specified field in the primary database.

For example, suppose you have two databases named Orders and Addresses. Both databases have a Customer ID field. Three lookups are defined as being dependent on the Customer ID field: Name, Mailing Address, and Phone. When a new order is taken, you create a new record in the Orders table and type a number into the Customer ID field. This triggers the three lookups, causing FileMaker Pro to search the Addresses table for a matching Customer ID number. When the ID number is found, the customer's name, address, and phone number are copied into the appropriate fields in the primary database.

Lookups have some drawbacks:

✦ The looked-up data is physically copied from the secondary database into the primary database, resulting in data duplication and additional storage requirements.

✦ If the data in the secondary file changes, the primary data does *not* change unless you reexecute the lookup.

✦ Even if multiple matches exist for the key field, FileMaker identifies only the *first* match that it finds and then uses its data.

On the other hand, lookups have one feature that's occasionally very useful. Looked-up data that is copied into the primary file will not change unless you trigger the lookup a second time or do a blanket relookup for the found set (described later in "Performing a relookup"). Sometimes this is exactly what you want. For example, looked-up price information in an invoice shouldn't change when the prices change. (You can't pass on an after-the-fact price increase.) Lookups are discussed in the second part of this chapter.

When lookups aren't the answer to your development needs, you can use relationships instead. The advantages of relationships include the following:

✦ Related data is not copied into the primary table; it is merely referenced. This avoids unnecessary duplication.

✦ Related data is automatically updated whenever it changes. You don't have to do anything to trigger an update.

✦ In addition to the one-to-one correspondence between records that is offered by lookups, relationships can be one-to-many. By using a general field, such as Department as a key field, multiple matching records can be drawn from the related table (all personnel in the Accounting Department, for instance).

✦ You can define relationships so there is two-way communication between the tables. For example, deletions in the primary table can be carried through to the related table.

✦ FileMaker Pro 7 introduced the ability to specify relationships based on conditions other than equality. For example, you can create a less-than-or-equal relationship matching all the secondary table records where the key field's value is no greater than the first table's key field value.

Perhaps the easiest way to understand the differences between relationships and lookups is by looking at an example. Figure 18-1 shows three databases — each containing one table — that a hypothetical video rental store uses to create and print customer invoices.

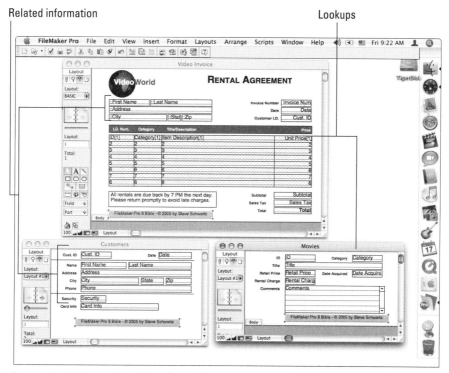

Figure 18-1: Three related database files.

On The Web Site

The example database depicted in Figure 18-1 is on this book's Web site in two forms: Traditional (multiple file) and Consolidated (using the multiple tables in one file feature).

In this example, Video Invoice (top) is the main database table. When a customer wishes to rent a movie, game, or piece of equipment, a clerk creates a new record in Video Invoice and then completes this form.

The Customers table (bottom left) contains only customer information, such as the name and address, phone number, customer identification number, and security deposit/credit card information. When a customer opens an account with Video World, the clerk records this information. Similarly, if the customer moves, changes his or her name, or wants to change the security deposit information (switching to a different credit card, for instance), the changes are made in the customer record. As the figure shows, the name and address are displayed in the Video Invoice table as relations. Thus, if a customer's address changes in the Customers database, the owner can be assured that every invoice for the customer displays the current address (making it easy to locate overdue rentals, if the need arises).

The Movies table (bottom right) contains a separate record for each rental item (movies, video games, and equipment). Each item has a unique identification number as well as its current rental price. As indicated in the figure, items in the Movies table are copied into each appropriate record in the Video Invoice file via lookups. This makes each invoice line item a permanent entry. When the rental charge for an item changes (because of a sale or a change in policy, for example), only new invoices will reflect the new price. Outstanding invoices will retain their original rental charges — as, of course, they must.

Tip   One way to determine whether you want a relation or a lookup is to decide whether you want the information's current state displayed or whether you want a snapshot-in-time displayed. In the former case, use a relation; in the latter, use a lookup.

Note   In the Invoice example, if the address information is used for shipping, you should probably use a lookup so that your records will indicate where the goods were shipped. This sort of decision-making is crucial to correctly deciding whether to use a lookup or relation. In some cases, you might want both on a layout even though they will often be redundant.

After defining the fields for the three tables, it is a simple matter to define the relationships between the tables. Be aware that fields in a related table can't be added to the layout until the relationship is created, so the customer's address information fields aren't yet on the layout.

STEPS: Defining Relationships When Tables Are in Separate Files

1. With your main (root) database open (Video Invoice), choose File ➪ Define ➪ Database and click the Relationships tab.

   The Relationships Graph appears, as shown in Figure 18-2.

Relationships Graph

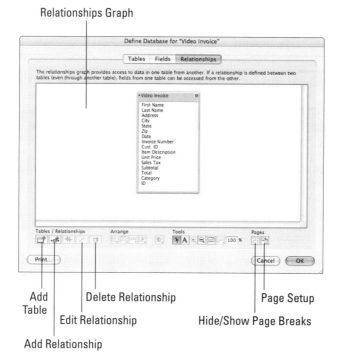

Add Table

Add Relationship

Edit Relationship

Delete Relationship

Page Setup

Hide/Show Page Breaks

Figure 18-2: You can define or revise relationships in the Relationships Graph.

2. Click the Add Table button to define the first relationship.

   The Specify Table dialog (see Figure 18-3) appears.

3. From the File pop-up menu/drop-down list, choose Add File Reference.

   An Open File dialog appears.

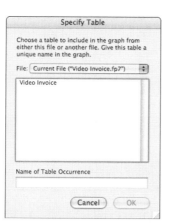

Figure 18-3: Specify tables to include in the Relationships Graph here.

4. Navigate to and select the database containing the table you wish to reference (Customers, in this case). The Specify Table dialog appears with the table selected.

5. Click OK to dismiss the Specify Table dialog.

The Customers table appears in the Relationships Graph.

Note   By default, tables in the graph receive the same name they had in the Specify Table dialog's list of tables; however, you can assign another name in the Relationships Graph by entering it in the Specify Table dialog's Name of Table Occurrence text box.

6. You can now drag the field on which the relationship will be based from one table onto its counterpart in the other table, as shown in Figure 18-4, resulting in the *key fields* (relationship-specifying fields) appearing in a pane at the top of the tables' field lists, with a line between them specifying the kind of relationship defined, as shown in Figure 18-5.

or

Click the Add Relationship button (refer to Figure 18-2), which presents the Edit Relationship dialog shown in Figure 18-6.

  a. Choose the tables you want joined from the Table pop-up menus/drop-down lists.

  b. Specify the type of relationship (this is usually an equality relationship, called an *equijoin*) from the pop-up menu between the two field lists.

  c. Select the pair of fields in the two databases that defines a set of matching records (in this case, Cust. ID and Cust. ID).

  d. Click the Add button.

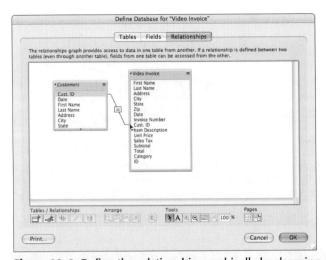

Figure 18-4: Define the relationship graphically by dragging the key field from one table to the other.

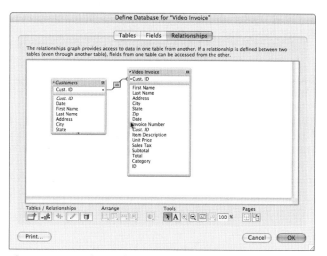

Figure 18-5: Relationship-defining fields appear in a scrollable area at the top of their tables and a line connects them.

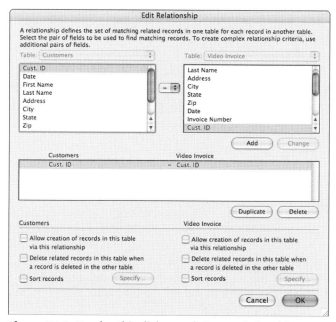

Figure 18-6: Employ this dialog to define a relationship between two tables.

The relationship appears in the list in the center of the dialog.

Note

There is no requirement that the matching fields have the same name — although in this instance, they do.

Note A small scroll arrow at the bottom of a table in the Relationships Graph indicates that not all fields are visible, as shown in Figure 18-5's Customers table (and/or at the top of the field list pane, if you've already scrolled down).

7. *Optional:* To enable the user to delete or create records in the related table (Customers) by making changes in the primary table (Video Invoice), select the appropriate check boxes below Customers at the bottom of the Edit Relationship dialog. (If the Edit Relationship dialog is not open, double-click the relationship's icon in the graph.) Analogously, if you have a layout where Customers is the primary table and you want the ability to create or delete invoice records (suppose you've archived the data and wish to remove it from the database), select the check boxes below Video Invoice.

8. *Optional:* If you'd like the related records to be sorted in a particular way when they are displayed, select one or both Sort Records check boxes. Establish a sort order in the Sort Records dialog (just as you do with the Records ⇨ Sort command), and click OK.

9. Click OK to record the first relationship.

10. Repeat Steps 2–9, defining the Video Invoice database's relationship with the Movies database. (In this example, the two matching fields are both named ID.)

After you define both relationships, the Relationships Graph looks something like Figure 18-7.

11. Click OK.

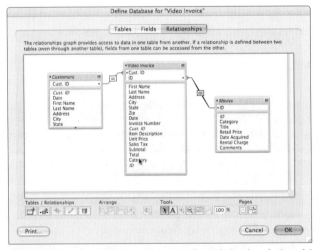

Figure 18-7: The Relationships Graph with both relationships defined.

When you create tables in a FileMaker Pro 8 database file, those tables automatically appear in the Relationships Graph, so there is no need to add file references to external files in order to define relationships between tables. The following steps, therefore, are going to be quite similar, albeit shorter.

STEPS: Defining Relationships When Tables Are in the Same File

1. With your database open, choose File ➪ Define ➪ Database and click the Relationships tab.

   The Relationships Graph appears.

2. You can now drag the field on which the relationship will be based from one table onto its counterpart in the other table, as shown in Figure 18-4, resulting in the *key fields* (relationship-specifying fields) appearing in a pane at the top of the tables' field lists, with a line between them specifying the kind of relationship defined, as shown in Figure 18-5.

   or

   Click the Add Relationship button, which presents the Edit Relationship dialog shown in Figure 18-6.

   a. Choose the tables you want joined from the Table pop-up menus/drop-down lists.

   b. Specify the type of relationship (this is usually an equality relationship, called an *equijoin*) from the pop-up menu between the two field lists.

   c. Select the pair of fields in the two tables that defines a set of matching records (in this case, Cust. ID and Cust. ID).

   d. Click the Add button.

   The relationship appears in the list in the center of the dialog.

3. *Optional:* To enable the user to delete or create records in the related table (Customers) by making changes in the primary table (Video Invoice), select the appropriate check boxes below Customers at the bottom of the dialog. Analogously, if you might have a layout where Customers is the primary table and you want the ability to create or delete invoice records (suppose you've archived the data and wish to remove it from the database), select the check boxes below Video Invoice.

4. *Optional:* If you'd like the related records to be sorted in a particular way when they are displayed, select one or both Sort Records check boxes in the Edit Relationship dialog (open it by double-clicking the relationship's icon if it isn't open). Establish a sort order in the Sort Records dialog (just as you do with the Records ➪ Sort command), and click OK.

5. Click OK to record the first relationship.

6. Repeat Steps 2–5, defining the Video Invoice table's relationship with the Movies table. (In this example, the two matching fields are both named ID.) After you've defined both relationships, the Relationships Graph looks like Figure 18-7.

These steps establish that there are two separate relationships: one between the Video Invoice and Customers tables and one between the Video Invoice and Movies tables, each relationship based on different match fields (Cust. ID and ID, respectively).

To specify the fields whose data will be copied to Video Invoice when matches are identified (in the case of rental item lookups) and the fields whose data will merely be displayed in Video Invoice (in the case of the customer name and address relations), options are set for the lookup fields in the Define Database dialog's Fields pane, and the related fields are placed in a layout for Video Invoice.

The Category, Item Description, and Unit Price fields will be defined as lookups, based on the Movies relationship.

STEPS: Defining the Lookups

1. Select the Video Invoice file, choose File ➪ Define ➪ Database, and select the Fields tab.

   The Fields pane appears.

2. Select the Category field in the field list and then click the Options button.

   The Options for Field Category dialog appears.

3. In the Auto-Enter section of the dialog, select the Looked-up Value check box.

   The Lookup for Field Category dialog appears, as shown in Figure 18-8.

4. In the Lookup from related table pop-up menu/drop-down list, choose the Movies table.

5. In the field list, choose Category as the field to copy from in the Movies table. Then click OK twice to return to the Define Database dialog's Fields pane.

Note

Fields accessed via a relationship (rather than a lookup) from a related table have a pair of colons added to the front of their names, allowing you to readily identify them when working in Layout mode.

6. Repeat Steps 2–5 to define the lookups for Item Description and Unit Price.

   The fields from which to copy data in the Movies database are Title and Rental Charge, respectively.

7. Click OK to close the Define Database dialog.

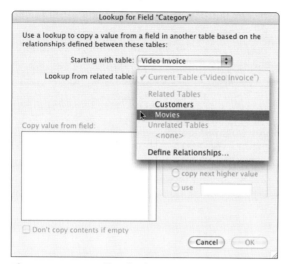

Figure 18-8: Specify a lookup in this dialog.

If you were to examine the Video Invoice file in Layout mode, you'd note that the field names in the line item section of the invoice are unchanged. They still appear as Category, Item Description, and Unit Price even though they will now be filled in via lookups triggered by typing an item's ID number at the beginning of each invoice line.

Related fields are defined a little differently from lookups. You have two options:

✦ Place the fields directly on the layout.

✦ Use the Portal tool to draw a rectangle on the layout and then place the fields in the portal.

In this example, you'll place the individual related customer name and address fields directly onto the Video Invoice layout. (Using a portal is explained later in this chapter.)

STEPS: Adding the Related Fields to the Layout

1. Bring the Video Invoice database to the front and switch to Layout mode.

2. Select the Field tool from the Tools palette and drag a blank field onto the layout.

   The Specify Field dialog appears, as shown in Figure 18-9.

Figure 18-9: The Specify Field dialog.

3. Choose Customers from the pop-up menu/drop-down list at the top of the dialog.

   This indicates that you are basing the selected field on the previously defined Customers relationship and that you will be choosing a field from the Customers file.

4. Choose the First Name field, remove the check mark from the Create field label check box, and click OK.

   The field you just placed on the layout is now labeled First Name. (A pair of colons precedes the name, indicating that it is a related field.)

5. Repeat Steps 2–4 to create and place additional fields for Last Name, Address, City, State, and Zip. Arrange the fields so that they form the address section of the layout.

If you were defining one-to-many joins rather than the one-to-one joins used here, you would place the related fields in a portal on the layout (drawn with the Portal tool). Related fields in a portal display *all* matches rather than just the first one found. For example, you could use a portal to show the names and rental charges of all inventory items of a given type (new movies or comedies starring Chevy Chase, for example).

Now that all the necessary fields have been defined and placed in the data entry layout for Video Invoice, here's what happens when a clerk creates a new customer invoice.

1. FileMaker Pro automatically fills in the invoice number and today's date.

2. The clerk asks for the customer's membership number, enters it in the Customer ID field, and presses Tab to move to the first line item.

3. Tabbing out of the Customer ID field causes FileMaker Pro to search for a matching ID number in the Customers database. When a match is found, the customer's name and address information is automatically filled in on the invoice. If a match is not found, the clerk creates a new record in the Customers database for this customer.

   If the Allow creation of related records check box was selected for this relationship definition, the clerk could enter the name and address information directly on the invoice form, thus simultaneously generating a new record for the customer in the Customers database.

Tip
It sometimes isn't a good idea to allow creation of a record for a related database, as was suggested earlier (creating a customer record from the Video Invoice form). Most of the time, not all the fields you want to record are displayed and enterable on the related database form. For example, the Video Invoice form does not include the customer's phone number—clearly an important field. Instead, it might be better to create a button with a script (see Chapter 15) on the Video Invoice form that takes you directly to the Customer form, where you can enter all the customer information. Then come back to the Video Invoice form and enter this customer's ID (which will then exist).

Here are some additional details concerning the design and use of the three related databases (Video Invoice, Customers, and Movies):

✦ The Video Invoice database has a single layout, devoted to creating the rental statements that customers receive when they rent movies, games, or video-related equipment (such as VCRs, DVD players, and video game systems).

✦ The Customers database contains customer-specific information, including a customer identification number, the date the customer record was created or last modified, name and address data, and information on the security deposit. The deposit information includes the form of the deposit (cash or a specific credit card) and a credit card number (if the deposit was made with a credit card). A unique customer identification number is automatically assigned whenever a new record is created: that is, when this information is taken from a new customer.

Note
The Cust. ID field is an auto-entry field. A new serial number is assigned to each record by incrementing the previous record's serial number by 13. The numbers assigned to the sample records are 1013, 1026, 1039, and 1052. (For more information on creating auto-entry fields, see Chapter 5.)

✦ The Movies database contains a separate record for every movie, video game, and piece of equipment the store rents. Every item gets its own identification number which, like Cust. ID, is automatically assigned when the record is created.

Note The ID field in the Movies database is also an auto-entry field. The ID numbers begin with 1000, and the number is incremented by 1 for each new record. The numbers assigned to the sample records are 1000–1009.

✦ Other information that can be recorded for each movie, game, or piece of equipment includes a category (Movie, Game, or Equipment) chosen from a pop-up menu, a title, the retail price, the date acquired, the current daily rental charge, and comments. (Equipment can optionally be identified by a serial number.)

All lookups and relationships are performed from the Video Invoice database. When a customer is ready to check out, the clerk chooses Records ➪ New Record or presses ⌘+N/Ctrl+N to create a new rental statement in Video Invoice. FileMaker Pro generates a new invoice number, and today's date is automatically entered on the form. Next, the clerk asks for the individual's customer number and enters it in the Cust. ID field. (If you want to try out the database, you can enter any of the following numbers into this field: 1013, 1026, 1039, or 1052.)

Cust. ID is the field used to define the relationship with the Customers database. The moment the clerk tabs out of the Cust. ID field or presses Enter, FileMaker Pro searches the Customers database for a record containing a match in the Cust. ID field. If it finds a match, the customer's name and address information are automatically filled in. On the other hand, if a match is not found, the clerk knows that the customer has an invalid number or that a search of the Customers database must be performed.

After FileMaker Pro has copied the address data onto the form, it automatically positions the cursor in the first ID field. When the clerk types the first item's identification number (a movie ID, for example) and tabs to the next field, this action triggers a lookup. (To ensure that a match is found in the sample data, you can enter any number between 1000 and 1009.) FileMaker Pro searches the Movies database for a record having a matching ID. When it locates that record, it fills in the rest of the information for that item (category, title, and daily price).

Note Both the Cust. ID and ID fields also have the Unique Value option selected (on the Validation tab of the field's Options for Field dialog). This prevents you from creating multiple customer records or having rental item records sharing IDs. This sort of relationship is called *one-to-many* because there could be many Video Invoice records related to a single customer, but only one customer can have the Cust. ID used on an invoice. This is denoted in the Relationships Graph (see Figure 18-7) by a single line going into the Customer table's Cust. ID field but a branched line going into the Video Invoice table's Cust. ID field.

If the customer wants to rent additional items, the clerk enters them in the same manner as the first item. Because the body of the rental agreement comprises repeating fields, every entry in the ID field triggers a lookup for that particular rental item. As the clerk enters items, the subtotal, sales tax, and total are instantly updated. (In this example, the sales tax is set as 7 percent on all video rental items, so it is calculated by multiplying the subtotal by .07 and rounding.)

After checking the rental statement to make sure it contains no errors, the clerk prints the customer's copy by choosing the File ⇨ Print command and selecting Current Record as the data to be printed. (If this database were used by an actual rental store, it would undoubtedly include a printing script that automatically chose Current Record — or possibly, one to e-mail a PDF of the current record to the customer.)

Whenever the rental price of an item changes (charging less for older movies than for current ones is a common practice, for example), the storeowner simply opens the Movies database, locates the record, and then enters the new rental price. Similarly, if a customer moves or loses rental privileges, the owner or a clerk can edit or delete a customer's record in the Customers database.

Among other things, these databases demonstrate the following:

✦ A relationship can cause multiple related or lookup fields to be displayed. When a Cust. ID is typed into a record in the Video Invoice database, all the following lookups are triggered: First Name, Last Name, Address, City, State, and Zip.

✦ A database can have multiple relationships, each one triggering one or several lookups and/or relations. The Video Invoice database contains two such fields: Cust. ID (which displays the customer's name and address) and ID (which looks up the category, title, and price information for each rental item).

✦ A single database can be linked (via relationships) to multiple databases. Video Invoice is linked to both the Customers database and the Movies database.

✦ When a repeating field is used as a match or key field, every repetition triggers another lookup or relationship. In Video Invoice, an entry in any of the eight repetitions of ID triggers a lookup for that invoice line.

✦ When tables are linked by a relationship, even to tables in other files, you do not have to open the other files before you use them. As long as the files have not been moved and the necessary disks are mounted, FileMaker Pro can access data in them.

Prior to FileMaker Pro 7, relationships had to be *direct:* That is, a layout based on Table A could access data from Table B only if Table A and Table B had a relationship defined between them. In FileMaker Pro 7 and later, the relationship can be *indirect,* meaning that if there is a sequence (path) of relationships between Table A and Table B, the data is accessible. A familiar analogy would be that in previous versions, you could only access tables that were immediate family; you can now communicate with cousins and in-laws as well.

Going Relational with FileMaker Pro

For end-users and developers who need the functionality FileMaker Pro's relational capabilities afford, there are fewer reasons to choose another database program. These features make FileMaker Pro a ready match for all but a few very expensive, high-end database management systems.

If you don't think you're ready for relational databases — many of us are very comfortable with FileMaker Pro's flat-file capabilities — there's nothing new you have to learn. The relational features are there if you need them and stay out of the way if you don't.

On The Web Site

Find a bonus on this book's Web site — a FileMaker Pro 8 version of Sean Lahman's baseball statistics database, previously only available in Microsoft Access 2000 and text (comma-separated values) form. Because Sean wants to make certain that you get the most up-to-date version of the data, you can find the data, ready for import, at www.baseball1.com. We are also providing Sean with the database in FileMaker Pro 8 format for inclusion on his Web site (in case you would rather download a fully populated database weighing in at over 40MB). See Appendix F for details about the Web site.

Defining a relationship

To work with related files in FileMaker Pro, you need to do just two things:

✦ Define the relationship (or relationships).

✦ Place the related fields in a layout in the current database.

STEPS: Defining a Relationship

1. Choose File ⇨ Define ⇨ Database and select the Relationships tab.

   The Relationships Graph appears (as shown previously in Figure 18-2). If this database already has any relationships, they are listed in this graph.

2. If the table to which you want to define a relationship is not already in the graph

   a. Click the Add Table button.

      The Specify Table dialog appears, and you can select a table from the pop-up menu/drop-down list or choose Add File Reference to locate the file containing the table(s) you seek.

   b. Choose a table from the list and click OK.

3. Click the Add Relationship button.

   The Edit Relationship dialog appears.

4. Choose the tables you wish to relate from the two Table pop-up menus/drop-down lists.

5. Choose a pair of match fields that will define the relationship — one from the left-hand field list (from the current database) and one from the right-hand field list (from the related database). Also, if your relationship is to be based on a condition other than equality, choose that condition from the pop-up menu between the two field lists.

When FileMaker Pro later uses the relationship to check for related records, it matches data from the first field with data in the second field, according to the comparison condition in effect.

6. *Optional:* To create a two-way link between the current table and the data in the related table, you can select the check boxes allowing creation and deletion of records.

7. *Optional:* If you'd like the related records to be sorted in a particular way when they are displayed, select the Sort records check box. Establish a sort order in the Sort Records dialog (see Figure 18-10), and click OK.

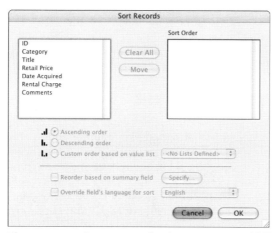

Figure 18-10: Set a sort order, just as you would if issuing the Records ➪ Sort command.

8. Click OK to save your changes and dismiss the Edit Relationship dialog. Otherwise, click Cancel to ignore all changes.

9. Repeat Steps 2–8 for any additional relationships you wish to define.

10. When you are through defining relationships, click OK.

If you later want to change a relationship (modifying its name, the match fields, or the options), choose File ➪ Define ➪ Database, click the Relationships tab, and double-click the relationship icon in the Relationships Graph to display the Edit Relationship dialog. You can also duplicate or delete existing relationships by selecting the relationship and clicking the appropriate buttons (Duplicate and Delete) in the Relationships pane.

In addition to using the Relationships Graph to specify relationships for a database, note that you can create them on the fly in almost any dialog containing a field list. Just choose Define Database from the pop-up menu/drop-down list above the field list, as shown in the example in Figure 18-11.

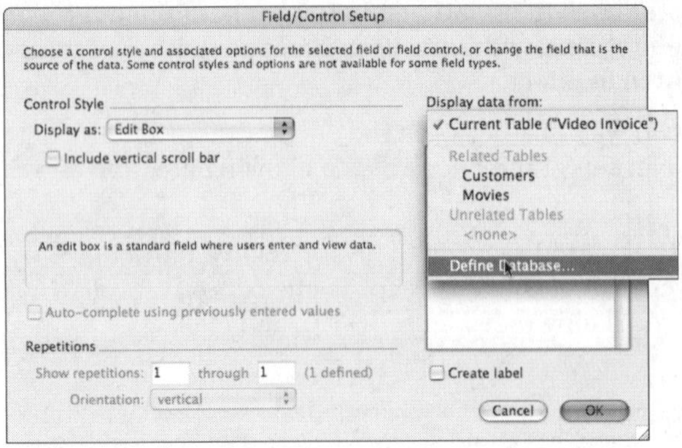

Figure 18-11: Defining a relationship from the Field/Control Setup dialog.

Placing related fields in a layout

One major difference (maybe the major difference) from pre-FileMaker Pro 7 versions is that a single database file on disk can now contain an arbitrary number of tables instead of exactly one table. One consequence of this change appears when you create a layout. In previous versions of FileMaker Pro, the layout's primary table was the file's table, without exception. In FileMaker Pro 7 and 8, when you create a new layout, the New Layout/Report dialog is headed by a Show records from pop-up menu/drop-down list, as illustrated in Figure 18-12. You choose the layout's primary table from this menu/list.

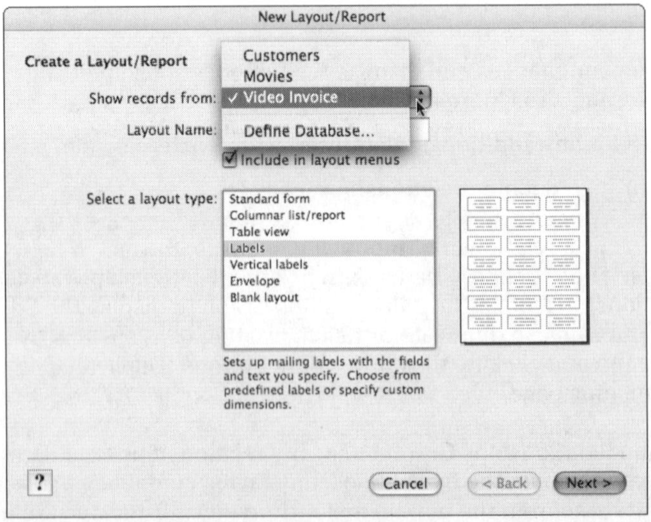

Figure 18-12: Specify a layout's primary table with the Show records from pop-up menu/drop-down list.

Here are two ways you can make data from a related table appear in a layout for the current table:

✦ Place related fields directly on the layout.

✦ Create a portal on the layout and then place the related fields in the portal.

The decision concerning which approach is best for a given relationship is not an arbitrary one, however. If records in the two databases have a one-to-one correspondence with each other (only one customer has the same ID number, for example), you should place the related fields directly onto the layout. On the other hand, if you are establishing a one-to-many relationship (you might have many contacts at a particular company, for example), you should place the related fields in a portal. Only a portal can display multiple matching records for the same key field.

STEPS: Placing Related Fields Directly on the Layout

1. Open the database that includes the defined relationship.

2. Switch to Layout mode by choosing View ➪ Layout Mode (or by pressing ⌘+L/Ctrl+L).

3. From the status area's Layout menu, choose the layout in which you want to display the related information.

4. Select the Tools palette's Field tool and drag a field rectangle on the layout.

   The Specify Field dialog appears (as shown previously in Figure 18-9).

5. From the pop-up menu/drop-down list above the field list, select the name of the related table.

   The field list changes to display only fields that have been defined for the related table (rather than for the current table). A pair of colons precedes the names of related fields: for example, ::Last Name.

6. Select the name of the related field you want to place on the current layout.

7. If you want a field label to be created for the field automatically, select the Create field label check box.

8. Click OK to place the chosen field on the layout, or click Cancel if you change your mind.

   The related field appears on the layout. You can now resize it, alter its formatting, or change its position, as necessary or desired.

STEPS: Placing Related Fields in a Portal

1. Open the database that includes the defined relationship.

2. Switch to Layout mode.

3. From the status area's Layout menu, choose the layout in which you want to display the related information.

4. Select the Portal tool from the Tools palette and then click and drag to create the portal. Release the mouse button when the portal is the correct size. (Every portal is rectangular.) FileMaker Pro opens the Portal Setup dialog. (See Figure 18-13.)

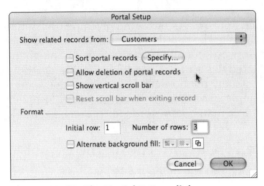

Figure 18-13: The Portal Setup dialog.

5. Use the Show related records from pop-up menu/drop-down list to choose the related table from which the portal's fields will be drawn. If no relationship is correct or you have yet to define the relationship, choose Define Database from the menu/list to create a new relationship (as discussed earlier in this chapter).

6. If you want to be able to delete related records in the portal by selecting them and choosing Records ⇨ Delete Record (⌘+E/Ctrl+E), select the Allow deletion of portal records check box. If you want the portal's records displayed in a particular order, select the Sort portal records check box (or click its accompanying Specify button) and define the sort as previously described.

7. *Optional:* If you want a vertical scroll bar displayed for use when there is more data than can be displayed in the space allocated, select the Show vertical scroll bar check box. You can select whether the scroll bar will be reset when exiting the current record—this is a choice between leaving the portal scrolled or resetting it to display the first matching record at the top.

8. In the Portal Setup dialog's Format section, specify the first row you want to show and the number of rows you want to show. You can also elect to alternate the rows of the portal with a background color and/or pattern. (Distinguishing the rows can make them easier to read.)

9. When you're done, click OK to dismiss the Portal Setup dialog.

10. Select the Field tool from the Tools palette and drag a field icon into the white, top row of the portal. It must reside completely within the top, white portal row for it to be represented in the portal.

The Specify Field dialog appears (as shown previously in Figure 18-9).

11. Choose the related table from the pop-up menu/drop-down list above the field list.

The field list changes to display only fields from the related table (rather than from the current table). A pair of colons precedes the names of related fields: for example, ::Last Name.

12. Select a related field to place on the current layout.

13. If you want a label for the field to be created automatically, select the Create field label check box.

14. Click OK to place the chosen field on the layout, or click Cancel if you change your mind.

15. Repeat Steps 10–14 to add other related fields to the portal, as required.

Figure 18-14 shows what a portal looks like in Layout mode and in Browse mode. To make it easy to determine which fields are being displayed in the portal, their field labels have been dragged above the portal. As you can see, each related record is displayed on a separate line in the portal. If there are many related records, the scroll bar at the right can be used to view records that are currently out of view.

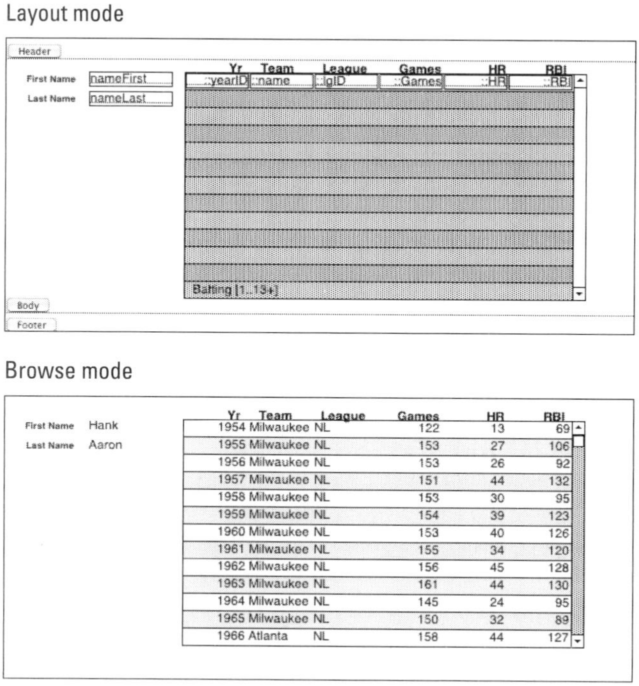

Layout mode

Browse mode

Figure 18-14: A fully defined portal in Layout mode (top) and Browse mode (bottom).

Tip

If you'd like to number the items displayed in a portal, issue the Insert ➪ Record Number Symbol command and drag the record number symbol (@@) into the portal. When viewed in Browse or Preview mode (and when printed), the portal records will automatically be numbered.

Self-joins

FileMaker Pro will also let you create a relationship within a single table rather than with a second table. This is referred to as a *self-join*. Understanding self-joins can be (at least) as difficult as understanding relationships. For example, under what circumstances would you want to create a self-join? When would you use one?

Here's a practical example: A realty company has a property listing database in which each home, office building, or lot is assigned to a primary salesperson. By defining the Sales Person field as *both* sides of the match and then adding a portal to the layout, whenever any of a given salesperson's listings are displayed, the portal could show *all* of that salesperson's listings (see Figure 18-15). The explanation of how to create this database is presented as follows.

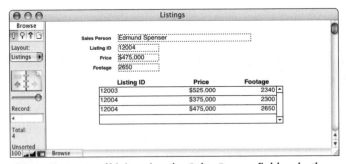

Figure 18-15: A self-join using the Sales Person field as both match fields conveniently displays all the salesperson's listings in the portal (sorted by the Listing ID).

STEPS: Creating the Listings Database

1. Create a new database named Listings.fp7.

2. Define the following fields (field types are shown in brackets): Sales Person [Text], Listing ID [Number], Price [Number], and Footage [Number].

3. Click the Relationships tab.

   The Relationships Graph appears (as shown in Figure 18-16).

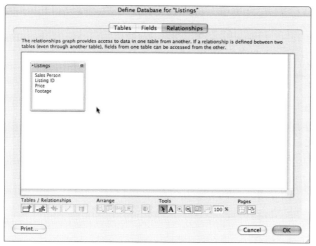

Figure 18-16: The Relationships Graph.

4. Click the Add Relationship button.

5. In the Edit Relationship dialog that appears, choose Listings from both Table pop-up menus/drop-down lists.

6. Select Sales Person and Sales Person as the match fields and click Add.

7. Select the right-hand Sort records check box.

   The Sort Records dialog appears.

8. Select Listing ID as the sort field, click Move, and then click OK.

9. Click OK to return to the Relationships Graph and then click OK.

   You're presented with the Add Relationship dialog. Click OK and then click OK again to dismiss the Define Database dialog

10. To make it simple to choose each salesperson's name when creating new records, you can create a value list based on and associated with the Sales Person field. Choose File ➪ Define ➪ Value Lists.

    The Define Value Lists dialog appears.

11. Click the New button.

12. In the Edit Value List dialog, name the value list Sales Person and select the Use values from field radio button.

    The Specify Fields for Value List dialog appears.

13. Choose the Listings table from the Use values from first field pop-up menu/drop-down list.

14. Select Sales Person as the field to use (in the left side of the dialog) and then click OK.

15. To dismiss the remaining dialogs, click OK and then click OK again.

16. Switch to Layout Mode by choosing View ⇨ Layout Mode.

17. Select the Sales Person field on the layout and choose Format ⇨ Field/Control ⇨ Setup (Opt+⌘+F/Ctrl+Alt+F).

18. In the Field/Control Setup dialog's Control Style section, choose Display as drop-down list and Display values from Sales Person. Click OK to dismiss the dialog.

19. Click the Portal tool and draw a portal beneath the current fields.

20. In the Portal Setup dialog, choose Listings 2 from the Show related records from pop-up menu/drop-down list and click OK.

    The Add Fields to Portal dialog appears.

21. Select the Listing ID, Price, and Footage fields. (Make sure that you are choosing from among the *related* fields. The pop-up menu/drop-down list should show the name of the relationship: that is, Listings 2.) Click OK.

22. Resize the fields in the portal (or the portal itself) as needed. Create text labels for the three portal fields above the portal, letting them serve as column headings.

23. To format the portal, double-click a blank area of the portal or choose Format ⇨ Portal Setup.

24. In the Portal Setup dialog, indicate the number of rows to show (4, for example) and other desired formatting options, such as displaying a scroll bar. Click OK when you are done.

25. Switch to Browse mode (View ⇨ Browse Mode) and create some records. All data should be entered in the top four fields: Sales Person, Listing ID, Price, and Footage. Create several records for each salesperson and be sure to use a given listing ID once. (If you were really going to use this database in business and wanted to prevent duplication, you would want to set the Listing ID field's Unique value validation option.)

26. To view all listings for a salesperson, all you have to do is display *any* of the salesperson's records. The portal at the bottom of the record will display all of her or his listings, sorted by the Listing ID.

Two other popular uses for self-joins are parts explosions and genealogies. For other self-join examples, search for *self-join* in the FileMaker, Inc. TechInfo Knowledge Base (www.filemaker.com/support/techinfo.html).

Many-to-many relationships

You can also establish many-to-many relationships in FileMaker Pro 8. For example, a school administrator might have two tables: Classes and Students. In each class are multiple students, and each student is enrolled in multiple classes. To manage such a situation, a third table is typically created (referred to as a *join table*). Relationships are established from each database to the intermediary join table. For an example of handling many-to-many relationships without using a join file, read the TechInfo Knowledge Base article 2949 at `http://filemaker.custhelp.com/cgi-bin/filemaker.cfg/php/enduser/std_alp.php`. (It's slightly dated, discussing the techniques employed with earlier, one-table-per-file FileMaker Pro versions, but those techniques still work.)

Working with Lookups

In order to execute a lookup, you need to have a pair of matching fields in two tables. As described previously in this chapter, you specify the matching fields by defining a relationship, just as you do when working with related data rather than lookups. Both fields must store the same kind of information, such as Social Security numbers. In general, the information in the matching fields should be unique because the lookup will access only the first match found.

The moment you enter or edit information in the field on which the lookup is based, FileMaker Pro automatically performs any lookups you have associated with that field. Often, a field triggers a single lookup. For example, typing an inventory part number could result in a lookup of the part's price. You can also associate multiple lookups with the same field. Entering an inventory part number could just as easily trigger lookups of the part name, color, description, and price, for instance.

Here's an extended example: Suppose you have two tables you want to link via lookups. The first is an Orders database. The order entry form serving as the main layout for Orders has a field in it called Customer Code. Customer information (including names and addresses) is kept in a separate table called Customers. A unique identification code, which is assigned when a customer first places an order, identifies each record in the Customers table. You define each of the name and address fields in Orders as lookup fields that are triggered by an entry in the Customer Code field.

Whenever a customer calls in a new order, a salesperson creates a new record in Orders and enters the customer's ID number into the Customer Code field. FileMaker Pro then checks the Customers database for a record containing a matching ID. If it finds a matching ID, it automatically copies the name and address information for that customer into the current order form. As this example shows, nothing prevents you from defining several lookup fields, all activated by the same match field — in this case, Customer Code.

Figure 18-17 shows an example of the Lookup for Field *field name* dialog in which you set options for a field you're defining as a lookup field. To reach this dialog, choose File ⇨ Define ⇨ Database (or press Shift+⌘+D/Shift+Ctrl+D) and click the Fields tab, create or select the lookup field, and click the Options button. In the Options dialog that appears, click the Auto-Enter tab at the top of the dialog and then select the Looked-up value check box. (Clicking the Specify button to the right of Looked-up value also works.)

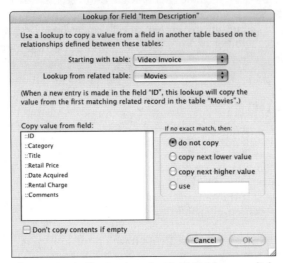

Figure 18-17: The Lookup for Field *field name* dialog.

You can learn several important things about lookups by examining Figure 18-17. First, when you define a field as a lookup field, you need to specify only three pieces of information:

✦ The table from which you start searching to locate the related table.

✦ The related table in which the data is looked up. (The relationship specifies the names of the two fields to be matched in the databases.)

✦ The field in the lookup file whose contents FileMaker Pro will copy into the current field.

Second, the Lookup for Field dialog enables you to specify what will happen if FileMaker does *not* find a match. (See the right-hand side of the dialog.) The default choice is to do nothing (do not copy). The next two choices (copy next lower value and copy next higher value) are often useful when you are performing lookups of numeric values. For example, when you want to determine the amount of postage that is necessary for a package, you could trigger a lookup in a postage rates database by entering a weight in the current database. Because postage is based on full ounces, you would use the Copy Next Higher Value option to take care of any weight that included a fraction of an ounce. Thus, entering **7.4** would return the value for 8 ounces.

The final option (use) enables you to specify a particular value or text string to enter when FileMaker Pro doesn't find a match. For example, if the lookup is supposed to return a consulting rate and you entered a new consulting code in the trigger field, you could instruct the lookup to return 100 (your usual hourly rate, right?). In the case of missing customer information, you could set this option to copy a message — such as New Customer or Client not found — into the field.

Finally, sometimes FileMaker Pro finds a match, but the field that's to be copied into the current file is blank. You can select the check box for Don't copy contents if empty (below the field list) to indicate what FileMaker Pro should do if it finds a match but the field to be copied is blank. This option is useful if you have hand-entered information into the current file and want to avoid having it replaced by blank data.

Defining lookup fields

Follow these steps to define a lookup field in your own database.

STEPS: Defining a Lookup Field

1. Open the database in which you want to define lookup fields.

2. Choose File ⇨ Define ⇨ Database (or press Shift+⌘+D/Shift+Ctrl+D) and click the Fields tab.

   The Define Database dialog's Fields pane appears.

3. In the field list, select the first field that you want to define as a lookup field and then click the Options button.

   The Options for Field *field name* dialog appears.

4. Click the Auto-Enter tab at the top of the dialog.

5. Select the Looked-up value check box (or click the Specify button to the right of the check box).

   The Lookup for Field *field name* dialog appears (as shown previously in Figure 18-17).

6. From the pop-up menus, select the starting table for the relation path and the related table you want FileMaker Pro to use.

The relationship defines the matching fields in the two files that will be used for the lookup. If you haven't already defined a relationship (as described in "Defining a relationship," earlier in this chapter), you can define one now by choosing Define Relationships from the pop-up menu above either field list.

7. Select the field to be copied from the Copy value from field list.

   The name of the chosen field does not need to be the same as the name of the field you're defining. What's important is that the fields contain similar content types.

8. Select a radio button in the right side of the dialog to indicate how you want to handle instances in which FileMaker Pro does not find an exact match.

   • Select do not copy if you want FileMaker Pro to do nothing at all. (This option is the default.)

   • Select copy next lower value or copy next higher value if you want FileMaker Pro to use the closest value it can find — either lower or higher (numerically or alphabetically). Be sure to use these options only in appropriate instances. If FileMaker Pro can't find a matching ID number, for example, would you really want it to copy data from the closest ID it can find?

   • Select use and then type a value or text string into the text box, specifying default data to be copied into the field.

9. To tell FileMaker not to copy a blank field into the current file, select the Don't copy contents if empty check box.

   Normally, if a lookup is performed and a match is found, FileMaker Pro copies the contents of the appropriate field into the field in the current file. Sometimes, however, the field from which data is to be copied from is blank or empty. If the field in the current file already contains data, copying an empty field into it would delete the contents of the current field. Selecting the Don't copy contents if empty option leaves the original data intact.

10. To accept the options you have set for the lookup field, click OK. To ignore any changes you have made to the field definition, click Cancel.

    You return to the Options dialog.

11. To accept this field as a lookup field, click OK.

    You return to the Define Database dialog.

12. When you have finished defining fields and setting field options, click OK.

If you ever want to change a field from a lookup field back to a normal field, choose File ➪ Define ➪ Database (or press Shift+⌘+D/Shift+Ctrl+D), click the Fields tab, select the field in the field list, click Options, and then deselect the Looked-up value check box. To edit the options for any lookup field, just click the Specify button to the right of Looked-up value.

Another idea for creating match fields

When FileMaker Pro executes a lookup, it presents data from the first matching record it finds. If, for example, you use Last Name as the trigger field and the lookup file contains five people who have the last name Hamilton, FileMaker simply selects the first Hamilton record that it finds. Other Hamiltons in the database would never be located by the lookup. For this reason, a match field should normally contain unique data, such as an ID number, Social Security number, or SKU.

Unfortunately, many databases contain no such field. With a little imagination, however, you can create trigger and match fields that are composites of other fields. To do so, you can create a Calculation field that *concatenates* two or more fields (combines them). In an address database, for example, you could create an ID number by combining an individual's last name with the last four digits of his or her phone number (as in Jones1247). Although this approach is not guaranteed to produce a unique ID, the only people you would normally expect to share the same composite number would be members of the same family.

In the table triggering the lookup, you would need to ask for two pieces of information: the last name (Last Name) and the last four digits of the person's phone number (Last4). The Calculation formula for the I.D. field would read as follows:

```
Last Name & Last4
```

The result type should be set to Text.

Because a matching field must also exist in the lookup table, you could create an ID Calculation field by using the following formula:

```
Last Name & Right (Phone, 4)
```

As in the first formula, the result type should also be Text. This formula assumes that you are already collecting a complete phone number (Phone) in the lookup table. The part of the formula that reads Right (Phone, 4) tells FileMaker Pro to consider only the last four digits of the phone number. Thus, you do not need to be concerned about whether some phone numbers in the database contain an area code while others do not. Similarly, it doesn't matter whether the phone number was typed with parentheses, dashes, spaces, or as a continuous string because only the final four digits are used, and they will always be digits.

Performing a relookup

Sometimes information in your lookup file changes. You update part descriptions and prices; contact names, addresses, and phone numbers can change. You can bring any values in the current file up to date by simply tabbing into or clicking in a match field and then issuing the Records ➪ Relookup Contents command.

Opening lookup files

When FileMaker Pro checks for a match in a related table from a different file (whether you are working with lookups or related data), it doesn't actually open the file. The file's name is displayed in the Window menu's Show submenu, surrounded by parentheses indicating that a link has been established to it. If you want to examine the file, you can choose it from the Window ⇨ Show submenu. The file opens just as it does when you choose the File ⇨ Open command. Note that files accessed via Lookup don't appear in the Show submenu until at least one lookup has been performed.

Therefore, when you are working with lookup or relational fields, you need to open only the file in which the relationship(s) have been defined. You don't need to open related files to access data; you only need to open them if you have some other reason (to enter or edit data, for example).

As an example, imagine that you have a small mail-order business selling tropical fish. You create a database called Catalog that can print an on-demand catalog listing the fish you have on hand and their prices. Catalog performs its lookups by searching an Inventory database containing description and price information for each type of fish currently in stock. As a small, specialized business, prices on particular fish can vary on a daily basis (depending on who your supplier happens to be today or what you recently caught). Whenever a customer requests a catalog, you perform a relookup to make sure that the prices are current.

You need to keep several important things in mind when executing a relookup:

✦ A relookup is performed for all records in the current found set. You can restrict the affected records by first selecting a particular record or group of records.

✦ Just as each match field in the current file triggers its own lookups, relookups are done only for the current match field (the one containing the cursor when you choose the Record ⇨ Relookup Contents command). Thus, if a file has several match fields, you can decide to perform a relookup for all or just some of the match fields.

✦ You cannot use the Undo command to undo a relookup. You might want to protect the integrity of the database by using the File ⇨ Save a Copy As command to create a backup of the database before you perform a relookup.

STEPS: Performing a Relookup

1. Open the database containing the match field (or fields) and display the appropriate layout.

2. Select the records that you want the relookup to affect.

    Use normal record selection techniques (such as the Find, Show All Records, and Omit commands) to select the appropriate records.

3. Tab into or click the first match field.

4. Choose Records ⇨ Relookup Contents.

The dialog in Figure 18-18 appears, showing the number of records in the current found set.

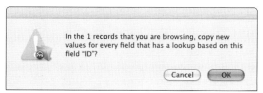

In the 1 records that you are browsing, copy new values for every field that has a lookup based on this field "ID"?

Cancel   OK

Figure 18-18: This dialog appears when you perform a relookup.

5. Click OK to replace the old values with new ones or click Cancel to leave the original values unchanged.

6. If you want to perform a relookup for additional match fields, repeat Steps 2–5.

You should always think carefully before executing a relookup. For instance, in an invoice database that pulls price information via a lookup field, performing a relookup on that field would effectively change the amounts due on outstanding invoices! Normal business practices dictate that you would seldom want to do a relookup on such a field.

Forcing a relookup for a single record

As mentioned previously, a relookup normally affects all records currently being browsed as well as all lookup fields associated with the current match field. Sometimes, however, you might want to update only a single record rather than the entire database or a subset of it. Although you can use Find requests to limit browsing to the one record of interest and then choose the Relookup command, here is an easier method you can use if you are updating only one record.

To perform the equivalent of a single-record relookup, display the appropriate record, select the data in the trigger field, cut it (by choosing Edit ⇨ Cut or by pressing ⌘+X/Ctrl+X), and then immediately paste it back into the same field (by choosing Edit ⇨ Paste or by pressing ⌘+V/Ctrl+V). Remember that editing the contents of a match field always causes a lookup to be performed. Because FileMaker Pro knows only that something has been done to the field, this cut-and-paste procedure forces a lookup to occur. If the data that is looked up has changed, the new values will appear in the lookup fields. (Another way to force a lookup is to delete a single character and then retype it.)

Additional Relationship/Lookup Options and Requirements

As we hope you've discovered, defining and using relationships and lookups isn't difficult. When you do use them, however, you should be aware of the following features and restrictions:

✦ If possible, entries in a lookup's match field should be unique. When FileMaker checks for a match, it simply shows the first that it finds. If there are several matches, the others will never be used. (This is precisely why it is dangerous in most databases to use Last Name as a match field.) You can avoid duplication in match fields by defining the field as an automatically generated serial number and/or specifying that the field must be unique. (For more information about setting field definition options, see Chapter 5.)

✦ A match field in the master file can be any type except Container or Summary; a match field in the related file can be any type except Container or Summary that doesn't have the Global Storage option selected. The match field in the related file must be capable of being indexed. Match fields must be of the same field type.

✦ When FileMaker is determining whether it has found a match in Text fields, it compares only the first 110 characters of each word in the trigger and match fields. Be sure that no word is longer than 110 characters — or that the match doesn't rely on any characters beyond the one-hundred-tenth. If you have two or more records differing only in the one-hundred-eleventh character or later, FileMaker will simply select the first one that it finds. Also, the order of words, capitalization, and punctuation are ignored when performing the comparison. Thus, *crosby* and *Crosby!* are considered the same, just as *Steve Simms* and *Simms, Steve* are treated as being the same. Finally, FileMaker ignores text in Number fields when it is checking for a match, just as it does when indexing a Number field.

✦ The match field in either file can be a Calculation field (so long as the calculation doesn't return a Container type). For instance, if the match field in the master file had the formula Sale > 1000, a relationship would be established with all records in the related file whose match field contained a number larger than 1,000.

✦ You can edit the information in a lookup field just as you can in any other field. However, a new lookup will occur only when you execute the Relookup command or edit the data in the match field.

✦ If possible, avoid selecting a repeating field as one from which you are copying (looking up) data. FileMaker simply copies the first entry from the repeating field.

✦ You can use the current file as the lookup or related file. That's right. Rather than looking in an external file, you can take values from other records in the same file. In the Video Invoice database, for example, the lookup field definitions could be changed so that when a Customer ID is entered, FileMaker Pro searches Video Invoice (rather than Customers) for a record with a matching Customer ID. As long as a previous invoice for that customer exists, FileMaker can simply copy the address information from that invoice into the current one. If no match is found, you're talking to a new customer, and you can fill in the information by typing it.

✦ You might have some older FileMaker Pro databases that rely on lookups. When you use these old databases with FileMaker Pro 3.0 through FileMaker Pro 6, the secondary files are converted as needed — either when you open and convert the primary file or as the files are referenced while using the primary file. To use one of these files with FileMaker Pro 8, you must perform an intermediate conversion with an older version (such as FileMaker Pro 6). However, a new lookup will occur only when you execute the Relookup Contents command or edit the data in the match field. During the conversion process, FileMaker Pro 8 automatically defines the relationships that were specified by the lookups in the original files and creates table entries in the Relationships Graph. Additionally, in the case of self-joins, FileMaker Pro 8 puts a second copy of the table into the Relationships Graph.

Summary

✦ A *relationship* (a pair of matching fields in two files) must be defined when working with related data and lookups. The names of the match fields in the two databases need not be the same.

✦ Relational joins can be one-to-one, one-to-many, many-to-many, or self-joins.

✦ Relations can be based on equality (equijoins), inequality, or comparison.

✦ Relationships can be indirect. That is, if TableA is related to TableB, then a TableA-based layout can access data from any tables related to TableB (directly or indirectly).

✦ Related data can be displayed as separate fields or grouped within a list box called a portal.

✦ By defining a field as a lookup field, you can copy its information from another database file. Related data, on the other hand, is merely referenced; it is not copied into the database.

✦ To trigger a lookup, simply type data into the match field or edit existing data in that field. Then exit the field by pressing Tab or Return/Enter.

✦ You can have one or many lookup fields associated with a single match field in the primary database.

✦ To bring records in the current file up to date, you can select the appropriate records and issue the Records ⇨ Relookup Contents command. Doing so causes a lookup to be executed for each of the records being browsed. (On the other hand, because related data is always up to date, there is no command necessary.)

✦ Every relookup is associated with a single match field. Only lookup fields that use that particular match field are affected by the relookup. Thus, if you have multiple match fields, you need to use multiple relookups to bring an entire record or found set up to date.

✦   ✦   ✦

Using FileMaker Pro in Workgroups

FileMaker Pro is not only network-compatible, but it also includes features enabling it to manage network traffic and control who sees which databases and who can modify them (regardless of whether the database is on a network or running in a single-user environment). In this chapter, we explain how to use FileMaker Pro on a network as well as how to password-protect and assign access privileges to sensitive data.

Those of you who have shared FileMaker databases using versions prior to FileMaker Pro 7 might be tempted to give this chapter a "once over lightly" perusal. Resist that temptation! Your task might actually be more difficult than that of FileMaker sharing neophytes — not only do you have new material to learn, but you have old habits and methods to unlearn. Virtually everything about sharing has changed to some extent. Some of it is minor, such as the maximum number of simultaneous connections, where the menu commands might be, or how dialogs are worded. Other changes are major, such as the access privileges model.

Running FileMaker Pro on a Network

Having your personal FileMaker Pro databases at your beck and call is great, but some data — particularly business information — is meant to be shared with others. Back in the old days (before networks were common), employees spent an inordinate amount of time unnecessarily duplicating and hand-distributing data or scheduling time on a shared computer system that stored their data. When a colleague down the hall needed a copy of your sales spreadsheet, for example, you made a copy of it on disk and carried the disk to his or her desk. Now that computer workstations can be linked via a company's network, you can share data without physically having to move or copy it. Files can stay right where they are, regardless of whether they're located on your hard disk or on a file server.

> **Note**   There are two ways you can share a database over a network. If no more than five users will ever need to simultaneously access the database, the built-in file-sharing features of FileMaker Pro will suffice. If more than five users (down from ten users in versions prior to FileMaker Pro 7) will ever simultaneously access the database, it *must* be hosted using FileMaker Pro Server. (Note that FileMaker Pro 7 and 8 databases *cannot* be served by FileMaker Server 6 or earlier.)

Right out of the box, FileMaker Pro 8 is a network-ready program. FileMaker Pro databases can be shared among the users of any TCP/IP (all platforms) network.

You establish whether your open files are shared via Transmission Control Protocol/Internet Protocol (TCP/IP) in the FileMaker Network Settings dialog (FileMaker Pro/Edit ⇨ Sharing ⇨ FileMaker Network) shown in Figure 19-1.

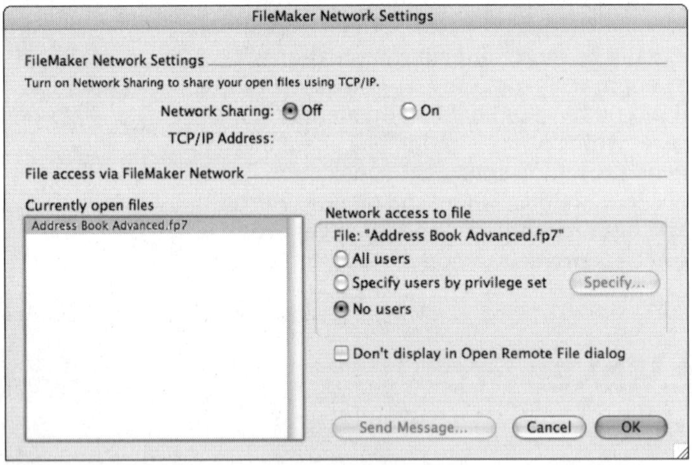

FileMaker Network Settings

FileMaker Network Settings
Turn on Network Sharing to share your open files using TCP/IP.

Network Sharing: ◉ Off   ○ On

TCP/IP Address:

File access via FileMaker Network

Currently open files
Address Book Advanced.fp7

Network access to file
File: "Address Book Advanced.fp7"
○ All users
○ Specify users by privilege set   (Specify...)
◉ No users

☐ Don't display in Open Remote File dialog

(Send Message...)   (Cancel)   (OK)

Figure 19-1: Turn sharing on or off here.

When discussing file sharing in the remainder of this chapter, please note that we are talking about individual users on the network hosting databases rather than having the databases served by FileMaker Server.

FileMaker Pro Server

FileMaker Server 8 and FileMaker Server 8 Advanced are capable of simultaneously hosting as many as 125 databases created in FileMaker Pro 7 or 8 for as many as 250 simultaneous guests. (Advanced also supports up to 100 simultaneous Web connections.) FileMaker Server 8 is designed to work on a cross-platform network, supporting Windows, Mac OS X, and Red Hat Linux.

If you have or are thinking about getting FileMaker Server, here are some useful bits of information:

✦ Macintosh and Windows versions are provided in the same box.

✦ FileMaker Server can be installed on any computer that's connected to your network. However, for optimum performance, install it on a dedicated computer — one that isn't used for other tasks.

✦ FileMaker Server's purpose is to host databases. To use any of the hosted databases, each person (client) must still have his or her own copy of FileMaker Pro installed on his or her computer.

✦ When you start FileMaker Server, it automatically opens all multi-user FileMaker Pro files found in the FileMaker Pro Server folder. (All databases to be hosted should reside on the computer on which FileMaker Server is installed.) To manually open other databases, choose File ➪ Administer and click the Open Database button. Other administrative tasks, such as closing databases and disconnecting guests, are also performed in the administer window.

✦ FileMaker Server 8 can automatically install updated versions of plug-ins on guest computers, ensuring that each user has an up-to-date copy of any plug-in required to use a particular database. (However, for this to work, the user must activate the Auto Update plug-in in his or her copy of FileMaker Pro's Preferences on the Plug-ins pane.)

✦ You can remotely administer FileMaker Server from any workstation on which FileMaker Pro is installed. In FileMaker Pro's Open dialog, click Remote, choose the server, and enter the requested password. Your administration capabilities depend in part on whether the Server Administration plug-in is installed on the computer you're using. (When it isn't installed, you'll be limited to viewing statistical information, guest lists, open files, and the like.)

✦ Any database containing fields that use the Today function must be closed and reopened in FileMaker Pro each day in order for the fields to be updated. Closing and reopening them in FileMaker Server will not accomplish this.

Hosts and clients

The person who opens a FileMaker Pro database and then declares it to be a multi-user database becomes the *host* for that database for the current session. To open a database for sharing, choose FileMaker Pro/Edit ➪ Sharing ➪ FileMaker Network, make sure Network Sharing is turned on, and then select the database file and assign network access capabilities for the file, as shown in Figure 19-2. If you select the Specify users by privilege set radio button, the Specify users by privilege set dialog (Figure 19-3) appears, allowing you to set access levels for different user classes. We discuss access privileges later in this chapter.

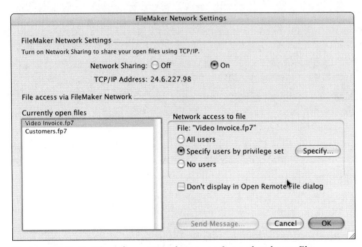

Figure 19-2: Setting the network access for a database file.

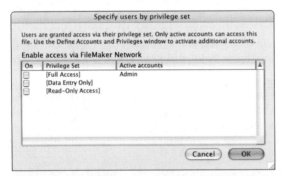

Figure 19-3: Setting access level by privilege class.

While the database file is open on the host, as many as five users on the network can simultaneously access it (including the host). These users are *clients*. (Previous versions called them *guests*, so you might encounter that term on the Web or in other FileMaker-related discussions.) The designer of the database—or in some cases, the database administrator—determines each client's specific privileges, either as an individual or as a member of a group.

If the previous host was someone other than you, you will see the changes made by that person as well as any changes made by clients. Because the host is in charge, only that person's changes to Sort, Find, Page Setup/Print Setup commands, and Global values are saved when the host closes the file.

Note

As shown in Figure 19-2, you can also specify that a file be shared but not displayed in the Open Remote File dialog. Choose this setting for files to which the user will need indirect access, such as files containing related tables that you don't wish the clients to be able to open independently. In previous versions, this option was the Multi-user (Hidden) radio button, grouped with the On (Multi-user) and Off (Single-user) radio buttons.

The host is in charge

Hosts and clients have different privileges and responsibilities. The following are some guidelines for being a host:

✦ Any related files required by the database must also be opened by the host.

✦ To minimize network congestion, the host should try to avoid running additional programs that might affect performance while he or she is serving as host.

✦ Only the host can close a shared file.

As you can see, the host is in charge of the big stuff: making certain that the database is ready to use, ensuring that his or her personal computer isn't overburdened, and making major changes to the structure of the database. Reserving these major privileges for the host makes good sense. If any of these actions were available to all users, no one would be able to get any work done. Imagine trying to enter a new record while several individuals were simultaneously shifting around the fields in a key layout. In fact, if the host attempts any of these actions, FileMaker Pro automatically asks all clients to close the file. After the host completes the necessary changes and reopens the database as shared, clients can reopen the file and resume their work.

When you — as host — finish using the file and want to close it, you can choose File ➪ Close (to close the file without quitting FileMaker Pro), FileMaker Pro ➪ Quit FileMaker Pro (Mac OS X) or File ➪ Exit (Windows), or select Off in the FileMaker Network dialog. If any guests are using the database, FileMaker Pro asks that you notify them, requesting that they close the database as well.

STEPS: Closing a Database as a Host

1. Do one of the following:

• Choose File ➪ Sharing, select the Single User radio button in the File Sharing dialog, and then click OK.

• Choose File ➪ Close (⌘+W/Ctrl+W).

• Choose FileMaker Pro ➪ Quit FileMaker Pro (Mac) or File ➪ Exit (Windows).

If clients are using the database, a dialog appears on the host's screen, as shown in Figure 19-4.

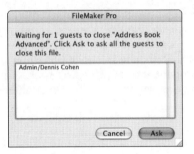

Figure 19-4: This dialog shows that others are still using the database.

2. Click Ask to send each client a message asking him or her to close the file.

A message appears on each client's screen (see Figure 19-5), stating that the host wants to close the file and that clients must relinquish access to it.

Figure 19-5: This message appears on clients' screens.

To acknowledge the message and relinquish the file, clients click the Close Now button.

3. After 30 seconds, FileMaker Pro automatically attempts to close the file.

If the file can be closed safely, FileMaker does so, regardless of whether guests have responded to the message. If the file cannot be closed safely, it remains open.

Saving a file's sharing status

When a host changes a file's sharing status from On to Off, or vice versa, that new status is saved along with the other database settings. If, for example, a host closes a file while it's still set as sharable, the next time the file is opened, the file is automatically marked as sharable and is ready to receive clients. On the other hand, if the file does not have sharable status set and is then closed, the next host — regardless of who that might be — must reset the file to sharable (assuming that you still want the file to be shared).

Client activities

To open a shared database as a guest, choose File ➪ Open (or press ⌘+O/Ctrl+O), click the Remote button in the file dialog that appears, select a host — and a file from that host — in the Open Remote File dialog (as shown in Figure 19-6), and then click Open. Only sharable files that a host has open appear in the Available Files list.

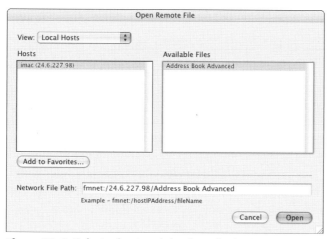

Figure 19-6: Select a host and database in the Open Remote File dialog.

Note FileMaker Pro 8 also has a command that will take you directly to the Open Remote File dialog: File ➪ Open Remote (Shift+⌘+O/Shift+Ctrl+O).

Each client can perform any action on the database that his or her privileges allow. At a minimum, each client can browse the file: Clients can examine records that haven't explicitly been marked off-limits to them but cannot change data in them.

Other normal activities, such as editing, adding, and deleting records, also might be permitted. For details, see "Protecting Databases and Setting Privileges," later in this chapter.

To avoid conflict between users, the following activities can be performed only by one person at a time: open ScriptMaker; define or modify relationships, tables, field definitions, account information/privileges, or value lists; or edit a given record or layout.

Notes on cross-platform database sharing

Both Macs and PCs can share FileMaker Pro databases on a network. In general, any typical task (such as entering and editing data, creating and deleting records, and sorting or issuing Find requests) can be performed on either platform (Mac or Windows). Data, graphics, and other elements that appear on one machine also appear on the other. In addition, the program commands used to work with databases are the same whether the user is running the Macintosh or Windows version of FileMaker Pro. However, here are a few important differences:

✦ Platform-specific tasks can be performed only on the appropriate platform. A Windows user, for example, cannot execute a script that relies on AppleEvents or AppleScript, and a Mac user can't execute scripts that execute Dynamic Data Exchange (DDE) commands.

✦ Fonts occasionally can pose a problem. Even common fonts, such as Times and Helvetica, can appear differently when viewed on a platform other than the one on which the database was created. Some fonts and changes in screen resolution can cause field labels to spill over into fields or wrap to a new line, for example.

✦ Special symbols used in entering data or creating layout text can produce unusual or unexpected results when viewed on the other platform.

✦ Container fields might exhibit differences between the two platforms. For example, Windows users can embed or link an Object Linking and Embedding (OLE) object in a Container field. Although Mac users can view, cut, copy, and paste OLE objects, they are not allowed to edit them.

For information concerning other differences between the Mac and Windows versions of FileMaker Pro, as well as the mechanics of sharing databases between these two platforms without a network, see Chapter 16.

Protecting Databases and Setting Privileges

Some databases are designed to be shared equally by all users on a network. It is not uncommon for a department to have a shared business contacts database, an inventory database, or a sales database, for example. Allowing such a database to be shared can save considerable time and energy compared with having every person maintain her or his own version.

However, not all company information is intended to be shared among all employees or even all members of the same department. A database containing employee salary information, for example, might well be available only to members of the Accounting Department and senior management. Also, within that database, certain layouts and data might properly be modified or viewed only by the head of the department.

Other information is often meant for no one other than the person who designed the database. A manager, for example, might create a database he uses to record comments about employee performance. Although the contents of this file might be extremely useful when the manager writes his annual employee evaluations, this sensitive information isn't meant to be viewed or edited by anyone else in the company.

FileMaker Pro anticipates the need for security and for assigning different types of privileges to different users. To this end, you can associate access privileges and database resources with specific privilege sets.

Versions prior to FileMaker Pro 7 adopted a password and privileges model where each password (or account group) had its access privileges independently managed. FileMaker Pro 7 completely replaced that model with an authentication approach where each user account is assigned a privilege set. This means that if an administrator changes a privilege set, all accounts assigned that privilege set inherit the changes. The group concept is completely eliminated in FileMaker Pro 7 and 8. Each account has a name, password, a named privilege set, and (optionally) a description.

Tip For those of you making the transition from an older version, you might think of FileMaker Pro 8's account as similar to the old password feature and the new password as an authentication mechanism for account access (just like logging into a Mac, Windows, or Unix system, where you supply an account name and an authenticating password). Just as your operating system account specifies what privileges you have, a FileMaker Pro 8 account has associated privilege sets.

A *privilege set* includes all the expected privileges from previous versions: edit records, edit layouts, delete records, and so forth. Additional privileges in FileMaker Pro 7 included specifying access to individual tables, layouts, and fields rather than just the record-level access of the old group model.

Note By default, access to tables, layouts, and fields is unrestricted so as to maintain compatibility with previous versions.

Creating accounts

Accounts determine which users can access a database and what actions they can perform within that database (through their assigned privilege set).

STEPS: Creating Accounts for a File

1. Open the file for which you want to define accounts.

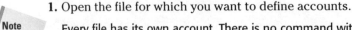

Note   Every file has its own account. There is no command with which you can create a universal account that works with all your databases other than the default Admin account or Guest account.

2. Choose File ➪ Define ➪ Accounts & Privileges.

The Define Accounts & Privileges dialog appears, as shown in Figure 19-7.

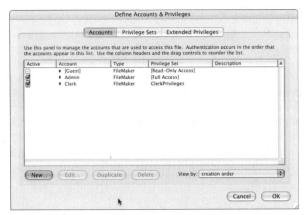

Figure 19-7: The Define Accounts & Privileges dialog.

3. If you have not yet created an Admin password for this database, do so now. Select the Admin account in the list and click Edit. The Edit Account dialog appears, as shown in Figure 19-8. Type a new password in the Password text box and then click OK.0

4. If this is the only account you want to create at this time, click OK (and skip the remaining steps).

or

Click New.

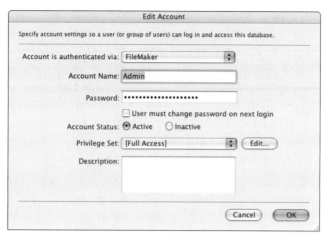

Figure 19-8: Edit account attributes and password in this dialog.

5. Name the account, assign a password, and choose a privilege set. You can choose one of the three predefined privilege sets: Full Access, Data Entry Only, and Read-Only Access. Or you can choose New Privilege Set from the Privilege Set pop-up menu/drop-down list, which presents the Edit Privilege Set dialog shown in Figure 19-9.

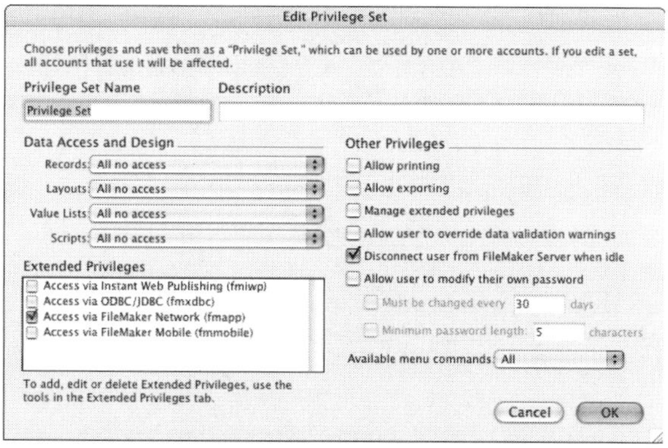

Figure 19-9: Establish the privilege sets' settings in this dialog.

If you choose the last-named option, you'll need to continue with the following steps:

> **a.** Name the privileges set and (optionally) give it a description to remind you (or other administrators) of the privilege set's purpose.
>
> **b.** Choose access levels for Records, Layouts, Value Lists, and Scripts from the correspondingly named pop-up menus/drop-down lists.
>
> **c.** Designate any extended privileges desired by selecting the check boxes in the Extended Privileges list.
>
> **d.** Select and deselect Other Privileges options, as desired.
>
> **e.** Choose what menu subset the privilege set is to have from the Available menu commands pop-up menu/drop-down list.
>
> **f.** Click OK (or Cancel, if you changed your mind) to close the Edit Privilege Set dialog.

6. Click OK to close the Edit Account dialog.

7. To create additional accounts, repeat Steps 4–6; otherwise, click OK to save the new accounts for the file.

Before closing the Define Accounts & Privileges dialog, FileMaker Pro makes sure that you know a Full Access account name and its associated password by displaying the Confirm Full Access Login dialog shown in Figure 19-10.

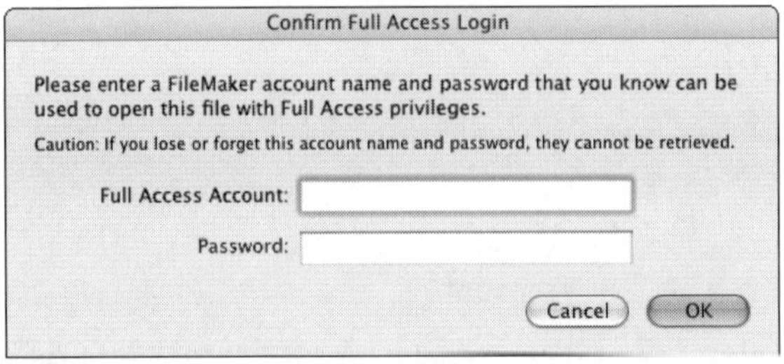

Figure 19-10: Enter a Full Access account name and password in this dialog to verify your right to make the preceding changes.

8. Type a full access account name and its password and then click OK.

At least one Full Access account must be active for a database. If only one account is enabled for a database, it is therefore a Full Access account. When more than one account is active, you will be asked for an account name and password to access the database. The only way to access a shared database without going through the login dialog is for the default Full Access account to be active and for it to not have an assigned password.

What happened to default passwords?

FileMaker Pro versions prior to FileMaker Pro 7 let you assign a default password to a database. When a default password existed, users were automatically logged into the database with that password and its associated privileges without ever seeing the login dialog. This feature is now controlled by the user rather than the administrator.

Choose File ➪ File Options. In the Open/Close pane, specify a default name and password to employ when attempting to open the file (log in). When the account name and password are valid, you don't see the login dialog; however, it will appear if the values you stored are invalid.

If you have enabled this auto-login option, you can force the login dialog to appear by holding down the Option (Mac) or Shift (Windows) key when choosing File ➪ Open (or using any of the other file-opening methods).

It is a major security risk to allow Full Access accounts to log in without a password assigned. Just to help you avoid that situation, if you try to exit the Define Accounts & Privileges dialog with multiple active accounts and no password on a Full Access account, FileMaker Pro 8 will warn you with the dialog shown here.

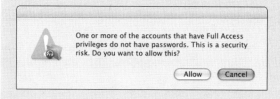

Note

To access fields from related files in the current database, you must have access privileges for the related file. If the related file uses the same accounts, FileMaker Pro will automatically reuse the account name and password. Storing multiple tables in a single file eliminates having to assign identical accounts to multiple files.

Note

You can also change your password by choosing File ➪ Change Password. In the Change Password dialog that appears, enter your old password, the new password you wish to use, and then enter the new password a second time as verification that it is really the password you want.

Tip

It is often advantageous to assign an initial password to new accounts; however, data security practices indicate that passwords should be private to the account. FileMaker Pro makes this easier by including the User must change password on next login check box in the Edit Account dialog. If you select this check box, users are presented with the dialog shown in Figure 19-11 upon their first subsequent access. Good security practice also advises that passwords should be changed periodically and should be of a minimum length. You can enforce both of these provisions in the Edit Privilege Set dialog shown in Figure 19-9, assuming that the users' privilege set allows them to modify their own password. (We recommend that you enable user-changeable passwords in all but a very few specific cases, such as an account shared by multiple users.)

Figure 19-11: You can force users to change their password at their next login to the file.

Record-level access privileges

You can restrict access to a database on a record-by-record basis. For instance, you can specify that users running with a particular privilege set can see only records that he or she created.

During the privilege set definition process, you'll note that the pop-up menu/drop-down list beside Records includes a Custom privileges choice. Choosing Custom privileges presents the Custom Record Privileges dialog shown in Figure 19-12. When you select a table from the list area, the various Set Privileges pop-up menus/drop-down lists become active. All five have Yes and No options, and all but the Create pop-up menu/drop-down list also include a Limited choice. Choosing Limited presents a Specify Calculation dialog. If the calculation evaluates to True (anything nonzero and non-empty), access is allowed to that record.

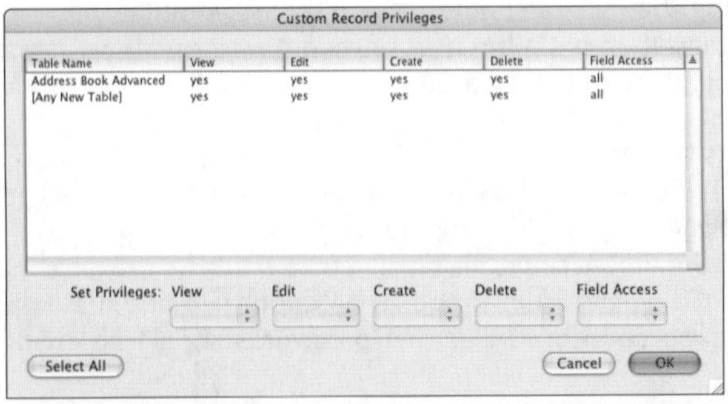

Figure 19-12: Set custom record access privileges here.

For example, to limit access to only the records that a user has personally created, you could define a User field for which Creator Name is set as the auto-entry option. The formula to restrict access would be

```
User = Get (UserName)
```

Tip
You can use the same formula for each of the four privilege types offering limited access (View, Edit, Delete, and Field Access), or you could use a different formula to apply a different condition. Before clicking OK to dismiss the Specify Calculation dialog, copy the formula in the middle of the dialog. When creating the formula for the other privileges, you can paste it (⌘+V/Ctrl+V) into the dialog.

Other Get calculations that you could create might be based on the record creation/modification date or a maximum number of concurrent guests — limiting a user's access to browsing only when Get (UserCount) exceeds a given number of users.

Tip
Think carefully about which of the options (View, Edit, Delete, and Field Access) should be set as Limited. For example, if you make viewing limited but neglect to do the same for deleting, you enable the user to delete records that he or she isn't allowed to *see* (by issuing the Delete All Records or Delete Found Records commands)! There are other limitations that you should also be aware of when creating limited-access privilege sets, especially when the solution is a relational one. Be sure to review the information in "Entering a formula for limiting access on a record by record basis" in FileMaker Pro Help.

Passing out accounts

When the database designer or administrator creates an account, the distribution could be handled on an individual or a group basis. For example, the department head might get an account, but the department staff might share an account.

When you create an account that will be shared by multiple people, you should probably not give them password-changing privileges lest one person lock out the remainder of the users sharing that account. All users know is that they have a passworded account giving them particular rights — not whether others also have the same password and privileges. You can, of course, create an individual accounts for users who really want a particular password or are paranoid about controlling their password, and then assign those accounts the same privilege set as you gave the communal account.

Modifying accounts

If you have a Full Access account, you can change or delete any account or password for the database as long as another Full Access account holder doesn't currently have the Define Accounts & Privileges dialog open. To modify an account, open the database using a Full Access account and choose File ➪ Define ➪ Accounts & Privileges. When the Define Accounts & Privileges dialog appears (previously shown in Figure 19-7), you can do the following in the Accounts pane:

✦ Delete an account by selecting the account and clicking Delete.

✦ Change an account's privileges and other settings by selecting the account, clicking Edit, and making your changes just as when creating a new account.

After deleting or modifying accounts, you have the responsibility of letting the affected individuals know about changes that could affect them, such as a password change.

Even if you don't have Full Access privileges to a database, you can change any password that has been assigned to you if a Full Access user enabled the Allow user to modify their own password option in your privilege set. Just choose File ➪ Change Password and proceed as described in the "Creating accounts" section, earlier in this chapter. (See Figure 19-11.)

Passwords for shareware templates

One handy use for accounts is when you are developing shareware or commercial templates you intend to sell to others. Before distributing the templates, you can create accounts with different privilege sets to address different customer needs. Here are some examples:

✦ *Guest:* This predefined account requires only that you enable it. Create a blank password with limited privileges (browse records and print/export records). This technique enables a prospective customer to examine the database and print reports, but he or she is restricted to using the records you included in the database.

✦ *Data Entry:* You could define this account's privilege set to allow the user to create new records or modify existing records.

✦ *Maintenance:* In addition to the privileges available to a Guest or Data Entry account, this account's privilege set could enable the user to customize layouts (perhaps inserting a corporate logo or other client-specific information). Offer to provide this account's password in exchange for a basic shareware fee. If they like your product, most customers will prefer this option.

✦ *Full Access:* This predefined account gives customers complete freedom to modify the template as they see fit, as well as the capability to modify or delete privilege sets and accounts. Because using this option is equivalent to selling a computer program's code, you might want to offer this master account's password for a higher fee. (Recognize, of course, that giving a user full access means that he or she has more opportunity to revise your scripts or use the template in ways you never intended, which can lead to technical support nightmares.)

Creating and deleting privilege sets

Before you create new accounts, you should consider defining a privilege set enumerating what that account should be capable of doing. FileMaker Pro 8 comes with three predefined privilege sets: Full Access, Data Entry, and Guest. Because each privilege set has specific capabilities and restrictions associated with it, you can be sure that all accounts assigned a specific privilege set have identical privileges.

Tip   Each of the three predefined privilege sets appears at the top of the list in brackets. These privilege sets are not modifiable. If you wish to create a similar privilege set, duplicate the one that is closest to what you seek and modify that.

Knowing whether you are creating a privilege set that will be shared by multiple accounts versus one that will be account-specific can be the determining factor on whether you create the account (specific) or the privilege set first (shared). As discussed earlier in this chapter, if the privilege set is to be specific to a single account, you can choose Custom Privileges from the Edit Account dialog's Privilege Set pop-up menu/drop-down list. However, if you intend to create a privilege set to be used by multiple accounts, you will be better placed to plan and create it first and then assign it to the various accounts to which it applies as you create them. Of course, you could create the privilege set while defining the first account that will use it; however, you are less likely to plan for generality if you do so.

Tip   You are not required to create additional privilege sets. If you simply want to prevent anyone else from opening a database that you designed, for example, just assign a password to the Full Access account.

Each privilege set is a cohesive set of capabilities. Any privilege not specified is denied. You can design privilege sets based on employee rank, departments in your company, or anything else you like. In most cases, "need to know" will be the most critical factor in determining which privileges to include. The key thing to remember is that any account assigned a specific privilege set has the same database privileges and can work with the same layouts and fields as any other account assigned that privilege set unless you set the privilege as limited and the determining calculation makes its decision based upon UserName or some other criterion unique to the account.

STEPS: Defining and Editing Privilege Sets

1. Open the database and supply the Full Access password if and when prompted for it.

   Only a person who has Full Access privileges can create or modify privilege sets.

2. Choose File ⇨ Define ⇨ Accounts & Privileges.

   The Define Accounts & Privileges dialog appears. Click the Privilege Sets tab to display the Privileged Set list, as shown in Figure 19-13.

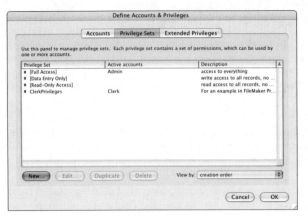

Figure 19-13: The Privilege Sets pane.

3. To create a new privilege set definition, click the New button to display the Edit Privilege Set dialog shown in Figure 19-14. Type a name for the set in the Privilege Set Name text box.

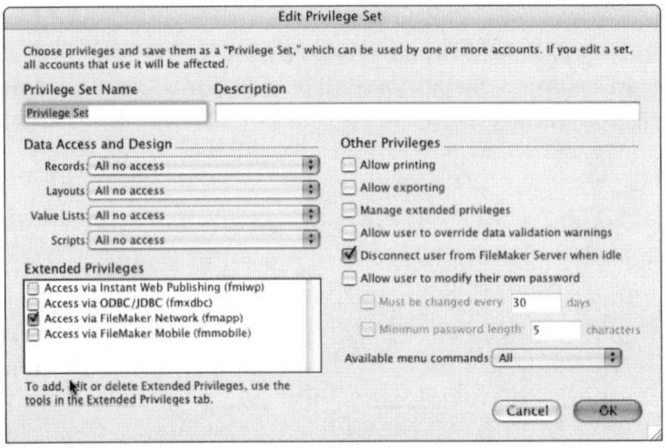

Figure 19-14: The Edit Privilege Set dialog.

or

To modify an existing privilege set, select it in the list and click the Edit button to display the same Edit Privileges dialog seen in Figure 19-14, except that it is already named and has some settings other than the defaults pictured.

Tip

Although not mandatory, it is generally a good idea to provide a description for the privilege set in the Description text box. One day, you might need to be reminded of why you created the set or you might hand the database off to another administrator who needs to know and understand the privilege set's purpose.

4. Use the Records, Layouts, Value Lists, and Scripts pop-up menus/drop-down lists to assign access privileges to the corresponding database items. In a new privilege set, all four default to All no access. (You saw an example of setting custom Record access privileges earlier in this chapter.)

   The Layouts, Value Lists, and Scripts menus/lists all offer four choices: All modifiable, All view only (or All execute only in the case of scripts), All no access, and Custom privileges.

5. To restrict access to particular layouts, choose Custom privileges from the Layouts pop-up menu/drop-down list. The Custom Layout Privileges dialog, similar to the one shown in Figure 19-15 (the list of layouts will vary from one database to the next) appears.

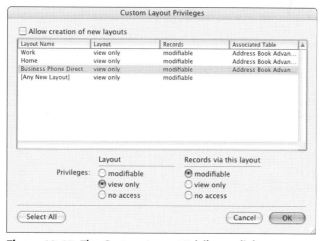

Figure 19-15: The Custom Layout Privileges dialog.

Select the Allow creation of new layouts check box if you want users with this privilege set to be able to create new layouts.

Select layouts from the list and use the radio buttons to set privileges for the specified layouts (one from each column). Click OK when done.

Note If Layout is set to no access, the right column is dimmed. (If you can't get to the layout, you can't see or modify the records, right?)

6. To control value list creation, modification, and even accessibility, choose Custom privileges from the Value Lists pop-up menu/drop-down list.

   Similar to the Custom Layout Privileges dialog, the Custom Value List Privileges dialog includes a check box permitting creation of new value lists and a list of existing value lists to which you can assign privileges on a case-by-case basis.

7. Choosing Custom privileges from the Scripts pop-up menu/drop-down list presents the Custom Script Privileges dialog, where you can select a check box permitting new script creation and specify on a script-by-script basis whether the user has no access, execute-only access, or modification access.

8. Click OK (back in the Edit Privilege Set dialog) to save the current settings and return to the Define Accounts & Privileges dialog, or click Cancel to discard any changes.

9. If you want to assign the newly (re)defined privilege set to any existing account, select that account in the Accounts pane and click Edit. Then choose the set from the Privilege Set pop-up menu/drop-down list.

10. When you finish defining and editing privilege sets and assigning them to accounts in the Define Accounts & Privileges dialog, click OK to save your changes and return to the database.

11. FileMaker Pro presents the Confirm Full Access Login dialog for you to verify your privilege to make the preceding changes.

You can delete any privilege set by selecting the privilege set name in the Define Accounts & Privileges dialog's Privilege Sets pane and then clicking Delete. Before you delete or modify privilege sets for a database that is currently being shared, however, users must close the file before the new privileges take effect.

Working with a protected file

When you attempt to open a protected file—whether that file is on a network or only on your personal computer—you immediately see the dialog shown in Figure 19-16. The Account Name is entered "in the clear," but as you enter the password, the characters are shown as bullets in the dialog. This extra bit of security keeps passersby from peeking at your password. If you make a mistake while typing the password, just press the Delete/Backspace key to remove the incorrect characters and then retype them (or select the whole password and retype it).

Figure 19-16: Use this dialog to access a protected database.

If you're running on a Mac, the login dialog, as shown in Figure 19-16, supports the Mac OS X Keychain, so you can add the login information to your system Keychain, and FileMaker will automatically fill the blanks with your account name and password. Although this is definitely a convenience, it can be a security risk if you leave your Mac running and unattended.

When you finish, click OK and press Return/Enter. If the account and password are correct, the database opens, and you're assigned the access privileges that are associated with the password.

If you type the password incorrectly (or are simply entering a guess), FileMaker Pro displays a dialog—shown in Figure 19-17—informing you that the account/password combination is incorrect. If you click OK in this dialog, the original login dialog reappears, and you can try again. If you don't know or can't remember the password, click Cancel in the login dialog. FileMaker Pro remains open, and you can select a different database with which to work until you can hunt down an Administrator to give you a hand.

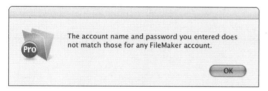

Figure 19-17: If you make a mistake in the account or password, this is what you'll see.

Opening a database as Guest

If the person who administers the database authorized Guest access, you'll see a slightly different version of the login dialog, as shown in Figure 19-18. You can then select the Guest account radio button, which disables the Account Name and Password text boxes, and then click OK. Now, to the limits of what Guests are allowed, you can access the file. As with actual accounts, a Guest also has specific access privileges assigned by the database designer or administrator. By default, the Guest account has the predefined Read-Only Access privilege set assigned.

Open "Baseball"

Open "Baseball" using:

- ● Guest Account
- ○ Account Name and Password

Account Name: Filemaker Bible

Password:

☐ Add to Keychain

(Change Password...)   (Cancel)   (OK)

Figure 19-18: A login dialog with a Guest option.

Changing a password

When accessing a database, you'll notice that the File ➪ Change Password command is enabled unless your account has the Allow user to modify their own password privilege deselected. Although you cannot alter your access privileges for the file unless you're a Full Access user, you can change your password whenever you want (with the above-mentioned exception).

STEPS: Changing a Password

1. Choose File ➪ Change Password.

   The Change Password dialog appears, as shown in Figure 19-19.

Figure 19-19: The Change Password dialog.

2. Type your current password in the Old Password text box.

3. Press the Tab key and type the new password in the New Password text box.

4. Press the Tab key and type the new password a second time (to verify it) in the Confirm New Password text box.

5. Click OK to save the new password.

Caution

Although security experts suggest that you change your password regularly, this FileMaker Pro procedure has one drawback. When you change a password for yourself, you're also changing it for anyone else who shares your account. In the event that your database administrator both assigns shared accounts and enables the Allow user to modify their own password option, it is your responsibility to notify all affected users of the database that you've changed the password.

A better approach is to leave password changes for shared accounts to the database administrator. Because that person has complete access to the database and can alter passwords at any time (even if a user has already changed the password), the Administrator is in a perfect position to handle this task. And because the Administrator also knows which users *share* each password, he or she can make sure that the new password is communicated only to the right people.

Extended Privileges

FileMaker Pro 7 and now 8 give you even more control over your shared files via Extended Privileges. Prior to FileMaker Pro 7, sharing was either on or off for a file. You can now specify whether it is on or off for network access, Instant Web Publishing, Open Database Connectivity/Java Database Connectivity (ODBC/JDBC), or any other external method defined.

FileMaker Pro 8 ships with support for network sharing, ODBC/JDBC data access, FileMaker Mobile, and Instant Web Publishing. If new access methods become available, you can exercise control over their use via the Define Accounts & Privileges dialog's Extended Privileges pane, shown in Figure 19-20.

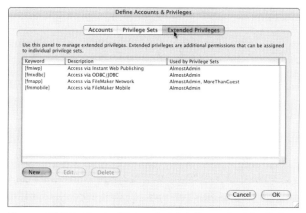

Figure 19-20: Control Extended Privileges in this dialog pane.

Click New to define a new access permission (or select one from the list and click Edit to modify an existing privilege). The Edit Extended Privilege dialog appears, as shown in Figure 19-21.

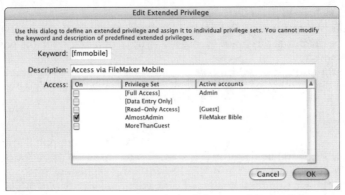

Figure 19-21: Create an extended privilege and assign it to privilege sets here.

The four predefined extended privileges cannot have their keywords or descriptions modified.

Summary

✦ If you are working on a TCP/IP network (any platform), FileMaker Pro 8 databases can be shared among users. As many as five users can simultaneously work in any shared database. However, each user must have his or her own copy of FileMaker Pro. If more than five users will ever simultaneously work in the database, you must use FileMaker Server 8 (or FileMaker Server 8 Advanced) to host the database. (Actually, because the database format hasn't changed from FileMaker Pro 7, you could also serve via FileMaker Server 7 if you're willing to forgo the additional features of FileMaker Server 8.)

✦ The first person to open a database for sharing during a computing session is the host. Although clients (other users) can view and edit data in the file, only the host's Page Setup, Find, and Sort changes are saved when the file is closed. The host is also responsible for closing the database.

✦ If they are on the same network, users of the Windows version of FileMaker Pro can share their databases with Mac users and vice versa.

✦ To protect a database or assign different privileges to different users or user classes, you can assign accounts to the database and define privilege sets associated with each account. Such privilege sets would then allow you to limit access to particular resources (such as records, layouts, value lists, scripts, and fields).

✦   ✦   ✦

Web Publishing with FileMaker Pro

Sharing a FileMaker Pro database with other FileMaker
Pro users on a network isn't the only way to share your
data. FileMaker Pro users (since 4.0) have been able to publish their databases on the World Wide Web or a corporate
intranet. Using a Web browser — such as Internet Explorer,
Mozilla, Firefox, or Safari — users around the globe can view
and interact with any sharable FileMaker Pro database, just as
they could if they were connected over a local area network.
FileMaker Pro 7 significantly expanded your ability to make
published databases look and act very similarly to how they
behave when used locally, and FileMaker Pro 8 adds a little
extra polish. One advantage of Web-based sharing is that the
users working with your data through their Web browsers
don't need a copy of FileMaker Pro to do their work — the
only copy required is the one you're running to publish
the database. This means that you can work with databases
you've shared from any location with an Internet connection
and a compatible Web browser.

Publishing Methods and Views

Unlike Web pages you post on an ISP's (Internet service
provider) Web server, when you use the FileMaker Pro 8's
Instant Web Publishing to host a database, your computer
acts as the server. People viewing and editing the database
are actually interacting directly with your computer and its
hard disk over a Transmission Control Protocol/Internet
Protocol (TCP/IP) connection.

Note   Users can view your published databases only when you are online, have the databases opened as shared, and also have the Instant Web Publishing extended privilege enabled. (See Chapter 19 for a discussion of Extended Privileges.) The IP (Internet Protocol) address of your computer serves as the Web address for the databases you are hosting. Thus, unless you have a permanent connection to the Internet, Web publishing might be impractical because modem connections are fragile, and your IP address might change each time you reconnect to your ISP. See the "About IP addresses" sidebar later in this chapter for additional information.

Instant Web Publishing enables you to put your database on the Web without programming or knowledge of HTML (HyperText Markup Language, the language used to create pages for the World Wide Web). All you do is select a handful of options from FileMaker Pro dialogs.

In FileMaker Pro 7 and 8, support for Cascading Style Sheets (CSS, the modern methodology for controlling formatting in HTML documents) enables Instant Web Publishing-accessed databases to look and behave almost identically to their FileMaker Pro appearance and behavior. Buttons that execute the Go to Layout script step still function on the Web, enabling users to switch layouts when in form view; or, users can choose a layout from the status area's Layouts pop-up menu. Multistep scripts can be attached to buttons on a layout; scripts can be of unlimited length up from a 3-step limit in previous versions but must consist only of supported steps (a 70+ step subset of the FileMaker Pro 7 and 8 script steps, up from the 22 script steps supported in FileMaker Pro 6).

Note   One consequence of the increased functionality is that only CSS-capable browsers are supported. FileMaker, Inc. no longer attempts to provide templates enabling pre-CSS Web clients to display data. Officially, FileMaker, Inc. supports only Internet Explorer 6 and later on Windows 98 or later (or Firefox, if your version of Windows supports it), Internet Explorer 5.1 or later on Mac OS X v. 10.2.8 or later, Safari 1.1 or newer on Mac OS X v. 10.2.8 or later, or FireFox 1.0 or later. Unofficially, Dennis was successful viewing a few sample databases with builds of Mozilla for the Mac on Mac OS X 10.4.2, so other CSS-compliant browsers might work as well. FileMaker, Inc. has not certified other browsers, so you'll be on your own to test them out.

Database layouts are available to all users, just as though they were shared over the network, dependent upon the user's access privileges. Even layout features such as drop-down calendars, tooltips, and tab controls are fully available. Users can switch between form, table, and list views; similarly, they can execute Find requests to locate particular records and (at your discretion) can sort the database to suit their needs if their access privileges allow those activities. There is also a built-in home page from which users can select a database to use, as well as a Help page that provides instructions for using and interacting with the databases.

Note   Web-shared list views display 25 records per page, and table views display 50 records per page, with controls to advance to the next page (when one exists) or to the previous page (when you're not at the beginning). Column headers in table view let users switch between an ascending and descending sort on the field whose header they click, assuming that you have enabled sorting in that layout's Layout Setup dialog (Table View Properties area).

All the account and permission restrictions (or lack thereof) that you can apply to databases shared over a network are applicable to Instant Web Published databases. Figure 20-1 shows a typical database created with Instant Web Publishing.

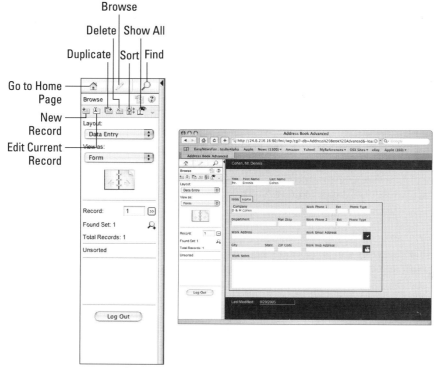

Figure 20-1: A database in form view published with Instant Web Publishing.

Versions of FileMaker Pro prior to FileMaker Pro 7 allowed up to ten guests in any 12-hour period. FileMaker Pro 7 and 8 impose no temporal restrictions but limit you to ten concurrently published files and five concurrent users. The increased functionality also eliminates the Custom Web Publishing feature present in FileMaker Pro 5, 5.5, and 6 — no more CDML (Claris Dynamic Markup Language, a set of proprietary HTML extensions created by Claris Corp., the old name of FileMaker, Inc.).

Note

If you anticipate more than sporadic traffic on your published databases (more than five concurrent guests or more than ten published files), you should consider another FileMaker, Inc. product: FileMaker Server Advanced. FileMaker Server Advanced can *host* (or serve) databases on the Web or an intranet to up to 250 concurrent network users and 100 concurrent Web users.

Instant Web Publishing

The quickest way to publish a FileMaker Pro database on the Web or an intranet — a way that will probably satisfy the needs of most users — is by using Instant Web Publishing.

FileMaker Pro 8 eliminates most of the differences between what a user sees when using an Instant Web Publishing database and one shared over the network. You no longer have to worry about themes or configuring a Web Companion plug-in and most scripting limitations have been removed. (There are no more script length limits, and over 70 script steps are supported.)

Publishing a database with Instant Web Publishing

Follow these basic steps to host a database with Instant Web Publishing (additional details are provided in the sections that follow).

STEPS: Publishing a Database with Instant Web Publishing

1. Open the existing database you want to publish (or create a new one).

2. Choose FileMaker Pro/Edit ➪ Sharing ➪ Instant Web Publishing.

   The Instant Web Publishing dialog (see Figure 20-2) appears.

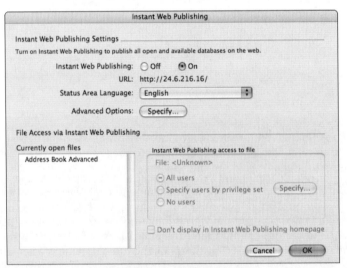

Figure 20-2: The Instant Web Publishing dialog.

3. Select the On radio button for Instant Web Publishing.

4. Select the file(s) you want to publish from the Currently open files list in the dialog's lower-left quadrant.

5. Specify which users can access the file by using the radio buttons under the Instant Web Publishing access to file section.

If you choose Specify users by privilege set, the Specify users by privilege set dialog shown in Figure 20-3 appears. Select the On check boxes next to those privilege sets that you want to grant access. FileMaker Pro will enable the Instant Web Publishing extended privilege to those privilege sets. Notice that each privilege set lists the active accounts having that privilege set. Click OK to dismiss the Specify users by privilege set dialog.

Figure 20-3: The Specify users by privilege set dialog.

The Don't display in Instant Web Publishing homepage check box (refer to Figure 20-2) makes the file sharable but disables direct user access by not listing it among the links on the Instant Web Publishing home page that FileMaker Pro creates. (See Figure 20-4 for an example of a home page.)

6. Click OK to dismiss the Instant Web Publishing dialog.

Instant Web Publishing defaults to using TCP/IP port 80. Mac OS X's security protocols require that an administrator account authorize the use of a port numbered lower than 1024. Therefore, the first time you attempt to share FileMaker databases via Instant Web Publishing, you may be prompted for an Administrator password and the desired port number. See the sidebar, "About IP Addresses," for more information.

The Instant Web Publishing dialog also sports a Specify button for Advanced Options. This button presents the Advanced Web Publishing Options dialog shown in Figure 20-5. The options available are pretty self-explanatory. Specify a port to use for Instant Web Publishing communication in the TCP/IP Port Number text box. Enumerate a list of acceptable IP addresses from which clients can connect. Keep logs of error messages using the Logging options check boxes. Set a time limit on how long a connection can be idle in the Session management section.

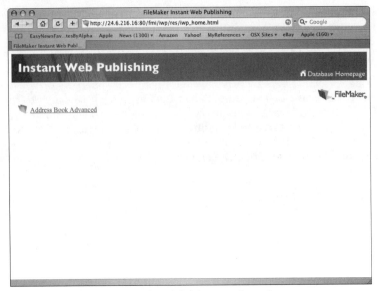

Figure 20-4: An Instant Web Publishing Database home page.

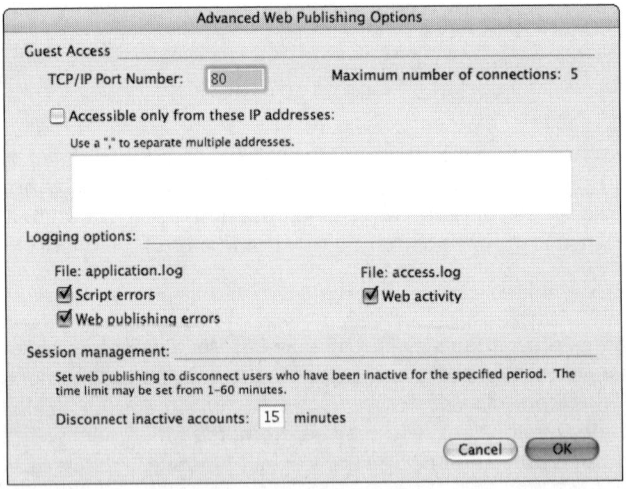

Figure 20-5: Set Advanced Web Publishing Options in this dialog.

Database considerations

When you use Instant Web Publishing, the layouts you make available in the status area's Layouts menu dictate the fields that appear — that is, *all* fields from the chosen layout(s) are used. Thus, if you want to omit some fields (Summary fields, for example), you must do so by making available only layouts containing just the desired fields.

About IP addresses

The *IP address* is the URL to which users connect when they go to your Web publishing home page. Every computer connected to the Internet or an intranet has a unique IP address in the form:

xxx.xxx.xxx.xxx

where the *x*'s represent numbers that contain from one to three digits, separated by periods (such as 207.254.25.117, for example). To open the home page for your Web publishing site, the user launches a Web browser, clicks in the browser's Address box, and types **http://**, followed by the full IP address of your home page, such as http://207.254.25.117 or http://207.254.25.117:591. (The latter method is used in the event that the special FileMaker Pro IP port, 591, has been designated instead of 80, which is the default port number.)

Many computers with a full-time connection to the Internet or a company intranet have a *static IP address.* That is, their IP address never changes, not even if the computer is temporarily disconnected from the Internet or intranet. The same IP address is assigned for each new connection. This sort of connection is ideal for Instant Web Publishing because your users will be able to bookmark your Instant Web Publishing Database home page (make a Favorite).

If you're like most Internet users, though, you are probably in a less enviable position. Most of you will have a *dynamic* IP address: namely, a new IP address that's assigned each time you log on to your Internet account. A dynamic address makes it extremely difficult for users to find your home page because its address changes each time you connect. With the increasing popularity and presence of cable and DSL service, even these full-time connections tend to be dynamic, but they rarely change, so you can treat them as static for most purposes. As an example, Dennis's IP address (for the iMac on which most of this book's screenshots were taken) has changed only twice in the last three-and-one-half years, and one of those occurrences was when the cable modem provider changed ownership from ATTBI to Comcast.

Nevertheless, if you still want to publish databases on the Web, all you do is find out what your IP address is when you log on and then communicate it to potential users. *How* you determine your IP address, however, might be a mystery to you. Regardless of whether you have a dialup or a permanent Internet connection, here are some methods you can use to find out your current IP address:

✦ **Macintosh OS X:** Connect to the Internet, open the Apple menu, and choose Location ⇨ Network Preferences. Your current IP address is shown.

✦ **Windows:** Windows 2000 and XP display this information when you select the Network Connections control panel.

✦ **All platforms:** Many Internet applications—with the notable exception of browsers and e-mail clients—show the current IP address somewhere within the program.

Continued

Continued

✦ **All platforms:** After logging on, send yourself an e-mail message. Open the returned message and examine the full header. You will find your current IP address there.

Note: The method of viewing the full header varies from one e-mail program to the next. For example, in Outlook Express (Windows), select the message, choose the File ➪ Properties command, and click the Details tab in the dialog that appears. To make the information easier to read, you can click the Message Source button. If you use Microsoft Outlook (Windows), open the message and choose View ➪ Options. In Entourage X, open the message and choose View ➪ Internet Headers. In Apple's Mail program, select the message and choose View ➪ Message ➪ Long Headers.

You can also subscribe to a service that redirects a (pseudo) static URL reference to your session's dynamic IP address. Some such services include No-IP (www.no-ip.com), DNS2Go (http://dns2go.deerfield.com), and DynIP (www.dynip.com). To find even more, run a Google search for **Dynamic DNS** (some services are platform-specific). You install a client (typically a *daemon*, or background process) that notifies their server when your IP address changes, such as when you first connect. This allows others to connect to your computer via a static URL, without having to remember four non-mnemonic numbers.

Layout design considerations

Because of the differences between the way Web browsers display text using Cascading Style Sheets, as well as the differences between how Web browsers display CSS and how an application like FileMaker Pro or Microsoft Word displays text, you are likely to encounter clipped text labels on fields, radio button groups that don't display all the buttons, and so forth. Design your layout elements so that there is sufficient space for the field element's content when displayed in a Web browser.

If your field labels are being clipped, allow more horizontal space to let the text fit.

Radio buttons and check boxes are displayed using standard HTML controls. These controls don't wrap well for vertical stacking. Horizontal rows are more likely to display properly. Similarly, the HTML equivalents require more space than the FileMaker Pro layout elements; allowing 50 percent more space vertically is a decent rule.

Rounded rectangles are displayed as standard rectangles, as are buttons. Similarly, the tabs in tab controls are all rectangular.

Text in buttons should be only one line in length.

Tip   Always check your layouts in as many supported Web browsers as you can. Display behavior will vary from one Web browser to the next, often even changing from one version to another of the same Web browser. For example, the Medical2004 database's relatively straightforward Medical2004 layout on the accompanying CD displays quite differently in Internet Explorer 6 (Windows), Internet Explorer 5.2 (Mac), and Safari 2.0 (Mac).

Testing your published database

To examine and interact with your database, you'll do what any other user would do — open it in your browser. Follow these steps to test your Web-published databases:

STEPS: Testing a Web-published Database

1. Launch FileMaker Pro and open the database you wish to publish. Make sure that Instant Web Publishing is turned on and that the database has its Instant Web Publishing extended privilege set.

2. With an active connection to the Internet or an intranet, launch your Web browser and type **http://** in the Address box, followed by your current IP address (such as **http://206.184.180.16**).

Note

If you are using any port other than 80, the port number must be appended to the IP address (for example, http://206.184.180.16:591).

or

If you don't have an active Internet connection, simply launch your browser and type

```
http://localhost
```

or

```
http://127.0.0.1/
```

in the Address box. This method enables you to test the database while working offline.

3. When the home page appears, click the link for your database. As you modify, add, and delete records on the Web pages, the changes are made to the FileMaker Pro database.

4. (Optional) You can enable logging options tracking user interaction with your published databases. You turn logging on in the Advanced Web Publishing Options dialog shown in Figure 20-5. These log files are plain text files that FileMaker Pro places in the Web logs folder within the FileMaker Pro application's folder.

Instant Web Publishing limitations

Although Instant Web Publishing is indeed a quick and easy way to get your databases onto the Web, there are some FileMaker Pro features and controls you must give up:

✦ Users cannot play sounds or display OLE (Object Linking and Embedding) objects in container fields (even in Windows) — a graphic placeholder is displayed.

✦ Users cannot insert graphics, sounds, movies, and so on into container fields.

✦ Items in Container fields are automatically shrunk to fit within the field.

✦ Users can't edit value lists by using an Edit item, nor can they enter unlisted values by using an Other item.

✦ If a field validation criterion is not met, a generic error message appears. Even if you have created custom error messages, they are not shown. For example, if data entered into a field fails a range test, there is no provision to explain to the user what the allowable range is.

✦ If a selected layout contains related fields from other files, Instant Web Publishing must be On for all such related files. However, you can prevent users from directly accessing the related files by selecting the Instant Web Publishing dialog's Don't display in Instant Web Publishing Database homepage check box for those files.

Interacting with a database published with Instant Web Publishing

When a user enters the URL for your home page, the current list of published databases appears. When a user clicks a link to a published database, the selected database appears. (If account-restricted access has been designated for the database, however, a login dialog appears first.)

The database opens displaying whatever layout you've specified as the default, in the view you've specified (Form, List, or Table), as shown in Figure 20-6. Depending on the permissions set, text links and buttons are provided that enable the user to edit or delete the current record, create new records, show all records, search, sort, summon help, and switch to list or table view.

Scripts and Web-published databases

You can attach user-executable scripts to buttons in Web-published database layouts — as long as the scripts meet certain requirements.

The primary requirement is that the script steps be among the more than 70 Web-compatible script steps. You can see which script steps are Web-compatible by selecting the Edit Script dialog's Indicate web compatibility check box. Incompatible steps are then dimmed (disabled) in the list of script steps and in your scripts. Chapter 15 covers scripting in more detail. In general, database-related script steps (such as Go to Next Field and Insert Text) are Web-compatible, and interface-related script steps (such as Adjust Window or Allow Toolbars) are not.

Scripts that create or modify records should have a Commit step to communicate that the user (or script) is done working with the record in question.

Form view

List view

Table view

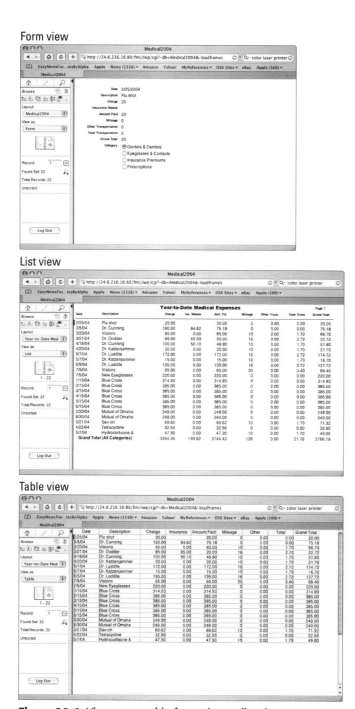

Figure 20-6: View a record in form view, a list view, or up to 50 records in table view.

What happened to Custom Web Publishing?

With the enhancements made to Instant Web Publishing in FileMaker Pro 7, support for Custom Web Publishing was eliminated. Custom Web Publishing is still available to users of the FileMaker Server Advanced product. Custom Web Publishing uses XML (eXtensible Markup Language) and XSLT (eXtensible Stylesheet Language Transformation) stylesheets to control data display, user interaction, and integration with other Web sites. See the FileMaker Web site at `www.filemaker.com` for more information on FileMaker Server Advanced and Custom Web Publishing.

Publishing Static Pages on the Web

Instant Web Publishing is designed for interaction between the user and the database hosted on your computer. If you just wish to make the data available for perusal, without the interaction where users might modify, sort, or search the data, you might prefer to publish your database as a static Web page. Using the Export command, you can export selected records, showing only the desired fields, and sorted in the same manner as in the original database.

Another time when you should prefer static Web pages is when you have an intermittent or low-bandwidth Internet connection (such as dialup). Placing static pages on a Web site that doesn't require your computer to be online makes the data available to more people and reduces your computing overhead.

The resulting output from this export procedure is an HTML or XML file laid out as a table. If you don't like the formatting, you can change or embellish it by opening the HTML file in any Web page editor. Then, you add the HTML (or XML/XSLT) to your Web site.

Mac OS X comes with the Apache Web server software (used by many ISPs) built-in, so you can host Web sites identical to those on major ISPs right from your Mac. Of course, this requires that your Mac be online at all times, just as if you were hosting via Instant Web Publishing, but without the five-user and ten-file restriction.

STEPS: Creating a Static Web Page

1. Open the database from which you want to create a Web page.

2. Use Finds and related procedures to select the desired records.

3. Using the Records ⇨ Sort Records command, sort the records in whatever order you like.

4. Choose File ⇨ Export Records.

   The Export Records to File dialog appears, as shown in Figure 20-7.

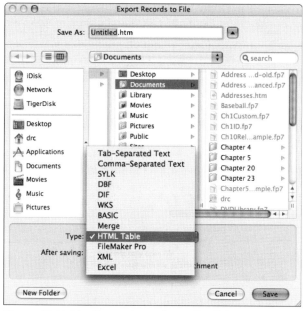

Figure 20-7: The Export Records to File dialog.

5. Navigate to the drive and folder where you wish to save the file and choose HTML Table from the Type pop-up/drop-down menu (see Figure 20-7) if you want a standard HTML table display or choose XML if you plan to transform the table using an XSLT stylesheet. Then name the file (retaining the `.htm` or `.html` extension for HTML table exports) and click Save.

The Specify Field Order for Export dialog appears. (See Figure 20-8.)

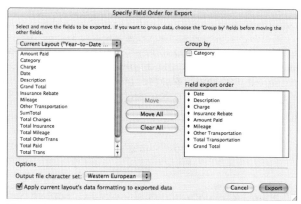

Figure 20-8: The Specify Field Order for Export dialog.

6. Move the desired fields from the left side of the dialog to the right side. Double-click each field, or select the desired field(s) and click the Move button.

   Note that you can simultaneously move multiple fields by Shift+clicking them (contiguous fields) or by ⌘/Ctrl+clicking them (noncontiguous fields).

7. The table will be created from the fields in the order that they are specified. If necessary, you can rearrange the fields in the Field export order list by dragging them up or down. (To move a field, position the pointer over the double arrow preceding a field name, click, and then drag.)

8. Click the Export button.

   The HTML (or XML) file is generated. (See Figure 20-9.)

Medical2004.htm

file:///Users/Shared/543474CDFiles/Medical2004.htm   Q⋅ Google

EasyNewsFav...tesByAlpha   Apple   Amazon   Yahoo!   News▾   MyReferences▾   OSX Sites▾   eBay

Medical2004.htm

Date	Description	Charge	Insurance Rebate	Amount Paid	Mileage	Other Transportation	Total Transportation	Grand Total
2/25/2004	Flu shot	20		20	0	0	0	20
3/5/2004	Dr. Cunning	160	84.82	75.18	0	0	0	75.18
3/20/2004	Visions	65	0	65	10	0	1.7	66.7
3/21/2004	Dr. Dodder	85	65	20	16	0	2.72	22.72
4/16/2004	Dr. Cunning	100	50.10	49.9	10	0	1.7	51.6
4/20/2004	Dr. Katzenjammer	20	0	20	10	0	1.7	21.7
5/7/2004	Dr. Luddite	172	0	172	16	0	2.72	174.72
5/7/2004	Dr. Katzenjammer	15	0	15	10	0	1.7	16.7
6/5/2004	Dr. Luddite	135	0	135	16	0	2.72	137.72
7/5/2004	Visions	65	0	65	20	0	3.4	68.4
7/5/2004	New Eyeglasses	220	0	220	0	0	0	220
1/15/2004	Blue Cross	314.93	0	314.93	0	0	0	314.93
2/15/2004	Blue Cross	385	0	385	0	0	0	385
3/15/2004	Blue Cross	385	0	385	0	0	0	385
4/15/2004	Blue Cross	385	0	385	0	0	0	385
5/15/2004	Blue Cross	385	0	385	0	0	0	385

Figure 20-9: The HTML file is formatted as a table, viewable in most browsers.

Note   Applying the field's formatting when exporting (Steps 6 and 7) does not include such attributes as justification or text color, as you can see in Figure 20-9. It does, however, include number of decimal places for numeric values, date, and time formats. In other words, it preserves data formatting attributes and not layout element formatting attributes.

Summary

✦ FileMaker Pro's Instant Web Publishing enables you to publish databases on the World Wide Web or an intranet. You host published databases directly from your computer, turning it into a Web server. Users connect to your computer by typing your IP address in their Web browser's Address box.

✦ Working with a published database is similar to using a database in FileMaker Pro. Data can be displayed in tables or lists for viewing multiple records, or in forms for working with one record at a time. Depending on the privileges assigned to them, users can add, edit, or delete records and can execute Find requests and sorts, for example.

✦ When you use Instant Web Publishing, all layouts accessible to that user via the status area's Layouts pop-up menu are presented almost identically to the way they appear in the FileMaker Pro application.

✦ You can set Instant Web Publishing options specifying which databases will appear on the built-in home page, choose a language for the interface, specify allowable user IP addresses, and set a different port for the Web server.

✦ The only officially certified browsers to work with Instant Web Publishing database pages are Internet Explorer 6 (or later) or Firefox for Windows and Safari 1.1 or later or Firefox on Mac OS X or later. Other browsers, assuming that they have sufficient Cascading Style Sheet support, might work.

✦ Published databases can be presented in record-creation order, presorted according to criteria you establish, or sorted by the user (but restricted to sort fields appearing on the layout).

✦ Published databases can incorporate a start-up script and scripts that are attached to buttons on your layouts. Script steps must be selected from the set of 70+ Web-compatible steps.

✦ Custom Web Publishing is no longer a feature of the FileMaker Pro product and is available only in FileMaker Server Advanced.

✦ Using the Export command, you can create an HTML table from any database, publishable on the Web or an intranet. Creating a static Web page in this manner, for instance, might be preferable for users who don't have a constant Internet connection or who merely want to include FileMaker data as a separate page in a larger Web site. Such Web pages can also be created by exporting XML and applying an XSLT stylesheet to format the data.

✦ ✦ ✦

Advanced Database Connectivity with XML and ODBC/JDBC

Unlike working with Open Database Connectivity (ODBC) and Java Database Connectivity (JDBC) (described in the "FileMaker and ODBC/JDBC" section, later in this chapter), exchanging data between applications as XML is easily within the grasp of most FileMaker users. Customizing the output, though, will take you into the basics of programming.

XML (eXtensible Markup Language) is a current standard for data interchange. The language is English-like and bears a similarity to HTML (HyperText Markup Language), the language used to display information in Web browsers. In fact, XHTML (eXtensible HTML) defines an XML implementation for Web browsers. (Check out www.w3.org/TR/xhtml1 for more details.) Although HTML is limited to a set of predefined tags (such as the <b> and </b> used to mark the beginning and end of some boldface text), XML users can create their own tags. As an example, here's the description of a single record, extracted from the msdso_elem.xml file, located in the FileMaker Pro 8 ⇨ English Extras ⇨ Examples ⇨ XML Examples ⇨ Import ⇨ MSDSO_ELEM folder, provided as XML sample data with FileMaker Pro 8:

```
<people>
  <Last>White</Last>
  <First>Mark</First>
  <Group>Red</Group>
  <Score>100</Score>
</people>
```

In this data file, `people` is the designator for a record. Everything between the opening `<people>` and `</people>` delimiters is data for a single record. The fields — each with its own set of delimiters — are `Last`, `First`, `Group`, and `Score`. `White`, `Mark`, `Red`, and `100` are the field data.

Fortunately, you don't have to know what a XML file looks like on the inside nor how an XSL stylesheet performs the transformations to give the data a new appearance any more than you have to know how to write HTML and JavaScript to create a Web page. Knowing a little more can let you customize the results, though, just as knowing HTML and JavaScript lets you customize your Web pages.

Note As you continue to use computers and modern applications, you frequently encounter XML documents. Apple, for example, uses XML extensively in OS X to define data structures. In fact, virtually every preference (`.plist`) file you have is an XML document. Similarly, Microsoft promotes XML heavily for document portability in its recent Office products. Your FileMaker Pro 8 label templates and layout themes are defined by XML documents.

Exporting and Importing XML

FileMaker Pro 8 can both import and export data in XML format. Data imported into FileMaker must conform to the FMPXMLRESULT grammar. FMPXMLRESULT contains specific information, such as the number of records in the database, field types, and field formats, necessary for creating the new records. If the XML data isn't in FMPXMLRESULT format, it can be modified by applying an XSLT (eXtensible Stylesheet Language Transformation) stylesheet.

Note An XSLT stylesheet is a set of rules for parsing and reformatting XML data based upon the tags and attributes used. Like a programming or scripting language, it contains both conditional (`If`) and looping (`For Each`, for example) constructs. If you're interested in all the technical jargon and a mathematically complete discussion of XSLT, check out `www.w3.org/TR/xslt`.

Tip XML and XSLT are large and interesting topics. If you feel the desire or need to learn more about them, we recommend *Applied XML: A Toolkit for Programmers* by Alex Ceponkus and Faraz Hoodbhoy (Wiley). It's a very good discussion with a lot of well-explained examples.

On XML export, FileMaker supports the FMPXMLRESULT and FMPDSORESULT grammars, the latter being a better choice when creating XML output intended for use with Cascading Style Sheets (CSS: commonly supported by most current Web browsers, such as Internet Explorer and Safari). As is the case with importing XML, you can also use an XSLT stylesheet to format or transform FileMaker data during the export process. In general, though, FMPXMLRESULT is the grammar recommended by FileMaker, Inc.

The following sections explain the procedures for exporting and importing XML data with FileMaker Pro 8.

Exporting XML data for use in other applications

The process of exporting data as XML is actually very similar to exporting using any other file format — HTML or tab-delimited text, for example. Think of XML as just another file format, and you'll be ahead of the game. The only decisions you have to make are

✦ Which grammar to use

- *FMPXMLRESULT:* When the data must be manipulable in the receiving application, additional information is provided about the database contents, such as the number of records, field types, and field formats.

- *FMPDSORESULT:* This is useful when the data's display relies on cascading stylesheets, commonly supported by most current Web browsers.

✦ Whether a stylesheet will be applied to format or transform the data

STEPS: Exporting XML

1. Open the FileMaker database from which you want to export data.

2. By performing Finds and related commands, select the records you wish to export. (Only the browsed set/found set will be exported.)

3. If desired, sort the records in the order that you wish them to be exported.

4. Choose File ➪ Export Records.

The Export Records to File dialog appears, as shown in Figure 21-1.

5. Choose XML from the Type pop-up menu/Save as type drop-down list (see Figure 21-1).

6. Navigate to the drive and folder in which you want to save the exported data.

7. In the Save As/File Name text box, enter a filename for the export file and click Save.

The Specify XML and XSL Options dialog appears. (See Figure 21-2.)

8. Select an output grammar from the Grammar pop-up menu/drop-down list.

9. (Optional) If you want to format the exported data using a stylesheet, select the Use XSL style sheet check box. Specify the stylesheet to use by doing either of the following:

- Select the File radio button and then select a stylesheet stored on your hard disk. Navigate to and select the XSL stylesheet from the file dialog that appears and then click Open.

or

- Select the HTTP request radio button and then enter the URL for the stylesheet's location on the Internet/intranet in the text box.

Figure 21-1: Export Records to File dialog.

Tip

If you'd like to see how stylesheets affect output, you'll find several sample stylesheets (with XSL extensions) in the FileMaker Pro 8 ⇨ English Extras ⇨ Examples ⇨ XML Examples ⇨ Export folder. Note that *without* an attached stylesheet, many applications are unlikely to know what to do with the data. Figure 21-3 shows just two examples of how stylesheets can affect output. You can find a large and growing number of XSLT stylesheets available for download at www.filemaker.com/products/technologies/xslt_library.html.

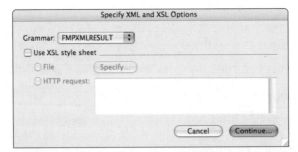

Figure 21-2: Select grammar and stylesheet options in the Specify XML and XSL Options dialog.

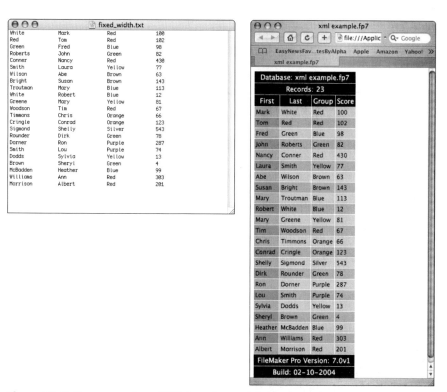

Figure 21-3: Two examples of XSL-transformed data.

10. Click Continue.

The Specify Field Order for Export dialog appears. (See Figure 21-4.)

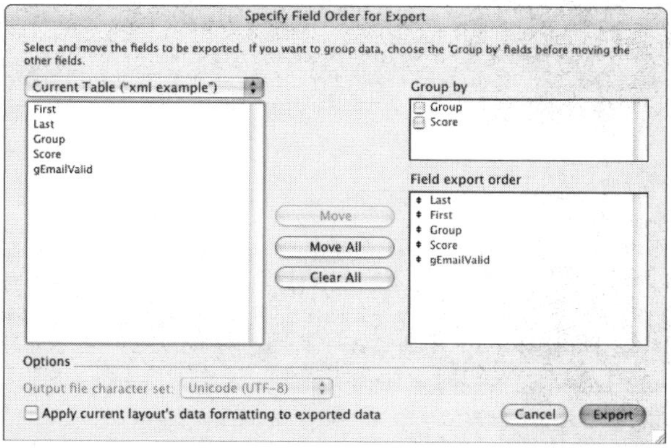

Figure 21-4: Select the fields you wish to export.

11. Select fields to include in the export and click Move to add them to the Field export order list box. To add related fields to the export, select a defined relationship from the pop-up menu/drop-down list above the left-hand list box.

12. The order in which the fields are listed corresponds to the order in which they will be exported. To change the position of any field in the list, move the pointer over the double arrow preceding the field's name and then drag the field up or down in the list.

13. Select the Apply current layout's data formatting to exported data check box to export the data using the field formatting specified in the current layout. (For example, a Number field formatted as currency might appear as $3,476.50 rather than 3476.5.)

14. To include grand summary or sub-summary values in the exported data, select the check boxes beside the desired field(s) in the Group by list box. (You must already have the database sorted before exporting for the grouping to occur.)

15. Click the Export button.

You can now open the exported data in any application that supports it. For example, after exporting data using the `complex_table.xsl` stylesheet, you could open the new file as an editable Excel worksheet (see Figure 21-5) or as a Web page containing a static table in Internet Explorer or Safari.

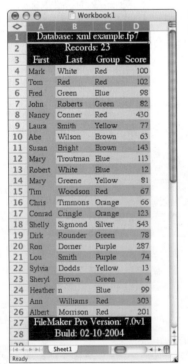

Figure 21-5: The exported data viewed in Microsoft Excel.

Note As is the case with any FileMaker export, only the *results* of calculations are exported — not the formulas. If this isn't sufficient, you might have to rebuild the formulas in the target application.

Importing XML data into FileMaker Pro

Here are the two ways to get XML data into FileMaker Pro:

✦ Open an XML data file and stylesheet, automatically creating a new FileMaker Pro database

✦ Import XML data into an existing FileMaker Pro database — adding new records, replacing the current found set, or updating the current found set

Regardless of the method you choose, the XML data must conform to the FMPXML-RESULT grammar. If necessary, you can apply a stylesheet to the data in order to make it conform to FileMaker's XML requirements.

Note As you saw in the previous section, exporting data as XML from within FileMaker is a snap — the capability is built into FileMaker Pro 8. All you need to do is choose the command and select a stylesheet. Now comes something that is slightly more complex. Importing XML data from another application requires that the application have an XML export feature and/or that you have access to (or can create) a stylesheet to transform the data into a form compatible with the FMPXMLRESULT grammar.

STEPS: Opening an XML Data Source to Create a New FileMaker Pro Database

1. Choose File ➪ Open (or press ⌘+O/Ctrl+O).

The Open File dialog appears.

2. From the Show pop-up menu /Files of type drop-down list, choose XML Data Source.

The Specify XML and XSL Options dialog appears. (See Figure 21-6.)

Note Even though this dialog has the same name as the dialog shown in Figure 21-2, it is a different beast.

3. Depending on whether the XML data is a local file or one located on the Internet/an intranet, perform one of these actions:

• Select the File radio button. In the standard Open dialog that appears, navigate to and select the XML data file stored on your hard disk and then click Open.

or

• Select the HTTP request radio button and enter the URL for the XML data's location on the Internet/intranet in the text box.

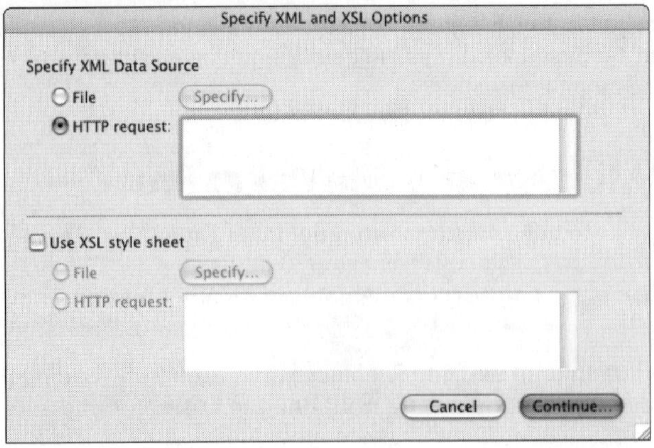

Figure 21-6: The Specify XML and XSL Options dialog.

4. To attach a stylesheet to the data (in order to convert it to FMPXMLRESULT or to format it), select the Use XSL style sheet check box and do one of the following:

   - Select the File radio button and select a stylesheet that is stored on your hard disk by navigating to and selecting the XSL stylesheet from the file dialog that appears and clicking Open.

   or

   - Select the HTTP request radio button and enter the URL for the stylesheet's location on the Internet/intranet in the text box.

5. Click Continue.

   The Create a New File Named dialog appears.

6. Name the new FileMaker database and click Save.

   The database is saved to disk and then opens in a new window.

STEPS: Importing XML Data into an Existing FileMaker Pro Database

1. Open the FileMaker database into which you want to import XML data.

2. (Optional) By performing Finds and related commands, select the records that you wish to replace or update. (Only the browsed set/found set will be replaced or updated.) You can skip this step if your intent is to merely add the XML as new records.

Caution   Replacing or updating records is irreversible. You are well advised to make a backup copy of your database before performing this type of data import.

3. Choose File ➪ Import Records ➪ XML Data Source.

The Specify XML and XSL Options dialog appears. (Refer to Figure 21-6.)

4. Depending on whether the XML data is a local file or located on the Internet/intranet, perform one of these actions:

- Select the File radio button, select the XML data file that is stored on your hard disk, and then click Open.

or

- Select the HTTP request radio button and enter the URL for the XML data's location on the Internet/intranet in the text box.

Caution

It may be necessary to choose a stylesheet transforming the XML to FMPXML RESULT form in order for the import to succeed. When in doubt, choose an FMPXMLRESULT stylesheet on imports.

5. Click the Continue button.

The Import Field Mapping dialog appears. (See Figure 21-7.)

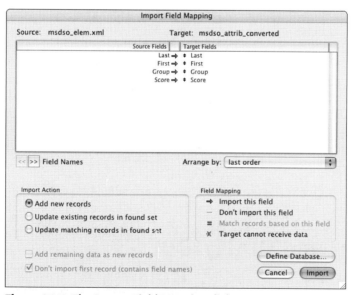

Figure 21-7: The Import Field Mapping dialog.

6. (Optional) To import fields for which there are currently no matching fields, click the Define Database button.

The Define Database dialog appears, enabling you to create the additional fields (in the Fields pane) in the current database. See Chapter 5 for details.

7. Select a radio button in the dialog's Import Action section.

- *Add new records* appends the imported records to the destination file.

- *Update existing records in found set* overwrites the records in the current found set.

- *Update matching records in found set* requires you to specify "match fields" in the two files (such as ID numbers, first and last names, or some other combination of fields that will identify matching records in the two data sets).

8. Match the fields that you want to import.

An arrow following a field name in the Map column indicates that the field will be imported into the field in the destination file. An equal sign (available only when Update matching records in found set is selected) marks a pair of match fields.

If you don't want to import a particular field, click its arrow. The indicator changes to a dimmed line, showing that the field will not be imported. (If Update matching records in found set is selected, you can click a second time to make the field a match field, changing the indicator to an equal sign.)

Because fields in the two files can be in any order, you might need to rearrange them manually so that they match. You can drag the arrows to the left of the field names in the destination file (on the right side of the dialog) to change their order.

9. (Optional) Click the double arrow buttons at the bottom left of the list box to review the matching fields in several records.

This is mainly a sanity check. By scanning several records, you can assure yourself that the fields do indeed match properly and that you have not omitted an important field.

10. Click Import.

The XML data is imported using the options and settings you've selected.

FileMaker and ODBC/JDBC

ODBC (Open Database Connectivity) is an API (application programming interface) enabling disparate database (or related) applications to access and use each other's data. Typical ODBC-compliant applications for which this method would be used include Microsoft Excel, Microsoft Access, and Oracle. JDBC (Java Database Connectivity) is an analogous, cross-platform API rooted in Sun's Java language.

Learning SQL (Structured Query Language) so as to query databases, configuring ODBC drivers, and the like is a subject far beyond the scope (and page count) of this book. You can find documentation on your FileMaker Pro 8 installation CD in the xDBC folder's Electronic Documentation subfolder. Much like learning to program a computer, if you aren't already working with ODBC databases, it's unlikely that you'll be doing so in the near future — and certainly not after reading a few pages in a manual or a book. If this indeed is something you wish to pursue, you should begin by reading about ODBC in FileMaker's manuals and Help files and then consult with your database administrator. For other data importing and exporting requirements (as explained in this chapter), you'll find that FileMaker's regular tools will easily meet your needs.

You might want to look through the electronic document, *FileMaker 8 ODBC and JDBC Developer's Guide,* to learn about interacting with an external database from within FileMaker Pro. This document is in the xDBC/Electronic Documentation folder on your installation CD as FM8_ODBC_JDBC_Developer.pdf. If you follow the instructions carefully, you'll successfully import data into the sample FileMaker database. In the process, you'll learn how simple composing queries from within FileMaker Pro 8 can be (see the upcoming discussion) after you've got the ODBC drivers configured. If you then move on to importing from your *own* data sources or importing FileMaker Pro data into a different application (such as Microsoft Excel) via ODBC, on the other hand, you'll also discover how complex it is when you're truly on your own.

The first step is to configure the ODBC driver for the file to be imported. Each file requires its own Data Source Name (DSN) entry, so if you have ten text files to import, you need to configure ten data sources. The preliminary driver configuration work, external to FileMaker Pro 8, is significantly different on Mac and Windows and from one ODBC driver to another. For these reasons and because the process is entirely external to the FileMaker Pro product and dependent upon the client chosen, we are forced to punt, referring you to the documentation on your FileMaker installation CD and from the client provider for references. As usual, after you're back in FileMaker Pro, the choice of platform will make no significant difference. After you have a driver installed and configured, all you need do is choose File ⇨ Import Records ⇨ ODBC Data Source, select your data source from the Select ODBC Data Source dialog that appears, and then use the FileMaker SQL Builder to formulate your queries.

Moral of the Chapter

Most of you will probably not want to tackle ODBC or JDBC on your own. How one prepares for ODBC importing or exporting depends on the particular ODBC driver you're using (and there are *many* of them, some of which cost a pretty penny) as well as the application you intend to use in combination with FileMaker Pro. If at all possible, we urge you to find someone who can do the set-up work for you. After the driver and data source are properly configured, the rest of the process is relatively simple.

Summary

✦ XML (eXtensible Markup Language) is a current standard for data interchange. FileMaker Pro 8 supports both exporting and importing of XML data.

✦ Exporting to XML requires only that you select an appropriate stylesheet to enable the exported data to be opened and displayed by the receiving application. Exporting as XML is very similar to exporting to any other data format.

✦ Importing XML into a FileMaker database requires that the data be generated as or converted to FMPXMLRESULT grammar. Thus, you'll either need an application that can generate such XML or a stylesheet that can convert it to FMPXMLRESULT grammar.

✦ FileMaker Pro's OBDC support allows two-way communication (using SQL queries) between FileMaker and other ODBC-compliant applications, such as high-end databases and spreadsheets. FileMaker Pro can be both the client and the data source for ODBC. After you configure the appropriate ODBC driver and the applications, you can use FileMaker's SQL Query Builder to create the necessary SQL (Structured Query Language) statements (assuming that you're importing data into FileMaker).

✦ FileMaker's JDBC driver enables FileMaker data to be extracted by Java applets and other JDBC-compliant applications.

✦ ODBC and JDBC sharing can be a very complex operation to set up because each driver can have different requirements. After it's established, though, the transfer of data via SQL Query is fairly simple (assuming you know what you want to ask for and are at least minimally proficient in SQL).

✦   ✦   ✦

Expanding FileMaker's Capabilities Using Plug-Ins

A plug-in's purpose (a *plug-in* being an application-specific software utility) is enhancing an application by giving it new or improved capabilities. Plug-ins are pervasive in today's software world. Many applications — such as desktop publishing programs, graphic applications, and databases — have been written to accept plug-ins. In fact, a great deal of the out-of-the-box functionality in such popular products as Photoshop and iPhoto exists because plug-ins are shipped as part of the product distribution. Using plug-ins provides a convenient method for the software publisher, as well as independent developers, to add new features to the application or update existing features without revising the basic product.

As a FileMaker Pro user, you might already be familiar with a few FileMaker plug-ins, whether you're aware that they're plug-ins or not. For example, Web Publishing is implemented via a plug-in (`Web.fmplugin`, in the Extensions folder within your FileMaker application folder, to be precise) enabling you to make your databases available to others over the Web. What you might not realize, however, is that FileMaker, Inc. isn't the only source of plug-ins. Many commercial plug-in developers might very well have the solution to what currently appears to be an insurmountable FileMaker problem. A few plug-ins are free.

To give you a better idea of the kinds of things you can do with plug-ins, as well as how they work, we'll examine a few plug-ins from one of the leading commercial plug-in developers — Troi Automatisering (www.troi.com).

Note   Because this is a new version of FileMaker Pro, you might wish to check with the plug-in publisher to ensure that a given plug-in is compatible with FileMaker Pro 8. We haven't encountered any FileMaker Pro 7-compatible plug-ins that weren't FileMaker Pro 8-compatible, but plug-ins from earlier versions are frequently incompatible with the later versions of the software. Obviously, you also want to make sure that the plug-in is compatible with your operating system, be it Mac OS X or Windows 2000/XP.

On The Web Site   Another leading developer of FileMaker plug-ins, 24U Software, has provided a sample plug-in that you'll find by browsing to the Web site accompanying this book. See Appendix F for details about the Web site.

Plug-in Licensing and Use

Like any other piece of software, unless a plug-in is distributed as free of restrictions, there are likely some restrictions concerning how you can use it. For example, using a plug-in is commonly restricted to a single computer. Although you may freely use the plug-in in conjunction with as many FileMaker Pro databases as you like, you might not be allowed to install your database/plug-in combination on a fellow worker's computer. In order to use your solution, each person will require a license for the plug-in. (Of course, if you intend to distribute your solutions, you'll find that most plug-in developers will happily sell you a broader license permitting you to distribute the plug-in in conjunction with your solution.)

Tip   Plug-in developers often offer their products as time-limited demos or on a "try before you buy" basis. If you aren't sure whether a particular plug-in will do what you need, visit the developer's Web site to see whether a downloadable demo version is available. For example, the Troi plug-ins discussed in this chapter can be downloaded for a 30-day trial.

FileMaker Pro plug-ins are not cross-platform software. Just as Windows programs will not run on a Mac (and vice versa), plug-ins also need to be platform-specific. You might also find, however, that a particular plug-in is available for only one platform, rather than both. This can be a result of a developer's greater programming proficiency on one or the other platform, or something as simple as one operating system being appropriate for a given plug-in while the other isn't. For example, there's little point in creating a plug-in for a particular computer if the plug-in's features are already available as part of the operating system. Sometimes, as in the case of the 24U SimpleSound plug-in (www.24usoftware.com), the developer distributes the plug-in as what is known as a *fat binary:* That is, a single file contains both the Mac and Windows versions. This results in a larger plug-in file, but it does ensure that you have what you require regardless of which platform you're using.

Installing the Troi Plug-Ins

To use any of the Troi plug-ins, they must first be installed for use by FileMaker Pro. With FileMaker Pro not running, proceed as follows:

✦ *On a Mac:* Copy the plug-in into the Extensions folder (found within the FileMaker Pro 8 folder). If the plug-in filename includes an extension, it will usually be .fmplugin.

✦ *On a Windows PC:* Copy the plug-in — the .fmx file — into the Extensions folder (found within the FileMaker Pro 8 folder). Assuming that you used the default setting when installing FileMaker Pro, the full path to the Extensions folder is probably

```
C:\Program Files\FileMaker\FileMaker Pro 8\Extensions
```

After it's installed, you can test the installation by launching FileMaker Pro 8 and choosing FileMaker Pro/Edit ⇨ Preferences. In the Preferences dialog (see Figure 22-1), click the Plug-Ins tab and see that your newly installed plug-ins are listed.

> **Note** When invoking a Troi plug-in that you haven't yet registered (that is, paid for and activated by entering the registration code), you'll see an alert reminding you to register. You can dismiss this dialog by clicking in it; then the plug-in will run.

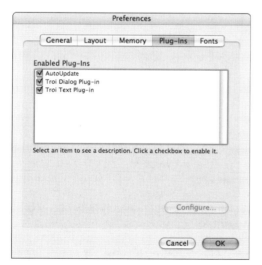

Figure 22-1: Installed plug-ins are listed on the Preferences dialog's Plug-Ins tab.

By default, the Troi plug-ins are automatically enabled. If you ever wish to disable any of them, open the Preferences dialog and remove the plug-in's check mark.

Plug-In Examples

Plug-ins work by creating new External functions you can include in FileMaker Pro script steps that can accept a calculation as part of their specification, such as the `Set Field` step. (See an example of this in the upcoming, "STEPS: Creating a Progress Bar.") To see a list of the External functions added by a new plug-in, display the Specify Calculation dialog (for example, by defining a Calculation field) and choose External Functions from the View pop-up menu/drop-down list. (See Figure 22-2.)

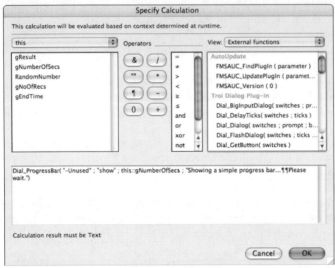

Figure 22-2: In the Specify Calculation dialog, choose External Functions from the View pop-up menu/drop-down list.

Note   Of course, seeing a list of the new External functions will show you only their names and syntax. It will *not* show you how to use them nor how to set options for them (if options are available). For that information, you'll have to refer to the plug-in's documentation and example files.

To give you an idea of the types of problems that plug-ins can help you solve, the rest of this chapter will show you two of the Troi plug-ins.

Tip   The names of External functions are case-sensitive. It is usually best to include a function in the calculation by double-clicking the function's name in the list rather than typing it directly in the large text box.

New Feature   In previous versions of FileMaker Pro, it was necessary to wrap external function references in parentheses as the argument to the External function. You no longer need to do so, as shown in the following examples, unless the function was written for a version of FileMaker Pro prior to FileMaker Pro 7. In other words, FileMaker Pro 7 (and 8)-native External functions are referenced exactly as if they were built-in FileMaker functions.

Troi Dialog plug-in

The Troi Dialog plug-in enables you to display a variety of different dialogs for different purposes:

✦ Gather user data for up to five fields (styled as text boxes, pop-ups, checklists, or password boxes)

✦ Request passwords

✦ Display a flashing dialog

✦ Present a list from which the user can choose an item

✦ Display a progress bar (either simple or barber-pole style)

In addition, other External functions included in the Troi Dialog plug-in allow you to set a delay time, determine which button was clicked, specify a custom icon to appear in the dialog (such as a note or warning icon), set default entries for input fields, and so on.

As an example, examine the Dial_ProgressBar function. When programs perform lengthy operations, they often display a progress indicator of some sort. Progress bars commonly appear, for example, when you download a file from the Internet, install software, extract files from an archive, and send or receive e-mail. By including the Dial_ProgressBar function in a time-consuming script, you accomplish two things:

✦ You let the user know approximately how long the operation will take.

✦ You assure the user that the operation has not stalled because the progress bar should continue to move.

To create a progress bar, you must insert the Dial_ProgressBar External function into the script three times:

1. Initialize the progress bar values and display it.

2. Increment the progress bar (telling it when to show an additional segment).

3. Halt the progress bar and dismiss it.

In the bookkeeping database mentioned earlier in this book, a script calculates an IRS 1040 Schedule C's line items by looping through the database one record at a time. Even with as few as 100 records, the process is hardly instantaneous. Normally, when performing a lengthy script, FileMaker just displays a cursor to indicate that the script is executing. However, using the ProgressBar function displays the considerably more informative dialog shown in Figure 22-3. The following steps explain how the original script was modified.

Processing records...

Records remaining: 15773

Figure 22-3: Example of a dialog generated by the ProgressBar function.

Tip

With this external function — or any other — you should read the accompanying documentation to learn what (if any) special parameter syntax is required. In the case of Dial_ProgressBar, you'll discover that it takes four arguments: a set of switches (frequently set to "-Unused" or left blank), a command ("show", "incr", or "stop"), an integer for the maximum or incrementation value, and a text argument for the text to display in the dialog.

STEPS: Creating a Progress Bar

1. In the Define Fields dialog, create two new Number fields with the Global storage attribute (click the Options button and then the Storage tab):

   - gCount: The number of records in the database

   - gResult: The field with which the ProgressBar function would be associated

2. Open ScriptMaker (choose Scripts ➭ ScriptMaker) and edit the existing 1040 script.

3. Use the Get(FoundCount) function to initialize gCount, setting it equal to the number of records in the current found set.

   ```
   Set Field [gCount, Get(FoundCount)]
   ```

   FoundCount returns the number of records in the *found set*, rather than in the entire database. To make it work correctly in this example, precede the initialization steps with a Show All Records script step.

4. Prior to the script's main loop, initialize the ProgressBar function with this Set Field script step:

   ```
   Set Field [gResult; Dial_ProgressBar( "-Unused";"show";"
   gCount";"Processing records . . .")]
   ```

   This step was specified for the gResult field. The show parameter indicates that the dialog should be displayed; gCount represents the maximum value for the progress bar (which, in this case, equals the number of records in the database or found set); and `Processing records . . .` is the text string to be displayed at the top of the dialog.

5. Immediately before the final steps of the loop, insert the following pair of `Set Field` steps to decrement gCount by one and to increment the progress bar:

```
Set Field [gCount; gCount-1]
Set Field [gResult; Dial_ProgressBar("-Unused";
"incr";1;"Processing records . . . ¶¶¶Records remaining: " &
gCount)"]
```

The Global field gCount is decremented by one to tell you that there is one fewer record remaining to be processed. In the second `Set Field` step, the incr parameter indicates that you are incrementing the progress bar; 1 is the amount of the increment; and the text message displayed above the progress bar (as shown previously in Figure 22-3) is

```
Processing records . . .
```

```
Records remaining:  x
```

where x is the current value of gCount. (Note that the ¶ symbols are used to add the blank lines between the two text strings.)

6. After all records have been processed, the following step is added to dismiss the progress bar:

```
Set Field ["gResult", Dial_ProgressBar("-Unused"; "stop";)]
```

Caution This last step is critical. If it is not present, the dialog will not go away, and you will find it necessary to force-quit from FileMaker Pro.

Tip In any calculation involving large numbers, you might prefer to increment the progress bar every 10 items or every 100 items rather than for every single item. To do so, you can use the Mod function within an `If` script step to test for a number that is divisible by 10 or 100 with no remainder. The progress bar is incremented only when the `If` test is true.

Troi File plug-in

If you need to perform more advanced file-handling than FileMaker allows, the Troi File plug-in will probably be up to the task. Some things you can do with this plug-in include

✦ Insert the contents of a text file into a field.

✦ Put data from FileMaker fields into an external file.

✦ Create, delete, copy, move, and rename external files.

✦ Display a file selection or save dialog.

✦ Locate or delete a folder, or display a folder's contents.

✦ Get file attributes, such as its size, modification date, and creator.

✦ Open a file with the application in which it was created.

✦ Create a thumbnail image from a graphics file and put it on the Clipboard.

Earlier in this book (Chapter 2), we describe a simple method for creating an auto-backup script to create a backup file of a database whenever you close it. Unfortunately, because the backup always has the same filename and is saved in the same location, it's necessary to manually rename the file each time. Using the Troi File plug-in, however, it's possible to rename the file as part of a script. To completely automate the renaming process, we've appended the current date to the backup file's name.

Note   To be bulletproof, the script described in the following steps needs error trapping added. As it is, there are no checks for the existence of the backup folder or that the user has read or write access to the folder. We've also assumed that it won't be run more than once in a day. Doing so would result in two backup files with identical names in the same folder, which is an operating system no-no.

STEPS: Creating an Enhanced Auto Backup Script

1. Create three additional fields in the Define Database dialog's Fields pane: gResult, Date, and FileName.

   • gResult is a field of type Text with the Global storage attribute set in the field's Options, which will be used to store the plug-in results.

   • Date is a Calculation field of type Date using the formula Get(CurrentDate). This sets the field equal to today's date.

   • FileName is a Calculation field of type Text that creates the text string representing the revised pathname of the backup file. It concatenates the original filename (through Address Book, followed by a space) with a text version of today's date and the .fp7 file extension, as follows:

   ```
   "Macintosh HD:Backups:Address Book " & GetAsText(Date)
   & ".fp7"
   ```

   Note   The preceding example is a Macintosh-specific file path. In a Windows implementation, the calculation would return a string similar to C:\Backups\ AddressBook.

2. Open ScriptMaker (Scripts ➪ ScriptMaker) and create a new script named RenameBackup. This script will use the Troi File plug-in to rename the copy of Address Book.fp7 to the designated backup name.

3. Add the `Set Field` step to the script, click Specify target field, and choose gResult. Then click the Specify button next to Calculated result to create the following formula using the TrFile_MoveFile External function:

```
TrFile_MoveFile("-Unused"; "Macintosh HD:Backups:Address
Book.fp7" ; Address Book Advanced::FileName)
```

This formula says to take the file `Address Book.fp7` (found on the Macintosh HD hard disk in the Backups folder) and to rename it to your calculated backup filename.

4. Click OK to complete the script definition.

5. Edit the original Auto Backup script by adding a Perform Script step that will execute the Rename Backup script as a subscript. (See Figure 22-4.)

6. Click OK to accept the revised script and then click Done to dismiss ScriptMaker.

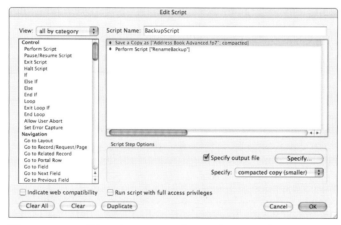

Figure 22-4: Editing the Auto Backup script to perform Rename Backup as a sub-script.

Note

There are a couple of other things (besides the error-checking noted earlier) that you should consider doing with the preceding "improved" backup script. First, because your default date format probably has slash (/) characters separating the parts of the date, you might want to reformat the text returned in GetAsText(Date) to not include slashes. A generic 8-digit number (4-digit year, 2-digit month, and 2-digit day) will also serve the purpose and keep the directory listing sorted chronologically. Second, you should probably ensure that the directory to which the backups are to be written is accessible to whatever user might run the script. On a Mac, that might be the `/User/Shared` directory, and in Windows, you might consider the `C:\Documents and Settings\All Users\Shared Documents` folder.

New Feature   FileMaker Pro 8 adds script variables, which allow you to create temporary variables that persist either through the life of the script or the FileMaker Pro session, depending upon how they are named. Using script variables obviates the need for global storage fields in many cases and are a boon to FileMaker Pro 8-specific solutions. However, if you want users of FileMaker Pro 7 to also access your database solutions, you should continue using global storage fields.

FileMaker Pro 8 significantly extends the definition of custom functions to include actual computations that can be used in calculations. You can't create or define them in FileMaker Pro 8 (that requires FileMaker Pro 8 Advanced), but you can employ them in calculations in any database where a FileMaker Pro 8 Advanced user has placed them. We discuss creating custom functions in Chapter 25.

More Plug-Ins

As mentioned at the beginning of this chapter, there are many commercial plug-in developers. To investigate some of the others, visit `http://solutions.filemaker.com` and enter **plugins** in the Search field.

Additionally, although it will require that you know how to write C or C++ code, 24U Software makes 24U FM Template freely available so that you have a shell for writing your own FileMaker Pro 7 and 8 plug-ins.

Summary

✦ Plug-ins are software add-ins that enhance FileMaker Pro's capabilities. A couple of plug-ins, Web and AutoUpdate, are included with FileMaker Pro 8. Others can be purchased from commercial software developers.

✦ Each user who needs a plug-in to run a particular FileMaker solution must have that plug-in installed on his or her machine.

✦ Plug-ins frequently add new External functions to FileMaker Pro. By including these functions in script steps, users can take advantage of a plug-in's capabilities.

✦   ✦   ✦

Developing Databases for Others to Use

Designing Databases for Others

No database is an island . . . actually, this statement is only occasionally true. You might create plenty of databases strictly for personal use—for example, a home financial database or one containing information about friends and business associates. At times, however, you might want to share your examples of database wizardry with friends, colleagues, or the public. Here are a few examples:

✦ *Sharing in-house business templates:* If your company doesn't have a network, employees can't access a central shared database. However, when someone in the company constructs a database that might be useful to other people in your department or to the company as a whole, you can distribute the template to everyone who needs it.

Suppose that as a sales associate, John creates a contact database that he uses to track sales leads, make follow-up calls, and record his successes and failures with each customer. The department decides to standardize, providing a copy of John's template to all salespeople so that they can install it on their own computers.

✦ *Sharing with friends:* Mark's club has an ongoing membership drive. Because several people on the membership committee use FileMaker Pro, Mark creates a template to record information about each prospective or new member and then passes out the template to the other people on the committee. Every month, each member e-mails Mark a copy of his or her current version of the database. Mark clicks a button on the template to execute a script that identifies which records have been added or modified during the past 30 days, exporting those records to a file. Mark then opens his master copy of the database and imports the records.

✦ *Sharing with the world:* After you develop a database to organize the contents of your wine cellar, to record the results of your biweekly gambling treks to Las Vegas or Atlantic City, or to track your huge CD and cassette collection, you might decide that the database is too good to keep to yourself. Because you have an Internet account or are a member of an online information service (such as America Online), you decide to offer the template to others. Depending on your personal philosophy or degree of entrepreneurial spirit, you can post the template as *freeware* (free to anyone who wants it) or *shareware* (software for which you request a fee from all users who decide to keep the template after trying it).

FileMaker Pro provides two means of sharing templates. The usual method is to use the Save a Copy As command to create a clone of the finished database, stripping it of all records. Each user has access to the scripts and layouts you have painstakingly created, but your personal data stays with you. This book's first 22 chapters discussed what you can do to create databases and templates using FileMaker Pro 8. Databases shared in this manner require that each user have a copy of FileMaker Pro.

The second approach is reserved for individuals who have purchased a special product called FileMaker Pro 8 Advanced (available from FileMaker, Inc.). Database templates that have been processed by Advanced can be run as standalone programs; the templates can be used on any Mac or Windows-based PC — without FileMaker Pro installed. For anyone who develops commercial templates, Advanced provides the enormous benefit of vastly expanding the potential market for those templates. Instead of being able to address the needs of only those individuals who already own FileMaker Pro — or who can be convinced to buy a copy of the program so that they can use your template — you can provide ready-made database solutions to virtually anyone who has a computer.

In Chapter 17, we introduce you to the procedures for creating a database template. This chapter carries the discussion further in four specific ways:

✦ Suggesting techniques that you can use to improve the user interface for your templates.

✦ Showing how to protect the structure of a template.

✦ Discussing different ways you can provide Help information for your databases.

✦ Explaining methods of restricting access to certain template features. (For example, you could distribute templates with some key features disabled as a way of encouraging users to send in the shareware fee so that they can obtain full access to features.)

Regardless of which FileMaker version you're using, you can employ the following techniques and strategies to improve the appearance, functionality, and marketability of your work:

✦ Simplify the interface with menus.

✦ Include buttons and scripts to handle common functions.

✦ Design for monitors of various sizes.

✦ Distribute shareware templates as demos or with selected features disabled.

✦ Provide Help files and other documentation that explain how your database works.

✦ Consider developing the template by using FileMaker Pro 8 Advanced.

Simplify the Interface by Using Menus

For any database containing more than just a simple data-entry layout, providing a menu layout to guide users to the different parts of the database is often a good idea. Menu layouts can be particularly helpful for computer novices and individuals who are unfamiliar with the database, ensuring that they can easily find their way around and readily access the functions they need.

Note
> The menus we're talking about here don't exist in the menu bar or as pop-ups or drop-downs in a window. In other words, they aren't menus in the Mac/Windows interface sense of the word. They closely resemble DVD menus, wherein you click buttons to move from one database layout or screen to another, just as clicking the buttons on a DVD menu moves you to another menu screen or plays a scene or movie. We apologize for any confusion that results, but the technology and its jargon drive the discussion. FileMaker Pro 8 Advanced introduces "real" custom menus, and we'll discuss those in Chapter 26.

Creating a main menu

If you want to use a main menu to control access to the different parts of a database, you can set the menu layout to be displayed automatically whenever the database is opened. To accomplish this, choose File ⇨ File Options. Click the Open/Close tab, if it isn't already selected. In the When opening this file section, select the Switch to layout check box and then choose the name of your menu layout from the pop-up menu/drop-down list. To save the new setting, click OK. From this point on, anyone who opens the database will immediately see the menu rather than the last layout used (the normal FileMaker Pro default).

Avoid button clutter

After you understand how easily you can assign actions to buttons, you might be tempted to go button crazy. If you check the online information services, you'll find many templates having layouts containing two or even three full rows of buttons. Just as using a dozen fonts in a document can make a desktop publishing effort look like a ransom note, presenting too many buttons in one place can slow down the user because finding the correct button for a function is difficult. Bad design or bad programming. . . .

If you really need that many buttons, either find a logical way to group them by function (as was done in the Want List database in Figure 23-3) or think seriously about creating a series of menu layouts rather than just a single menu. Additionally, with FileMaker Pro 8's introduction of tab controls, you probably won't need quite so many layouts, so the number of buttons will diminish naturally.

Menu layouts are most useful when the database is divided into several different modes, each associated with a particular layout or set of layouts. In a parts inventory database, for example, you might have separate layouts for entering parts sales, generating order forms when the inventory for a part drops below a critical level, and printing a status report showing the optimal number, number on hand, and reorder level for every part. A simple menu with three choices (Sales Entry, Order Parts, and Status Report) can help users move directly to the section of interest.

Of course, the more logical sections your database contains, the more helpful (and appropriate) a menu layout can be. In databases that include dozens of layouts, you can create additional submenu screens as needed. For example, if you've created layouts for half a dozen different types of reports and labels, you might want to design separate Report and Label menus, placing each set of menus on a separate layout.

Tip   Don't overdo menu nesting, however. Although additional menus are helpful to novices and new users, the added time and button-clicking required to navigate through unnecessary menu layers can get old very quickly.

Figure 23-1 shows a menu created as a separate layout in the New Buttons database. In this example, clicking any of the three buttons in the Main Menu area carries the user to a different database layout. Separate layouts are devoted to blank buttons, over-sized (large) buttons, and navigational buttons. This same menu type could enable users to select from several types of reports or to switch between several primary database functions, such as executing a Find, generating mailing labels, or opening an associated database.

Note   Many of the databases mentioned in this chapter, as well as a number of other examples provided in this book, are available on the CD accompanying this book.

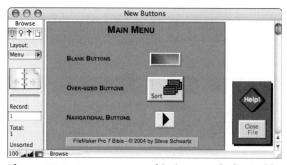

Figure 23-1: A menu created in its own dedicated layout.

In the Medical Expenses database (shareware, downloadable from www.
siliconwasteland.com), the menu is incorporated into the Data Entry layout.
(See Figure 23-2.) Because users spend the majority of their time in this layout,
the menu palette enables them to click buttons to perform a variety of functions
related to data entry and browsing. Several of the buttons duplicate menu commands in order to help novice users execute commands without having to remember the keyboard shortcut or the menu in which the command is located.

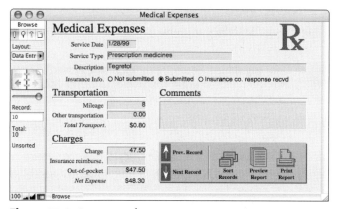

Figure 23-2: A menu palette.

The menu at the bottom of the database shown in Figure 23-3 is a variation on the
type of the menu palette displayed in Medical Expenses. Instead of restricting itself
to browsing functions, it presents all major functions that a user might want to
perform with the database. Such functions include selecting important subgroups,
generating onscreen and printed reports, clearing out old records, and summoning
Help. Although this type of menu could easily have been created as a separate layout (as was the one for New Buttons), placing it in the most common layout (Data
Entry) eliminates having to add an additional layer of complexity to a full-featured
database. Parsimony is a good thing!

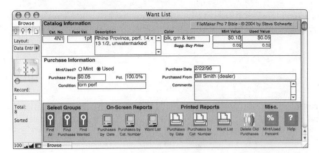

Figure 23-3: A menu incorporated into an existing layout.

Creating a Navigation Menu

As mentioned throughout this book, buttons — such as those used in the menu examples — gain their functionality by having ScriptMaker scripts or a script step attached to them. In the following series of steps, we explain how to design a navigation menu like the one used by the New Buttons database (refer to Figure 23-1).

STEPS: Creating a Navigation Menu

1. Open the database and switch to Layout mode (by choosing View ⇨ Layout Mode or by pressing ⌘+L/Ctrl+L).

2. Create a new layout to hold the menu by choosing Layouts ⇨ New Layout/ Report (or by pressing ⌘+N/Ctrl+N). Choose the Blank Layout style, name the layout, and allow the New Layout/Report Assistant to create the layout.

   or

   If you like, you can create the menu as part of an existing layout. (Refer to Figures 23-2 and 23-3.) If you decide to do so, switch to the appropriate layout and go to Step 3.

3. In Layout mode, use the Button tool to create text buttons. If you prefer graphic buttons, you can paste, import, or draw the graphics that will serve as the buttons in FileMaker Pro.

Note   If the Status area is hidden, you will need to click the Show Status Area button at the bottom of the window to make the Status area and Button tool accessible.

4. Arrange the buttons on the layout as desired.

5. Select a button by clicking it; then choose Format ⇨ Button Setup.

   The Button Setup dialog appears, as shown in Figure 23-4.

6. Choose the Go to Layout step from the scrolling list. From the Specify pop-up menu/drop-down list in the Options area, select the layout to which you want to go.

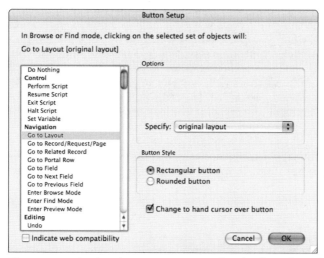

Figure 23-4: Setting the Go to Layout action for the selected button.

New Feature FileMaker Pro 8 allows you to specify whether the buttons should be rectangles or rounded rectangles in the Button Setup dialog's Button Style section.

7. Repeat Steps 5 and 6 for each menu button you want to define, selecting a different destination layout for each button.

8. If you always want the menu layout to appear immediately when you open the database, see the sidebar, "Creating a main menu."

Not all buttons must be icons

Although buttons are cool and lend a professional appearance to most databases, not everyone is a graphics wizard. Nor is everyone an icon lover. In FileMaker Pro, *any* object can be a button.

In Layout mode, you can use the Button tool to create 3-D buttons with standard text labels. You can use normal editing procedures to change the size of the button as well as the font, style, size, and color of the button text. You can also define a static text string as a button. The following figure shows a text button and a text string that perform the same function.

Sort   Sort

Providing Instant Access via Buttons and Scripts

Anything increasing a template's ease of use simultaneously increases its worth. Why ask users to do things the hard way (manually selecting sets of sort instructions, for instance), when you can create scripts and buttons that perform the tasks for them when they click a button or choose a command from the Scripts menu?

Think carefully about how others will want to use your template. If you know that many users will perform common sort procedures, focus on specific subgroups, or generate the same kinds of reports, you should create layouts and appropriate scripts to automate these activities.

To make scripts user-accessible, you can assign them to buttons, list them in the Scripts menu, or do both. See Chapter 15 for more information on creating scripts and defining buttons.

Consider Screen Real Estate

When you're designing templates for others, you might want to consider the size/resolution of the user's display. For example, users with a large display commonly design layouts that fill the screen. Unfortunately, when such templates are opened on computers with a smaller screen, significant portions of the window will be offscreen.

You have several options:

✦ Restrict the template dimensions to fit the smallest screen size that you want to support. At the time of this writing (October 2005), you can pretty much count on FileMaker Pro 8 users having monitors that support at least 1024 x 768 resolution.

✦ Assume that a user who has a small screen will be willing to scroll to reach parts of any layout that are offscreen.

✦ Provide several versions of the template, each optimized for a particular display.

✦ Divide a large layout into several smaller ones, and switch between the different layouts by using menus or buttons. Alternatively, you can employ FileMaker Pro 8's new tab controls to conserve screen real estate.

Tip   If you just want to expand the window to completely fill whatever screen the user has, you can use the following step in an opening script:

```
Adjust Window [Maximize]
```

Even more considerately, you can determine the resolution (in pixels) of any user's display by using the Get (ScreenHeight) and Get (ScreenWidth) functions as parameters to the Move/Resize Window script step.

Protecting a Template

When you design a template for in-house use, you might want to prevent others from changing it. For example, regardless of whether the person who is changing the locations of fields in a data layout is an expert or a novice who selected Layout mode by mistake, you might want to prevent changes to the field locations or formatting. Similarly, if a database contains sensitive information, such as salaries, you might want to prevent other users from accessing the database at all or restrict who has access rights to such layouts.

By choosing File ➪ Define ➪ Accounts & Privileges, the designer can establish privilege sets and accounts with those privileges.

Note   Although access privileges are more commonly associated in people's minds with products installed on a network, you can set access privileges for *any* FileMaker Pro database, including databases that will be run on standalone Macs or PCs. For more information, refer to Chapter 19.

In addition to protecting your template from unwanted changes, you can restrict access to some of its features when you create a demo or shareware version. To restrict access, you assign one or more accounts for the database and have each privilege set limit the particular features available to the account. By taking this approach, you give users an added incentive to buy the full version or to pay the requested shareware fee.

Label those buttons!

Although the Mac and Windows PCs are graphically oriented computers, and icons are a common part of the user interface, you might frequently be tempted to design buttons as unlabeled icons. Resist this temptation at all costs! Although the meaning of a button might be obvious to you, it might not be apparent to other people who will use your database or template. (A new computer user might not even understand the use of a question mark as a Help button, for example.)

When you're designing a template for others, you should avoid anything that slows people down by making them guess what you had in mind, search for the Help file, or reach for a manual. As the examples in Figures 23-1 through 23-3 clearly show, adding a label to a button takes little screen space.

For example, you could define three different privilege sets and accounts for a database. At the lowest level, access could be limited to basic features, allowing users to do no more than browse and edit the sample records included in the database. This level of access provides the equivalent of a demo, giving the user a feel for the database's capabilities. This account and password could be supplied in the documentation included with the template or set as a default login that would automatically (and transparently) be used by FileMaker Pro every time the database was opened. For instructions on setting a default password, use the Open/Close pane of the File Options dialog as described in Chapter 19.

As an alternative, FileMaker Pro also enables you to define a Guest account. To do this, you simply enable the Guest account in the Define Accounts & Privileges dialog's Account pane. When new users open the file, they can select the login dialog's Guest radio button and be granted Read-Only access to the database.

Note   By default, Guest access and Read-Only access are synonymous; however, you can edit the Guest account's privilege set just as you would any other. We recommend using a default login rather than Guest access if you want other privileges, though, because that will provide greater consistency by keeping Guest and Read-Only paired in users' minds.

Another predefined privilege set is Data Entry Only. Assigning an account the Data Entry Only privilege set simultaneously restricts users to Browse mode and allows them to do no more than create new records, edit existing records, and execute scripts.

On receipt of a basic shareware fee, you can supply a second account name and password that enables the user to print and export records, create new records, delete records, and override data-entry warnings. Assuming the users are happy with the way the database is designed (as you hope they will be), this level of functionality will be all the person requires. For an additional charge, you could offer a master password (with Full Access privileges), enabling the user to also modify the database structure (adding/deleting tables, defining fields, defining relationships, changing and designing layouts, editing scripts, and so on). Advanced users might want to take advantage of this ultimate password so that they can freely customize and modify the template in ways that make it more useful to them.

The Medical Expenses shareware template (refer to Figure 23-2) illustrates another approach to creating shareware templates. Medical Expenses contains a set of ten sample records. Users can freely try out any basic operation in the template (executing scripts, viewing and printing reports, and replacing the sample data). However, they cannot add new records, modify or create scripts, nor change the layouts. After the shareware fee is received, the user is sent the master account and password — enabling her or him to bypass or remove the limitations and change the template in any way desired. This approach to crippling a shareware template has the advantage of leaving all functions intact while still giving the user an important reason for sending the shareware fee.

Creating Help Systems for Your Databases

Do any of the following scenarios sound familiar?

✦ You've just spent half an hour downloading an interesting-sounding FileMaker Pro template from AOL or the Internet. You discover that it contains no instructions whatsoever — no Read Me file, no help screens, no descriptive text. Now what?

✦ Bill, one of your co-workers at XYZ Corp., is on vacation. While he's away, the boss asks whether you can fill in by entering customer orders, printing mailing labels, and generating daily reports. Although you know that Bill accomplishes these tasks with extraordinary ease using a FileMaker Pro database that he designed, you haven't got a clue as to how he does it.

✦ A couple of years back, you designed an elaborate database with dozens of scripts and buttons. Recently you realized that with just a few modifications, you could put the database to work for a new task. Unfortunately, when you designed the database, documenting how it worked didn't seem important. Now you can't remember what half the scripts do or what data the field named Extra was meant to collect. (It's surprising how easily you can forget. . . .)

✦ You've created a whiz-bang FileMaker Pro template that you think every Mac and Windows user will want. In your rush to share it with the world, you deposit copies of it all over the Internet and ask for a $10 shareware fee. Because you didn't bother to explain how the template works, it doesn't sell as well as you'd hoped, and the people who *are* sending you the shareware fee are also pestering you with questions.

Of course, not every database needs elaborate documentation. But if you spend a little time creating a simple Help system or Read Me file, you can avoid some headaches later on. The following sections discuss appropriate (and sometimes essential) topics you should include and suggest several approaches that you can take in creating help systems.

Suggested Help topics

A carefully thought out Help system anticipates the user's needs. The better you anticipate, the happier the user will be and the less time you will spend supporting or explaining the template. Here is a brief list of some material that is appropriate for inclusion in a Help system or a Read Me file:

✦ A description of the purpose of the database.

✦ An explanation of the purpose of each field, the type of data it should contain, and any restrictions and/or validation options that have been set. (See Chapter 5 for information on data validation options.) The Comments text box in the Define Database dialog's Fields pane is a good starting point for this information. Another solution is to use FileMaker Pro 8 Advanced to associate tooltips with layout elements (our personal choice, but it does require that you do your development with Advanced).

✦ An explanation of the purpose of each layout, as well as any special preparations the user must make before using the layout (changing the Page Setup or printer selection, for example).

✦ An explanation of what each script does and how to execute the script (by selecting it from the Scripts menu or pressing a button).

✦ Suggestions for customizing the template (for example, selecting different fonts, changing screen colors, creating new reports and mailing labels, and adding features).

If you want people to treat your template as a serious business product rather than as something you just knocked together in a free moment, make it look like a business product. Documentation and/or a Help system are a must.

Note   The Tools ⇨ Database Design Report command in FileMaker Pro 8 Advanced produces a HTML or XML report on your database, giving you a good start on the Read Me file suggested above. We discuss the Database Design Report in more detail in Chapter 25.

Different approaches to providing help

You can present help information and documentation in several ways. In choosing a method, consider who is the intended reader of the information (you, other developers and technical people, or end users and customers) and how often you expect the reader to refer to the information. For example, does it make sense to create an elaborate, context-sensitive online Help system for information that the reader might need to see only once?

Approach 1: A Read Me file

Creating a separate Read Me file in a word processing program or text editor is obviously the easiest way to document a template. And having the full text-formatting capabilities of a word processor at your disposal can make the writing go quickly.

Arguably, the Read Me approach is best for providing information needed only once—such as installation instructions and minor customization notes—or when you create a database only for personal or limited in-house use. In the case of a personal template, if you later decide to share it with others, your notes can form the basis of an in-template Help system.

Choosing Help topics

Need and common sense should dictate the types and quantity of help you provide. If you're writing a Help system for a database that will be used only by the accounting department in your company, for example, you should offer help with common data-entry and report-generation questions you expect to occur. Because everyone will be using the same version of the database, you can omit information about customizing the database.

When deciding the types of help to offer, try to put yourself in the place of a new user. Think about field labels you've used that might not be immediately understood. When it could be unclear what type of information should be entered in a field, explain it. (If you're really smart, you'll give the database and mockups to some people to test — and ask them to tell you what kind of help they need — *before* you distribute it. Think of these as mini-focus groups.)

To get more ideas about the types of help to include, you might want to download some of the shareware templates available from FileMaker, Inc., AOL, and other sources on the Internet. You're sure to find several excellent (as well as many horrid) examples of help information.

If you intend to distribute your database as shareware, a Read Me file is certainly better than no documentation, but it isn't the best method. See Approaches 2 and 3, later in this chapter, for more appropriate means of providing Help information for shareware.

If you want others to be able to read and print your Read Me file, you should give careful thought to which word processor or text editor you'll use to create the file or whether you wish to provide it as a PDF file or an HTML file. Obviously, if you write the documentation in an obscure program, you will prevent many people from being able to open and read the file. The following sections offer some suggestions for creating a Read Me file.

Text editors

Text editors — such as BBEdit (Macintosh) and Notepad (Windows) — are essentially bare-bones word processing programs. Fancy formatting commands usually aren't provided, nor is there support for multiple fonts and styles. As the name implies, a *text editor* is a program for editing text. Files created in a text editor are stored in Text-Only format and, as such, can be opened by any other text editor or word processing program. This is precisely the reason why so many Read Me files are created in text editors.

Tip   *TextEdit,* a text editor included with Mac OS X, can also be used to create Text-Only files. To do so, set its New Document Format preference to Plain Text. Similarly, you can create plain text documents in WordPad by choosing Plain Text from the

Save as type drop-down list when saving the document. Both of these applications use RTF (Rich Text Format) as their default, however, so you now have a standard format available supporting the fonts, styles, and other formatting you might desire.

If you intend to distribute a template on the Internet and online information systems, you can keep your documentation compact by creating it in a text editor. (No one wants to waste half an hour downloading a few pages of documentation that grew to several hundred K because of the format selected. This is sometimes a problem with standalone documents, as you will see in the following section.)

Caution

When it comes to cross-platform documentation, Text-Only isn't necessarily only text. Some text editors include style information and end-of-paragraph characters that are different on Mac and Windows, resulting in ugly boxes interspersed in your text. If you want your Read Me file to be readable on both platforms, it is critical that you test it on both platforms. Do not assume compatibility.

PDF files

As evidenced by the number of software publishers who use this method, perhaps one of the best ways to create documentation is to distribute them as PDF (Portable Document Format) files. You can use the Adobe Acrobat commercial program to convert existing formatted documents into PDF files. The documents can readily be opened on a Mac, a Windows PC, or even a Unix workstation with a free Adobe program called Acrobat Reader (called Adobe Reader in some incarnations).

To create a PDF file, you can print the document to disk (by using a special print driver); you can generate it in Adobe InDesign, QuarkXPress, or many other popular desktop publishing programs; or you can generate a PostScript file and then convert it to PDF format with Acrobat Distiller. Acrobat offers several advantages: It supports all normal formatting, graphics, and fonts; its files can be published on the World Wide Web; and documents can include features such as a live, clickable table of contents or multimedia clips.

If you have a Mac running OS X, the ability to create PDF files from *any* document is built right into the operating system! To create a PDF file from an OS X word processing, text editor, or desktop publishing program, open the document you want to convert, choose File ➪ Print, and click the Save As PDF button (see Figure 23-5) in OS X 10.3.x or the PDF button in OS X 10.4.

Web page documents

One documentation solution gaining increasing popularity is to use HTML (or XML) to create Web pages documenting your product. You can include graphics, hyperlinked references to related material, tables, and all the other formatting that Web browsers support. Additionally, you can be certain that if the user has a computer that will run your solution, he or she has a Web browser.

Panther

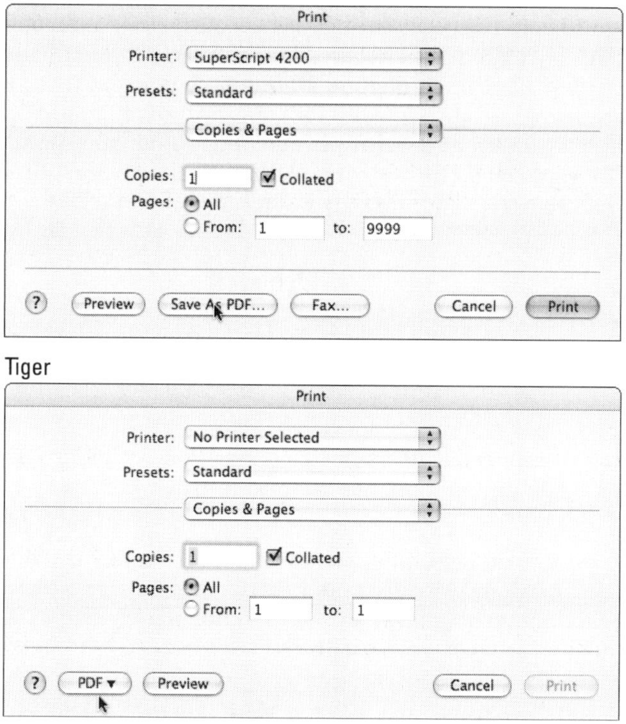

Tiger

Figure 23-5: In the Mac Print dialog, you can generate a PDF file from any printable document.

Word processing programs

If you're creating documentation that will be distributed, the least desirable method is to use a standard word processing program (Microsoft Word, for example). One exception to this general rule is when you develop a template solely for in-house use and everyone in the company uses the same word processing program. Although many word processing programs can read documents created in other such programs, a sizable number of people might still be unable to read the file, and even those who can open it with their word processor are likely to encounter formatting differences or some features that either aren't supported or display differently. Additionally, you have to hope that they have the fonts you're using. However, authors who distribute documentation in a word processing format can increase the odds that users can read it by including copies of the documentation in several formats. Microsoft Word, Rich Text Format, and Text-Only are the most common choices. (TextEdit on Mac OS X 10.3 and 10.4 and WordPad on Windows can read Word files.)

Paper-only documentation

Of course, you might want to skip the compatibility issues altogether and simply include printed instructions with the template. You can distribute the template on information services but offer the printed documentation only to users who send in the shareware registration fee. Most authors who take this approach, however, are obliged to also include at least a stripped-down version of the documentation in a Read Me file. If you don't give users some idea of how the template works, they might not explore it enough to determine whether it does something useful for them.

Approach 2: A Help layout

Another method is to include the documentation or help information in the template itself. The advantages of placing this material in a FileMaker Pro template include the following:

✦ *No compatibility problems:* Because users need a copy of FileMaker Pro in order to use the template, by definition, they have all the software they need to read the Help text, too.

✦ *Ready access:* Users who need help don't want to hunt for it; they usually want it right away. And because Read Me files take up disk space, users frequently delete them after reading them, so such files aren't immediately accessible (or they might no longer be accessible at all).

Figure 23-6 shows an example of help text in a FileMaker Pro database. This Expense Report template is, in fact, one of the many templates included with FileMaker Pro 8, all of which have an Information layout similar to the one pictured. All the Help information is contained in a single layout. If the information is too long to fit on a single screen (as it is in this example), users can click the scroll bar to see it all.

As you can see in this figure, a Help layout might contain no fields at all. It can be constructed entirely of static text and graphics, so you never have to worry about the user inadvertently changing what's onscreen. When this layout is displayed, even if the user clicks the book icon to flip from one record to the next, the Help screen doesn't change.

To create a Help screen similar to the one shown in the figure, follow these steps.

STEPS: Creating a Help Screen

1. In a new or existing database, switch to Layout mode.
2. Choose Layouts ➪ New Layout/Report (or press ⌘+N/Ctrl+N).

   The New Layout/Report Assistant appears, as shown in Figure 23-7.

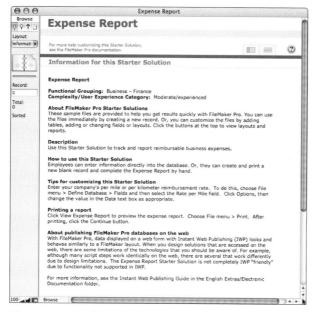

Figure 23-6: Help text as a separate layout.

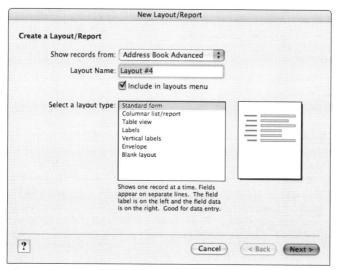

Figure 23-7: The New Layout/Report Assistant.

3. Enter an appropriate name for the layout (Help, for example), select Blank layout as the type, and click Finish to create the layout.

Because you usually don't display fields in a help layout, choosing Blank layout saves time. (You can optionally include the layout in the Layout pop-up menu.)

4. Select the Text tool (the uppercase A) from the Tools palette to add text blocks to the layout. Resize the text blocks as necessary.

If you have already prepared Help text in a word processing document, you can copy and paste it into the layout. And if your word processing program supports it, you can also drag and drop the Help text into the layout.

5. (Optional) Add graphics by copying them from a graphics program and then pasting them into the layout.

You can also import graphics directly into the layout by choosing the Insert ⇨ Picture command. (See Chapter 6 for additional information on adding and importing graphics into a layout.) In addition, some graphics programs, such as the graphics environments of AppleWorks, support drag-and-drop. You can use this feature to drag graphics directly onto FileMaker Pro layouts.

6. (Optional) Create scripts that switch from the Help layout to the data-entry layout and vice versa (via the Go to Layout script step).

Although you can place the scripts in the Scripts menu, assigning them to buttons on the layout is more convenient. (See the "Using a button to summon help" sidebar in this chapter.)

As you design the Help layout, remember that you can mix fonts, styles, and colors in the same text block. When you're designing for other users, however, getting fancy with fonts doesn't pay. Unless users have the same fonts installed on their computers, different fonts will automatically be substituted. Also, although you can create the help text as one long text block, you might want to break it into a series of smaller, more manageable chunks. When you use this approach, you can easily intersperse graphics (such as screen captures, illustrations, and clip art) in the text.

Tip   Another approach is to take a screen shot of an important layout, edit and embellish it with callouts in your favorite graphics program, and then paste the image into the help layout. (To take a screen shot on a Mac, press Shift+⌘+3. This captures the entire screen and saves it on your hard disk. To capture just a single window, press Shift+⌘+4, press the spacebar, and then click the window you want to capture. To take a full-screen shot on a PC, press the Print Screen key. This copies the screen to the Clipboard. Then open a graphics program and choose Edit ⇨ Paste or press Ctrl+V.) If you're going to be taking a lot of screen shots and want more flexibility, commercial products such as Ambrosia Software's Snapz Pro X (www.ambrosiasw.com) for the Mac or No Nonsense Software's ScreenGrab (www.no-nonsense-software.com) for Windows are recommended acquisitions.

Approach 3: Data-entry assistance

Setting data validation options makes it easy to ensure that users enter only the correct type of information for each field. If you want to help them do so, you can present a custom error message whenever incorrect data is entered for a field. As an example, Figure 23-8 shows how to create a custom message that is displayed if a user neglects to enter data into a required field or enters the wrong type of data into a field whose Validation options include Strict data type. Thus, if you choose the Display custom message if validation fails option in a field's Validation options, you can create a unique, helpful message for any field whose intended contents might not be immediately obvious. (See Chapter 5 for instructions on setting validation options for fields.)

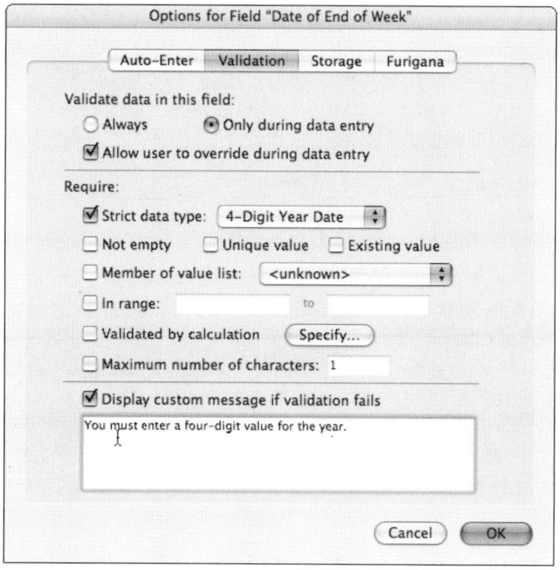

Figure 23-8: You can set the Display Custom Message . . . option to present an alert whenever a field's validation fails.

If you don't want to tie a custom message to a field's validation options, you can use the Show Message script step to present field-related help by attaching the script to a button. To enable users to summon such help, you might place a tiny "?" button at the end of each field and then associate the appropriate message script with each button. Figure 23-9 shows an example of one type of message associated with a Number field help button.

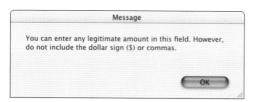

Figure 23-9: The Show Message script step can be used to present custom messages, such as this one.

In FileMaker Pro 8, you can take data-entry assistance even further. By using the Show Custom Dialog script step and attaching it to a button beside a particular field, you can prompt for the information required for that field, as shown in Figure 23-10. The button definition dialogs are shown in Figure 23-11.

Figure 23-10: Using a custom dialog like this one, you can give detailed instructions concerning the data expected and prompt for it at the same time.

Using a button to summon Help

To make it easy to move from any layout in the database to your help layout (and back again), you can create buttons for the different layouts. The script attached to each navigation button in the database consists of this single line:

```
Go to layout <x>
```

where <x> is the name of the data-entry or Help layout. (In the data-entry layout, use the name of the Help layout. In the Help layout, use the name of the data-entry layout.) To attach the command to a custom button, switch to Layout mode, select the button, and choose Format ⇨ Button Setup. Or you can use the Button tool to create and define a button simultaneously. (See Chapter 15 for more information on creating scripts and defining buttons.)

This approach can also be used with multiple help layouts. In a complex database, you might want separate Help screens for providing help with specific functions, such as data entry, performing Find requests and sorts, and printing reports. Having several specific Help layouts serves several purposes:

✦ The user doesn't have to scroll through multiple screens of information.

✦ Your Help screen more closely approximates the type of specific, context-appropriate help that users have come to expect from programs.

For example, a data-entry screen could have separate buttons for data entry and sorting Help; a reports screen could have a single button that summons help for preparing and printing a report.

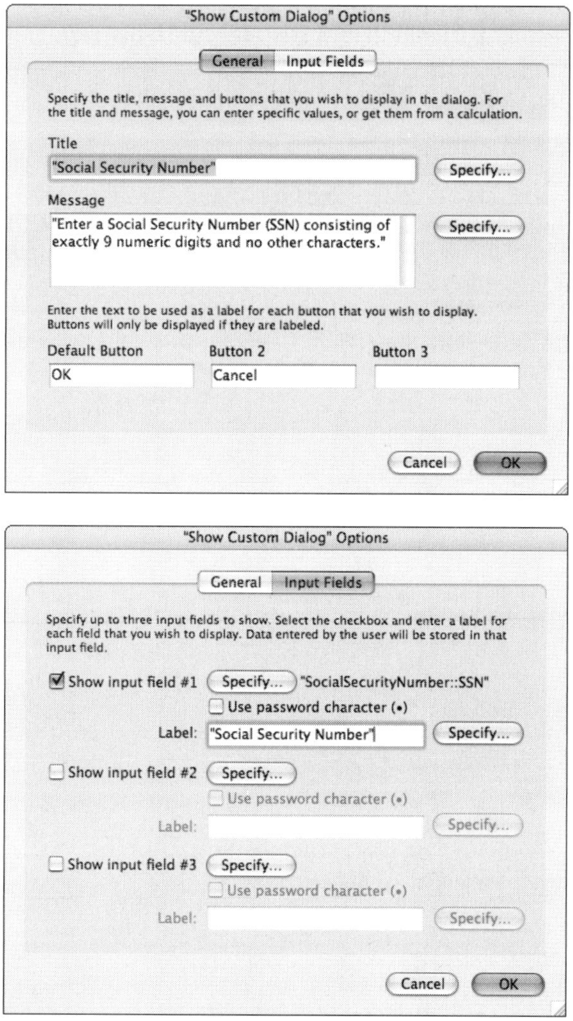

Figure 23-11: Specifying the makeup of the custom dialog.

Approach 4: Script-guided help

FileMaker Pro scripts can make your Help system fancier and more helpful. By creating simple scripts and button definitions, you can design a series of Help layouts having the following features:

✦ Your users can page through the Help screens. Each left-arrow and right-arrow button can have an attached script telling FileMaker Pro to go to the previous or next Help layout.

✦ Your users can access the Help screens through a menu. Each button or text string on the Help menu can cause a different Help layout to display.

✦ You can access the Help screens through an index. You can link each index entry to a specific Help layout.

For example, here is a database named Callable Help. Instead of forcing the user to jump back and forth between a help layout and other layouts in the database, Callable Help stores the help information in a second database file. Because the Help information is in a different file, you can view it while you're still working in the main database.

Clicking the Help button in the main database (Help Caller, in this case) opens the help database (Books Help). Figure 23-12 shows the two database files.

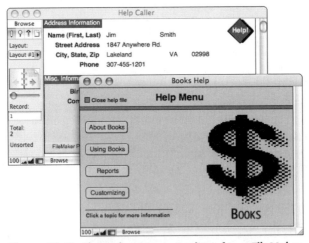

Figure 23-12: The Help system consists of two FileMaker Pro databases: The main file (Help Caller) and the Help file (Books Help).

Here's how the two databases interact. As a user, to access Help, you simply click the Help button in the main database. The Help button executes the Open File script step, where you specify Books Help, as shown in Figure 23-13.

When the Help file opens, several actions that are set in the File Options automatically occur. The Help database displays the first layout (called Help Menu) and then hides the status area (the book pages and Tools palette) by executing the script named Open Script. (See Chapter 7 for more information on setting Document General preferences.)

In Books Help, you move to a particular help topic by clicking the name of the topic in the Help Menu, which is the first layout (refer to Figure 23-12). In fact, you use a Go to Layout script step to make *every* movement — whether to a Help topic, to the main menu, or to a new page in the same Help topic. You can then execute a script and make an appropriate layout appear by clicking any of four help topic text strings in the Help Menu layout.

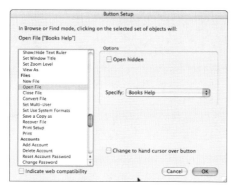

Figure 23-13: Specifying the button script step that opens the Help file.

A set of buttons appears at the top of every Help layout. In each layout except that of the Help Menu, the upper-left button (Help Menu) returns the user to the Help menu. In the Help Menu layout, the Help Menu button is replaced with the Close Help File button, which closes the Help file in the same manner as clicking the close button/box.

In Help topics that span more than one layout (such as Using Books), one or two arrow buttons occupy the upper-right corner of each layout. (See Figure 23-14.) Clicking an arrow executes a script that switches to the previous or next layout for that Help topic. The number of layouts for a Help topic appears in the lower-right corner of each layout.

More help with Help

Regardless of the method you use to incorporate Help information into your database, you might find the following tips useful.

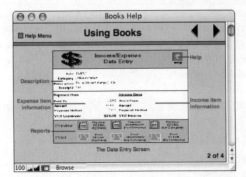

Figure 23-14: Click an arrow to navigate between multiple layouts for the same help topic.

Using headers and footers in Help screens

If you want some help information to remain onscreen at all times, put it in the Help layout's header or footer. As the user scrolls the window, the header and footer stay in place.

Figure 23-15 shows a Help layout from the Apple Events Reference database (found in the FileMaker Pro 8 ⇨ English Extras ⇨ Apple Events folder in the Mac version) in which the header keeps critical information and navigation buttons onscreen.

Type	User Terminology	Object Class	Event Suite	Event
Event	Class Info		kAECoreSuite	kAEGetClassInfo
Event	Close		kAECoreSuite	kAEClose
Event	Count		kAECoreSuite	kAECountElements
Event	Create New		kAECoreSuite	kAECreateElement
Event	Data Size		kAECoreSuite	kAEGetDataSize
Event	Delete		kAECoreSuite	kAEDelete
Event	Do Menu		kAEMiscStandards	kAEDoMenu
Event	Do Script		kAEMiscStandards	kAEDoScript
Event	Duplicate		kAECoreSuite	kAEClone
Event	Event Info		kAECoreSuite	kAEGetEventInfo
Event	Exists		kAECoreSuite	kAEDoObjectsExist
Event	Find		kAEFileMaker	kAEFind
Event	Get Data		kAECoreSuite	kAEGetData
Event	Get Remote URL		kAEFileMakerSuite	kAEOpenRemoteURL
Event	GetURL		kAEURL	kAEGetURL
Event	Go To		kAEFileMaker	kAEGoto
Event	Open		kAECoreSuite	kAEOpen
Event	Open Application		kAERequiredSuite	kAEOpenApplication
Event	Open Documents		kAERequiredSuite	kAEOpenDocuments
Event	Print (files)		kAERequiredSuite	kAEPrintDocuments
Event	Print (objects)		kAECoreSuite	kAEPrint
Event	Quit		kAERequiredSuite	kAEQuitApplication
Event	Save		kAECoreSuite	kAESave
Event	Set Data		kAECoreSuite	kAESetData
Event	Show		kAEMiscStandards	kAEMakeObjectVisibl
Event	Sort		kAEDatabaseSuite	kAESort
Object	Application	cApplication		
Object	Cell	cCell		
Object	Database	cDatabase		
Object	Document	cDocument		
Object	Field	cColumn		
Object	FileMaker Script	cFileMakerScript		
Object	Layout	cTable		

For more information click an event or object.

Figure 23-15: You can keep essential Help information or controls onscreen by placing them in the header and/or footer parts.

Cheking yer riting and speling

Don't forget that FileMaker Pro has a built-in spelling checker. You might be a database whiz, but if your documentation or Help text is riddled with spelling errors and typos, your skills as a developer might also be questioned. To check spelling for the entire Help layout, change to Layout mode, switch to the Help screen layout, and choose Edit ➪ Spelling ➪ Check Layout. (See Chapter 12 for more information on using the spelling checker.)

Creating a credits screen or a registration form

Using the same method you use to provide in-template help, you can create a credits screen, copyright screen, or a shareware registration form for your template. Without such a screen, you are likely to lose credit for the work you've done or miss out on shareware fees that are due to you.

In the case of a shareware template, you want to make it as convenient as possible for the user to pay for the template. Creating the registration form as a separate layout ensures that

- ✦ When ready to pay, the user never has to search the hard disk for a separate file containing your name and address.

- ✦ The user is repeatedly reminded that the template isn't public domain and that payment is expected.

- ✦ When the template is copied and given to others, the registration information is also copied.

Figure 23-16 is an example of a layout that provides credit and registration information.

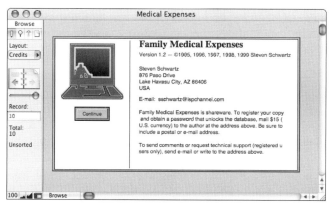

Figure 23-16: This opening screen explains what the user must do to register his or her copy of a shareware template.

Using FileMaker Pro 8 Advanced

As mentioned at the beginning of this chapter, FileMaker Pro 8 Advanced can compile FileMaker Pro templates, changing them into royalty-free, standalone FileMaker Pro databases that will run on the Mac or in Microsoft Windows. If you intend to create commercial templates, using Advanced offers three direct benefits when compared to creating normal FileMaker Pro templates:

✦ *It increases the size of the potential market.* To use a normal template, an individual must already own or be willing to buy FileMaker Pro. When you're selling an expensive, vertical-market database (such as a video store rentals database), customers might consider the cost of a copy of FileMaker Pro to be a drop in the bucket. When you're attempting to sell an inexpensive, general-purpose template, on the other hand, you cannot expect customers to shoulder the cost of a program just so that they can use the template.

✦ *It allows you to include features unavailable in the base FileMaker Pro 8 product.* The main features include layout tooltips (offering help information when the pointer hovers over a layout element), custom menus in the menu bar specific to your solution, and creating custom functions to expedite calculation development.

✦ *It protects your investment while preventing tampering.* Providing an unprotected FileMaker Pro template to customers is tantamount to handing them the source code for your product. If you have used special techniques to create the template, Advanced keeps them safe from prying eyes and prevents customers from inadvertently or deliberately modifying the way the template works.

FileMaker Pro 8 Advanced includes some tools (the Script Debugger and Database Design Report) to facilitate your efforts in addition to the Developer Utilities that create the standalone database applications. These tools will be the subject of the next three chapters (Chapters 24–26).

Summary

✦ Templates that are good enough for your personal use might not be ready to market commercially or give to others. You should consider many factors when designing templates for distribution.

✦ When developing a template for the widest possible audience, you can easily add features that enhance ease of use and enable the template to be used on a variety of monitors.

✦ Shareware and demo templates can use FileMaker Pro's privilege sets and accounts to restrict access to template parts or features.

✦ Even if you don't want to implement a formal Help system for your database, you can easily create a Read Me file.

✦ You can add help, credit or copyright, and shareware registration screens to any database as separate layouts. Use the Go to Layout script step to switch between any of these screens and the database's main menu or data-entry layout.

✦ When you embed help information in layouts, you can create a single scrolling text screen or break the information into discrete chunks and place them in a series of layouts.

✦ You can attach the Show Message script step to buttons and use it to display custom Help messages. A data validation option can display a custom message automatically if a field's validation fails, like when a user neglects to enter information into a required field.

✦ By attaching the Show Custom Dialog script step to a button, you can simultaneously specify the type of data expected for a field and prompt for it.

✦ You can use text strings — as well as graphics objects — as buttons. Clicking a text string in a Help menu, for example, can cause a specific Help layout to display.

✦ To keep a database as small as possible, you can create a separate Help database that the user can display and then dismiss when it is no longer needed. Keeping the Help separate from the main database also enables users to view the Help in a separate window while they're entering data, creating reports, or constructing new layouts.

✦ If you're interested in becoming a commercial template developer, you should consider purchasing a copy of FileMaker Pro 8 Advanced.

✦   ✦   ✦

Debugging Scripts

Although ScriptMaker relieves you of writing code in a text editor, FileMaker scripting really is programming. ScriptMaker pretty much eliminates *syntax* errors (errors in the programming language's grammar), but ScriptMaker can't protect you from making logical errors, such as leaving out a step, using the wrong command for what you want to do, doing things in the wrong order, or referencing the wrong layout/field/request/record or whatever.

To help you catch these logical errors, FileMaker Pro 8 Advanced includes a useful tool, the Script Debugger, that lets you execute a script one script step at a time, run a script until you reach a predetermined *breakpoint* (a place where you want to start *stepping,* or executing a script one step at a time), change the order of execution, terminate the script's execution, or return to ScriptMaker to modify the script while it's running.

Tip In your FileMaker Pro 8 Advanced directory's English Extras folder, you will find a very informative and helpful PDF document, `FMPA8_Development.PDF`, otherwise entitled *FileMaker Pro 8 Advanced Development Guide*. We highly recommend this electronic booklet as a reference to developing with FileMaker Pro 8 Advanced.

Introducing the Script Debugger

If you open the FileMaker Pro 8 Advanced Tools menu, you'll see a Debug Scripts menu item. This command is a toggle — select it, and it gains a check mark, indicating that when you execute a script, the Script Debugger (shown in Figure 24-1) will be in control. In fact, executing a script opens the Script Debugger, patiently waiting at the first script step for you to tell it what to do.

Figure 24-1: The FileMaker Pro 8 Advanced Script Debugger.

Note In the spirit of full disclosure, the preceding paragraph slightly overstates the case. Two other conditions must be met for the Script Debugger to display and let you debug a script. Your access privilege set must include the ability to edit scripts, and the script you invoke mustn't be executable-only (per the current user's Access Privileges). Of course, you wouldn't ever mark a script you're developing as execute-only until after you had fully verified its efficacy, would you?

Note It is probably at least as cumbersome for you to continue reading *FileMaker Pro 8 Advanced* as it is for us to keep typing it. Therefore, for convenience, we'll just use *Advanced* for the product name from this point forward.

Using the Script Debugger

Table 24-1 shows the nine buttons residing at the top of the Script Debugger window and their purposes. The table also displays the keyboard equivalents for both Mac and Windows for the Tools ➪ Debugging Controls submenu items.

	Table 24-1		
	The Script Debugger Control Buttons		
Button	*Name and Description*	*Mac Key Equivalent*	*Windows Key Equivalent*
	Step: Execute the current script step. If the current step is a Perform Script step, that sub-script will be run in its entirety and control returned at the next step in the current script. If you wish to step through the sub-script(s), use the Step Into button instead.	F5	F5

Button	Name and Description	Mac Key Equivalent	Windows Key Equivalent
	Step Into: Perform the current script step. If the current step is a Perform Script step, the Script Debugger will enter the sub-script, stopping at the first step in the sub-script. The Active Scripts list will be updated to indicate the nesting level, as shown in Figure 24-2.	F6	F6
	Step Out: Perform all remaining steps in the current script until either the (sub)script ends or a breakpoint is encountered.	F7	F7
	Run: Perform all script steps until the script ends, a pause condition is reached, or a breakpoint is encountered.	F8	F8
	Halt Script: Cease executing the script and exit /close the Script Debugger.	⌘+F8	Ctrl+F8 or ⌘+. (period)
	Set Next Step: If you select a step in the list of script steps and click this button, the selected step will become the current step (next to be executed).	Shift+⌘+F5	Shift+Ctrl+F5
	Set/Clear Breakpoint: If you select a step in the list of script steps and click this button, FileMaker Advanced will mark it as a point to pause script execution when you choose the Run or Step Out command. If the selected step is already marked as a breakpoint, clicking this button will remove the breakpoint mark. (Note: You can clear all breakpoints at one time by choosing Tools ⇨ Debugging Controls ⇨ Remove Breakpoints or pressing Shift+⌘+F9/Shift+Ctrl+F9.)	⌘+F9	Ctrl+F9
	Go to ScriptMaker: This button combines clicking the Halt Script button with choosing Scripts ⇨ ScriptMaker, selecting the current script, and clicking ScriptMaker's Edit button.	⌘+F10	Ctrl+F10
	Open Data Viewer: This button invokes the new Data Viewer, allowing you to monitor variables, field values, and other expressions while executing scripts. (This is new in FileMaker Pro 8 Advanced.)	<none>	<none>

Note

Certain script steps are ignored when debugging. Setting Hide or Minimize in an Adjust Window script step is ignored because the window would no longer be visible for you to view the result of subsequent script steps operating on said window. Similarly, setting a script as non-abortable (Allow User Abort set to Off) is ignored so that Halt Script and Go to ScriptMaker will function properly.

Figure 24-2: Stepping into a sub-script displays the script nesting in the Active Scripts list.

New Feature

In this book's previous edition, we lamented the lack of a data inspector and suggested that readers request said functionality. Well, either FileMaker, Inc. was thinking along the same lines or a sufficient number of readers (and other users) requested an inspector capability because Advanced introduces the Data Viewer, shown in Figure 24-3. You can invoke the Data Viewer either by clicking the Data Viewer button at the far right of the Script Debugger window's row of buttons or by choosing Tools ➪ Data Viewer. Initially, there is nothing in the expression list.

Figure 24-3: The Data Viewer window lets you monitor the values of variables, fields, and expressions.

To add an expression to the list, click the green + button to invoke the Edit Expression window shown in Figure 24-4. (Compare the Edit Expression window with the very familiar Edit Calculation dialog — the similarities are intentional.)

Clicking the Monitor button adds the expression to the Data Viewer window.

Note

The positions of the Monitor and Cancel buttons are reversed between the Mac and Windows versions.

You can click the Data Viewer's Refresh Values button to re-evaluate expressions; however, they update automatically when you're debugging a script.

Figure 24-4: Define and edit expressions just as you define and edit calculations.

New Feature

Also new to Advanced's Script Debugger is the ability to disable (and re-enable) script steps during the debugging process, but not while the script is actually executing. When a disabled script step is encountered, it is skipped. You disable a script step, without removing it from the script, by selecting the script in the Define Scripts dialog, clicking Edit, selecting the step(s) in the Edit Script dialog, and clicking the Disable button. Disabling a script step is equivalent to commenting-out code in a traditional programming language — in fact, the // characters preceding disabled steps will be very familiar to C and C++ programmers. When you print a script, disabled steps are italicized.

Summary

✦ You can use Advanced's Script Debugger to step through scripts and into sub-scripts in order to find errors in your scripting logic.

✦ The Data Viewer allows you to evaluate and monitor the values of fields, variables, and other expressions, both while working in a database and (more importantly) while debugging a script.

✦ You can disable script steps for testing purposes without having to remove them from a script.

✦ The Script Debugger lets you set breakpoints (run until encountered) and halt execution of run-away scripts.

✦   ✦   ✦

Generating Database Reports

When you develop databases for others to use, especially as the databases become more complex via relationships, lookups, privilege sets, layouts, value lists, scripts, and so forth, you're going to find that maintaining, modifying, and enhancing your product can get increasingly complicated. Just as with a major software, hardware, or construction project, you need to document what you're doing.

In fact, even if you're designing complex database projects for your own use, you'll find documentation an invaluable aid in maintaining and optimizing the performance of your database. You'll see where replication of functionality occurs, where redundant or unnecessary fields take up space, and where overly complicated calculations might be simplified.

The Database Design Report in FileMaker Pro 8 Advanced (hereafter, just *Advanced*) documents how all the pieces of your database tie together. This overall detail is the *database schema*. The Database Design Report generates your choice of an HTML or XML document, and you have control over which database elements are documented.

Specifying a Database Design Report

As you can see in Chapter 2, FileMaker Pro 8 includes Print buttons in ScriptMaker and the Define Database dialogs, enabling you to get printed documentation concerning your database's scripts, tables, fields, and relationships. These reports are a good start, but they are just the beginning. For example, the report from ScriptMaker doesn't tell you how the layouts and scripts are related, which accounts have access to a given script, or any of a myriad of other interesting details. A sample page from a Define Database report is shown in Figure 25-1, and the equivalent portion from a Database Design Report is shown in Figure 25-2, showing just how much more information the Database Design Report provides.

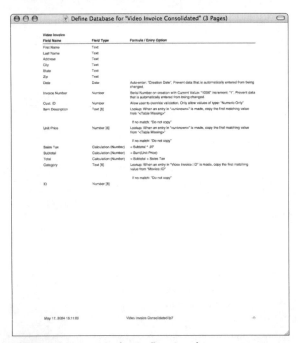

Figure 25-1: Here's the Define Database report on a table.

Not only does the Database Design Report give you a hyperlinked set of tables and pages — allowing you to follow a logical chain between scripts, layouts, and fields — but you also get statistics concerning how many items of each kind you're using. Of course, if you want a hard copy, you can print this report from your Web browser, but that will lose the interactive links. Similarly, if you create an XML report, you could employ an XSLT (eXtensible Stylesheet Language Transformation) to transform the report into any other format you might require.

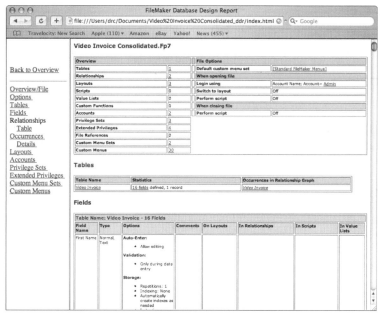

Figure 25-2: Here's the start of the Database Design Report on that same table.

To create a Database Design Report, proceed as follows.

STEPS: Creating a Database Design Report

1. Open the database(s) of interest in Advanced. Make certain you open the database using an account with full access privileges; otherwise, you won't be able to generate the report.

2. Choose Tools ➪ Database Design Report.

   The dialog shown in Figure 25-3 appears.

3. From the Available files list, select the files on which you want a report.

   Tables from a file selected in the Available files list appear in the Include fields from tables in selected file list. Deselect the check boxes for the tables you want omitted from the report.

4. Select the check boxes for the items you want included in the report in the Include in report section.

5. Select either the HTML or the XML Report Format radio button.

6. If you want the generated report to be displayed automatically, select the Automatically open report when done check box.

7. Click the Create button.

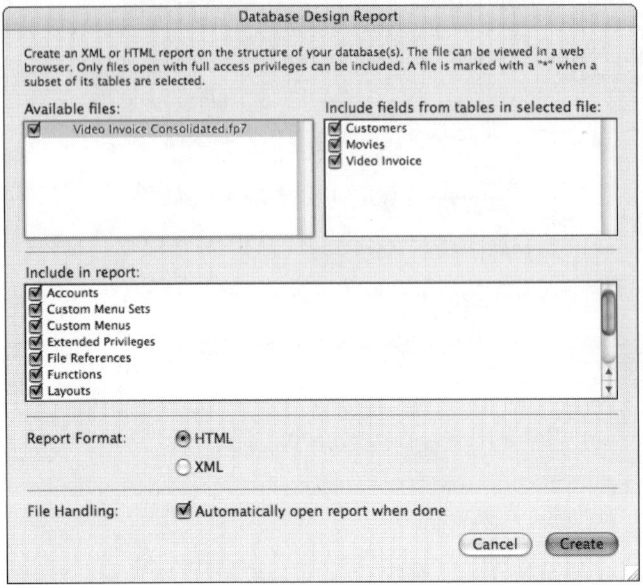

Database Design Report

Create an XML or HTML report on the structure of your database(s). The file can be viewed in a web browser. Only files open with full access privileges can be included. A file is marked with a "*" when a subset of its tables are selected.

Available files:
- ☑ Video Invoice Consolidated.fp7

Include fields from tables in selected file:
- ☑ Customers
- ☑ Movies
- ☑ Video Invoice

Include in report:
- ☑ Accounts
- ☑ Custom Menu Sets
- ☑ Custom Menus
- ☑ Extended Privileges
- ☑ File References
- ☑ Functions
- ☑ Layouts

Report Format: ⦿ HTML
                    ◯ XML

File Handling: ☑ Automatically open report when done

(Cancel)   (Create)

Figure 25-3: Specify your Database Design Report in this dialog.

A typical HTML Report opens to a Summary page, as shown in Figure 25-4. The Summary page includes links to reports on the individual files (in the File Name column). Clicking a filename links to a page consisting of two frames, a narrow navigation frame on the left, and a larger content frame on the right, as shown in Figure 25-5. The Back to Overview link returns you to the Summary page. There's a dividing line beneath that link, followed by links to the various tables in the report.

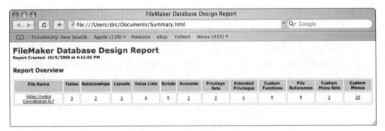

Figure 25-4: A Database Design Report's Summary page.

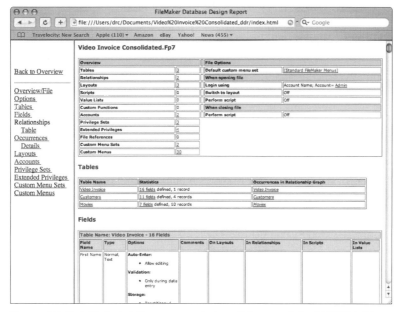

Figure 25-5: A file's details are reported on this page full of HTML tables.

Note

HTML reports will open in your default Web browser. XML reports will open in whatever your system has set for XML files. Under Mac OS X, this might default to the Property List Editor, in which case Property List Editor will launch, but nothing will display — or it might be Pages, which will generate an error alert that the file is not in Word format. If you attempt to open the XML file in Safari, you might get either a blank page or an error message. You can then choose View ➪ Source to look at the raw XML source. If you are running OS X, we recommend that you have Firefox as your default for XML files because it will display the XML document tree, as shown in Figure 25-6. On Windows, your XML file is likely to default to Internet Explorer, in which case the source (that is, document tree) will display in the main window. In either case, there will actually be two XML files — the Summary file and the details file — which will have as its name the name of the database with _fp7.xml appended. The bulk of the information is in the details file.

New Feature

New in this version's Database Design Report is support for two new Advanced features: Tooltips and Custom menus/menu sets, both of which are covered in Chapter 26.

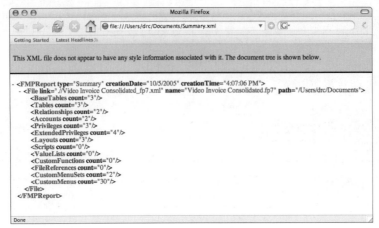

Figure 25-6: A Summary `.xml` file displayed in Firefox.

Although direct table import (see Chapter 26) is a new feature in Advanced, obviating most of the need for a tool like New Millennium Communications' FMRobot utility, FMRobot exemplifies how a third-party tool can leverage a Database Design Report to generate tables, layouts, or other database features. Similarly, you can create custom reports by applying an XSLT to the XML output.

Summary

✦ By using printed reports from the ScriptMaker and Define Database dialogs and HTML (or XML) Database Design Reports, you can document your database's design and operation.

✦ An XML Database Design Report can be used with third-party tools and XSLTs to re-create tables in new files or repurpose the report contents.

✦   ✦   ✦

Creating Custom Database Solutions

You've created your tables, value lists, forms and reports; implemented and debugged your scripts; established the privilege sets necessary to compartmentalize access and created the accounts that make use of those privilege sets; and documented the whole process. You're just about ready to deploy your database solution to an eagerly waiting world — or at least to a known customer or two.

As we discuss in Chapter 23, you can do your entire development in FileMaker Pro 8 and produce a marketable product. Of course, if you don't have FileMaker Pro 8 Advanced, you won't have access to the Script Debugger (Chapter 24) or the Database Design Report (Chapter 25), nor will you be able to insert tooltips (discussed later in this chapter) or create your own menus (also discussed later in this chapter), and your customers will have to own a copy of FileMaker Pro 8 to make use of your solution. But if you spring for the extra cost of FileMaker Pro 8 Advanced, you have the opportunity to sell to a much larger customer base by creating a runtime solution that will be usable by anyone running relatively current versions of Windows or Mac OS X, whether or not they own a copy of FileMaker Pro.

In addition, with FileMaker Pro 8 Advanced, you can make your development chores simpler by defining *custom functions,* encapsulating and parameterizing sequences of calculations you use throughout your database.

When running the Windows version of FileMaker Pro 8 Advanced, you cannot simultaneously run FileMaker Pro 8 on that machine.

Working with Custom Functions

The Custom Functions feature in FileMaker Pro 8 Advanced gives you the opportunity to create reusable functions that can be employed anywhere in a database that built-in functions are used: in calculations, field specifications, and so forth.

FileMaker Pro 7 added text-formatting calls to the list of functions used in calculations. However, using those functions to set the font, size, and style of a text string requires that you include code something like the code shown in Figure 26-1 every time you want to perform conditional formatting. And if — as in Figure 26-1 — other functions are invoked in creating the string you want to format, the formula can rapidly become a convoluted, virtually indecipherable mess. On the other hand, you could define a custom function TextAttribs (as shown, for example, in Figure 26-2) that would take a text argument, a font, size, and color and return the formatted text.

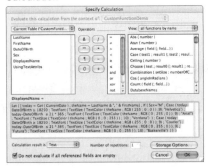

Figure 26-1: Using a calculated field to produce variable text formatting.

Not only were custom functions a new feature added in version 7, but Let statements were added to the calculation lexicon. This allows you, as shown in Figure 26-2, to consolidate frequently occurring constant expressions into variables that are evaluated at the beginning and whose subsequent use make your calculation more readable. Variable names are case-insensitive.

Custom Function

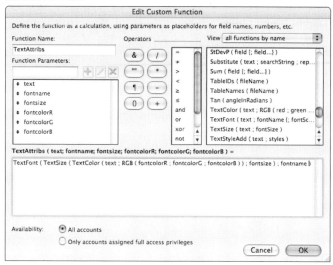

Using Custom Function

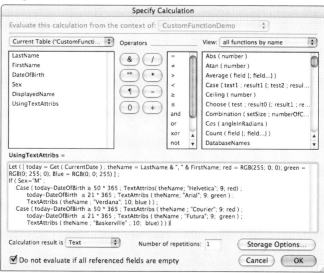

Output

Figure 26-2: Defining a custom function, you can create a more readable calculation, resulting in the same output.

Defining a custom function

To create your own custom function definitions, choose File ➪ Define ➪ Custom Functions. The Define Custom Functions for "<*databasename*>" dialog appears, such as the one shown in Figure 26-3.

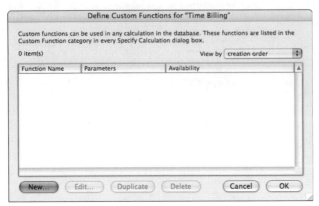

Figure 26-3: The Define Custom Functions for "<*databasename*>" dialog.

Click the New button to define a new custom function or select an existing custom function from the displayed list and then click the Edit button to modify that function. If you wish to create a slightly modified version of an existing function, you can make a copy of an existing custom function by selecting that function and then clicking the Duplicate button. The Edit Custom Function dialog is shown in Figure 26-4, as it would appear if you were creating a new function. If you're editing an existing function, the Function Name text box, the Function Parameters list, and the New Function text box display the function's current name, parameter list, and definition (as it does in the top part of Figure 26-2).

Proceed as follows to define your new function.

STEPS: Defining Your New Function

1. Enter a name in the Function Name text box (unless you want it to be called New Function).

   Function names must be unique and less than 100 characters in length. Also, they can contain neither spaces nor other special characters: That is, only letters, digits, and underscores are permitted.

   Note   In addition to the allowable character restrictions, function names cannot begin with a period (although periods may appear within the name). If you attempt to give a function an illegal name, an alert will appear telling you what is not allowed.

2. Enumerate (specify) your function's parameters by entering them in the Function Parameters text box and then clicking the plus button (or pressing Return/Enter).

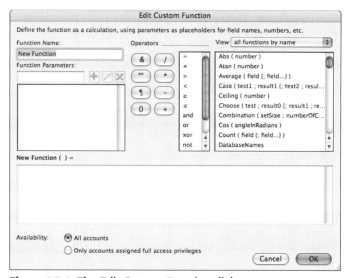

Figure 26-4: The Edit Custom Function dialog.

You can drag the parameters up and down in the parameter list to change the order in which they should appear. Selecting a parameter in the list makes its name appear in the Function Parameters edit box, allowing you to modify the name, and clicking the pencil button accepts your edits. Selecting a parameter and clicking the X button removes the parameter from the list.

3. Build a formula in the formula text box at the bottom of the dialog, just as you would define a calculation. See the top part of Figure 26-2 for an example of a formula definition.

4. You can restrict the custom function's visibility to Full Access users by selecting the Only accounts assigned full access privileges radio button; otherwise, the custom function is visible to all users of the database.

5. Click OK to dismiss the Edit Custom Function dialog. Click OK again to dismiss the Define Custom Functions for "*<database>*" dialog (or create/edit additional functions).

Invoking custom functions

If you haven't restricted custom function access to just Full Access accounts, any user of the database will see your custom function(s) in the Function list at the right of any Specify Calculation dialog. The custom functions appear under the obviously named Custom functions category in the Specify Calculation dialog's View pop-up menu/drop-down list, as shown in Figure 26-5.

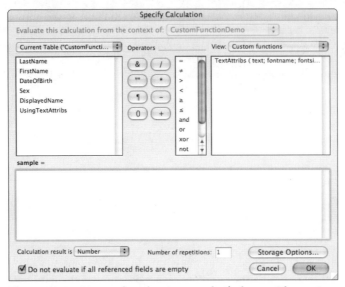

Figure 26-5: Custom functions appear in their own View category in a Specify Calculation dialog.

Note   If the custom function is restricted to Full Access accounts only and you are using the database without full access privileges, you will see the string <Private Function> rather than the custom function in any script or calculation employing it, and you will also be unable to edit the calculation or modify the script step where it occurs.

Importing Tables from Other FileMaker Databases

The most profound change that occurred in FileMaker Pro 7 was the ability to maintain multiple tables in a single database file. You no longer had to manage multiple files to provide a relational solution, and the single file approach also reduces the operating system overhead concomitant with keeping multiple files open simultaneously. Unfortunately, version 7 provided no convenient method to consolidate existing multiple-file solutions into single-file solutions — you either had to manually reconstruct the tables in your new database, or you had to purchase a third-party utility (such as New Millennium's FMRobot) to automate the table re-creation based upon a Database Design Report (see Chapter 25).

New Feature

FileMaker Pro 8 Advanced introduces built-in table import functionality, eliminating the tedium of manually reconstructing tables or the cost of purchasing a third-party utility to consolidate existing multiple-file solutions into a single-file solution.

In keeping with the KISS principle (Keep It Simple, Stupid!), the easiest way to replicate a table schema (structure, but not data) is to open the original file, select it in the Define Database dialog's Tables pane, and choose Edit ➪ Copy (or press ⌘+C/Ctrl+C) and then move to the destination file and choose Edit ➪ Paste (or press ⌘+V/Ctrl+V).

More generally, though, you can import table schemas, either with or without their data, as follows.

STEPS: Importing a Table

1. Open the file into which you wish to import a table by using any of the standard methods for opening a database file (choosing File ➪ Open, double-clicking, and so on).

2. Choose File ➪ Define ➪ Database and select the Tables tab. Using the Video World example's Video Invoice file would present the screen shown in Figure 26-6.

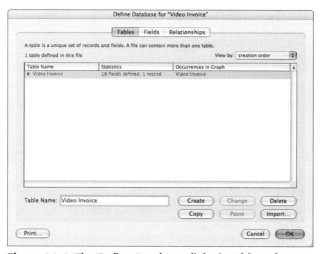

Figure 26-6: The Define Database dialog's Tables tab.

3. Click the Import button near the dialog's bottom-right corner. You will see an Open File dialog as appropriate to your operating system (Mac OS X or Windows).

4. Select the file from which you wish to import tables. The Import Tables dialog shown in Figure 26-7 appears. (In our case, we're selecting the Movies.fp7 file.)

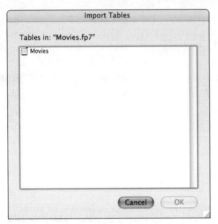

Figure 26-7: Select the tables you wish to import.

5. Select the check box(es) associated with the table(s) you wish to import and then click OK. The Import Summary dialog, shown in Figure 26-8, appears. If you have items renamed, if you have errors, or if you're interested in a more detailed description of the import, click the Open Log File button; otherwise, click OK. (The Log File will open in your system's default text editor — usually TextEdit on a Mac or Notepad on a Windows system.)

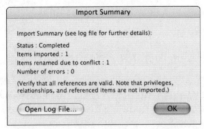

Figure 26-8: Check the results of your import operations.

6. Repeat Steps 3–5 for any additional database files from which you wish to import tables.

Note
As you are informed in the Import Summary dialog (see Figure 26-8), relationships and privilege sets are not imported. You will need to re-create those in the Relationships tab and Define Accounts & Privileges dialog, respectively.

Adding Tooltips to Your Layouts

One form of help that is pervasive in modern graphical user interfaces is the *tooltip*, those little (usually yellow) rectangles of text that appear over interface elements when you pass or rest your mouse pointer above them, as shown in Figure 26-9.

Figure 26-9: A tooltip in the Mac OS X Finder and on a FileMaker Pro 8 layout.

Associating a tooltip with a layout element in FileMaker Pro 8 Advanced is simplicity itself. Proceed as follows:

STEPS: Adding a Tooltip

1. Display the layout containing the element(s) requiring a tooltip.

2. Enter Layout mode.

3. Select the element to which you wish to attach a tooltip.

4. Choose Format ➪ Set Tooltip. The Set Tooltip dialog, shown in Figure 26-10, appears.

5. Enter a text string or click the Specify button to display the familiar FileMaker Pro Specify Calculation dialog, where you define a calculation to generate the tooltip you wish displayed. Click the Specify Calculation dialog's OK button to enter the calculation and return to the Set Tooltip dialog.

6. Click OK to dismiss the Set Tooltip dialog.

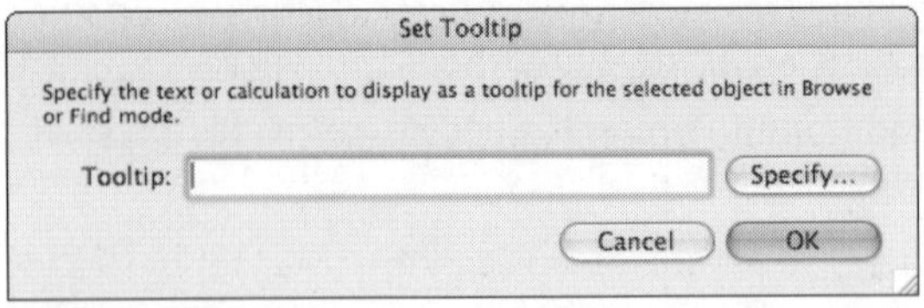

Set Tooltip

Specify the text or calculation to display as a tooltip for the selected object in Browse or Find mode.

Tooltip: [   ] (Specify...)

(Cancel) (OK)

Figure 26-10: Enter your tooltip's text here (or click the Specify button).

Now, when you (or one of your users) use this layout in Browse or Find mode, hovering the mouse pointer over the layout element displays a tooltip as shown previously in Figure 26-9.

Tip   You can group layout objects and have a tooltip apply to the group. This can be handy when you wish to describe interrelated objects.

Creating Custom Menus

Heretofore, creating a custom solution had one serious limitation — you were constrained to using the FileMaker Pro set of menus. FileMaker Pro 8 Advanced breaks new ground by allowing you to replace the standard FileMaker Pro menus with customized menus specific to your solution or to just tweak the existing menus to provide desired functionality or eliminate inappropriate commands. You can even create menu sets that appear, for example, only when specific layouts are active.

Probably the simplest customization is to modify a menu command, such as New Record, to match your solution: for example, renaming the command New Employee for a Human Resources database or New Contact for a contact manager.

Just so we're all in terminology lockstep, the following terms have specific meaning in this discussion of custom menus:

✦ **Menu bar:** The area at the top of a Windows window or the Mac screen that displays the active menus.

✦ **Menu set:** A group of menus that appears in the menu bar.

✦ **Menu:** A name in the menu bar and a set of items that appear when the name is selected.

✦ **Menu item:** One entry in a menu. Menu items can be enabled or disabled. Disabled items, such as separators or inactive items, cannot be selected.

✦ **Submenu:** A menu that appears subordinate to another menu when a specific menu item is selected.

✦ **Shortcut:** Also called a *keyboard shortcut,* this indicates keys that can be pressed to invoke the action as selecting the menu item.

✦ **Separator:** A (disabled) line dividing menu items into groups of related commands.

✦ **Standard FileMaker menus:** The menu set consisting of the default FileMaker menus.

Menu customization generally falls into two broad classes, as follows:

✦ Modification of existing FileMaker menus

✦ Creation of a new menu from scratch

All menu customization activities originate in the Define Custom Menus dialog, which you invoke by choosing File ➪ Define ➪ Custom Menus and then selecting the Custom Menus tab. The Define Custom Menus dialog is shown in Figure 26-11.

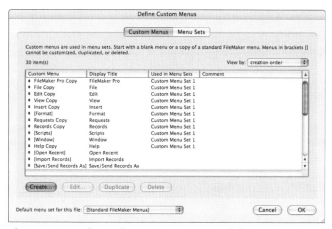

Figure 26-11: The Define Custom Menus dialog

Note

Menus whose names are enclosed in square brackets are locked and cannot be customized.

In the Define Custom Menus dialog, you can

✦ Select an existing menu from the list of menus and click Edit to present the Edit Custom Menu dialog (see Figure 26-12).

✦ Click the Create button to (surprise!) create a custom menu. The Create Custom Menu dialog, shown in Figure 26-13, appears.

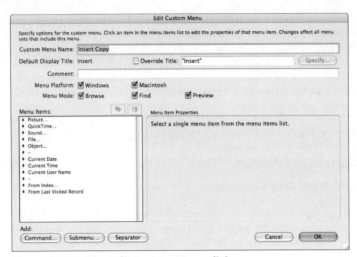

Figure 26-12: The Edit Custom Menu dialog.

Figure 26-13: The starting point for Custom Menu creation and modification.

1. Select either the Start with an empty menu radio button (to begin from scratch), or select the Start with a standard FileMaker menu radio button and then select a menu from the list to create a menu based on one of the existing FileMaker menus.

2. Click OK to present the Edit Custom Menu dialog (refer to Figure 26-12).

You specify all the custom menu's settings in the Edit Custom Menu dialog. As you can see in Figure 26-12, you give the menu a name (100 characters or shorter) that will identify it in the Define Custom Menus dialog (but is not the name that appears in the menu bar), a menu title (this is what appears in the menu bar), an optional comment to help you document what you're doing, the platform or platforms (Windows, Macintosh) on which your menu will be used, and the FileMaker modes in which the menu will appear.

Note   You cannot display custom menus in Layout mode.

At this point, you're ready to start the actual work of populating your menu with its menu items. You can delete items by selecting them and clicking the trash can button at the top right of the Menu items list or duplicate an item by selecting it and clicking the double-plus button just to the left of the trash button. To add an item to the list, do one of the following:

✦ *Add a menu command*

   1. Click the Command button at the bottom left of the Edit Custom Menu dialog, which displays the Specify FileMaker Command dialog shown in Figure 26-14.

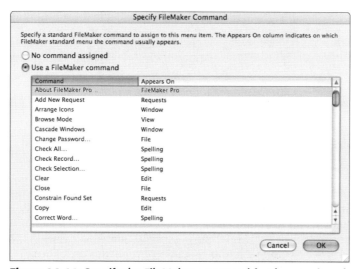

Figure 26-14: Specify the FileMaker command for the new item here.

2. Select the command you wish to add in the list or select the No command assigned radio button to have FileMaker add an Untitled menu item. Click OK to return to the Edit Custom Menu dialog.

3. The item you just added will appear at the bottom of the list or immediately below any item that was selected when you clicked the Command button.

4. Set the properties for the menu item in the Menu Item Properties area.

✦ *Add a submenu*

1. Click the Submenu button at the bottom left of the dialog, which presents the Specify Submenu dialog shown in Figure 26-15.

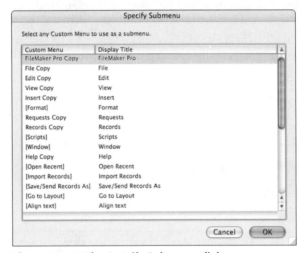

Figure 26-15: The Specify Submenu dialog.

2. Select the menu you wish to include and click OK.

✦ *Add a separator*

1. Select the item beneath which you want the separator line to appear.

2. Click the Separator button near the bottom left of the Edit Custom Menu dialog (refer to Figure 26-12).

For each item in the list, select it and specify its properties as follows:

✦ To specify what command the item executes, click the Specify button at the right end of the Command line. The Specify FileMaker Command dialog, shown previously in Figure 26-14, appears.

✦ Select the Windows check box, the Macintosh check box, or both to specify on which platform(s) the menu item will be available.

✦ Specify the menu item's title. This can be either a text string or a calculation created in the Specify Calculation dialog that appears if you click the Specify button.

If you wish to associate an access key (the key that, in conjunction with the Alt key, selects the item), precede that character with an ampersand (&) in the menu title. For example, you could enter Current &Date to make D the access key. You can even assign the access key on a Mac, but you won't see the result except when using the database in Windows.

✦ Specify the keyboard shortcut, if any, you wish associated with the menu item. The Specify Shortcut dialog is shown in Figure 26-16.

Figure 26-16: Enter your keyboard shortcut when this dialog is showing.

✦ Specify whether a script or script step is executed when a user selects the menu item by selecting the Action check box and then choosing either Script or Script Step from the pop-up menu/drop-down list. Depending upon whether you chose a script or script step, you will see either the Specify Script Options dialog or the Specify Script Step dialog (both shown in Figure 26-17).

Creating custom menus, as just described, is only part of the equation in creating your custom solution. Defining when those menus appear is every bit as critical as creating the custom menus in the first place, and that is where menu sets enter the picture.

Script

Script Step

Figure 26-17: Specify your script or script step actions in these dialogs.

To define a menu set, proceed as follows.

STEPS: Defining a Menu Set

1. Choose File ➪ Define ➪ Custom Menus and select the Menu Sets tab. The Menu Sets pane is shown in Figure 26-18.

2. Either create a new menu set by clicking the Create button or select an existing menu set and click the Edit button. In either case, the Edit Menu Set dialog, shown in Figure 26-19, appears.

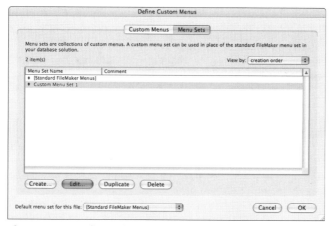

Figure 26-18: The Define Custom Menus dialog's Menu Sets pane.

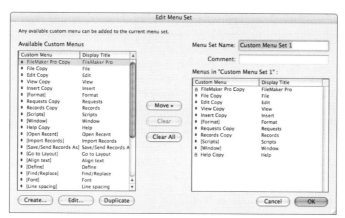

Figure 26-19: Construct your custom menu sets in the Edit Menu Set dialog.

3. Enter a name for your custom menu set in the Menu Set Name text box (upper right of the dialog) and (optionally) a descriptive comment in the Comment text box. Comments appear in the Define Custom Menus dialog's list of custom menu sets (Menu Sets pane).

4. Add and/or remove menus from your custom menu set using the Move, Clear, and Clear All buttons. Clicking the Create button will take you to the Edit Custom Menu dialog described earlier (refer to Figure 26-12) if you wish to create a new menu at this time. Similarly, you can select an existing menu in the Available Custom Menus list and duplicate it by clicking the Duplicate button or modify it by clicking the Edit button.

You can also double-click menus in the list of available menus to move them to the list of menus in the custom set.

Note

Menus in the custom menu set appear in the order they occupy in the custom menu list. You can reorder this list by dragging the little handles to the left of the names, just as in other FileMaker Pro dialog-based lists.

5. When you've finished defining your menu sets by repeated applications of Steps 3 and 4, click OK to dismiss the Edit Menu Set dialog and then OK again to dismiss the Define Custom Menus dialog.

After you have defined your custom menu sets, you are still left with the task of telling FileMaker when they are to be displayed. Menu sets can be

✦ Used as a database's default menu set. Choose File ➪ Define ➪ Custom Menus; in the Custom Menus pane, choose the set from the Default menu set for this file pop-up menu/drop-down list at the bottom of the dialog.

✦ Attached to a specific layout: Switch to Layout mode, choose Layouts ➪ Layout Setup, select the General tab, and choose a menu set from the Menu Set pop-up menu/drop-down list (as shown in Figure 26-20).

Figure 26-20: The Layout Setup dialog's General pane is where you attach a menu set to a layout.

✦ Changed in response to scripts: You can check which menu set is currently active with the Get(CustomMenuSetName) function and instantiate a different menu set with the Install Menu Set script step.

Tip

As with any software development exercise, liberal use of Get(LastError) to check for problems after an Install Menu Set invocation and rigorous testing of your solution are strongly recommended. Experience (both ours and that of every developer we've ever known) indicates that failure to test something is a virtual guarantee that the untested functionality *will have bugs!*

When operating in the FileMaker Pro 8 Advanced environment, you can switch menu sets on the fly by choosing Tools ⇨ Custom Menus and then choosing the desired custom menu set from the submenu that appears.

> **Note** Remember, custom menu sets are not accessible in Layout mode, so you must be in Browse, Find, or Preview mode to switch custom menu sets.

In both FileMaker Pro 8 and FileMaker Pro 8 Advanced, you can choose FileMaker Pro ⇨ About FileMaker Pro (Mac)/Help ⇨ About FileMaker Pro (Windows) and then click Info in the ensuing dialog to see whether custom menus are installed.

> **Note** There are a number of platform-dependent restrictions and caveats relating to the use of custom menus and custom menu sets. These concerns are well described in the FileMaker Pro 8 Advanced Development Guide booklet that comes with your copy of FileMaker Pro 8 Advanced. In fact, they are so well and clearly enumerated that attempting to reiterate them here would be either redundant or an act of plagiarism — so, this is a rare instance where we will direct you to the manual.

Using the File Maintenance Command

A menu command that is available only in FileMaker Pro 8 Advanced is Tools ⇨ File Maintenance. Choosing this command presents the dialog shown in Figure 26-21.

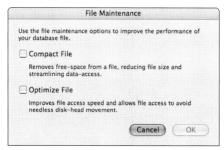

Figure 26-21: The File Maintenance dialog.

Selecting Compact File reduces the file's disk footprint (size) by rewriting the file and removing free space (such as that left by deleted records, indexes, and the like). Selecting Optimize File operates similarly to a disk defragmenter, rewriting the file so that the physical order of the data matches the logical (described) order. In other words, records become contiguous, with the data order matching the field order, thus minimizing disk activity when retrieving records.

Note   The Compact File option has the same result as doing a Save As, choosing Compacted File, and then deleting the original. The difference is that you do not require the extra (temporary) disk space required for the copy because the compaction occurs in place.

You will be notified by an alert when the selected maintenance activity completes.

Using the Developer Utilities

Choosing Tools ⇨ Developer Utilities presents the dialog shown in Figure 26-22. As you can see, this dialog's major focus is on creating a runtime solution; however, there are a few capabilities independent of whether you're maintaining a standard FileMaker Pro database or creating a runtime package.

Figure 26-22: The Developer Utilities dialog offers a plethora of choices.

You employ the Developer Utilities to manipulate database solution files. You can use the Developer Utilities to create an entirely new set of (possibly renamed) files, add customized About or Help dialogs, or create runtime solutions.

The first requirement in employing the Developer Utilities is to ensure that all the database solution set files on which you intend to operate are closed. Follow these steps to use the Developer Utilities on your solution.

STEPS: Using the Developer Utilities

1. Choose Tools ⇨ Developer Utilities.

   The dialog seen in Figure 26-22 appears.

2. Click Add.

   A standard Open dialog, entitled Add a File, appears. Navigate to and select the file(s) you wish to add. You can select multiple files at one time using standard selection techniques (Shift+clicking for contiguous selections and ⌘/Ctrl+clicking for noncontiguous selections).

   The selected files are added to the Solution Files list, as shown in Figure 26-23. You can remove files from the list by selecting them and clicking the Remove button.

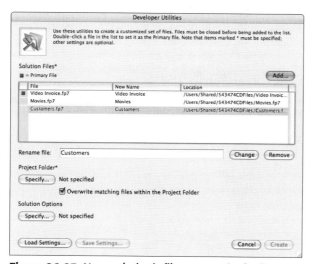

Figure 26-23: Your solution's files appear in the list.

3. (Optional) Double-click a file in the list to designate it as the primary file in your solution.

4. (Optional) Rename a file by selecting it in the list and entering the new name in the Rename file text box. Do *not* include the filename extension (such as .fp7).

5. Specify a Project Folder (the destination folder for your solution).

   The Choose a folder for this project's files dialog appears. Create a new folder or select an existing folder and click Choose/OK.

You can deselect the Overwrite matching files with the Project Folder check box if you don't want FileMaker to replace existing files with the same name. This decision is pertinent only when writing to an existing folder (because a new folder won't have any pre-existing contents).

6. (Optional) Customize your files or create a runtime solution by following the steps in "STEPS: Specifying Solution Options."

7. (Optional) If this is a solution that you might need to update, you can click Save Settings and choose a location for your settings file. This settings file can be reloaded, saving you a great deal of time and eliminating some possibility of error when re-creating the solution's settings.

8. Click Create.

Developer Utilities copies all the selected files — making all specified modifications — to the designated Project Folder.

Database Utilities' real power comes in creating a runtime solution. Proceed as follows to create a runtime solution (starting after Step 5 of the preceding step list).

STEPS: Specifying Solution Options

1. In the Developer Utilities dialog (refer to Figure 26-22), click the Specify button under Solution Options.

The Specify Solution Options dialog (see Figure 26-24) appears. If you select an option's line in the list, a description and associated settings appear in the bottom half of the dialog.

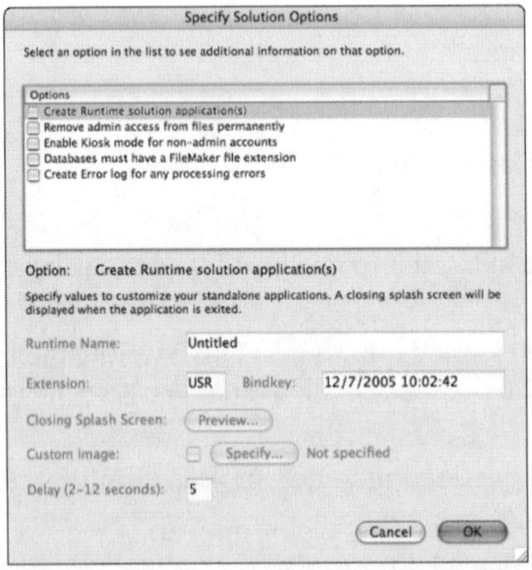

Figure 26-24: The Specify Solutions Options dialog.

2. Select the check boxes for the options you desire.

Some options are mutually exclusive. For example, if you select Create Runtime solutions application(s), the Databases must have a FileMaker file extension option becomes unavailable.

The various options are described in Table 26-1.

3. Click OK.

<table>
<tr><td colspan="2" align="center">Table 26-1
Solution Options</td></tr>
<tr><td>*Option*</td><td>*Description*</td></tr>
<tr><td>Create Runtime solution application(s)</td><td>This tells FileMaker Pro 8 Advanced to create double-clickable applications that users can run without a copy of FileMaker Pro (or FileMaker Pro 8 Advanced). No FileMaker Pro 8 Advanced-specific features are available in a runtime application, and many FileMaker Pro menu options (such as the File ➪ Define submenu choices) are also unavailable.[†]</td></tr>
<tr><td>Remove admin access from files permanently</td><td>Selecting this option permanently strips the solution files from being opened by an administrative (full access) account. This option, after it's employed, is not undoable — you cannot restore an Admin account to the database.</td></tr>
<tr><td>Enable Kiosk mode for non-admin accounts</td><td>This option forces accounts lacking full access privileges to run the application in Kiosk mode. (See the "Kiosk mode" sidebar for more information.)</td></tr>
<tr><td>Databases must have a FileMaker file extension</td><td>Add the .fp7 file extension to the names of database files that don't already have the extension. This option is disabled if you have selected to create a runtime solution.</td></tr>
<tr><td>Create Error log for any processing errors</td><td>Selecting this option creates a text log (which you can name), describing all errors encountered during the process of applying the other selected options. An error alert might or might not also be presented during processing.</td></tr>
</table>

[†]You can open these standalone applications in FileMaker Pro and/or FileMaker Pro 8 Advanced to gain access to the File ➪ Define submenu choices or FileMaker Pro 8 Advanced-specific features. However, if you have permanently removed Admin access, much of the functionality will still be unavailable.

New Feature In FileMaker Pro 7's Developer version (and earlier Developer versions), you could only customize the Help, About, and Scripts menus. With FileMaker Pro 8 Advanced, the special check boxes for dealing with those three cases have disappeared in favor of the more general custom menu and custom menu set capabilities described earlier in this chapter.

Planning for a runtime solution

It's not enough to just say, "I want a runtime solution." You need to plan ahead if you want your customers to have full functionality without the FileMaker Pro envelope surrounding the database. For example

✦ Unlike a standard database file that can be used with either the Mac or Windows version of FileMaker Pro, a runtime solution is bound to a particular platform, as described in the *FileMaker Pro 8 Advanced Development Guide* booklet. You can bind for Mac on a Mac and for Windows under Windows. Because of the differences in operating system functionality (packages and resources on a Mac and DLLs on Windows), you will need to bind on each separately, Windows first, using the same binding key and three-character extension if you want a cross-platform solution. Binding keys and extensions are case-sensitive.

✦ Runtime solutions don't provide Open or Close options in the File menu, so you need to provide scripts (or buttons) to open any needed auxiliary database files. The auxiliary files will also need a layout with a button or script that returns control to the primary database file.

✦ Whenever possible, you should consolidate tables into a single file rather than managing multiple files. This makes resolving file references moot and improves performance. If you opt to maintain multiple-file solutions, you must ensure that every file reference includes a path that is just the name of the sought file, indicating that it is in the same directory as the primary file (because the Developer Utilities moves all solution files into a single folder).

✦ Use a binding key that you'll remember. If you forget your binding key or use a different one (even if it varies just in capitalization) when making a modification, you'll have to redistribute all files *including the runtime file* for your update.

✦ ScriptMaker is not available in a runtime solution, so you need to anticipate all the scripting needs your clients might have.

✦ Layout mode is unavailable in a runtime solution; therefore, you must create all the forms and reports your clients might require or desire.

✦ If you feel that you might need to add or modify layouts or scripts in a runtime solution, do not permanently remove Admin access because you can open a runtime solution in FileMaker Pro or FileMaker Pro 8 Advanced and make the modifications if full access is still available. If you eliminate full access accounts, you'll have to open and modify the original files and rebind the entire solution.

Note FileMaker Pro and Advanced Help is usually pretty useful in describing product functionality and some of the things that you should consider when using specific features, assuming you know which questions to ask. Conversely, the printed documentation is usually fairly sparse. When it comes to preparing for and implementing a runtime solution, though, these generalities both get stood on their heads. The *FileMaker Pro 8 Advanced Development Guide* booklet actually does a very good job of covering the process of planning and creating a runtime solution. In fact, once again, it's difficult for us to do an equally good job without flirting with plagiarism, so we're going to refer you to the FileMaker Advanced Development manual for additional details.

Note that custom functions you've defined in the database are still accessible in a runtime application. However, the user will not be able to edit them (no File ➪ Define ➪ Custom Functions menu item) nor create new calculations using them (no File ➪ Define ➪ Database menu item).

You cannot share a runtime solution, either over a network or on the Web, nor can a runtime solution communicate with Java applets.

Runtime applications do not support OLE automation on Windows; however, AppleScript/AppleEvent support is still present in Mac runtime solutions.

Some other runtime solution changes include

✦ In the Preferences dialog, the Layout tab is called the Color tab, with a concomitant decrease in options. (Only the Color Palette section remains.)

✦ The File Options dialog has only one tab: Spelling.

✦ The Recover command is absent from the File menu; however, the functionality is still present if you press Option+⌘/Ctrl+Shift while launching the runtime solution.

✦ Various script steps are ignored, including (but not limited to) Open ScriptMaker, Set Multi-User, Execute SQL, Open Sharing, and New File.

Writing your own plug-ins

You'll find the source code for a sample plug-in on your FileMaker Pro 8 Advanced CD (the Plugin Examples folder at the root of the CD). The example is written in C++, and both Mac and Windows versions are present (Xcode for Mac and CodeWarrior Development Studio for the Mac; Microsoft Visual Studio .NET 2003 for Windows). Support is not provided for other languages or development systems.

Kiosk mode

Not only can you create database solutions that your users employ like a standard Mac or Windows application; you can also create solutions that run in *Kiosk mode.* This means that the solution takes over the entire screen, hiding the menu bar, toolbar(s), and the Dock/taskbar. In short, your application turns the computer into a standalone information kiosk. Touchscreen interfaces are also supported as are all other tasks normally performed by choosing from a menu (including quitting).

Kiosk solutions are often found (at least in our experience) in corporate lobbies for auto-mated visitor login/logout, and generally include functionality for name badge printing and sometimes for paging the person being visited. Another fairly common Kiosk solution is to use the solution in place of a store's Information Desk; for example, the database has the store's inventory, and you can search for an item by entering data into search fields and clicking Search. The database then lists what's available, matching your request, and shows where those items can be found. (This solution is very popular in book or video stores.)

All navigation is done via buttons and scripts. Note that this means you must add a button allowing application termination; otherwise, the only way to exit the runtime solution is to force-quit the application, possibly resulting in data loss or file corruption. ***Warning:*** If the Kiosk application is run on a Windows system, users can press Alt+F4 to force-quit; how-ever, there is no Mac keyboard equivalent (not even ⌘+Option+Esc), and users would be forced to shut down the computer using the power button (or unplugging the computer). Similarly, if deployed on a Windows-based platform, users can press Alt+Tab to switch to another application, but the equivalent (⌘+Tab) is not available on the Mac — no operating system access is available on the Mac when in Kiosk mode.

You should also be aware that running in Kiosk mode does not scale layouts nor perform any clever tricks to position content. Your layouts are displayed at the size and location saved in the non-runtime solution. The remainder of the screen is filled with black, resulting in a display similar to that shown in the following figure.

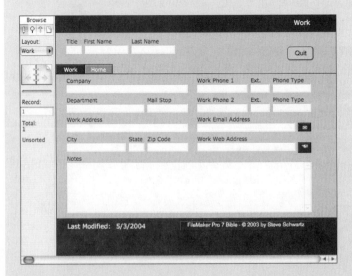

Therefore, be sure to size and position your layouts as you want them to appear in a Kiosk solution. At a minimum, size and arrange the layout elements to fill a full-screen window: Large fonts, large buttons, and an uncrowded arrangement complement a Kiosk solution. *Remember:* This is a situation where the computer screen is likely to be sitting on a podium or other pedestal, and the user is unlikely to be positioned at as comfortable a viewing distance and angle as would be the case for a typical workstation solution.

Alternatively, you could (as FileMaker, Inc. suggests) include a startup script that invokes the Adjust Window and Set Zoom Level script steps to size and position the window, and then zoom in to fill the space. (Be careful to get the current screen size and perform the appropriate scaling calculation if you don't know beforehand what the display size and resolution will be.)

Branding your layout themes

FileMaker uses Theme XML files to describe its layout themes. These XML documents specify fonts, sizes, styles, fills, and patterns for the various layout parts. They do not specify object positioning information. You can modify existing themes or create your own theme files, putting your brand (or your client's brand) on the layouts in your solution.

Tip Although you certainly can create the Theme XML files from scratch, their structure is quite well defined, and you will save a lot of time and aggravation by starting with a copy of one of the presupplied theme files.

The FileMaker Theme XML files are text files with an `.fth` file extension, located in the FileMaker Pro 8 Advanced (or Pro) folder's Themes folder (`C:\Program Files\FileMaker\FileMaker Pro 8\Extensions\English\Themes`) on a Windows system or the Themes folder within the Mac application package. Ctrl+click the application icon, choose Show Package Contents, and then drill down to Contents ➪ Resources ➪ English.lproj ➪ Themes.

Note Although Web browsers will display as much of a syntactically incorrect HTML file as they can parse, XML files must be syntactically correct (well-formed) for FileMaker to parse them. Any error, such as a missing end tag, results in an unusable document.

Theme XML file format

A *FileMaker Theme XML file* (.fth) is an XML document that can contain one or more theme descriptions. Because FileMaker places a limit of 50 on the number of theme files you can have, you might find it advantageous to include multiple custom theme descriptions in a single file. In addition to staying below the 50-file cap, you control the order in which the theme names appear. (The order matches the order in which they're declared in the file.)

A theme file contains, at a minimum, the following elements (in the order listed):

✦ The XML declaration

```
<?xml version="1.0" standalone="yes" ?>
```

✦ The FMTHEMES start tag

```
<FMTHEMES>
```

✦ One or more FMTHEME declarations

```
<FMTHEME>
...<THEMENAME VALUE="put a unique themename here" />
</FMTHEME>
```

✦ The FMTHEMES end tag

```
</FMTHEMES>
```

Within the FMTHEME block, you include XML elements for each of the layout parts, describing how that part is to be rendered. Similarly, you can include XML descriptions for the formatting of text in files, labels, and text boxes within each layout part. FileMaker Pro 8 Advanced uses default values for any absent element formats. If you define multiple instances for an element, the last one listed is the one FileMaker uses. The *FileMaker Pro 8 Advanced Development Guide* lists valid elements and what subordinate elements they can contain — as well as value constraints — starting near the end of page 34.

Summary

✦ You can create custom functions to augment the functions that FileMaker, Inc. and plug-ins provide.

✦ You can import tables directly, either via copy and paste or via the File ➪ Import Records command.

✦ You can employ tooltips to provide non-modal help to your customers concerning layout objects that might be unfamiliar or that have special constraints.

✦ Use custom menus (and menu sets) to provide targeted menu choices for your solutions.

✦ Use the File Maintenance command to compact or optimize your database's internal storage.

✦ Enhance your solution's branding with custom layout themes.

✦ If you're comfortable programming in C++, you can create your own plug-ins to extend FileMaker's capabilities.

✦ The Developer Utilities command lets you create runtime solutions for your customers.

✦   ✦   ✦

Appendixes

P A R T

VII

◆ ◆ ◆ ◆

In This Part

Appendix A
Macintosh Keyboard
Shortcuts

Appendix B
Windows Keyboard
Shortcuts

Appendix C
FileMaker Pro
Function Reference

Appendix D
Glossary

Appendix E
Resources

Appendix F
About the Web Site

◆ ◆ ◆ ◆

Macintosh Keyboard Shortcuts

This appendix contains keyboard equivalents for FileMaker Pro commands and actions on the Macintosh. These commands are organized according to the various kinds of tasks you might want to perform. Note that the tables in this appendix do not contain all the commands the program offers; they merely list the commands that have keyboard shortcuts.

Table A-1
General Commands

Command	Key	Menu	Comments
Cancel an operation or dismiss a dialog	⌘+. (period)		You can also dismiss a dialog by pressing Esc.
Close a window	⌘+W	File ⇨ Close	You can also click the close button on the document window. Option+⌘+W closes all open application windows.
Define database	Shift+⌘+D	File ⇨ Define ⇨ Database	
Help	⌘+? or Help	Help ⇨ FileMaker Pro Help	You can also Control+click and choose FileMaker Help from the shortcut menu that appears.
Open Remote	⌘+Shift+O	File ⇨ Open Remote	You can also click Remote in the Open File dialog.
Open a database	⌘+O	File ⇨ Open	
Play a sound or movie in a Container field	Spacebar or double-click the field		
Preferences	⌘+, (comma)	FileMaker Pro ⇨ Preferences	
Print	⌘+P	File ⇨ Print	
Print without a dialog	⌘+Option+P		This is the Print One command.
Stop playing a movie in a Container field	Spacebar or single-click the field		
Quit	⌘+Q	FileMaker Pro ⇨ Quit FileMaker Pro	

Table A-2
Mode-Selection Commands

Command	Key	Menu	Comments
Browse	⌘+B	View ⇨ Browse Mode	You can also choose this command from the Mode pop-up menu or click the button in the status area.
Find	⌘+F	View ⇨ Find Mode	You can also choose this command from the Mode pop-up menu or click the button in the status area.
Layout	⌘+L	View ⇨ Layout Mode	You can also choose this command from the Mode pop-up menu or click the button in the status area.
Preview	⌘+U	View ⇨ Preview Mode	You can also choose this command from the Mode pop-up menu or click the button in the status area.

Table A-3
Document Window Control Commands

Command	Key	Menu	Comments
Close a database	⌘+W	File ⇨ Close	
Hide FileMaker Pro	⌘+H	FileMaker Pro ⇨ Hide FileMaker Pro	
Minimize the current window	⌘+M	Window ⇨ Minimize Window	
Resize window	Shift+⌘+Z		This command is the same as clicking the window's zoom button.
Scroll to top of current record or preview page	Home		
Scroll to bottom of current record or preview page	End		

Continued

Table A-3 *(continued)*

Command	Key	Menu	Comments
Scroll up one page in current record, report, View as List, or View as Table	Page Up		
Scroll down one page in as List, current record, report, View or View as Table	Page Down		
Scroll to first record with View as List or View as Table checked	Home		
Scroll to last record with View as List or View as Table checked	End		
Status area (hide/show)	⌘+Option+S	View ➪ Status Area	You can also click the status area control.

Table A-4
Layout Mode Commands

Command	Key	Menu	Comments
Align bottom edges of selected objects	⌘+Option+↓	Arrange ➪ Align ➪ Bottom Edges	
Align left edges of selected objects	⌘+Option+←	Arrange ➪ Align ➪ Left Edges	
Align right edges of selected objects	⌘+Option+→	Arrange ➪ Align ➪ Left Edges	
Align top edges of selected objects	⌘+Option+↑	Arrange ➪ Align ➪ Left Edges	
Bring forward	Shift+⌘+[	Arrange ➪ Bring Forward	
Bring to front	⌘+Option+[	Arrange ➪ Bring to Front	
Button format	Double-click a button	Format ➪ Button Setup	
Constrain lines to vertical/ horizontal	Press Shift while drawing		

Command	Key	Menu	Comments
Constrain lines to 45-degree increments	Press Option while drawing		
Constrain ovals to circles and rectangles to squares	Press Option while drawing or resizing		
Constrain resizing to vertical/horizontal	Shift+drag a handle		
Copy selected object	⌘+C	Edit ⇨ Copy	Places a copy of the object or text on the Clipboard.
Cut selected object or text	⌘+X	Edit ⇨ Cut	Places a copy of the object or text on the Clipboard.
Date format	Option+double-click a Date field	Format ⇨ Date	
Delete layout	⌘+E	Layouts ⇨ Delete Layout	
Display field or object's format	Option+ double-click the field or object		See also specific object and field types listed in this table.
Drag selected layout part past an object	Option+drag		
Duplicate an object	⌘+D (or Option+ drag the object)	Edit ⇨ Duplicate	
Field borders	⌘+Option+B	Format ⇨ Field/ Control ⇨ Borders	
Field setup	⌘+Option+F	Format ⇨ Field/ Control ⇨ Setup	
Field behavior	⌘+Option+K	Format ⇨ Field/ Control ⇨ Behavior	
Graphic format	Option+double-click a Container field or graphic object	Format ⇨ Graphic	
Group objects	⌘+R	Arrange ⇨ Group	
Insert current date	⌘+− (hyphen)	Insert ⇨ Current Date	
Insert current time	⌘+; (semicolon)	Insert ⇨ Current Time	

Continued

Table A-4 *(continued)*

Command	Key	Menu	Comments
Insert current user name	Shift+⌘+N	Insert ⇨ Current User Name	
Lock object	⌘+Option+L	Arrange ⇨ Lock	
Merge field	⌘+Option+M	Insert ⇨ Merge Field	
Move an object with Object Grids on	⌘+drag the object		Allows object dragging to positions other than those provided by the grid.
Move selected object one pixel	Arrow keys		Moves the object in the direction of the arrow key.
New layout	⌘+N	Layouts ⇨ New Layout/Report	
Next layout	Ctrl+↓		
Number format	Option+double-click a Number field	Format ⇨ Number	
Object Grids	⌘+Y	Arrange ⇨ Object Grids	Works as an on/off toggle.
Paste text or object from Clipboard	⌘+V	Edit ⇨ Paste	
Portal setup	Double-click a portal	Format ⇨ Portal	
Previous layout	Ctrl+↑		
Redefine field on layout	Double-click the field		
Reorder selected layout part	Shift+drag the part		Only certain parts, such as sub-summaries, can be reordered.
Reorient part labels	⌘+click a part label		You can also click the control at the bottom of the document window.
Reset default format based on current object	⌘+click the object		

Command	Key	Menu	Comments
Resize an object with Object Grids on	⌘+drag a handle while resizing		Allows object sizes other than those provided by the grid.
Rotate	⌘+Option+R	Arrange ➪ Rotate	Rotates a selected text string or object in 90-degree increments.
Save layout	⌘+S	Layouts ➪ Save Layout	
Select an object	Tab, Shift+Tab		Continue until object is selected.
Select all	⌘+A	Edit ➪ Select All	
Select objects by type	⌘+Option+A		An object must first be selected.
Send backward	Shift+⌘+]	Arrange ➪ Send Backward	
Send to back	⌘+Option+]	Arrange ➪ Send to Back	
Set alignment	Shift+⌘+K	Arrange ➪ Set Alignment	Opens the Alignment dialog.
Sliding/printing	⌘+Option+T	Format ➪ Sliding/ Printing	
Square the object being resized	Option+drag a handle		
Switch between current tool and Pointer tool	Enter		
Text format	Option+double-click a Text field or label	Format ➪ Text	
Time format	Option+double-click a Time field	Format ➪ Time	
T-squares	⌘+T	View ➪ T-Squares	Works as an on/off toggle.
Undo	⌘+Z	Edit ➪ Undo	
Ungroup object	Shift+⌘+R	Arrange ➪ Ungroup	
Unlock object	Shift+⌘+ Option+L	Arrange ➪ Unlock	

Table A-5
Text Formatting Commands[†]

Command	Key	Menu	Comments
Align center	⌘+\	Format ⇨ Align Text ⇨ Center	
Align full	Shift+⌘+\	Format ⇨ Align Text ⇨ Full	
Align left	⌘+[	Format ⇨ Align Text ⇨ Left	
Align right	⌘+]	Format ⇨ Align Text ⇨ Right	
Bold	Shift+⌘+B	Format ⇨ Style ⇨ Bold	
Italic	Shift+⌘+I	Format ⇨ Style ⇨ Italic	
Plain	Shift+⌘+P	Format ⇨ Style ⇨ Plain	
Underline	Shift+⌘+U		
Next larger point size in menu	Shift+⌘+>	Format ⇨ Size	
Next smaller point size in menu	Shift+⌘+<	Format ⇨ Size	
One point larger	Shift+⌘+ Option+>	Format ⇨ Size ⇨ Custom	
One point smaller	Shift+⌘+ Option+<	Format ⇨ Size ⇨ Custom	
Select all	⌘+A	Edit ⇨ Select All	
Subscript	Shift+⌘+− (hyphen)	Format ⇨ Style ⇨ Subscript	
Superscript	Shift+⌘++ (plus sign)	Format ⇨ Style ⇨ Superscript	
Underline	Shift+⌘+U	Format ⇨ Style ⇨ Underline	

[†]Text formatting commands can be used in Browse mode (to format user-entered text) or Layout mode (to set default field formatting or selected text). Many of these commands can also be chosen from the Text Formatting toolbar or from the pop-up menu that appears when you select and Ctrl+click a text string.

Table A-6
Data Entry and Editing Commands

Command	Key	Menu	Comments
Clear a field	Clear	Edit ⇨ Clear	Clears entire field without storing the material on the Clipboard.

Command	Key	Menu	Comments
Clear selected text or object	Delete		Clears object or selected text within a field without storing it on the Clipboard.
Copy	⌘+C	Edit ➪ Copy	Copies selected text or object to the Clipboard.
Correct Word	Shift+⌘+Y	Edit ➪ Spelling ➪ Correct Word	The File Option, Spell as you type, must be on.
Cut	⌘+X	Edit ➪ Cut	Cuts selected text or object and stores it in the Clipboard.
Delete next character	Del		Not available on all keyboards.
Delete next word (or delete to end of current word)	Option+Del		Not available on all keyboards.
Delete previous character	Delete		
Delete previous word (or delete to beginning of current word)	Option+Delete		
Enter a Tab character	Option+Tab		
Find or replace x character	Shift+⌘+F	Edit ➪ Find/Replace ➪ Find/Replace	
Find again	⌘+G	Edit ➪ Find/Replace ➪ Find Again	
Find selected text string	⌘+Option+H	Edit ➪ Find/Replace ➪ Find Selected	
Insert current date	⌘+– (hyphen)	Insert ➪ Current Date	
Insert current time	⌘+; (semicolon)	Insert ➪ Current Time	
Insert current user name	Shift+⌘+N	Insert ➪ Current User Name	
Insert from index	⌘+I	Insert ➪ From Index	
Insert from last record	⌘+' (apostrophe)	Insert ➪ From Last Record	

Continued

Table A-6 (continued)

Command	Key	Menu	Comments
Insert from last record and move to next field	Shift+⌘+' (apostrophe)		
Next field	Tab		
Nonbreaking space	Option+spacebar		
Paste	⌘+V	Edit ⇨ Paste	Pastes text or object from the Clipboard.
Paste without text style	⌘+Option+V		
Previous field	Shift+Tab		
Replace a field's values	⌘+= (equal sign)	Records ⇨ Replace Contents	
Replace this instance and then find next occurrence of data	⌘+Option+G	Edit ⇨ Find/Replace ⇨ Replace & Find Again	
Reverse direction of a Find Again	Shift+⌘+G		
Reverse direction of a Find Selected	Shift+⌘+Option+H		
Reverse direction of a Replace & Find Again	Shift+⌘+Option+G		
Select all	⌘+A	Edit ⇨ Select All	
Undo	⌘+Z	Edit ⇨ Undo	

Table A-7
Commands for Working with Records

Command	Key	Menu	Comments
Copy all text in a record†	⌘+C		You must not have anything selected within the record.
Copy found set	⌘+Option+C		Copies all records in the found set to the Clipboard as text.

Command	Key	Menu	Comments
Delete Record or Find Request†	⌘+E	Records ⇨ Delete Record, or Requests ⇨ Delete Request	This command is
Delete immed-iately Find	⌘+Option+E		This command bypasses the confirmation dialog.
Duplicate Record or Request†	⌘+D	Records ⇨ Duplicate Record, or Requests ⇨ Duplicate Request	This command is mode-specific.
Omit a record	⌘+T	Records ⇨ Omit Record	In Find mode, this shortcut toggles the state of the Omit check box.
Omit Multiple	Shift+⌘+T	Records ⇨ Omit Multiple	
Modify Last Find	⌘+R	Records ⇨ Modify Last Find	
New record or Find request†	⌘+N	Records ⇨ New Record, or Requests ⇨ Add New Request	This command is mode-specific.
Next record, Find request, or report page	Ctrl+↓		
Previous record, Find request, or report page	Ctrl+↑		
Select a record by number	Esc		
Show all records	⌘+J	Records ⇨ Show All Records, or Requests ⇨ Show All Records	
Sort records†	⌘+S	Records ⇨ Sort	Specific sort commands can be chosen by Control+ clicking within the desired sort field.

†These commands can also be chosen from the shortcut menu that appears when you Control+click in a blank area of the layout.

✦   ✦   ✦

Windows Keyboard Shortcuts

This appendix contains keyboard shortcuts for FileMaker Pro commands and actions in the Windows environment. These commands are organized according to the various kinds of tasks you might want to perform. Note that the tables in this appendix do not contain *all* the commands the program offers; they merely list the commands that have keyboard shortcuts.

Note FileMaker Pro 8 for Windows supports the Microsoft IntelliMouse. You can use it in all modes to zoom in or out. And, by using its wheel, you can flip through records in Browse mode. For additional information, see *IntelliMouse support* in the Help file.

Table B-1
General Commands

Command	Key	Menu	Comments
Cancel a dialog or operation	Esc		
Close a database	Ctrl+W, Ctrl+F4	File ⇨ Close	You can also click the document window's Close button.
Define database	Ctrl+Shift+D	File ⇨ Define ⇨ Database	
Exit	Alt+F4 or Ctrl+Q	File ⇨ Exit	
Help	F1	Help ⇨ FileMaker Pro Help	
Open Remote	Ctrl+Shift+O	File ⇨ Open Remote	You can also click the Remote button in the Open dialog.
Open a database	Ctrl+O	File ⇨ Open	
Play a QuickTime movie or sound	Spacebar or double-click a selected Container field		
Print	Ctrl+P	File ⇨ Print	
Print without a dialog	Ctrl+Alt+P		
Stop a QuickTime movie or sound	Spacebar or single-click the Container field		

Table B-2
Mode Selection Commands†

Command	Key	Menu	Comments
Browse mode	Ctrl+B	View ⇨ Browse Mode	
Find mode	Ctrl+F	View ⇨ Find Mode	
Layout mode	Ctrl+L	View ⇨ Layout Mode	
Preview mode	Ctrl+U	View ⇨ Preview Mode	

†You can also choose these commands from the Mode pop-up menu at the bottom of any FileMaker document window.

Table B-3
Document Window Control Commands

Command	Key	Menu	Comments
Cascade windows	Shift+F5	Window ⇨ Cascade	
Close a window	Ctrl+W, Ctrl+F4		
Resize window	Ctrl+Shift+Z		
Scroll to top of current view/report	Home		
Scroll to bottom of current view/report	End		
Scroll up one screen/page in current view/report	Page Up		
Scroll down one screen/page in current View/report	Page Down		
Scroll to first record in View as List	Home		
Scroll to last record in View as List	End		
Scroll left in the document window	Ctrl+Page Up		
Scroll right in the document window	Ctrl+Page Down		
Status area (show/hide)	Ctrl+Alt+S		You can also click the status area control at the bottom of the document window.
Tile windows horizontally	Shift+F4	Window ⇨ Tile Horizontally	
Zoom in	F3	View ⇨ Zoom In	
Zoom out	Shift+F3	View ⇨ Zoom Out	

Table B-4
Layout Mode Commands

Command	Key	Menu	Comments
Align bottom edges of selected objects[†]	Ctrl+Alt+↓	Arrange ⇨ Align ⇨ Bottom Edges	
Align left edges of selected objects[†]	Ctrl+Alt+←	Arrange ⇨ Align ⇨ Left Edges	
Align right edges of selected objects[†]	Ctrl+Alt+→	Arrange ⇨ Align ⇨ Right Edges	
Align top edges of selected objects[†]	Ctrl+Alt+↑	Arrange ⇨ Align ⇨ Top Edges	
Align text to the center	Ctrl+\	Format ⇨ Align Text ⇨ Center	
Align text to the left	Ctrl+[	Format ⇨ Align Text ⇨ Left	
Align text to the right	Ctrl+]	Format ⇨ Align Text ⇨ Right	
Align text using full	Ctrl+Shift+\	Format ⇨ Align Text ⇨ Full	
Bring forward	Ctrl+Shift+[	Arrange ⇨ Bring Forward	
Bring to front	Ctrl+Alt+[	Arrange ⇨ Bring to Front	
Clear object from layout	Del	Edit ⇨ Clear	Clears without storing it on the Clipboard.
Constrain lines to vertical/horizontal	Shift+drag while drawing		
Constrain lines to 45-degree angles	Ctrl+drag while drawing or resizing		
Constrain ovals to circles and rectangles to squares	Ctrl+drag while drawing or resizing		
Constrain resizing to vertical/horizontal	Shift+drag a handle		
Copy selected object or text	Ctrl+C	Edit ⇨ Copy	Places a copy of the object or text on the Clipboard.

Command	Key	Menu	Comments
Cut selected object or text	Ctrl+X	Edit ⇨ Cut	Places a copy of the object or text on the Clipboard.
Date format	Alt+double-click a Date field	Format ⇨ Date	
Delete layout	Ctrl+E	Layouts ⇨ Delete Layout	
Display object's format	Alt+double-click the object		See also specific object and field types in this table.
Drag selected layout part past an object	Alt+drag		
Duplicate selected object	Ctrl+D or Ctrl+ drag the object	Edit ⇨ Duplicate	
Field behavior	Ctrl+Alt+K	Format ⇨ Field/ Control ⇨ Behavior	
Field borders	Ctrl+Alt+B	Format ⇨ Field/ Control ⇨ Borders	
Field format	Ctrl+Alt+F	Format ⇨ Field/ Control ⇨ Setup	
Graphic format	Alt+double-click a Container field or graphic image	Format ⇨ Graphic	
Group objects	Ctrl+R	Arrange ⇨ Group	
Insert current date	Ctrl+– (hyphen)	Insert ⇨ Current Date	
Insert current time	Ctrl+; (semicolon)	Insert ⇨ Current Time	
Insert current user name	Ctrl+Shift+N	Insert ⇨ Current User Name	
Lock object(s)	Ctrl+Alt+L	Arrange ⇨ Lock	
Merge field	Ctrl+M	Insert ⇨ Merge Field	
Move an object with Object Grids on	Alt+drag the object		Allows object dragging to positions other than those provided by the grid.
Move selected object 1 pixel	Arrow keys		Moves in the direction of the arrow key.

Continued

Table B-4 (continued)

Command	Key	Menu	Comments
New layout	Ctrl+N	Layouts ⇨ New Layout/Report	
Number format	Alt+double-click a Number field	Format ⇨ Number	
Object Grids	Ctrl+Y	Arrange ⇨ Object Grids	Works as an on/off toggle.
Paste text or object from Clipboard	Ctrl+V	Edit ⇨ Paste	
Portal format	Double-click, Ctrl+double-click, or Alt+double-click a portal	Format ⇨ Portal	
Redefine field on layout	Double-click or Ctrl+double-click the field		
Reorder selected layout part	Shift+drag the part		
Reorient part labels from horizontal to vertical	Ctrl+click any part label		You can also click the label control at the bottom of the document window.
Resize an object with Object Grids on	Alt+drag a handle while resizing		Allows object sizes other than those provided by the grid.
Rotate an object	Ctrl+Alt+R	Arrange ⇨ Rotate	
Select all objects on layout	Ctrl+A	Edit ⇨ Select All	
Select an object	Tab, Shift+Tab		Continue until object is selected. Tab moves forward; Shift+Tab moves backward.
Select objects by type	Ctrl+Shift+A		An object must first be selected.
Send backward	Ctrl+Shift+]	Arrange ⇨ Send Backward	

Command	Key	Menu	Comments
Send to back	Ctrl+Alt+]	Arrange ⇨ Send to Back	
Set alignment	Ctrl+Shift+K	Arrange ⇨ Set Alignment	
Text format	Alt+double-click a Text field	Format ⇨ Text	
Time format	Alt+double-click a Time field	Format ⇨ Time	
T-squares	Ctrl+T	View ⇨ T-Squares	Works as an on/off toggle.
Ungroup objects	Ctrl+Shift+R	Arrange ⇨ Ungroup	
Unlock object	Ctrl+Alt+Shift+L	Arrange ⇨ Unlock	

†Layout commands from the Arrange menu can also be selected from the Arrange toolbar. To display this toolbar, choose View ⇨ Toolbars ⇨ Arrange.

Table B-5
Text Formatting Commands†

Command	Key	Menu	Comments
Align center	Ctrl+\	Format ⇨ Align Text ⇨ Center	
Align left	Ctrl+[	Format ⇨ Align Text ⇨ Left	
Align right	Ctrl+]	Format ⇨ Align Text ⇨ Right	
Align with full justification	Ctrl+Shift+\	Format ⇨ Align Text ⇨ Full	
Bold	Ctrl+Shift+B	Format ⇨ Style ⇨ Bold	
Italic	Ctrl+Shift+I	Format ⇨ Style ⇨ Italic	
Plain	Ctrl+Shift+P	Format ⇨ Style ⇨ Plain Text	
Underline	Ctrl+Shift+U	Format ⇨ Style ⇨ Underline	
Next menu point size larger	Ctrl+>		
Next menu point size smaller	Ctrl+<		
One point larger	Ctrl+Shift+>		
One point smaller	Ctrl+Shift+<		
Select all text in a field	Ctrl+A	Edit ⇨ Select All	
Underline	Ctrl+ Shift+U	Format ⇨ Style ⇨ Underline	

†Text-formatting commands can be used in Browse mode (to format user-entered text) or Layout mode (to set default field formatting or static text elements such as field labels). Many of these commands can be chosen from the Text Formatting toolbar or from the pop-up menu that appears when you select and right-click a text string.

Table B-6
Data Entry and Editing Commands

Command	Key	Menu	Comments
Clear selected text or object	Del	Edit ➪ Clear	Clears without storing it on the Clipboard.
Copy	Ctrl+C or Ctrl+Insert	Edit ➪ Copy	Copies selected text or object to the Clipboard.
Correct Word	Ctrl+Shift+Y	Edit ➪ Spelling ➪ Correct Word	Option to Spell as you type must be on.
Cut	Ctrl+X or Shift+Del	Edit ➪ Cut	Cuts selected text or object and stores it in the Clipboard.
Delete next character	Del (or Backspace)†		
Delete next word	Ctrl+Del or Ctrl+Backspace		
Delete previous character	Backspace		
Enter a Tab character	Ctrl+Tab		
Find or replace data	Ctrl+Shift+F	Edit ➪ Find/Replace ➪ Find/Replace	
Find again	Ctrl+G	Edit ➪ Find/Replace ➪ Find Again	
Find selected text string	Ctrl+Alt+H	Edit ➪ Find/Replace ➪ Find Selected	
Insert current date	Ctrl+− (hyphen)	Insert ➪ Current Date	
Insert current time	Ctrl+; (semicolon)	Insert ➪ Current Time	
Insert current user name	Ctrl+Shift+N	Insert ➪ Current User Name	
Insert from index	Ctrl+I	Insert ➪ From Index	
Insert from last record	Ctrl+' (apostrophe)	Insert ➪ From Last Record	
Insert from last record and move to next field	Ctrl+Shift+' (apostrophe)		
Next field	Tab		

Command	Key	Menu	Comments
Non-breaking space	Ctrl+spacebar		
Paste	Ctrl+V	Edit ⇨ Paste	Pastes text or object from the Clipboard.
Paste without text style	Ctrl+Shift+V		
Previous field	Shift+Tab		
Replace a field's value in records in found set	Ctrl+= (equal sign)	Records ⇨ Replace Contents	
Replace this instance and then find next occurrence of data	Ctrl+Alt+G	Edit ⇨ Find/ Replace ⇨ Replace & Find Again	
Select all	Ctrl+A	Edit ⇨ Select All	
Undo	Ctrl+Z or Alt+ Backspace	Edit ⇨ Undo	

†Note that the Del/Delete and Backspace keys perform the same functions when used in FileMaker Pro.

Table B-7
Commands for Working with Records

Command	Key	Menu	Comments
Copy found set	Ctrl+Shift+C		Copies records to Clipboard as text.
Copy record or Find request†	Ctrl+C		Nothing must be selected.
Delete record or Find request†	Ctrl+E	Records ⇨ Delete Record or Requests ⇨ Delete Request	Command is mode-specific.
Delete record or Find request immediately	Ctrl+Shift+E		Bypass confirmation dialog.
Duplicate record or Find request†	Ctrl+D	Records ⇨ Duplicate Record or Requests ⇨ Duplicate Request	Command is mode specific.
Modify last Find	Ctrl+R	Records ⇨ Modify Last Find	

Continued

Table B-4 *(continued)*

Command	Key	Menu	Comments
New record or Find request[†]	Ctrl+N	Records ➪ New Record, or Requests ➪ Add New Request	Command is mode-specific.
Next record or Find request	Ctrl+↓ or Shift+Page Down		
Omit current record	Ctrl+T	Records ➪ Omit Record	
Omit multiple records	Ctrl+Shift+T	Records ➪ Omit Multiple	
Open the layout drop-down list	F2		This won't work if you have an insertion cursor blinking in the field's text box.
Perform Find requests	Enter		
Previous record or Find request	Ctrl+↑ or Shift+Page Up		
Replace a field's value	Ctrl+= (equal sign)	Records ➪ Replace	
Show all records	Ctrl+J	Records ➪ Show All Records or Requests ➪ Show All Records	
Sort records[†]	Ctrl+S	Records ➪ Sort	

[†]These commands can also be chosen from the pop-up menu that appears when you right-click a blank area of a layout in Browse or Find mode.

✦   ✦   ✦

FileMaker Pro Function Reference

FileMaker Pro includes scores of predefined functions you can use to define formulas for Calculation fields (as explained in Chapter 14). The purpose of each of these functions is summarized in Table C-1.

New Feature

The names of functions introduced in FileMaker Pro 8 are shown in bold in Table C-1. This includes functions whose names have changed in FileMaker Pro 8. Functions new to FileMaker Pro 8.5 are introduced in the special Quick Start (look for the gray section in this book).

On The Web Site

If you are coming to FileMaker Pro 8 from a version prior to FileMaker Pro 7, you are going to see a lot more functions that are new to you in the following table than the few introduced with FileMaker Pro 8. (FileMaker Pro 7 introduced dozens of new functions.) For that reason, we are including a PDF file of this appendix from *FileMaker Pro 7 Bible* on the accompanying Web site. See Appendix F for details about the site.

Caution

One of the unheralded changes introduced in FileMaker Pro 7 was that semicolons became the separators for function parameters instead of commas, which were used in earlier versions. If you're accustomed to typing function argument lists, you should break the habit of using commas and switch to semicolons. If FileMaker Pro 8 is set to a language/locale that employs the comma as a list separator (such as U.S. English), the comma will continue to work, and FileMaker will do the conversion to semicolon for you when saving the calculation, but doing things correctly yourself is always good practice.

Table C-1
FileMaker Pro's Built-In Functions

Function Name	Purpose
Abs	Calculates the absolute value of an expression.
Atan	Calculates the arc tangent of an expression, in radians, and returns a value between −π and π.
Average	Computes the average value (the arithmetic mean) of all values in one or more fields.
Case	Performs a series of tests and selects one answer (or the default answer, if no test is found to be true).
Ceiling	Returns the smallest integer greater than or equal to the argument.
Choose	Selects one answer from a series.
Combination	Computes and returns the number of unique ways to select a given number of items from a collection of a specified size.
Cos	Calculates the cosine of an argument expressed in radians, returning a value between −1 and 1.
Count	Counts the number of valid, nonempty values in one or more fields.
DatabaseNames	Returns the filenames of all currently open FileMaker Pro databases.
Date	Converts numeric values for month, day, and year into a valid date.
Day	Displays the day of the month, 1–31, for a given date.
DayName	Displays the weekday name for a given date.
DayNameJ	Returns a Japanese (Kanji) text string for the weekday name.
DayofWeek	Displays the number of the day within a week, 1–7, for a given date.
DayofYear	Displays the number of the day within a year, 1–365, for a given date.
Degrees	Converts a value in radians into degrees.
Div	Returns the integer part of a division result.
Evaluate	Returns the result of treating a text expression as a calculation. You can include a list of fields as arguments so that when any are modified, the expression is reevaluated.

Function Name	Purpose
EvaluationError	Returns the error code for any syntactic or runtime errors resulting from evaluating the argument.
Exact	Returns True if two text expressions match exactly (including case).
Exp	Returns the antilog (base e) of an expression.
Extend	Makes a nonrepeating field a repeating field (with the identical value in each place) for use in calculations with other repeating fields.
External	When a plug-in is installed, these functions let you employ the plug-in's capabilities.
Factorial	Returns the product of multiplying all integers between 1 and the first argument — or, if a second argument is present, between the first argument and (the first argument through the second argument +1): For example, factorial(9;3) returns 9*8*7 (504).
FieldBounds	Returns the location and rotation angle of a given field in a particular layout of a database.
FieldComment	Returns the field definition's comment text.
FieldIDs	Returns a list of all unique field ID numbers (including related fields) in the specified database and layout.
FieldNames	Returns the names of all fields used in a particular layout or in the default table.
FieldRepetitions	Returns the number of repetitions of a given repeating field as it is formatted on a particular layout of a database, as well as whether it is displayed vertically or horizontally.
FieldStyle	Returns information about how a field in a particular layout is formatted as well as the name of any value list associated with the field.
FieldType	Returns the field definition for a specified field in a particular database.
Filter	Returns a string containing only those characters in the second argument that appear in the first argument, in the order they occur in the first argument.
FilterValues	Returns a list containing only those values in the first argument that appear in the second argument, in the order they occur in the first argument.

Continued

Table C-1 *(continued)*

Function Name	Purpose
Floor	Returns the largest integer less than or equal to the argument.
FV	Computes an investment's future value for a given payment amount, interest rate, and number of periods.
Get(AccountName)	Returns the name of the account currently using the database.
Get(ActiveFieldContents)	Returns the contents of the field in which the cursor currently resides. If the field is a repeating field, the current repetition is returned. Replaces the GetField function from previous version.
Get(ActiveFieldName)	Returns the name of the field in which the cursor currently resides.
Get(ActiveFieldTableName)	Returns the name of the table containing the current active field.
Get(ActiveModifierKeys)	Returns an integer corresponding to the codes for the keyboard modifier keys currently being pressed. The Mac has five modifier keys (⌘, Shift, Option, Control, and Caps Lock); Windows has four (Shift, Alt, Ctrl, and Caps Lock).
Get(ActiveRepetitionNumber)	Returns the number of a repeating field's active repetition.
Get(ActiveSelectionSize)	Returns the number of characters in the current selection.
Get(ActiveSelectionStart)	Returns the position within the field where the current selection begins, or lacking a selection, where the cursor resides.
Get(AllowAbortState)	Returns 1 if the Allow Abort script step is present; 0, otherwise.
Get(AllowToolbarState)	Returns 1 if toolbars are allowed to be visible; 0, otherwise. (The Allow Toolbars script step toggles this state.)
Get(ApplicationLanguage)	Returns the primary language name.
Get(ApplicationVersion)	Returns the name and version number of the application currently in use.
Get(CalculationRepetitionNumber)	Returns the repetition of the current calculation field.

Function Name	Purpose
Get(CurrentDate)	Returns the current date as specified by the system clock. Replaces the Today function.
Get(CurrentHostTimestamp)	Returns the date and time according to the system clock of the computer hosting the database.
Get(CurrentTime)	Returns the current time as specified by the system clock on the client computer.
Get(CurrentTimestamp)	Returns the current date and time as specified by the system clock of the client computer.
Get(CustomMenuSetName)	Returns the name of the currently active custom menu set (a null string if the current menu set isn't a custom set).
Get(DesktopPath)	Returns the path to the current user's Desktop folder.
Get(DocumentsPath)	Returns the path to the current user's Documents (Mac) or My Documents (Windows) folder.
Get(ErrorCaptureState)	Returns whether the Set Error Capture script step is on (1 = yes; 0 = no).
Get(ExtendedPrivileges)	Returns a list of extended privileges (separated by carriage returns) possessed by the currently active account.
Get(FileMakerPath)	Returns the path to the currently running FileMaker Pro application.
Get(FileName)	Returns the basename (no path or file extension) of the currently active database file.
Get(FilePath)	Returns the full operating system-dependent path to the currently active database file, including the filename.
Get(FileSize)	Returns the size (in bytes) of the currently active database file.
Get(FoundCount)	Returns the number of records in the current found set.
Get(HighContrastColor)	Returns name of the current Windows high-contrast default color scheme. (Returns empty string if used on a Mac or if Use High Contrast is unavailable.)
Get(HighContrastState)	Returns 1 if Use High Contrast is available and on; 0, otherwise. Useful only on Windows.
Get(HostIPAddress)	Returns the IP (Internet Protocol) address of the machine hosting the current database.

Continued

Table C-1 *(continued)*

Function Name	Purpose
Get(HostName)	Returns the (network-) registered name of the computer hosting the currently active database file.
Get(LastError)	Returns the numeric code for the error (if any) resulting from the most recently executed script step.
Get(LastMessageChoice)	Returns the numeric ID of the button clicked in the last Show Custom Dialog script step.
Get(LastODBCError)	Returns string specifying the ODBC error state (also known as the SQLSTATE), as per ODBC standards.
Get(LayoutAccess)	Returns 0 if the accounts privileges do not allow access to the layout, 1 if access is View only, and 2 if access is Modifiable.
Get(LayoutCount)	Returns the number of layouts in the current database file.
Get(LayoutName)	Returns the name of the current layout.
Get(LayoutNumber)	Returns the current layout's number as specified in the Set Layout Order dialog.
Get(LayoutTableName)	Returns the name of the current layout's primary table.
Get(LayoutViewState)	Returns 0 if Form view, 1 if List view, and 2 if Table view.
Get(MultiUserState)	Returns 0 when sharing is off, 1 when on and you're accessing from the host, and 2 when on and you're accessing from a remote computer.
Get(NetworkProtocol)	Returns the name of the current network protocol — always TCP/IP in FileMaker Pro 8.
Get(PageNumber)	Returns the page number of the page currently being printed or previewed; 0 if not printing or previewing.
Get(PortalRowNumber)	Returns the number of the currently selected portal row (or 0).
Get(PreferencesPath)	Returns the path to the folder containing the current user's preferences and options settings.
Get(PrinterName)	Returns the queue name and IP address (Mac) or the printer, driver, and port names (Windows).
Get(PrivilegeSetName)	Returns the name of the current account's privilege set.
Get(RecordAccess)	Returns 0 if record is inaccessible to current account, 1 if viewable, 2 if editable.
Get(RecordID)	Returns the FileMaker-internal (unique) ID number, assigned when the record is created.

Function Name	Purpose
Get(RecordModificationCount)	Returns the number of times changes to the current record have been committed.
Get(RecordNumber)	Returns the sequence number for the record in the current found set.
Get(RecordOpenCount)	Returns the number of unsaved records in the current found set.
Get(RecordOpenState)	Returns 0 if the record is closed/committed, 1 for a new record that hasn't been committed, and 2 for an existing record that has been modified but not yet committed/saved.
Get(RequestCount)	Returns the current table's total number of defined Find requests in the current window.
Get(RequestOmitState)	Returns 1 if the Omit check box is selected; 0, if not.
Get(ScreenDepth)	Returns the number of bits available to represent a color at the current main monitor display setting.
Get(ScreenHeight)	Returns the number of pixels vertically onscreen containing the active window.
Get(ScreenWidth)	Returns the number of pixels horizontally onscreen containing the active window.
Get(ScriptName)	Returns the name of the currently active script.
Get(ScriptParameter)	Returns the argument(s) passed to the current script step.
Get(ScriptResult)	Returns the script result of the most recently performed subscript of the current script. Returns a null string if there were no subscript or if the subscript didn't return a result.
Get(SortState)	Returns 0 if the active table is unsorted, 1 if the active table is sorted, and 2 if the active table is partially sorted.
Get(StatusAreaState)	Returns 0 if hidden, 1 if visible, 2 if visible and locked, and 3 if hidden and locked.
Get(SystemDrive)	Returns the volume name (Mac) or drive letter (Windows) for the currently active OS.
Get(SystemIPAddress)	Returns a list of all machines connected to a Network Interface Controller (NIC) card.
Get(SystemLanguage)	Returns the primary language of the local system.

Continued

Table C-1 *(continued)*

Function Name	Purpose
Get(SystemNICAddress)	Returns the hardware address of all the machine's NIC cards (six hexadecimal bytes, separated by colons).
Get(SystemPlatform)	Returns −1 if Mac, −2 if Windows.
Get(SystemVersion)	Returns 5.0 for Windows 2000, 5.1 for Windows XP, 10.3 for Mac OS X (Panther), and 10.4 for Mac OS X (Tiger).
Get(TextRulerVisible)	Returns 1 if the text ruler is being displayed; 0, otherwise.
Get(TotalRecordCount)	Returns the number of records in the current table.
Get(UserCount)	Returns 1 plus the number of remote clients accessing a database file via Network Sharing.
Get(UserName)	Returns the name of the current user (as set in Preferences ⇨ General).
Get(UseSystemFormatState)	Returns 1 if the Format menu's Use System Formats command is selected (checked); otherwise, returns 0.
Get(WindowContentHeight)	Returns the height, in pixels, of the currently visible layout content area.
Get(WindowContentWidth)	Returns the width, in pixels of the currently visible layout content area plus, if visible, the status area.
Get(WindowDesktopHeight)	Returns the height in pixels of the Desktop minus the menu bar and Dock (Mac) or inside the MDI window (Windows).
Get(WindowDesktopWidth)	Returns the width in pixels of the Desktop area minus the Dock (Mac) or of the MDI window (Windows).
Get(WindowHeight)	Returns the height in pixels of the window on which the script is operating.
Get(WindowLeft)	Returns the distance from the left edge of the monitor to the left edge of the window on which the script is operating.
Get(WindowMode)	Returns 0 for Browser, 1 for Find, 2 for Preview, or 3 if printing is active.
Get(WindowName)	Returns the name for the window on which the script is operating.
Get(WindowTop)	Returns the distance in pixels from the bottom of the menu bar to the top of the window on which the script is operating.

Function Name	Purpose
Get(WindowVisible)	Returns 1 if the window is visible, 0 if it has been hidden by the FileMaker Pro Hide Window command.
Get(WindowWidth)	Returns the width in pixels of the window on which the script is operating.
Get(WindowZoomLevel)	Returns the magnification (zoom) percentage for the currently active window. (On Windows, if the Enlarge window contents to improve readability option is selected in Preferences' General pane, the percentage will be followed by an asterisk.)
GetAsBoolean	Returns 0 if the expression evaluates to 0 or is null; 1, otherwise.
GetAsCSS	Returns the argument, formatted with CSS (Cascading Style Sheet) instructions.
GetAsDate	Converts text strings to dates for use in calculations.
GetAsNumber	Returns the argument converted to a number (non-numeric characters are stripped).
GetAsSVG	Returns the argument, formatted per Scalable Vector Graphics (SVG) syntax.
GetAsText	Returns the argument converted to text. If a container field, either a ? (question mark) for embedded content or a path for external content.
GetAsTime	Converts the argument to a Time value.
GetAsTimeStamp	Converts the argument to a Timestamp value.
GetField	Returns the contents of the field specified as an argument.
GetNextSerialValue	Returns the next serial number for the specified field in the specified database.
GetNthRecord	Returns the value in the specified field of the numerically specified record.
GetRepetition	Presents the contents of a particular repetition in a repeating field.
GetSummary	Calculates the value of a particular Summary field when the database has been sorted by the specified break field.
GetValue	Returns the numerically specified value from the named value list. (This calculation is useful in calculations that loop or are recursive.)

Continued

Table C-1 *(continued)*

Function Name	Purpose
Hiragana	Converts Katakana text to Hiragana.
Hour	Displays the number of hours in a time expression.
If	Performs a logical test and completes one action if it is true, another if it is false.
Int	Returns the integer portion of a numeric value.
IsEmpty	Determines whether a value or field is blank.
IsValid	Determines whether a related field can be found and contains valid data, and whether a related file can be found.
IsValidExpression	Returns 1 if expression argument is syntactically correct, 0 if there are syntax errors.
KanaHankaku	Converts Zenkaku Katakana to Hankaku Katakana.
KanaZenkaku	Converts Hankaku Katakana to Zenkaku Katakana.
KanjiNumeral	Converts Arabic numbers to Kanji numbers.
Katakana	Converts Hiragana text to Katakana.
Last	Shows the last valid, nonempty entry in a repeating field.
LayoutIDs	Returns a list of all layout ID numbers for the specified database.
LayoutNames	Returns the names of all layouts in a specified database.
Left	Returns the specified number of characters of a text string, counting from the left.
LeftValues	Returns the number of paragraphs specified by the second argument from the carriage return-delimited first argument.
LeftWords	Returns the specified number of words from a text string, counting from the left.
Length	Finds the number of characters in a given text string.
Let	Assigns values to identifiers for the duration of the calculation.
Lg	Computes the binary (base 2) logarithm of an expression.
Ln	Computes the natural (base e) logarithm of an expression.

Function Name	Purpose
Log	Computes the common (base 10) logarithm of an expression.
Lookup	Returns the contents of a lookup, based upon the current relationship graph.
LookupNext	Returns the looked-up value or the next higher/lower if no match is found.
Lower	Converts a text string to all lowercase.
Max	Displays the greatest value among those in specified fields.
Middle	Returns a portion of a supplied text string, starting at a given position and extending a specified number of characters.
MiddleValues	Returns the values/paragraphs, specified by the third parameter, from the first parameter, starting at the value indicated by the second parameter.
MiddleWords	Returns the specified number of words from a text string, counting from the specified starting word.
Min	Displays the smallest value among those in specified fields.
Minute	Returns the minute portion of a time expression.
Mod	Returns the remainder when an expression is divided by a given number.
Month	Displays the number of the month in a date expression, within the range 1–12.
MonthName	Displays the name of month in a date expression.
NPV	Finds the net present value of an investment (also known as *discounting cash flow*), using values in repeating fields as unequal payment values and the given interest rate.
NumToJText	Converts Arabic (Roman) numbers to Japanese (Kanji) with optionally specified separators.
PatternCount	Returns the number of instances of a specified text string found within another text string or field.
PI	Returns the value of the mathematical constant pi.

Continued

Table C-1 *(continued)*

Function Name	Purpose
PMT	Calculates a loan payment, using the given principal, interest rate, and term.
Position	Scans text for the specified string starting at the given position and returns the location of the first occurrence of the string, or (if a fourth parameter is present) the occurrence specified by that fourth parameter.
Proper	Converts the first letter of each word in the text string to uppercase (used to capitalize names, for example).
PV	Calculates the present value of an investment, using a given payment amount, interest rate, and periods. Compound interest is an example of a present value calculation.
Quote	Returns the argument, surrounded by quote marks, escaping special characters (such as carriage returns or quotes).
Radians	Converts a degree value to radians (for use with trigonometric functions).
Random	Generates a random number between 0 and 1.
RelationInfo	Returns information about a particular relationship that has been defined for the current database.
Replace	In a text string, starts at the given position, moves the specified number of places, and replaces the existing text with the specified new text string.
RGB	Returns a 24-bit color value, comprising the specified 8-bit red, green, and blue (RGB) components.
Right	Counting from the right, returns a given number of characters in a text expression.
RightValues	Returns the specified number of values/paragraphs from the first argument, starting from the end.
RightWords	Returns the specified number of words from a text string, counting from the right.
RomanHankaku	Converts from Zenkaku to Hankaku characters.
RomanZenkaku	Converts from Hankaku to Zenkaku characters.
Round	Rounds off a numeric expression to the specified number of decimal places.
ScriptIDs	Returns a list of all script ID numbers for the specified database.

Function Name	Purpose
ScriptNames	Returns the names of all scripts that have been created for a given database, separated by carriage returns.
Seconds	Displays the seconds portion of a time expression.
SerialIncrement	Returns the text argument with the numeric characters incremented by the specified amount.
SetPrecision	Specifies the number of decimal places for calculations (of nontrigonometric functions).
Sign	Examines a numeric expression and returns 1 for positive, −1 for negative, or 0 for 0.
Sin	Computes the sine of an angle expressed in radians.
Sqrt	Computes the square root of a numeric expression (the same as expression ^ 0.5).
StDev	Examines all values in any repeating or nonrepeating field and gives the sample standard deviation.
StDevP	Examines all values in any repeating or nonrepeating field and gives the population standard deviation.
Substitute	Substitutes one set of characters in a text string for another.
Sum	Totals all values in specified fields.
TableIDs	Returns a list of FileMaker's internally assigned (unique) ID numbers for all tables in the current database file.
TableNames	Returns a carriage return-delimited list of all tables occurring in a database file's Relationships Graph.
Tan	Computes the tangent for a given angle expressed in radians.
TextColor	Changes the argument's text display color to match the RGB argument.
TextColorRemove	Removes all color or, if an optional RGB second parameter is specified, the specified color from the current text's display attributes.
TextFont	Changes the argument's text display font to the specified font name.
TextFontRemove	Returns the text display to the default font for the layout element or, if a font is specified, just reverts any text in that font to the default.
TextFormatRemove	Removes any (or specified) text formatting applied to a field, returning the display to the default formatting for that layout field.

Continued

Table C-1 *(continued)*

Function Name	Purpose
TextSize	Changes the argument's text display size to that specified.
TextSizeRemove	Reverts the text to the layout's default size or, if a specific size is passed as the optional second parameter, only the text in the specified size is reverted to the layout element's default.
TestStyleAdd	Changes the argument's text display to include the specified style attribute (bold, underline, and so on).
TextStyleRemove	Changes the argument's text display to not include the specified style attribute.
Time	Converts three given numeric values into a time equivalent.
Timestamp	Converts given date and time values into a timestamp.
Trim	Strips the specified text expression of leading and trailing spaces.
TrimAll	Returns the text argument with leading and trailing spaces removed, and other spacing performed as per the additional arguments.
Truncate	Truncates a number to the specified number of decimal places.
Upper	Converts a text expression to all uppercase.
ValueCount	Returns the number of values in a (carriage return-delimited) list.
ValueListIDs	Returns a list of all value list ID numbers for the specified database.
ValueListItems	Returns the items in a particular value list for a given database.
ValueListNames	Returns the names of all value lists that have been defined for a given database.
Variance	Returns the square of the standard deviation.
VarianceP	Returns the square of the population standard deviation.
WeekofYear	Determines the number of the week in the year, 1–54, for the specified date expression.

Function Name	Purpose
WeekofYearFiscal	Determines the number of the week in the year, 1–53, for the specified date expression (in accordance with the particular day that is considered the first day of the week).
WindowNames	Returns a list of currently open windows' names, whether visible, hidden, or minimized.
WordCount	Returns the total number of words found in a text expression or field.
Year	Returns the year part of the specified date expression.
YearName	Returns the Japanese year name for the date passed as an argument.

The functions are divided into 15 categories: aggregate, date, design, external, financial, get, logical, numeric, repeating, summary, text, text formatting, time, timestamp, and trigonometric. This appendix provides a detailed explanation for each of FileMaker Pro's built-in functions. The functions are listed alphabetically within the category to which they belong. In addition to an explanation of each function's purpose and an example of how the function is used (except for those that return Japanese text), the sections include a statement showing how to phrase the function and its arguments. (The order for arranging the function and its arguments is the *syntax* of the function.) Special notes and cautions, as well as references to related functions, are included in the explanations of some of the functions.

To use a function in a Calculation field definition, double-click its name in the function list in the upper-right section of the Specify Calculation dialog box. Then replace the function's arguments with the appropriate field names or expressions.

Aggregate (Statistical) Functions

These functions compute statistics on repeating and nonrepeating (normal) fields. The result can be either repeating or nonrepeating. Although the arguments are often Number fields, Date and Time fields can also be used.

The aggregate functions are as follows:

✦ Average

✦ Count

✦ Max

✦ Min

✦ StDev

✦ StDevP

✦ Sum

✦ Variance

✦ VarianceP

Average

Purpose: Computes the average value of all values in the specified field or fields. The fields may be repeating, nonrepeating (normal), or a combination of the two; and the result type can be repeating or nonrepeating. The average is calculated by adding all the appropriate values together and then dividing by the number of values added. The result is a numeric value or, in the case of a repeating result, a series of numeric values.

Syntax: Average (*field . . .*)

where *field . . .* is a list of one or more valid fields containing only numeric values.

Example: Suppose that Prices is a repeating field containing the extended price of each item in an order. The following expression displays a message about the cost of these items:

```
"On average, the items you ordered cost $" & NumToText(Average(Prices))
```

If Prices contains 5.00, 10.00, and 30.00, the expression produces the following message:

```
On average, the items you ordered cost $15.00
```

Using aggregate functions with repeating and nonrepeating fields

Although aggregate functions are commonly used with repeating fields, FileMaker Pro also enables these functions to be used with nonrepeating fields as well as with a mixture of repeating and nonrepeating fields. Each aggregate function discussed in this section accepts a single repeating field or series of repeating and/or nonrepeating fields as arguments. Regardless of the result data type chosen (Number or Date, for example), you can optionally specify that the result be a repeating value and display a particular number of repetitions. The fields can be in the main table or any related table.

Example: If the nonrepeating fields F1, F2, and F3 contain 4, 6, and 8 in a given record, the formula Average (F1; F2; F3) returns 6.

See also: Max, Min, StDev, StDevP, Sum

Count

Purpose: Determines the number of nonblank entries in a repeating field, a series of nonrepeating fields, or a mixture of the two field types, returning the result or results as numeric values.

Syntax: Count (*field* . . .)

where *field* . . . is a list of one or more valid, nonempty repeating fields of any type or a series of repeating and/or nonrepeating fields.

Example: If the repeating field Prices, formatted to contain up to ten values, actually contains 5.00, 10.00, and 30.00, the following expression yields a message about the items ordered:

```
"You ordered " & Count(Prices) & " items. Thank you!"
```

In this case, the expression produces the following message:

```
You ordered 3 items. Thank you!
```

Max

Purpose: Finds the highest, latest, or greatest value among all values in a nonempty repeating field or in a series of nonrepeating and/or repeating fields. The result is returned in the appropriate format.

Syntax: Max (*field* . . .)

where *field* . . . is either a list of one or more nonempty, valid fields of any type or a series of repeating and/or nonrepeating fields.

Example: Suppose that Dates is a repeating field containing dates of orders in an invoice record. Suppose, further, that it contains three values: 03/17/2005, 04/18/2005, and 05/19/2005. In that case, the expression

```
"Your last order was on " & Max(Dates)
```

produces this message:

```
Your last order was on 05/19/2005
```

See also: Min

Min

Purpose: Finds the lowest, oldest, or smallest value among all values in a nonempty repeating field or in a series of nonrepeating and/or repeating fields. The result is returned in the appropriate format.

Syntax: Min (*field . . .*)

where *field . . .* is a list of one or more nonempty, valid fields of any type.

Example: If Dates is a repeating field containing the three values 03/16/2005, 04/17/2005, and 05/18/2005, the following expression

```
"Your first order was on " & Min(Dates)
```

produces the following message:

```
Your first order was on 03/16/2005
```

See also: Max

StDev

Purpose: Computes the standard deviation for all values in a nonempty, numeric repeating field, a series of nonrepeating fields, or a mixture of the two field types. The standard deviation is a measure of how the values in a sample depart from the average value.

Note

The formula formerly used to calculate StDev in FileMaker Pro 2.1 is the one that is now used to calculate StDevP. If you have older FileMaker databases and want them to calculate a sample standard deviation, be sure you use StDev in the formula rather than StDevP.

Syntax: StDev (*field . . .*)

where *field . . .* is the name of a valid, nonempty repeating field containing either numeric data only or a series of repeating and/or nonrepeating fields.

Example: If the repeating field TestScores contains the values 98, 76, and 90, the expression StDev (TestScores) yields 11.136, which is the standard deviation of these test scores.

See also: StDevP

StDevP

Purpose: Computes the population standard deviation for all values in a nonempty, numeric repeating field, a series of nonrepeating fields, or a mixture of the two field types. The difference between StDev (described previously) and StDevP is that the former is assumed to be based on a sample, whereas the latter is a population statistic. (That is, StDevP is not based on a sample.)

Note
The formula formerly used to calculate StDev in FileMaker Pro 2.1 is the one that is now used to calculate StDevP. If you have older FileMaker databases and want them to calculate a sample standard deviation, be sure that StDev is used in the formula rather than StDevP.

Syntax: StDevP (*field . . .*)

where *field . . .* is either the name of a valid, nonempty repeating field containing numeric data only or a series of repeating and/or nonrepeating fields.

Example: If the repeating field TestScores contains the values 98, 76, and 90, the expression StDevP (TestScores) yields 9.09, which is the population standard deviation of these test scores.

See also: StDev

Sum

Purpose: Adds the contents of each nonblank entry in a numeric repeating field or in a series of nonrepeating and/or repeating fields. The result returned is a numeric value.

Syntax: Sum (*field . . .*)

where *field . . .* is the name of either a valid, nonempty repeating field containing numeric values only or a series of nonrepeating and/or repeating fields.

Example: If the repeating field Prices contains the values 5.00, 10.00, and 30.00, the expression

```
"Your item total is $" & Sum(Prices)
```

produces the following message:

```
Your item total is $45.00
```

See also: Average

Variance

Purpose: Computes the variance for all values in a nonempty, numeric repeating field, a series of nonrepeating fields, or a mixture of the two field types. The variance is a measure of how the values in a sample depart from the average value.

Syntax: Variance (*field . . .*)

where *field . . .* is either the name of a valid, nonempty repeating field containing numeric data only or a series of repeating and/or nonrepeating fields.

 Note   The variance is the square of the standard deviation.

Example: If the repeating field TestScores contains the values 98, 76, and 90, the expression Variance (TestScores) yields 124, which is the variance of these test scores.

See also: StDev, StDevP, VarianceP

VarianceP

Purpose: Computes the population variance for all values in a nonempty, numeric repeating field, a series of nonrepeating fields, or a mixture of the two field types. The difference between Variance (described previously) and VarianceP is that the former is assumed to be based on a sample, whereas the latter is a population statistic. (That is, VarianceP is not based on a sample.)

Syntax: VarianceP (*field . . .*)

where *field . . .* is either the name of a valid, nonempty repeating field containing numeric data only or a series of repeating and/or nonrepeating fields.

Note   The VarianceP is the square of the population standard deviation.

Example: If the repeating field TestScores contains the values 98, 76, and 90, the expression StDevP (TestScores) yields 82.667, which is the population standard deviation of these test scores.

See also: StDev, StDevP, and Variance

Date Functions

Date functions are used to find out various facts about dates entered by the user, to determine the current date from the system clock, and to convert date data into text format.

The date functions are as follows:

- ✦ Date
- ✦ Day
- ✦ DayName
- ✦ DayNameJ
- ✦ DayofWeek
- ✦ DayofYear
- ✦ Month
- ✦ MonthName
- ✦ MonthNameJ
- ✦ WeekofYear
- ✦ WeekofYearFiscal
- ✦ Year
- ✦ YearName

Date

Purpose: Determines the calendar date associated with three numbers, interpreted as days, months, and years, computed since January 1, 1 AD.

Syntax: Date (*month; day; year*)

where *month* is the number of the month, *day* is the number of the day, and *year* is the number of the year. (All are numeric expressions.)

Example: In a database, the fields DueMonth, DueDay, and DueYear are used to specify the due date of an invoice. If the fields contain 12, 19, and 2005, the following expression

```
"Your invoice was due on " & Date(DueMonth; DueDay; DueYear)
```

produces the following message:

```
Your invoice was due on December 19, 2005
```

 Note The result type for the formula must be set to Date. If it is set to Number, the displayed result is a serial number (732299) rather than the date previously shown.

See also: Day, Month, Year

Day

Purpose: Returns the number of the day in the month, from 1–31, for a specified date. The value returned is numeric.

Syntax: Day (*date*)

where *date* is a valid expression with a date format.

Example: If the field InvoiceDate contains the value 02/26/2005, the expression Day (InvoiceDate) returns 26.

See also: Month, Year

DayName

Purpose: Returns a text string with the name of the day of the week for the specified date expression. The text returned is capitalized.

Syntax: DayName (*date*)

where *date* is a valid date.

Example: The following expression could be used as part of a message in a form letter:

```
"We missed you on " & DayName(Appointment Date)
```

If the Appointment Date field in the formula contains 10/23/2005, the following message is displayed:

```
We missed you on Sunday
```

See also: MonthName

DayNameJ

Purpose: Returns a Japanese text string containing the specified date expression's day of week name.

Syntax: DayNameJ (*date*)

where *date* is a Date field or an expression yielding the Date data type.

Example: The following expression defines a Calculation field with text results, giving an invoice date after the text "This invoice was prepared on":

```
"This invoice was prepared on " & DayNameJ (Invoice Date)
```

See also: DayName

DayofWeek

Purpose: Returns a number representing the day of the week (from 1–7) on which the specified date falls. The number 1 is returned for Sunday, 2 for Monday, 3 for Tuesday, and so on.

Syntax: DayofWeek (*date*)

where *date* is a valid date expression.

Example: If a Birthday field contains 10/5/2005, the expression DayofWeek (Birthday) returns 3, which represents Tuesday. To display the name of the day rather than a number, you could use the formula DayName (DayofWeek (Birthday)).

See also: DayofYear, WeekofYear

DayofYear

Purpose: Returns the number of days elapsed in the appropriate year since the specified date. The result is a numeric value.

Syntax: DayofYear (*date*)

where *date* is a valid date expression.

Example: Assuming that today is February 9, 2005, the expression DayofYear (Today) returns 40 because February 9th is the 40th day of 2005.

Example: The following expression can be used to print a message about the Yuletide holiday:

```
"Only " & NumToText(358 - DayofYear(Today)) & " days until Christmas!"
```

If today's date were 7/31/2005, the expression would produce the following message:

```
  Only 146 days until Christmas!
```

See also: DayofWeek, WeekofYear

Month

Purpose: Returns a numeric value in the range 1–12, corresponding to the month in the specified date expression.

Syntax: Month (*date*)

where *date* is a valid expression in date format.

Example: If the Date field contains 03/16/2005, the expression Month (Date) yields 3.

See also: Day, Year

MonthName

Purpose: Returns a text value with the proper name of the month in the given date expression. The text returned is capitalized.

Syntax: MonthName (*date*)

where *date* is a valid date expression.

Example: If the field Date contains the value 08/10/60, the following expression

```
  MonthName(Date) & " was a great month! You were born."
```

produces the following message:

```
  August was a great month! You were born.
```

See also: DayName

MonthNameJ

Purpose: Returns a Japanese text value with the proper name of the month in the given date expression. The text returned is capitalized.

Syntax: MonthNameJ (*date*)

where *date* is a valid date expression.

See also: DayNameJ

WeekofYear

Purpose: Calculates the number of weeks that have elapsed for a specified date in a given year. Fractional weeks at the start or end of a year are treated as full weeks, so possible values can range between 1–54. The value returned is in numeric format.

Syntax: WeekofYear (*date*)

where *date* is a valid date expression.

Example: If the Date field contains the value 2/9/2006, the expression WeekofYear (Date) returns the value 7.

See also: DayofYear, WeekofYearFiscal

WeekofYearFiscal

Purpose: Calculates the number of weeks that have elapsed for a supplied date in a given year, assuming that the week starts on a particular day. WeekofYearFiscal considers the first week of the year as the first one that contains at least four days. That is, when January 1 falls on a day between Monday and Thursday, that week is considered the first week of the year; otherwise, the next week is considered the first week. The returned numeric value is between 1–53.

Syntax: WeekofYearFiscal (*date; starting day*)

where *date* is a valid date expression and *starting day* is a number (1–7) that represents the day of the week that is to be treated as the first day of the week (1 is Sunday, 2 is Monday, and so on).

Example: January 1, 2006, fell on a Sunday. If the Date field contains the value 3/12/2006, the expression WeekofYearFiscal (Date; 1) returns the value 11.

See also: DayofYear, WeekofYear

Year

Purpose: Extracts the year portion of a date expression. The value returned is in numeric format and can be used in calculations.

Syntax: Year (*date*)

where *date* is a valid date expression.

Example: If the Date field contains the value 3/16/2005, the expression Year (Date) yields the result 2005.

The following expression yields the person's age after this year's birthday:

```
Year(Get(CurrentDate)) - Year(Birthday)
```

See also: Day, Month

YearName

Purpose: Returns a Japanese text value with the proper year name for the given date expression. You have a variety of formats you can specify.

Syntax: YearName (*date; format*)

where *date* is a valid date expression, and *format* is 0, 1, or 2 depending upon which Japanese date format to apply. See FileMaker Pro Help for further details of Japanese date formats.

See also: DayName

Design Functions

The design functions enable you to obtain information about the current database or any other database that is open, such as the names of all open databases, items in a value list, or the names of all fields used in a particular layout. The design functions are as follows:

✦ DatabaseNames

✦ FieldBounds

✦ FieldComment

✦ FieldIDs

+ FieldNames
+ FieldRepetitions
+ FieldStyle
+ FieldType
+ GetNextSerialValue
+ LayoutIDs
+ LayoutNames
+ RelationInfo
+ ScriptIDs
+ ScriptNames
+ TableIDs
+ TableNames
+ ValueListIDs
+ ValueListItems
+ ValueListNames
+ WindowNames

Caution
Database, layout, value list, field, and relationship names used in Design function expressions *must* be enclosed in quotation marks, such as LayoutNames ("Sales") or FieldNames ("Invoices"; "Data Entry"). If you neglect to include quotation marks around these elements, the formula will *not* work!

FileMaker Pro databases must be open at the time they're referenced in Design functions.

DatabaseNames

Purpose: Returns the names of all currently open FileMaker Pro database files at the time the record is created. Filenames are listed alphabetically (without filename extensions) and are separated by carriage returns.

Syntax: DatabaseNames

Note that the DatabaseNames function takes no arguments.

Example: If the currently open FileMaker Pro databases are named Invoices and Sales.fp7, the expression DatabaseNames returns the text strings Invoices and Sales, each on a separate line within the Calculation field.

FieldBounds

Purpose: Returns the location, size, and angle of rotation of a given field in a particular database layout. The result is type Text and in the form *a b c d e* (with each item separated from the others by a single space), where

- ✦ *a* is the distance from the field's left edge to the layout area's left edge.
- ✦ *b* is the distance from the field's top to the top of the layout area.
- ✦ *c* is the distance from the field's right edge to the layout area's left edge.
- ✦ *d* is the distance from the field's bottom edge to the top of the layout area.
- ✦ *e* is the field's angle of rotation (clockwise).

Items *a–d* are given in pixels. An unrotated field returns a rotation result of 0.

Syntax: FieldBounds (*database filename; layout name; field name*)

Example: The expression FieldBounds ("Invoices"; "Data Entry"; "State") returns 42 267 85 283 0. The first four items represent the distance of various edges of the State field from the top and left edges of the Invoices database's Data Entry layout. The final number (0) shows that the field is unrotated.

See also: FieldNames, FieldRepetitions, FieldStyle, FieldType

FieldComment

Purpose: Returns the specified field's comment, as entered in the Define Database dialog's Fields tab.

Syntax: FieldIDs (*database filename; field name*)

Example: The expression FieldComment ("Sales"; "CustomerID") returns "Customer's ID code," if that is what was entered in the CustomerID field's Comment text box.

See also: FieldNames

FieldIDs

Purpose: Returns a list of all unique fields in the current database or, if a layout is specified, in that particular layout. Fields are identified by number rather than by name. Successive field names are separated by carriage returns; that is, each field ID number is listed on a separate line. Specify Text as the calculation result type.

Syntax: FieldIDs (*database name; layout name*)

Example: The expression FieldIDs ("Sales"; "Report") returns the ID numbers of all fields used in the layout named Report in the database named Sales.fp7. To view a list of all unique fields in the default table, as well as related fields, you would omit the *layout name* portion, as in: FieldIDs ("Sales"; " ").

See also: FieldNames

FieldNames

Purpose: Returns the names of all fields used in a particular layout (or in all layouts) of a specified database. The result is of type Text. Successive field names are separated by carriage returns. To retrieve the names of all fields in the default table, enter a pair of quotation marks as the layout name, as in FieldNames ("Sales"; " ").

Syntax: FieldNames (*database filename; layout name*)

Example: The expression FieldNames ("Invoices"; "Data Entry") returns the names of all fields used in the layout named Data Entry in the database named Invoices.fp7. Each field name is listed on a separate line within the field.

See also: FieldIDs, FieldBounds, FieldRepetitions, FieldStyle, FieldType

FieldRepetitions

Purpose: Returns the number of repetitions and the orientation of a given repeating field as it is formatted on a particular layout of a database. The result is of type Text, and the orientation returned is either vertical or horizontal.

Syntax: FieldRepetitions (*database filename; layout name; field name*)

Example: If a field named Rept is a repeating field formatted to display three repetitions in a vertical array, the expression FieldRepetitions ("Invoices"; "Data Entry"; "Rept") returns 3 vertical.

See also: FieldBounds, FieldNames, FieldStyle, FieldType

FieldStyle

Purpose: Returns a text string describing the specified field's format (Format ⇨ Format Field). Results can be Standard (a standard field), Scrolling (standard field with a vertical scroll bar), Popuplist, Popupmenu, Checkbox, or RadioButton. If the field has a value list associated with it, the name of the value list is also returned (separated from the returned style by a space).

Syntax: FieldStyle (*database filename; layout name; field name*)

Example: The expression FieldStyle ("Invoices"; "Data Entry"; "State") returns Standard if State is an ordinary text field. If State were formatted as a pop-up list and had a value list named State Names associated with it, the returned text would be Popuplist State Names.

See also: FieldBounds, FieldNames, FieldRepetitions, FieldType

FieldType

Purpose: Returns information about the defined type of the specified field as a text string containing these four items, in order:

- ✦ Standard, StoredCalc, Summary, UnstoredCalc, or Global.
- ✦ The field type (Text, Number, Date, Time, Timestamp, or Container).
- ✦ Indexed or Unindexed.
- ✦ The maximum repetitions defined for the field. (If the field is not a repeating field, 1 is returned.)

Syntax: FieldType (*database filename; field name*)

Example: The expression FieldType ("Invoices"; "State") returns Standard Text Unindexed 1, showing that the storage options have not been changed for the State field, it is of type Text, it is not indexed, and it is not a repeating field.

See also: FieldBounds, FieldNames, FieldRepetitions, FieldStyle

GetNextSerialValue

Purpose: Returns the next serial number for the specified field in the specified database. Specify Text as the calculation result type.

Syntax: GetNextSerialValue (*database filename; field name*)

Example: You have a CustID field in the database named Customer and have set "Serial number" as an auto-enter option. To determine the serial number that will next be assigned to the CustID field, you would use the expression GetNextSerialValue ("Customer"; "CustID").

GetValue

Purpose: Returns the item from a value list, based upon an index value into the list.

Syntax: GetValue (*valuelist; n*)

Example: The expression returns the *n*th item from the specified valuelist.

LayoutIDs

Purpose: Returns a list of the ID numbers of all layouts in the specified database, separated by carriage returns. Note that the database must be open on your computer (or opened as guest on another computer) in order for this function to return values. Specify Text as the calculation result type.

Syntax: LayoutIDs (*database filename*)

Example: The expression LayoutIDs ("Invoices") returns a list of the ID numbers of all layouts that are currently defined for the database named Invoices.fp7. (This assumes that Invoices is open when this Calculation field is evaluated. If Invoices is not open, the expression returns nothing.)

See also: LayoutNames

LayoutNames

Purpose: Returns a list of the names of all layouts in the specified database, separated by carriage returns. Note that the database must be open on your computer (or opened as guest on another computer) in order for this function to return values.

Syntax: LayoutNames (*database filename*)

Example: The expression LayoutNames ("Invoices") returns a list of the names of all layouts that are currently defined for the database named Invoices. (This assumes that Invoices.fp7 is open when this Calculation field is evaluated. If Invoices is not open, the expression returns nothing.)

See also: LayoutIDs

RelationInfo

Purpose: Returns information about a specified relationship. The four returned values are separated by carriage returns and consist of the name of the related database, the name of the match field in the master database, the name of the match field in the related database, and options that have been set for the relationship. Possible options include Delete ("When deleting a record in this file, also delete related records" has been set), Create ("Allow creation of related records" has been set), and Sorted ("Sort related records" has been set).

Syntax: RelationInfo (*database filename; name of related table*)

Example: In the expression RelationInfo ("Invoices"; "Cust ID"), Invoices is the current database for which the relationship Cust ID has been defined. The result might be Call Log, ID, CustNum, and a blank line (separated by carriage returns), indicating that Call Log is the related database filename, ID is the match field in the master database (Invoices), CustNum is the match field in the related database (Call Log), and no options have been specified for the relationship.

ScriptIDs

Purpose: Returns a list of all script ID numbers in the specified database, separated by carriage returns. Note that the database must be open on your computer (or opened as guest on another computer) in order for this function to return values. Specify Text as the calculation result type.

Syntax: ScriptIDs (*database filename*)

Example: The expression ScriptIDs ("Customers") returns a list of the ID numbers of all scripts that have been defined for the `Customers` database.

ScriptNames

Purpose: Returns the names of all scripts that have been created for a given database, separated by carriage returns.

Syntax: ScriptNames (*database filename*)

Example: In the expression ScriptNames ("Books 2005"), a list of all scripts that have been defined for the Books 2005 database is presented, separated by carriage returns.

TableIDs

Purpose: Returns a list of all table ID numbers in the specified database, separated by carriage returns. Note that the database must be open on your computer (or opened as guest on another computer) in order for this function to return values. Specify Text as the calculation result type.

Syntax: TableIDs (*database filename*)

Example: The expression ValueListIDs ("Customers") returns a list of the ID numbers of all tables defined in the Customers database file.

TableNames

Purpose: Returns a list of all table occurrences in the specified database's relationships graph, separated by carriage returns. Note that the database must be open on your computer (or opened as guest on another computer) in order for this function to return values. Specify Text as the calculation result type.

Syntax: TableNames (*database filename*)

Example: The expression ValueListIDs ("Customers") returns a list of the ID numbers of all tables defined in the Customers database file.

ValueListIDs

Purpose: Returns a list of all value list ID numbers in the specified database, separated by carriage returns. Note that the database must be open on your computer (or opened as guest on another computer) in order for this function to return values. Specify Text as the calculation result type.

Syntax: ValueListIDs (*database filename*)

Example: The expression ValueListIDs ("Customers") returns a list of the ID numbers of all value lists that have been defined for the Customers database.

ValueListItems

Purpose: Returns the items in a particular value list for a given database, separated by carriage returns.

Syntax: ValueListItems (*database filename; value list name*)

Example: The expression ValueListItems ("Customers"; "MemberClass") returns the list of items in a value list named CustType from the Customers database. The items returned, in this instance, might be Regular, Business, Gold.

See also: ValueListNames

ValueListNames

Purpose: Returns the names of all value lists that have been defined for a given database, separated by carriage returns.

Syntax: ValueListNames (*database filename*)

Example: In the expression ValueListNames ("Sales"), the names of all currently defined value lists for the Sales database would be returned.

See also: ValueListItems

WindowNames

Purpose: Returns a list of names for all currently open FileMaker Pro windows. A window can be open even if not visible, for example, when related data from it is being retrieved or displayed.

Syntax: WindowNames

Example: The expression WindowNames returns Video Invoice, Customers, and Movies in our Video Invoice example from this book's companion CD.

External Functions

The purpose of external functions is to allow installed, enabled plug-ins to exchange data with FileMaker Pro. All installed, enabled plug-ins that support external functions will automatically be listed in the External Functions category when you are creating or editing a calculation in FileMaker Pro. To enable or disable any installed plug-in, choose FileMaker Pro/Edit ➪ Preferences and click the Plug-Ins tab.

Plug-ins written specifically for FileMaker Pro 7 and later define their own calling sequence and are invoked in the same manner as a native FileMaker Pro function. Plug-ins written for previous versions of FileMaker Pro (6 and earlier) continue to work but must be invoked as arguments to the External function. The function name is the first argument, and the second argument is a text string comprising the function's argument list (conventionally separated by pipe — | — symbols).

As you'll note when viewing the list of external functions in the Specify Calculation dialog, only some plug-ins provide external function support.

Note   In addition to the plug-ins that ship with FileMaker Pro 8, some commercial plug-ins may also support external functions. Refer to the plug-in's documentation for instructions concerning the syntax and use of the supported external functions.

Auto Update external functions

Purpose: The Auto Update plug-in enables networked FileMaker Pro users to automatically receive updates to plug-ins from FileMaker Server. To use external functions, the Auto Update plug-in must be enabled and FileMaker Server must be available on the network.

Syntax: External (*"function name"; parameter*)

where *function name* is surrounded by quotation marks and is the name of any external function supported by the plug-in. The supported Auto Update external functions are as follows:

✦ External ("FMSAUC-Version"; *parameter*)

✦ External ("FMSAUC-FindPlugin"; *parameter*)

✦ External ("FMSAUC-UpdatePlugin"; *parameter*)

✦ External ("FMSAUC-SaveVersion"; *parameter*)

✦ External ("FMSAUC-SaveAsMacBin"; *parameter*)

Example: External ("FMSAUC-Version"; 0) returns the version number of the Auto Update plug-in that's in use.

Financial Functions

These functions perform investment-related calculations. They are used to determine loan specifications, how investments will grow over time, and the amount that investments are worth in constant money. They duplicate functions found on many financial pocket calculators.

The financial functions are as follows:

✦ FV

✦ NPV

✦ PMT

✦ PV

FV

Purpose: Computes the future value of an investment, based on the provided payment value, interest rate, and number of compounding periods. A numeric value is returned. The result is not the future value of an investment, starting with a certain balance; rather, it is the amount that accrues when equal payments are made over time to an account that bears a particular rate of interest.

Syntax: FV (*payment; rate; periods*) where *payment* is the amount of each payment, *rate* is the interest rate per period, and *periods* is the number of payment periods.

Example: The following expression

```
FV(100; .05/12; 360)
```

returns $83,225.86, which is the value of an account if $100 payments are made each month for 30 years at an annual interest rate of 5 percent (.05/12).

Note   Payments are assumed to be made at the end of a period. Be sure to give the interest rate per period. Divide the annual rate by 12, as shown in the example, to obtain the monthly rate if employing a period of one month.

The following formula returns the future value of a continuously compounded investment, assuming a certain starting value:

```
Future Value = Present Value * (1 + Rate)^Periods
```

See also: NPV, PV

NPV

Purpose: Calculates the *net present value* (value in today's dollars) of a series of unequal payments made at regular intervals to an account bearing fixed interest per period over the life of the payments.

Syntax: NPV (*payment; rate*)

where *payment* is a payment amount or the name of a valid field containing the numeric value of each payment, and *rate* is a numeric value indicating the interest rate per period.

Example: The following expression yields the profit on the transaction in today's dollars with an interest rate of 3 percent:

```
NPV(LoanAmt; .03)
```

When the repeating field LoanAmt contains the values –1000, 500, 600, 400, and 700, the result is $1,008.73. Note that the LoanAmt field contains five values that represent an initial loan of $1,000 (expressed as a negative value) and the values for the four annual payments.

See also: FV, PV

PMT

Purpose: Calculates the payment needed to fully amortize a loan, given the loan amount, the interest rate per payment period, and the number of periods.

Syntax: PMT (*principal; rate; periods*)

where *principal* is a number representing the amount of the loan, *rate* is the interest rate per period, and *periods* is the number of payments.

Example: The following expression

```
PMT(34100; 10.2005/12; 60)
```

yields a payment of $744.55, which is the amount required to finance $34,100 at 10.2005 percent annual interest over 60 months.

PV

Purpose: Calculates the present value of a series of equal payments, made at regular intervals, to an account bearing a fixed rate of interest.

Syntax: PV (*payment; rate; periods*)

where *payment* is the numeric amount of each payment, *rate* is the interest rate per period, and *periods* is the number of payments.

Example: The following expression

```
PV (500; .03; 5)
```

yields the value of five annual $500 payments in today's dollars ($2,500 gross amount), assuming a 3 percent interest (or inflation) rate—in this case, $2,289.85.

See also: NPV, FV

Get Function

The Get function can provide information about the current system on which FileMaker Pro is running, the number of records in the current file, the name of the current user, and more than 60 other useful tidbits. Unlike other function categories, the Get category consists of just one function, but it takes more than 70 preset arguments. The result of the Get function varies with the argument used.

Although you can type the argument to the Get function after choosing Get from the alphabetical function list presented in the Specify Calculation dialog, you might find it difficult to remember the exact spelling and wording of the argument. The easy way to create an expression using the Get function is to choose Get functions from the View pop-up menu/drop-down list and then select the correct argument.

The following section provides a general description of the Get function and its arguments. For a more detailed explanation of the Get function arguments and the meaning of the data they return, choose Get functions from FileMaker Pro Help.

Tip   The variations of the Get function are extremely useful as script steps. (Several, in fact, are *only* useful as parts of scripts.) For example, the expression Get (SystemPlatform) is used to determine whether the database is running on a Macintosh or under Windows. Depending on the result of the Status (SystemPlatform) check, you could have the script execute an AppleScript (if running on a Mac) or do something else (if running under Windows). Note that the Set Field step is often useful for adding Get functions to a script to make certain the desired field is active/selected.

When using the Get function, be sure to set the result type correctly, given the type of data that is returned. Get (CurrentTime), for example, returns 16:19:23 when the result type is Time but returns a numeric string if the result type is set to Number.

Get

Purpose: Performs a check on the state of the database, hardware in use, and so on, and then returns this information in an appropriate form based on the result at the time of calculation.

Syntax: Get (*status flag*)

where *status flag* is one of the preset arguments supplied by FileMaker Pro 8. The Get function can return a text string, a number, or a date, depending on its purpose and the argument passed. The Get function accepts no parameters other than the preset arguments shown here:

✦ *Get(AccountName):* Text string containing the name of the account accessing the database.

✦ *Get(ActiveFieldContents):* The contents of the field containing the cursor.

✦ *Get(ActiveFieldName):* Name of the field containing the cursor.

✦ *Get(ActiveFieldTableName):* Name of the table containing the currently active field.

✦ *Get(ActiveModifierKeys):* Number representing the current modifier key being pressed by the user, where 1 = Shift, 2 = Caps Lock, 4 = Control/Ctrl, 8 = Option/Alt, and 16 = ⌘ (Mac).

✦ *Get(ActiveRepetitionNumber):* A number telling the current instance of the active repeating field (or 1, if not repeating).

✦ *Get(ActiveSelectionSize):* Number of characters currently selected in the active field.

✦ *Get(ActiveSelectionStart):* Position in the current active field of the cursor or the start of the current selection.

✦ *Get(AllowAbortState):* Returns 1 if the Allow User Abort script step has been executed or 0 if not.

✦ *Get(AllowToolbarState):* Returns 1 if toolbars are allowed to be visible per the Allow Toolbars script step; 0, otherwise.

✦ *Get(ApplicationLanguage):* Text string returning the application's current language default (for example, "English").

✦ *Get(ApplicationVersion):* Text telling what version of FileMaker Pro is running.

✦ *Get(CalculationRepetitionNumber):* A number representing which repetition of a repeating calculation field is currently being evaluated.

✦ *Get(CurrentDate):* The current date, according to the system clock.

✦ *Get(CurrentHostTimestamp):* The current date and time on the computer hosting the database being used.

✦ *Get(CurrentTime):* The current time on the computer being used to the nearest second.

✦ *Get(CurrentTimestamp):* The current date and time on the computer being used.

✦ *Get(CustomMenuSetName):* Returns a null string if the current menu set is not a custom menu set; otherwise, it returns the name of the active custom menu set.

✦ *Get(DesktopPath):* Returns a text string indicating the path to the current user's desktop folder starting with the startup volume name (Mac) or the drive letter (Windows).

✦ *Get(DocumentsPath):* Returns a text string indicating the path to the current user's Documents (Mac) or My Documents (Windows) folder starting with the startup volume name (Mac) or the drive letter (Windows).

✦ *Get(ErrorCaptureState):* 1 if the Error Capture script step is active; 0, otherwise.

✦ *Get(ExtendedPrivileges):* A carriage return-delimited list of the current account's extended privileges.

✦ *Get(FileMakerPath):* Returns a text string indicating the path to the currently running copy of FileMaker Pro starting with the startup volume name (Mac) or the drive letter (Windows).

✦ *Get(FileName):* The name of the currently active database file, minus the file extension.

✦ *Get(FilePath):* The full operating system path to the currently active database file, including the filename extension.

✦ *Get(FileSize):* The size of the currently active database file in bytes.

✦ *Get(FoundCount):* The number of records in the current found set.

✦ *Get(HighContrastColor):* The name of the Windows OS's current high-contrast default color scheme. (Returns empty string if running on a Mac or if Use High Contrast is not selected in Windows Accessibility Options dialog.)

✦ *Get(HighContrastState):* True (1) if running on Windows and Use High Contrast is selected; False (0) otherwise.

✦ *Get(HostIPAddress):* Returns the IP address (nnn.nnn.nnn.nnn) of the computer hosting the currently active FileMaker database.

✦ *Get(HostName):* The name of the computer (as registered on the local network) hosting the currently active database.

✦ *Get(LastError):* The error code from the most recently executed script step, if any. A list of all error codes can be found in the online Help files. AppleScript errors return AppleScript error codes, and ODBC errors return SQLSTATE error codes.

✦ *Get(LastMessageChoice):* The number of the button (1, 2, or 3) clicked in the alert presented by the Show Custom Dialog script step.

✦ *Get(LastODBCError):* An error state/message that is returned by ODBC.

✦ *Get(LayoutAccess):* Access privileges for the current layout: 0 = current account doesn't have any access to the layout, 1 = Read-only access, 2 = Modifiable access.

✦ *Get(LayoutCount):* Number of layouts that are defined in the database file.

✦ *Get(LayoutName):* Name of the current layout.

✦ *Get(LayoutNumber):* Number of the current layout, according to the order reflected in the Set Layout Order dialog.

✦ *Get(LayoutTableName):* The name of the current layout's primary table.

✦ *Get(LayoutViewState):* 0 if in Form view, 1 if in List view, 2 if in Table view.

✦ *Get(MultiUserState):* Number representing the current sharing status of the database, where 0 = single user; 1 = multi-user and the user is the host; and 2 = multi-user and the user is a guest.

✦ *Get(NetworkProtocol):* Name of the current network protocol (always returns TCP/IP in FileMaker Pro 8).

✦ *Get(PageNumber):* Number of the page currently being printed or previewed onscreen; 0 if not printing or previewing.

✦ *Get(PortalRowNumber):* Number of the row that is selected in a portal. If a portal is not selected, 0 is returned.

✦ *Get(PreferencesPath):* Returns a text string containing the path to the current user's Preferences folder starting with the startup volume name (Mac) or the drive letter (Windows).

✦ *Get(PrinterName):* Name of the current (default) printer.

✦ *Get(PrivilegeSetName):* The current account's Privilege Set name ([Full Access] if using default Admin account).

✦ *Get(RecordAccess):* Access privileges for the current record: 0 = current account doesn't have any access to the record, 1 = Read-only access, 2 = Modifiable access.

✦ *Get(RecordID):* The unique ID number of the current record.

✦ *Get(RecordModificationCount):* Number of times that the current record has been modified. This number is incremented only when changes to the record have been committed: that is, when you switch to a different record, change to Find mode, or exit all fields in the record (pressing Enter on a Macintosh, for example). If the record has never been modified, 0 is returned.

✦ *Get(RecordNumber):* Current record's position in the found set.

✦ *Get(RecordOpenCount):* Returns the number of open/uncommitted records in the current found set.

✦ *Get(RecordOpenState):* Returns 0 if the current record is closed or committed, 1 if the current record is a new record that hasn't been committed, and 2 if the current record is an existing record that has been modified but not yet committed.

✦ *Get(RequestCount):* Number of find requests that are defined for the current table.

✦ *Get(RequestOmitState):* Returns 0 if the Omit check box is not currently selected, 1 if the Omit check box is selected.

✦ *Get(ScreenDepth):* Given the display settings of the current computer, this is the number of data bits required to represent the color of a pixel. (When in 256-color mode, for example, the result is 8; in thousands mode, the result is 16.)

✦ *Get(ScreenHeight):* Height (in pixels) of the current monitor on which the database is being run.

✦ *Get(ScreenWidth):* Width (in pixels) of the current monitor on which the database is being run.

✦ *Get(ScriptName):* Name of the script that is currently running or paused.

✦ *Get(ScriptParameter):* The parameter string passed to the current script step.

✦ *Get(ScriptResult):* Returns the result returned by the most recently executed subscript of the current script, a null string if the subscript did not return a result or if no subscript has been executed.

✦ *Get(SortState):* A number indicating the sort status of the database: 0 = unsorted, 1 = sorted, or 2 = semi-sorted.

✦ *Get(StatusAreaState):* Current state of the status area: 0 = hidden, 1 = visible, 2 = visible and locked, or 3 = hidden and locked.

✦ *Get(SystemDrive):* Returns the volume name (Mac) or the drive letter (Windows) for the currently running operating system. Obviously, for Windows users, this will almost always be C.

✦ *Get(SystemIPAddress):* List (carriage return-delimited) of all devices connected to a NIC.

✦ *Get(SystemLanguage):* Primary language on current system.

✦ *Get(SystemNICAddress):* List of the hardware addresses for all NICs on the current system.

✦ *Get(SystemPlatform):* A number indicating the current platform (–1 for Mac OS X and –2 for Windows 2000 or Windows XP).

✦ *Get(SystemVersion):* System software version number currently in use, such as 10.4.2 (Mac OS X 10.4.2) or 5.1 (for Windows XP).

✦ *Get(TextRulerVisible):* Returns 1 if the text ruler is being displayed, 0 if it isn't.

✦ *Get(TotalRecordCount):* Number of records in the current table.

✦ *Get(UseSystemFormatState):* Returns 1 if the Use System Formats command is set in the Formats menu; 0, otherwise.

✦ *Get(UserCount):* Number of users currently accessing the file: 1 if in single-user mode, actual number plus one when the file is being shared on a network.

✦ *Get(UserName):* Name of the current user, as specified in Preferences.

✦ *Get(WindowContentHeight):* Height, in pixels, of the current layout window's content area.

✦ *Get(WindowContentWidth):* Width, in pixels, of the current layout window's content area (includes Status Area, if visible).

✦ *Get(WindowDesktopHeight):* Height, in pixels, of the Desktop space (not including menu bar, Dock, and so on).

✦ *Get(WindowDesktopWidth):* Width, in pixels, of the Desktop space.

✦ *Get(WindowHeight):* Height, in pixels, of the current layout window.

✦ *Get(WindowLeft):* Distance, in pixels, from the left edge of the current window to the left edge of the main screen (Mac) or application window (Windows).

✦ *Get(WindowMode):* 0 for Browse, 1 for Find, 2 for Preview, 3 for printing.

✦ *Get(WindowName):* Name of the current layout window to which the calculation is applied.

✦ *Get(WindowTop):* Distance in pixels from the top of the window to the bottom of the menu bar or (if present) bottom-most toolbar.

✦ *Get(WindowVisible):* True (1) if the window is visible, false (0) if not.

✦ *Get(WindowWidth):* Width, in pixels, of the current layout window.

✦ *Get(WindowZoomLevel):* Returns the zoom percentage (magnification) for the currently active window. If you are running on Windows and have the General Preferences pane's Enlarge window contents to improve readability option selected, the percentage returned will have an asterisk appended.

Logical Functions

In early versions of FileMaker Pro, If was the only logical function. Logical functions return one of two values (0 for False and 1 for True). In FileMaker Pro 3.0 through FileMaker Pro 6, there were six. FileMaker Pro 8 expands that to 15:

✦ Case

✦ Choose

✦ Evaluate

✦ EvaluationError

✦ GetAsBoolean

✦ GetField

✦ GetNthRecord

✦ If

✦ IsEmpty

✦ IsValid

✦ IsValidExpression

✦ Let

✦ Lookup

✦ LookupNext

✦ Quote

Case

Purpose: Evaluates a series of expressions and returns the result supplied for the first true expression that is found.

Syntax: Case *(test1; result1 [; test2; result2; default result] . . .)*

where *test* is any text or numeric expression and *result* is the result that corresponds to the expression.

Example: The Payment field is examined in the following expression:

```
Case (Payment="V"; "VISA"; Payment="M"; "MasterCard"; "Other")
```

If the Payment field contains a V, the result is VISA. If it contains an M, the result is MasterCard. If it contains anything else or is blank, the default result (Other) is returned.

See also: If, Choose

Choose

Purpose: Selects one of a series of results based on an index value.

Syntax: Choose *(expression; result0 [; result1; result2] . . .)*

where the *result* of an *expression* yields a number (between 0 and the number of the last result specified) that indexes into the result list that follows, and *result* is one or more results. Choose can return text, a number, a date, a time, or a container.

Note   As indicated in its syntax, Choose is a zero-based index. A result of 0 is needed to select the first result in the list.

Example: The following expression returns a random four-character string comprising the letters a–d:

```
Choose(Int(Random*4); "a";"b";"c";"d")
```

See also: If, Case

Evaluate

Purpose: Evaluates its first argument as a calculation. Subsequent (optional) parameters are fields whose modifications should trigger a reevaluation, and the optional fields list is enclosed in brackets.

Syntax: Evaluate (*expression {;[field1; field2; . . .; fieldn]}*)

Example: The following expression returns 16 when CommissionRate contains "0.04 * SalesPrice" and the SalesPrice field contains 400.

```
Evaluate(CommissionRate; [SalesPrice])
```

See also: EvaluationError

EvaluationError

Purpose: Returns an error code, if any, resulting from evaluating *expression*. If *expression* includes the Evaluate function, syntax errors will also be returned.

Syntax: EvaluationError (*expression*)

Example: If calcField contains commission + 10 but the commission field is not accessible (not present), the following will return error code 102, which means Field Missing.

```
EvaluationError(calcField)
```

See also: Evaluate

GetAsBoolean

Purpose: Returns whether the argument exists and is nonzero (or non-null).

Syntax: GetAsBoolean (*expression*)

Returns 0 if the expression (or field) is 0, a null string, or empty — any other evaluation returns a 1.

Example: If the container field — aContainer — is empty, GetAsBoolean(aContainer) returns 0; however, if aContainer holds a picture, movie, or anything else, GetAsBoolean(aContainer) returns 1.

GetField

Purpose: Returns the contents of the specified field. It is best to set storage options for the results as not indexed and not stored (calculate only as necessary).

Syntax: GetField (*field*)

To return the actual contents of the specified *field,* surround the field name in quotes, as in GetField ("Sales Total"). If you include *field* without quotes — Getfield (Sales Total) — it is treated as a reference to another field. That is, the Sales Total field would be checked for the presence of a valid field name (such as Quantity), and the contents of the Quantity field would be returned. When concatenating two unquoted (referenced) field names, such as GetField (A & B), the result must be a valid field name.

GetNthRecord

Purpose: To obtain the contents of a specified field from a numerically specified record number.

Syntax: GetNthRecord (*fieldname; recordnumber*)

Example: GetNthRecord (Surname; Get(RecordNumber)+1) returns the value in the Surname field from the record immediately following the current record in the current table.

If

Purpose: The If function is used when you want to perform one of a set of alternative actions based on the results of a logical test. Normally, the If function is used to choose between two actions; however, you can nest If functions within each other to add choices.

The If function works with the other logical operators, such as less than, equals, OR, AND, and NOT. You combine these operators to create a test that is evaluated for each record.

Syntax: If (*Test; Expression1; Expression2*)

where *Test* is a logical or numeric expression yielding a logical or numeric result, *Expression1* is an expression to be evaluated and whose value is assigned to the field if the test is true or is not equal to zero, and *Expression2* is an expression to be evaluated and whose value is assigned to the field if the test is false or is equal to zero.

Example: Consider this simple example:

```
If(Number > 0; "The number is positive."; "The number is less
than or equal to zero.")
```

If the Number field contains 35, the expression produces this text:

```
The number is positive.
```

If the Number field contains –11, the expression produces this text:

```
The number is less than or equal to zero.
```

Remember, the function returns the value of the first expression if the test is true, and it returns the value of the second expression if the test is false.

You can put Ifs inside Ifs *(nesting)* to add choices. The following example, derived from the first, can handle the additional case where the value in the Number field is equal to zero:

```
If(Number > 0; "The number is positive."; If(Number = 0; "The
number is zero."; "The number is negative."))
```

Note   The test does not have to be a logical expression. If you use a numeric expression, the first action will be performed if the test result is not zero, and the second action will be performed if the test result is zero.

The values of the two expressions should be the values that you want for the field as a whole, depending on which condition is met. For example, you can use the If function to define a Calculation field that gives the tax rate for mail order shipments. The following expression assigns a tax rate of 6 percent to shipments within the state if you're shipping from New Mexico; otherwise, the rate is zero:

```
If(State = "NM"; .06; 0)
```

If the Calculation field using the preceding expression has the name Rate, you can use it in calculations as follows:

```
Tax = Rate * Total
```

Sales tax is then automatically computed and added for in-state shipments and omitted (set to zero) for out-of-state shipments.

IsEmpty

Purpose: Determines whether a particular field or expression is empty. It returns 1 (true) if the field or expression is empty or 0 (false) if it is not empty.

Syntax: IsEmpty *(field)*

where *field* is a field name or a text or numeric expression.

Example: The following expression returns 1 if the Last Name field for the current record is blank; otherwise, it returns 0 (false), indicating that the field contains data:

```
IsEmpty(Last Name)
```

See also: IsValid

IsValid

Purpose: Checks a related file for the presence of a given field. It returns 0 (false) if the field is missing or contains invalid data; otherwise, it returns 1 (true).

Syntax: IsValid (*field*)

where *field* is the name of a field.

Example: The following expression checks for a Customer Number field in the file specified by the relationship named ID:

```
IsValid(ID::Customer Number)
```

A result of 0 (false) is returned if any of the following conditions occur:

 ✦ The related file cannot be found.
 ✦ The field in the related file does not exist.
 ✦ The value contained in the field in the matching record is invalid — that is, it is the wrong data type.

See also: IsEmpty

IsValidExpression

Purpose: Returns 1 if *expression* is syntactically correct; 0, otherwise.

Syntax: IsValidExpression (*expression*)

Example: If textField contains 12 +, the following would return 0 (false) because the second addend is absent.

```
IsValidExpression(textField)
```

Let

Purpose: Sets identifiers to calculated results for the duration of an encompassing calculation. If more than one identifier is being assigned, the assignments must be enclosed in brackets.

Syntax: Let({[}*var1=expression1*{;*var2=expression2*. . .]}; *calculation*)

Example: The following example would return 15.

```
Let([x=25; y=10]; if (x>y; x-y; x+y))
```

Lookup

Purpose: Returns the contents of the field specified by the first argument, using the relationships defined in the Relationships Graph. If the lookup fails and a *failexpression* parameter is provided, the value of *failexpression* will be returned.

Syntax: Lookup (*sourceField* {;*failExpression*})

Example: If the table Person with fields Name and ZIP with record Spenser and 94085 as field values and the table ZIPCode with fields ZIP and City has 94085 and Sunnyvale as field values, the following calculation will return Sunnyvale for Spenser's record.

```
Lookup(ZIPCode::City; "not present")
```

LookupNext

Purpose: Returns the contents of the field specified by the first argument, using the relationships defined in the Relationships Graph. If the lookup fails, the preceding or next record will be returned based upon the value of *flag* (Lower or Higher).

Syntax: LookupNext (*sourceField* ;*flag*)

Example: If the table Person with fields Name and ZIP and with records Spenser and 94086 and Don and 95054 as field values for its two records and the table ZIPCode with fields ZIP and City has 94085 and Sunnyvale and 95054 and Santa Clara as field values for its two records, the following calculation will return **Sunnyvale** for Spenser's record.

```
LookupNext(ZIPCode::City; Lower)
```

Quote

Purpose: Returns the text argument, surrounded by quotes, and with any special characters escaped.

Syntax: Quote (*text*)

Example: If the field LastName contains the string Cohen, the following example will return Cohen.

```
Quote(LastName)
```

Numeric Functions

These functions perform standard mathematical computations on numeric fields and expressions.

The numeric functions are as follows:

- ✦ Abs
- ✦ Ceiling
- ✦ Combination
- ✦ Div
- ✦ Exp
- ✦ Factorial
- ✦ Floor
- ✦ Int
- ✦ Lg
- ✦ Ln
- ✦ Log
- ✦ Mod
- ✦ Random
- ✦ Round
- ✦ SetPrecision
- ✦ Sign
- ✦ Sqrt
- ✦ Truncate

Abs

Purpose: Returns the absolute value of a numeric expression. This function changes negative values to positive ones and leaves zero and positive values alone.

Syntax: Abs (*expression*)

where *expression* is a numeric expression or the name of a field containing a numeric value.

Example: If the field Difference contains 125 or –125, the following expression returns 125:

```
Abs(Difference)
```

See also: Sign

Ceiling

Purpose: Returns the smallest integer greater than or equal to a numeric expression's result.

Syntax: Ceiling (*expression*)

where *expression* is a numeric expression or the name of a field containing a numeric value.

Example: If the field Price contains 125.01, the following expression returns 126:

```
Ceiling(Price)
```

See also: Floor, Truncate, Int

Combination

Purpose: Returns the number of unique groupings of numChoices taken from a set of numItems items.

Syntax: Combination (*numItems*; *numChoices*)

where *numItems* and *numChoices* are non-negative integral numeric expressions or the names of a field containing such values.

Example: The following expression returns 20:

```
Combinations(5; 3)
```

See also: Factorial

Div

Purpose: Returns the result of integer division. The result is identical to Floor(dividend/divisor).

Syntax: Div (*dividend*; *divisor*)

where *dividend* and *divisor* are numeric expressions or the names of fields containing numeric values.

Example: The following expression returns 12:

```
Div(64; 5)
```

See also: Floor

Exp

Purpose: Returns the Naperian (often called *natural*) antilog of the given numeric expression. This value is the result obtained when Euler's constant, e, is raised to the power of the expression; e is approximately 2.7182818.

Syntax: Exp (*expression*)

where *expression* is a numeric expression or a field containing a numeric value.

Example: The following expression calculates the number that has base e logarithm 2 (which is what is meant by the antilog 2):

```
Exp(2)
```

returns 7.389, rounded to three decimal places.

See also: Lg, Ln, Log

Factorial

Purpose: Returns the factorial (product of sequential integer values) starting with number and descending until numFactors (default is number) multiplicands.

Syntax: Factorial (*number {;numFactors}*)

where *number* is a positive integer or a field containing a positive integer and *numFactors* is a numeric expression or field telling how many factors to multiply.

Example: The following expression returns 11880 (12 * 11 * 10 * 9):

```
Factorial(12; 4)
```

See also: Combination

Floor

Purpose: Returns the greatest integer less than or equal to a numeric expression's result.

Syntax: Floor (*expression*)

where *expression* is a numeric expression or the name of a field containing a numeric value.

Example: If the field Price contains 125.99, the following expression returns 125:

```
Floor(Price)
```

See also: Ceiling, Truncate, Int

Int

Purpose: Returns the integer portion of a numeric expression. This portion is the part to the left of the decimal point. The portion to the right, if any, is simply dropped.

Syntax: Int (*expression*)

where *expression* is a numeric expression or a field containing a numeric value.

Example: The expression Int (Pi) is equal to 3.

See also: Round, Truncate

Lg

Purpose: Returns the binary (base 2) logarithm of the expression.

Syntax: Lg (*expression*)

where *expression* is a positive numeric expression or the name of a field containing a positive numeric value.

Example: The following expression returns 6:

```
Lg(64)
```

See also: Ln, Log

Ln

Purpose: Returns the Naperian (natural) (base e) logarithm of the expression.

Syntax: Ln (*expression*)

where *expression* is a positive numeric expression or the name of a field containing a positive numeric value.

Example: The following expression returns 0.99999998 (to eight decimals):

```
Ln(2.7182818)
```

See also: Lg, Log

Log

Purpose: Returns the decimal (base 10) logarithm of the expression.

Syntax: Log (*expression*)

where *expression* is a positive numeric expression or the name of a field containing a positive numeric value.

Example: The following expression returns 6:

```
Log(100000)
```

See also: Ln, Lg

Mod

Purpose: Performs modulo arithmetic, which returns the remainder when a given number or expression is divided by another number.

Syntax: Mod (*expression, divisor*)

where *expression* is a numeric expression or numeric field, indicating the number to be divided, and *divisor* is a numeric expression or numeric field, indicating the number by which to divide. (Note that the expression determines the sign of the result. If the expression is positive, the result is positive; if the expression is negative, the result is negative.)

Example: The following expression is equal to 1, which is the integer remainder when 10 is divided by 3:

```
Mod(10;3)
```

Random

Purpose: This function returns a random value in the range 0–1, inclusive. This function takes no arguments.

Syntax: Random

Example: The following expression yields a random integer between 1–52, inclusive:

```
Int(52 * Random) + 1
```

Such a number might represent a card drawn from a standard deck of playing cards.

Any of the following conditions causes the generation of a new random number:

- ✦ A new record is created.
- ✦ The Random function is newly assigned to a formula.
- ✦ Data is changed in any of the fields that are referenced by the formula containing the Random function.

Round

Purpose: Rounds off a numeric result to the specified number of decimal places.

Syntax: Round (*expression*; *places*)

where *expression* is a numeric expression or a field that contains a numeric value, and *places* is a numeric expression that indicates the number of decimal places to retain. A negative places parameter rounds to the left of the decimal point: For example, Round(1234; 2) returns 1,200.

Example: The following expression returns the value of Pi to four decimals, or 3.1416.

```
Round(Pi;4)
```

See also: Int, Truncate

SetPrecision

Purpose: Evaluates any mathematical expression to the specified number of decimal places (up to 400). This does not include trigonometric functions.

Syntax: SetPrecision (*expression* ; *precision*)

where *expression* is a numeric expression or the name of a field containing a numeric value, and *precision* is an integer.

Example: The following expression returns 6.66667:

```
SetPrecision(20/3 ; 5)
```

See also: Round, Truncate

Sign

Purpose: Returns one of three values, depending on the value of the expression. If the expression is greater than zero (positive), Sign is equal to 1. If the expression is equal to 0, Sign is also equal to 0. If the expression is less than 0, Sign is equal to –1.

Syntax: Sign (*expression*)

where *expression* is a numeric expression or a field containing a numeric value.

Example: The expression Sign (163) has the value 1.

See also: Abs

Sqrt

Purpose: Returns the square root of the given expression. The square root is the number which, when squared, equals the original expression.

Syntax: Sqrt (*expression*)

where *expression* is a numeric expression or a field containing a numeric value.

Example: The expression Sqrt (9) is equal to 3.

Other roots can be extracted by using the exponentiation operator (^). The *n*th root of a number is equal to that number raised to the reciprocal of n. Thus, the cube (or third) root of 27 can be calculated using the expression: 27 ^ (*f* ⅓).

Truncate

Purpose: Returns a number that is truncated to the specified number of decimal places. Numbers in additional decimal places (to the right) are dropped, not rounded off.

Syntax: Truncate (*number, precision*)

where *number* is a numeric expression or a field containing a numeric value, and *precision* is the number of decimal places.

Example: The expression Truncate (9.75621; 3) returns 9.756. The expression Truncate (9.75621; 10) returns 9.75621. (Because the additional decimal places do not exist, the original number is returned.) Similarly, Truncate(321; –2) returns 300.

See also: Int, Round

Repeating Functions

Repeating functions enable you to convert a normal field so it can be treated as a repeating field in a calculation, reference a particular repetition in a repeating field, or find the last valid entry in a repeating field.

The repeating functions are as follows:

- ✦ Extend
- ✦ GetRepetition
- ✦ Last

Extend

Purpose: Extends a nonrepeating field for use in calculations with repeating fields. Every value in the extended field is identical; that is, the original value is simply duplicated.

Syntax: Extend (*nonrepeating field name*)

where *nonrepeating field name* is the name of a valid, single-entry field.

Example: The following expression enables you to calculate series of tax amounts, where Prices is a repeating field, and TaxRate is a normal field that contains the state sales tax rate:

```
Prices * Extend(TaxRate)
```

GetRepetition

Purpose: Enables you to obtain the value of a specific repetition in a repeating field.

Syntax: GetRepetition (*repeating field name*; *repetition number*)

where *repeating field name* is the name of a valid, nonempty repeating field of any type, and *repetition number* is the number of the specific repetition within the field.

Example: If Prices is a numeric repeating field containing three values, 5.5, 10, and 30, the expression GetRepetition (Prices; 2) returns 10 (the value in the second repetition).

See also: Last

Last

Purpose: Finds the last valid, nonempty entry in a repeating field. The entry is returned in the appropriate format.

Syntax: Last (*repeating field name*)

where *repeating field name* is the name of a valid, nonempty repeating field of any type.

Example: If Prices is a numeric repeating field containing the values 5, 10, and 30, the following expression

```
"The last item you ordered cost $" & Last(Prices)
```

yields the following result:

```
The last item you ordered cost $30.00
```

See also: GetRepetition

Summary Functions

FileMaker Pro 8 contains only one summary function: GetSummary.

GetSummary

Purpose: Returns the values for a particular Summary field when the database is sorted by the break (grouping) field.

Syntax: GetSummary (*summary field; break field*)

where *summary field* is the name of the Summary field, and *break field* is the name of the field that is used to group the records (the *when sorted by* field). The break field can be a Text, Number, Date, Time, or Calculation field.

Example: Suppose you want to see year-to-date sales totals for the individual members of your company's sales force. After the database has been sorted by the Salesperson field, the following expression displays a different value for the Sales Total field for each salesperson in the database:

```
GetSummary (Sales Total; Salesperson)
```

Note   To display a grand total for a Summary field rather than individual subtotals, use the name of the Summary field as both arguments to the function:

```
GetSummary (Sales Total; Sales Total)
```

Text Functions

Text functions are used to compare text strings and to extract pieces of text strings. They can also be used to insert text into a string.

The text functions are as follows:

- ✦ Exact
- ✦ Filter
- ✦ FilterValues
- ✦ GetAsCSS
- ✦ GetAsDate
- ✦ GetAsNumber
- ✦ GetAsSVG
- ✦ GetAsText
- ✦ GetAsTime
- ✦ GetAsTimestamp
- ✦ Hiragana
- ✦ KanaHankaku
- ✦ KanaZenkaku

- ✦ KanjiNumeral
- ✦ Katakana
- ✦ Left
- ✦ LeftValues
- ✦ LeftWords
- ✦ Length
- ✦ Lower
- ✦ Middle
- ✦ MiddleValues
- ✦ MiddleWords
- ✦ NumToJText
- ✦ PatternCount
- ✦ Position
- ✦ Proper
- ✦ Replace
- ✦ Right
- ✦ RightValues
- ✦ RightWords
- ✦ RomanHankaku
- ✦ RomanZenkaku
- ✦ SerialIncrement
- ✦ Substitute
- ✦ Trim
- ✦ TrimAll
- ✦ Upper
- ✦ ValueCount
- ✦ WordCount

Exact

Purpose: Compares two text expressions or fields and determines whether they are exactly the same. The comparison is case-sensitive, so capitalization counts. The returned result is a logical value: true (1) if the two strings are exactly the same, false (0) if they are not.

Syntax: Exact (*first text; comparison text*)

where *first text* and *comparison text* are Text fields, expressions, or constants.

Note   To create a text constant—such as Saturday, in the following example—you must surround it with quotation marks.

Example: The following expression is true if today's date is July 29, 2006:

```
Exact(DayName(Get(CurrentDate)); "Monday")
```

Tip   You can adapt the Exact function to perform a test that isn't case-sensitive. Use either the Upper or Lower function to convert both text strings to all uppercase or lowercase, as in:

```
Exact(Upper(Field1); Upper(Field2))
```

See also: Position

Filter

Purpose: Returns the characters in *text,* in order of occurrence, that also exist in *filter.*

Syntax: Filter (*text; filter*)

where *text* is a text expression or text field, and *filter* is a text expression or field. This is a handy way to strip formatting characters from phone numbers, dollar amounts, and so on.

Example: The expression Filter ("(800) 555-1212"; "0123456789") yields 8005551212.

See also: FilterValues

FilterValues

Purpose: Returns the values in *text,* in order of occurrence, that also exist in *filter.*

Syntax: Filter (*text; filter*)

where *text* is a text expression or text field, and *filter* is a text expression or field. Values are delimited by carriage returns.

Example: The expression Filter ("Red¶Green¶Blue"; "Blue¶Red") yields Red¶Blue.

See also: Filter

GetAsCSS

Purpose: Returns the specified text expression or field, formatted per CSS (Cascading Style Sheet) standards.

Syntax: GetAsCSS (*text*)

where *text* is a text expression or text field.

Example: Assuming that the Field is formatted as 18-point Arial, italic, and blue on your layout and contains the text Spenser, GetAsCSS(theField) would return

```
<SPAN STYLE = "font-family: 'Arial'; font-size: 18px;
color:#0000FF; font-style: italic; text-align: left;", Begin:
1, End: 7>Spenser</SPAN>
```

See also: GetAsSVG

GetAsDate

Purpose: Changes a text date value directly into date format. The supplied text must be in the same format as the date format on the machine being used for this function to work correctly.

Syntax: GetAsDate (*text*)

where *text* is a text constant or text expression in date format.

Example: The following expression converts a text constant into date format:

```
GetAsDate ("11/18/2005")
```

This expression yields the following result in date format:

```
11/18/2005
```

See also: GetAsNumber, GetAsTime, GetAsTimestamp

Note   GetAsDate is a good way to enter a date constant into a formula requiring a date parameter, such as DayofYear and DayName.

GetAsNumber

Purpose: Converts the number part of a text expression into numeric format. The non-numeric characters are ignored.

Syntax: GetAsNumber (*text*)

where *text* is a text constant or a text expression.

Example: The following example defines a Calculation field in which non-numeric data — such as a dollar sign and commas — are stripped from a price:

```
GetAsNumber(Price)
```

If the information in Price (a Text field) had been entered as $19,995.95, the Calculation field would contain 19995.95.

See also: Filter

GetAsSVG

Purpose: Returns the specified text expression or field, formatted per SVG (Scalable Vector Graphics) standards.

Syntax: GetAsSVG (*text*)

where *text* is a text expression or text field.

Example: Assuming that the Field is formatted as 18-point Arial, italic, and blue on your layout and contains the text Spenser, GetAsSVG(theField) would return:

```
<StyleList>
<Style#0>"font-family: 'Arial'; font-size: 18px; color:#0000FF; font-style:
italic; text-align: left;", Begin: 1, End: 7</Style>
</StyleList>
<Data> <Span style="0">Spenser</Span></Data>
```

See also: GetAsCSS

GetAsText

Purpose: Converts numeric, date, time, timestamp, or container values to a text string.

Syntax: GetAsText (*data*)

where *data* is any numeric, date, time, timestamp expression or a number, date, time, timestamp, or container field.

Example: The following expression, if the field currentAge contains 54, returns 54 as text.

```
GetAsText (currentAge)
```

GetAsTime

Purpose: Converts a text value or expression into time format. The results can then be passed on to a calculation that requires data in time format.

Syntax: GetAsTime (*text*)

where *text* is a text constant or text expression. The data supplied must be in the form HH:MM:SS. Seconds are optional, and AM and PM may be used as suffixes.

Example: The following expression yields 14:15:00:

```
GetAsTime ("2:15 pm")
```

Tip   The formatting of the converted text is initially determined by the result type that you select. If you select Time as the result type, the result returned is 2:15 p.m. rather than the military time format used when Text is selected as the result type.

See also: GetAsTimestamp, GetAsDate

GetAsTimestamp

Purpose: Converts a text value or expression into time format. The results can then be passed on to a calculation that requires data in timestamp format.

Syntax: GetAsTimestamp (*text*)

where *text* is a text constant or text expression, formatted as a date followed by a time. A single integer is interpreted as the number of seconds since 00:00:00 on 01/01/0001.

Example: The following expression yields 5/28/2002 14:15:00:

```
GetAsTimestamp ("05/28/2002 2:15 pm")
```

See also: GetAsTime, GetAsDate

Hiragana

Purpose: Converts Katakana (Zenkaku and Hankaku) into Hiragana.

Syntax: Hiragana (*text*)

where *text* is a text expression or text field.

See also: Katakana, KanaHankaku, KanaZenkaku

KanaHankaku

Purpose: Converts Zenkaku Katakana into Hankaku Katakana.

Syntax: KanaHankaku (*text*)

where *text* is a text expression or text field.

See also: Katakana, Hiragana, KanaZenkaku

KanaZenkaku

Purpose: Converts Hankaku Katakana into Zenkaku Katakana.

Syntax: KanaZenkaku (*text*)

where *text* is a text expression or text field.

See also: Katakana, KanaHankaku, Hiragana

KanjiNumeral

Purpose: Converts Arabic numerals into Kanji numerals.

Syntax: KanjiNumeral (*text*)

where *text* is a text expression or text field.

See also: Filter

Katakana

Purpose: Converts Hiragana into Zenkaku Katakana.

Syntax: Katakana (*text*)

where *text* is a text expression or text field.

See also: Hiragana, KanaHankaku, KanaZenkaku

Left

Purpose: Returns a text result equaling the left-most part of a given Text field or expression, including only the specified number of characters.

Syntax: Left (*text*; *number*)

where *text* is a text expression or text from which the left-most part is to be taken, and *number* is a numeric expression or field specifying how many characters to use.

Example: The expression Left ("photocopy"; 5) yields photo.

See also: LeftWords, Right, Middle

LeftValues

Purpose: Returns the first *number* of values found in *text*. Values are carriage-return-delimited strings.

Syntax: LeftValues (*text*; *number*)

where *text* is a text expression or text from which the left-most (beginning) part is to be taken, and *number* is a numeric expression or field specifying how many values to use.

Example: LeftValues ("Red¶Orange¶Yellow¶Green¶Blue¶Indigo¶Violet"; 3) returns Red¶Orange¶Yellow.

See also: FilterValues, MiddleValues, RightValues

LeftWords

Purpose: Returns a text result that equals the left-most part of a given Text field or expression, including only the specified number of words.

Syntax: LeftWords (*text*; *number*)

where *text* is a text expression or text from which the left-most part is to be taken, and *number* is a numeric expression or field specifying how many words to use.

Example: LeftWords ("The worst years of your life"; 3) returns The worst years.

See also: RightWords, MiddleWords, Left

Length

Purpose: Returns a numeric result that indicates the number of characters the specified text contains. When text length is calculated, alphanumeric characters, spaces, numbers, and special characters all contribute to the total.

Syntax: Length (*text*)

where *text* is a text expression, constant, or field that contains a text value.

Example: The expression Length ("photocopy") returns 9.

See also: Trim

Lower

Purpose: Converts the specified text string into all lowercase letters.

Syntax: Lower (*text*)

where *text* is a text expression, constant, or field containing a text value.

Example: The expression Lower ("PrintMonitor") yields printmonitor.

See also: Upper, Proper

Middle

Purpose: Extracts a specified number of characters from a given text string, starting at a certain position.

Syntax: Middle (*text*; *start*; *number of characters*)

where *text* is a Text field, text constant, or text expression; *start* is a numeric value indicating where to begin extracting characters; and *number of characters* is a numeric value indicating how many characters to extract.

Example: The following expression returns the letter Q:

```
Middle("John Q. Public"; 6; 1)
```

Tip   Remember that spaces are characters, too.

See also: Left, Right, MiddleWords

MiddleValues

Purpose: Returns the *number* of values, starting with the specified *startValue,* found in *text.* Values are carriage return-delimited strings.

Syntax: MiddleValues (*text*; *startValue*; *number*)

where *text* is a text expression or text from which part is to be taken; *startValue* is a number, numeric expression, or field containing a numeric value indicating the value (paragraph) at which to start extracting; and *number* is a numeric expression or field specifying how many values to use.

Example: MiddleValues ("Red¶Orange¶Yellow¶Green¶Blue¶Indigo¶Violet"; 3; 3) returns Yellow¶Green¶Blue.

See also: FilterValues, LeftValues, RightValues

MiddleWords

Purpose: Enables you to extract a consecutive group of words from any text string, regardless of the starting position of the target word group.

Syntax: MiddleWords (*text*; *starting word*; *number*)

where *text* is the text expression or text from which the specified portion is to be extracted; *starting word* is a numeric expression or field that contains the number of the first word to be extracted; and *number* is a numeric expression or field specifying how many words to extract.

Example: The expression MiddleWords ("Baby animals must fend for themselves"; 2; 3) returns animals must fend.

See also: RightWords, LeftWords, Middle

NumToJText

Purpose: Converts Roman (Arabic numerals) numbers to Japanese text.

Syntax: NumToJText (*number*; *separator*; *characterType*)

where *number* is a numeric expression or field; *separator* is a number from 0–3 representing a separator type; and *characterType* is a number from 0–3 indicating whether to use Hanakaku (0), Zenkaku (1), Kanji (2), or Traditional Kanji (3) characters.

See also: KanjiNumeral

PatternCount

Purpose: Returns the number of instances that a specified text string is found within another text string or field.

Syntax: PatternCount (*text; pattern*)

where *text* is the text expression or text to be searched, and *pattern* is the particular text string for which you are searching.

Example: The expression PatternCount ("You are the apple of my eye"; "e") returns 5 because there are 5 e's in the text string.

Position

Purpose: Scans a specified text expression in an attempt to locate a particular instance of a search string, starting at a given position, and returns a numeric value equal to the position at which the search string starts within the larger string. If the search string is not found, the result is zero.

Syntax: Position (*text; search string; start; occurrence*)

where *text* is a text constant, field, or expression in which to search; *search string* is the text for which to search; *start* is a number that indicates at what character position to begin the search; and *occurrence* is a number, numeric expression, or field containing a number that indicates the particular occurrence of the string you want to find.

Examples: The expression Position ("bewitching beauty"; "be"; 1; 1) returns 1; Position ("bewitching beauty"; "be"; 1; 2) returns 12, as does Position ("bewitching beauty"; "be"; 10; 1).

See also: LeftWords, RightWords, MiddleWords

Proper

Purpose: Returns a text string in which the first letter of each word of the supplied text expression has been capitalized; all others are converted to lowercase. Some word processing programs refer to this as *title case*.

> **Note** A true title case won't capitalize articles, conjunctions, or prepositions unless they are the first word of a sentence. That's why this isn't really a title case.

Syntax: Proper (*text*)

where *text* is a Text field, constant, or expression.

Example: The expression Proper ("SURF AND TURF") returns Surf And Turf.

See also: Upper, Lower

Replace

Purpose: Inserts a specified text string into another text string, starting at a specified position and replacing a given number of characters. The number of characters replaced need not be equal to the number inserted.

Syntax: Replace (*text*; *start*; *size*; *replacement text*)

where *text* is a Text field, constant, or expression; *start* is a numeric value indicating the position at which to begin replacing; *size* is a numeric value that indicates the number of characters to replace; and *replacement text* is a Text field, constant, or expression to insert in the place of the specified characters.

Example: The expression Replace ("Clinton R. Hicks"; 9; 2; "Robert") returns Clinton Robert Hicks.

See also: Substitute

Right

Purpose: Starting at the right, extracts the specified number of characters from the specified text expression.

Syntax: Right (*text*; *number*)

where *text* is a Text field, expression, or constant from which to extract characters, and *number* is a numeric value that indicates how many characters to extract.

Example: The expression Right ("Rosanna"; 4) returns anna.

See also: Left, Middle, RightWords

RightValues

Purpose: Returns the last *number* of values found in *text*. Values are carriage return-delimited strings.

Syntax: RightValues (*text*; *number*)

where *text* is a text expression or text from which the right-most (end) part is to be taken, and *number* is a numeric expression or field specifying how many values to use.

Example: RightValues ("Red¶Orange¶Yellow¶Green¶Blue¶Indigo¶Violet"; 3) returns Blue¶Indigo¶Violet.

See also: FilterValues, MiddleValues, RightValues

RightWords

Purpose: Returns a text result that equals the right-most part of a specified Text field or expression, including only the specified number of words.

Syntax: RightWords (*text; number*)

where *text* is a text expression or text from which the right-most part is to be taken, and *number* is a numeric expression or field specifying how many words to extract.

Example: The expression RightWords ("These are the best days of our lives"; 5) returns best days of our lives.

See also: LeftWords, MiddleWords

RomanHankaku

Purpose: Converts character symbols and numerals from Zenkaku to Hankaku.

Syntax: RomanHankaku (*text*)

where *text* is a text expression or text field.

See also: RomanZenkaku

RomanZenkaku

Purpose: Converts character symbols and numerals from Hankaku to Zenkaku.

Syntax: RomanZenkaku (*text*)

where *text* is a text expression or text field.

See also: RomanHankaku

SerialIncrement

Purpose: Convert the text string by incrementing the numeric portions by the specified amount.

Syntax: SerialIncrement (*text; number*)

where *text* is a text expression or text field, and *number* is a numeric expression or field specifying by how much the numeric portion should be incremented.

Example: SerialIncrement("Spenser-33BT34"; 100) would return Spenser-34BT34.

See also: Filter, GetAsNumber

Substitute

Purpose: Enables you to substitute one text string for another.

Syntax: Substitute (*text*; *search string*; *replacement string*)

where *text* is a text expression or Text field, *search string* is the text that is to be replaced, and *replacement string* is the text that is to be used as the replacement.

Example: The expression Substitute ("Paul was the walrus."; "Paul"; "I") returns I was the walrus.

See also: Replace

Trim

Purpose: Removes leading and trailing spaces from a text expression or field.

Syntax: Trim (*text*)

where *text* is a Text field, constant, or expression.

Example: The expression Trim ("   Johnny   ") returns Johnny (with no surrounding spaces).

See also: Left, Right, Middle, Position

Tip   Some programs and computer systems require a set number of characters per field. Unused spaces in such fields may be padded with blanks. You can use the Trim function to remove these blanks when you import data from such programs and systems.

TrimAll

Purpose: Removes leading, trailing, and (optionally) other spaces from a text expression or field.

Syntax: Trim (*text*; *trimSpaces*; *trimType*)

where *text* is a Text field, constant, or expression; *trimSpaces* is 0 or 1; and *trimType* indicates what trimming style you want to employ:

✦ 0 removes spaces between Roman and non-Roman characters.

✦ 1 leaves a half-space between non-Roman and Roman characters.

✦ 2 removes spaces between non-Roman characters (consolidating multiple spaces into a single space).

✦ 3 removes all spaces everywhere.

See also: Trim

Upper

Purpose: Converts a given text string into all uppercase letters.

Syntax: Upper (*text*)

where *text* is a Text field, constant, or expression.

Example: The expression Upper ("Honorable") returns HONORABLE.

See also: Lower, Proper

ValueCount

Purpose: Returns the number of values (paragraphs) in a text expression or field.

Syntax: ValueCount (*text*)

where *text* is a Text field, constant, or expression.

Example: The expression ValueCount ("Red¶Orange¶Yellow¶Green¶Blue¶Indigo¶Violet") returns 7.

See also: Left, Right, Middle, Position

WordCount

Purpose: Returns the total number of words in a text string.

Syntax: WordCount (*text*)

where *text* is a Text field or expression.

Example: The expression WordCount (Comments) returns the number of words in the Comments field.

Text Formatting Functions

The Text Formatting functions provide you with tools to change a text value's display font, color, size, and style.

The text formatting functions are as follows:

- ✦ RGB
- ✦ TextColor
- ✦ TextColorRemove
- ✦ TextFont
- ✦ TextFontRemove
- ✦ TextFormatRemove
- ✦ TextSize
- ✦ TextSizeRemove
- ✦ TextStyleAdd
- ✦ TextStyleRemove

RGB

Purpose: Combines red, green, and blue components to return a (24-bit) color value. The color value is the red component × 65,536 plus the green component times 256 plus the blue component. (0 is black, and 16777215 is white.)

Syntax: RGB (*red*; *green*; *blue*)

where *red*, *green*, and *blue* are numeric expressions between 0–255, inclusive.

Example: RGB(0; 255; 255) returns 65535.

TextColor

Purpose: Applies the specified color to the text when displayed.

Syntax: TextColor (*text*; *color*)

where *text* is a text field or expression, and *color* is an integer in the RGB color space.

Example: TextColor("Spenser"; RGB(0; 0; 0)) returns the word Spenser in black.

See also: TextColorRemove, TextFont, TextSize, RGB

TextColorRemove

Purpose: Removes all (or specified) color embellishments applied by calls to TextColor from the text when displayed.

Syntax: TextColorRemove (*text; color*)

where *text* is a text field or expression, and *color* is an integer in the RGB color space.

Example: TextColorRemove(Surname; RGB(255; 0; 0)) reverts anything in red within the Surname field to whatever color the Surname field has as its layout default.

See also: TextColor, TextFont, TextSize, RGB

TextFont

Purpose: Applies the specified font to the text when displayed.

Syntax: TextFont (*text; fontName {;fontScript}*)

where *text* is a text field or expression, *fontName* is the name of a font, and *fontScript* (optional) is the name of a character set containing the glyphs for writing in a given language. Font names are case-sensitive.

Example: TextFont("Spenser"; "Baskerville") returns the word Spenser in Baskerville font.

See also: TextColor, TextSize, RGB

TextFontRemove

Purpose: Removes font customizations applied by calls to TextFont.

Syntax: TextFontRemove (*text {; fontName ;fontScript}*)

where *text* is a text field or expression, *fontName* is the name of a font (optional), and *fontScript* (optional) is the name of a character set containing the glyphs for writing in a given language. Font names are case-sensitive.

Example: TextFont("Spenser"; "Baskerville") returns the word Spenser in the default font if it was in Baskerville or unchanged if it was in a different font.

See also: TextFont, TextColor, TextSize, RGB

TextFormatRemove

Purpose: Removes all formatting customizations from the referenced text.

Syntax: TextFormatRemove (*text*)

where *text* is a text field or expression.

Example: TextFormatRemove (Surname) removes all font, color, size, and style customizations from the Surname field to display it in the layout's default style.

See also: TextColor, TextFont, TextSize, RGB

TextSize

Purpose: Applies the specified size to the text when displayed.

Syntax: TextSize (*text*; *size*)

where *text* is a text field or expression and *size* is an integer representing the point size (72 points per inch).

Example: TextSize("Spenser"; 72) returns the word Spenser in 72-point type.

See also: TextFont, TextColor, RGB

TextSizeRemove

Purpose: Removes size customizations from the referenced text or field.

Syntax: TextSizeRemove (*text* {; *size*})

where *text* is a text field or expression and *size* is an (optional) integer representing the point size (72 points per inch).

Example: TextSizeRemove ("Spenser"; 72) returns the word Spenser with any 72-point customizations removed. In other words, if "Spenser" were currently displayed in 36-point type, nothing would change, but if any characters were in 72-point type, those characters would now display in whatever the default size for that layout element specifies.

See also: TextFont, TextColor, TextSize, RGB

TextStyleAdd

Purpose: Applies the specified styles (multiple styles can be enumerated, separated by plus signs) to the text when displayed.

Syntax: TextStyleAdd (*text*; *style*)

where *text* is a text field or expression, and *style* is an expression consisting of one or more style identifiers joined by plus signs.

Example: TextStyleAdd ("Spenser"; SmallCaps+Bold) returns the word Spenser.

See also: TextStyleRemove

TextStyleRemove

Purpose: Removes the specified styles (multiple styles can be enumerated, separated by plus signs) from the text's formatting when displayed.

Syntax: TextStyleRemove (*text*; *style*)

where *text* is a text field or expression, and *style* is an expression consisting of one or more style identifiers joined by plus signs.

Example: If you have a field, Name, set to display its contents as underlined, bold, in small caps and the record to be displayed contains Spenser in that field, TextStyleRemove (Name; Underline) returns the word Spenser.

See also: TextStyleAdd

Time Functions

The Time functions are analogous to the Date functions described earlier in this appendix. You can use them to extract elements from a time expression or to convert number results into valid times, even if the numbers don't fall into the 0–60 and 0–24 ranges normally required for minutes and hours.

The time functions are as follows:

✦ Hour

✦ Minute

✦ Seconds

✦ Time

Hour

Purpose: Extracts the hour part of a time expression or field, yielding a numeric result.

Syntax: Hour (*time*)

where *time* is a Time field or expression.

Example: If Current is a time field containing 12:30 PM, the expression Hour (Current) is equal to 12. If the field contained 12:30 AM, on the other hand, the result would be 0.

See also: Minute, Seconds

Minute

Purpose: Extracts the minute part of a time expression or field, yielding a numeric result.

Syntax: Minute (*time*)

where *time* is a Time field or expression.

Example: If Current is a Time field containing 8:23:17, the expression Minute (Current) returns 23.

See also: Hour, Seconds

Seconds

Purpose: Extracts the seconds part of a time expression or field, yielding a numeric result.

Syntax: Seconds (*time*)

where *time* is a Time field or expression.

Example: If Current is a Time field containing 8:23:17 PM, the expression Seconds (Current) yields 17.

See also: Hour, Minute

 Tip

The Hour, Minute, and Seconds functions can be used together to obtain the decimal equivalent of a time value. You must divide the Minute result by 60 and the Seconds result by 3,600, as shown in the following expression:

```
Hour(Current)+(Minute(Current)/60)+(Seconds(Current)/3600)
```

Time

Purpose: Returns a time value containing the specified number of hours, minutes, and seconds counted from midnight. The function compensates for fractional values, extracting seconds from fractional minutes and minutes from fractional hours.

Syntax: Time (*hours*; *minutes*; *seconds*)

where

- ✦ *hours* is a numeric expression indicating the number of hours.
- ✦ *minutes* is a numeric expression indicating the number of minutes.
- ✦ *seconds* is a numeric expression indicating the number of seconds.

Example: The expression Time (13; 70; 71) is equal to 2:11:11 p.m.

See also: Date

Timestamp Functions

The lone Timestamp function is analogous to the Date or Time functions described earlier in this appendix. You can use to convert date and time results into valid timestamps.

The time function is Timestamp.

Timestamp

Purpose: Returns a timestamp value resulting from combining date and time arguments.

Syntax: Timestamp (*aDate*; *aTime*)

where

- ✦ *aDate* is a properly formed Date value.
- ✦ *aTime* is a properly formed Time value.

Example: The expression Timestamp (Date(3; 20; 2006); Time (19; 20; 00)) is returns 3/20/2006 7:20:00 p.m.

See also: Date, Time

Trigonometric Functions

This group of functions enables you to work with angles, degrees, and other geometric data. Note that the trigonometric functions are designed to work in radians. (There are 2π radians in 360 degrees.) You can use the Degrees function to convert radian results into degrees.

The trigonometric functions are as follows:

- ✦ Atan
- ✦ Cos
- ✦ Degrees
- ✦ Pi
- ✦ Radians
- ✦ Sin
- ✦ Tan

Atan

Purpose: Returns the arc tangent (in radians) of the specified expression.

Syntax: Atan (*number*)

where *number* is a Number field, numeric expression, or constant. The returned value is between $-\pi$ and π.

Example: The expression Atan (Pi) is equal to 1.2626, rounded to four decimal places.

See also: Tan, Degrees

Cos

Purpose: Gives the cosine of the specified expression (assumed to be provided in radians).

Syntax: Cos (*number*)

where *number* is a Number field, numeric expression, or constant — in radians.

Example: The expression Cos (Pi) is equal to –1.

See also: Sin, Degrees

Degrees

Purpose: Converts a value given in radians into degrees. There are 2π radians in 360 degrees.

Syntax: Degrees (*number*)

where *number* is a Number field, numeric expression, or constant — in radians.

Example: The expression Degrees (Pi) is equal to 180.

See also: Radians

Pi

Purpose: Returns the value of the mathematical constant pi. *pi* is defined as the ratio of a circle's circumference to its diameter. It is an irrational/transcendental number (one whose fractional part neither repeats nor terminates). This function takes no arguments.

Syntax: Pi

Example: If R is equal to 2, the following expression is approximately equal to 12.57:

```
Pi * R ^ 2
```

This expression gives the area of a circle with a radius equal to R.

Radians

Purpose: Converts a value in degrees into radians, for use with calculations expecting a value in that form.

Syntax: Radians (*number*)

where *number* is a Number field, constant, or expression containing a value expressed in degrees.

Example: The expression Cos (Radians (45)) is equal to 0.707, rounded to three decimal places.

See also: Degrees

Sin

Purpose: Returns the sine of the given expression, interpreted as an angle expressed in radians.

Syntax: Sin (*number*)

where *number* is a Number field, constant, or expression given in radians.

Example: The expression Sin (Pi) is equal to 0.

See also: Cos

Tan

Purpose: Returns the tangent of the specified angle, assumed to be expressed in radians.

Syntax: Tan (*number*)

where *number* is a numeric field, constant, or expression given in radians. Avoid odd multiples of pi/2 because that involves dividing by zero — and meaningless, large values will be returned.

Example: The expression Tan (Pi) is equal to 0.

See also: Atan

✦   ✦   ✦

Glossary

Although this book assumes you're familiar with the basics of operating a computer (using the mouse, choosing menu commands, selecting objects and text, and printing), everyone can use a little help now and then. This glossary includes definitions of some additional common terms that you might run into while using FileMaker Pro and reading this book.

access privileges Activities a user is allowed to perform after opening a database using a particular account.

account A name (and, usually, an associated password) that allows access to a database and specifies the access privileges and extended privileges the account user possesses.

Admin The default account name (without an initial password) provided with access to a newly created database. The Admin account has Full Access privileges. Any account assigned the Full Access privilege set is considered an Admin account. See also *Full Access*.

alert A program or system software dialog that notifies you when something important has occurred or is about to happen. See also *dialog*.

algorithm A series of steps for accomplishing a specific task.

alias A Macintosh stand-in icon for a program, file, folder, or disk. Double-clicking an alias results in the same action that occurs when you double-click the original icon. Under Windows, *shortcuts* serve similar functions to Macintosh aliases.

alphanumeric data Information consisting of letters of the alphabet, numbers, or a mixture of the two (for example, 1911 Oak Street).

Apple menu (🍎) The menu at the far left side of the Macintosh menu bar. System-wide choices (independent of the frontmost application) can be found in the Apple menu. See also *Dock*.

AppleEvents Messages sent between Macintosh applications that enable the applications to interact. An application can also send AppleEvents to itself. See also *AppleScript*.

AppleScript A programming language from Apple Computer (Macintosh only) that enables within- and between-program communications via AppleEvents. See also *AppleEvents*.

Application menu Found to the immediate right of the Apple menu in the Macintosh's menu bar, this menu bears the name of the current (frontmost) application and lists application-wide commands, such as Quit and Preferences.

archive An archival copy of one or more files; frequently compressed. Archives can be created to save disk space, to reduce the time it takes to transmit (upload) and receive (download) the files by modem, or to serve simply as a backup copy (a personal safety net). See also *self-extracting archive*.

argument A value supplied to a function from which the function's value is calculated. See also *expression* and *function*.

arrow keys Keys on a standard keyboard that when pressed, move the text insertion cursor within a FileMaker Pro database field or move a selected object when in Layout mode.

ascending sort A sorting order that starts with the smallest or oldest value and ends with the largest or most recent value. For numbers, values begin with the smallest value and proceed in numerical order. For text, values are arranged according to the current language's collating sequence (ASCII for English, for example). Dates and times are sorted in chronological order. See also *descending sort*.

ASCII Abbreviation for *American Standard Code for Information Interchange;* a code that associates a numerical value (0–255) with a character or control code. Control codes, letters, punctuation, and numbers are found in codes 0–127. Codes 128–255 (commonly referred to as *Extended ASCII*) consist of symbols and foreign language characters. See also *Extended ASCII* and *Unicode*.

auto-entered value A value, text string, date, calculation, or other item that is automatically entered into a particular field when a new record is created. You specify auto-entry options for a field when you wish to establish a default entry.

auto-entry field A database field that FileMaker Pro automatically fills in for each new or modified record.

auto-incrementing field A field that is automatically filled in when you create a new record. The entry in the field is based on an increment over the contents of that field in the previous record. This feature is useful for generating new invoice numbers, check numbers, record numbers, and so on. See also *Serial Number field.*

Avery A manufacturer of specialized stock for printing a variety of labels, including disk and address labels.

backup *n:* An exact copy of a file (folder or disk).

back up *v:* To create a duplicate of one or more files.

bitmap A collection of individual picture elements (pixels or dots) that together constitute a graphic item. See also *pixmap.*

body A FileMaker Pro layout part typically containing the bulk of any given record's data.

book An icon in a FileMaker Pro database window's status area. In Browse mode, you use the book to flip through database records. In Find mode, the book is used to view multiple Find requests. In Layout mode, it is used to view different database layouts. In Preview mode, the book enables you to see additional pages of the current report.

Boolean A type of algebra in which expressions are evaluated for their truth values. Results are either true or false.

browsed records Those records in a FileMaker Pro database that are currently visible (not hidden). See also *found set.*

button (1) An object in a FileMaker Pro database layout having a script or script step associated with it. Clicking the button makes the script action or series of actions occur. (2) A user interface element found in many dialogs and windows that you click to select, confirm, or cancel an action.

cache An area in the computer's memory set aside for temporarily storing data that is on its way to and from a disk. Using a cache can greatly speed up operations because RAM is much faster to access than a disk.

Calculation field A field type used to generate within-record computations. Formulas in Calculation fields can reference other fields in the current record or related records, use FileMaker Pro's built-in functions, and contain constants.

check box A small box associated with an option in a dialog or a type of field format in a FileMaker Pro layout. Clicking the box changes the state of the option from selected to deselected (and vice versa). Normally, you can select multiple check boxes.

click To press the mouse button once and then immediately release it. See also *double-click*.

client Any user (identified by the computer he or she is using) who opens a shared database after the host has opened it. See also *guest* and *host*.

Clipboard An area in memory that is used to store the most recently copied (⌘+C/Ctrl+C) or cut (⌘+X/Ctrl+X) object or text string. The contents of the Clipboard can be pasted (⌘+V/Ctrl+V) into other locations in the same document, another document, or even into the document of another application.

clone An exact copy of a database—including all layouts, field definitions, and scripts—but without records. A clone is used as the basis for a new, empty database. FileMaker often refers to clones as *templates*.

Close button/box The tiny red button in the upper-left corner of some Macintosh windows or the tiny x in the upper-right corner of some Windows windows that when clicked, closes or dismisses the window and any document it contains.

conditional test A logical test that when executed, causes a script to take a particular action, depending on the result of the test.

constant A value *guest*—typically within a calculation—that does not change. Pi, e, and 274 are all examples of constants.

constrain To reduce the found set by adding additional Find criteria. (Essentially, constraining the found set is the same as performing an AND search.) See also *extend*.

Container field FileMaker Pro fields of this type can be used to store graphics, QuickTime movies and audio, OLE objects, sound clips, or other files.

cosine The cosine of an angle is the ratio of the adjacent side in a right triangle to the hypotenuse, where the adjacent side and hypotenuse form the angle in question.

crash The cessation of functioning by a computer or a program. Signs that a computer has crashed include system dialogs on the Macintosh (which often suggest that the ". . . application has unexpectedly quit"), General Protection Fault error messages under Windows, and keyboard and mouse lock-ups.

current field The database field that is presently selected (by tabbing or clicking in the field). Only the current field can be modified.

current record The record that is presently selected. Only the current record can be modified.

cursor An onscreen indicator that moves in response to movements you make with the mouse or another pointing device. The cursor changes its shape to reflect the activity you are currently performing.

database An organized collection of information, normally with one central topic.

database program (or database management program or DBMS) A program for entering, editing, and otherwise managing data records.

Data Entry One of three predefined privilege sets. An account with this privilege set can create, view, edit, and delete records; execute scripts; print; export; and access menu commands. The account cannot create nor modify layouts, scripts, or value lists.

data-entry keys Keys (such as the alphabetic, numeric, and punctuation keys) that when pressed, add data at the insertion point. See also *modifier key*.

data validation User-specified criteria that instruct the database program to check a particular field's contents for allowable and unacceptable data. Validation criteria can include range checking and required fields, for example.

DDE Abbreviation for *Dynamic Data Exchange;* a Windows-based command sent to a program, instructing it to perform one or more specific commands. FileMaker Pro for Windows can send DDE commands (via the DDE Execute script step) but cannot receive them.

default The initial "factory setting" for a changeable value. This setting determines how an option or preference behaves if you never change the setting.

default value A value that is automatically entered in a field when you create a new record. Using a default value saves typing time and ensures that information is entered consistently.

descending sort A sorting order that starts with the largest (or most recent) value and ends with the smallest (or oldest) value. An alphabetic sort in descending order begins with Z. See also *ascending sort*.

Desktop The main work area on the computer screen.

dialog A special type of window that applications and the system software use to present information and instructions enabling you to make choices and supply additional information. See also *alert*.

dimmed command A menu command that cannot presently be selected usually because it is irrelevant to the current operation. Dimmed items are also referred to as *grayed-out* and can appear in dialogs as well as in menus.

Dock On a Macintosh, the Dock serves as a launcher for frequently used programs, documents, and system utilities and an indicator of which programs are currently running. Whenever you launch a program or minimize a document, an icon for that program or document appears on the Dock. To view that particular program or document, you can click its icon on the Dock. (In Windows, the taskbar, tray, and Start menu perform similar functions to the Dock.)

dot matrix A type of printer technology in which a print head that has many pins, each corresponding to one picture element (pixel or dot), is passed rapidly over a page, hammering out an impression through a ribbon. This type of printer is becoming more rare as inkjet printer prices continue to drop. Dot matrix, however, is still the primary technology employed for dealing with multipart forms.

double-click To press the mouse button twice in rapid succession. See also *click*.

download The process of using a modem or network connection to retrieve a program or document file from the Internet, an online information service, a bulletin board system, or another user's computer. See also *upload*.

drag To hold down the mouse button while moving the mouse pointer.

drag and drop Applications that support drag-and-drop technology enable you to drag text and graphics from one place in a document to another, from one document to another, as well as between documents in different applications. In essence, drag and drop is simply a direct way of accomplishing a single cut-and-paste or copy-and-paste operation without using the Clipboard as an intermediary.

drop-down list A user interface element, common on Windows but used more sparingly in Mac OS (where pop-up menus are more frequently employed for the same purpose), allowing you to type in a text box or click an adjoining button to choose from a list of options. See also *pop-up menu*.

export To create a file in one program that can be read by other programs. To ensure compatibility with the program that will receive the data, most programs that export data can write it in a number of different file formats. See also *import*.

expression A statement consisting of one or more operators (such as + or * or &) joining at least two variables or constants. See also *argument, constant, function,* and *variable*.

extend Working from the current found set or browsed records, you can expand the set by adding additional Find criteria. (Essentially, expanding the found set is the same as performing an OR search.) See also *constrain*.

Extended ASCII Any ASCII character with a value higher than 127 but less than 256; the upper half of the ASCII character set. Special symbols and foreign language characters are found in Extended ASCII. See also *ASCII* and *Unicode*.

extended privileges A set of values describing methods by which a database can be accessed. Examples are Network, Web, and Mobile.

External A function used to invoke other functions — those supported by installed plug-ins. The functions supported by plug-ins written specifically for FileMaker Pro 7 or later do not require the External function for invocation.

external script A script in another FileMaker Pro database file that is executed via the Perform Script step. When an external script is performed in this manner, the database containing the script automatically opens. See also *internal script.*

field The building blocks of which database records are composed. Each field is meant to store one particular type of information, such as a Social Security number or a birth date. See also *field type.*

field type Set in the Define Database dialog's Fields pane, a field type specifies the type of information a particular field is intended to collect and display. Some common field types are Text, Number, Date, and Time. The main reason for declaring field types is to enable the database program to screen for invalid data so it can warn you if, for example, you have entered something other than a date in a Date field.

file Any named collection of information or instructions that is stored on disk. Programs, documents, and system software components are examples of files.

file dialog Any dialog designed to enable file-handling tasks, such as opening, saving, importing, and exporting files.

file format A specification for the way data is stored on disk and interpreted. The file format determines which particular programs can open and interpret the data.

file reference A collection (carriage return-delimited list) of paths FileMaker Pro will search to locate an external file, table, script, or value list. The first one found terminates the search.

filter To extract a data subset. For example, you can filter a text field to extract just the numeric portions (for example, extracting *1234* from *Ab1cde2fg34*).

Find A FileMaker Pro mode for locating a record or group of records based on criteria you establish. For example, you might want to find the address record for Ames Corporation or identify the records of all salespeople who earned more than $40,000 last year. Most database programs — including FileMaker Pro — enable you to set multiple criteria when performing a Find. Some other applications (such as Excel) call such operations *filtering*. See also *Find request.*

Find request A set of search criteria entered on a single FileMaker Pro layout. One Find request can consist of a single search criterion (Sales > 15000) or multiple criteria (an AND search, such as Sales > 15000 *and* Division = "St. Louis"). To conduct an OR search—in which at least one set of criteria must be satisfied—you create multiple Find requests. See also *Find.*

flat-file database A flat-file database consists of a single table in a single file. Every field that is necessary must be contained in that table. See also *relational database program.*

folder A holder of documents, applications, and other folders on a given disk, CD, or other computer data storage medium. Also called a *directory.*

footer A FileMaker Pro layout part appearing at the bottom of every record or report page. Page numbers and the current date are frequently placed in the footer. If you want to put special information on just the first or cover page of a report, use a Title Footer part. See also *header.*

Force Quit command A Macintosh keyboard command (⌘+Option+Esc) you can use to present a dialog where you can select a program to quit. Option+Control+ clicking an application's Dock icon offers a Force Quit option in the menu that appears. The equivalent command under Windows is Ctrl+Alt+Delete, which gives you an option of closing any current Windows task or program.

found set The remaining visible (or browsed) records following a find operation, such as a find request, Omit command, or Omit Multiple command. See also *Find* and *browsed records.*

freeware Programs, plug-ins, documents, or templates offered to users free of charge. Freeware might be copyrighted and include conditions concerning further dissemination. See also *shareware.*

Full Access A predefined privilege set providing complete access to a FileMaker Pro database, including permission to change the design of the database, set or change passwords and access privileges, and establish or change groups. See also *privilege set.*

function An operation performed on zero or more values (parameters) yielding a unique result for that value set. The function result for two different value sets can be the same, but the function result for a given value set can never differ from the original result. See also *argument* and *expression.*

Global storage field A field used to hold the same value for all records in the database. Any value that must be constant throughout the database is a candidate for Global storage (set in a field definition's Options dialog on the Storage pane). Examples might include a fixed shipping charge, a user's name, a state's sales tax percentage, and various preference settings. A field with the Global storage option set can also be used to temporarily store script results although the introduction of script variables in FileMaker Pro 8 has made using global fields for temporary storage unnecessary.

grayscale Objects and text are displayed in shades of gray rather than in color. As with color, most displays can support multiple gray shades (4, 16, and 256, for example).

group A set of objects in a layout to which you have applied the Group command so you can treat them as a single entity rather than as a collection of objects. To work again with the individual components of a group, use the Ungroup command. Groups can contain other groups.

guest A user account, created (but disabled) by default, that can open a shared database assigned the Read-Only privilege set. See also *privilege set, client,* and *host.*

handle A black dot that appears at the corners of an object when it is selected in Layout mode. You can drag the handles to resize the object.

header A FileMaker Pro layout part appearing at the top of every record or report page. The report title is often placed in the header. If you want to put special information on just the first or cover page of a report, use a Title Header part. See also *footer.*

header record A special first record frequently included as part of an exported file. The header identifies (by name) all fields present in the file and indicates the order in which they can be found. The header record can also specify the separator (such as tab- or comma-delimited text) and field types and sizes (as found in a dBASE file, for example). See also *export.*

hierarchical menu A menu in which one or more menu items contain a submenu.

host The user who first opens a FileMaker Pro database and turns on FileMaker Network Sharing (FileMaker Pro/Edit ⇨ Sharing ⇨ FileMaker Network), enabling other users on the network to share that database. In subsequent sessions, other users may become the host. See also *guest.*

HTML Abbreviation for *HyperText Markup Language;* the simple language used to create pages for the World Wide Web. See also *XML.*

import To bring data from another program into the current program. Importing saves you the effort of needlessly retyping data. FileMaker Pro, for example, can read any tab-delimited text file, regardless of what program actually created the file. See also *export.*

index FileMaker Pro maintains an internal list of data that includes the contents of selected Text, Number, Date, Time, Timestamp, and Calculation fields. Indexes are responsible for the speed with which FileMaker Pro executes find requests. In versions of the program prior to 3.0, indexing was automatically performed for every appropriate field type. In FileMaker Pro 3.0 and higher, indexing is an option that must be turned on individually for desired fields on the Storage pane of their Options dialog. See also *sort.*

inkjet A type of printer technology in which ink is forced at high pressure onto the page. Inkjet printers are frequently inexpensive, predominately color, while being capable of matching or surpassing the resolution and quality of many laser printers. The cost per page can be significantly higher for inkjets as opposed to laser print-ers because of the cost of the ink cartridges.

insertion point A blinking vertical line that indicates the point where the next typed, pasted, or imported data will appear.

installer A special program provided to enable users to copy a program, templates, and supporting files to their hard disks. Sometimes called a *set-up program*.

Instant Web Publishing Publishing a FileMaker Pro database to the Internet or a company intranet for access via a Web browser.

internal script A script that is contained in and executed from the current FileMaker Pro database file. See also *external script*.

invalid data Information that does not adhere to the specific format for a given field or that falls outside the acceptable range of values for that field. This term also refers to data of the wrong type, such as character data in a Number field.

Java A programming language developed by Sun Microsystems and designed to create applications that can be deployed on multiple platforms without recompiling.

JDBC Abbreviation for *Java Database Connectivity;* provides a Java-based means of exchanging data with Web-published databases. See also *ODBC*.

join See *relationship*.

keyboard shortcut Keys you press as an alternative to using the mouse to select a command from a menu or a dialog box option. Also called a *keyboard equivalent*.

laser printing A printing technology in which laser light creates an image of a page on a rotating photosensitive drum, applying an electrostatic charge to the drum. Toner particles adhere to the charged drum and are then transferred onto paper, where they are fused at high heat. This technology works like a conventional photocopier.

layout In FileMaker Pro, a particular arrangement of fields, graphics, and static text. An unlimited number of layouts can be designed for each database, each with a dif-ferent purpose. For example, some layouts may be used for data entry and others for generating printed or onscreen reports.

layout parts The major sections in a database layout. Depending on the purpose of the layout, it might contain a body, a header, a footer, and a summary, for example.

List view Using the View as List command, you can display records in a continuous scrolling list rather than one record per screen. See also *Table view*.

lock A Layout mode option that enables you to lock selected fields, labels, graphics, and the like in place on the current layout, thus preventing them from being moved, deleted, or their formatting or properties modified.

lookup A field option instructing FileMaker Pro to search another table for the first record containing a match to the data entered in the current table's key field. If a match is found, data from another field in the other table is automatically copied into a field in the current database. For example, entering an inventory part number in one table can trigger a lookup in another table for that part's price and description.

lookup field A field in the current table into which data will be copied when a lookup is triggered. See also *match fields*.

lookup table The table in which data is looked up (in response to data being entered or edited in the trigger field in the current table).

mail merge Combining address and other personal or business information (usually from a database) with a form letter to generate a series of personalized letters. You can generate a merge directly within a FileMaker Pro layout.

match fields When performing a lookup or certain imports, the fields in the two database files that are compared. These fields define the relationship between the files. To identify matching records, a key field such as a Social Security or customer identification number might serve as match fields in the two files. See also *lookup field*.

menu A list of choices, presented by a program or the operating system, from which you can choose an action. A menu opens when you click its title in the menu bar.

menu bar In a Macintosh program or in the Finder, the horizontal strip at the top of the screen containing the menu titles; in a Windows program, the horizontal strip at the top of a window containing the menu titles.

merge The process of combining information from a database with a text document, such as for a form letter (also known as a *mail merge*). See also *mail merge*.

modal dialog Any dialog that you must respond to before you can continue working. See also *modeless dialog* and *sheet*.

mode A state of a FileMaker Pro database in which you can perform only a single set of related activities. The four modes are *Browse, Find, Layout,* and *Preview*.

modeless dialog A dialog that you can leave open while you attend to work in other window or applications; it does not require an immediate response or dismissal. See also *modal dialog* and *sheet*.

modifier key A key or keys that, when pressed in combination with a letter, number, or punctuation key, change the meaning of the second key. When you are typing text, for example, the Shift and Option/Alt keys frequently act as modifier keys. Similarly, pressing the ⌘ (Macintosh) or Ctrl key (PC) in combination with a second key issues a program command. On a Macintosh keyboard, modifier keys include Shift, Option, ⌘, and Control. On a PC, modifier keys include Shift, Alt, and Ctrl. See also *data-entry keys.*

monochrome Refers to a two-color display (typically black-and-white).

ODBC Acronym for *Open Database Connectivity;* a protocol used to interact with and request data from other databases. FileMaker Pro 8 can act as an ODBC client program and request data from other sources, such as Oracle or Sybase databases. FileMaker can also respond to ODBC queries from other applications. Some non-database applications, such as Microsoft Word and Excel, can also import data via ODBC. See also *JDBC.*

OLE Abbreviation for *Object Linking and Embedding;* a Microsoft technology that enables objects to be inserted into OLE-compliant programs, such as FileMaker Pro. Using Windows, OLE objects can be inserted and edited. When using a Macintosh, however, OLE objects can only be viewed, cut, copied, or pasted; they cannot be inserted nor edited in any manner.

omit To remove a record from a found set, temporarily hiding it from view. If you select the Omit option when performing a Find request, FileMaker Pro shows only the records that do *not* match the search criteria. For example, if the search criterion were State = CA, clicking the Omit option would result in a found set of records from all states *except* California (that is, the request becomes a *Find not*). You can also manually omit records from the found set — without performing a Find — by choosing the Records ⇨ Omit Record or Records ⇨ Omit Multiple commands.

open To load a copy of a document from disk into a program. You can also open folders and Desktop windows for disks by double-clicking the icons representing them or single-clicking their entries on the Macintosh Dock or Windows taskbar.

operator A symbol indicating that a certain action should be performed on the entities surrounding the operator symbol. Both + and / are examples of mathematical operators, and & is an example of a string operator.

operator precedence See *order of operations.*

options See *preferences.*

order of operations (or precedence) Refers to the way in which algebraic expressions in formulas are evaluated. Exponents are evaluated first, then multiplication and division, and then addition and subtraction. When operators are of equal precedence, they are evaluated from left to right. You can include parentheses in an expression to alter the order of operations. Expressions in the innermost set of parentheses are evaluated first. See also *expression*.

password A string of characters associated with an account name that a user must type when opening a protected FileMaker Pro database.

pixmap An uncompressed graphics format where each *pixel* (picture element) is represented by a number signifying its color.

platform A particular computer/operating system combination. Mac OS X (Panther 10.3 and Tiger 10.4) on Macintosh and Windows 2000 and XP on Intel (sometimes called *Wintel*) are common platforms and platforms on which FileMaker Pro 8 will run.

plug-in A software add-on enhancing FileMaker Pro by giving it new capabilities. For example, Auto-Update is a FileMaker Pro plug-in. Other programs, such as Adobe Photoshop and InDesign, also support plug-ins. Plug-ins are typically specific to the application for which they were created: For example, FileMaker Pro will not recognize Photoshop plug-ins and vice versa.

pop-up menu A user interface element commonly employed in Mac OS. It is typically presented as a button with an up-down arrowhead pair at its right end.

portal A rectangular area on a layout created with the Portal tool; used to display multiple records from a related table. Think of a portal as a window into a related table.

precedence See *order of operations*.

preferences Program-specific or document-specific options you set to govern how certain aspects of a program behave. Preferences are often referred to as *options*.

Preview A FileMaker Pro mode enabling the user to see what a printed report or other document will look like onscreen prior to committing it to paper.

print driver A software program used to control a specific printer. Macintosh print drivers and supported printers are accessible the Printer Setup Utility. Specific printers can also be selected in any Print dialog. Windows print drivers can be selected in either the Print or Print Setup/Page Setup dialogs. See also *Printer Setup Utility*.

Printer Setup Utility In Mac OS X (Panther and later), Printer Setup Utility (a system software component in the /Applications/Utilities folder) is used to specify a default printer, locate connected printers, and manage print queues.

questionable spelling The term that FileMaker Pro's spelling checker uses to identify a word that is not contained in the current main or user dictionaries.

QuicKeys A Macintosh macro utility from CE Software that enables users to automate functions in most programs. When you use the Send Apple Event script step, QuicKeys macros that access other programs can be executed from within FileMaker Pro.

QuickTime An Apple-created system extension enabling you to play or display video, picture, and sound data on any Macintosh or Windows PC. QuickTime movies and audio clips can be inserted into Container fields.

radio button In dialogs, buttons that present a series of mutually exclusive options or settings (for example, enabling or disabling background printing). Fields can be formatted as radio buttons in FileMaker Pro in order to present a set of distinct choices.

RAM Abbreviation for *Random Access Memory;* the memory the computer uses to run programs, temporarily store data, and so on.

range checking A database validation feature that prevents input errors by making certain each entry in a particular field is within acceptable ranges. For example, numeric entries for student grades might have to be between 0–4.

reader (or viewer) A utility program that enables the contents of a document to be read, regardless of whether or not the user has his or her own copy of the program in which the document was created. A reader typically provides the user only with *read* privileges: That is, the user can read documents created with a particular program but cannot *write* (create new documents of that type). Adobe/Acrobat Reader is a common reader application for both Macs and PCs.

Read Me file A text file that provides information about a program or template. Manufacturers of commercial programs often include a Read Me file on disk to inform users about important topics that are not covered in the program's manual. Although these files do not have to be named Read Me, such a name encourages users to open the file and examine its contents.

record The basic unit of every table. All tables are composed of records, each storing information for a single entity, such as a person, catalog item, videotape, or recipe.

relational database program A program in which key fields link information in multiple tables, enabling you to generate reports and display information based on data from more than one table. See also *flat-file database*.

relationship A relationship between two FileMaker Pro tables is defined by a pair of matching fields in the files, such as a customer ID number or Social Security number. When a relationship has been defined, either table can draw/display data from the other for viewing onscreen or use in reports. Additionally, data from other tables that are also related via an intermediate table can be accessed/displayed. For example, using Customer Email Address as the matching field between two databases (Tech Support and Customers), a case record in the Tech Support database could display contact information for each customer by pulling it from the related record in the Customers database. See also *self-join.*

Relookup A Records menu command that causes all lookups for a database to be executed again (for every record currently being browsed). Choosing this command ensures that all lookup fields contain current data.

repeating field A field option enabling a single field to store and display multiple values, such as the names of purchased items in an invoice table.

report A copy of selected information from a database, consisting of specified records in a certain layout, often presented in a particular sort order.

required field (not empty) A field with this validation setting must be filled in before finalizing the information for the record. The record is checked for completeness only when you press Enter; attempt to switch to a different record, layout, or mode; close the database; or try to quit FileMaker Pro while the database is still open.

reset switch A hardware switch or button that causes the computer to go through its start-up sequence. Refer to your owner's manual for the availability and location of the switch or button. Normally, the reset switch should only be pressed to recover from a system crash when less drastic measures (such as Force Quit) have failed.

resources In a FileMaker Pro database, these are the layouts, value lists, scripts, and the fields. When defining access privileges associated with a particular group, the database designer or administrator can prevent users from modifying or even seeing particular resources.

root The top or highest level of any disk or volume. When a disk icon is initially opened, the root is the part of the disk you first see.

save To store a current copy of a document on disk.

script A user-defined sequence of commands and actions that automates FileMaker Pro tasks. A script consists of one or more commands associated with a specific database that FileMaker will execute automatically or when instructed to do so by the user. External (non-FileMaker) scripts can be created in other applications and programming environments, such as Visual Basic for Applications (Windows) and AppleScript (Mac).

ScriptMaker The FileMaker Pro component you use to design scripts.

scroll arrow The arrow icon at either end of a scroll bar (or one of the two arrows at the bottom or left of a Macintosh scroll bar, if you have the System Preference set to display the arrows together). When you click the arrow, the window's contents move in the opposite direction of the arrow.

scroll bar A rectangular bar along the right side or bottom edge of a window. Clicking or dragging in a scroll bar changes your view of the window's contents. Document windows, portals, and large text fields often have scroll bars.

scroll box The box in a scroll bar. The position of the scroll box indicates the position of what is displayed in the window relative to the entire document.

SCSI (pronounced *skuz*-zee) Abbreviation for *Small Computer Systems Interface.* Enables devices, such as hard disks, CD-ROM drives, tape drives, and scanners to be connected in series to a computer. SCSI used to be the standard hardware interface on new Macintoshes, and it could be found on some PCs. In current hardware, SCSI is almost completely supplanted by IDE, FireWire, and USB.

search criteria Information used as a reference in search or find operations.

self-extracting archive One or more compressed files that contain a built-in file extraction program. When a user double-clicks the icon of a self-extracting archive, a file dialog appears enabling the user to select a destination disk and folder for the expanded (normal) files. See also *archive.*

self-join A relationship in which a file is related to itself. See also *relationship.*

Serial Number field A field whose Auto-Entry options are set to be Serial Number. Such fields have an automatic increment amount that operates on the (filtered) numeric portion.

set-up program See *installer.*

shareware Programs or templates that are distributed to users on the honor system. If you decide to keep the program or template, you send the author the requested fee. See also *freeware.*

sheet A Macintosh user interface dialog that acts like a modal dialog for the window to which it is attached and a modeless dialog for any other window. In most applications, a Save dialog or Print dialog is presented as a sheet. See also *modal dialog* and *modeless dialog.*

shortcut A Windows stand-in icon for a program, file, folder, or disk. Double-clicking a shortcut results in the same action that occurs when you double-click the original icon. On a Macintosh, *aliases* serve similar functions to Windows shortcuts.

shortcut menu On a Macintosh or Windows PC, you can Control+click/right-click database fields and layout elements to display a menu of commands relevant to the item clicked. These context-sensitive menus are also available in many other programs, as well as on the Desktop and within open document folders. Historically, Mac users might see them referred to as *contextual menus.*

Shut Down A command in the Mac's Apple menu and Windows' Start menu that you use to shut down the computer and devices that are connected to and drawing power from it.

sine For a right (90-degree) triangle, the ratio of the side opposite the angle to the hypotenuse.

size box Refers to the box in the lower-right corner of most Macintosh windows. Dragging the size box changes the size of the window. (In recent versions of the Mac OS, three diagonal lines in the lower-right corner of the window have replaced the size box. In Windows, you can change the size of windows by clicking and dragging any window corner or edge.) Occasionally, you will encounter a size box on an object within a window, such as a list or display pane.

sort To rearrange database records in a different order than the one in which they were originally entered. Most database programs — including FileMaker Pro — can simultaneously sort on multiple fields. The more powerful database programs enable you to specify key or index fields (special sort fields that are automatically maintained by the program). Indexes are particularly useful for very large databases, where a normal sort would be extremely time-consuming. Indexing can be specified for most types of FileMaker Pro fields. See also *index*.

sort order The order in which a field is sorted. Every FileMaker Pro database field can be sorted in one of three sort orders: ascending, descending, or according to the entries in a value list.

source code In a computer program, the set of instructions that makes a program do what it was intended to do. The instructions are in a human-readable form (usually in a programming language such as Pascal, C, C++, BASIC, Java, or assembly language). In a FileMaker Pro template, script definitions, DDE instructions, and AppleScript instructions can be considered the equivalent of source code.

standalone document A document that contains its own reader and hence, does not require the user to own a specific program to open and read the document. The document is a program. For example, on the Macintosh, all documents created in the shareware program DOCMaker are standalone documents.

standalone program After FileMaker Pro 8 is used to compile a template, the template becomes a standalone program. It can be run on any suitable Mac or Windows PC, and the program does not require that a copy of FileMaker Pro be installed. Such standalone databases are sometimes called *run-time applications*.

status area The area on the immediate left of a FileMaker Pro database window. In Browse mode, the status area contains controls that enable you to select a different layout, navigate among records, change the magnification (zoom), and show or hide the status area. Information on the current state of the database (such as whether it is sorted, the number of records being browsed, and the current record number) is also displayed in the status area.

step (or script step) A single action in a FileMaker Pro script.

sub-script Any FileMaker Pro script that is performed by another script.

Summary field A type of field used to summarize the information in a specified field across all currently browsed (visible) records.

system software Software that supports application programs by managing system resources, such as memory and input/output devices.

tab control A layout element used to group fields and other layout objects on separate panes. Tabs conserve screen space and avoid having to maintain separate layouts when the objects on the different panes do not have to be simultaneously available. You frequently encounter tabbed dialogs in FileMaker Pro and other programs, particularly for setting preferences — these dialogs inspired the tab control implementation.

table A collection of data applicable to a specific subject, such as contact information or current inventory. A database consists of one or more tables although FileMaker Pro 8 allows you to create a database file with no tables — just layouts that are based on tables in other files.

Table view In Table view, data is displayed in spreadsheet format. Each row corresponds to a record and each column to a field. See also *List view*.

tangent In a right (90-degree) triangle, the ratio of the opposite side to the adjacent side for one of the two non-right angles.

TCP/IP Abbreviation for *Transmission Control Protocol/Internet Protocol;* a network protocol (supported by FileMaker Pro 4.0 and higher) that is used to connect to the Internet. TCP/IP is the only connection protocol supported by FileMaker Pro 8.

template (or stationery document) A partially completed document that serves as a starting point for other documents. In a word processing program, for example, you might create a memo template containing appropriate headers and text formatting, making it simple for you to create each new memo without having to retype basic text. The equivalent document in FileMaker Pro is known as a *clone* and is created using the File ➪ Save a Copy As command. See also *clone*.

text box (or text-edit box) A rectangular area in a dialog or layout that is used to enter or edit information. A common example is the space provided for a filename in Export or Save dialogs.

text file (also called text-only file) A file saved without formatting (a single font and no style or size options). Most text editors, such as BBEdit on the Macintosh and Notepad under Windows, automatically save documents in this format. You can usually create such files by using a word processing program's Save As command

and choosing Text-Only or Text as the format. In general, you create pure-text files so other programs or other types of computers can read them.

title bar The horizontal bar at the top of a window that shows the name of the window's contents. You can move a window by dragging its title bar.

trigger field A field in the current table that when data is entered or modified, initiates a lookup in another table.

uncompressing (or extracting) To shorten the length of time required to download files from an information service or to transmit e-mail attachments, a utility program is often used to compress the files into an archive (making the files smaller). Uncompressing or extracting the contents of an archive restores the files to their original size and format. See also *archive*.

Unicode An international character-encoding table providing a unique value for every character in known human languages.

unique field A field that can contain only data that is not duplicated in any other record.

upload To transfer data from your computer to another computer. See also *download*.

URL Abbreviation for *Uniform Resource Locator;* an Internet standard expression specifying a protocol and address for communicating with another computer.

user name A unique name assigned to a computer or its primary user; normally used to distinguish that computer from others on a network.

value list A user-defined list of choices or values. Using value lists can help speed data entry and ensure the consistency of information presentation. Value lists can be displayed as pop-up lists, pop-up menus, radio buttons, or check boxes.

variable A value in an expression that can change, usually indicated by a letter or name. A field can be considered a variable because its contents might change from record to record.

windoid A tiny, special-purpose window type that is typically provided as a user-control tool. FileMaker Pro's Size tool and the various tear-off palettes, such as the ones used to apply colors or textures to objects, are examples of windoids.

Web page A page on the World Wide Web, frequently consisting of a mixture of text, graphics, and multimedia elements (such as sound and movie clips).

World Wide Web A graphically rich portion of the Internet, consisting of billions of pages programmed in HTML. Users can move from page to page by clicking text or graphic links.

XML Abbreviation for *eXtensible Markup Language,* an emerging standard for next-generation documents delivered via the Internet. As the standard evolves, you can track it on the Internet at www.xml.com and at www.w3.org/xml.

XSLT Abbreviation for *eXtensible Stylesheet Language Transformation;* a technology employed to repurpose (transform) data in XML format for use in applications expecting a different format. For example, XSLTs can be used to convert XML into HTML, tab-delimited text, or Word or Excel documents.

zoom Changing the magnification level of a database, enlarging or reducing your view of all elements on a layout.

zoom button/box On a Macintosh, the green plus icon in a window's upper-left corner. Under Windows, this box is beside the close box (the tiny x) and is referred to as Maximize/Restore. Click the box to expand the window to its most recent manually expanded size. A second click returns the window to its original size.

✦   ✦   ✦

Resources

In addition to using this book and the material that came with your copy of FileMaker Pro, you can turn to many other resources for more information about the product. These resources can help you accomplish the following:

+ Learn new database programming techniques and tricks.

+ Work around or discover solutions to problems you've encountered while using FileMaker Pro.

+ Find out about utilities and plug-ins that enhance the program.

+ Purchase ready-to-run FileMaker Pro templates that are designed for your particular business.

+ Hire a specialist to create a database template for you.

+ Try out free and inexpensive templates.

Technical Support and General Help

If you need help with a problem that isn't explained in this book or in the FileMaker Pro online Help system, the best source of information is the FileMaker Technical Support Department (408-727-9004). Have your access code or product serial number handy when you call.

If you have Internet access and a Web browser, you should visit the FileMaker Web site at www.filemaker.com. In addition to helpful tips and troubleshooting notes, you will find the site an invaluable source of FileMaker Pro templates, plug-ins, and other FileMaker-related add-ons. You can also download user manuals, reviewer's guides, sample files, and FileMaker-related white papers at

www.filemaker.com/downloads/index.html#manuals

Custom Programming and Vertical Applications

Because FileMaker Pro is such a popular database program, you probably won't be surprised to learn that many individuals and companies make their living by providing after-market materials, such as database templates, custom programming, and training materials.

FileMaker publishes a guide (*FileMaker Resource Guide,* 13th Edition) to third-party companies that provide FileMaker Pro solutions. A copy is included in the box with FileMaker Pro or FileMaker Pro 8 Advanced.

If your intent is to provide some FileMaker Pro solutions of your own, you can join the FileMaker Solutions Alliance (FSA) program for an annual fee of $249 (Subscriber), $599 (Associate), or $799 (Partner) with a varying list of benefits, by calling 800-325-2747 or 408-987-7162.

Just in case you haven't yet purchased your copy of FileMaker Pro 8, all three membership categories include a free copy of FileMaker Pro 8 and FileMaker Mobile. The Subscriber membership, which costs the same as the suggested retail price of FileMaker Pro 8, makes the membership quite cost-effective.

Design Tips and Programming Tricks

In 1995, an enterprising FileMaker Pro developer named Matt Petrowsky decided that the best way to spread the word about FileMaker Pro was to use it in a manner that FileMaker, Inc. never intended—to publish and distribute an electronic magazine, namely *ISO FileMaker Magazine.* Dedicated to FileMaker Pro topics, this gorgeous monthly database contains scads of excellent design and programming tips. To download sample issues or to subscribe ($25 quarterly), you can visit ISO Production's Web page at www.filemakermagazine.com or contact them at the mailing address shown later in this section.

Tip   Be sure to check out the enormous resource list compiled by ISO at www.filemakerworld.com.

ISO is also the publisher of several FileMaker-related CDs, including the *Everything CD for FileMaker Pro, Volume 5* and *Scriptology.* You can order from the ISO Web site or by phone or mail at the following address:

ISO Productions, Inc., 4049 First Street, Suite 141 Livermore, CA 94550. Phone: 877-958-8999 or 925-454-0187.

In addition to the articles available to subscribers, you'll find a number of online tutorials and videos providing you with tips and techniques.

FileMaker Internet Mailing Lists

If you have a FileMaker Pro programming problem, want to pick up some great tips, or have an interest in some particular aspect of FileMaker Pro development, you should check out the links at www.filemaker.com/support/mailinglists.html. You'll find a veritable cornucopia of both general and targeted lists for FileMaker users and developers linked from this page.

Magazines: An Additional Source for Tips

Several computer magazines occasionally provide FileMaker Pro tips and techniques. In addition to featuring in-depth reviews of new versions of programs (such as FileMaker Pro), they sometimes publish user tips and feature articles that explain how to get more out of FileMaker Pro.

Macworld magazine focuses primarily on the needs of business users. *Macworld* is the primary source of Mac information for many users. *MacTech*, a publication formerly directed at Mac programmers, has broadened its charter and covers a panoply of power-user topics; among the favorites are articles covering advanced FileMaker topics. *Mac Home Journal* caters more to novice users and the needs of individuals who have Macs at home. You should be able to pick up a copy of these magazines at a local newsstand, or you can contact the magazines directly for subscription information at the addresses that follow.

If you're not satisfied with scanning magazines for the occasional FileMaker article, give *FileMaker Pro Advisor* a try. This magazine is dedicated to FileMaker Pro and contains user success stories, technical articles, and tips and tricks.

✦ *Macworld* magazine: Subscription Services P.O. Box 54529 Boulder, CO 80322-4529. Phone: 800-288-6848 in U.S.; 303-604-7445 outside the U.S. Web site: www.macworld.com.

✦ *MacTech* magazine: Xplain Corporation, 850-P Hampshire Road, Westlake Village, CA 91361-2800. Phone: 805-494-9797. Web site: www.mactech.com.

✦ *MacHOME* magazine: 703 Market Street, Suite 535 San Francisco, CA 94103. Phone: 800-800-6542. Web site: www.machome.com.

✦ *FileMaker Pro Advisor* magazine. P.O. Box 429002, San Diego, CA 92142. Phone: 800-336-6060. Web site: http://filemakerAdvisor.com.

More Internet Resources

FileMaker developers are keenly aware of the need for an Internet presence; many have their own Web sites. To make it easy for you to find them, we've compiled a list of FileMaker-related sites and sites offering products based upon or developed in FileMaker that we think you'll find useful.

Table E-1
FileMaker-Related Web Sites

Company	Web Address
3D Audio	www.3daudioinc.com
Altasoft Corporation	www.bizpack.com
Applied Arts	www.a2soft.com
Arsene Software	www.arsene.com
OmniPilot Software.	www.omnipilot.com/default.html
Buttons & Things	www.lunsfordfamily.com/bandt
Database Pros	www.databasepros.com
DW Data Concepts	www.dwdataconcepts.com
Epigroove	www.epigroove.com
FileMaker, Inc. (FTP site)	ftp.filemaker.com/pub
FileMaker, Inc. (Web site)	www.filemaker.com
FileMaker Pro Advisor (magazine)	http://filemakeradvisor.com
FileVille	www.fileville.com
FMPro.org	www.fmpro.org
FMPtraining.com	www.fmptraining.com
FMWebschool	www.fmwebschool.com
HPO SOFT	www.amug.org/~hposoft
Inaka Software	www.inakasoftware.com
ISO Productions *(FileMaker Magazine)*	www.filemakermagazine.com
K–12 MicroMedia Publishing	www.k12mmp.com
Kinetic Synergy Inc.	www.ksi.ca
Krische Database Systems	www.krischesystems.com
DwayneWright.com (formerly LeSaux Media Services)	www.dwaynewright.com/lesaux, www.dwaynewright.com/afa/index.html
Lupien Limited Consulting	www.databasediva.com
Medical Databases	www.practicemaker.com
New Millennium Communications	www.nmci.com
Northwestern Consulting Group	www.deepscreen.com

Company	Web Address
Schwartz, Steve (*FileMaker Pro Bible co-author*)	www.siliconwasteland.com
Spinfree	www.spinfree.com
SumWare Consulting	www.sumware.co.nz
Tokerud Consulting Group	www.tokerud.com/FileMaker.html
Trackware Corporation	www.trackware.com
Troi Automatisering	www.troi.com
Waves in Motion	www.wmotion.com, www.iSurveys.com
Web Broadcasting Corporation	www.macweb.com
Working Solutionz Software	www.bizbasics.net
X2max Software	www.x2max.com

✦　　✦　　✦

About the Web Site

This appendix provides you with information on the contents of the Web site that accompanies this book. To get to the Web site, browse to www.wiley.com/compbooks/ filemaker8.5bible. Here is what you'll find:

+ System requirements

+ Using the CD with Windows and Mac

+ What's on the CD

+ Troubleshooting

System Requirements

Make sure that your computer meets the minimum system requirements listed in this section. If your computer doesn't match up to most of these requirements, you could have a problem using the files on the Web site.

For Windows 2000 or Windows XP:

+ PC with a Pentium III processor running at 600 MHz or faster

+ At least 128MB of total RAM installed on your computer; for best performance, we recommend at least 256MB

+ At least 200MB of hard drive space

For Mac:

✦ Mac OS computer with a 500 MHz Power Macintosh G3 or faster processor running OS X 10.3 or later

✦ At least 128MB of total RAM installed on your computer; for best performance, we recommend at least 256MB

✦ At least 200MB of hard drive space

What's on the Web Site

The following sections provide a summary of the software and other materials that you'll find on this book's companion Web site.

Author-created materials

All specified author-created material from the book, including code listings and samples, are in the `Author` folder. Each chapter's files are in separate folders named for the chapter.

Chapter 4 contains the Address Book Advanced example, which is referenced frequently throughout this book.

Chapter 5 contains the Summary Field Tester example and the InvoiceUsingRepeatingFields example.

Chapter 18 contains the Video World database example in both "separate file" and "consolidated" forms so that you can compare the design approaches. Also present is the (empty) database for Sean Lahman's baseball statistics, ready for you to import the data from his Web site at `www.baseball1.com`.

Chapter 20 contains the Medical 2004 database with some dummy records.

Chapter 23 contains the Callable Help Example.

FileMaker Pro 7 Bible items contains Chapter 4 from the previous edition, the old (non-tabbed) version of the Address Book Advanced example, and Appendix C from the previous edition.

Applications

You can access the following trial applications through the book's Web site as well:

FileMaker Pro trial versions (Mac and Windows) are fully functional, time-limited demonstration versions of FileMaker Pro.

FileMaker XSLT Library (from FileMaker, Inc.) is a collection of XSL translators that you can specify when importing XML from various sources or when exporting a database to XML.

FMRobot is an automated tool from New Millennium Communications for importing tables from other FileMaker Pro 6, 7, and 8 database files into a FileMaker Pro 8 or higher database file.

DialogMagic is a plug-in from New Millennium Communications for creating and managing dialogs in your FileMaker Pro database.

MediaManager is a multi-faceted plug-in from New Millennium Communications that allows you to manage and manipulate content, such as images, in container fields, access file system metadata, create Web pages, and much more.

Troi Text Plug-in from Troi Automatisering is a handy plug-in for creating and managing flexible dialogs for use with your FileMaker Pro database.

24U FM Template from 24U Software is an Xcode project for creating external function plug-ins.

24U SimpleHighlight plug-in project from 24U Software is an example project employing the 24U FM template for creating plug-ins. The plug-in implements two functions for highlighting text or rectangular areas of the layout with a user-specified color.

Shareware programs are fully functional, trial versions of copyrighted programs. If you like particular programs, register with their authors for a nominal fee and receive licenses, enhanced versions, and technical support. *Freeware programs* are copyrighted games, applications, and utilities that are free for personal use. Unlike shareware, these programs do not require a fee or provide technical support. *GNU software* is governed by its own license, which is included inside the folder of the GNU product. See the GNU license for more details.

Trial, demo, or evaluation versions are usually limited either by time or functionality (such as being unable to save projects). Some trial versions are very sensitive to system date changes. If you alter your computer's date, the programs will "time out" and no longer be functional.

Troubleshooting

If you have difficulty installing or using any of the materials on the companion Web site, try the following solutions:

✦ **Turn off any antivirus software that you might have running.** Installers sometimes mimic virus activity and can make your computer incorrectly believe that it's being infected by a virus. (Be sure to turn the antivirus software back on after the installation is finished.)

✦ **Close all running programs.** The more programs you're running, the less memory is available to other programs. Installers also typically update files and programs; if you keep other programs running, installation might not work properly.

If you still have trouble with the Web site materials, please call the Wiley Product Technical Support phone number: (800) 762-2974. Outside the United States, call (317) 572-3993. You can also contact Wiley Product Technical Support at www.wiley.com/techsupport. Wiley Publishing will provide technical support only for installation and other general quality-control items; for technical support on the applications themselves, consult the program's vendor or author.

To place additional orders or to request information about other Wiley products, please call (800) 225-5945.

✦   ✦   ✦

Index

Continued

Continued

Continued

Continued

Continued

Continued

Continued

Continued

Continued

Continued

S

Continued

Continued